GOD, THEOLOGY & COGNITIVE MODULES

A General Theory of Human Thought

by Lorin Friesen

ISBN: 978-0-9879785-0-9

Published by Lorin Friesen

Second Printing, 2025

https://www.mentalsymmetry.com

Contents

✵ Introduction

Imagine that you are driving down the street in your car and that you hear a strange noise. What do you do? You listen and try to determine which part of your car is making the noise. Is it the brakes? Is it the tires? Is it the transmission? Is it a wheel bearing?

In order to figure out which part is causing the noise, one must first know the various parts of a car and have an idea of how they function. For instance, if the noise is coming from the tires, then the noise will stop when the vehicle is not moving. If the noise is coming from a wheel bearing, then it will probably be louder when the vehicle is turning left or right. If one is not familiar with how a car is put together, then the only option is to take it to a service station and to complain in some vague way that 'the car is making a strange noise'.

Going further, the purpose of localizing a car noise is not to construct a general theory about car noises. Instead, the ultimate purpose is to fix the car so that it stops making the noise. Notice that the noise itself is not the problem. Instead, the noise is a sign that some part in the car needs fixing or replacing. If this part is not repaired, then the car will eventually break down and stop functioning. Gaining an understanding of car parts and learning to identify car noises plays an essential intermediate role in the process of repairing a car, because it allows one to identify a potential problem and deal with it before it becomes serious.

That describes how this book will be approaching the topic of God and religion. The scientific world tends to regard religious doctrine as mental 'noise', and so it ignores it. My premise is that this so-called noise provides valuable information. But in the same way that one must know the various parts of a car and how they work in order to analyze a car noise, so one must know the various cognitive modules of the mind and how they function in order to analyze religious doctrine.

So how *does* a cognitive module function? One can answer this question by looking at the example of the *right parietal lobe*, a module within the human brain which is reasonably well understood. The functions of the right parietal lobe all seem to relate to objects and spatial connections, but in different ways and at different scales. Damage here can lead to:

- Constructional apraxia: an impairment in constructing physical objects.
- Impaired spatial relations: an inability to relate one physical object with another.
- Impaired body image: an inability to deal with the object of the physical body.
- Anosognosia: an impairment in constructing the mental object of self-image.
- Impaired problem-solving: an inability to manipulate objects mentally.

One sees that a single cognitive module is dealing with physical objects, mental objects, conceptual objects, and subjective objects. In other words, the part of the mind that deals with objects does not care about whether that object is a thing, a person, a concept, or a physical body. All that matters is that it is a type of object and can be analyzed as an object.

Science is quite different, because it restricts its analysis to physical phenomena and it takes an objective approach which avoids dealing with the subjective. Thus, science will only handle objects if they describe things or physical bodies. When science encounters mental objects or subjective objects, then it relegates them to the fields of philosophy, psychology, or religion.

Notice that science is making a distinction which the physical brain does not make. This suggests that it is possible to explain topics such as religion by taking scientific thought and extending it into the realm of the *internal* and the *subjective*. That is what we will be doing in this book. We will be looking at the cognitive modules that are responsible for producing rational thought and scientific analysis. Then, we will be using those *same* cognitive modules to analyze the internal and subjective topic of religion, as well as taking a look at philosophy and psychology.

Let me tie this down with the help of another analogy. When I buy a personal computer, I can use that computer to do 'scientific' tasks such as manipulating physical data or storing pictures from my camera. But, I can also use the same computer to do social networking or to play games involving supernatural creatures and imaginary worlds. When I run a virus checker on my computer, I do not limit my virus checking to physical data and pictures of the real world. Instead, I virus check my *entire* file system, including the social networking programs and the games. In fact, it is precisely in the area of social networking and games that I am most likely to get a computer virus. And, when I check my e-mail files and my game files for computer viruses, I do not simply erase all of the files. Instead, I treat files that deal with subjective and non-physical information in the same way that I approach files that contain real, objective data.

Similarly, it does not make sense to limit the mental 'virus checker' of rational and scientific education to the realm of the physical and the objective, because that leaves most of the mental 'hard drive' vulnerable to mental 'viruses'. Instead, I suggest that one should use rational education to analyze all topics—even those that are imaginary and subjective. That is because demagogues, prophets, and dictators *are* inserting 'viruses' into these imaginary and subjective regions of thought and these mental 'viruses' *are* causing people to behave in destructive ways that are very real and very physical.

Applying this concept to religion, even if God does not exist, a mental concept of God has sufficient power to destroy civilizations. However, by taking a *cognitive* approach and analyzing the subject in terms of cognitive modules, one can study topics such as God and religion in a rational manner—even if God does not exist. Going further, if one uses these same mental mechanisms in a positive manner, then one can create a mental concept of God which has sufficient power to build a civilization—even if that God does not exist.

This does not mean that I am trying to prove that there is no God, or that I am attempting to prove the existence of God. Instead, I am suggesting that it is possible to *postpone* dealing with this question and still do meaningful research. When the scientist tries to 'delete' mental files because 'they are not real', or the religious believer places arbitrary information into the mind because 'it is important', then I suggest that this is counterproductive. Instead, both of these sides need to stop squabbling and start asking what type of mental files are *appropriate* for the region of the mind that deals with the subjective and the imaginary. For, real or not, subjective or not, this region of thought desperately needs to be scanned by a 'virus checker'.

What is a computer virus? It takes control of your computer, it slows it down, it makes your computer do things that you do not want it to do, it hides itself, it pretends to be what it is not, and it harms your computer. I suggest that the same attributes apply to a mental 'virus'. Thus, whatever causes cognitive modules to function better and in a more integrated manner is a helpful mental 'program'. In contrast, mental programming that shuts down part of the mind, turns one cognitive module against another, or leads to destructive thought or behavior, can be regarded as a mental 'virus'.

Curiously, when one takes this approach of deferring the question of the existence of God, focusing upon the task of cognitive development, and defining morality in functional terms, then one ends up with concepts which are being taught as religious doctrine by major religions. It then becomes possible to approach the topic of God and religion in a more intelligent manner. For, instead of religious belief being merely an existential leap into the unknown, cognitive principles can now be used to point belief in a specific direction.

In this book, we will be subdividing the human mind into seven cognitive modules. These seven modules come from a system of cognitive styles which my brother Lane Friesen encountered in the late 1970s. As I assisted my brother in working out the traits of these seven cognitive styles, it became clear to me that these seven ways of thinking describe the functioning of seven different major regions of the human brain, leading to the concept of cognitive modules. As neurology has progressed, it has continued to confirm the initial hypotheses which I made back in the early 1980s. The exact boundaries of these various cognitive modules may still be uncertain, but these modules definitely do exist within the human brain.

Here are the seven cognitive modules. Four of them are located in the cortex of the brain:

Right parietal lobe: Deals with objects. The right hippocampus also does spatial processing, and the right parietal lobe is connected via the superior fasciculus with the right dorsolateral frontal cortex.

Left parietal lobe: Deals with actions and sequences. The left hippocampus also handles sequential processing, and the left parietal lobe is connected via the superior fasciculus with the left dorsolateral frontal cortex.

Right temporal lobe: Deals with experiences and non-verbal language. This region is connected with the right amygdala as well as the right orbitofrontal region.

Left temporal lobe: Deals with words and sentences. This region is connected with the left amygdala in addition to the left orbitofrontal region.

It appears that each of these four cognitive modules has an automatic region in the back of the cortex together with an 'internal world' in the front of the cortex.

The last three cognitive modules are located primarily in the subcortex, though they also appear to access and possibly use regions of the cortex:

Nucleus Accumbens and the Dopamine circuit: This cognitive module is associated with urge and desire. The exact extent of this module is uncertain but it definitely includes the striosomes and/or direct path of the basal ganglia.

Basal Ganglia, Subthalamus, and possibly Supplementary Motor Area: This cognitive module is associated with planning, control, decision, and optimization. Again, one could argue over the precise extent of this module.

Thalamus: This cognitive module handles mixing and balancing for the rest of the mind and is itself controlled from the reticular nucleus of the thalamus.

In addition, there are also brain regions, such as the medial frontal cortex or the angular gyrus, which appear to act as interfaces between one cognitive module and another, as well as regions, such as the hypothalamus or the insula, which interface between mental state and physical state. And regions such as the occipital cortex or the central sulcus deal purely with physical input and output.

This book will *not* be discussing neurology. However, I want to mention the neurology in order to demonstrate that the seven cognitive modules which we will be using in our analysis of cognition and religion appear to have a solid basis in the physical brain. And, because I will be using the *same* cognitive theory to analyze both *brain* regions and thinking activity which is traditionally assigned to the *mind*, I will not be making a sharp distinction between mind and brain within this book, but instead I will be treating them as overlapping domains. Exactly where the one stops and the other one starts I do not know, but it appears that a *single* theory can be used to analyze them both.

Using neurology to prove that these are the 'right' cognitive modules is rather difficult. However, it is possible to use neurology to show that these are *valid* cognitive modules, and if one uses these cognitive modules as the starting point then it is possible to construct a logically self-consistent model of human thought which can explain a number of seemingly unrelated topics, including many concepts which people seem to have problems explaining.

The first five chapters of this book will lay the cognitive foundation for our discussion of religion, while the remaining chapters will use these concepts to analyze God and religion, as well as scientific thought. The end of the book contains a number of appendices that explain additional topics which are only covered briefly in the main text. The following is a very terse summary of what will be covered in each chapter:

The first chapter will describe the cognitive model that we will be using as well as introduce the concept of left hemisphere emotion and right hemisphere emotion. This distinction between theoretical emotion and experiential emotion will play a major role in our analysis of science, education, personal development, and religion.

The second chapter will discuss mental networks. We will suggest that emotional memories behave in a different manner when they combine to form a network of memories than when they exist as isolated memories, and that mental networks generate feelings which are more potent than normal emotions. This will lead us to the topics of habit, desire, violence, and sex. We will then use mental networks to explain Theory of Mind, a concept which plays a major role in cognitive science. Finally, we will produce a cognitive explanation for the Agency Detector, a concept which lies at the heart of the emerging field of cognitive science and religion.

The third chapter will examine the two cognitive modules that use right hemisphere thought. This will lead us to a discussion of truth and emotions, and we will see that the mind uses two incompatible methods to define belief. We will then use these two methods of defining belief combined with the concept of mental networks to explain the categories of intuitive physics, intuitive biology, intuitive psychology, and intuitive religion. We will also discuss the way in which cognitive style modifies Theory of Mind.

In the fourth chapter we will extend our look at the relationship between belief and emotions in the direction of the subjective, which will lead us to the concept of personal identity. We will look at the ways in which emotions affect self-image, as well as examining the fundamental role that the physical body plays in defining personal identity. This will lead us to the two mental mechanisms of identification and denial. Finally, we will examine the Ten Commandments in the light of mental networks, personal identity, and identification.

In the fifth chapter we will turn our attention to science and abstract thought. We will observe that scientists can be quite dogmatic and do not always pursue the scientific method, leading us to a discussion about the interaction between mental networks and abstract thought. We will introduce Thomas Kuhn and *The Structure of Scientific Revolutions.* Guided by Kuhn, we will look at the role that emotions play in evaluating and changing paradigms. We will examine what happens when one paradigm comes into contact with another and explain Kuhn's observation that the winning paradigm rewrites history.

We will then see that competing paradigms can coexist peacefully if one is translated into the language of the other in a way that preserves both meaning and emphasis. We will look at the difference between a translation and a paradigm shift. We will examine

Kuhn's concept of incommensurability and suggest that the theory of mental symmetry provides a way of reconciling competing paradigms. Finally, we will see how identification and denial occur with abstract thought.

In chapter six, we will examine how the mind forms an image of God, beginning with an extension of the argument used by the cognitive science of religion. We will come up with a cognitive definition for monotheism, as well as explaining why science avoids talking about God. We will introduce the three stages of learning. We will look at the type of image of God that emerges during the first stage of overgeneralization, and we will observe that the second stage of technical knowledge is associated with an attitude of religious skepticism. We will see that worship and irrationalism can be used to reinforce a concept of God that is based in overgeneralization, which will lead us to a discussion of Eastern mysticism.

We will examine the cognitive basis for Nietzsche's pronouncement that 'God is dead' and look briefly at the rise of 19th century German liberal theology. We will suggest that a concept of Deity does not remain 'dead' but tends to return to life, and that when 'God is dead', this provides an opportunity to rebuild religious thought upon a more solid mental foundation. We will look at the field of the cognitive science of religion and see how it is using the theory of evolution to rebuild a mental concept of God. Finally, we will describe cognitive motivations for believing in the theory of evolution.

Chapter seven will begin by analyzing the mental power that is wielded by a concept of God, and we will see that an image of God harnesses the emotional might of a mental network. We will explain why the mind poses the question of the existence of evil and why the religious adherent believes in hell. We will look at Eastern mysticism and examine why it replaces hell with the concept of karma.

We will then take a closer look at concrete thought and see the role that is played by the mental map, using golf as an illustration. This will lead us to a discussion of value and economics, and we will look at the mental relationship between cause-and-effect, conscience, and economic activity. We will examine how mental networks give emotional power to the voice of conscience and relate this to different kinds of money. We will then turn our attention from concrete thought to abstract thought and look at the role which abstract mental networks play in fiat money, common sense, and an image of God that is based in conscience. This will lead us to discuss the mental effect which miracles have upon an image of God as well as the relationship between common sense and a belief in the supernatural. We will suggest that it is natural for a mental concept of God to emerge, and we will note that when a person or group becomes a source of societal order, then it will naturally claim to be the mouthpiece of God.

In chapter eight, we will examine the process of education, and we will show how education uses the two mental shortcuts of revealed truth and verbal understanding to develop abstract thought. We will look at the ways in which identification and denial can derail the path of education, and we will see that Western education tries to avoid dealing directly with personal identity. We will suggest that effective education should begin with rote learning and blind faith but that it must lead to critical thinking and rational understanding, and we will see what happens when one of these is emphasized to the exclusion of the other. We will discuss how the development of critical thinking makes it mentally possible to emerge from the educational shortcut of rote learning, how this is similar to a paradigm shift, and the major role that the book plays in this process.

We will then extend these educational principles into the realm of religion by adding the element of personal identity. We will come up with a cognitive definition for a holy book, and look at the relationship between critical thinking and a mental concept of God. We will examine the difference between religious and scientific education and point out that religious education uses personal honesty to develop abstract thought, whereas scientific education uses common sense. We will examine how religious worship can either assist or hamper learning, and discuss the concept of conditional acceptance. Finally, we will examine how the religious fundamentalist responds when his faith is analyzed rationally.

Chapter nine will examine the difference between math and science. We will analyze how the mind approaches a mathematical problem, and we will look at the mental basis for science. This will lead us back to Kuhn and his description of scientific learning, which we will compare with the approach taken by philosophy. We will look at Kuhn's concept of the exemplar and analyze scientific problem-solving. We will see how action can be used to apply verbal theory and how action can act as a basis for verbal theory. We will look at the difference between 'works' and 'righteousness', describe the mental role that is played by altruism, and relate this to Kant's categorical and hypothetical imperative. Finally, we will contrast a math-like concept of God with a science-like concept of God.

Chapter ten will describe the process of applying the theory of mental symmetry, examine Hume's is-ought problem in the light of mental symmetry, and analyze the golden rule from a cognitive perspective.

We will then turn our attention back to concrete thought and examine the cognitive mechanism behind the Platonic Form and the Form of Good. This will lead us to the religious concept of the Holy Spirit, as well as a cognitive basis for a belief in heaven. We will look at the cognitive reason for religious self-denial and the role that this plays in motivating monastic behavior. We will examine the emotional difficulty of adding application to theory, and see how technology makes it easier to combine these two by making action more general and experiences more Form-like. We will conclude by examining how the partial transformation produced by the Industrial Revolution is currently being extended to create mental images of God.

Chapter eleven will examine the difference between normal abstract thought and technical abstract thought, and we will use this to explain Kuhn's two categories of revolutionary science and normal science. We will see that technical thought uses concentration to limit thinking to a specific mental context. We will look at the leap of knowing which the mind takes when entering technical thought along with the epistemological crisis that occurs when technical thought realizes that it has built its rigorous thinking upon a non-rigorous foundation. We will examine how the mind can move between the total certainty of technical thought and the partial certainty of normal thought. We will then extend Kuhn's distinction between revolutionary science and normal science to concrete thought, we will look at the relationship between technical abstract thought and technical concrete thought, we will relate this to Michel Foucault's three *epistemes* of Western thought, and we will use this distinction to describe the three stages of learning in more detail.

We will see the role that action and speech play in separating these two forms of technical thought, and we will analyze how the path of education makes it possible to bring these two forms of technical thought together, resulting in a technical mindset that combines abstract and concrete thought, leading us to the concept of R&D, or research and development. We will look more closely at the Industrial Revolution and the societal rebirth that occurs when applied education challenges traditional culture.

We will then derive the religious equivalent by adding the personal element. We will see how the relationship between abstract technical thought and concrete technical thought allows us to come up with a cognitive explanation for the religious doctrine of incarnation, and we will describe the various stages of following the path of religious education.

Chapter twelve will focus upon the concept of personal rebirth. Following the path of education leads to the possibility of a new identity or culture, which will collide with existing identity or culture. Rebirth occurs when the new replaces the old. We will note that parallels can be made between the Christian story of incarnation and the path of education. We will introduce Justin Barrett's minimally counterintuitive concept, and see how the field of the cognitive science of religion uses this to explain the anthropomorphic nature of religious doctrine. We will examine Kant's concept of radical evil, and we will see how the concepts of domain and function make it possible to come up with a cognitive explanation for the Christian 'prayer of salvation'. We will compare the short-term solution of the 'prayer of salvation' with the long-term solution of personal rebirth, using school as an illustration.

We will then examine the implications of viewing salvation-through-rebirth as a paradigm, which will lead us to a discussion of teleology. We will examine the cognitive reasons for avoiding the concept of teleology as well as the cognitive reasons for believing in the theory of evolution. We will look at the cognitive need that the theory of evolution attempts to address, and we will evaluate how well a belief in evolution meets this cognitive need. We will examine the cognitive implications of regarding the theory of evolution as a universal theory and discuss the relationship between evolution and revolution. We will finish by taking another look at the Ten Commandments, comparing them with the process of education.

Chapter thirteen, the final chapter, will look at three systems of thought that emphasize left hemisphere time and sequence while downplaying right hemisphere objects and facts. We will begin with the philosophy of *Martin Heidegger*, who reinterpreted human existence in terms of time and personal action, and we will discuss his analysis of objects, space, self-image, and abstract thought. We will suggest that his left hemisphere viewpoint is a valid alternative, but conclude that his refusal to develop right hemisphere thought has cognitive and moral consequences. We will then use our understanding of the path of education to analyze Heidegger's description of personal rebirth, angst, and authenticity, and compare this with the path of religious education.

Next, we will look at the religion of *Judaism*. We will see that the Jewish mind connects God with the actions and rituals that are contained within the Jewish Torah. Thus, while Christianity associates religion with believing, Judaism associates religion with doing. We will compare the Christian focus upon the individual with the Jewish emphasis upon the group and the country and see how this contrast can be used to explain many of the theological differences between these two religions. We will examine the Jewish Exile in the light of Heidegger's path of authenticity through angst. We will come up with a cognitive definition for 'chosen race' and apply this to Judaism. Finally, we will see that Christianity and Judaism emphasize different aspects of the path of education and that the two concepts of 'holy book' and 'chosen race' make it difficult for one to extend into the realm of the other.

Finally, we will address the topic of *aliens*. We will see that the human mind contains two symmetrical circuits and that the influence of the physical body and the physical world causes these two circuits to appear as concrete thought and abstract thought. We will suggest that if the human mind were placed within a mirror-image body that inhabited a mirror-image universe, then concrete thought and abstract thought would switch places, and when one explores this possibility, one comes up with predictions that sound like popular descriptions of angels and UFOs. We will examine the mental reason why science debunks alien life and why humans are terrified of alien encounters. We will see that even if such creatures do not exist, human specialization combined with legislation has a natural tendency to create an artificial environment in which concrete thought and abstract thought *do* switch places. We will examine what would happen if these two modes of existence were to come into contact with each other, and we will see that the Industrial Revolution has created a technical world of science and technology in which these two modes of existence partially coexist. We will end by looking briefly at the religious implications of alien life.

In the appendices, we will flesh out the theory of mental symmetry in several directions that are only covered briefly in the main text. We will describe technical thought in more detail, we will analyze math as an example of abstract technical thought that is based in concrete technical thought, and we will analyze music as an illustration of concrete technical thought that has been expanded by abstract technical thought. We will use the theory of mental symmetry to explain Piaget's theory of childhood development, Maslow's hierarchy of needs, Kohlberg's stages of conscience, and Foucault's three epistemes. We will show that the theory of mental symmetry can be used to clarify a number of the current unexplained problems in philosophy. Finally, we will do a detailed analysis of Quine's book, *The Web of Belief*, translating almost every concept in his book into the language of mental symmetry.

I would like to end this introduction by discussing the matter of sources, references, and methodology. Normally, a researcher will read the literature extensively before attempting to do original research. For me, the process tended to occur in reverse. My research began in the 1980s with an extensive study of personality types and character traits. My brother, Lane Friesen, gathered much of the initial data from analyzing biographies, while I focused upon neurology and psychology. This biographical data is available in written form and I will occasionally be referring to it in order to expand or illustrate some concept.[1] The result of this research into personality was what I call the 'diagram of mental symmetry', which was originally used as a psychological model to describe human behavior. Because my brother and I collaborated for so many years, it is difficult to recall exactly who came up with what idea during this time. However, if I distinctly remember that my brother worked out a concept, then I have acknowledged Lane Friesen in a footnote.

In the summer of 2008, I realized that this model made it possible to perform a comprehensive analysis of religious thought. This book is the *seventh* version of my original attempt to put this analysis down on paper. During the third try I focused upon highlights and attempted to write as simply as possible. That version has been the most successful so far. The main feedback that I received from academia about the third version was a concern over my lack of references. Obviously, when one is doing an original analysis of religion based upon an original model of the mind which is itself based upon original research into personality traits, then most of the references have long been forgotten. Therefore, I took some time to compare my work with the research of others, and the result is this book. The number of references may still not be that numerous, but instead of merely referring to others, I have actually expanded my cognitive model in order to include as an integral part the findings of individuals who played major roles in defining a field of thought.

I know that academic researchers tend to regard Wikipedia as beneath their dignity, but I found it to be quite useful as a starting point, because the articles are usually comprehensive and well written. The Internet Encyclopedia of Philosophy was very helpful, and I also spent a considerable amount of time at the Stanford Encyclopedia of Philosophy, though occasionally I found the writing to be too academic. For most general topics, I simply 'googled' the subject until the concepts became clear.

---

[1] I have some information on my website at http://www.mentalsymmetry.com and Lane Friesen has published several books which contain extensive personality descriptions based upon biographical data. His current edition is titled *All Sorts of People: Ordered Complexity.*

My knowledge of Christianity comes from years of Sunday School (back when that still existed) combined with a year of Bible School. Over the years, I have had a fair bit of exposure to Judaism and I have checked my conclusions with those who are more knowledgeable than I. For many years I played in a string quartet with a couple who is immersed in Israel and Judaism and we had many long conversations on the way to and from musical gigs. I also speak Hebrew passably. My knowledge of Buddhism comes from books on Zen and meditation that I read back in the 1980s combined with eight years of recent encounters with Buddhism in South Korea (which gives one quite a different picture). As for Islam, I have read through the Quran three times, so I am at least familiar with the theological source.

I should emphasize that I will not be approaching philosophy as a philosopher. I will not be quoting from the experts in order to determine precisely what a certain philosopher said or referring to the various interpretations of a certain school of philosophy. Instead, my purpose is to examine philosophy in order to discover cognitive principles. I will assume that the philosopher is studying his mind and that he is attempting to describe this process as accurately as possible. Thus, by analyzing philosophy, one can come up with clues as to how the mind functions.

Likewise, I will not be approaching theology as a theologian. I will not be quoting from the commentaries or referring to various theological schools of thought. Instead, my purpose is to examine theology in order to discover cognitive principles. I will assume that the theologian is trying to develop his mind and that he is attempting to describe this process as accurately as possible. Thus, if one analyzes theology, one can come up with clues as to how the mind functions.

These are not trivial distinctions. Instead, they lead to major differences in methodology, which I will describe here and explain later on in the book. Let us look first at philosophy. As far as I can tell, the main purpose of philosophy today is to explore abstract thought in a rigorous manner. (The following statements apply primarily to analytical philosophy. Continental philosophy is more all-encompassing and also less rigorous.) In contrast, I find philosophy useful because it examines human thought—the same topic which I am studying.

As we shall see later, rigorous logic emerges when one particular cognitive module takes control of thought and begins to operate the mind in a technical manner that limits the expression of other cognitive modules. Thus, the *method* of rigorous logic cannot be used to understand the *entire* mind for the simple reason that rigorous logic is only one aspect of mental functioning. Saying this another way, it is not possible to use a method which *limits* mental functioning to analyze *all* mental functioning. Since my goal is to decipher how the *entire* mind functions, one must use an approach that is *consistent* with how the entire mind functions, which means using a form of logic which is looser than rigorous logic.

This explains why the philosopher can become annoyed when I present him with my cognitive model. I may be using his data, but according to him, my thinking is muddled and unclear. However, I suggest that the real problem lies with the analytical philosopher, because he is attempting to extend the use of rigorous logic beyond where it can be legitimately applied. When he does so, then he ends up concluding, like the young Wittgenstein, that the method of philosophy cannot say anything meaningful about the topic of philosophy. The answer, I suggest, lies in distinguishing between the method of philosophy and the topic of philosophy. The method of analytical philosophy is useful for developing clear thinking and for exploring the limits of rigorous logic. The topic of philosophy is human thought, which includes rigorous logic as well as other modes of thought. When philosophy examines aspects of human thought that are not rigorous, then it must respect the way in which human thought operates and not insist upon attempting to squeeze all of human thought into a subset of human thought. If this conclusion seems unwarranted, then please read the appendix on Willard Quine's *Web of Belief*, because he says the same thing.

So, if the method of rigorous logic is not available, then what is left? Must all logic be thrown out of the window? Not at all. I suggest that a number of logical tools still remain. Let me begin, though, with one tool that cannot be used.

Karl Popper says that a theory which cannot be disproven is not a scientific theory. This intellectual standard makes sense when using technical thought to analyze physical phenomena—though as Thomas Kuhn states, it usually takes far more than one or two counterexamples to topple a scientific theory. However, how can one disprove a general theory of human thought, when many of the facts upon which it is based are vague and uncertain?

The answer is to use lesser methods of disproving a theory, methods that are specifically tailored to studying the mind. First of all, we know from neurology that every normal person has a similar brain, and that people use the same brain to study different topics. Presumably, the mind, however it relates to the brain, functions in a similar manner. Thus, by combining completeness with consistency, we can error-check a theory of the mind.

What is the most complete record of human thought? A library. It contains the entire range of topics that the human mind has covered and describes all of the mental approaches that the human mind has taken. Obviously, it is not possible to analyze every book in the library. But, it is possible to look at every genre and analyze every major topic. Any valid theory of the mind must be able to explain every genre and deal with every topic.

Thus, in the spirit of Popper, if a theory of human thought does not, will not, or cannot explain certain 'books in the library', then that theory must be incomplete. For instance, using a strictly scientific approach to build a theory of the mind is incomplete because science only deals with the 'books in the library' that contain physical and natural data. Similarly, an economic theory of humanity is incomplete because economics refuses to analyze the subjective emotions that lie behind value, effectively ignoring the 'romance section'. Similarly, the method of theology is incomplete when it fixates upon a single holy book and focuses upon the 'religious section'. Notice that I said *incomplete* and not incorrect. An incomplete theory of human thought may still be valid within the section of the library that it addresses.

How can one test if a partial theory is valid? By comparing one partial theory of human behavior with another. If two theories of human behavior *independently* come up with similar observations, then this increases the probability that these two theories are accurate, especially if these two theories approach the mind from completely different perspectives.

Notice that completeness and independent confirmation both require an interdisciplinary approach. Comparing one theory with another means becoming competent in more than one discipline, while evaluating the entire library is the antithesis of the specialization that is found today. These days, the typical person who wants to earn a PhD has to apply technical thought to a narrow area of expertise for several years. Thus, he ends up acquiring skills which are not optimized for deciphering the mind, for he learns the wrong method and uses the wrong focus. Hyper-specialization may be appropriate for incremental development in a technological society, but it does not help when analyzing human thought.

Rigorous logic and specialization appear to be mentally bound together, for when the mind enters its technical mode of operation, it also restricts thinking to a limited context. Thus, when a person who uses rigorous logic reads this book, not only will he regard my thinking as muddled, but he will also accuse me of being scattered in my writing and jumping continually from one topic to another. But that is precisely how one performs error-checking when studying the *entire* mind. One dare not stick to a single topic but instead one must jump from one seemingly unrelated topic to another in order to demonstrate completeness and independent confirmation.

Moving further, I suggest that there are also *internal* tests which can be applied. If all human thought is being carried out by the same type of brain, then a model of human thought will have to be *internally consistent*. If a model of the mind explains one aspect of thought in one way and another aspect in another way, then something is wrong with that model. For instance, it is currently popular in the West to make a mental distinction between objective and subjective thought. But, both of these are being generated by the *same* mind, which means that similar mental mechanisms must be responsible for both objective and subjective thought.

In addition, a model can be internally evaluated by its *simplicity and elegance*. If a model of the mind has to develop a specialized set of terms that can only explain thought through the use of complicated and convoluted language, then it is either incomplete or inaccurate. That is because normal words were developed as a result of people using their minds in normal circumstances. Thus, it should be possible to describe how the mind functions by using normal words. It may be necessary to define these words in a more technical manner, but one should not have to throw away normal words, define an entirely new vocabulary, and adopt a writing style that is turgid and incomprehensible. I suggest that Martin Heidegger is an example of someone who violates this rule of simplicity and elegance, and we will take a few pages to look at his philosophy in the final chapter.

Another internal test which can be applied is that of *mechanism.* The mind does not just sit there. It *functions.* Therefore, a theory of the mind must go beyond mere description to explanation. In other words, describing a personality trait is good, but outlining a mental mechanism or a mental process which could generate that trait is better. In addition, the mechanism that is being described must be an *internal* mechanism. For instance, the theory of evolution is sometimes used to provide an *external* mechanism for the development of certain mental traits. However, this does not explain how the mind *itself* generates that trait. In order to be regarded as a *theory* of the mind, an explanation must be a theory of the *mind.*

What makes analyzing the mind different than any other topic of study is that the mind is studying *itself.* This leads to both an advantage and a difficulty, which I will introduce by referring to Immanuel Kant. This will also illustrate what happens when the *method* of rigorous logic is followed too far. Kant's transcendental argument says that the mind naturally interprets sensory information using categories such as space and time. The philosopher who is following rigorous logic reads this and concludes that it is impossible to know anything about external reality.

However, I suggest that the philosopher is making a *cognitive* error. The mind *is* capable of using rigorous logic to examine a self-contained subset of thought—which describes what the philosopher is doing. But, the mind does not use rigorous logic when evaluating sensory data. Instead, it uses multiple sensory modes, it correlates, it compares, it fills in the blanks, it looks for simplicity, and then it jumps to a conclusion based upon this limited information. All of this mental processing is being applied to sensory data which has only partial certainty. Using these non-rigorous methods, the philosopher, like any other normal human being, manages to navigate his way through physical reality quite successfully. But when the philosopher uses rigorous logic to examine his non-rigorous human existence, he declares that rigorous logic must apply, even though it doesn't apply and even though the philosopher himself seldom applies rigorous logic to normal life. And when the philosopher discovers that rigorous logic doesn't apply, he concludes that knowledge is impossible, even though he still continues to function quite adequately as a human being on the basis of partial knowledge.

In contrast, the person who is using attempting to decipher the mind looks at the transcendental argument of Kant and sees a *clue.* Kant is actually using 18th century language to describe how the mind works. He is saying that the mind contains a mode of processing which analyzes sensory data for spatial information as well as a mode of processing that looks for temporal information. The theory of mental symmetry refers to these processing modes as *cognitive modules.* Kant came up with a number of assumptions which he says that the mind implicitly makes. He then generalized from there to a list put together by Aristotle. Kant's personal observations fit in well with the theory of mental symmetry. Aristotle's list does not. In addition, Kant's transcendental argument actually makes it *easier* for the mind to understand itself, because it will naturally think in ways that are consistent with its functioning.

Let us turn our attention now to the concept of Kant that makes it more *difficult* for the mind to understand itself. That is Kant's concept of *radical evil.* In simple terms, this says that people naturally behave in ways that are inconsistent in order to gain personal advantage in specific situations. In addition, we know that the human mind has a strong tendency to *rationalize*, coming up with semi-logical theories that legitimize inconsistent behavior. But, we have just concluded that one of the tests of a valid theory of the mind is internal consistency, especially between one mental context and another. Thus, we conclude that radical evil combined with rationalization will limit the mind's ability to understand itself.

And that brings us finally to the *theologian.* I mentioned earlier that I will be discussing theology, but not from the viewpoint of a theologian. We have just seen that understanding the mind is a tricky business, because one has to overcome a natural tendency towards emotionally driven self-deception. Religion deals with 'truth' that applies to the subjective, and it talks a lot about 'knowing oneself' and 'overcoming personal self-deception'. Any sincere attempt to truly understand the mind will be interested in not only analyzing but also applying such principles.

When the typical theologian examines subjective truth, he focuses upon the *source* of this truth. He turns to holy books, commentaries, respected religious leaders, religious traditions, historical context, and doctrinal schools of thought in order to determine precisely what is being said by a certain passage or meant by a specific doctrine. For, he wants truth in its purest form without any of the distortion that Kant's radical evil combined with rationalization produces.

However, what the theologian tends to neglect is the greatest source of distortion of all, which is his *own* mind. What is the point of discovering ultimate truth if I myself am unable to hold on to it? If one wishes to analyze accurately how the mind functions, then one must face the human tendency for emotionally driven self-deception and rationalization, and come up with a method of overcoming this cognitive barrier.

That explains why I ended up writing a book on theology. My initial goal was *not* to study theology. Instead, I simply wanted to understand how the mind works. But I knew that this meant pursuing a path of brutal personal honesty. Thus, I was forced to deal with topics such as radical evil, self-deception, and rationalization. As I continued on my path of self-discovery, I realized that the cognitive principles which I was discovering were being taught as religious doctrine. That is when I began to approach religious doctrine from a cognitive perspective.

I then came to the realization that not all religious doctrine is equally useful. From a cognitive perspective, religious doctrine seems to deliver what it claims, for if one applies these principles personally, then one experiences the cognitive results that are promised. But some of these doctrines are like magic tricks, because they stop working if one attempts to analyze how they work. In contrast, other doctrines work even better when subjected to cognitive analysis, and treating them as magical incantations lessens their mental effectiveness.

This provides us with a cognitive method for error-checking religious doctrine. If a religious belief only works when it is *not* rationally understood, then one can conclude that it is an inferior doctrine which has at best temporary validity. However, if a religious doctrine works better when presented in rational terms, then one can conclude that it is a superior doctrine that is worth holding on to.

One final point. It may appear at first glance that the development of functional brain scanners makes all of these principles obsolete, but I suggest that this is not the case. Neurological knowledge has doubled or tripled since I began learning about the brain back in the 1980s, and this knowledge provides invaluable clues and constraints about how the mind functions. However, because science focuses upon physical phenomena, it will only see the part of the mental 'iceberg' that sticks up above the surface of physical reality. The principles that I have described are still required to work out the rest of the 'iceberg'. And because the mind is still studying itself, the researcher will tend to see only the part of the 'hidden iceberg' which he himself is personally acknowledging.

This principle is illustrated by current work on the thalamus, a subcortical brain region that corresponds to one of the cognitive modules used in this book. Neurologists now know the wiring and the structure of the thalamus reasonably well. They also know in fair detail how the lateral geniculate nucleus works, because this is the subregion of the thalamus that works with *physical* data: It transfers visual input from the eyes to the cortex. However, when it comes to the *rest* of the thalamus, then researchers can only suggest that it probably functions like the lateral geniculate nucleus, but they do not know exactly what this means, because the rest of the thalamus handles internal mental traffic. In other words, researchers know that an 'iceberg' exists, and they understand the part of the 'iceberg' that lies above the surface. The approach that I have outlined allows one to fill in the rest of the picture by using information from other sources to look 'below the surface of the water'.

Addendum

I read through this book in 2019 in order to see how well the content has stood up over time. I have corrected typos and fixed grammar mistakes, but the ideas appear to be sound. The biggest change is that mental symmetry can now be mapped onto neurology with much greater precision, and a paper on neurology can be accessed using the doi: 10.13140/RG.2.2.28982.24641.

I now refer to abstract technical thought and concrete technical thought and tend to avoid the cryptic labels Ci and Cp, but that is just terminology. Finally, this book recognizes the importance of the Scientific and Industrial Revolutions and mentions R&D, but neglects to mention the Consumer Revolution, which started around 1880.

Theology
is Cognitive Science
in Emotional Garb

Technical Definitions

In this book, I have assigned technical definitions to a number of terms. Because these definitions may not match up precisely with common usage, I include a brief list of defined terms here:

Abstract Thought: Thought that looks behind sensory information for general principles.

Analytical: Left hemisphere thought that deals with time, sequences, and order in a linear fashion.

Associative: Right hemisphere thought that works with objects, space, and random connections.

Belief: The label which Perceiver thought attaches to a Perceiver fact.

Ci: (Intellectual Contributor) A technical circuit of abstract thought controlled by Contributor mode.

Concrete Thought: Thought that deals directly with specific items in the physical environment.

Confidence: The mental ability to handle emotional pressure without falling apart.

Cp: (Practical Contributor) A technical circuit of concrete thought controlled by Contributor mode.

Emotional 'Belief': Belief that is the result of emotional pressure overwhelming Perceiver mode.

Emotional 'Knowing': A fact that is regarded as true because of emotional 'belief'.

Fact: A set of connections that describes the relationship between various elements within either a situation or a sentence.

General Theory: A set of symbols upon which Teacher mode can continue to concentrate; a paradigm.

Love: Mutually beneficial personal interaction; an emotion that is associated with Mercy generality.

Mercy Emotion: An emotional label that is attached to memories of experiences.

Natural Law: A sequence that one finds occurring repeatedly, consistently, and inescapably in the physical world.

Object: A collection of Mercy items held together by Perceiver connections.

Paradigm Shift: Using a different general Teacher theory to explain the same Perceiver facts.

Personal Identity: The set of mental networks within Mercy thought upon which I can continue to focus.

Righteousness: The Server skill of acting in a way that is consistent with general Teacher understanding.

Teacher Emotion: Emotion that comes from order-within-complexity.

Technical Thought: Cp, the concrete technical circuit, and Ci, the abstract technical circuit.

Truth: A set of connections that is repeated in many places and many times.

Cognitive Styles

The cognitive model used in this book began with a system of cognitive styles. Each cognitive style is conscious in a specific cognitive module and emphasizes the traits of that cognitive module. Here is a very brief description of each of the seven cognitive styles (which also illustrates the behavior of the corresponding cognitive module):

Contributor: Aware of opportunities; naturally creative. Enjoys feeling confident; hates losing control. Bothered by small talk and small expenses. Gives to the needy; competes with peers. Good at developing and implementing plans; naturally attracted to business.

Exhorter: Loves excitement; thrives in emotional crisis. Learns lessons from life; wants theory that is practical. Naturally clumsy; must learn fine motor control. Tends to exaggerate; remembers how things 'should have been'. Superb imagination; capable of daydreaming. Hates being frustrated or bored.

Facilitator: Mixes and balances between people and situations. Has many acquaintances; connects people and projects. Naturally good at science and psychology; likes experimenting. Likes to organize; enjoys working on committees. Adaptable; hates feeling muddled. Finds it easy to observe and analyze himself and others.

Mercy: Continually reminded of experiences and feelings; learns mainly through experience. Aware of non-verbal speech. Emotionally sensitive; emphasizes love. Good at developing novel solutions. Hates insincerity. Able to focus on a situation.

Perceiver: Continually reminded of facts and beliefs. Good with maps and spatial connections. Believes in truth and justice. Able to work with uncertain information. Hates hypocrisy. Finds it hard to concentrate. Tells puns and 'one liners'.

Server: Lives in the present; learns practical skills. Better at doing than delegating. Emotionally stable unless the future is uncertain. Trustworthy; finishes jobs. Likes to converse; can be verbose with friends. Has a quiet dignity and elegance.

Teacher: Emotionally driven to learn general theories; wants to know why. Rejects uncertain information. Able to concentrate on intellectual work. Capable of original thought. Remembers words and speech but has a poor memory for experiences.

✸ 1. Two Emotions and a Diagram

A trough with a semi-circular cross section is being filled with water. The trough is 4 meters long and the cross section has a radius of 50 cm. Water is flowing into the trough at a rate of 0.05 cubic meters per second. After 20 seconds, how fast is the level of water rising in the trough?

This type of question has to be solved by using calculus and is known as a 'related rates' type of problem. Don't worry. This is not a book about calculus. Instead, my goal in presenting the problem was to provoke an emotional reaction. How did you *feel* when reading that paragraph? As we all know, the average person does not enjoy mathematics. That is why I immediately followed the calculus problem with an assurance that this is not a mathematical book, for I want the average person to *read* this book and not just set it aside after encountering the first paragraph. True, the topic of math will occasionally come up, but we will keep the equations very simple. That is because we want to focus upon what is happening within the mind.

And when we look at the mind, we notice that some people actually *enjoy* doing math. Give them the description of the water flowing into the trough and they immediately think of the steps that are needed to solve the problem, take out a pencil, and write out the appropriate equations. I know, because I am one of those people. In fact, I taught high school calculus for several years. And for those people, I have included an appendix in which math is discussed at length.

So, what can we conclude? First, the average person dislikes math. Second, some people enjoy math. Let me add to this a third point: It is actually possible to learn to enjoy math. Like most delicacies, it is an acquired taste. It may take time to acquire an appreciation for math, but it is possible.

My students would often ask me why they had to study mathematics. In response, I generally told them that the goal of teaching math is to wake up a part of the brain. For many students, this aspect of mental processing never fully activates. But when this form of thought does kick in, it is as if a light suddenly goes on inside. You explain a concept, the student's face brightens and he says, "Teacher, I understand." It is these 'aha' moments which bring joy to the instructor. They can occur in all subjects, but they exhibit themselves in purest form when teaching abstract topics such as mathematics. For, once this internal light goes on, then the attitude of the student changes; instead of detesting the subject, he starts to enjoy it.

Notice that we have been talking about emotions, pleasure, and joy. It may seem strange to equate math with emotions, but something has to motivate mathematicians and other types of theoreticians. Think, for instance, of another type of theoretical activity which the average person abhors: bureaucracy and the filling out of forms. I may enjoy math, but I certainly do not derive pleasure from filling in all of the boxes with the relevant information, standing in line in front of the appropriate counter, and then waiting for my information to be processed.

But some people must enjoy this, because they make a career out of being part of a bureaucracy. Math and bureaucracy have a lot in common. Math has equations; bureaucracy has forms. Both involve words, numbers, and symbols. Mathematical equations have variables into which one plugs the appropriate numbers; forms have blank spots into which the correct information is entered. Equations are solved; forms are processed. And, the relationship between these two fields is not just theoretical. In fact, for hundreds of years, a person who performed mathematical calculations was known as a computer. When working out complex mathematical problems, calculations would be broken down into steps and these various steps would be assigned to a group of human computers to solve, reducing math to a bureaucratic like system of filling out forms and passing these forms on to the appropriate individuals.

But imagine working as a human computer or a government clerk. What would keep a person going emotionally? Where would the pleasure be? The human brain gives us a clue. Neurologists have discovered that there is a part of the brain, known as the *amygdala*, which is responsible for processing emotions. But the brain contains *two* of these emotional processors, one in the verbal left hemisphere and the other in the experiential right hemisphere, and researchers are beginning to realize that these two emotional processors do not function in the same way.

My research into human personality began back in the 1980s with a study of personality types.[2] When we began our research, it was immediately obvious that one cognitive style strongly emphasizes experiences and emotions. But the brain contains *two* amygdalae and not just one. One is located in the non-verbal right hemisphere, while the other is in the *verbal* left hemisphere. This suggested to us that there is *another* cognitive style which functions emotionally, using *words*. And, when we examined the behavior of the cognitive style associated most with words, we discovered feeling and emotion.

And so, let me introduce you to these two cognitive styles, which we will call Mrs. Mercy and Mr. Teacher. The Mercy person, like any cognitive style, can be either male or female, but the emotional traits are most prominent in the female mind, whereas they tend to be more subdued in the male. And, when I talk about Mr. Teacher, I am not referring to an instructor in a school. Instead, I am describing a person with the cognitive style that combines words and emotions.

If these labels bother you, then I am afraid that it is too late to do anything about it now. We have been using them for thirty years and we actually got them originally from

---

[2] My brother, Lane Friesen, began the research into cognitive styles and I initially worked as his research assistant. However, much of the initial work on the theory of mental symmetry, as well as all of the recent work, was done by myself.

someone else. Besides, they have the important attribute of each starting with a different letter of the alphabet, so instead of writing Teacher, Mercy, Perceiver, Server, Exhorter, Contributor, and Facilitator, one can write T, M, P, S, E, C, and F. And when one uses letters, then one does not have to feel disturbed about labels. After all, one of the most famous men in the world is called Charles Philip Arthur George, and that does not seem to bother him, even though his first wife called him Philip Charles Arthur George at their wedding ceremony when saying her wedding vows.

We will begin with Mrs. Mercy, because the type of emotion that she uses is the familiar kind. She lives in a mental world of experiences, each colored by an emotional label. Whenever she encounters a new experience, it reminds her of similar events from her past and these memories influence how she responds to the present. So, if she goes to a restaurant and finds a hair in her food, then from then on this unpleasant experience will come to mind when dining out at any similar eating establishment. She is not naturally attracted to theory. Instead, when you tell her some abstract principle, she will ask you *who* you are talking about, and when you describe a theory to her, she will ask you for a practical example. She remembers birthdays and special occasions and likes to be remembered on her birthday, for this triggers pleasant memories. When cooking, she does not usually follow the recipe. Instead, the tasting spoons multiply, and that is where the true genius of the Mercy person lies. She—or he, is better than anyone else at coming up with unorthodox solutions which work. Occasionally, these unconventional methods backfire spectacularly, but most of the time they are both original and successful.

Yes, I know. We *all* think this way. To some extent this is true, for all of our brains have Mercy modules. But, the Mercy person *lives* in that module; it defines her identity. Those who are Mercy persons or who have spent some time with Mercy persons know the difference between having a Mercy module and being conscious within that module. It is like the difference between the native speaker of a language and someone who has merely studied the language as an adult.

Before we move on to Mr. Teacher, let me make some technical remarks. The theory of mental symmetry suggests that human intelligence is composed of seven interacting mental modules, and that each of these modules corresponds to a specific region of the brain. Of course, these are not the only mental modules. It is also possible to break up each of these seven modules into more specific sub-regions, and there are also brain regions that handle the coordination between various modules, as well as modules that process sensory information. However, this cognitive model of seven interacting high-level modules really seems to work. I have used this approach to examine numerous fields of thought over a period of two decades, and it has not failed me yet.

Stated in the briefest of terms, the Mercy module uses *associative* processing with *concrete* experiences, applying a label of *emotion* to each experience. For instance, finding a hair in some food is a concrete experience with an emotional label. When a person enters a similar restaurant, the Mercy module associates to the unpleasant encounter with the hirsute hash, making the current meal also feel unpleasant.

Let us move on now to Mr. Teacher. He is a strange creature, for he loves theory. While others are chatting about the day's events, he is sitting quietly in the corner pondering the recent financial crisis and the impact that this will have upon the global economy. As a child, he often has a socially inappropriate grin on his face. His sister may be crying because he is killing ants with a magnifying glass, but he is fascinated by the process of amplifying light and the effect that this has upon living organisms, and it is this fascination which produces the grin. Others may view his emotional pleasure as socially inappropriate, but he regards the feelings of 'normal' people as intellectually improper, for he is convinced that emotion should be related to understanding. And so he distances himself socially from the irrational emotions of others in order to contemplate matters of significance, such as the course of the global economy. For, what is the point of conversing about what a person ate for lunch when the fate of the entire world is hanging in the balance?

I think that we can agree that most people do not think this way. Teacher thought must be developed, and the Teacher person appears to be the rarest of the seven cognitive styles. But I assure you that the Teacher person definitely exists. Now that we have been introduced to Mr. Teacher, let us describe how Teacher emotion works in more formal terms.

But first a small matter of verbal housekeeping. We have introduced two different types of thought, which I will refer to as *modules* or *modes*. A module is a mental structure which functions in a specific manner. When referring to the functioning of the Mercy module, I will talk about Mercy *thought*. The two modules that we have introduced so far both function emotionally. When talking about Teacher emotion or Teacher feeling, I am referring to the emotion that is being produced by Teacher thought within the Teacher module. And, when I say Teacher *person*, I mean the person who has the cognitive style of Teacher. In such a person, the Teacher module is conscious while the other modules are subconscious.

Cognitive Style	Other Modules that can be Seen
Mercy	None
Teacher	None
Server	Teacher
Perceiver	Mercy
Exhorter	Teacher and Mercy
Contributor	Perceiver, Server, Exhorter
Facilitator	Some Awareness of All Modules

Each cognitive style is conscious in only one cognitive module, but some cognitive styles can also 'look through a window' into adjacent modules. This secondary awareness is summarized in the table above, and is also shown by the lines and arrows on the diagram of mental symmetry.

Now that we have that out of the way, let us return to our description of Teacher emotion and compare it with Mercy feelings. First, Teacher emotion comes from *generality*. It thinks about mathematical theorems and the state of the global economy. Mercy emotion, in contrast, is very specific. It remembers your birthday and prepares a special gift just for you. Teacher emotion does not care about someone's birthday, for a birthday has no universal significance. It is just a single occurrence in a vast array of similar events. However, if one could come up with some general conclusions about how birthday purchases affect the shopping patterns of people, then this might attract the attention of Teacher thought. But general statements about shopping patterns do not interest Mercy thought, for they are far too impersonal. Instead, Mercy thought wants to know whether or not the young boy living next door received the red bicycle that he requested for his twelfth birthday.

Second, Teacher emotion is primarily *verbal*. Here we must be careful, because speech also has a Mercy component. Teacher thought deals with the words themselves and what they mean. Teacher mode feels good when a complex concept can be conveyed using precisely the right technical term. Mercy thought, in contrast, notices *how* the information is conveyed, the tone of voice that is being used, and the accompanying body language. Using more technical language, Teacher thought deals with *verbal* speech, whereas Mercy thought is aware of *non-verbal* communication. Normally, the verbal component of speech is dominant, and we ignore whether a lady is speaking with a soprano voice or a man is talking with a basso profundo. But when *singing*, then tone of voice plays the dominant role and the words themselves play second fiddle.

Third, Teacher emotion is *unnatural*. Everyone knows about Mercy feelings. Even babies know that food feels good and hunger feels bad. One does not have to attend school to learn that some experiences are pleasant and other experiences are unpleasant. However, whenever I tried to tell my students that theory and understanding can also feel good, most of them would look at me as if I was a strange person from another planet. Why is that? The deficiency does not seem to lie in the human brain. We all have two brain hemispheres and two amygdalae.[3] Presumably these are all equally capable of functioning. Instead, the problem seems to lie with the physical body.

Does a newborn baby wake up in the middle of the night and yell out '$E=mc^2$'? No, but a baby does awake when everyone else is sleeping and start crying because of unpleasant experiences. In other words, the physical body teaches the mind about Mercy experiences and Mercy feelings by filling the mind with experiences that feel physically

---

[3] This may give the impression that a brain scan of a typical person will reveal that only the right amygdala is operating. The right amygdala is more active in children. But Teacher emotion comes from order-within-complexity, which can appear in many different forms. The left amygdala appears to be sensitive to order-within-complexity. However, one cannot prove this, because neurology describes Teacher emotion, but it does not recognize what it is describing.

pleasant or unpleasant. As a result, the Mercy module is the first to develop in the infant mind. It is only later that the Teacher module begins to grasp the concept of words, and even more time elapses before Teacher thought in the child starts to formulate rules of grammar. As for using Teacher thought to construct general theories, that ability often does not emerge until college. Meanwhile, Mercy mode has experienced infancy, childhood, and adolescence, each with its own complete world of Mercy experiences and personal emotions. For those who want more details, one of the appendices contains an analysis of Piaget's stages of development. But don't try reading it now, because it includes a number of concepts that we have not yet discussed.

So what exactly *is* Teacher emotion? I have mentioned that it is general, verbal, and unnatural, but what exactly makes Teacher mode feel good? I suggest that it is the presence of *order-within-complexity*. When there are many individual items and these items all fit together, then Teacher mode feels good.

For instance, suppose that I want to give someone directions to my house. The complicated way is to give a detailed set of instructions: "Turn left at the first light. Go six blocks. Then turn right. Continue straight for 2.5 km." Pretty soon my head is swimming and I don't know whether I have gone five blocks or seven blocks. This type of complexity does not bring joy to Teacher thought.

I live near Vancouver in Canada, which uses a much simpler and more elegant way of determining location. All avenues run west to east and all streets run north to south. In addition, most of the main roads have numbers instead of names. All of the road numbers and all the house numbers begin from Main street in Vancouver in the west and the American border in the south. Thus, 16th Avenue is sixteen blocks north of the American border, while 320th Street is 320 blocks east of Main street. So, if my address is 28012 30th Avenue (a number I pulled randomly out of the air), people know that my house is located 280 blocks east of Main street and 30 blocks north of the US border.

It is that sort of order-within-complexity which brings emotional pleasure to Teacher thought, because it covers the complexity of many addresses with the general umbrella of a simple system. But I suspect that many of the people living in the Vancouver area are not aware of this system, and that illustrates one of the main reasons why the average person is also not aware of Teacher emotion. Mercy emotion reaches out and grabs you by the throat—quite literally. When your body needs something to drink, you can feel that your throat is parched. Teacher order-within-complexity, on the other hand, seems to lie around the corner and just behind the bend. If one looks for it, one will discover it, but it is also possible to live in the middle of Teacher order-within-complexity and never realize that it exists. But, once this order-within-complexity is discovered, then the Teacher emotion comes as well. However, even then it is noticed more often by its absence. There may be a period of intellectual delight when the metaphorical light first goes on, but that is generally followed by the steady background glow of a general understanding—an emotional glow that is easy to take for granted.

However, if the structure ever falls apart, then the lack of order-within-complexity will be felt quite keenly.[4]

Because the way in which Mercy emotions are produced is so different than the way in which Teacher emotions are generated, one would think that it would be easy to distinguish one from the other. However, that is not the case. Emotions are emotions, regardless of their source, and Mercy emotions feel the same as Teacher emotions. Therefore, if I want to tell whether an emotion that I experienced was produced by Mercy mode or by Teacher mode, then I have to analyze the situation which provoked the emotional response in order to determine the cognitive source of that feeling. And as we shall see in a later chapter, the mind finds it rather difficult to perform cognitive analyses when confronted with strong emotions.

As a result of this inherent uncertainty, those who work with general theories and Teacher emotions generally try to protect intellectual thought by using *external* methods to avoid personal experiences with their subjective Mercy emotions. This explains why most intellectuals insist upon being objective and why they lock themselves up in ivory towers of higher learning and limit their intellectual interaction to colleagues who share similar theories. They are attempting to avoid being 'contaminated' by Mercy feelings. It is very easy for subjective bias to affect intellectual thought. When a researcher comes up with a new general theory, this brings him emotional pleasure. But, what is the *source* of this feeling? Does it come from the Teacher emotions of a general understanding, or is the theory triggering an emotional memory of a situation within Mercy thought? The most obvious solution is to isolate Teacher thought as much as possible from the wider world of Mercy experiences and Mercy emotions.

The research of Sigmund Freud provides a classic example of confusing Teacher emotion with Mercy feelings. Freud came up with general theories of human personality, and he thought that his theories were universal and that they explained behavior in *all* people. But the colleagues of Freud looked at his ideas and observed that many of Freud's supposedly universal concepts were in fact based in specific traumatic memories from Freud's childhood. Thus, much of the emotion which Freud thought was coming from Teacher thought was actually being provided by Mercy thought.

That is one reason why a scientist subjects his new theories to *peer review*. Because Mercy emotions are based in *specific* experiences, then the Mercy feelings felt by one individual should be different than the Mercy feelings felt by other researchers. Therefore, if one

---

[4] Kant divides emotions into the four categories of the agreeable, the beautiful, the sublime, and the good. Translating this into the language of mental symmetry, the *agreeable* relates to Mercy emotions and physical sensations. The *beautiful* occurs when specific items produce Teacher feelings of order-within-complexity. The *good* describes the Teacher feeling that occurs when some situation is a specific example of a general Teacher law. The *sublime* is a combination of Teacher pleasure and Mercy pain, because it generates Teacher feelings of generality but also threatens the integrity of Mercy mental networks. For instance, watching an atomic explosion feels sublime.

person evaluates the theories of another person, then between the two of them, they should be able to recognize their personal biases and be able to eliminate them.

But, what if the topic *itself* involves Mercy emotions? Then there is no easy way of emotionally distilling the theoretical Teacher essence from the subjective Mercy noise. And the scientific system—as a whole—will instinctively reject the topic, because it contains Mercy feelings. Peer review will not work because all of the researchers will share the *common* personal bias of distrusting Mercy feelings. That is what happens when one attempts to study subjective topics such as God, religion, and personal identity. One must find *other* methods of separating rational understanding from personal bias, and one will have to do this research *outside* of the university system.

So how can one protect oneself from emotional self-delusion when working outside of the university system? One way is by continually corroborating one's research with the findings of others. If the facts that one finds are consistent with what is being discovered by others, then one is subjecting one's research to a form of peer review. The other way is to develop the principles that are contained within this book. Much of what is described in the rest of this volume was discovered as a result of my personal quest to avoid deceiving myself, and the end result was a general Teacher theory that appears to be free of personal Mercy bias.

The Diagram of Mental Symmetry

I have suggested that Teacher thought uses words to construct general theories. The general theory described in this book takes the form of a *diagram*, known as the diagram of mental symmetry, which contains several words connected by various lines and arrows. Starting from this diagram, we will be using logic to analyze how the human mind forms an image of God and how this internal image relates to personal identity.

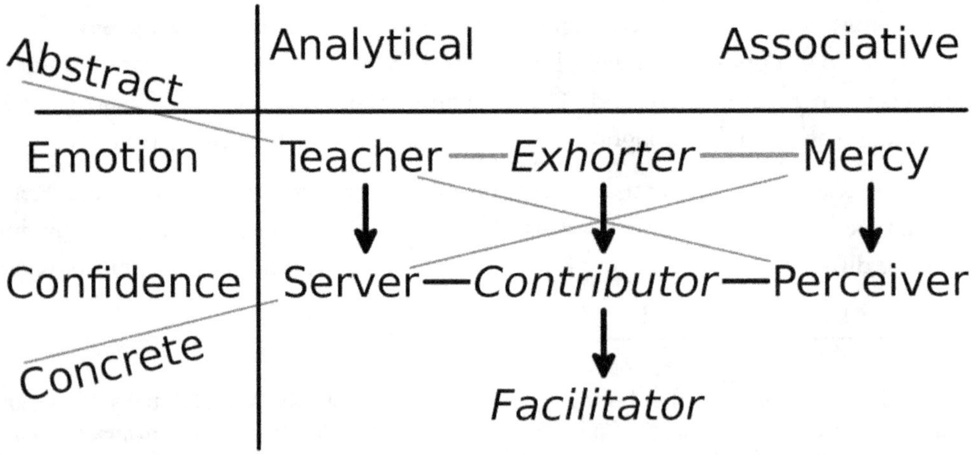

No, it is not that complicated. As far as diagrams go, it is rather simple and obvious. In fact, it is possible to explain much of this diagram using simple common sense. Think first of the external world. Every item that exists has a *nature* and it has a *location*. For instance, the spherical object in front of my face is an apple; that is its nature. The apple is on the table next to the banana; that is its location. The same division appears at atomic levels: Here is an oxygen atom; that is its nature. It is connected to two hydrogen atoms; that is its location, though things start to become vague at this scale because of the Heisenberg uncertainty principle. If I look at the apple in more detail, then I can focus either on nature or location. The apple is red and crispy with a waxy appearance. That describes its nature in more detail. But, I can also use location to determine that there is a stem on top of the apple and that there are seeds in the middle of the apple. I can then zoom in on one of the seeds and make further statements about either nature or location.

The right hemisphere of the brain deals with objects and experiences. The two mental modules that are located within the right hemisphere are shown on the *right* side of the diagram of mental symmetry: Mercy and Perceiver. Mercy mode, with its emotional processing, examines the *nature* of items, whereas Perceiver mode looks for connections that describe the *location* of items: The apple is connected to the banana because they are physically close together. However, this is not a solid connection, because when you move the apple, the banana stays put. In contrast, the connections between the seeds and stem of the apple are reasonably solid. Pick up the apple, and the seeds and the stem both follow along. These solid connections allow Perceiver thought to conclude that the apple is an object—all of its parts are solidly connected, therefore they belong together.

Why are Perceiver and Mercy modes *associative*? Because the physical world is already filled with objects. Therefore, these two mental modules can associate between one pre-existing object and another. And because the world already consists of objects, Perceiver and Mercy thought are both primarily *input* modules. They observe the physical world and come up with mental conclusions.

Move now to the left side of the diagram, and the two mental modules called *Teacher* and *Server*. These are located in the left hemisphere of the brain, which deals with time and sequence. These two modules handle physical *output*. What sort of output is the physical body capable of producing? It can *talk* and it can *do*. That's basically it. Teacher mode generates speech, and Server mode produces action. Teacher thought is the *talking* module, and Server thought is the *doing* module. And the one-way linear nature of time means that I have to say something one word at a time, and I am forced to carry out a sequence of actions one step at a time. That is why Teacher and Server thought are *not* associative. It is easy to associate mentally from one item to another when they are all laid out in front of me. It is far more difficult when the objects pass in front of my vision one item at a time and I have to keep mental track of what happened when.

As I mentioned in the introduction, those of you who have read Immanuel Kant may recognize that we have arrived at a version of his transcendental argument. Kant pondered why the world is full of objects and why sequences exist, and he concluded that it is our minds which divide what we see into distinct objects and arrange events into sequences. In essence, I am taking Kant's conclusions and turning them into mental modules: Why do we see objects in the external world? Because our minds contain a mental module known as Perceiver thought which looks for objects. Why do we perform actions as sequences? Because the mental module of Server thought works with sequences and actions.[5]

So, are there *really* objects in the physical world? Does time *really* exist? We cannot know for certain, because the human mind is only capable of thinking in terms of space and time, but if we examine the evidence, it does appear that our physical bodies, our minds, and the physical world have all been constructed in a way that makes them work together very well. Thus, we can be *reasonably certain* that a real world exists which is composed of space and time.

Look now at the middle column of the diagram. These three mental modules are responsible for operating the mind, using a three-step process that follows the arrows from the top of the diagram to the bottom. First, we *want*, then we *decide*, then we *implement.* The Exhorter module generates the *desire*, the Contributor module makes the *decisions*, and the Facilitator module is in charge of *implementation.* Think, for instance, of the apple and the banana sitting on the table. I look at the fruit and I realize that I am hungry; that is a desire. Desire comes from emotion: I examine the apple and it looks good—the Mercy module gives it a positive emotional label; this emotion leads to a desire within the Exhorter module (notice the line on the diagram connecting Mercy to Exhorter). Desire is followed by decision: Should I eat the apple or the banana? Should I consume it now or wait for a while? Does the fruit belong to me or do I need to take it to the store counter and pay for it? After decision comes implementation: Suppose that I decide to eat the apple now; this then determines the context for my subsequent behavior. When thought or behavior is limited to adjusting parameters within a specific context, then the Facilitator module takes charge.

Summary

One of the things I learned when teaching in a high school is that whenever one comes to the end of a chapter then it is time for a review. So, we will be finishing each chapter in this book with a review of what was covered.

We began the book with a simple calculus problem in order to introduce the concept of intellectual emotion. We realized that emotion comes in two forms: Experiences can be emotional, but so can theories; it feels good to eat ice cream, but it also feels good to understand a theory. These two types of emotions are contrasted in the following table:

---

[5] I first analyzed these findings of Kant many years after I had worked out the nature of the various mental modules. I was surprised to find out how well his observations fit into the theory of mental symmetry. Evidence suggests that Kant had the cognitive style of Perceiver person.

	Mercy Emotion	Teacher Emotion
Appears as	A label attached to an experience	Order-within-complexity
Related to	Specific events	General theories
Based mainly in	Experiences	Words
Acquired	From the physical body	Through education and observation
Begins	At birth	As order-within-complexity is noticed

I then suggested that the mind is comprised of seven interacting modules, and that two of these modules function emotionally. The Mercy module works with experiences; the Teacher module handles words and theories. One can also divide *people* into seven different categories or cognitive styles. Each cognitive style has the same brain and the same seven interacting modules, but each cognitive style is conscious in only one of these seven modules. The Teacher person, for instance, is conscious in Teacher mode.

I then pointed out that there is no easy way of distinguishing Mercy emotion from Teacher emotion. Instead, emotion feels the same, regardless of its source. Therefore, when people work with theories, they often use external means to block off Mercy emotions so that their theoretical judgments are not colored by personal bias.

However, it is not possible to follow that option when dealing with emotional topics such as God, religion, or personal identity. Therefore, the only other alternative is to learn how to think clearly and rationally in the presence of subjective emotion.

Words can be used as building blocks to construct general theories within Teacher thought. These theories may take the form of logical premises or mathematical equations. The general theory contained within this book places words within a *diagram* which I call the diagram of mental symmetry. This diagram describes the seven mental modules that make up the mind and indicates the manner in which they interact. There are two *associative* modules: Mercy mode examines the *nature* of experiences; Perceiver mode looks at the *connections* between experiences. There are two *analytical* modules: Teacher mode works with *speech*; Server mode produces *action*. Finally, there are three mental modules that *operate* the mind: Exhorter mode generates desire, Contributor thought produces decision, and Facilitator mode handles implementation.

One final point. If this book is to make sense, then the diagram of mental symmetry *must* be memorized in order to have a clear mental picture of what each cognitive module does. We will be introducing these modules one by one so this should not be that difficult. At the beginning of the book, we will only be looking at the function of one or two modules. But as the book progresses, we will be dealing with increasingly complicated mental circuits. Having a clear mental picture of the diagram will help to reduce confusion.

✵ 2. Mental Networks

They had been married for over forty years. He knew exactly how she would respond in most situations, and at times she would start a sentence and he would be able to finish it for her. When she passed away, he felt as if something inside of him had died as well. He would come across something in the newspaper that she would have found interesting, he would start telling her about it and then realize that she was no longer there to respond to what he was saying. He visited her gravesite regularly, carefully placing some of her favorite flowers on the tombstone. He would stand there quietly for a while, or sing a song that she had enjoyed. Others found his graveside visits morbid, but for him they were a celebration of life, for one of the things that kept him going emotionally was the belief that someday, somehow, they would meet again. Until then, he tried to keep alive the memory of his beloved wife.

I think that you get the picture. While I am not referring to any specific couple, I am sure that everyone has encountered or read about situations like this. In this chapter, I would like to address the question of what it was exactly that perished. Obviously, the wife died physically. That we know for certain. But that was not the only life that was affected. In addition, something was 'alive' within the mind of the husband, and that something continued to exist even after his wife had physically passed away.

Mental life is one of those emotional topics which researchers like to avoid, and cognitive scientists have always been rather dismissive of any explanation which requires the presence of some internal 'little man' or *homunculus*. But when we examine situations such as the passing away of some loved one, then we conclude that the wife not only lives alongside her husband, but in some cognitive manner, she also lives *inside* of her husband's mind.

So, I would like to present a *cognitive* explanation for how the mind represents people and other living creatures, one which does not require the presence of homunculi. We will examine the mental framework in this chapter and add some more details later on. However, if we are going to come up with a cognitive explanation, then that will require looking at some theory.

I have mentioned that emotional experiences are stored within Mercy thought, and that whenever the mind encounters a new experience or thinks of some experience, related memories will come to mind. For instance, if I go to dine at a certain franchise of eating establishments, Mercy mode may be reminded of the delicious chicken fajita dinner that I had at one of their restaurants, but it might also be reminded of the incident in which I took a forkful of hash browns and a blonde hair emerged from the midst of the hash.

That is the nature of associative Mercy memory. It brings to mind related experiences, especially those with emotional overtones.

If enough similar emotional memories connect together, then a different mental effect will emerge. Instead of existing as isolated incidents, the memories will 'band together' and begin functioning as an integrated mental unit. The field of Artificial Intelligence is talking about a similar concept when it refers to the idea of *neural networks*. Individual Mercy experiences can feel good or bad. This describes normal emotion. Emotional memories that combine to form a mental network will produce a completely *different* type of emotion that is related to integration and fragmentation. Whatever builds or strengthens a mental network will produce the *hyper*-pleasure of integration, whereas anything which threatens to tear apart a mental network will lead to the *hyper*-pain of fragmentation. Any mental network that continues to be suppressed will gradually fade and start to fall apart, leading to the hyper-pain of impending fragmentation. On the other hand, any event that activates and enhances a mental network will lead to feelings of hyper-pleasure.

Before I lose my audience, let me tie this down with an example. Think of a simple habit, such as clearing my throat. The emotions that are associated with such a habit are fairly minimal. A sore throat is not very painful and clearing my throat produces only a modicum of pleasure. However, if this action is repeated enough times, then it will form an integrated mental network, and as a mental network it will try to express itself when triggered. As long as I continue to clear my throat, then the integrity of this mental network will not be threatened. But, if I try to *stop* clearing my throat, then this mental network will eventually fade to the point where it starts falling apart. I will then feel a very strong need to clear my throat. If I do, then the unpleasant feeling will immediately go away, because the mental network has been activated. However, if I suppress the urge to clear my throat, then the hyper-pain of impending mental fragmentation will increase until the intensity is almost unbearable, and may even express itself as a sense of dread or panic. If I persist in suppressing the urge, then eventually it will go away, indicating that the mental network has fallen apart and no longer functions as a set of integrated memories.

If one did not know any better, one might consider such a mental network as being alive, because it looks and acts like a 'little man' or homunculus living within my mind. However, it is basically a network of emotional memories that generates emotions based upon its status as a unit, and this causes it to exhibit many of the attributes that are characteristic of life. Like any living organism, it must be treated as a single unit, and it responds with strong feelings of self-preservation if its integrity is threatened. A mental network requires a 'diet' of compatible information, and if it is 'fed' experiences that contradict the network, then this will eventually threaten the integrity of that network. In biological language, it must be 'fed' food and not poison, and it will get 'hungry' and eventually 'starve' and 'die' if it is not 'fed' properly.

With that in mind, think back to the example at the beginning of this chapter. Obviously, the husband's emotional memories of his wife have integrated within his mind and have formed a mental network within Mercy thought. Whenever he encounters an emotional situation that brings to mind one of these emotional memories, then this triggers that mental network and it becomes mentally *activated* and reminds him of his wife and how she behaves. Every time his wife responds in a familiar fashion, then her behavior *reinforces* the mental network within his mind that represents his wife and 'feeds' it.

For instance, suppose that his wife likes hazelnut-flavored instant coffee. This preference will form one emotional element within the mental network that represents his wife. Whenever he sees hazelnut-flavored instant coffee in the store, the mental network representing his wife will come to mind. Similarly, every time that his wife drinks a cup of hazelnut-flavored instant coffee, her behavior will reinforce this mental network. Now suppose that she decides to drink black tea instead. Her behavior will be inconsistent with the mental network within his mind that represents her. If she exhibits many unfamiliar traits, then he will feel that he no longer knows his wife, which will threaten the integrity of the mental network that represents her. Finally, if she dies, then all of the emotional experiences that used to lead to emotional responses from his wife will now be followed by different results. For instance, if he buys hazelnut-flavored instant coffee, this will no longer be followed by experiences of her opening the tin and having a cup. If he leaves her room untouched as a shrine, then this will help to prevent new and incompatible experiences from altering the memories of his departed beloved. Similarly, if he visits her grave and leaves a tin of hazelnut-flavored instant coffee, then he is helping to reinforce the mental network that represents his wife.

Does this mean that life after death is purely a figment of the imagination? Not necessarily. I am simply suggesting that it is natural for the mind to believe that life continues after physical death, regardless of whether or not this actually occurs. I am also suggesting an alternative way of defining the term 'natural'. If one bases one's definition of 'natural' upon what happens in the external world, then obviously life after death will be rejected as unnatural because one does not see people physically rising from the dead. However, if 'natural' means what occurs naturally within the *mind*, then the concept of life continuing after physical death becomes quite natural, and it is mentally unnatural to believe that life ceases at the moment of physical demise.

Justin Barrett, one of the researchers in the field of the cognitive science of religion, makes this argument in his book *Why Would Anyone Believe in God*: "When someone dies, our living-thing describer tells us that the person will never function biologically again. Our ToM [Theory of Mind], however, keeps generating predictions about what the deceased thinks, believes, hears, and feels. Such continued production of predictions and inferences may be especially likely when it is someone close to us who has died."

Hyper-emotion and Normal Emotion

Let us return to the topic of mental networks. Before we continue, though, I should point out that since we are dealing with an emotion which goes beyond normal emotion, the examples that we use will tend to be emotionally intense.

The hyper-emotion that is produced by a mental network appears to be independent of normal feeling. Emotion comes from the pleasantness or unpleasantness of individual experiences. Hyper-emotion is produced when these experiences come together to form a functioning unit. This means that it is possible to build a mental network out of painful experiences. Think, for instance, of a phobia. I may be terrified of spiders, but if I have a number of unpleasant encounters with arachnids, then these emotional memories will come together to form a mental network within Mercy thought, and that mental network will respond with hyper-pain if its integrity is threatened.

This leads to a situation where a person is emotionally caught between a rock and a hard place. On the one hand, the individual with arachnophobia cannot face spiders, because they are emotionally terrifying. On the other hand, he cannot let go of his fear of spiders, because digesting this phobia leads to the hyper-pain of mental fragmentation. If that conclusion seems strange, then think of the individual who is in an abusive relationship. If that person stays in the relationship, then he experiences pain. But, if he leaves the relationship, then he will be treated in a way that is inconsistent with his mental network, leading to hyper-pain. It is common for such individuals to remain within an abusive relationship even if this means suffering substantial personal pain.

The number of emotional experiences that is required to create a mental network depends upon the emotional intensity of those experiences. If a situation is sufficiently traumatic, then it will only take one or two incidents for that situation to begin 'living' within my mind. For instance, compare pre 9/11 America with post 9/11 America. The events of that single morning brought something to life within the mind of the average American which changed the social fabric of an entire nation. Even now, a decade after this event, that situation still continues to 'live' within most American minds as a mental network. In contrast, it may take years of living within a house before the emotional memories associated with that location integrate within Mercy thought to form a mental network.

The hyper-emotion that is produced by a mental network takes precedence over normal emotion. Given a choice between feeling bad and falling apart, the average person would rather experience mental pain than go through the hyper-pain of mental fragmentation. We already saw this illustrated by the abusive relationship. An even more extreme example can be found in the barbaric practice of female circumcision. This is a painful, personal procedure whose sole purpose is to limit a women's ability to experience pleasure. However, in some societies, female circumcision helps to define culture. Thus, the hyper-pleasure of maintaining this practice takes precedence over the intense emotional pain that this procedure creates. Stated in blunt terms, parents would rather mutilate their daughters than have a mental network that is associated with their culture fall apart.

Obviously, not all mental networks are emotionally that intense. Think, for instance, of the habit of clearing my throat. The emotional memories associated with that action have formed a mental network within Mercy thought which becomes activated when my throat starts to itch. However, the hyper-pain that must be endured in order to break such a habit is not that intense. But if one responds emotionally to such a mental 'molehill', then these intense feelings can turn the 'molehill' into an emotional mountain. Suppose, for instance, that a person is ashamed of some small habit and that he goes to great lengths to hide it from others or to disguise its appearance. This will turn an innocuous mental routine such as counting numbers in one's head or touching objects as one passes them into a full-blown psychological compulsion or obsession, protected by major levels of hyper-emotion.

Exhorter Mode

A distinction must be made between a mental network and the desire or urge which comes from that mental network. In order to explain this point, I need to introduce another cognitive module, known as *Exhorter* mode. Networks of emotional experiences reside within the Mercy module; they emerge when emotional Mercy memories combine into groups. But the desire or urge that is associated with such a mental network is being produced by the Exhorter module, which operates 'next door' to Mercy thought. This interaction between the Mercy module and the Exhorter module is indicated on the diagram of mental symmetry by a line connecting Mercy with Exhorter. Extensive research has been done in neurology on the topic of desire and addiction, and how these mental urges are being generated by a brain circuit that is linked to the neuromodulator *dopamine*. I suggest that the dopamine based desire circuit is the brain location for the mental module of Exhorter thought.[6]

You will notice on the diagram of mental symmetry that Mercy, Teacher, and Exhorter all lie on the row that is labeled *emotion*. While Exhorter drive or excitement is based in emotion, it differs from emotion in two very important ways: First, emotion finds pain unpleasant and pleasure pleasant. Exhorter excitement, in contrast, finds both pain and pleasure equally stimulating. Second, while emotion remains constant over the long term, excitement gets bored. In psychological terms, Exhorter thought will habituate to any situation which remains static and does not change.

Now consider our example of arachnophobia. Mercy mode does not want to think about spiders because these experiences are unpleasant. But Exhorter mode finds traumatic memories of spiders exciting, and Exhorter mode is the mental module that provides drive and motivation for the mind. So, whenever unpleasant memories combine to form a mental network within Mercy thought, then thinking about these memories will bring pain, but the mind will also feel driven to focus upon these painful memories because they are exciting, just as a person finds it exciting to go on a terrifying roller coaster ride.

---

[6] I am not sure exactly how far the Exhorter module extends within the brain. The relationship between the dopamine circuit, located within part of the basal ganglia, and Exhorter thought is quite solid. But I do not know which *other* related brain regions, if any, also belong to the Exhorter module. In a similar vein, evidence suggests that Serotonin is related to the function of Contributor mode and Noradrenaline to the function of Facilitator mode.

Theory of Mind

So far, our examples may have given the impression that a mental network is something undesirable. However, this is definitely not the case. For instance, emotional experiences from my physical body will combine within Mercy thought to form an emotionally potent mental network, and this mental network provides the basis for my sense of self-preservation. Contemplating any action which might harm me physically will bring to mind the mental network that represents my physical body and will trigger strong hyper-emotions of impending mental fragmentation. Thus, the mental network that is associated with my physical body acts as an internal advance warning system, emotionally repelling my mind from behavior that might produce physical harm.

Similarly, every person with whom I have had significant emotional interaction will be represented within Mercy thought as a mental network, for emotional experiences involving that person have come together within my mind and they function as an integrated unit within Mercy thought. When I interact with such a person, the mental network within my mind that represents that person will respond emotionally to my behavior, allowing me to mentally predict what that person would enjoy and what would that individual would hate. In addition, if I consider behaving in a way that would harm the personal integrity of that individual, then the corresponding mental network within my mind will respond with hyper-pain.

This provides a cognitive explanation for what researchers refer to as *Theory of Mind*—the mental ability to guess or predict what is happening within the mind of another individual. This term came up a few pages back in a quote regarding mental life. Theory of Mind states that whenever I interact with another person, I am continually trying to determine how he is responding internally to what I am saying or doing: Does he find my words interesting? Does he know something which I am trying to keep hidden? Does he want to change the topic or talk with someone else? As I speak with this person, Mercy thought within my mind will associate to various emotional mental networks, and these mental networks allow me to guess how the other person is responding to my words. Obviously, if I am friends with the person with whom I am conversing, then my primary guide will be the mental network within my mind that is composed of emotional memories that involve that person. However, other mental networks may be triggered as well. For instance, I may have a more general mental network within Mercy thought that contains memories of gestures and mannerisms made by people who are trying to be polite but who are secretly bored with what I am saying.

Mental networks also explain why interacting emotionally with another individual makes it harder for me to hurt that person. It is relatively easy to harm or destroy a person if he does not 'live' within my own mind, for as far as I am concerned, he is a thing and not a person. Thus, there is no emotional trauma in killing an enemy when this means pushing a button and having some nameless foe crumple silently in the distance. It is much harder to pull the trigger when the victim is a living, breathing entity who screams when shot and who cries 'mommy' as he twitches in agony on the floor and gasps his last breath.

And by using these emotionally charged words, I am probably triggering a mental network within the mind of the reader. That is why euphemisms are used in activities which deal with the well-being of people. If I talk about 'killing a 21 year old youth', then I will mentally trigger an emotional mental network and have to deal with the hyper-emotions that threatening this network produces. But if I refer to 'taking out a target', then no mental network within Mercy thought will be activated.

But located adjacent to Mercy mode and its mental networks is the Exhorter module, and Exhorter mode can find excitement in the Mercy hyper-pain of impending self-destruction. War may be hell, but it is also exciting, as is climbing up a sheer cliff without a rope where one misstep means certain death. If a person continues to perform such behavior, then his repeated actions will *themselves* form a mental network. Notice the progression: Emotional experiences from my physical body create a mental network that mentally represents my physical existence. Threatening this mental network with fragmentation produces an emotion of hyper-pain. Exhorter mode can find excitement in this painful hyper-emotion, driving the individual to act in ways that threaten his personal existence, such as climbing cliffs, racing cars, or fighting in wars. If the person physically survives for long enough, then the emotional memories generated by threatening personal existence will themselves form a mental network—which will attract the attention of Exhorter thought. The person has now become addicted to the mental network formed out of emotional experiences that involve threatening his personal existence. If he performs death-defying actions, then this mentally threatens the integrity of the emotional network that represents his physical body. But if he does *not* perform death-defying stunts, then his behavior is inconsistent with the mental network that has formed as a result of his life-threatening acts, threatening the integrity of *that* mental network. It is possible for such an individual to reach the state where normal life is mental death, and he is only fully alive mentally when he is on the verge of physical death.

So far, we have focused upon the hyper-*pain* that results from mental or physical fragmentation. It appears that worship and sex are the primary means of generating hyper-*pleasure*. When I worship an object or individual, then a form of mental integration is occurring between the mental network that represents myself and the mental network that represents my object of worship. Similarly, when two people have sex, then the mental networks that represent their physical bodies are experiencing the hyper-pleasure of integration. This provides a cognitive reason for placing sex within the framework of a long-term relationship. For, if hyper-pleasure is produced by *integration* and hyper-pain is generated by *fragmentation*, then it makes sense that sex can only continue to produce hyper-pleasure if the relationship between the partners remains integrated and does not fragment.

Moving on, as far as I can tell, a mental network does not actually activate itself. Instead, it has to be triggered in some way in order to become activated. For instance, suppose that I love dark chocolate and that pleasant experiences involving cocoa butter and cane sugar have formed a mental network within Mercy thought. As long as I do not see any chocolate, read or hear anything that reminds me of chocolate, associate mentally to the concept of chocolate, or experience any hunger pangs which cause me to think of chocolate, then my mental network involving my love of chocolate will not be activated. Of course, we all know that choosing not to think about something is not so straightforward. That is because *trying* not to think about something generates intense emotions, and Exhorter thought is attracted by strong feelings. Thus, the more I try to suppress a certain memory, the more I am driven to focus my attention upon it.

Tourette Syndrome

The mental futility of attempting to defeat an Exhorter urge is illustrated by *Tourette syndrome*, a medical condition. The person with Tourette syndrome feels driven to make verbal noises or perform motor tics, usually involving the head, neck, or face muscles. These various tics are internally sensed as an urge that can be temporarily suppressed, but which must eventually be expressed. Once the movement is carried out or the sound is spoken, then the urge will temporarily go away. On the other hand, if an urge continues to be suppressed, then when the urge is finally released, the tic will have to be carried out more extensively before the urge goes away.

Some individuals with Tourette syndrome also feel driven to say words or make gestures that are dangerous or socially inappropriate, consistent with the suggestion that Exhorter thought finds emotional pleasure and emotional pain equally stimulating. Forbidden words and expressions have strong negative emotional labels. Therefore, they lead to Exhorter urges and desires.

Only a small portion of the population suffers from this disorder, but I suggest that Tourette syndrome is an abnormal expression of a normal mental circuit. Exhorter mode generates urges and desires within every mind. The individual who attempts to suppress his Exhorter urges will find that this is a self-defeating task, because the emotional intensity that is generated by fighting an urge simply makes that urge more compelling for Exhorter thought. And there is also a relationship between Exhorter urges and novelty. Expressing an Exhorter urge causes it to lose its novelty and become boring for a while. However, if an urge is suppressed, then it will gradually stop being boring and become regarded again by Exhorter thought as something novel and exciting.

It is the relationship between Mercy emotions and Exhorter excitement that makes a mental network appear to be 'alive'. An isolated emotional memory is like a piece of paper, 'sitting silently' on the desk, waiting to be picked up. If one chooses to ignore this piece of paper, then there are no emotional repercussions. A mental network, in contrast, behaves more like the cat walking between one's legs that is pestering for attention and complaining that it wants to be fed. If one examines the situation in detail, then it appears that a mental network still has to be triggered in some way and that it does not actually appear out of nowhere. And it also appears that the mental 'pestering' is actually being done by Exhorter thought as it attempts to fixate upon this mental network. However, if one combines Exhorter urge, Exhorter novelty, and Exhorter habituation with the hyper-emotion that a mental network is capable of producing, then the behavior that is generated definitely feels 'alive'.

For instance, think of a network of emotional memories involving chocolate. As long as I can avoid thinking about chocolate—or anything that is related to chocolate—then this mental network will not be triggered. But once it comes to mind, the Mercy emotions will lead to Exhorter desire, and any attempt to suppress this set of memories will increase the strength of this Exhorter urge. In the short term, the only way to remove this Exhorter desire is to 'feed' the mental network, which in this case means physically feeding my face with chocolate. In the long term, if an urge is suppressed for long enough, then the mental network will eventually fall apart and the urge will go away. What generally happens is that after fighting the urge for days or weeks, a person will wake up one morning and not think about the subject. He will only realize that the desire is gone when something else causes him to think about the subject and he notices that the urge which used to drive him is no longer present.

The Cognitive Science of Religion

There is a new field of research known as the cognitive science of religion. One of the basic concepts of this field is the discovery that the mind has a natural tendency to ascribe a personal cause to events. Thus, if I hear a noise in the middle of the night, my mind will instinctively think that some person or animal caused this noise. Cognitive researchers refer to this mental behavior as an ADD, or Agency Detection Device. In this book, I will refer to it as the Agency Detector.

The basic argument of the cognitive science of religion is that the mental mechanism of the Agency Detector leads naturally to a belief in God. The logic goes as follows: If I see some event, my internal Agency Detector will automatically attempt to determine who or what caused that event. If I cannot come up with any natural agent or natural cause, then I will conclude that the event was caused by some supernatural being. In a later chapter, I will be using a variation of this argument to begin our discussion of how the mind constructs an internal image of God.

But remember that cognitive scientists do not like explanations which involve the concept of a homunculus. Simply *describing* the Agency Detector without suggesting how it might function leaves one with the impression that there is a tiny little trigger-happy man with his hand on a big red button living inside the brain who is continually scanning the world for the presence of intelligent agents. However, if one wants to work out how the mind *detects* the presence of life, then it appears to me that one must first step back and address the more basic question of how the mind *represents* the presence of life, which is what we have attempted to do in this chapter.

And once one understands how the mind *represents* life, then it becomes possible to come up with a cognitive explanation for 'the fleeing caveman', the scenario that lies at the heart of the field of the cognitive science of religion. Imagine that a person lives in the jungle and is surrounded by wild animals. Obviously, he will have unpleasant encounters with ferocious beasts, and these emotionally painful memories will form mental networks within Mercy mode. Now suppose that he hears a twig snap in the middle of the night. This will provoke a cascade of mental events: First, a mental network involving emotional memories of wild beasts will be triggered within Mercy thought, bringing to mind a collection of emotional associations involving stalking, leaping, clawing, tearing limb from limb, and consuming. The intense negative emotions contained within this mental network will immediately attract the attention of Exhorter thought. But this mental association will be quickly followed by an even stronger mental leap. What will be triggered next is the mental network associated with the physical body, and that mental network will start 'screaming' the hyper-pain of impending personal demise, causing Exhorter thought to fixate upon the emotional crisis of personal survival. The intense feelings that are involved will ensure that all of this occurs within a fraction of a second: Mercy thought, guided by Exhorter urges, will go from 'sound of twig' to 'behavior of wild animals' to 'I am about to be killed'.

Summary

And after your heart stops pounding, let us make the mental jump from talking about wild animals to summarizing the contents of this chapter. We began by looking at the death of a loved one. When a close friend of mine dies, then I am actually faced with two different kinds of death. Obviously, a *biological* death has occurred, because the physical body of my friend has ceased functioning. But within my own mind, something dies as well. That leads us to the question of how life is represented within the mind.

I then introduced the concept of mental networks and hyper-emotion. Individual Mercy experiences can feel good or bad. However, when a number of related emotional memories come together, then they will form a mental network and begin to function as an integrated unit. Anything that threatens the integration of this mental network will create a hyper-pain of fragmentation, while anything that leads to further integration will generate feelings of hyper-pleasure.

We then observed that the mental network within the mind which represents another person will remain in existence even when that person physically passes away, which led us to pose the question of whether is it is 'natural' to believe in life after death. The answer depends upon one's definition of the word 'natural'. From a biological perspective, life after death is unnatural; from a cognitive viewpoint, though, it is natural to believe that life continues after physical death.

We then looked at mental networks in more detail. The number of emotional experiences that it takes to form a mental network depends upon the strength of the emotions. If a situation is sufficiently traumatic, then a single event may suffice to create a mental network. But, if the feelings are weak, then it takes many reoccurrences for a mental network to form.

Hyper-emotion is independent of normal feeling, and these two types of feelings can oppose one another. This is what happens when emotionally painful experiences combine to form a mental network. Facing these memories will lead to pain, whereas questioning these memories will generate hyper-pain. Hyper-emotion takes precedence over normal emotion. Given a choice between feeling bad and falling apart, a person will usually choose to feel bad.

We then introduced the Exhorter module, which is responsible for generating mental drive, excitement, and energy. Exhorter mode has access to memories within Mercy mode and creates urges based upon memories with strong emotions. Exhorter urges are strengthened by novelty. A lack of change, in contrast, leads to boredom and an absence of mental energy. Mental networks provide potent emotional input for Exhorter mode, which transforms these strong feelings into personal drives and motivations.

The most important mental network is the one is that is initially programming by emotional experiences from the physical body. Preserving the integrity of this mental network generates a person's sense of self-preservation. Similarly, the mental networks that a person has which represent other individuals motivates him to preserve their personal integrity as well. Mental networks also allow a person to predict the emotional behavior of other individuals, leading to what psychology calls *Theory of Mind.*

It is possible for Exhorter excitement and mental networks to interact in a manner that actually threatens personal integrity. If Exhorter mode finds excitement in life-threatening experiences, then these emotional experiences will themselves form a mental network which can only be preserved by continuing to behave in life-threatening ways.

Worship and sex are related to hyper-pleasure, because in both cases, the mental network that represents a person is becoming integrated with another mental network. This hyper-pleasure will turn into hyper-pain if the mental relationship becomes fragmented.

We then turned our attention to Exhorter thought and the relationship between Exhorter urges and Mercy emotions. Suppressing an Exhorter urge is counterproductive, because the effort involved in suppressing a desire creates potent emotions which will end up making the Exhorter urge stronger. Tourette syndrome provides an extreme example of what happens when a person attempts to suppress Exhorter urges.

Finally, we looked at the field of the cognitive science of religion and I suggested that mental networks provide a cognitive explanation for what is referred to as ADD, or the Agency Detector Device.

✵ 3. Truth and Objects

Do you remember when you first found out that your parents were not omniscient? I recall very little from my childhood, but I distinctly recall asking my father a question and instead of receiving an answer, being informed that fathers do not know everything. This must have been a shock to my system, because that memory fragment has remained with me. Fast forward a few years to the teenage years and an entirely different scenario emerges. The typical teenager no longer thinks that his parents are all-knowing. Instead, he is often convinced his parents are imbeciles who know nothing.

What happened? Do parents automatically lose their cognitive abilities when their offspring reach a certain age? Obviously, the parents have not changed. Instead, the shift has occurred within the mind of the teenager.

Imagine what it is like to be a small child. Adults loom over you like giants; they have the power to pick you up with a single hand and they shield you from danger; they have lived seemingly for eons and they provide for all of your physical needs. In the previous chapter, we examined how the mind represents people: Emotional experiences that are related combine to form mental networks within Mercy mode. In most children's minds, emotional memories of father and mother form the largest mental networks, because parents are the primary source of emotional experiences for the child.

The situation is quite different for the teenager. Physically, he is now the same size as his parents, he has lived for a while, and he is now stronger than many adults. In addition, he has spent a lot of time outside of the home, interacting emotionally with his peers. These emotional memories have created a new set of mental networks within Mercy thought that are oriented around peers instead of parents.

Two Definitions of Truth

If we step back and analyze this situation, we can come up with one possible definition for truth: Truth is determined by individuals who have emotional significance within Mercy thought. If the emotions associated with a person are positive, then whatever that person says will be accepted as true. In contrast, if Mercy thought feels negatively about that individual, then anything spoken by that person will be rejected as false. Stated more simply, someone who is good is right; someone who is bad is wrong; people who lack emotional significance do not affect truth.

Thus, the child believes everything that he is told by his parents because they have great emotional significance within his mind. When he becomes a teenager, then his peers take on this role. Because he assigns positive emotional significance to his peers, he believes whatever his friends tell him. In contrast, he now regards his parents in a negative light, and so he concludes that anything they tell him is wrong.

Is truth so simplistic? For many people, yes. For instance, a significant portion of the American populace is convinced that political truth boils down to the question of Republican versus Democrat. Anything spoken by a Republican is true, while anything that comes out of the mouth of a Democrat is false—or vice versa. In a similar vein, the fundamentalist religious believer is often convinced that truth comes exclusively from adherents to his religious faith. Similarly, I have met professors who are equally certain that truth only comes from individuals who have the emotional status of a doctoral degree, or that anything which is associated with a religious mindset is by definition false.

However, it is also possible to approach truth from the viewpoint of *common sense*. Suppose that I ask you to define a tree. You may respond that trees have wooden trunks, roots which extend into the ground, and green leaves that gather sunlight. If I ask you how you *know* that this is *true*, you will not refer me to any expert or guide me to any political party or religious dogma. Instead, you will tell me that you know what a tree is because you have seen many trees, and every tree that you encountered had the same combination of trunk, roots, and leaves.

Thus, it is possible to come up with another definition for truth: Truth is based in repeated connections. If certain elements consistently go together, then that combination describes a fact which is true. Because we have all had numerous encounters with trees, rocks, cars, bananas, books, and myriads of similar items, we all share a set of common facts that are based in common sense. Science formalizes this method of knowing by searching for physical connections which are repeated.

Notice that only one of these two methods of defining truth actually *deals* with truth. If truth is based in connections that are repeated, then the only way to test a fact is by *examining* that fact to see if the connections which it describes actually *are* repeated. For instance, suppose that I say that overeating leads to obesity. In order to prove this connection, I have to observe obese individuals and see if they have been overeating, and I have to look at those who are overeating and see if they are gaining weight.

In contrast, when truth is determined by people with emotional status, then there is no need to examine the facts. One does not have to 'open up the letter' and read the message. Instead, one can judge the veracity of the contents simply by glancing at who the letter is from. Thus, we can conclude that when the method of repetition is being used, the mental module that analyzes facts is functioning, whereas when emotional status defines truth, then the mental module that works with facts is *not* functioning, but instead it is being overruled by the mental module that determines emotional status.

Let us state this in more formal terms. The Mercy module remembers experiences with emotional labels. The Perceiver module looks for connections between experiences that are repeated. This was mentioned back in the first chapter when we introduced the diagram of mental symmetry. If the emotions associated with some person or experience are sufficiently intense, then Perceiver mode will be overwhelmed and will not be able to function. Instead, any facts or connections that are contained within this *specific* situation will be accepted blindly by Perceiver thought as truth.

For instance, suppose that parents tell their little children about Santa Claus. The emotional status that memories of parents have within a child's Mercy module will mesmerize the child's Perceiver module into knowing that Christmas is connected with a fat man with a long white beard wearing a red suit.

When Perceiver belief is determined by emotional status, then it is possible to know instantly both *what* is true and *that* it is true. That is because Perceiver mode is being mesmerized into accepting with absolute certainty the connections of a *specific* situation. This mental mechanism provides the basis for many kinds of belief. For instance, 'love at first sight' occurs when the emotions of a single encounter between him and her mesmerize Perceiver thought in their minds into knowing beyond a shadow of a doubt that 'they belong together forever'. Similarly, if I have a scary encounter with a thief in a back alley, then the trauma of that incident may convince Perceiver thought that all back alleys are connected with personal danger. Or, in a similar vein, if a major terrorist attack occurs on 9/11, then people may become convinced that all swarthy foreigners who speak with strange accents are terrorists. Finally, if I assign sufficient emotional status to a group of experts, then I will accept their words or writings as 'gospel truth'.

Examining the facts, in contrast, takes time. In order to know with confidence which connections are repeated and which ones are not, one must examine many situations and many connections, and science has worked out statistical procedures for determining whether a possible connection or significant or not. Ironically, it is when Perceiver mode is being mesmerized by Mercy feelings that a person 'knows' for certain what is true and what is false. In contrast, when an individual is using Perceiver thought to determine truth, then it is not possible to be 100% certain. That is because, as a finite being, one can never evaluate all of the facts, and so there is always a possibility that new information will arise that will contradict existing data. That is why statistical analysis assigns *probability* to its conclusions. I may know that it will rain tomorrow with 80% certainty, but I cannot be 100% sure. However, if my knowledge is based in blind faith in the pronouncements of some expert, then even though I 'know' the facts with absolute certainty, there is no guarantee that this 'knowing' corresponds in any way to actual truth. And before we move on, I should mention that this problem of absolute certainty is not limited merely to the realm of emotional 'truth', for we will see that it shows up again in a few chapters when discussing *technical thought.*

Truth and Emotions

Emotions also play a role when Perceiver thought is *functioning*. However, instead of adding certainty to belief, strong feelings make it more difficult to determine what is true. For instance, some people find it difficult to write exams. They may study hard and know all of the answers at home, but when they sit down in front of the examination paper, their minds go blank and they cannot recall anything. This is because the emotional intensity is temporarily disabling Perceiver thought and preventing it from functioning.

Emotionally induced uncertainty can occur even when dealing with simple spatial objects. Determining visually whether a switch is off or on should be a straightforward task for Perceiver thought. However, if that switch controls the iron or the stove, then the emotions of potential disaster can overwhelm Perceiver thought: "Did I leave the stove on? What if there is a fire?" How does a person deal with this uncertainty? Through *repetition.* It is possible to increase Perceiver certainty by examining the stove *again.* But, for some people with compulsive disorders, it is difficult for Perceiver thought to achieve certainty no matter how many times the stove is checked.

We have introduced a number of new concepts. Let us now put them together. Right hemisphere thought is composed of two mental modules: Mercy mode looks at the *nature* of items; it remembers experiences along with associated emotions. Perceiver mode looks at the *connections* between items; a connection that is repeated is remembered as a fact. Perceiver facts that describe the arrangement of external matter are known as physical *objects.* For instance, if Perceiver thought notices the repeated occurrence of a trunk plus roots plus leaves, it will conclude that there exists an object which we know as a tree. Of course, in order to *talk* about trees, then one has to use the mental module that generates words, but generic concepts such as trees, cars, breakfast, France, restaurants, and examination papers are all stored within Perceiver thought as sets of repeated connections.

On the diagram of mental symmetry, there is an arrow running from Mercy to Perceiver. This indicates that there is a flow of information *from* Mercy mode *to* Perceiver mode. Mercy experiences provide the raw material for Perceiver facts; Perceiver facts are based upon connections between Mercy experiences.

This arrow also indicates that Perceiver thought is influenced by Mercy emotions. The Perceiver module can only function if it has sufficient *confidence* to handle the current level of emotions. On the one hand, if the emotions are sufficiently intense, then Perceiver thought will be overwhelmed, and Perceiver mode will remember a *specific* set of connections as *universal* truth. On the other hand, if the level of Perceiver confidence is sufficiently high, then Perceiver mode will be able to work out the connections despite the emotional pressure. If the emotional intensity is close to the level of confidence, then Perceiver thought will feel uncertain because it is 'half-awake', neither asleep nor awake. If Perceiver thought manages to hold on to the facts in a situation, then the level of Perceiver confidence will rise and Perceiver thought will become 'more awake'. However, if emotions are allowed to determine truth, then the level of Perceiver confidence will fall, and Perceiver thought will become 'more asleep'.

It is important to realize that gaining Perceiver confidence is quite different than remaining objective. The person who is attempting to remain objective will stay away from personal feelings and will avoid using words with emotional connotations. In contrast, one builds Perceiver confidence by accepting feelings and realizing that facts are *independent* of feelings. I may love apples and hate bananas, but that does not change the fact that there is an apple on the table sitting to the left of a banana. Or, for a more relevant example, I may love eating chocolate and hate being fat, but that does not change the fact that overeating will make me fat. Once I can mentally acknowledge that Perceiver connections are independent of Mercy substance, then I have acquired sufficient Perceiver confidence to handle the emotional pressure. And building Perceiver confidence is like exercising a muscle. It is not gained overnight. Instead, it is only acquired gradually, one successfully handled emotional crisis at a time.

One sees this mental struggle in *societal* form when citizens attempt to free themselves from a dictatorship. On the one side, the dictator is using various forms of emotional pressure to impose his version of truth upon the citizens. On the other side, the individual citizens are attempting to wake up from their political passivity and determine the facts for themselves. What matters to the people is *repeatability*—do the same Perceiver truths apply to both the people and their leaders. In contrast, the dictator will maintain that he is above the law—his emotional *status* is the source of Perceiver truth. The media play a critical role in such a struggle. If they parrot the propaganda of the regime, then the dictator will probably win. But if individual citizens are able to determine the facts and share the facts, then the dictator will eventually have to step down. Of course, in such a struggle, there is always the danger that one dictator will be replaced by another. When that happens, Perceiver thought remains 'asleep' but it is now being mesmerized by a new emotional master.

Technically Speaking

Philosophy talks a lot about facts, truth, and belief. Therefore, in order to satisfy the more rigorous mind, we will take a few paragraphs to describe these concepts clearly and carefully, which means plowing through some technical definitions. However, I will try to keep this material as simple as possible.

Perceiver thought works with facts. A *fact* describes the set of connections that are contained within a situation or a sentence. Thus, if I see a banana sitting next to an orange, then the connection between banana and orange will be remembered as a fact. Or, if someone tells me that the moon is made of green cheese, then the connection between 'moon' and 'green cheese' will be remembered as a fact. Note that a fact is a piece of information that is stored within Perceiver thought. This piece of information might be correct or it might be incorrect. Maybe the lighting was poor and I mistook a grapefruit for an orange. But, in my mind, what connects together is the orange and the banana, and a fact describes what connects together *within my mind.*

A *belief* is the label of certainty which Perceiver thought applies to a fact. This Perceiver label can vary all of the way from 'definitely correct' to 'maybe correct' to 'uncertain' to 'probably incorrect' to 'definitely incorrect'. Belief says nothing about the actual validity of a Perceiver fact, but rather reflects what Perceiver thought *thinks* about that fact. Thus, if the lighting was poor, I may remember the fact that an orange was next to a banana, but only place a label of 'maybe correct' upon this fact.

Belief can be increased through *repetition.* This repetition can occur in the *present.* This happens when I look again or ask someone to repeat a sentence. For instance, if I look at the apple and orange again and still see an apple and an orange, then my belief in that fact will go up. Or, I may respond to someone's words by saying, "I thought that was what you said, but I wasn't sure and so I asked you to repeat yourself." Repetition can also occur in the *past.* This happens when a new fact reminds me of existing facts that are similar. Because the new fact is a repetition of existing facts, then it will be given a label of belief which is fairly certain. So, if ten people have already told me that the moon is made of green cheese and I hear it for the eleventh time, then my belief in this fact will be much stronger than when I heard it for the first time. Finally, repetition can occur in the *future.* A fact that already exists within Perceiver thought will become more believable if it is encountered again in the future. For instance, if I look at the scene later when the lighting is better and see an apple next to an orange, then I will conclude that I *was* seeing the situation clearly when the light was indistinct. Because the label of belief that is assigned to a fact depends upon which related facts come to mind and the beliefs which have been assigned to those facts, one can speak, as Willard Quine does, of a *web* of belief. Thus, we can define *knowledge* as a network of similar facts together with their associated interrelated labels of belief.

Very seldom is a repeated situation *exactly* like the ones which came before. Instead, when Perceiver thought encounters a new fact, it will usually be reminded of a range of similar facts, some of which may be quite similar while others have only a few characteristics in common. For instance, the first time I see the apple and the orange, I may see it out of the corner of my eye at eye level, while the closer look I take later on may be looking down from above. Obviously, repetition that is quite similar will affect belief more strongly than repetition which is only somewhat similar.

Strengthening belief through repetition takes *time*, because the fact must be encountered several times and not just once. However, it is possible to acquire *instant* 'belief' if the fact that is encountered is accompanied by strong emotions. When this happens, then the belief is not being worked out by *Perceiver* thought but rather is being imposed upon Perceiver mode by *Mercy* thought. For instance, suppose that Dr. Rev. Smith, whom I respect greatly, tells me that the moon is made of green cheese. The emotional status that Mercy thought in my mind gives to this person will cause me to 'believe' strongly that moon and green cheese belong together. Or, suppose that I encounter a burglar in the house at night and see an apple next to an orange out of the corner of my eye. The emotional intensity of the situation will burn the arrangement of that fruit into my mind and Perceiver thought will 'believe' with great certainty that there was an apple next to an orange. Maybe I saw things wrong and the orange is really a grapefruit, but the emotions will mesmerize Perceiver thought into 'believing' that apple and orange go together, whether or not they actually did, and whether or not they actually do.

Because emotional 'belief' is an instant *shortcut* to belief which suppresses Perceiver thought and does not require repetition, I will put the word 'belief' in quotes. When Perceiver thought is functioning, then the very concept of emotional belief is a contradiction in terms, because belief comes from Perceiver thought, whereas emotions are produced by Mercy thought. However, when Mercy thought overwhelms Perceiver mode, then emotions become synonymous with belief and good will be equated with right and bad with wrong. For instance, if I am a Republican and I hate Democrats and Joe Democrat tells me that the moon is made of green cheese, then because Mercy thought labels Joe Democrat as bad, Perceiver thought will be mesmerized into 'believing' that Joe Democrat is wrong.

Belief and emotion *interact.* The level of belief determines the emotional intensity that a fact can handle without falling apart, while the *overall* level of belief within some context determines the emotional intensity that Perceiver thought can handle in that context without falling apart. For instance, suppose that I look at the moon through a telescope and see no evidence of green cheese. If my father insists that the moon is made of green cheese, then my belief in the fact that I observed may be sufficient to survive the emotional influence of my father. But if Dr. Jones, who is a world expert upon lunar matters, declares that the moon is made of green cheese, then the emotional status that my mind gives to Dr. Jones may cause me to doubt the fact that I saw with my own eyes. Because belief determines the ability to handle emotion, the diagram of mental symmetry uses the label *confidence* rather than belief or certainty.

If Perceiver thought is *functioning*, then the Perceiver label of belief will be the result of Perceiver thought. However, if Mercy emotions overwhelm Perceiver mode and prevent Perceiver thought from functioning, then belief will be determined by Mercy emotions and will be *imposed* upon Perceiver thought. When belief is determined by Mercy emotions, then I will put the word 'belief' in italics or refer to blind faith.

So far, we have only looked at what is happening within the mind. Facts and beliefs both refer to mental concepts and may or may not be correct. A fact is *true* if it *is* correct. Thus, *truth* is the *ideal* to which Perceiver thought aspires, something which Perceiver thought would *like* to acquire but struggles to achieve. If a fact is a mental set of connections within Perceiver thought and if the label of belief that is applied to a fact is based upon repetition, then truth is a fact that really *is* repeated, a set of connections which actually *can* be found in many places and at many times.

Discovering truth with *absolute* certainty does not appear to be possible. But it is possible to become increasingly certain of truth through careful investigation. However, when Mercy emotions overwhelm Perceiver thought, then a person may 'believe' with absolute certainty that he has acquired truth, whether he actually has or not. When a Perceiver fact acquires absolute certainty through emotional means, then I will refer to this as 'knowing' or emotional 'knowing'. 'Belief' refers to the label of absolute certainty which is applied to the fact; 'knowing' describes the fact together with the sense of absolute certainty.

I suggest that there are two *primary* sources of truth. One primary source of truth is *observation.* If a set of connections occurs repeatedly in the external world, then this set of connections is *true.* This definition applies even to a single incident, such as a car accident at the corner of Main Street and First Avenue on the morning of April 18. In this case, the repetition comes from related situations that occurred *before* the incident, such as the black subcompact car speeding through the intersection, and related situations which occurred *after* the incident, such as the black subcompact sitting smashed at the side of the road, as well as the numerous people who either saw or could have seen the accident. Determining the exact truth with total certainty is impossible, but by examining enough physical evidence and questioning sufficient relevant witnesses it is possible to become reasonably certain of the truth. Observation is the primary source of truth for science, which looks to the *external* world to find connections which are repeated.

The theory of mental symmetry suggests that the structure of the mind is another primary source of truth. The premise of this book is that the same inescapable cognitive connections keep showing up repeatedly in different topics. Even though different people are examining different situations, they are all using minds which are composed of the same cognitive modules connected together in the same way, and that common structure provides an *internal* reference point for checking facts.

Books and experts can act as *secondary* sources of truth. A secondary source of truth can be wrong, but if it is carefully chosen it can be reliable. Obviously, a primary source of truth takes precedence over a secondary source, but if it is not possible or feasible to examine a primary source, then one must be satisfied with a secondary source of truth.

Finally, *absolute* truth or *universal* truth describes Perceiver connections which can be found at all times and in all situations. For instance, atoms describe absolute truth, because the same relationship between protons, neutrons, and electrons can be found throughout the physical universe. Similarly, I suggest that mental structure acts as absolute truth for a human being, because a person cannot exist without his mind.

Many people assume that religion consists solely of emotional 'belief'. Because religion addresses topics that are highly emotional, this is often the case. However, the premise of this book is that if Perceiver thought gains sufficient confidence, then it is possible to approach religious topics rationally.

Similarly, science assumes that it is only possible to discover rational truth if subjective emotions are either suppressed or avoided. Thus, the average person equates science with *objective* science. But, I suggest that it is possible to deal rationally with emotional subjects, if Perceiver thought gains sufficient confidence.

As a Perceiver person, I can assure you that pursuing Perceiver thought in the midst of emotional pressure is not easy. Most people learn how to think somewhat rationally when dealing with fairly emotional subjects. However, if one wants to acquire the ability to deal rationally with *all* emotional subjects, then it appears that one must follow a specific *path* of mental development. And if one analyzes the cognitive steps which make up this mental path, then one discovers that these cognitive steps actually correspond to specific religious *doctrines*. Thus, even though religion appears to be emotionally driven and irrational, if one gains sufficient Perceiver confidence to analyze religious content, then one realizes that hidden within these emotional trappings are cognitive principles which are highly rational. Hence, my suggestion at the beginning of this book that 'religion is cognitive science in emotional garb'.

Finally, I should mention that after reading Quine's *Web of Belief*, I realized that my terminology was insufficiently precise. Therefore, I have tweaked my definitions in order to make my use of the words *belief*, *truth*, and *knowledge* consistent with Quine's usage of these terms. For those who want to know more, a detailed analysis of Quine's *Web of Belief* can be found in an appendix.

Childhood Development

Now that we have finished plowing through the technical definitions, let us continue with our main discussion and examine how the relationship between Mercy emotions and Perceiver thought develops in the mind of the typical child. We have already seen in a previous chapter how Mercy mode develops: The physical body programs Mercy thought with experiences of physical pain and pleasure. Any experience that is similar to an emotional experience becomes associated with it and emotionally colored by it. Thus, experiences of mother acquire good emotional labels because they remind the baby of pleasant experiences of being fed and cleaned. In addition, whenever a sufficient number of similar emotional memories combine, then these memories begin functioning as an integrated network, generating hyper-emotion based upon integration and fragmentation.

Perceiver thought develops most easily in situations where repetition is obvious and emotions are low. This is the case when dealing with *physical objects*. A rock does not emote and a tree does not produce emotions, and it is obvious that one rock is similar to another rock and that rocks are different than trees. Similarly, it is equally obvious that 'letting go of an object' is always followed by 'the object falling to the ground', making it easy for Perceiver thought to connect these two experiences. This leads to the realm of thought which cognitive science refers to as *intuitive physics* and which the average person calls *common sense.*

Mental networks form most easily when dealing with *biological* entities, such as people and animals, because living creatures *do* emote and they respond violently when they are not treated as integrated units. When a child picks up a rag doll, the doll does not respond. But when the child attempts to grab the family cat, then the cat reacts emotionally. Even more dramatically, the rag doll will not protest if the child pulls off a leg, but if the child attempts to perform the same procedure on the cat, then the cat will protest quite vigorously. The mental result is what cognitive researchers refer to as *intuitive biology.*

If a biological entity is treated as an *integrated* unit, then the emotions that it produces are fairly low, making it possible for Perceiver thought to function. Perceiver thought will treat living entities as objects, looking for common connections in order to classify them and organize them: These are cats. Those are dogs. Cats purr when they are happy.

Dogs wag their tail. But if Perceiver thought attempts to vivisect a biological entity into its various components, then the resulting hyper-pain will overwhelm Perceiver thought.

However, even though living creatures respond emotionally, their functioning is guided by rational principles. Saying this more simply, a physical body is a very complicated machine. Therefore, if one wants to cure a sick or injured person or animal, then one must gain sufficient Perceiver confidence to think rationally (along with sufficient Server confidence to act rationally) in the midst of personal trauma. Those who enter the medical profession and who acquire this mental confidence are paid highly for this ability and are given great respect. Putting this more bluntly, what is the primary difference between a butcher and a surgeon? They both cut meat, but a butcher cuts dead meat, whereas a surgeon cuts meat that is still alive. The surgeon is paid more because he has greater Perceiver knowledge, increased Server skill, and much higher mental confidence. The history of medicine shows that this knowledge, skill, and confidence were not acquired easily. For, medicine has not always been guided by rational thought, and it is only comparatively recently that people realized that biological life is guided by rational principles.

A mental network forms within Mercy thought whenever a group of similar emotional memories become connected, even when there is no corresponding biological entity. Think, for instance, of writing an exam, getting a job promotion, or hiking through the forest. All of these activities are capable of forming mental networks within Mercy thought, because they contain a number of similar emotional events. But none of these mental networks is associated with any specific person or animal. This describes the realm of *intuitive psychology*. In the previous chapter, we looked at the *Mercy* side of intuitive psychology. Here, we are viewing the same mental landscape from the vantage point of Perceiver mode.

As far as Perceiver thought is concerned, intuitive psychology is like attempting to distinguish one partially obscured object from another in the twilight while being hit by frequent earthquakes. The objects are partially obscured because one is dealing with fragments of desire and ill-defined clusters of personal feeling. The light is dim because these internal networks do not correspond to any physical objects. And the mental 'ground' of solid facts is continually being shaken by emotional outbursts which disrupt the functioning of Perceiver thought.

Mental Objects

The previous paragraph extends the concept of object from the physical world to the mental realm. In simplest terms, an object is a collection of Mercy items held together by Perceiver connections. A *physical* object contains atoms that are connected by chemical bonds. A *mental* object contains Mercy experiences that are connected by Perceiver connections. Perceiver thought forms a mental object whenever it decides that certain Mercy experiences belong together. But, emotional 'belief' also leads to the formation of a mental object. However, in this case emotional pressure is being used to determine Perceiver connections. If Perceiver thought is to evaluate these connections, then it must 'wake up' and develop sufficient confidence to function within this emotional pressure.

Finally, a mental network is also a kind of mental object, because emotional experiences are *combining* to form an integrated network. Here, any attempt by Perceiver thought to alter the connections will have to deal with the hyper-emotions of fragmentation and integration. Anyone who has attempted to be rational when dealing with hyper-emotionally charged situations such as 'falling in love' knows that this is rather difficult. Because these various forms of mental objects come from different sources, use different methods of forming connections, and involve different levels of emotion, the natural tendency is to regard them as different and incompatible. However, in each case, it appears that the same two mental modules are being used: Mercy mode and Perceiver mode.

The previous chapter introduced another psychological concept that is related to intuitive psychology, known as *Theory of Mind*, which is basically one person attempting to guess what is taking place within the mind of another. This too can be viewed simply as another form of object recognition, because Perceiver thought in one person is attempting to recognize which *mental* objects are currently active within another person.

Each cognitive style will naturally emphasize the aspect of Theory of Mind that relates to the cognitive module in which he is conscious. For instance, the Perceiver person emphasizes the *object recognition* aspect of Theory of Mind. As a Perceiver person, Theory of Mind guides me when I am attempting to explain a concept to another person. Based upon clues from that person's appearance, age, culture, education, religion, values, and personal background, I will try to guess which Perceiver facts they know, and then tailor my explanation to begin from that starting point. For example, if I am conversing with someone who is technically inclined, then I may use computer terminology; if I am talking to a school teacher, then I will use illustrations from the field of education. I can also use Theory of Mind to detect which *mental networks* are currently active within the mind of my audience so that I know which topics to *avoid*. That is because I have learned through repeated experience that mental networks generally prevent Perceiver thought from functioning.

The typical Mercy person uses the same mental circuit for a rather different purpose. He is not interested in the relationship *between* one mental object and another, but rather in the emotional content that is contained *within* a mental object. In addition, he views emotional content and mental networks as entities to embrace rather than obstacles to avoid. Thus, Theory of Mind gives the Mercy person the ability to *empathize* with other individuals. The various clues that he receives from another person will remind subconscious Perceiver thought within his mind of some mental network, and he will use the emotions of this mental network to guide him in his interaction with the other individual. Saying this another way, he does for the other person what he would like that person to do for him if he were in the same shoes. For instance, suppose that the Mercy person appreciates chocolate when feeling depressed. If he senses that another person is feeling down, then the Mercy person may respond with a gift of chocolate. Notice, by the way, the *identification* that is present in the Mercy version of Theory of Mind. We will look at this in more detail later on.

And extending this look to a cognitive style which we have not yet discussed, the Contributor person puts a practical spin upon Theory of Mind, because he adds Server actions to Perceiver facts. As a result, whenever subconscious Perceiver thought within his mind performs some type of object recognition, Contributor thought adds an action to this mental object. Thus, instead of attempting merely to determine which Perceiver facts are known by another individual, the Contributor person will try to guess what *plan* the other person is carrying out, and he will tailor his response to fit the current step in that plan. As a result, the Contributor person has a natural talent of seeing exactly what needs to be *done* within a specific situation. For instance, one of my nieces is a Contributor person. When she was young, she would watch her father working on the car. He often commented that she had an uncanny ability to know what he was doing and hand him exactly the right tool at the appropriate time.

Theory of Mind takes yet another form for the Facilitator person, another cognitive module which we have not yet discussed. Facilitator mode is the *final* mental module, which adjusts and balances the operation of other mental modules. In the right hemisphere, Perceiver thought sets the mental *context* for Facilitator thought. Thus, when the Facilitator person enters a situation, subconscious Perceiver thought within his mind attempts to guess which mental objects are relevant and these mental objects then provide the 'world' within which Facilitator thought functions by adjusting and balancing the various aspects of these mental objects. For instance, suppose that the Facilitator person attends a dinner function for the ambassador from some Asian country. Subconscious Perceiver thought within his mind will access mental objects related to 'ambassadors', 'dinner functions', and 'Asian countries', and these mental objects will set the context for Facilitator thought, bringing to mind everything that the Facilitator person knows or has experienced about these various subjects. Facilitator thought will then adjust his behavior in real time by internally sampling various tidbits from this smorgasbord of cognitive possibilities, mixing the various mental hors d'oeuvres in order to suit the palette of the moment. Thus, in a sense, one could say that Facilitator thought *is* Theory of Mind, because it does the actual adjusting. And when one examines the cognitive styles of those who practice psychology, one finds a preponderance of Facilitator persons.

We have looked at intuitive physics, intuitive biology, and intuitive psychology. To these three, I would add two additional areas of intuitive *religion* and intuitive *government.* Stated in a single sentence, religion deals with topics and experiences that involve the destruction and integration of *mental* networks, whereas government deals with topics and experiences which involve the destruction and integration of *physical* networks. When people are falling apart inside, then they turn to religion for help; when they are threatened externally, then they turn to government for assistance. When a baby is born, a couple gets married, or a person dies, then this is usually marked by a religious ceremony. The purpose of such a ceremony is to help people to cope with the *mental* disruption that such major change produces. Government, in contrast, maintains that it has the exclusive right to administer *physical* force: Governments maintain armies; they send people to prison; and they execute criminals.

However, a human being combines mind and body. Thus, religion and government both lay claim to the human individual. Religion attempts to regulate his mind, while government tries to rule his body, leading to a natural conflict between church and state. When one of these two invades the intuitive realm of the other, then this leads to major human oppression. On the one hand, if the church uses physical force, then this results in the tyranny of a theocracy. On the other hand, when the state tries to control how people think, then the result is a totalitarian dictatorship. The reason that this struggle has such profound effects is because both religion and government are dealing with the *hyper*-emotions of personal integration and fragmentation.

Automatic Thought and Chains of Reasoning

This book is focusing upon the relationship between the mind and religious thought. We will be looking at strongly held beliefs, why the mind holds on to such beliefs, and how they can be changed. As I mentioned very briefly in the introduction, it appears that each of the four cortical cognitive modules of Mercy, Teacher, Perceiver, and Server has an *automatic* region in a specific part of the back of the cortex as well as an internal world in a region of the frontal lobes. The frontal lobes establish the internal framework that guides thought and behavior, while the specific memories that fill this mental framework reside within the posterior regions of the brain. What will concern us most in this book is the internal framework and not the specific memories.

The type of processing that occurs in automatic thought is similar to what occurs within the internal world, but it is less dogmatic and it happens automatically. For instance, suppose that I ask you what you ate for breakfast during the last month. In order to answer this question you will have to sort through a number of vague memories within automatic thought.

If you ate a certain type of cereal that you enjoy, then the emotions of eating this food may bias your answer and you might respond, "I usually eat cereal." Or, if you remember putting bread into the toaster quite often, then this repetition may cause you to say, "I usually have toast for breakfast."

Notice that the same two categories of emotional 'knowing' and repeated connection show up, but in weaker form. That is how automatic thought works. It leads to emotional biases and factual hunches, but not solid opinions. However, these biases and hunches can provide the *starting* point for stronger opinions. For instance, suppose that you are trying to follow a strict diet. In this case, you will probably know exactly what you had for breakfast, because you had to learn facts about foods and you had to decide what you would and would not eat. Now we are dealing with belief and discovering truth, and not just opinions and vague facts.

This explains why debate *solidifies* belief. When people do not think about issues, then the facts that they hold tend to reside within automatic thought, and these facts can be overruled fairly easily. However, when one person argues with another over an issue, then Perceiver thought must decide what is right or wrong, either by referring to some emotional source, or by looking for connections which are repeated. For example, in North America, abortion is a hotly debated issue. Therefore, people have strongly held views about the subject, and it is very difficult to change someone's opinion. When I lived in South Korea, I discovered that the situation was different, because the average South Korean had not thought deeply about the topic of abortion. As a result, it was easier to change someone's views about this subject.

This process can also work in *reverse*, because strongly held beliefs can determine how a person responds to new information. For instance, suppose that I am encountering the theory of mental symmetry for the first time. The only way that I can evaluate these new facts is by relating them to what I *do* know. Therefore, if I have decided that cognitive styles do not exist, then I may conclude that the theory of mental symmetry is invalid because it reminds me of cognitive styles. Or, if applying rational thought to religious topics reminds me of apostate professors, then I may instinctively reject the theory of mental symmetry as untrue.

Notice that associative labeling always works its way back to some starting point. For instance, the reader may decide that mental symmetry is wrong because he knows that the concept of cognitive styles is wrong. He may know that the idea of cognitive styles is wrong because he tried a personality test and it did not describe him accurately. He may know that this test did not describe him because—well, because it did not describe him.

In the language of logic, every system of proofs is based upon a fundamental set of axioms that cannot be proven. It is possible to pick a set of axioms at random. However, that is rarely done. Instead, axioms are invariably chosen by one of the two methods of belief described earlier in this chapter: First, the emotions associated with some defining experience or expert may mesmerize Perceiver thought into accepting an axiom. Second, repetition that comes from some *other* system may provide the initial set of facts. For instance, for the religious mystic, the defining experience of feeling 'one with the Universal' provides the starting axiom for religious thought. For the fundamentalist believer, the initial Perceiver beliefs usually come from the words of a holy book. For the more typical believer, the primary Perceiver facts come from the words of a religious guru or a famous professor. In contrast, most of the initial facts for the scientist come from observing what is repeated in the external environment. In this book, the diagram of mental symmetry provides the starting point, and it came from observing repeated patterns in human behavior.

In a formal system of logic such as mathematics, everything can be proven by starting from a few fundamental axioms. In normal thought, the method of proof is much less formal, the chains of logic are much shorter, and the number of axioms are much greater. This type of informal logic defines how Perceiver thought functions. Whenever I, a Perceiver person, encounter a new situation, I always begin by asking myself what I know for certain—based either in repetition or the opinions of experts. Then, starting from those known facts, I attempt to decipher the rest of the information.

When Perceiver facts are evaluated emotionally, then good and bad will be equated with right and wrong, and chains of reasoning will not cross emotional boundaries between good and bad. Thus, if mental symmetry reminds the fundamentalist believer of skeptical intellectualism, then it will be labeled as both wrong and bad—regardless of the actual content. In contrast, if some favorite preacher makes a dogmatic statement, then it will be accepted instinctively as both right and good. Or, for the non-religious person, if Carl Sagan or Stephen Hawking makes some pronouncement about God and religion, then this may be accepted instinctively as both right and good, while anything said by the dogmatic preacher will be discarded as both wrong and bad.

For the Perceiver person, this type of associative thinking comes naturally and forms a major part of normal thought. For other cognitive styles, it occurs subconsciously and is not subject to either conscious control or conscious awareness. However, it still provides the mental mechanism whereby the mind determines what is reasonable and what is unreasonable, and we will examine it further when looking at the minimally counterintuitive concept.

The Perceiver *person* is consciously aware of automatic Perceiver thought, and this content acts as a sort of mental 'tool shed' full of factual fragments which provide the raw material for thought. Similarly, the Server person is consciously aware of automatic Server thought, the Mercy person of automatic Mercy thought, and the Teacher person of automatic Teacher thought. As far as I know, each of these four cognitive styles has a conscious awareness of information that is not possessed by other cognitive styles, and this conscious awareness makes it possible for these four cognitive styles to work with incomplete and inadequate information within their specific realm of thought.

Summary

Let us summarize. We began this chapter by looking at how the childish mind defines truth. Anything that is spoken by a person with *emotional status* is automatically accepted by the child as true. Initially, parents act as the main source of truth. As a person grows up, he looks to other emotional sources for truth. The teenager often bases his truth in the emotional status of his peers. And for many adults, truth is defined primarily by religious dogma, political affiliation, or cultural heritage.

We then suggested that truth can also be based in *repetition*. Whenever the mind notices that certain elements repeatedly occur together, then this set of connections becomes accepted as truth. This definition of truth forms the basis for both common sense and science.

Comparing these two methods of establishing truth, we notice that one method examines the message itself, while the other focuses upon the emotional status of the messenger while ignoring the message. Thus, we conclude that the truth of facts can be determined either by *using* the mental module that works with facts or else by using emotional pressure to *override* this module. Saying this in the language of mental symmetry, the Perceiver module stores and evaluates facts by looking for connections that are repeated. However, if a situation contains sufficiently strong emotions, then these feelings will overwhelm Perceiver thought. The connections that are contained within that *specific* emotional situation will then be accepted as *universal* truth.

Extreme emotions overwhelm Perceiver thought, resulting in *emotional 'belief'*. Feelings that are less intense will confuse Perceiver mode, leading to mental uncertainty. Perceiver thought assigns a level of certainty or belief to each fact. The overall level of belief within a context can also be referred to as *confidence* because this determines the level of emotional intensity which Perceiver thought can handle within that context while continuing to function. It is possible to increase confidence by successfully holding on to facts when faced with emotional pressure.

Objective science tries to protect Perceiver thought by *avoiding* emotional pressure. Religion, in contrast, deals with emotional topics. Thus, religion tends to define truth by using strong emotions to overwhelm Perceiver thought.

In most general terms, an object is a group of Mercy experiences held together by Perceiver connections. The interaction between Mercy feelings and Perceiver confidence causes the mind to form different classes of objects: Physical objects such as trees, stones, and automobiles occur repeatedly and they do not produce emotions. Therefore, Perceiver thought finds it easy to form mental objects based upon repeated connections, leading to common sense and *intuitive physics*. People and animals, in contrast, do produce strong emotions, especially when they are not treated as integrated units, causing the mind to represent them as emotional mental networks, leading to *intuitive biology*. Because a mental network forms whenever a group of emotional experiences combine, Mercy thought contains many mental networks that do not correspond to any physical entity, such as 'love', 'justice', 'taking a vacation', or 'asking my boss for a raise'. *Intuitive psychology* deals with this realm of invisible, emotional objects. Perceiver thought usually has sufficient confidence to *categorize* and *recognize* emotional mental networks, but it generally lacks the confidence that is required to *subdivide* a mental network into its component parts. Perceiver or Mercy content that lies outside of these three main categories falls into the generic realm of facts and experiences.

Neurologically speaking, it appears that these generic objects and experiences are processed automatically by the *posterior* half of the right hemisphere, whereas truth and experiences with strong emotions are processed by the right *frontal* lobe.

Theory of Mind is one person using object recognition to try to guess which mental networks are currently active within the mind of another person. Each cognitive style naturally focuses upon the aspect of Theory of Mind which relates to the mental module in which he is conscious.

Going further, I suggested that intuitive *religion* focuses upon the destruction and integration of *mental* networks, whereas intuitive *government* deals with the destruction and integration of *external* structures. Because there is often a strong relationship between mental structure and external structure, church and state have a tendency to invade the territory of one another.

Finally, we took a brief look at automatic Perceiver thought and chains of reasoning. On the one hand, the repetition and emotions of everyday experiences can provide the starting point for more solid conclusions. On the other hand, known facts are used to evaluate new information which the mind encounters.

✵ 4. Childish Identity

Consider the teddy bear, or more precisely, consider the teddy bear being clutched by the sobbing little girl. Is it alive? Physically speaking, no. And, as far as the father is concerned who is trying to take the teddy bear from his little daughter, it *definitely* is not alive. But within the mind of the crying child, this ragged little bag of cloth and stuffing is not only alive, but it forms a vital part of her personal identity.

In a previous chapter, we saw that the mind represents people as mental networks of emotional memories within Mercy thought. Obviously, the most critical mental network is the one that represents my own personal identity. But, *why* is this obvious, what makes personal identity so significant, and how is it different than other mental networks?

We can begin answering these questions by comparing the response of the child with the actions of her father. The child is focusing upon *feelings*. Emotional experiences associated with her teddy bear have formed a potent mental network within Mercy thought, and the emotional strength of that mental network is motivating her struggles. Obviously, her father does not share this emotional bond. As far as he is concerned, the teddy bear is only a dirty old stuffed toy. That is because he is looking at the *facts*. He knows that this bear is not physically attached to his daughter's body and that she will not suffer any physical pain if it is taken away from her. Therefore, he finds it strange that she is holding on to the teddy bear and emotionally protecting it as if the teddy bear is physically part of her body.

In other words, we are seeing a mismatch between the child's *physical* identity and her *mental* identity. *Externally* speaking, the child and the teddy bear are physically distinct, because one can easily be separated from the other. Within the *mind* of the child, though, the teddy bear is an inseparable part of the mental network that represents personal identity. The actions of the father are being guided by his child's *physical* identity, whereas the responses of the child are being motivated by her *internal* identity.

This distinction between physical and mental identity provides a partial explanation for the situation, but it still does not tell us how the mind distinguishes one mental network from another and how it chooses which mental network will represent personal identity.

The answer is quite simple, but in order to work it out, we have to take one mental step back from the situation, which is why I brought in the teddy bear. How is the child treating her teddy bear? She is *clinging* to it; she is trying desperately to hold on to it without letting go; she is attempting to keep it close to her so that she can continue focusing upon it.

And that explains why there is such a strong connection between physical identity and mental identity. My physical body always follows me around. Wherever I go, it goes. In fact, I cannot go anywhere without moving my physical body.

Personal Identity

Thus, I suggest the following formal definition for personal identity: Personal identity consists of the mental networks upon which I can continue to focus. Personal identity differs from other mental networks simply by being the one that always repeats itself. Every time I look in the mirror, I see the same body reflected in the glass. Every time I wake up, I find myself occupying the same physical body. Thus, the child in our illustration considers the teddy bear to be part of her personal identity because it *also* follows her around wherever she goes.

This means that Mercy thought and Perceiver thought *cooperate* to define personal identity. On the Mercy side, personal identity is composed of mental networks within Mercy thought. As I have mentioned previously, the physical body provides the mind with experiences that are physically pleasurable or physically painful. These are stored within the Mercy module as emotional experiences. The steady stream of emotionally charged experiences from the physical body leads to the formation of mental networks within Mercy thought, and these mental networks provide the raw material for personal identity.[7]

Perceiver thought then uses *repetition* to decide which of these mental networks define personal identity. And which mental network is *always* repeated? The one that represents my physical body, because wherever I go, my physical body is always present. This may seem like a strange way of describing the situation, but remember that everything is being processed by the *mind.* Therefore, if we want to comprehend human intelligence, then we must approach situations like these from the viewpoint of the mind.

We have seen how emotional experiences from the physical body provide the raw material for personal identity. The physical body also *limits* personal identity in two major ways. First, it limits what can be *removed* from personal identity. My physical body follows me around wherever I go because I am literally attached to it. I can let go of objects such as teddy bears, but I cannot get rid of my physical body. Therefore, the father in our illustration might take his child's teddy bear away from her, or ask her to remove her clothes when she is taking a bath, but he would never attempt to remove an arm or a leg from his daughter.

Second, the physical body limits what can be *acquired* by personal identity, primarily by placing me within a specific physical location. When I am physically *here,* I cannot

---

[7] In the previous chapter, we made a distinction between automatic thought and the internal world. Obviously, personal identity involves the *internal* world of Mercy thought because we are dealing with deep feelings and strong emotions. Automatic Mercy thought remembers experiences that feel fairly good or somewhat unpleasant.

experience *there*, because I am here and not there. In order to experience there, I must first move my physical body from here to there, and that takes both time and effort. And once I have arrived there, then I can no longer experience here, because I am now there and not here. Saying this another way, Perceiver thought works out which items are close by and which ones are far away, and that determines which Mercy experiences are capable of being *connected* with my personal identity and which ones are not.

Notice that the *same* physical body is both a physical object and the source of emotional experiences for Mercy identity. On the one hand, my body is a physical object with a solid shape that I always find present; this incessant repetition programs Perceiver thought. On the other hand, my body is also a constant source of pain and pleasure that I cannot avoid, and these emotional experiences develop mental networks within Mercy thought. These two aspects always go together, because the physical sensations of pain and pleasure that I feel are produced by my body and only by my body. Thus, when dealing directly with my physical body, gaining the Perceiver confidence that is required to handle emotional pressure is for me literally a matter of physical life and death.

But, it is difficult to gain the Perceiver confidence that is required to handle the emotional intensity associated with mental networks. Therefore, any aspect of personal identity which does not deal directly with the physical body will be naturally governed by emotional 'knowing'. And that, I suggest, describes the core problem facing childish identity.

Let me say this another way. When dealing with *physical* identity, Perceiver thought and Mercy thought must learn how to work together, because physical feelings of pain and pleasure come exclusively from the physical object that is my physical body. However, when working with *mental* identity, then Perceiver thought and Mercy thought do *not* naturally work together, because the strong emotions that are produced by mental networks overwhelm Perceiver thought.

Physical Identity and Mental Identity

Now that we understand the relationship between the physical body and personal identity, we can clarify what is meant by *physical* identity and *mental* identity. Technically speaking, there is no such thing as 'physical' identity because both of these exist as mental networks within the Mercy module. Therefore, my physical identity refers to the mental network that directly represents my physical body. Any mental attempt to disregard either the demands or limitations of my physical body will be met by immediate and severe physical consequences—which will impose themselves forcefully upon the mind. Thus, the mental network that represents my physical body forms the core of my personal identity. Mental identity, in contrast, refers to the aspects of personal identity that extend *beyond* my physical body.

For instance, I am a violinist. I started playing violin when I was three years old, and so violin forms a major part of my personal identity. The connection between the violin and my personal identity began as a *physical* extension, just like the girl with her teddy bear, because I was often holding a violin or walking around clutching a violin case, and whenever I went on a trip, my violin usually accompanied me. But the connection between the violin and my personal identity is now primarily a mental connection. I consider myself to be a violinist because I have the *ability* to play a violin. Whenever I pick up a carved wooden box and pull the horsehair across the catgut, I can make music. Thus, what I can continue to focus upon now is not a specific physical instrument but rather the skill of creating music using a violin. And because I can continue to focus upon this, it forms a part of my personal identity.

Similarly, I am also an engineer. Originally, I considered myself to be an engineer because I attended Engineering school and because I have the diploma on my wall and an engineer's ring on my little finger. But since then, I have come to realize that I am an engineer because I have learned to think like an engineer and approach problems with the mindset of an engineer. It is this mental ability which is repeatable and which I can continue to focus upon.[8]

Mercy thought also contains memories and mental networks that are *related* to personal identity but are not directly a part of personal identity. My physical body is responsible for forming the core of my personal identity because it is *always* present. Family members, while not part of personal identity, are closely related to personal identity because they are *frequently* present. Similarly, friends are also related to personal identity, though usually not as closely. As with personal identity, friends and family members are represented within the mind as mental networks. The connection between physical body and personal identity also explains the strong emotional attachment that a mother has for her child, because that infant began its existence as a part of the mother's physical body. When the mother gives birth, what was a part of her body now becomes separated from her body, and the process by which all of this occurs contains sufficient emotional trauma to form strong mental networks within the mind of the mother.

Inanimate objects such as cars, violins, and teddy bears can also become related to personal identity. Sometimes, they form emotional networks and are treated by the mind as people—like the child's teddy bear. But usually they are connected with personal identity through the concept of *ownership*. When I own an object, then Perceiver thought within my mind knows that it is possible for me to choose to focus upon this object whenever I wish. Similarly, when an object is owned by someone else, then Perceiver thought knows that it is *not* possible for me to choose to focus upon this object. Ownership requires stable Perceiver connections: Perceiver connections between owners and the objects that they own must remain present, and Perceiver connections between non-owners and the objects that they do not own must remain absent. These Perceiver connections can be provided either internally or externally. If people have

---

[8] An aspect of personal identity also resides within Server mode, based upon my personal skills and what I can *do*. However, because the human mind is so intimately attached to the Perceiver object of a physical body, Server-based personal identity plays a secondary role. We will discuss this further in the final chapter.

sufficient Perceiver confidence to know what belongs to whom, then ownership can be determined *mentally*. However, if this Perceiver confidence is absent, then ownership can only be maintained through the use of *external* barriers which separate non-owners from objects through the use of walls and fences.

Thus, one can determine the relationship between Perceiver facts and Mercy emotions within a particular society by examining their physical walls. If rich people live beyond high walls topped with barbed wire and patrolled by armed guards, then one can conclude that Perceiver thought within the average individual lacks the confidence that is needed to handle emotional pressure. In contrast, if valuable objects are left out in the open and people do not seem to be concerned, then this indicates that at least some mental networks within the minds of citizens are being defined by Perceiver facts. Because people from different societies tend to develop Perceiver confidence in different areas of thought, this is not an absolute indicator, but it does provide a strong clue.

Defining Mental Identity

We have looked at *physical* identity—the aspect of personal identity that directly represents the physical body. Any person who does not use Perceiver thought here will quickly damage or destroy his physical body. We will now examine *mental* identity, the aspect of personal identity that extends beyond the physical body, focusing upon the role that Perceiver thought plays in defining personal identity and what happens when Perceiver thought is *not* applied to an aspect of personal identity.

First, there is the matter of *repetition.* Perceiver thought defines personal identity as the mental networks that are consistently repeated. But the formation of a mental network is *not* based primarily upon repetition, but rather upon emotional intensity. The more emotional a situation, the less repetition it takes for that situation to form a mental network, the harder it is for Perceiver thought to function within that context, and the more intensely Exhorter thought will be attracted to that mental network. Putting this all together, one concludes that the mind will naturally attempt to focus upon mental networks that are not repeated.

For instance, suppose that I have an encounter with a famous individual, come across a new electronic gadget, or see a beautiful girl or attractive guy. Depending upon my age and gender, emotional situations such as these will create mental networks within Mercy thought. If the Perceiver module is functioning, then it will examine incidents like these, notice that they are not repeated, and conclude that they are not a part of personal identity. But if Perceiver thought is not functioning, then that mental network will *become* an aspect of personal identity, for the simple reason that the mind will succeed in continuing to focus upon this isolated situation. Looking at our three examples, the chance encounter with the famous individual will form a significant part of my identity: "I shook hands with the president of the United States." Similarly, I will obsess over the new gadget: "That cellphone has so many amazing features." Or, I will start fantasizing about the girl or guy, imagining that this individual has an intimate connection with my personal identity.

Saying this more simply, whenever the mind encounters an item, person, or situation that is emotionally attractive, the natural tendency is for Mercy thought to *identify* with that item and pretend that it is an aspect of personal identity. Saying this another way, the mind is equating 'good' with 'true'. 'Good' is a Mercy label; 'true' is the presence of a Perceiver connection. If an experience feels sufficiently good, then these emotions will overwhelm Perceiver thought into believing that this desirable experience is connected with personal identity.

Notice the fundamental problem: I am mentally rehearsing emotional situations that I cannot repeat externally. The presence of that little word 'I' is critical, because we are not trying to determine whether an item or individual exists or not. That is a question for Perceiver thought to decide. Instead, we are examining whether it exists *for me*. One applies this mental distinction all the time when dealing with ownership. If I am surrounded by houses, then Perceiver thought within my mind will come up with the mental category of 'house' and will be able to know facts about houses with great certainty. But, if I do not *own* a house, then a house does not exist *for me*—it is not mine. When I do not *own* a house, then it will not be possible for my mind and my body to focus upon the object of house, because whenever I get too close to a house, then authorities will impose laws of ownership upon me by coming and taking me away from that house.

A similar distinction applies to personal identity. Suppose, for instance, that I travel with a musical group as an assistant. Perceiver thought within my mind will notice people playing music and will come up with the category of 'musician'. But even though I am in the company of musicians and am surrounded by music, I myself am not a musician, because my mind and my body are incapable of creating music. At most, I can consider myself to be a friend of musicians or an assistant to musicians.

When the mind identifies with emotional experiences that it cannot repeat, then it is setting itself up for future hyper-pain. The reason for this is simple. A mental network wants to be 'fed' with compatible input. If it is not activated regularly, then it will eventually 'starve' and 'die'. But 'feeding' a mental network means repeating the experience, which in this case is not possible. If I have had a chance encounter with the president of the United States, I cannot stroll into the White House and expect him to have an extended conversation with me. Similarly, if I do not own the new and improved gadget, then I cannot take it into my hands and use any of its fancy features. As for the attractive person, my relationship with that person must remain a fantasy, because I cannot turn imagination into reality.

In addition, identifying with isolated incidents prevents the mind from enjoying experiences that *can* be repeated. If I spend my time thinking about my single encounter with the president, then I will not enjoy interactions with friends who are willing to converse with me. If I mentally drool over the new gadget, then I will no longer enjoy my current devices. And fantasizing over attractive individuals prevents me from enjoying the long-term relationship that I have with my spouse.

Moving on to the second point, Perceiver thought determines which emotional experiences can be *acquired* by personal identity. When dealing directly with the physical body, this principle is obvious. I do not reach out and try to grab a spoon that is sitting on a shelf in a different city, because Perceiver thought within my mind has learned that it is only possible to grab items which are physically close by. If I want to take a spoon, then I must move my physical body to the vicinity of that spoon so that I can reach out and grab it.

When Perceiver thought is not functioning, then the natural tendency is to use *identification* to pretend that a desirable object, experience, or person is part of personal identity. For instance, suppose that I am a fan of some sports star. I can buy posters of that athlete and hang them up in my room, I can learn about that individual and his professional statistics, I can watch the games in which he plays, and I can even buy a jersey that has been signed by that player and hang it up in a prominent location. The repeatability is there, because I am surrounded by memorabilia that visually remind me of my hero. And these external objects will continue to 'feed' the mental network within Mercy thought that represents that person. But, physically and mentally speaking, the sports star is very distant from my personal identity. If I try to get physically close to him, then his bodyguards will push me away. And my mind and body lack the skills, knowledge, and physical ability to reproduce his maneuvers. Thus, identification performs the mental equivalent of attempting to grab a spoon that is located in a different city.

The major problem with identification is that it aborts personal movement. Suppose that I actually could reach out to the other city and grab the spoon. There would then be no need for me get up from my chair and go anywhere. And that is precisely what happens with the 'couch potato'. By pressing a few buttons, he can repeatably and reliably identify with all manner of experiences, allowing him to create and 'feed' mental networks upon demand. But this identification prevents him from gaining knowledge, acquiring skills, or even moving his body from where it is slumped in the easy chair. Similarly, a professional sports event has been described as 50,000 people in desperate need of exercise watching twenty people in desperate need of rest.

Identification is much easier for the individual who has wealth and power, because he can either pay someone or force someone to go to the next city and grab the spoon for him. The end result, again, is a lack of personal movement, because he does not have to move his body physically or develop his mind. One is reminded of the joke in which the doctor tells the rich man that he needs to exercise, and the rich man turns to his butler and says, "Jeeves, run around the block a few times for me." In other words, despite knowing that identification does not work with the physical body, we often practice it with mental identity.

Moving on to the third point, Perceiver thought also determines which experiences can be *removed* from personal identity. When dealing with physical identity, I can take off my shirt, but I cannot remove my finger. For the average person, this distinction is totally obvious. But it is only obvious because feedback from the physical body forces Perceiver thought to learn this principle. However, when dealing with *mental* identity, then the typical individual often does attempt to remove mental 'fingers' and 'arms' from personal identity through the process of *denial*.

Denial says that 'bad' equals 'false'. 'Bad' refers to a Mercy feeling; 'false' is the absence of a Perceiver connection. If a personal situation or memory is sufficiently unpleasant, then the emotions will overwhelm Perceiver thought into believing that this situation has no connection with personal identity. In simple terms, if I do not like an experience or person, then I will try to avoid focusing upon that experience or person.

For example, suppose that I have a deep relationship with some 'significant other' and that this relationship turns sour. The person that I used to love dearly I now hate intensely. The natural tendency is for these negative experiences to lead to physical separation—for the bad Mercy feelings to be followed by false Perceiver connections. Therefore, my boyfriend will turn into my ex-boyfriend, whom I no longer have anything to do with, or my marriage will break up and lead to divorce.

The problem is that denial leaves mental networks intact. Using colloquial terms, denial fills my mind with 'emotional baggage'. The mental mechanism behind 'emotional baggage' is quite simple. Suppose that I try to deny a mental network because it contains unpleasant experiences. Any situation which is similar to that mental network will bring it back to mind. Whenever it is reactivated, it will produce a contradictory emotional effect. On the one hand, this mental network is filled with painful emotions—that is what caused me to deny it in the first place, and this emotional pain will motivate me to continue denying this mental network. On the other hand, if I continue to deny the mental network, then it will eventually start to fragment, leading to hyper-pain. Thus, thinking about the mental network will produce emotional pain, whereas not thinking about it will eventually generate emotional hyper-pain. This emotional clash is illustrated by the typical cycle of repeated bad relationships. In the short term, emotional pain causes a person with emotional baggage to avoid his previous partner, while in the long term, emotional hyper-pain drives him to find a new partner who is similar to the previous one. That is because a mental network can only be 'fed' by providing it with experiences that are *compatible* with its structure.

The way out of this vicious circle is to use Perceiver thought to *digest* the emotional baggage by analyzing the mental network that is being denied and breaking it up into its various components. However, that is the mental equivalent of taking the family cat and pulling it apart limb from limb. Any attempt to vivisect the creature will cause it to put up an intense struggle for survival, which is how mental networks respond when Perceiver thought tries to divide them into various pieces.

An additional difficulty emerges when attempting to digest emotional baggage that includes sexual encounters. First, the act of sex produces feelings that extend beyond normal emotion to include hyper-emotions related to personal integration. Second, sex is very closely related to the physical body. Now suppose that a person attempts to deny a mental network that was created through sexual activity. This mental network cannot be ignored, because sexual desire from the physical body will continue to bring it to mind. And it cannot continue to be suppressed because this will eventually cause the mental network to fall apart, generating intense hyper-pain. But it also cannot be analyzed because its mental structure is being reinforced by the same physical body that is responsible for creating the core of personal identity.

An additional mental effect comes into play when a person has multiple sexual partners. The easiest way to describe this is through the use of an example. Suppose that John has sex with Jane. Like any human being, Jane occupies a physical body with distinctive physical appearance and distinctive mannerisms. Therefore, John's intense relationship with Jane will create a mental network within the mind of John that corresponds specifically to the body and behavior of Jane. Now suppose that John has sex with Jill. Jill looks and acts different than Jane, therefore the mental network within John's mind that is associated with Jill will be *different* than the mental network that is associated with Jane. Whenever John has sex, both of these mental networks will come to mind and each one will want to be 'fed' with its own version of reality. Thus, when John has sex with Jane, the mental network that is associated with Jane will feel activated, whereas the mental network that is associated with Jill will feel suppressed, because it is being 'fed' with incompatible information. The result is that John will be mentally distracted from his interaction with Jane and will only feel partially satisfied. And because Jane and Jill each occupy unique physical bodies, it is not possible to integrate the two mental networks that represent them, because this mental integration will be contradicted by evidence from the physical body—evidence which the mind finds very difficult to ignore. Saying this in a single sentence, because sex directly involves the physical body, any mental network that is produced by sex must take into account the fundamental fact that each human mind is trapped for its entire lifetime within a unique physical body.

This chapter will cover one more topic, but before we begin, I would like to make some general observations. First, it appears that the human mind is a simple, but general, computing device. So far, most of our analysis has been limited to two cognitive modules: the Mercy module which stores emotional experiences and the Perceiver module which builds connections. And yet, using only these two modules and the interaction between them, we have managed to explain a number of core elements of human behavior. Second, the physical body plays a crucial role in developing and defining human identity. Placing the human mind within a different type of physical container would result in a radically altered form of personal identity. We like to fantasize about occupying different bodies or having supernatural abilities, but if fantasy ever turned into reality, then we would fall apart inside and suffer deep hyper-pain because the integrity of core mental networks would be threatened.

Third, childhood leaves personal identity in a partially developed state. When dealing directly with the physical body, Perceiver thought is forced to gain the confidence that is required to handle Mercy emotions. Plus, the ever-present solidness of the physical body gives Perceiver mode the repetition that is needed to acquire this Perceiver confidence. However, when dealing with aspects of personal identity that go beyond the physical body, then the natural path is for Mercy emotions to disable Perceiver thought. Here, the mind uses identification to focus upon isolated emotional encounters that cannot be repeated, and it uses denial to suppress unpleasant situations that are repeated. Because *mental* identity—the part of personal identity that does not deal with the physical body—naturally exists in a semi-fragmented state, this book will refer to Mercy mental networks of childish identity in the *plural*, rather than talking about a *single* Mercy mental network of childish identity.

These various factors bring us back to the familiar categories of intuitive physics, intuitive biology, and intuitive psychology. Intuitive physics occurs where repetition is obvious and emotions are low. Because there are no strong emotions, Exhorter thought feels no desire to focus upon these areas, and thus they do not form a part of personal identity. In the area of intuitive biology, strong emotions are produced, but these feelings are always combined with the solid objects of physical bodies. Thus, personal identity exists and it is well defined. Finally, there is the nebulous mental region of intuitive psychology which is filled with random mental networks acquired mainly through identification and denial. Here, personal identity is not defined but rather triggered, as events and objects from the external world bring to mind mental networks which then determine personal identity for that moment. Perceiver thought here is forced to classify from a distance, repelled from closer analysis by a lack of confidence and an excess of emotion.

The Ten Commandments

Moving on now to our final topic, I pointed out in an earlier chapter that religion deals primarily with the assembling and disassembling of mental networks. I have also suggested that it is possible to make sense of religious doctrine if one approaches theology from a cognitive viewpoint. Therefore, I would like to finish this chapter by using the concept of mental networks to analyze the Ten Commandments, a set of moral rules that were written over 3000 years ago which form the basis for three of the world's major religions.

The first three (or four, depending upon how one counts) of the Ten Commandments cover concepts that we have not yet discussed, so we will begin here with the commandment regarding *parents*, which says "Honor your father and mother." We saw in an earlier chapter that the most potent mental networks within the mind of the child are those that represent father and mother. Therefore, it makes sense from a cognitive viewpoint that these mental networks need to be treated with respect.

The next commandment is a prohibition against *murder*. The mind represents people as mental networks, and personal identity is also formed out of mental networks.

Therefore, from a mental perspective, a prohibition against murder protects the existence of all mental networks which are similar to the one that represents personal identity.

Next comes the prohibition against *adultery*. We have just covered this commandment in our look at 'mental baggage'. Sex generates hyper-emotion and creates a strong mental network. Adultery uses sex to program Mercy thought with *incompatible* mental networks.

This is followed by the commandment which prohibits *stealing*. We discussed ownership earlier on in this chapter. When a person steals, he is acquiring new experiences for personal identity in a manner that violates ownership. First, he identifies with the object emotionally, and then he disregards existing Perceiver connections between that item and personal identity.

The next commandment tells a person not to 'bear false witness against his neighbor'. As with the prohibition against stealing, this commandment is stated in a manner that specifically references mental networks. 'My neighbor' is represented within the mind as a mental network that is closely related to personal identity, because physically speaking, he lives next-door to me. The individual who is honest about his neighbor uses Perceiver facts to govern the relationship between the mental network that represents personal identity and adjacent mental networks. In contrast, the person who 'bears false witness against his neighbor' attempts either to improve personal identity or else damage neighboring mental networks by suppressing Perceiver thought.

Finally, there is the last commandment (or according to some numbering schemes, the last two commandments). The first part tells a person not to covet his neighbor's wife. This prohibition combines sex, identification, and mental networks that are adjacent to personal identity. In the language of mental symmetry, it says that even when dealing with the strongest hyper-pleasure, and even when the possibility for experiencing this hyper-emotion is directly adjacent to personal identity, Perceiver ownership should still be respected and identification should not be used.

The second part of this commandment generalizes this into a prohibition against coveting anything that belongs to one's neighbor. In other words, even when dealing with mental networks that are mentally adjacent to personal identity, the method of identification should not be used to improve personal identity.

So what is the alternative to identification? In order to answer this question, we must refer to the mental circuit of *concrete thought* which we will be discussing later on in this book. The basic process is as follows: Suppose that a mental network exists that is physically within reach of personal identity. Exhorter thought will notice the strong emotions and create a desire to focus more fully upon these emotional experiences. Stated in concrete terms, I will see my neighbor's healthy cow and want to steal it. If Perceiver thought has sufficient confidence in the facts of private property, then it will know that a connection does not exist between my personal identity and my neighbor's property, and this Perceiver knowledge will prevent Exhorter thought from focusing upon my neighbor's goods. In simple language, I will no longer want to have my neighbor's cow. Perceiver confidence in the facts of ownership does not *remove* Exhorter desire but rather *redirects* it. Instead of wanting my neighbor's cow, I now want to have my own cow. This rechanneling of desire activates the *mental circuit* of concrete thought, a circuit that uses Contributor planning and Server actions to acquire Mercy goals. In addition, Contributor thought can mentally reassign ownership, making it possible for me to earn the money that is needed to *buy* my neighbor's cow. In the words of Ludwig von Mises, the famous economist, "The foundation of any and every civilization, including our own, is private ownership of the means of production. Whoever wishes to criticize modern civilization, therefore, begins with private property."

Thus, our hypothesis that the Ten Commandments regulate mental networks appears to be valid. The six commandments that we have examined tell a person not to block off the mental networks that initially defined his mental existence, not to destroy any mental networks that are similar to personal identity, and to accept Perceiver truth and not pursue identification when attempting to improve personal identity. These commandments are stated in terms that apply directly to mental networks and they focus upon the mental networks that contain the strongest emotions.

If one were to apply these standards to Western civilization, how would it rate? Not very well. In fact, it appears that there are entire industries whose primary purpose is to violate one or more of these commandments. Consider the *entertainment* industry. Entertainment centers upon emotional identification. When a person watches a movie, he is supposed to forget about himself and focus completely upon what is being portrayed on the screen. And he is also supposed to 'suspend critical reasoning' and not allow his knowledge of Perceiver facts to hinder his enjoyment of the moment. Similarly, the sounds, sights, and lights of today's typical musical performance are also designed to provide an environment within which the listener mentally immerses himself.

Consider next the industries of *advertising and marketing*. If one analyzes the typical ad or marketing campaign, it is attempting to use emotional means to create a mental network associated with a specific product within the mind of the consumer, in order to ensure that the consumer will continually be reminded of that product. In other words, it tries to manipulate personal identity using emotional methods that overwhelm or confuse Perceiver thought.

Identification also plays a key role in the field of *professional sports*. The sports fan does not say, "I watched an amazing game in which two very skilled teams played each other." Instead, he says, "We Won!!!", even though all he did was sit on a bench and jump up and down as someone else played a game. And much of the marketing of professional sports is geared towards increasing both the intensity and the extent of this emotional identification.

Finally, there is the *legal* field. Officially, its purpose is to apply Perceiver thought to the area of personal identity, and to some extent, this still occurs. However, in practice, a significant portion of current legal maneuvering falls under the category of 'bearing false witness against my neighbor'—attempting to distort or spin Perceiver facts in order to acquire something for personal identity or else bring harm to the personal identity of another.

Related to the legal field is the realm of *politics.* As I mentioned in a previous chapter, American politics have become largely reduced to emotionally identifying with one party while denying anything that is connected with the other party. As for Perceiver thought, it has become replaced by emotionally-driven image and spin. As a result, political identity is determined by the latest emotional event, while long-term issues are ignored.

It is interesting to note that a number of the 'captains of industry' within these fields are adherents to religions that verbally assert the supremacy of the Ten Commandments. This illustrates that there is often a major cognitive disconnect between the religious doctrine that a person verbally pronounces and the religious rules which he actually obeys. Justin Barrett, along with other researchers in the field of the cognitive science of religion, have performed a number of experiments which demonstrate that theological religion is quite different than folk religion, and that what a person *says* that he believes is often overruled by what he believes in *practice.* In the next chapter, we will show how words can be turned into a form which is capable of changing the mental networks that are associated with personal identity and folk religion.

Summary

We began this chapter with the child clutching her teddy bear while her father was attempting to take it away from her, which led us to divide personal identity into physical identity and mental identity. The child is holding on to the bear because it forms part of her mental identity, while her father is trying to take it away because it does not form a part of her physical identity.

I then suggested that personal identity can be defined as the mental networks upon which I can continue to focus. My physical body forms an inseparable part of my personal identity for the simple fact that it *is* inseparable from my personal existence. The pain and pleasure that it produces creates mental networks within Mercy thought, while its continued presence both helps Perceiver thought to gain the confidence that is needed to handle this emotional pressure and punishes the mind severely when the Perceiver module does not function.

Personal identity begins by representing the physical body but it extends beyond this to represent knowledge and skills that I have acquired. In addition, mental networks which are *often* but not always repeated define my family and friends. Moving in the other direction, items whose presence is continually repeated but which do not form mental networks define my possessions. Ownership involves Perceiver thought, because it forms a solid connection between an object and the mental network of its owner. If these Perceiver connections are not provided internally, then they must exist externally in the form of walls and gates.

When dealing with aspects of personal identity that do not relate directly to the physical body, the natural tendency is for the mind to identify with emotional situations and events that do not occur repeatedly. That is because the emotional content causes a mental network to form, and this mental network attracts the attention of Exhorter thought while disrupting the operation of Perceiver thought.

When Perceiver thought is not functioning, then experiences will be acquired by personal identity through identification and removed from personal identity through denial. Identification confuses 'good' with 'true', whereas denial equates 'bad' with 'false', because Perceiver connections are being determined by emotional pressure. Identification aborts personal growth by pretending that I have already arrived at my goal, whereas denial fills the mind with 'emotional baggage'. Emotional baggage leads to a vicious circle of denying and re-embracing; the immediate pain of focusing upon emotional baggage leads to denial, whereas the long-term hyper-pain caused by this denial motivates a person to embrace new situations that are similar to the ones which he denied.

Sexual content magnifies the difficulty of dealing with emotional baggage, because it is closely connected with the physical body. In order to deny or digest these memories, one must mentally suppress or alter memories which are directly related to the mental network that represents the physical object whose continued presence and form defines human life itself. In a similar vein, when an individual has more than one sexual partner, sex then becomes mentally associated with mutually incompatible mental networks, making it difficult to focus upon the current sexual partner and enjoy the feelings of the moment.

We ended this chapter by using the concept of mental networks to analyze the last six of the Ten Commandments, and we noticed that all of these commandments address mental networks, focus upon mental networks with intense emotional content, prohibit denial and identification, and prescribe the use of Perceiver thought.

Finally, we looked at Western society and noticed that identification, together with the suppression of Perceiver thought, define the norm in the areas of entertainment, advertising, marketing, professional sports, the legal field, and politics. We then observed that many of the leaders in these various fields adhere to religions that verbally assert the supremacy of the Ten Commandments. That brought us to the conclusion that what a person says that he believes often has very little effect upon what he believes in practice, an observation that is backed up by extensive data from the field of the cognitive science of religion.

✵ 5. Science and Teacher Thought

We all know the story of Galileo and his struggle with the Catholic Church. Medieval Christianity taught that the earth is the center of the universe and that the stars and planets are embedded in celestial spheres which rotate around the earth. Galileo, in contrast, advocated the heliocentric model which states that the planets revolve around the sun, and he used observation to support his model. The telescope had just been invented, and when Galileo used an improved version which he had developed to observe the planet Jupiter, he saw four moons orbiting the massive planet, proving that celestial objects exist which do not orbit around the earth. However, Galileo was eventually called to Rome to defend his new theory, he was accused of heresy and forced to recant, and he spent the rest of his life under house arrest forbidden from publishing any new books.

Galileo is lifted up as one of the great heroes of science, and his conflict with the church is usually portrayed as a fight between scientific observation and religious dogma. As the story is typically told, Galileo applied the scientific method by carefully observing the real world, rejecting a theory which did not fit the facts, and proposing a paradigm that was consistent with objective data, whereas the Catholic Church clung to outdated theories supported by religious dogma based in blind faith in ancient Christian tomes.

However, if one probes further, one discovers that Galileo himself was quite capable of promoting dogma and ignoring scientific research. When it came to explaining the tides, for instance, it was Johannes Kepler who correctly realized that the tides are caused by the gravitational pull of the moon, an idea which Galileo rejected as 'useless fiction'. Albert Einstein, looking back at this dispute several centuries later, concluded that Galileo had been driven to come up with his unscientific explanation by his desire to prove that the earth moves and does not stay still. Similarly, Galileo also dismissed Kepler's discovery that the planets move in elliptical orbits. In this case it was Kepler's model that was based in the careful observations of Tycho Brahe, whereas Galileo was convinced that the circle is the 'perfect shape' for a planetary orbit.

As for Johannes Kepler, he also came up with theories which today would be considered quite unscientific. For instance, he explained the distances between the orbits of the planets in terms of geometrical solids, the scientific version of using apples to explain oranges. And he regarded the universe as an image of God, with the Sun corresponding to God the Father, the celestial spheres to God the Son, and the space separating the spheres to God the Holy Spirit.

My goal is not to belittle the scientific method, but rather to show that even the heroes of science only partially live up to the ideals of science. Science states that its general theories are built upon careful observation and logical thought and it claims that, unlike religion, it does not cling blindly to outdated theories but instead is willing to abandon a hypothesis and search carefully for a new and improved model if even a single counter-example is discovered. What happens in practice, though, is quite different, for the typical scientist clings to his theories with a tenacity that matches the fervor of the religious dogmatist, and his intellectual world generally has to come crashing down around him before it is possible to pry his fingers away from clutching on to his current paradigm.[9]

Thomas Kuhn

If these conclusions sound excessive, then I highly recommend reading *The Structure of Scientific Revolutions* by Thomas Kuhn, a classic written in the 1960s. Because I will be quoting rather extensively from Thomas Kuhn's volume throughout this book, I need to mention that I encountered the research of Kuhn for the first time in 2011. I then took several weeks to analyze his book and was amazed to discover that his findings match up closely with what I have discovered. His book helped to clarify a number of concepts that I had independently uncovered as well as provide corroborative evidence for a significant portion of my research. As I mentioned in the introduction to this book, when one is studying the mind, then one must use independent confirmation to error-check a theory. Therefore, when one discovers that the contents of an *entire book* written by one of the main figures in the philosophy of science can be placed within the theory of mental symmetry, then that provides strong independent confirmation. Of course, Kuhn didn't talk about 'general Teacher theories'. He used the term 'paradigm'. However, it appears that what Kuhn calls a paradigm has the same meaning as what mental symmetry calls a general Teacher theory, and this book will be treating these two terms as equivalent. Similarly, while editing this volume, I encountered *The Web of Belief* by Willard Quine for the first time, and realized that it also fits very well into the theory of mental symmetry—another example of independent confirmation. That analysis can be found in an appendix.

Before we begin looking at Kuhn, I need to reiterate my statement in the introduction that I will not be approaching philosophy as a philosopher. My goal is to understand the mind, and not to apply an ironclad system of formal logic to human thought. Later on, we will be looking at how the mind generates formal logic, and I have included an appendix suggesting how and why the mind constructs the formal thinking of math, but we still will not be using formal logic to analyze the mind. In fact, as I stated in the introduction, I suggest that it is *impossible* to use formal logic to analyze human thought for the simple reason that formal logic is only one aspect of human thought. Thus, I view Kuhn's work on paradigms as *empirical* data, and not as a system of formal logic.

---

[9] Paradigms involve the *internal* world of Teacher thought. Automatic Teacher thought, in contrast, deals with specific words, conversations, and theoretical notions. These Teacher fragments help to 'flesh out' a paradigm and can provide the starting point for Teacher thought.

He observed how scientists behave and tried to describe this as accurately as he could. I too have observed human behavior, originally from the perspective of cognitive styles, and I also have tried to describe it as accurately as I know how.

As I have attempted to share my understanding with others over the years, I learned from firsthand experience what happens when paradigms interact, and I used my cognitive model to try to understand the reaction that I was experiencing. When I read Thomas Kuhn, I discovered that he was describing precisely the same sort of intellectual behavior that I had personally encountered. Because he came up with the same data from a different perspective, his descriptions provide independent confirmation for the cognitive model of mental symmetry, and I have used his careful observations to clarify and expand this model. Thus, I will not be looking at how others have interpreted Kuhn, or even at how Kuhn himself eventually felt about the concepts that he unleashed upon the public. Instead, I will simply be taking Kuhn's remarks and fitting them into the cognitive model of mental symmetry.

Kuhn notes "what scientists never do when confronted by even severe and prolonged anomalies. Though they may begin to lose faith and then to consider alternatives, they do not renounce the paradigm that has led them into crisis. They do not, that is, treat anomalies as counterinstances, though in the vocabulary of philosophy of science, that is what they are." In a similar vein, the famous scientist Max Planck wrote in his *Scientific Autobiography* that "a new scientific truth does not triumph by convincing its opponents and making them see the light, but rather because its opponents eventually die, and a new generation grows up that is familiar with it."

Thus, if one compares the typical behavior of science to the parable of Galileo and the church, historians of science conclude that science tends to play the role of the church more often than it displays the intellectual rigor and observational honesty attributed to Galileo.

Why is this the case? I suggest that the answer can be found by combining two concepts from previous chapters. We began this book by comparing Teacher emotion with Mercy emotion. We then took some time to look at mental networks and how they relate to Mercy thought. This discussion assumed that all mental networks are based in Mercy experiences. However, a mental network forms whenever emotional memories combine to function as a unit. Because the body provides the mind with emotional *experiences*, most mental networks are composed of Mercy experiences. But it is also possible for *Teacher* memories to combine to form a mental network.

A mental network that forms within the Teacher module will act like any other mental network—it will want to be 'fed' and it will want to 'stay alive'. The method by which one 'feeds' a Teacher-based mental network can be worked out by looking at how Teacher emotions are formed. Remember that Teacher emotion comes from order-within-complexity. It feels good when a simple theory can be used to explain many individual items, situations, or occurrences, and it feels bad when a situation is encountered which a theory cannot explain. Therefore, a Teacher-based mental network is 'fed' simply by providing it with data that it can explain. In contrast, whenever a situation is encountered that contradicts the theory, then the Teacher-based mental network will feel pain. If a general theory encounters sufficient counterexamples, then it will begin to fall apart and generate the hyper-pain of fragmentation.

Science and Emotions

Thomas Kuhn describes some of the emotions that are felt by scientists when their general theories fall apart: "Wolfgang Pauli, in the months before Heisenberg's paper on matrix mechanics pointed the way to a new quantum theory wrote to a friend, 'At the moment physics is again terribly confused. In any case, it is too difficult for me, and I wish I had been a movie comedian or something of the sort and had never heard of physics.' That testimony is particularly impressive if contrasted with Pauli's words less than five months later: 'Heisenberg's type of mechanics has again given me hope and joy in life.'"

This explains why scientists, mathematicians, philosophers—and theologians—cling to their general theories. Once a theory forms a mental network within Teacher mode, it becomes difficult to dislodge this theory. Kuhn himself comments that "almost always the men who achieve these fundamental inventions of a new paradigm have been either very young or very new to the field whose paradigm they change...obviously these are the men who, being little committed by prior practice to the traditional rules of normal science, are particularly likely to see that those rules no longer define a playable game and to conceive another set that can replace them."

Saying this another way, objective science attempts to protect Perceiver thought by *avoiding* subjective Mercy emotions. But, it does not realize that a general theory within Teacher thought is *also* emotional and that it *too* can form a mental network. Thus, objective science may win the battle against emotions but it ends up losing the war. For if a person *avoids* learning how to deal rationally with emotional issues, then once he acquires a Teacher understanding and his understanding turns into a mental network, then he will become emotionally locked in to his current paradigm, unable to change. In contrast, if a person gains the Perceiver confidence that is needed to be logical in the midst of subjective Mercy feelings, then this same Perceiver confidence will also give him the ability to evaluate or re-evaluate a general Teacher theory.

In essence, the *objective* scientist is like the typical blank CD or DVD disk. A general theory can be placed into his mind *once*, but if a new theory comes along, then the only alternative is to throw him away and pick a fresh 'blank mind' from the next generation. If that sounds harsh, then I am simply paraphrasing Kuhn: "Scientific training is not well designed to produce the man who will easily discover a fresh approach. But so long as somebody appears with a new candidate for paradigm—usually a young man or one new to the field—the loss due to rigidity accrues only to the individual. Given a generation in which to effect the change, individual rigidity is compatible with a community that can switch from paradigm to paradigm when the occasion demands."

In addition, Mercy emotions are very difficult to avoid. The typical scientist may start out by being objective, but once he acquires the personal status of a high-paying job at a prestigious university, then Mercy emotions have re-entered the scene, especially if the scientist becomes publically recognized as an important person. These secondary Mercy emotions will make it even more difficult for the once-objective scientist to question the intellectual status quo.

Even when a person has sufficient Perceiver confidence to evaluate his Teacher theories, history shows that Perceiver facts by themselves are insufficient to cause a person to drop a general theory. In other words, the myth of the logically driven scientist abandoning his scientific theory because he discovers a counterexample appears to be—a myth. Instead, the person who has acquired a general Teacher theory will only let go of this theory if he is given another theory to take its place. According to Kuhn, "once it has achieved the status of paradigm, a scientific theory is declared invalid only if an alternate candidate is available to take its place. No process yet disclosed by the historical study of scientific development at all resembles the methodological stereotype of falsification by direct comparison with nature. That remark does not mean that scientists do not reject scientific theories, or that experience and experiment are not essential to the process in which they do so. But it does mean—what will ultimately be a central point—that the act of judgment that leads scientists to reject a previously accepted theory is always based upon more than a comparison of that theory with the world. The decision to reject one paradigm is always simultaneously the decision to accept another, and the judgment leading to that decision involves the comparison of both paradigms with nature *and* with each other."

We can understand this mental constraint better by comparing Teacher emotions with Mercy emotions. Mercy feelings are ubiquitous; Mercy mode is continually being flooded with emotional experiences from the physical body. Thus, if some human hero or defining experience falls from its pedestal, there are dozens of alternatives clamoring to take its place. Potent Teacher emotions, in contrast, are rare. In order to feel a strong Teacher emotion, one must either construct or learn a general theory, a process that takes time and energy. The result is that when a general Teacher theory crumbles, then the choice is often between something and nothing, and once Teacher mode has begun to function, it cannot return to the state of not functioning. As Kuhn points out, "Once a first paradigm through which to view nature has been found, there is no such thing as research in the absence of any paradigm. To reject one paradigm without simultaneously substituting another is to reject science itself."

This leads us to the following general observation: I have suggested that tearing apart a mental network leads to the hyper-pain of fragmentation. However, there is an emotional horror which is even deeper than mental fragmentation and that is mental *annihilation.* This is the sense of angst that emerges when core mental networks within either the Mercy or Teacher module start to fall apart, because this threatens the continued functioning of the cognitive module itself. Fragmentation is horrifying, but annihilation is unthinkable for Teacher thought and inconceivable for Mercy thought.

Normally, the hyper-agony of angst is associated with core *Mercy*-based mental networks falling apart, because these are the ones that usually define personal existence. However, for the scientific mind, Teacher-based mental networks play a much greater defining role than they do in the mind of the typical individual, thus the scientist can feel the loss of a paradigm quite keenly.

For instance, in the last chapter, we saw that the physical body is responsible for forming and supporting core mental networks of personal identity within Mercy thought, because every living creature is inseparably connected with a specific physical body for its entire lifetime. Now imagine meeting intelligent creatures who did *not* live within physical bodies. Obviously, an encounter such as this would threaten the integrity of these core mental networks. This explains the emotional response of those who claim to have been 'abducted by aliens'. What concerns us here is not the validity of these reports but rather the emotional reactions of those who are making the claims, for they describe a sensation of utter horror and nameless dread. That is what it feels like when core mental networks start to fall apart, and that also describes what it is like for a scientist to attempt to function without a general theory—it is unthinkable.

This explains why the typical scientist recoils with horror at the religious concept of *miracles*, for a miracle is an *exception* to the universal rules of science, and general Teacher theories hate exceptions. However, that is precisely how the typical religious believer portrays a miracle: "The doctors took another X-ray and they saw that the cancer had completely disappeared. Medical science has no rational explanation for what happened. It must be a miracle." Thus, the average religious believer portrays a miracle as the *absence* of a general Teacher theory, and he expects the scientist to embrace religion by throwing away his Teacher-based mental networks and replacing them with—nothing. For the scientist, that describes intellectual suicide; it is unthinkable.

Teacher Mental Networks

Before we continue, we should clarify the precise difference between a general Teacher theory and a Teacher-based mental network. And from now on, instead of using the clumsy term 'Teacher-based mental network', we will use the slightly less awkward 'Teacher mental network'.

A general Teacher theory provides the *raw material* for a Teacher mental network, because a mental network requires emotional memories, and the way to create emotional memories within Teacher thought is by constructing a general theory. In addition, a mental network forms when many related memories come together, and a general theory ties together many related memories. However, while a Teacher mental network is based upon a general theory, it goes *beyond* it.

This is similar to the way in which a habit goes beyond a mere urge. I may have an urge to scratch my chin, but when I think about my chin, I still have to choose to scratch it. In contrast, when a habit develops, then when my chin comes to mind, I have to choose *not* to scratch it. And if I continue to choose not to scratch my chin, then the urge to scratch will become stronger and stronger. Likewise, it feels good when I can use a general Teacher theory to explain many situations, even if this theory has not reached the level of a mental network. But if I choose not to think about this theory or decide to interpret the situation using some other general explanation, then I will not experience mental pain or feel driven to use the theory.

However, if I *continue* to study or use a general theory, then it will eventually acquire sufficient emotional content to turn into a mental network. And once a general theory passes this threshold, then it will demand the right to interpret any incident which falls within its domain. When a theory which has turned into a mental network comes to mind, then I will *want* to study more about it, and I will have to choose *not* to think about it.

This is the transition that every instructor hopes to achieve within the minds of his students. The student who lacks a general Teacher theory usually does not want to learn and would rather be somewhere else. The one who gains a general Teacher understanding of the subject enjoys learning—as long as he is sitting in class or doing assigned homework. However, if the general Teacher understanding within the mind of the student turns into a mental network, then the student becomes self-motivated and will choose to learn even when he is not being driven by his teacher.

I still remember passing that mental threshold in my research of mental symmetry, way back in the 1980s. I had spent several months helping my brother work out some of the basic traits of the Perceiver person. Even though I found the topic interesting, I was still doing it partially for the sake of my brother. But one day I began to experience a curious mental phenomenon. I would mentally respond to some situation and then a second or two later something within my mind would explain why I had reacted in that manner. Looking back, I realize that the general theory of mental symmetry had formed a Teacher mental network. After that point, it distinctly felt as if the theory of mental symmetry gradually but inexorably 'ate up my mind'.[10]

Was the theory of mental symmetry actually 'alive'? Was it *choosing* to activate itself? I do not think so. Instead, it was the *predictability* of my behavior that was continuing to trigger the theory. As a Perceiver person, I am conscious within Perceiver mode. This means that whenever I use conscious thought, I can only use *Perceiver* thought. Therefore, if I learn about a general Teacher theory that explains Perceiver thought, then it will be activated whenever I use conscious thought, regardless of the situation or location. A similar principle would apply to every cognitive style.

This leads us to an alternate source for personal identity, one that is rooted in an *internal* Teacher theory rather than an *external* physical body. In the last chapter, I defined personal identity as the set of experiences upon which I can continue to focus. The mental network that represents my physical body forms the core of my personal identity

---

[10] Kant says that the 'faculty of reason' seeks to unify all particulars under more general principles of knowledge—even when this generalization goes beyond the existing evidence.

for the simple reason that my body follows me around wherever I go. However, what is even more closely bound to personal identity is *conscious thought.* As a Perceiver person, I cannot escape the fact that I am a Perceiver person. Wherever I go, this mode of thought follows me around. But my mind will only realize this if Teacher thought constructs a general Teacher theory that explains conscious thought.

We will return to this concept in a moment, but let us look first at the behavior of a Teacher mental network and compare it with Mercy mental networks. The primary difference between these two types of mental networks is that Mercy mental networks are rooted in specific private experiences whereas Teacher mental networks are produced by general theories.[11] And everyone knows that an army has many privates but only a few generals. This may be a bad joke but it does illustrate the point. Mercy mental networks are bountiful not just because we live in physical bodies but also because we are surrounded by many individual people who live in physical bodies. Teacher mental networks are rare not just because they must be constructed but also because they are general. A general theory ties together many separate items, thus in the same way that the world contains far less countries than inhabitants, and far fewer generals than privates, so the mind has far fewer general Teacher theories than specific Mercy experiences.

Competing Theories

Countries and armies also illustrate the relationship between one general theory and another. For instance, suppose that I am an American citizen living in South Korea. Which national law governs my behavior? Normally, I would be expected to obey Korean law, but if I live on an American army base, then I am subject to American law. However, what happens if an American soldier commits a crime against a Korean when he is not on an American army base? This happened in 2002 when an American bridge-laying tank ran over two Korean girls while returning from a military exercise. The American soldiers were tried in an American court and acquitted and this led to major protests by the Korean population as well as a general backlash against foreigners living in Korea.

A similar question of jurisdiction occurs whenever two general theories collide. Just as it is not possible for two countries to rule over the same section of land, so it is not possible for two competing theories to continue explaining the same situation. Suppose, for instance, that an American citizen moves to Korea. Obviously, he will be expected to submit to Korean law. If he refuses, then he will either be made to submit or else expelled from the country. Similarly, whenever a general Teacher theory experiences an exception to the rule, then this produces feelings of Teacher pain. In order to stop the

---

[11] It is also possible for Mercy thought to deal with generality and Teacher thought to work with specifics. While that type of mindset is compatible with the mind, it is *not* compatible with human existence, and we are looking here at the type of mental structures that emerge in the naturally developing human mind.

pain, the exception must either be removed or else forced in some way to conform. Now suppose that the rebellious American insists that he does not have to conform to Korean regulations because he is an American citizen who has the backing of the American state. This is what happens when one general theory comes into contact with a conflicting theory. If one theory attempts to fit the incident into its general scheme, then this will end up creating an exception for the other general theory. The result is a zero-sum interaction in which intellectual joy from one general theory is always accompanied by mental pain from the other.

When this type of stalemate continues within the political arena, then situations turn into international incidents. In terms of our illustration, what began as a traffic accident in which two girls were killed by a passing military vehicle became a major event in which heads of state were involved and thousands of citizens demonstrated. Likewise, if two competing theories continue to attempt to explain the same situation, then eventually the Teacher pain of a simple counterexample will turn into the Teacher hyper-pain of a crumbling theory, for the very existence of the one general theory will threaten the integrity of the other. The two theories are now locked in a life and death struggle in which only one can continue to survive. And when one theory wins, then it will eliminate Teacher pain by removing any remaining traces of any competing theories.

A similar escalation and resolution occurs in science when there are competing general theories. Kuhn elaborates upon the initial escalation from local problem to 'international incident': "When...an anomaly comes to seem more than just another puzzle of normal science, the transition to crisis and extraordinary science has begun. The anomaly itself now comes to be more generally recognized as such by the profession. More and more attention is devoted to it by more and more of the field's most eminent men. If it still continues to resist, as it usually does not, many of them may come to view its resolution as *the* subject matter of their discipline. For them the field will no longer look quite the same as it had earlier." And he also describes the victory of one general theory over another: "When it repudiates a past paradigm, a scientific community simultaneously renounces, as a fit subject for professional scrutiny, most of the books and articles in which that paradigm had been embodied."

But, a general theory does not just explain current situations, it also explains memories of past situations. Thus, if a victorious general theory is to remove all exceptions to its rule, it must also rewrite history to make it appear as if no other general theory ever existed. As Kuhn states, "For reasons that are both obvious and highly functional, science textbooks (and too many of the older histories of science) refer only to that part of the work of past scientists that can easily be viewed as contributions to the statement and solutions of the texts' paradigm problems. Partly by selection and partly by distortion, the scientists of earlier ages are implicitly represented as having worked upon the same set of fixed problems and in accordance with the same set of fixed canons that the most recent revolution in scientific theory and method has made seem scientific. No wonder that textbooks and the historical tradition they imply have to be rewritten after each Scientific Revolution."

So far we have described what happens when one general theory *competes* with another. However, it is possible for two theories to coexist on peaceful terms, but only if one of these theories is *translated* into the language of the other. For instance, Canada has two official languages, English and French. Therefore, all Canadian laws are written in both languages. Similarly, it is possible to describe the laws of physics using mathematical models that appear on the surface to be quite different, but which can be shown mathematically to be equivalent.

That is why I began this book by suggesting that theology is cognitive science in religious garb. What I really mean is that it is possible to *translate* the principles of theology into the language of cognitive science. If one looks at the diagram of mental symmetry, one sees that Teacher and Perceiver are labeled as *abstract*. When translating abstract concepts and general theories from one language to another, I suggest that both of these mental modules play a major role. The Perceiver side of translation deals with the meanings of words, whereas the Teacher side of translation conveys the overall understanding. A good translation preserves both the specific words as well as the overall intent of the original passage.[12]

Let us look at these two aspects to translation, using first an example from theology and then one from the cognitive science of religion. We will begin with the Perceiver side of specifics words and their meanings.

Consider, for instance, the Greek word ἁμαρτία or 'hamartia', which is translated as 'sin' in the English Bible. Originally, this word was taken from archery, and it had the meaning of shooting an arrow at a target and missing. In Greek tragedies, it refers to an error in judgment, in which a person tries to achieve a good goal but ends up provoking disaster through a lack of knowledge. For the modern religious believer, the word 'sin' conveys the concept of becoming emotionally tainted through personal association with places, events, or situations that are disapproved. As for the objective scientist, the word 'sin' does not form part of his normal vocabulary, but instead is mentally connected with irrational subjective thought. Finally, mental symmetry describes 'sin' as cognitive behavior that is supposed to produce a good result but ends up being harmful because mental modules are either undeveloped, controlling each other, or working in isolation—a meaning that matches up fairly closely with the original Greek intent. Notice how each culture group has associated the word 'sin' with a different set of Perceiver facts and Mercy experiences. That illustrates the fundamental *Perceiver* problem when attempting to translate a word from one language into another language.

Hidden behind the obvious Perceiver problem of choosing the correct word is the deeper issue of conveying the same general Teacher understanding. For instance, I

---

[12] The precise circuit is as follows: Words are stored within Teacher thought. These Teacher memories acquire Server stability as words are repeated. Contributor thought then connects each Server pattern with a specific Perceiver meaning. This will be discussed several chapters later when looking at the technical circuit of Ci.

recently took a look at the field of the cognitive science of religion, and the book *Minds and Gods* by Todd Tremlin, a well known researcher in this emerging area, provides a good example of the issues that are involved in the Teacher side of translation. Tremlin examines the cognitive basis for a belief in God, similar to the approach that is being taken in this book, and I found it very helpful to go through Tremlin's book in detail and to translate his concepts into the language of mental symmetry.

At the Perceiver level of words and meanings, Tremlin examines a number of religious terms and attempts to translate them carefully into the language of cognitive science. However, at the level of general Teacher theory, one discovers that the emphasis of Tremlin is quite different than the emphasis of the typical theologian. For the theologian, what matters is doctrine and holy books. Tremlin, in contrast, ignores doctrine and focuses upon religious practice.

For instance, Tremlin says that theology has mistaken concepts about God: "So from the perspective of cognition, the real attributes of gods turn out to be rather different from those provided by theology, such as the list of divine properties drawn from Christianity in the last chapter." Tremlin also states that theology has no connection with cognitive science: "This, of course, is to enter into the realm of theology—an interesting enterprise but one wholly irrelevant to understanding the way minds think." He concludes that theology is basically background noise which needs to be tuned out: "It is sometimes all too obvious that the religious system works quite well without depending to any significant degree upon such theological notions. Sometimes theology seems to do little more than provide soothing background noise. Even if this is an unnecessarily harsh characterization of theology's place in religious systems, at least it must be said that such notions are not the motor that drives religious ideas and the practices these ideas inform, nor does it play any significant role in the growth and decline of religious traditions."

Tremlin *replaces* theology with the scenario of primitive men living in the jungle fleeing from wild animals, a story that we analyzed from a cognitive viewpoint in an earlier chapter. In essence, Tremlin's model suggests that humans today look for intelligent causes behind unexplained events because our distant ancestors developed this ability in order to recognize and flee from wild beasts. Thus, a scenario that the typical theologian would regard as rather trivial, Tremlin views as fundamental, whereas facts and books that the theologian would consider to be foundational, Tremlin dismisses as irrelevant. That is what it means to alter the Teacher emphasis when attempting to translate. Because Tremlin changes the emphasis so radically, one concludes that at the Teacher level of general theory, he is *not* translating religion into cognitive science.

We can tie down this concept of Teacher emphasis with a situation which I repeatedly encountered in Korea. Suppose that one asks someone a negative question such as "You do not have any bananas, do you?" A Westerner will respond, "*No*, we have no bananas," whereas an Asian will reply, "*Yes*, we have no bananas." That is because the Westerner is mentally emphasizing the *question*, and so he responds negatively to the information. The Asian, in contrast, is emphasizing the *person*, therefore he agrees with the individual.

According to Kuhn, this type of change in emphasis occurs when one scientific theory *replaces* another: "Since new paradigms are born from old ones, they ordinarily incorporate much of the vocabulary and apparatus, both conceptual and manipulative, that the traditional paradigm had previously employed. But they seldom employ these borrowed elements in quite the traditional way. Within the new paradigm, old terms, concepts, and experiments fall into new relationships one with the other."

Formulating a general theory could be compared to carrying out an election, because one concept is being chosen from the entire population in order to explain all of the other concepts. If that 'leader' cannot bring order to rest of the population, then it is 'deposed' and another potential leader is chosen. This process continues until a successful 'leader' is found. This analogy corresponds quite closely to the way in which Teacher thought operates. For the typical theologian, the core concept may be God revealing himself to humankind through the process of written revelation. For Tremlin, it is the jungle dweller hiding from predators. For mental symmetry, it is the concept of interacting cognitive modules.

When a concept becomes a 'successful leader', it acquires positive Teacher emotion because, like any good leader, it brings order to complexity. And because Exhorter mode is connected to *both* Mercy *and* Teacher thought, these strong *Teacher* emotions have the ability to draw the attention of the Exhorter module away from emotional Mercy situations to general Teacher theories. This is what happens when a paradigm is discovered for the *first* time in some area of thought. When such a mental transition occurs within the mind of the Exhorter *person*, he discovers—often to his surprise—that he is capable of abstract thought and that grand theories can be both exciting and addictive. But, what attracts Exhorter thought is general theories and *not* petty details. Therefore, these Exhorter urges will cause a person to focus upon fundamental concepts while ignoring ideas that are trivial, just as television news focuses more upon what the leader of the country is saying or doing in Metropolis than upon what is happening to Joe Average in Smallville.

A *change* in paradigm can be compared to a change in government, in which the original leaders are deposed and replaced by a new set of leaders. In the words of Kuhn, "Led by a new paradigm, scientists adopt new instruments and look in new places. Even more important, during revolutions scientists see new and different things when looking with familiar instruments in places they have looked before. It is rather as if the professional community had been suddenly transported to another planet where familiar objects are seen in a different light and are joined by unfamiliar ones as well."

Translation versus Paradigm Shift

We can now describe more clearly the relationship between a translation and a paradigm shift. Translation includes the two aspects of Perceiver meaning and Teacher emphasis.

The core element of a paradigm is the Teacher emphasis, because a paradigm takes a collection of concepts and elevates some of them into significance while demoting other ones into insignificance. When the Perceiver meanings stay the same but the Teacher emphasis changes, then there is a *paradigm shift.* When the Perceiver meanings are the same *and* the Teacher emphasis is the same, then there is a *translation* of the original paradigm.

This distinction may seem unimportant, but it is actually quite significant. For instance, compare the way in which the average Christian or Jew reads the Bible with the method of higher criticism that is applied by the typical Biblical scholar. Because both the layman and the scholar are studying the same religious book, the assumption is that their methods are *equivalent.* After all, they are both reading precisely the same words. However, one method is actually a major paradigm shift from the other. The average reader is emphasizing Biblical passages that bring him emotional comfort and personal guidance. Higher criticism, in contrast, is attempting to decipher the source of Biblical passages by comparing them with other manuscripts from similar periods. When the layman reads about a miracle, he regards this as significant, because in his mind it represents the hand of God. In contrast, higher criticism downplays the miracle and focuses instead upon passages which match the writings of other authors from that period. Thus, what one focuses on, the other tends to ignore. That is the sign of a paradigm shift.

As Kuhn describes it, "One perceptive historian, viewing a classic case of a science's reorientation by paradigm change, recently described it as 'picking up the other end of the stick,' a process that involves 'handling the same bundle of data as before, but placing them in a new system of relations with one another by giving them a different framework.'"

Notice that the Perceiver side of translation is more basic than the Teacher side, because Perceiver facts are used to construct general Teacher theories. This is what makes the *interpretation* suspect. It claims to preserve a general Teacher theory while presenting it using a new set of Perceiver facts, but there is no way of telling whether the interpretation is the same as the original or different. Thus, the interpretation often turns into another example of one general theory attacking and replacing another. Saying this more simply, in order to compare one general theory with another, one must first define words clearly and carefully.

A translation is never perfect. When two competing theories are radically different, then it becomes quite difficult to translate from one theory to the other. Because each theory emphasizes a different set of facts, Perceiver thought will work out categories and meanings with great care and precision in areas that are regarded as significant, whereas in areas that are regarded as trivial, Perceiver facts will remain vague and categories will be unclear. Thus, the translator may discover that Perceiver facts exist within one theory for which there are no corresponding terms in the other theory.

For instance, the Korean language has numerous words for family members for which there is no English equivalent. When a younger sister refers to her oldest brother, she will call him 'Opa', whereas a younger brother will refer to the same person as 'Hyong'. These precisely defined categories exist because Korean society is heavily influenced by Confucianism, which places a major emphasis upon family relationships and familial duties.

At an even more basic level, the process of translation assumes that Perceiver thought is functioning, for Perceiver thought defines the categories that are used to apply meanings to words, and Perceiver thought also compares the categories within one language to the categories within another language in order to determine which word—or set of words—in one language is equivalent to a word in another language. However, we learned in a previous chapter that it is possible for Mercy emotions to overwhelm Perceiver thought and prevent it from functioning. When this is the case, then words tend to have emotional connotations instead of precise meanings. This is often true when dealing with religious words. For instance, in *American Jesus: How the Son of God Became a National Icon*, Stephen Prothero describes some of the ways in which various social groups have redefined the historical Jesus in order to meet their emotional needs.

In addition, emotional pressure will prevent the mind from translating between 'us' and 'them', because 'good' in Mercy thought becomes equated with 'true' in Perceiver thought, while 'bad' in Mercy thought is regarded as the equivalent of 'false' within Perceiver mode. Perceiver thought may compare one 'good' concept with another 'good' concept, or relate one 'bad' idea with another 'bad' idea, but if Perceiver thought attempts to compare a 'bad' fact' with a 'good' fact, then the strong emotional contrast will prevent Perceiver thought from functioning.

This is often the case when dealing with religious books and religious doctrines. A Christian believer, for instance, might compare the words and theories of one Christian theologian with those of another theologian, because both of these theories come from emotional sources that are labelled as 'good' within Mercy thought. Similarly, he might compare the views of one Buddhist author with those of another, because he regards both of these authors as 'bad'. However, the Christian believer probably will not compare a Christian theory with a Buddhist theory, because one is associated with 'good' Mercy experiences while the other is mentally connected with 'bad' Mercy experiences. In some religions, the very concept of translation is regarded with suspicion. For instance, the Muslim Quran can be 'interpreted' but it cannot be 'translated', and until fairly recently, the Catholic mass was celebrated in Latin, without being translated into the local language.

The primary goal of this book is to translate theology into the language of mental symmetry. Will the result be a translation that is equivalent to the original or will it be a paradigm shift? I suggest that this depends upon whether one is focusing upon the *approach* or the *content* of religion. If the fundamental concept of religion is blind faith in the words of a holy book, then the theory of mental symmetry represents a paradigm shift. However, if one examines the *content* of theology, then I suggest that we are indeed dealing with an equivalent translation and not a paradigm shift.

Kuhn talks at length about the difficulties of translating one theory into the language of another, and he refers to this problem as *incommensurability*: "We have already seen several reasons why the proponents of competing paradigms must fail to make complete contact with each other's viewpoints. Collectively these reasons have been described as the incommensurability of the pre- and postrevolutionary normal-scientific traditions, and we need only recapitulate them briefly here."

Let us examine Kuhn's concept of incommensurability in a little more detail. We have seen that it is difficult to compare one paradigm with another, and we have also seen that a person who uses a paradigm has emotional reasons for holding on to his existing paradigm and refusing to examine alternative theories. Some people have concluded from this that scientific thought is emotional and not logical, while others have argued that if one paradigm cannot be compared with another, then it is not possible to say that one paradigm is better than another, which means that all paradigms are essentially equivalent and that there is no such thing as a good paradigm or a bad paradigm.

I suggest that the solution lies in realizing that a paradigm involves an *interaction* between logic and emotion. A paradigm is constructed out of factual Perceiver bricks using logical steps. Neither the bricks nor the process of construction is emotional. But when the bricks are combined to form a structure, then that structure *will* generate an emotion. As a result, either questioning a paradigm or comparing one paradigm with another will produce unpleasant Teacher feelings, because this threatens the overall structure. However, evaluating a paradigm still means using logical facts that are independent of emotions. As we have seen, learning how to use Perceiver facts in the midst of emotional pressure is difficult, but it is an ability that can be acquired.

The skill of evaluating or comparing paradigms has several components: First, building Perceiver confidence makes it possible for a person to question a paradigm in *deeper* and more fundamental ways. If a person avoids emotional pressure by remaining objective, then he will find even trivial challenges to his paradigm emotionally overwhelming. In contrast, the individual who learns how to hold on to Perceiver facts in the midst of emotional pressure can continue to use logic to evaluate a paradigm even when Teacher thought is expressing significant emotional discomfort.

Second, understanding the process of evaluating paradigms makes it emotionally *easier* to carry out this process. That is because understanding produces positive Teacher emotions, and these positive Teacher feelings will help to balance the negative Teacher feelings that are being generated by the paradigm which is being questioned. Taking this one step further, it is possible to represent the process of evaluating paradigms *itself* as a general paradigm—a general theory that describes the process of comparing general theories. And, jumping ahead to concepts which we have not yet discussed, if one continues to successfully complete the process of comparing one paradigm with another, then this repetition will lead to the growth of *Server* confidence, which will make it easier to compare one paradigm with another. Saying this another way, it is possible to develop the *skill* of being able to compare paradigms. These factors will be discussed later on in the book.

Third, an emphasis upon rigorous logic and specialization will make it more *difficult* for a person to compare one paradigm with another. As we shall see later—and as Kuhn makes clear—it is not possible to use rigorous logic to compare one paradigm with another. Instead, rigorous logic can only be used within a paradigm. Therefore, when a scholar is taught that he must use *only* rigorous logic, then he will mentally suppress the type of thinking that is needed to step outside of his paradigm and compare it with another. And if a person only learns about one paradigm, then how can he compare this paradigm with other paradigms?

If rigorous logic cannot be used to compare one paradigm with another, then what logical tool *can* be used? Translation. Translating one paradigm into the language of another makes it possible to compare one paradigm with another, which explains why we have taken the time to examine the process of translation. If one wishes to use logic to compare one paradigm with another, then one must first translate one paradigm into the language of another. As I mentioned in the introduction, one of the primary tools that I have used to error-check the theory of mental symmetry is to translate related theories into the language of mental symmetry. That explains why the main text of this book deals with so many seemingly unrelated subjects, why a number of appendices have been added that cover even more subjects, and why I often repeat a concept two or three times using different words. I am continually trying to translate.

The process of translation involves an *interaction* between logic and emotions. Translating specific *terms* from one language to another is a logical process which uses Perceiver mode to search for common meanings. But, comparing the *emphasis* of one theory with another is an *emotional* process. There is always emotional pressure to change the emphasis of one theory to match the emotional emphasis of the other, instead of allowing the emotional emphases of both theories to remain intact when comparing them. But if one shifts the emotional emphasis of a theory when translating that theory, then one is actually performing an implicit paradigm shift and not a valid translation.

Comparing one paradigm with another is like taking two fragments of a map and attempting to fit one onto the other. The specific meanings could be compared to the places on the map: Here is a town, there is a river, and so on. The emotional emphases could be compared to the height of the landscape: Here is a mountain that is being emphasized; there is a valley that is being ignored. It is *much* easier to compare one map fragment with another if one has three dimensional maps which include height and depth and not just two dimensional maps that have only places and locations.

In contrast, replacing the topography of one map fragment with assumed topography based upon the other map fragment will make it much more difficult, if not impossible, to see how one map fragment fits in with the other. When one instinctively adjusts the emotional topography of a supposedly translated map fragment and finds that it does not fit, then the natural tendency is to go one step further emotionally and reject the entire modified map fragment as invalid and unworthy of consideration.[13]

Kuhn muses that it might be possible to avoid the difficulties of translation if it were possible to discover a *neutral* language based in something which all scientists had in common, such as direct sensory impressions: "It might, for example, be conducted in terms of some neutral observation-language, perhaps one designed to conform to the retinal imprints that mediate what the scientist sees." Similarly, Willard Quine suggests that scientific thought is based in *observation sentences*, simple descriptions of external events upon which all observers to an event can agree. This is useful when dealing with physical situations that are objective, but it does not help when examining the sort of topics that we are addressing in this book.

However, if all humans share the same mental structure, then by using the language of cognitive modules, it is also possible to find a common language for *internal* and *emotional* situations. Whenever people think, they are using their minds, and it appears that every human mind has access to the *same* mental 'toolbox' of seven cognitive modules. Over the years, I have been amazed at the number of diverse fields that can be analyzed and integrated using the lingua franca of mental symmetry. Saying this another way, I have used the theory of mental symmetry to look at many different sections within the 'library' of human knowledge, and the theory has survived intact.

Learning to speak this 'international mental language' is not easy, for it requires extensive Perceiver confidence as well as a general Teacher understanding. However, the person who acquires this confidence gains the mental ability to handle the emotional trauma that is generated when comparing alternate Teacher theories, and the theory of mental symmetry gives Teacher thought a general framework to hold on to emotionally while other theories are being questioned. Plus, if the *process* of questioning a paradigm can itself be analyzed in terms of the theory of mental symmetry, then this lends additional emotional support.

In terms of our map analogy, I suggest that the theory of mental symmetry is like a global map of human thought. When one uses it to compare one paradigm with another, then each paradigm is treated as a map fragment and placed within the appropriate location in the 'global map', providing an underlying structure that can be used to relate these two paradigms.

Of course, the 'international language' which I am proposing is *itself* a paradigm, and my discussion about paradigms is itself being couched in terms of the general theory of

[13] Notice that an emotional mountain could be produced by either Teacher feelings of generality or Mercy feelings of importance. It does not matter, for if one understands how Mercy thought functions and if one is able to use Perceiver mode in the presence of these Mercy emotions, then this provides additional clues for matching up one map fragment with another. When I am trying to evaluate a paradigm, one of the first things that I look for is the presence of Mercy-driven emotional bias, because that usually gives me a rough idea of where the paradigm fits.

mental symmetry. Saying this another way, whenever one uses *words* to discuss a theory, one is using the words of some *language*, and each language has its own presuppositions and rules of grammar. Saying this yet another way, when it comes to evaluating general Teacher theories, there is no such thing as 'remaining objective'.

When dealing with the concrete world, one can be objective because *objects exist.* One can talk about trees in an objective manner, for instance, because we are all surrounded by trees. But when dealing with abstract theories, there is no 'objective' world. Instead, one must evaluate a theory either by jumping into that theory, 'going native' and 'living within the culture', or else by translating it into the language of another theory—in essence visiting the 'land' as a foreigner whose native tongue is another language. Kuhn makes this point very clearly: "When paradigms enter, as they must, into a debate about paradigm choice, their role is necessarily circular. Each group uses its own paradigm to argue in that paradigm's defense."

In order for the theory of mental symmetry to act as a paradigm of paradigms, I suggest that it must remain at the relatively vague level of comparing cognitive modules and mental networks. If rigorous logic is used to 'tighten up' the theory of mental symmetry, then it will lose its usefulness. As a Perceiver person who is used to working with uncertain facts, I find it difficult to imagine exactly how rigorous logic could be used to ruin the theory of mental symmetry, but based upon the experience of what the application of rigorous logic has done to Kuhn's theory, I suspect that something similar could occur, and I am trying to take a pre-emptive strike. We will discuss this in more detail when comparing Kuhn's normal science with his revolutionary science.

For instance, in Kuhn's 1970 postscript to his book, he mentions that one 'helpful' reader noted that he used the term *paradigm* in at least twenty-two different ways. When one is attempting to step outside of a specific paradigm, then I suggest that this type of vagueness is essential. Insisting upon a single rigorous definition of the word *paradigm* turns the general concept into a specific paradigm which is no longer capable of being used to compare paradigms. Therefore, I have attempted to give technical definitions to the terms which I use, but I have also tried to keep these definitions as general as possible in order to avoid locking myself into any one specific paradigm.

If an intentionally semi-rigorous theory is being used to compare one paradigm with another, then a translation from one paradigm to another will always be imperfect. Again, this does not mean that it is impossible to compare one paradigm with another, but rather that one is dealing with uncertain information and that one is reduced to using probabilities and educated guesses. However, when one is comparing paradigms that describe aspects of human thought, then these paradigms will share a common *cognitive* basis, because they are all observing the *same* human mental architecture at work.

In my experience, it tends to be easiest to translate one paradigm of human thought into another when looking at the *original* research done by the person who *started* a field. That is because the thinking of the original author was being guided by the human thought that he was observing, and his mental processing was not affected by the presence of an already existing paradigm. In contrast, those who follow tend to use rigorous logic to 'tidy up' an existing theory—which often ends up making the theory less true to the underlying cognitive structures.

Results of Translation

When one theory is successfully translated into the language of another, then there are several possible results. One may discover that the two theories are *equivalent*. This occurs when the Perceiver facts are similar, the Teacher emphases are the same, and both theories include the same high level concepts. For instance, if one studies Canadian legislation in French and Canadian legislation in English, one will discover that the two are equivalent.

Another alternative is for one theory to be a *subset* of the other, similar to the way in which a conquered monarch can become a vassal of another king, or a subjugated country can become a client state of another. Turning a theory into a subset does not make it wrong, it simply makes it more *specific*. A theory that is more specific covers less ground than a more general theory, but in the area where they overlap, it is possible to translate between one theory and the other.

For instance, I suggest that Kuhn's theory of scientific research is a *subset* of the theory of mental symmetry. That is because mental symmetry covers more areas than the theory of Kuhn. Both Kuhn and mental symmetry analyze scientific thought, and in this area of overlap there is extensive agreement between them. But because mental symmetry *also* covers subjects such as God and personal identity, it is more *general* than the theory of Kuhn. By *extending* the theory of Kuhn, it is possible to cover these additional subjects.

Subsets are very necessary. The central planning of Communism shows us what happens when a single general theory attempts to rule over every aspect of society without allowing subset theories to exist. The result is disaster, because the central plan is being imposed upon every situation without being adjusted to fit the local circumstances. The role of state and municipal governments is to act as 'subsets' of the national government that adjust the central plan to meet local needs.

It is also possible for one theory to be an *approximation* of another theory. This usually happens when the Perceiver meanings and categories of one theory are more precisely defined than those of another. For instance, Newton's three laws of motion are an approximation of Einstein's theory of relativity. The equations used by Newton are simple enough to be taught in high school physics, while Einstein's field equations require a knowledge of advanced calculus. Newton's laws give approximate answers to normal problems. However, if one wants a more accurate solution, or if one is dealing with extreme situations, then one must turn to the equations of Einstein.

In the area of cognitive styles, I suggest that the theory of MBTI® is an approximation of the theory of mental symmetry. Like mental symmetry, it also divides people into different cognitive categories, but these categories are less precise. MBTI® Thinking, for example, is very close to Perceiver thought, and MBTI® Feeling is almost the same as Mercy thought. However, Thinking describes Perceiver thought that *avoids* Mercy emotions, while Feeling refers to Mercy thought that is controlling Perceiver facts through the use of emotional 'knowing'. In contrast, mental symmetry analyzes the various ways in which Perceiver thought and Mercy thought can interact instead of simply describing the two extreme situations in which one functions at the expense of the other.

One theory can also be a *paradigm shift* of the other. When this happens, then it is possible to translate the specific concepts of one theory into another, but there is no correspondence at the more general level. This is like taking the same set of bricks and using them to construct totally different buildings. Each brick in one building may correspond to a brick in the other building, but the relationship between the bricks is quite different.

For instance, the theory of mental symmetry represents a paradigm shift from the field of the cognitive science of religion. The facts and the research described by the cognitive science of religion fit quite well into the theory of mental symmetry. But the cognitive science of religion assembles these facts in a manner that is different than the theory of mental symmetry. For the cognitive science of religion, what matters is primitive human ancestry combined with environmental pressure. In contrast, mental symmetry focuses upon cognitive modules and the ways in which they interact.

Finally, one theory may end up being obviously *superior* to the other. This usually happens when one theory is simpler or more elegant than the other. Simplicity and elegance are Teacher emotions, because Teacher emotion comes from order-within-complexity. When many items can be placed neatly into an uncomplicated intellectual package, then there is more order within greater complexity, and thus increased Teacher emotion. Simplicity refers to the form of the package, whereas elegance emphasizes the way in which everything fits together easily without having to bend or squeeze anything in order to force it to fit.

Kuhn refers to this sense of elegance: "There is also another sort of consideration that can lead scientists to reject an old paradigm in favor of a new. These are the arguments, rarely made entirely explicit, that appeal to the individual's sense of the appropriate or the aesthetic—the new theory is said to be 'neater,' 'more suitable,' or 'simpler' than the old." Kuhn also describes the lack of elegance that helped to convince astronomers in Galileo's day to reject Ptolemy's system of concentric crystal spheres: "Given a particular discrepancy, astronomers were invariably able to eliminate it by making some particular adjustment in Ptolemy's system of compounded circles. But as time went on, a man looking at the net result of the normal research effort of many astronomers could observe that astronomy's complexity was increasing far more rapidly than its accuracy and that a discrepancy corrected in one place was likely to show up in another."

When one theory is obviously superior to another, then there is a strong emotional drive—from Teacher thought—to drop the old theory in favor of the new. However, remember that general theories can form mental networks, and abandoning a mental network leads to the hyper-pain of mental fragmentation. Thus, even though holding on to an inferior theory produces Teacher pain, letting go of the theory will generate the even greater hyper-pain of mental fragmentation.

In the previous chapter, we noted that the presence of strong emotions combined with the absence of confidence causes childish identity to be driven by the two primary mental mechanisms of *identification* and *denial.* A similar situation arises when dealing with competing general theories. When faced with a new theory, the instinctive response is to protect Teacher emotions by refusing to examine the new theory. And when one does embrace a new paradigm, then this is commonly accompanied by a dropping of the old paradigm. Both of these responses are examples of intellectual *denial.* It is emotionally draining to translate one theory into the language of another, and it takes mental confidence to be able to handle this emotional pressure. Plus, there is always the possibility that there will be a collision between these two theories which will turn into an 'international incident' in which one theory threatens the existence of the other.

Intellectual *identification* can occur when one is working with a theory that is a *subset* of a more general theory, because the temptation is to ignore the more specific theory and focus directly upon the strong emotions of the more general theory. Intellectual identification leads to the fatal trap of the central plan, so vividly illustrated by the history and demise of Communism. On the one hand, it is exciting to deal with national issues and global directives. On the other hand, anyone who has struggled to maintain a shoddily constructed vehicle knows that a general theory will not survive unless careful attention is paid to details. If a car is to continue functioning, then it must be constructed out of specific parts that are carefully designed and manufactured.

Intellectual identification exists in many guises: It 'solves' the problems of the world at the local pub while ignoring the leaky faucet in the bathroom. It follows national politics avidly but does not know the name of the local mayor. It has memorized the game statistics of sports legends but has no clue how the children are doing in their various subjects at school. It engrosses itself in the lifestyles of the rich and famous, but does not know the names of the next door neighbors. The problem with intellectual identification is that it is self-defeating, because lasting order-within-complexity is only created through an attention to details.

Summary

At this point, we have paid enough attention to details, and it is time for us to review. This chapter has focused upon the relationship between science and Teacher thought. Science uses Perceiver facts to build general Teacher theories, and science promotes this ideal as the scientific method. However, if one examines the history of science, one notices that Teacher emotions play a far greater role than is commonly acknowledged.

A general theory forms within Teacher mode when one general concept is used to explain many other concepts, similar to a king ruling over his subjects. If a general theory passes a certain threshold of order and structure, then it will turn into a mental network that produces hyper-emotions of integration and fragmentation. Before this threshold is passed, one has to choose to think about a theory; after this threshold, one must choose *not* to think about it. A general theory that has turned into a mental network is very difficult to dislodge or question, turning scientific inquiry into intellectual conservatism.

Questioning a theory requires mental confidence. If the student of science constructs his theories by *avoiding* emotional topics, then he will lack the confidence that is needed to question his general theories once they turn into mental networks. Mental confidence gives an individual the ability to question a general theory, compare one theory with another, and if necessary let go of one theory and replace it with another. However, once a person develops a mental network within Teacher thought, then it is not possible for him to go back to the state of having *no* general theory, for that would face Teacher mode with mental annihilation.

When two *competing* theories collide, then each will attempt to put its own explanation upon specific situations. If one theory succeeds in explaining a situation, then this will be seen as a contradiction by the other theory, leading to Teacher pain. If this state of contradiction continues to exist, then the pain of contradiction will eventually turn into the hyper-pain of theoretical fragmentation. When that point is reached, then the conflict between the two theories will become a life and death struggle for existence in which only one theory can survive. The theory that wins this conflict will then remove all traces of the competing theory, to the extent of rewriting history to pretend that the other theory never existed.

However, it is also possible for two competing theories to coexist peacefully with one another. In order for this to occur, one of the two theories must be translated into the language of the other. Translation has both a Perceiver and a Teacher component. The Perceiver side of translation deals with the meanings of words. The Teacher side of translation ensures that the same elements are being emphasized and trivialized in both the original and the translation. A paradigm *shift* occurs when a *different* general Teacher theory is used to explain the *same* set of Perceiver meanings and facts.

Translating between one paradigm and another is difficult because each paradigm will spend time clarifying Perceiver facts and meanings that it considers to be important while ignoring concepts that it regards as trivial. Thus, facts will exist within one theory for which no corresponding terms exist in the other theory. Translation is very difficult when Perceiver facts and 'beliefs' are determined by Mercy emotions. First, words will not have precise meanings, but instead will be 'defined' by their emotional connotations. Second, Perceiver thought will lack the confidence that is needed to build mental connections between theories that come from 'good' people and those which are taught by 'bad' people.

Translating or evaluating a paradigm involves a combination of logic and emotions. The Perceiver 'bricks' that are used to build a paradigm or to establish common meanings when translating from one paradigm to another are based in logic and do not have emotional content. In contrast, the general structure that appears when one places Perceiver 'bricks' together does generate Teacher feelings, and the emphasis that determines which facts are highlighted and which facts are ignored is also the result of Teacher emotions modified by Mercy feelings. Thus, even though building a general theory or translating a theory requires logic and not emotions, emotions will be triggered by this logical process, and Perceiver mode must have confidence to be able to handle these emotions. The emotions then become an aspect of the translation which can assist in comparing theories more accurately.

Whenever a general theory is being translated, it is always translated *into* the language of some general theory and evaluated *using* the concepts of that theory. This, combined with the absence of any 'objective' external world of theory, means that evaluating a theory involves some form of circular reasoning.

A cognitive theory such as mental symmetry can act as a sort of common language when attempting to translate theories that involve human thought, because all such theories share the common feature of using the human mind. However, mental symmetry can only act as a paradigm of paradigms if it remains sufficiently vague and is not 'tidied up' by using excessive rigorous logic.

When one theory is translated into the language of another, then there are several alternatives. One theory may end up being *equivalent* to another. This occurs when the Perceiver meanings and Teacher emphases are the same, and what is regarded as general in one theory is also regarded as general in the other theory. One theory may also be a *subset* of the other. In this case, the Perceiver meanings and Teacher emphases are the same, but the more specific theory contains a 'zoomed in' view of only part of the more general theory. One theory can also be an *approximation* of the other. In most cases, an approximate theory will be simpler, but it will also give answers that are only partially correct. One theory can also be a *paradigm shift* of the other. This occurs when the same Perceiver facts are assembled in a different way. Finally, translation may reveal one theory to be obviously *superior* to the other, which will cause the old theory to be dropped in favor of the new—unless the hyper-pain of abandoning the old theory is too intense.

Childish Mercy identity is driven by identification and denial. Similar mechanisms exist within Teacher thought. Teacher *denial* occurs when a person clings to an existing general theory without evaluating an alternative or else drops an existing theory in order to embrace a new theory. Teacher *identification* can occur when one is working with a theory that is a subset of a more general theory, because it feels better to ignore the more specific theory and focus upon general concepts. However, the robustness of a general theory depends upon the quality of its details; a theory which is not well thought out will not last very long.

❋ 6. The Birth, Death, and Rebirth of God

What do you do when you hear the doorbell ring? You go to the door to see who is there. And when you open the door, you expect to see a person standing on the doorstep. But what if nobody is there? Then, you look around the corner or peer into the bushes to see if the person who rang the doorbell is walking away or possibly hiding. But you still assume that someone rang the doorbell.

So far we are on familiar ground, for I am simply describing the function of the Agency Detector that we mentioned in an earlier chapter. When an event occurs which could be caused by a person and which cannot be attributed to some natural effect, then the mind looks for some personal cause: "Who rang the doorbell?"

In that earlier chapter we also described the mental mechanism behind the Agency Detector. A person is a cluster of intelligent, emotional responses contained within a physical package. When I spend time with a person, I experience his likes and dislikes, interests, reactions, thoughts, responses, and habits. These emotional memories combine easily within Mercy thought to form a mental network that represents that person. Perceiver thought then classifies and organizes these various mental networks, leading to further mental networks such as 'the typical person in my neighbourhood', 'people who go door-to-door promoting their religion', and 'that ten year old brat down the street who does childish pranks'. Whenever a mental network is triggered, then it will attempt to remain activated in order to process information. Hearing the doorbell ring will bring to mind the mental networks that I have mentioned along with various others, and each will mentally clamour for attention. Opening the door and looking outside will then give Perceiver thought the facts that are needed to decide which mental network within Mercy thought is the appropriate one. If a mental network is repeatedly triggered but never allowed to be activated, then it will eventually produce feelings of hyper-pain: "I am waiting for my aunt Betsy to show up. Every time the doorbell rings, I think that it will be her. I hope that she is fine and that nothing has happened to her."

Now let us alter the situation, using a variation of the argument that lies at the heart of the cognitive science of religion. Suppose that I go to the door, and instead of seeing someone, I hear a voice. My first instinct will be to look for the 'ten year old brat from down the street'. But suppose that he is nowhere within sight. I will then be left with a nagging question in my mind. What did I hear? Was it a person? Going further, suppose that the phone rings and I answer it and hear the *same* voice. And suppose that I turn on the radio and hear the same voice talking, and that I change the station on the radio and the same voice keeps talking. And when I turn on the television set, I see no picture but

I hear the same voice—on every channel. If this process continues, then at some point I will feel as if I have entered 'the twilight zone', because I will become convinced of two things: First, some intelligent person is attempting to communicate with me. Second, this intelligent person is not a normal human being.

Obviously, this sort of freaky situation does not occur externally, but I suggest that it *does* happen within the mind. When we looked at the Agency Detector, we assumed that *all* mental networks involve emotional experiences within Mercy thought. But we saw in the last chapter that a mental network will also form within the Teacher module whenever a general theory acquires sufficient emotions. And a general theory acts like a voice that is heard everywhere. Teacher theories are based in words, and a general theory applies the *same* explanation to a number of specific situations. People are limited to specific locations. A person cannot simultaneously be at the front door, the back door, on the phone, and on every radio frequency and every television channel. But it is possible to come up with a single Teacher theory that can explain *all* of these situations. And if that Teacher theory turns into a mental network, then it will attempt to 'speak' in every situation which it is capable of analyzing—past, present, and future. And, unlike a Mercy mental network which is connected with the physical body of some specific person, it is not possible to assign a physical body to a Teacher mental network. For instance, where is the 'law of gravity'? It is nowhere; it is everywhere; it has no location; it applies to every location.

If this continues, then the mind will eventually conclude that a person exists who is based in words, a person who does not live in a physical body and who transcends space and time. And, like any general Teacher theory, this imaginary 'person' will be driven emotionally by feelings of order-within-complexity. A general theory feels bad when it experiences an exception to its rule. Therefore, this imaginary individual will respond with emotional displeasure whenever it encounters behavior that violates its general theory. And if personal behavior continues to violate the general rule, then this 'disembodied voice' will eventually feel personally threatened and produce hyper-emotions of impending fragmentation.

A Mental Image of God

As most of you have surmised by now, we have described a cognitive basis for a belief in God. In simple terms, a mental image of God forms when a general Teacher theory affects personal identity within Mercy thought. In the previous chapter, we examined how a general Teacher theory behaves, guided by Thomas Kuhn's analysis of scientific thought. But science is by nature *objective*. It avoids personal emotions and attempts to stay away from subjective feelings. As a result, the general theories of science do *not* create mental images of God. However, if one were to *extend* the theories of science to include the subjective, then the result would be an image of God.

Science, along with its folk version of common sense, does form Teacher mental networks, and these Teacher mental networks do clamor for mental attention when some unknown incident occurs. For instance, suppose that I hear a banging noise on the side of the house in the middle of the night. This may bring to mind the Mercy mental network of an intruder attempting to break in. But it may also bring up the *natural explanation* of the wind blowing against a tree and causing a tree branch to hit the wall of the house. That natural explanation comes from a Teacher mental network based in common sense, which wants to activate itself by *explaining* the situation.

Officially, the general Teacher theories of science ignore personal emotions and avoid attributing any event to a homunculus or 'invisible little man'. However, the Teacher theories of science do have a major *indirect* effect upon personal identity. This combination leads to the paradoxical un-image of God known as *Nature*. Verbally, science insists that Nature is not a personal deity—while at the same time indirectly ascribing most of the attributes of a personal deity to Nature.

Moving further, a mental image of God will only emerge in personal areas where a general Teacher theory of the subjective *does* speak. Areas where this general Teacher theory does not apply will be viewed as *secular*, or independent of God. And it is also possible for different areas of the subjective to be explained by different general Teacher theories. As long as these various theories do not come into contact with one another, then they will coexist within the mind and a person's image of God will depend upon the social context. For instance, a person may have one image of God when attending a religious service while subscribing to a rather different concept of deity when enjoying entertainment.

The concept of *monotheism* emerges when a person believes that a *single* universal Teacher theory describes *all* of personal existence. Higher religions, such as Islam, Judaism, and Christianity, teach the doctrine of monotheism and most adherents to these religions *say* that they believe in a monotheistic God. However, if one examines behavior more closely, it usually becomes apparent that personal existence is fragmented into various domains, each explained by its own general theory and its own image of God. That is because talking about a universal theory of the subjective is quite different than actually *having* a universal theory of the subjective.

For instance, some of you may have read the *Foundation Trilogy* by Isaac Asimov, a fascinating science fiction series that describes 'galactic history' being guided by 'the Hari Seldon plan', a universal theory of human society. However, even though these books talk extensively *about* such a theory, very little of this theory is actually presented, for the simple reason that Asimov himself did not possess a universal theory of human society but only knew a few general concepts. Similarly, modern man possesses a number of *general* theories of human existence, but so far no detailed cognitive model of human thought and behavior has been developed. Therefore, this book will usually describe God as the mental image of an invisible 'person' that emerges when a *general* theory explains personal experiences, for that describes the situation today. However, if a universal theory of the subjective is ever developed, then this will encourage people to stop *talking* about monotheism and start *believing* in monotheism.

That explains one of my primary motivations for working on the theory of mental symmetry, for my goal is to develop a universal theory of human behavior, and so far, the theory of mental symmetry appears to be a valid candidate. Obviously, such a theory has the potential to create a rather potent image of God, which is why it becomes both possible and imperative for the theory of mental symmetry to explicitly include an analysis of God and religion.

Moving on, I have suggested that words form the basic building blocks for general Teacher theories. If one compares the way in which the mind of the child handles words, I suggest that it corresponds to the way in which the childish mind forms a belief in God.

Linguists tell us that children learn the rules of grammar by first *overgeneralizing* and then learning exceptions to the general rule. For instance, the young child will typically say "I goed to the store, I buyed a candy bar, and then I runned home." That is because the general rule in English is to turn the present tense into the past tense by adding an '-ed' to the verb. The child will learn this rule and apply it *everywhere*. Once this general rule has been acquired, then the child will learn the specific exceptions to the rule, such as 'went', 'bought', and 'ran'.

Translating this into the language of mental symmetry—and we now know what it means to translate from one paradigm into the language of another—when Teacher mode comes up with a theory, it will try to make its statement as general as possible. That is because a general theory feels good. The greater the generality, the better it feels. Exhorter mode provides the *motivation* for generalizing a theory, because it transforms strong emotions into mental drives and urges. Perceiver thought, with its solid facts and unforgiving categories, acts as the mental 'policeman' that places limits upon how far a Teacher theory can be generalized: "You can't say that, because it contradicts this fact. You can't apply that principle here, because you are dealing with two completely different situations." Thus, Perceiver thought takes the *overgeneralized* initial theories proposed by Teacher thought and limits them.

One sees this mental interaction illustrated by the behavior of the Perceiver and Exhorter *persons*. On the one hand, the Perceiver person sticks with the facts and reacts strongly when they are embellished or 'spun' by others. The Exhorter person, on the other hand, is prone to exaggeration. The Perceiver person views this exaggeration as dishonesty. The Exhorter person, in contrast, sees it more as stating the situation as it could have been, or how it should have been. And if one examines the statements of the Exhorter person more carefully, one sees that there are actually limits to his stretching of the facts. He may bend the truth, but he will not break it; he may tread into territory that Perceiver mode finds unreasonable, but he will not step into regions which Perceiver thought considers to be impossible.

One could compare Perceiver facts to jigsaw puzzle pieces. If the pieces are all similar or do not have solid edges, then, like plastic building blocks, they can be put together in many ways. That corresponds mentally to an overgeneralized Teacher theory. It takes a pile of poorly defined facts and forces them to fit together. Perceiver thinking defines these puzzles pieces by working out the exact shape of each piece as well as the precise differences between one puzzle piece and another. This Perceiver precision destroys an overgeneralized Teacher theory by pointing out all of the numerous ways in which puzzle pieces have been jammed together. But defining the puzzle pieces more carefully also makes it clear how they *should* fit together, and the big picture that emerges when puzzle pieces are connected properly makes a lot more sense that the jumble of fragmentary images that result from forcing pieces to fit. Similarly, in the short term, Perceiver thought may destroy the ill-formed theory, but in the long term it also makes it possible to construct a far more solid and stable intellectual structure.

Justin Barrett and others have discovered that a similar mental transition occurs in the concepts that children have concerning God. Based upon a number of experiments carried out with pre-school children, Barrett concludes in *Why Would Anyone Believe in God*: "In childhood, our standard, default assumption is that people and God are superknowing, superperceiving, and superpowerful. We must work to learn that this is not so of people, whereas theologically appropriate notions of God come with little struggle." He continues, "Until children outgrow this stage and begin to appreciate human fallibility, God is just another human who just happens to live in the sky. After children understand that humans do not, in fact, possess Godlike properties, God is left as the only member of the pantheon. God is thus a residual of childhood naïveté supported by theological instruction."

Notice that the childish mind's approach to God and people is a *personalized* version of the childish mind's treatment of grammar. Grammar builds general Teacher theories about words, whereas an image of God is a general Teacher theory affecting *people*. Grammatical theories are applied universally until the development of Perceiver thought restricts these universal Teacher theories. Similarly, the childish mind develops universal theories about people until these too are restricted by Perceiver facts. Thus, according to the child, every adult is a god who knows everything and can do anything. However, as Perceiver thought learns about the finite nature of human beings, these universal Teacher theories become restricted and humans are dethroned from their divine pedestals.[14]

Three Stages of Learning

These same three stages seem to occur in *all* areas of learning. First, there is the initial stage of overgeneralization, during which grand Teacher theories are built upon random collections of poorly defined facts. The facts are poorly defined because Perceiver mode lacks content and confidence. The content is missing because the student is just *beginning* to learn, and when Perceiver thought has only a few facts to work with, then it can only

---

[14] Teacher thought may be overgeneralizing in the childish mind, but Piaget's stages of development make it clear that Mercy mental networks are still in control of thought.

make crude mental distinctions between one fact and another. The confidence is lacking because Perceiver confidence is based upon *repetition* and the student is encountering most facts for the first time. This combination places Perceiver mode in a vulnerable state in which it can easily be swayed by emotions. And when Perceiver thought is uncertain, then it is also possible for Teacher thought to come up with general theories which combine elements that do not really fit together. The Exhorter person naturally excels at this first stage of learning, because he combines Teacher thought with Mercy thought. Therefore, he finds it natural to go directly from specific Mercy situation to general Teacher theory.[15]

As Perceiver mode acquires content and gains in confidence, it is able to work out facts more precisely and assert these facts with greater certainty. This signals the emergence of the *second* stage of learning. When Perceiver thought discovers which pieces fit together and which ones do not, then the crudely constructed intellectual edifices that were erected during the first stage of learning usually come crashing to the ground, because the facts will point out flaws in the general theories. During the second stage of learning, Perceiver facts usually have the power to dismantle Teacher theories, because the typical Teacher theory that is developed during the first stage of learning has not progressed to the point of forming a mental network. But if it does form a mental network, then a person can become emotionally locked into the first stage of learning, driven by Teacher hyper-emotion to cling to his crude theory and to reject Perceiver facts: "Don't confuse me with facts because my mind is already made up." In fact, if the Teacher theory is sufficiently irrational, then Perceiver mode itself can be viewed as a threat to Teacher understanding.

The second stage of learning is characterized by a multiplicity of disconnected facts. The Contributor *person* shines at this second stage of technical expertise, because Contributor thought ties together Perceiver mode and Server mode, connecting specific Server steps with specific Perceiver facts. Unlike the first stage overgeneralizing student who tends to feel that he 'knows everything', the Teacher understanding of the second stage technical student is usually far more limited.

Finally, there is the third stage of the expert. This is when the fragmented knowledge of the second stage reintegrates. The first stage formed overgeneralized Teacher theories that lacked Perceiver facts. The second stage acquired Perceiver facts but these facts ended up destroying the general theories. Finally, the third stage uses Perceiver facts to build general Teacher theories. In terms of our puzzle illustration, the first stage jams together poorly formed puzzle pieces, the second stage defines the puzzle pieces—which probably tears the puzzle apart, while the third stage places each puzzle piece in its proper location.

---

[15] The personality traits of the seven cognitive styles were initially worked out by Lane Friesen, a Teacher person, and myself, a Perceiver person. Lane Friesen got the initial idea of seven cognitive styles from an Exhorter person who emphasizes the first stage of learning.

Science has the potential of operating at the third stage of learning, for it gathers Perceiver facts through careful observation and then uses these facts to build general Teacher theories. But because of specialization, the typical scientist often remains largely at the second level of fragmented technical knowledge without truly entering the third level of general Teacher theories. We will explore this in greater detail later on.

A branch of science that lacks a general theory can only function at the second stage of fragmented knowledge and partial understanding, and it will tend to regard general theories with great suspicion because they will be mentally associated with the first stage of learning. This is especially true of the social sciences in general and the field of theology in specific. On the one hand, there are the pop psychologists and the televangelists who epitomize the first stage of learning, sharing grand theories with great enthusiasm that are supported by a minimum of facts. On the other hand, there are the scholars who are attempting to move beyond this first stage by making cautious conclusions backed up by experimental data. The goal of the theory of mental symmetry is to move beyond the second stage of detailed facts to the third stage of integrated understanding. However, in my experience, those who are in the first stage of learning typically complain that mental symmetry contains *too many* facts and details, whereas those who are in the second stage complain because it goes *beyond* facts and details.

The underlying assumption of the third stage of learning is that all of the puzzle pieces *can* be put together, and that it *is* possible to go beyond a detailed focus upon specific facts and return to the 'big picture'. When one purchases a jigsaw puzzle, there is an image of the finished result on the cover of the box. However, when learning tries to progress from the second to the third stage, then there is no guarantee that the various pieces will fit together. Not only is the picture not provided, but there might not even *be* a picture. However, as we quoted from Kuhn in the previous chapter, science cannot exist without a paradigm. It assumes the existence of a 'big picture' or general theory. Has science succeeded in its quest? In the hard sciences, this goal is within sight, whereas in the soft sciences only fragments of the puzzle have been assembled. A single 'unified theory of everything' still eludes the social scientist.

A God of Overgeneralization

Now let us extend these various concepts to a person's belief in God. I have suggested that a mental image of God emerges when a general theory in Teacher thought explains personal identity in Mercy thought. This makes a belief in God both natural and obvious during the first stage of learning. It is natural because the Teacher module is forming general theories, and it is obvious because subjective Mercy emotions play a major role during the first stage of learning.

But what *type* of image of God emerges during this first stage? One that speaks in grand yet vague platitudes, a God who cannot handle being exposed to the light of Perceiver facts. However, if a person focuses sufficiently upon God at this first level of learning, then this vague general theory of the subjective will form a mental network within

Teacher thought, and like any mental network, it will attempt to 'stay alive', and will respond to impending fragmentation with hyper-pain.

But how does one preserve the 'integrity' of a vague universal theory of God? How can a partially assembled puzzle be kept in a state in which the pieces do *not* fit together properly? The two primary means are *worship* and *irrationality*. Worship uses emotions from one mental network to enhance the integrity of another mental network. In religious language, 'God lives in the praises of his people'. Worshipping God works because Mercy emotions feel the same as Teacher emotions—even though they are defined quite differently. Mercy emotions are associated with specific experiences, such as a wonderful meal, a marvelous evening, a horrid dog, or a painful toothache. Teacher emotions, in contrast, come from *generality*; Teacher mode feels good when many items fit together. Because Teacher emotion feels the same as Mercy emotion, it is possible for one to augment the other. Therefore, if one uses words—the basic building blocks for Teacher theories, and adds intense Mercy feelings to these words, then Teacher mode will interpret these Mercy feelings in terms of Teacher generality.

For instance, suppose that I say phrases like "God is marvelous, God is amazing, God is incredible, God is omnipotent," and that I accompany these words with beautiful pictures and inspiring songs. I have not constructed a general Teacher theory because I have not used these words to explain anything. But because I have added emotions to words, I have created the mental *illusion* of a general Teacher theory. Teacher thought will *feel* that these words describe order-within-complexity because they are emotional, and according to Teacher thought, emotion equals order-within-complexity. In terms of our puzzle illustration, it is as if painting one piece of the puzzle with bright colors gives the impression that this specific piece is the *entire* puzzle.

A vague concept of God is also preserved through *irrationality*. That is because Perceiver facts are the enemy of overgeneralization, and a vague concept of God that emerges during the first stage of learning is based in overgeneralization. Worship *builds up* a vague image of God; irrationality *protects* that image from being attacked. This religious irrationality will express itself in several forms, all of which are designed to minimize the intrusion of Perceiver thought. God will be described using poorly-defined words with emotional connotations. The feeling will be that defining God in human terms limits God—which is precisely what happens when a vague image of God comes into contact with Perceiver facts and meanings that are based in normal existence.

There will also be a lack of *curiosity*. Normally, a general theory in Teacher thought leads to curiosity, because Teacher thought feels good when a theory expands and becomes more general. Therefore, a person with a theory will want to learn facts, because they add to his understanding. But during the first stage of learning, facts are the *enemy* of theories; instead of making theories more general, they limit them. Thus, Teacher emotions will drive a person *not* to learn and to *avoid* new and potentially threatening information. When presented with factual data, the religious worshipper will insist that 'God is beyond rational thought'. However, such an individual *will* be intensely curious about situations that connect God with the *absence* of Perceiver facts, such as someone deciding to abandon rational thought in order to 'live by faith' and discovering that 'God provided for him', or someone having a medical ailment and receiving a 'miraculous healing' that the medical establishment cannot explain.

I suggest that a *physical* version of these four factors of worship, irrationality, a lack of curiosity, and connecting God with unusual events occurs with the idol worship of the jungle native. The starting point is some physical object, such as a tree or a rock. Using *worship* to attach Mercy emotions of religious fervor to this physical object will give Teacher thought the feeling that this tree or rock possesses Teacher generality and is actually godlike. But a tree or rock is a *specific* object just like any other tree or rock; it does not possess Teacher generality. However, if a *fence* is placed around the object of worship, then Perceiver thought will be prevented from mentally comparing this tree or rock with other trees and rocks, allowing Teacher thought to maintain its illusion of generality. The sanctity of this fence will be protected by a *taboo*; any person who connects the idol with normal objects or everyday experiences will be punished. However, people with emotional status such as priests or tribal leaders will be permitted to interact with the idol in a *ritualistic* manner.

Notice how all four factors show up in physical form: The worship is applied to a physical object; irrationality is preserved by putting a fence around the idol; a lack of curiosity is enforced through the taboo; and the idol is emotionally enhanced through special rituals carried out by special people.

This *physical* combination of idols, fences, taboos, and rituals can also be found in 'higher religions'. One thinks, for instance, of the wine and the bread being stored in the chancel of a church, separated from the lay worshipper by a railing which only the clergy may cross. The doctrine of transubstantiation states that during the religious ceremony of the Eucharist, this wine and bread becomes miraculously transformed into the blood and flesh of God in human form.

However, in modern religion, it is more typical to find the *internalized* version of worship, irrationality, a lack of curiosity, and the miraculous event. I suggest that this internal version occurs in its purest form in Eastern mysticism as practiced by Buddhism and similar religions. The starting point is the ultimate overgeneralization, a theory which states that 'everything fits together', or 'all is one', which gives Teacher thought the *illusion* of a universal theory. This 'universal' theory is then turned into an image of God by 'applying' it to personal identity through the childish Mercy method of *identification*: "You are God." Once this mental connection has been formed, then this 'universal' theory can be emotionally supported through the worship of meditation: "Forget about yourself. Focus upon God. Quiet your mind. Embrace infinity. Identify with infinity. You are infinity." This vague concept of God is then protected by a taboo against Perceiver thought: "God is beyond facts. You must let go of logic in order to discover God." Even making factual statements about the process of going beyond facts will be religiously suspect, for it indicates that Perceiver thought is still functioning, and as long as it functions, it will limit the overgeneralization that forms the basis for Eastern mysticism. Combined with this suppression of Perceiver thought will be a denial of Perceiver *content*: "The world is illusion. Your senses tell you that the chair is different than the table. That is illusion. They are all ultimately the same. Do not believe your senses." In contrast, mentally fixating upon objects and sounds in a hypnotic way will be encouraged, because this helps to disable Perceiver thought.

One can illustrate this with the way that one typically encounters Buddhism in South Korea. As one is walking into a subway station, one sees a person sitting on the steps. His—or her—head is shaved and he is wearing a shapeless, colorless, grey uniform. He is beating on a drum at a rate of about one beat per second. He continues this repetitive beating for hours: bang, bang, bang... He says nothing, he does nothing, he hands out no literature, he helps no one; he simply continues to bang on his little drum, giving the impression that religion can be reduced to a ticking metronome painted grey.

Notice that we see again the presence of the two fundamental childish attitudes of *identification* and *denial*. This is happening within the *Teacher* module: Teacher thought is emotionally identifying with an overgeneralized theory and Teacher thought is denying other theories which might contradict this theory. It is also occurring within the *Mercy* module: Mercy thought is identifying with the image of God, and it is denying the existence of Mercy mental networks which would point out that finite personal identity is different than universal understanding.

Using our puzzle illustration, Eastern mysticism takes the various puzzle pieces of existence, dumps them into a blender, presses the purée button, pours out the resulting sludge, and then declares that the picture has been assembled and that each individual puzzle piece can now 'identify' with the entire puzzle. But that leaves one rather significant question. What exactly is the *cup* holding the sludge that was the puzzle, and how does it fit into the overall scheme? It is *different* than the sludge and it is more *solid* than sludge. In other words, an overgeneralized theory of cosmic unity is too vague to be able to explain the mental mechanisms that generate these feelings of cosmic unity. But without these mental mechanisms, the feelings of cosmic unity could not exist.

However, I also need to emphasize that the combination of overgeneralization, worship, and irrationality *works*. From a cognitive perspective, religion that is based in the first stage of learning makes perfect sense. It does produce a mental image of God, and it does generate the feeling of being united with God and/or one with the universe—a very calming and intoxicating emotion. In addition, if one persists in performing irrational worship, then personal identity will become associated with mental networks that are independent of the physical body and physical reality, leading to what is known as altered states of consciousness. And these changes in consciousness can be seen on brain scans. For instance, one researcher found that frontal lobe activity increases during Buddhist meditation while right parietal lobe activity decreases.[16] Translating this into the language of mental symmetry, activity increases in the internal world of thought, while the part of Perceiver mode that interacts with the physical world becomes less

---

[16] http://www.andrewnewberg.com/research.asp

active, consistent with the suggestion that meditation creates mental networks which are independent of Perceiver facts that are based in physical reality.

Notice that this form of religion only works as long as it is *not* understood—as long as one focuses completely upon the sludge *in* the cup and not upon the cup itself. For when one understands the method of irrational worship, then one realizes that the *structure* of the mind contradicts the *content* that has been placed in the mind, and one also senses that the theory of cosmic unity—which supposedly is more universal than any other theory—has now become a *subset* of the theory that describes the *structure* of the mind.

If that sounds confusing, then simply think of the fable of the Emperor who had no clothes. An overgeneralized theory is like an emperor parading with invisible clothes, and a logical explanation of this overgeneralization is like a boy pointing out the nakedness of the emperor and deflating his pomposity with a simple observation. However, when viewed from a cognitive perspective, invisible apparel feels just like the real thing, and until the little boy shows up, everyone will sincerely feel—and believe—that the emperor really is clad in magnificent garments.

This idea of comparing mental *content* with mental *structure* may seem unusual, but it is this cognitive approach that makes it possible to evaluate a religious system. For if the general Teacher theory upon which an image of God is based cannot explain how the mind works, then there will be an irreconcilable contradiction between brain *hardware* and brain *software*, leading to two opposing mental images of God, one based in mental structure and the other in mental content. In contrast, if one wishes to build an image of a monotheistic God and avoid the mental trauma of duelling general Teacher theories, then the only cognitive option is to construct an image of God that is consistent with the structure and functioning of the mind.

Religious Skepticism

Let us move on now to the *second* stage of learning. This stage is entered when the student develops Perceiver thought and learns Perceiver facts. As we have just seen, facts are the enemy of overgeneralized theories. Thus, when the student starts learning solid facts, then the general theories that were developed during the first stage of learning usually come crashing to the ground. This has major religious implications, for an image of God is based in a general theory. Thus, the second stage of learning is strongly associated with religious skepticism. In plain English, when students start thinking logically, then they stop believing in God. This describes the typical situation for the college student who 'loses his faith' as a result of 'higher learning'.

Science has a destructive effect upon the overgeneralized theories of the childish mind, but *objective* science is doubly corrosive because it also avoids subjective *Mercy* emotions. An image of God emerges when a general Teacher theory explains personal identity in Mercy thought; objective science demolishes overgeneralized theories *and* it suppresses subjective emotions. Thus, the religious adherent is left with an emotional vacuum: His overgeneralized concept of God has been logically dismantled *and* his personal identity is being ignored; his primary Teacher mental network is being verbally demolished by his professors, while the Mercy mental network that represents his person is either being ignored or else explained away in objective terms. Given this combination, one can see why religious faith that is based in the first stage of learning tends to view objective scientific knowledge as Public Enemy Number One, for like the proverbial dog in the manger, objective learning chases away all living creatures but does not provide an alternative.

I suggest that Friedrich Nietzsche was describing a similar transition in Western society when he declared in 1882 in *The Gay Science* that 'God is dead'. It was around this time that the average person in the street began to experience the new facts of scientific technology in his personal life. The first machine gun was invented in 1861, the electric dynamo in 1871, the telegraph in 1874, and the first primitive telephone in 1876. Thomas Edison invented the phonograph in 1877 and the light bulb in 1879, while the automobile engine was invented by Karl Benz in 1879. Imagine encountering these various consumer marvels for the first time—technological wonders that took the form of solid Perceiver objects embodying logical Perceiver facts. One can see that first stage learning with its overgeneralized view of God would not survive long in such a mechanistic personal environment, and it is interesting to note that Michel Foucault dates the beginning of his *Modern episteme* to precisely this time period—which we will discuss later on in the book.

The third stage of learning begins when general Teacher theories are discovered that tie the various Perceiver facts together. The flimsy overgeneralized theories that came crashing down during the second stage of learning are now replaced by *general* theories that explain the facts instead of ignoring them. As I have mentioned before, it is this *combination* of solid Perceiver facts and general Teacher theories which is the hallmark of scientific thought. However, when science protects Perceiver thought by suppressing Mercy feelings, then the general Teacher theories that science discovers will *not* cause a mental concept of God to re-emerge. Instead, the objective theories of science will gradually but inexorably grow at the *expense* of peoples' images of God.

This growth of scientific thought will be driven by scientific *curiosity*. Exhorter mode within the mind of the scientist will find it exciting to discover new Perceiver facts because these facts lead to better understanding accompanied by greater Teacher emotions. Thus, in the same way that the growth of civilization encroaches upon the territories of wild animals, so religious thought will find its domain increasingly limited by the growth of scientific thought, for each time that science discovers a new Perceiver fact, the second stage precision of science will subdivide this mental landscape into regular, rectangular plots, while the third stage rational understanding of scientific theory will replace the wild, emotional flora and fauna of first stage religious thought with the straight roads, manicured lawns, and droning lawn mowers of suburbia. Eventually, religious belief will find itself restricted to the emotional swamplands of subjective identity, for that is the one place where objective science refuses to go.

For instance, consider the story of Moses parting the Red Sea and the Israelites crossing on dry land. Science looks at this account and either comes up with a natural explanation for it, such as a strong wind or an earthquake, or else discounts the story as wishful thinking and primitive exaggeration. Because science knows how to use Perceiver thought, and because the facts of science are emotionally supported by the theories of science, this type of naturalistic explanation will become widely accepted. The religious believer will then be forced either to accept the interpretation given by science or else insist that God is capable of acting irrationally despite the rational facts and theories of science.

The same German cultural milieu that prompted Nietzsche to declare that 'God is dead' also led to the rise of liberal Christian theology. Friedrich Schleiermacher is regarded as the father of liberal theology and his approach has two basic threads. First, he stated that a belief in God stands apart from rational thought and is ultimately based in the emotion of 'utter dependence'. Schleiermacher says in *The Christian Faith* that this religious affection can be interpreted as finite identity contemplating universal understanding but that it goes beyond a mere verbal description of this: "It is possible to give a non-religious explanation of the sense of absolute dependence; it might be said that it only means the dependence of finite particulars on the whole and on the system of all finite things, and what is implied and made the center of reference is not God but the world. But we can only regard this explanation as a misunderstanding. For we recognize in our self-consciousness an awareness of the world, but it is different from the awareness of God in the same self-consciousness."

Saying this in the language of mental symmetry, Schleiermacher is basically reiterating the concept that an image of God emerges when a general theory impinges upon personal identity, but he is also insisting that this sensation of the divine occurs prior to words and language and that reducing this feeling to a mere logical formula ruins the feeling. Thus, liberal theology as a whole attempted to protect its belief in God from being destroyed by scientific facts by asserting that this emotion is *independent* of scientific facts. This describes what happens when Christian belief in God is forced to retreat to the 'emotional swampland' of subjective feeling by the encroachment of scientific facts upon its 'natural habitat'. And when religious belief is forced to retreat to its emotional core, it gradually turns into a form of Eastern mysticism.

Second, liberal theology led to what is known as 'higher criticism', which applies scientific analysis to religious writings. Given the story of Moses and the crossing of the Red Sea, for instance, higher criticism either attempts to come up with a rational, scientific explanation for the event, or else views it as a myth driven by sociologic factors—the aspect of higher criticism that was described in a previous chapter.

Notice how liberal theology responds to the growth of objective science by splitting into two incompatible fragments. The aspects of theology that can be explained rationally are emotionally 'cleansed' of their subjectivity and brought within the folds of objective science, whereas the personal side of theology is divorced from rational thought and portrayed in purely emotional terms. In essence, the wild animals from the forest that can be tamed are adopted as pets, while those which cannot be tamed are placed within a wildlife preserve free from the intrusions of mankind.

In nature, this leads to the contradiction of the caged wild animal. In religion, it creates the mental paradox of the finite God. A God is, by definition, a *general* being, for an image of God emerges as a *general* theory explains personal identity—and a mental image of a monotheistic God results from a *universal* theory of the subjective. But we have just seen that the growth of the *objective* theories of science will limit the concept of God to shrines, clergy, services, Bibles, churches, worship songs, and other religious paraphernalia. Thus, while the religious believer may still *say* that God is a universal being, in practice, his image of God has become caged within a small religious ghetto. Cognitively speaking, such an image of God is 'clinically dead'. At this point the only remaining choices are to 'pull the plug' and let the image of God die, or attempt to keep the image of God alive on the 'artificial life support' of irrational worship.

One could compare this situation to that of an absolute monarch whose domain has been taken over by a foreign power and whose rule is now restricted to a few square blocks surrounding the royal palace. If the royal attendants continue to flatter the king with obsequious praise, then he can maintain the illusion of still being the supreme lord of his nation, but anyone who steps outside of the palace walls and walks for a few minutes will know that this is all an empty façade. That describes the mental predicament of a limited image of God.

The growth of secular scientific thought will be greatly facilitated by the continuing development of new consumer technology. For instance, I remember as a child reading a fable about a medieval king who asked a local holy man to prove the existence of God with a miracle. In response, the holy man caused strawberries to grow in the middle of winter and presented the doubting king with a bowl of fresh strawberries. The underlying assumption of this tale is that miracles, God, and personal excitement can be found by violating the general Teacher laws of nature. Compare that fable with the actual situation today, in which it is possible to go down to the local supermarket and purchase fresh strawberries every single day of the year thanks to the wonders of modern technology. Thus, modern technology continually demonstrates that *submitting* to the rational laws of science leads to a cornucopia of daily, ever-present, growing wonders. What is more desirable, an exciting experience that *might* occur if the universal laws of nature are violated, or an exciting experience that will *always* occur as long as principles of natural cause and effect are followed?

A belief in irrational miracles will be kept alive by the fact that science is *objective.* Because science is objective, the benefits that it brings are always one step removed from personal identity. For instance, medical advances benefit the body, but not the mind that lives within that body. Similarly, consumer conveniences have transformed physical existence but they have done little for personal welfare. Thus, when people are facing situations in which personal identity itself is being threatened, then they will still turn to God and religion for help.

And that brings us to an aspect of this struggle which we have not yet discussed—the presence of mental networks. Thomas Kuhn mentions that it usually takes an entire generation to complete a paradigm shift in science, because the older generation is unable to let go of its existing general Teacher theories. If that is the case when dealing with mental networks which only involve Teacher thought, then obviously the emotional bond will be even stronger when Teacher mental networks *combine* with Mercy mental networks—which is what happens when an image of God forms within the mind and becomes 'alive'.

When objective science and technology grow at the expense of religion, then religious thought will become equated with conservatism. Older religious people will be tempted to regard newfangled gadgets as 'works of the devil', because the existence of these new technological marvels threatens the integrity of their mental networks of religious faith. For younger religious people, the story will be quite different. They have grown up surrounded by these new gadgets, and therefore the mental networks that exist within their minds *assume* the existence of this new technology. Thus, what the older people cannot live *with*, the younger people cannot live *without*. When mental networks are defined so differently within the minds of old and young, then the natural result will be a 'generation gap'. Meanwhile, technology will continue to progress, inevitably turning the present younger generation into the old codgers who resist the innovations of the next generation.

This succession of steps from one generation to the next will bring about a major shift from religious to secular existence. For Nietzsche, the concept that 'God is dead' was accompanied by mental trauma and angst, signs that fundamental mental networks within his mind were collapsing and expressing hyper-pain. Thus, Nietzsche insisted that people needed to replace their mental image of God with mental images of 'supermen'—substituting one super-human mental network for another. However, for many people today, the concept that 'God is dead' seems both obvious and archaic, for within their minds, God has never been 'alive'. Instead, God is a foreign concept, unrelated to any existing mental network. For Nietzsche, the concept of God was like a habit that he was trying to break or an ex-lover that he was attempting to forget, because the mental network that represented God within his mind was in its death-throes. For the typical Westernized individual today, the concept of deity does not play a role in normal thought.

However, I suggest that an image of God *never* stays dead. Instead, an image of God will *always* come back to life—because of the inherent nature of human existence. Humans are finite creatures with limited knowledge and skills who depend upon other people and an external environment to provide for their needs. Thus, a human being will always find himself living as a finite creature within a more general environment. And this combination of living as a specific being within a general environment will lead in some way to a concept of God.

When an image of God dies, then this is not necessarily a tragedy, because it presents the individual with the rare opportunity of being able to *choose* the type of image of God that will be reborn within his mind. For it is only a matter of time before another image of God forms, and when that new image of God turns into a mental network, then it will start to control the mind. Kuhn suggested that for the average scientist, acquiring a paradigm is a *onetime* process, for once the typical scientist acquires his paradigm, he becomes incapable of changing it. If that is true about a general theory that does *not* affect personal identity, imagine how much stronger the mental bondage is to a general theory that *includes* personal identity.

This means that when 'God is dead', one can either passively *float* through life until societal forces cause an image of God to re-emerge, *submit* to some system of personal organization which will lead to the formation of a mental image of God, or else consciously *choose* to build a mental image of God that is compatible with personal fulfilment. One of the goals of this book is to use the theory of mental symmetry to work out what type of God *is* compatible with personal happiness and mental wholeness.

We have seen that objective science naturally 'kills' overgeneralized concepts of God. However, objective science will eventually lead to the formation of an image of God as objective research converges upon the core of personal identity. For instance, identity and thought are both internal, but by observing the external behavior of an individual, *psychology* is able to infer what is happening within the mind. Similarly, thought is invisible, but it occurs within the physical brain, which is visible. Therefore, by measuring, analyzing, and imaging the brain, *neurology* can turn invisible thought into visible data. In a similar manner, tampering directly with human thought is not possible, but *computer science* makes it possible for us to construct artificial minds that can be analyzed, taken apart, and reprogrammed. Thus, computer science allows us to model what happens within the human mind. As a result, the objective theories of science will eventually become close enough to personal identity to tip the mental scale and lead again to a concept of God.

Evolution as an Image of God

The book *Minds and Gods,* by Todd Tremlin, which we discussed earlier, provides a good illustration of this mental transition back to an image of God and the contrast that often exists between what the objective scientist says explicitly and what he is communicating implicitly. As I mentioned before, *Minds and Gods* examines the cognitive reasons for a belief in God, and it contains a number of insights that we are using within this book.

Tremlin concludes his book with the following comforting words: "The cognitive science of religion does not set out to challenge the veracity of religious thought and behavior but, rather, to better understand them...Nor does the cognitive science of religion seek to overturn religion. Religious belief persists *because of* not *in spite of* the reasons described in this book. It might even be pointed out that little of what has been discussed here is fundamentally at odds with religious teaching, save perhaps to fundamentalists for whom the idea of an evolutionary model (in any form) is anathema."

Thus, Tremlin leaves us with the impression that his scientific approach to religion is compatible with existing religious thought, as long as the religious individual is willing to adjust his religious beliefs to accommodate the theory of evolution.

However, if one understands that an image of God emerges when a general theory explains personal identity, then a rather different conclusion emerges, one which illustrates the sort of thing that happens when objective science uses cognitive science to invade the final remaining territory of religion. First of all, Tremlin does not regard the theory of evolution as merely a minor modification of existing religious thought, for he devotes the first thirty pages of his book to a description of the theory of evolution and the next thirty pages to describing the various ways in which the structure of the mind was formed by the process of evolution.

Second, Tremlin tells us that he regards the theory of evolution as a *universal* theory of human behavior: "Understanding the processes and products of the mind therefore requires close attention to their evolutionary background. As Robert Wright says, 'if the theory of natural selection is correct, then essentially everything about the human mind should be intelligible in these terms'. True to such predictions, the work of evolutionary psychology is yielding striking insights into the architecture of the mind and human behavior alike."

Third, Tremlin extends the theory of evolution to *personal* identity: "At first glance there may seem to be little point of contact between evolutionary history and the thoughts you are entertaining at this very moment. Even if the ins and outs of natural selection are accepted, it remains hard to see how ideas we humans ponder here in the twenty-first century have anything to do with the thoughts of strange hominids eking out a living millions of years ago. Likewise, it is difficult to clearly relate the physical structures and functions of the brains that we carry around inside our heads with the amorphous ideas that spring so naturally from them. Yet the connections between ancient past and present day, and between gray matter and invisible thought, are direct and paramount."

Thus, we conclude that the theory of evolution has formed an image of God within Tremlin's mind, and that he views religious practice as a mere subset of the God of evolution.[17] This helps us to understand why Tremlin disregards theology and limits his analysis to the subjective experiences associated with religion. He already *has* a universal theory of the subjective in the theory of evolution, and there is only room in Teacher thought for one universal theory.

---

[17] One reaches the same conclusion if one compares Tremlin's description of a mental concept of God in *Minds and Gods* with the attributes that he ascribes to the theory of evolution within that same book. Curiously, Tremlin himself does not make this connection. However, Justin Barrett states in *Why Would Anyone Believe in God*: "One of the embarrassing realities for evolutionary theorists is the difficulty of consistently thinking or talking about natural selection without using mental-states language. At an implicit level, natural selection amounts to a sanitized and scientifically sanctioned 'God' that may displace God."

But why would Tremlin, together with countless other scientific thinkers, reject traditional theology and rebuild a concept of God upon a universal theory of evolution? Before we address this question, I need to say a few words regarding the theory of evolution. At the beginning of this book, I suggested that it is possible to defer the question of the existence of God and focus instead upon the mental concept of God. We will be taking a similar approach with the theory of evolution. This book will focus entirely upon the cognitive reasons for believing in the theory of evolution as well as the cognitive implications of holding on to such a theory.

I suggest that this cognitive approach is warranted for two basic reasons: First, the theory of evolution has very little bearing, if any, upon *physical* existence. Suppose that the theory of gravity were suddenly repealed and that the law of gravity no longer applied. The repercussions would be immediate and overwhelming, for earth would turn into a sort of spaceship in which every object drifted freely. In contrast, what difference would the validity or non-validity of the theory of evolution have upon normal human life? As far as I can tell, nothing would change. Second, the theory of evolution does have a major *cognitive* impact. A person's belief or non-belief in the theory of evolution does affect the way that he thinks and behaves. And in many groups, a person will be essentially excommunicated if he makes unacceptable statements regarding either the validity or non-validity of the theory of evolution.

Having said that, let us continue with our cognitive look at the theory of evolution. I know of *five* cognitive reasons for accepting the theory of evolution, two of which will be discussed in later chapters. The first reason is that evolution is *natural.* It explains all of existence in terms of *natural* processes. Instead of appealing to miraculous intervention, it attempts to explain everything as a function of natural law. Thus, it respects the general Teacher theories of science. Second, evolution is *objective.* It says that all life evolved as a result of external, environmental forces. This is consistent with the attitude of *objective* science, which discovers its Perceiver truths by ignoring subjective feelings and looking to the external environment for patterns that are repeated. The third reason for believing in evolution is that technical thought tends to belittle anything that lies outside of the current theory, and evolution is the current theory of origins. One sees this type of belittling, for instance, in Tremlin's dismissal of theology. The fourth reason has to do with the Facilitator filter of reasonableness and Justin Barrett's concept of the minimally counterintuitive item. These third and fourth reasons will be described later on.

The fifth reason for believing in the theory of evolution is that the alternative theory of creation is generally connected with the overgeneralized concept of God that forms during the first stage of learning. That type of religious thinking talks about universality, but it does not actually respect Teacher thought, for it takes specific experiences and *over*-generalizes from them in order to form general theories, following a method of thought which has been described as 'proof by example'. Similarly, it claims to know truth, but it suppresses Perceiver thought and ignores Perceiver facts. One can see why the typical scientist would find evolution attractive and traditional religion repulsive.

Summary

Let us summarize. We began by answering the door, which brought us back to the concept of the Agency Detector. The cognitive mechanism responsible for detecting the presence of agents is the *mental network*. People are represented within the mind as mental networks, and when some experience brings a mental network to mind within Mercy thought, then that mental network will attempt to interpret that experience.

However, mental networks can also form within *Teacher* thought, based upon general theories. If a general theory explains subjective experiences, and if that general theory turns into a mental network, then, like the Mercy mental networks that represent people, it too will clamour for attention when subjective experiences come to mind. But a *Teacher* mental network is based in *words*, it explains *many* situations, and it responds emotionally to *order* and *disorder*. This provides the cognitive basis for a mental image of God.

A mental image of God behaves precisely like any other general theory within Teacher thought. The only difference is that people and personal behavior fall within the domain of the theory. The general theories of objective science do not create a mental image of God because they are *objective*. A universal theory of the subjective will form the image of a *monotheistic* God. Because the theory of mental symmetry appears to be a universal theory of the subjective, it has the potential to form a monotheistic image of God.

The process of learning appears to go through three stages. During the first stage of learning, Perceiver mode lacks both content and confidence. Therefore, Mercy emotions will tend to determine Perceiver facts, and Teacher mode will be free to overgeneralize without being restricted by Perceiver facts. This combination will lead to the type of thinking known as 'proof by example'. The second stage of learning focuses upon the acquisition of Perceiver facts, which will tend to ruin the overgeneralized theories that were formed during the first stage of learning. Finally, the third stage of learning uses Perceiver facts to build general Teacher theories. The first stage describes the beginner, the second the technician, and the third the expert.

Because an image of God emerges as a general theory explains personal identity, belief in God will reflect these three stages of learning. The first stage of learning will lead naturally to a belief in God, but this will be a vague, overgeneralized concept of deity that is mentally supported through worship and irrationality. Worship uses Mercy emotions to inflate Teacher words and make them feel universal, whereas irrationality protects an overgeneralized theory from being limited by Perceiver facts.

An image of God that is based in an overgeneralized theory is mentally vulnerable. However, if this overgeneralized Teacher theory turns into a mental network, then the religious believer will be driven by hyper-emotion to protect the 'integrity' of his inadequate concept of God.

A physical version of Teacher overgeneralization, worship, and irrationalism occurs in the worship of idols. However, the ultimate overgeneralized image of God can be seen in religions that practice a form of Eastern mysticism, because the worshipper identifies emotionally with a cosmic theory of oneness, while denying all Perceiver facts as illusion. This method of worship will produce emotional benefits, as long as the process is not understood and facts remain suppressed. But if a 'universal' theory cannot explain itself, then it cannot claim to be universal.

The second stage of learning will lead to religious skepticism. The assumption will be that learning facts causes a person to stop believing in God. When a student learns Perceiver facts from *objective* science, then the mental result will be an emotional vacuum, because his understanding of God is being attacked in Teacher thought *and* his personal identity is being suppressed in Mercy thought. If one examines Nietzsche's seminal statement that 'God is dead', one notices that he lived in a time when consumer gadgets first began to transform society.

During the third stage of learning, Teacher thought takes the Perceiver facts that were acquired during the second stage of learning and uses them to build general theories. This is the type of thinking that science proclaims—and often practices. However, science gathers its Perceiver facts by ignoring subjective experiences and by looking for repeated patterns in the physical world. Thus, the paradigms that are discovered by science will not cause a mental image of God to re-emerge. Instead, science will use its objective theories to provide rational natural explanations for any Perceiver facts that are associated with a belief in God. And as objective science removes Perceiver facts from the realm of religion, religious worship will be forced to become increasingly like Eastern mysticism in order to survive. Meanwhile, on the practical side, the objective theories of science will lead to a continual stream of new consumer objects, diverting the attention of Mercy thought away from people to things.

Because humans are finite creatures with limited abilities, they require assistance from other people as well as from the environment. This combination of living as a specific individual within a general social and physical environment will lead to a concept of God. Therefore, a mental image of God cannot stay dead but will eventually come back to life. When God 'dies', then this is an opportunity to choose the type of image of God that will re-emerge.

Objective science itself will eventually create an image of God as objective research encroaches upon personal identity. But because objective science avoids human emotions, the resulting image of God will be inhuman. And it will probably be based upon the theory of evolution, because this theory is natural and objective.

✵ 7. The Power of God

When one thinks of the word God, the attribute of awesome power usually comes to mind. But how can an invisible person who might not even exist have power? Physical power is obvious because it is visible and tangible. We speak of a powerful storm or a powerful earthquake. In physics, power describes the rate at which physical energy is being expended. Political power is also easy to explain because it usually boils down to physical power. Sometimes, this connection is made explicit. In Chairman Mao's words, 'political power grows out of the barrel of a gun'. More commonly, the iron fist is in a velvet glove. But is the power of the state *only* physical power, or is there more to the story? After all, most people obey the state even when a policeman is *not* around.

I suggest that it is this 'more to the story' that relates to the power of God. For instance, when a major disaster strikes, it is commonly referred to as an 'act of God'. Similarly, religious people talk of God coming in power to judge the world, or having the power to create the universe. But has anyone actually *seen* God doing any of these things? When Fred hits me with a powerful punch, I know that Fred is responsible because he is standing in front of me when his fist connects with my jaw. But when a natural disaster strikes, how does one distinguish an 'act of God' from a random natural occurrence? In fact, even if the entire world were to become engulfed in a conflagration corresponding to the four horsemen, the seven plagues, and the seven vials as described by the Apostle John in the Apocalypse, how would one *know* that this global cataclysm was being caused by the hand of God? And yet, people *do* equate overpowering events with the hand of God, and the religious believer insists that God is far more powerful than any human could ever hope to be.

This leads us to conclude that it is our *minds* that are causing us to connect massive events with God. Thus, in order to understand the power of God, one must take a cognitive approach. Whether God exists or not, people do ascribe incredible power to God, and a belief in God has sufficient power to give birth to entire civilizations. Therefore, when people talk about the power of God, I suggest that it is fundamentally an *image* of God which is exerting *cognitive* power: Cognitive mechanisms are causing people to believe that natural events are being caused by God, and these same cognitive powers are being harnessed by leaders of nations and founders of civilizations. After all, we speak of powerful ideas, and we are told that 'the pen is mightier than the sword'.

I suggest that the cognitive power of an image of God emerges when a general theory of the subjective turns into a *mental network* within Teacher thought. Until then, God can be discussed in an abstract, objective manner, and religious belief can be either accepted or rejected. But once the theory within Teacher thought becomes 'alive', then the rules of the game change, for now an image of God will use hyper-emotion to protect itself and to impose itself upon the rest of the mind. This explains why religious fervor is so difficult to comprehend for those who are 'outside of the faith'. They may understand the doctrines, but these 'puzzle pieces' have not coalesced to form a mental network within their minds.

To begin with, there is the inherent emotional power of the mental network. As I have pointed out several times, whenever a mental network is triggered, then it wants to function by being 'fed' compatible information. For instance, if I think about my close friend, then I will want to meet him, talk with him, or interact with him in some way. If a mental network comes to mind and is not permitted to function, then it will feel suppressed, and if it continues to be suppressed, then it will produce the hyper-pain of fragmentation.

But the mental network that lies behind an image of God does not just represent some finite person within Mercy thought. Instead, it is ultimately based in a *universal* theory that claims to explain *everything*. Obviously, a theory which claims to explain everything will *always* be triggered. Like the illustration of the disembodied voice at the beginning of the previous chapter, a universal theory will speak at the front door, the back door, on every television channel, and *everywhere* else—because it applies universally. If an image of God is only based in a *general* theory, then this mental effect will not be as strong, but it will still be present. The voice of God may not speak at *all* times and in *all* places, but it will still speak in *many* places and at *many* times, and the mind will continually have to choose between activating this theory or suppressing it. If you want a personal example, imagine taking the proverbial meddling mother-in-law and multiplying her interference.

In addition, a mental image of God is—by definition—difficult to *ignore.* Remember that personal identity is defined as the set of experiences that repeatedly come to mind, and an image of God emerges as a general theory explains personal identity. If a general theory explains experiences that repeatedly come to mind, then that theory will also repeatedly come to mind. Saying this in terms of an analogy, if all of my close friends enjoy hockey, then it will be rather difficult for me to avoid the topic of hockey.

If this is the case, then why does the topic of God come up so seldom in normal conversation? I suggest that the answer lies in the nature of personal identity combined with the impact of objective science. In an earlier chapter, we saw that my personal identity develops from the mental network that represents my physical body. That is because I am stuck for my entire life within a body which is both a physical object and a source of emotions. But objective science studies physical objects and events while ignoring personal feelings. Therefore, objective science leads to a mindset which treats the human individual purely as a physical object while ignoring the emotional and personal side of humanity.

For instance, when modern man gets sick, then he usually goes to a doctor and not to a pastor or priest. And a doctor will apply scientific theories that are objective and thus do not mentally connect with a concept of God. Similarly, if someone has psychological problems, then he will probably visit a psychologist and not a pastor or priest. And psychology, like medicine, is also rooted in objective science.

A mental concept of God emerges when general understanding explains *personal* identity. Modern man can ignore a concept of God because he defines both general understanding and personal identity in *objective* terms. But if the doctor or the psychologist cannot cure a person, or if emotional disaster strikes, then modern man will start thinking about God. Pastors and priests will tell you that much of their time is spent counselling people and helping them with their personal emotional problems. Before the development of objective science, the concept of God played a major role in society, and the pastor, priest, medicine man, or witchdoctor was consulted frequently.

Finally, an image of God is *unique.* The world contains billions of people but only a handful of higher religions. As was mentioned in a previous chapter, mental networks within Mercy thought are common, whereas mental networks within Teacher mode are rare. And we also saw what happens when one general Teacher theory comes into conflict with another: They fight to the death, and the winner rewrites history.

When a mental network is unique, then it cannot be allowed to fall apart, because there is no alternative to replace it. If it does fall apart, then the result is not fragmentation but rather *annihilation.* That is what happens when a cognitive module stops functioning. As Kuhn points out, science cannot exist without a paradigm. Once Teacher thought develops a general theory and thinking begins to be guided by that general theory, it is not possible to return to the situation of not having a general theory, because that would face Teacher mode with mental annihilation.

Let us now apply these three points to religious thought: First, one can see the motivation that drives *missionary* activity. It feels good when a general theory can expand and explain more specific situations. Obviously, a general theory that explains personal identity can expand by *gaining converts.* This principle applies to any human organization. A bureaucracy is driven by Teacher emotion to grow larger, and a government wants to expand.

Second, one can also see why the mind naturally attributes super-human events to the hand of God. I have mentioned that an image of God emerges as a general Teacher theory explains personal behavior. When an image of God turns into a mental network, then this theory becomes emotionally driven to interpret personal behavior. Obviously, a general theory of the subjective will focus upon *personal* behavior because it is a general theory of the *subjective,* it will emphasize events that are big and powerful because it is a *general* theory of the subjective, and it will zero in on situations that preserve order and structure because it is a general *theory* of the subjective.

We saw earlier that mental networks in Mercy thought try to interpret specific situations that could be caused by agents. But behind all of these specific Mercy mental networks lies the Teacher mental network of a universal theory which is *also* attempting to explain personal events. Thus, if some human agent does not appear to be responsible for an event, then the universal Teacher mental network will claim responsibility, especially if that event felt personal, powerful, or preserved structure. And even if a specific person or animal *did* cause the event, then the universal Teacher mental network may still claim that it *influenced* the behavior of that person or animal.

Using a simple example, suppose that I hear the doorbell ring and I go to the door and see a plate of freshly baked cookies sitting on the doorstep. I will then think of all of my neighbors who are generous and who are good cooks in order to figure out *who* delivered the cookies, and that will remind me of Mrs. Field living just down the street who loves to bake sweets and give unexpected treats to others. But suppose that Mrs. Field is out of town. Because receiving a plate of cookies is a fairly trivial event, my gut feeling will be that God is too busy with important matters to stoop to delivering a plate of cookies. Besides, common sense tells me that cookies are baked by people. But I might think that God *motivated* either Mrs. Field or some stranger to bake the cookies and leave them on my doorstep, especially if I was feeling down and really needed some personal encouragement in order to keep going. In contrast, I will be much more prone to attribute a flood, volcano, or other natural disaster to the hand of God, because it is too big to be caused by finite humans and it feels big enough to merit the personal attention of a universal being.

This mental mechanism will also lead people to pose the question of 'Why does God allow people to suffer?' For instance, suppose that a volcano erupts and the inhabitants of a nearby village are all asphyxiated by pyroclastic flow. Because this event is big and because it affected human life, there will be a natural tendency to blame God for it. But the eruption brought chaos and not order and structure, leading naturally to the mental quandary of 'why God permits suffering'. In response, the typical believer in God will conclude that the volcano *does* fit into God's general plan and that we will eventually know the answer, just as the typical scientist who is faced with a counterexample to his general theory that he cannot explain will usually set the problem aside for a later date. Quoting Kuhn: "How...do scientists respond to the awareness of an anomaly in the fit between theory and nature?...There are always some discrepancies. Even the most stubborn ones usually respond at last to normal practice. Very often scientists are willing to wait, particularly if there are many problems available in other parts of the field."

Third, these factors provide a cognitive basis for a belief in *hell*. Suppose that an individual with an image of God attempts to remove thoughts of God from his personal life. By definition, personal life falls within the domain of an image of God. Thus, the general Teacher theory that produces the image of God will feel suppressed, and because personal identity contains the experiences that *repeatedly* come to mind, this general theory will *repeatedly* feel repressed. And any mental network that is repeatedly repressed will eventually start to fall apart, generating emotions of hyper-pain. Where will that emotional hyper-pain be felt? If the theory behind the image of God is *universal*, then it will be felt in all situations and at all times, because a universal theory applies in all situations and at all times. And because a universal theory is *unique*, Teacher thought will not just project the hyper-pain of fragmention, but rather the more intense hyper-pain of impending annihilation. Thus, attempting to live apart from the concept of God will face the religious believer with a mental sensation of inescapable, universal, personal hyper-anguish. And that defines hell: It is a 'place' apart from God that is filled with inescapable, eternal, personal hyper-anguish.

Now suppose that the believer in a universal God becomes friends with someone who does not share his concept of God and religion. Experiences with this friend will eventually form a Mercy mental network within the mind of the believer, and this mental network will *contradict* the believer's concept of deity. As a result, the believer will feel driven by internal emotions to warn his 'pagan' friend that if he does not start believing in God, then he will face eternity in hell.

This mental effect will be strongest when a religious believer has a concept of God that is based in a *universal* theory which is subject to *contradiction.* For the average Western individual today, his image of God is *not* universal, it *can* be successfully ignored for most of the time, and living without an image of God does *not* lead to feelings of mental annihilation. That is because objective science has largely displaced religion. Therefore, if one wants to see the power that an image of God has historically wielded, then one must either read literature from several hundred years ago or else examine the way that *science* is currently treated. First, science *is* universally accepted throughout the world. Every country has universities and other institutes of higher learning and *all* of these schools teach essentially the same content—especially when dealing with the hard sciences such as physics, mathematics, chemistry, and biology. Second, science is impossible to ignore. If a person wants a good job, then he must have an official degree from an accredited university. Finally, science is unique. There is no alternative to the officially recognized international network of universities. That is what it means to have the concept of a universal God. Take the *external* ubiquity, pervasiveness, and exclusivity of the university system, *internalize* this, and apply the resulting universal system to personal identity.

The God of Buddhism

If the concept of hell is related to the impending demise of a universal image of God, then this helps us to understand why the idea of hell is not present in the religion of Buddhism, because a universal theory that is based upon the *absence* of logic cannot be threatened by either facts or logic. One of the key concepts of Eastern mysticism is the premise that Perceiver thought, Perceiver facts, and Perceiver logic stand in the way of attaining emotional union with God. Perceiver mode places confidence in facts; it looks for solid connections that are repeated. Therefore, avoiding the use of Perceiver thought means keeping facts vague and indefinite. As the platitudes spoken by the typical politician illustrate, it is difficult to find a logical contradiction in speech that is vague and indefinite. And if the ultimate goal is to go 'beyond logic', then, as the Zen *koan* demonstrates, a logical contradiction actually helps to *build* an image of God and not tear it down.

Saying this in terms of the puzzle analogy, if someone points out to the Eastern mystic that he has put some of the pieces together incorrectly, then the mystic will respond that puzzles need to be 'assembled' by placing them in a blender. The mystic will then add that the person who is trying to fit the pieces together is still mentally operating at the logical level of 'putting pieces together' and that he needs to 'graduate' to the blender method which goes 'beyond logic'.

As I mentioned in the previous chapter, the growth of objective science drives religions in the direction of Eastern mysticism and Buddhism for the simple reason that whenever religion *does* say something definite, objective science will attempt to analyze that fact, remove it from the domain of religion, and bring it within the domain of objective science. Thus, religion eventually learns that the way to survive is by remaining vague and indefinite, and when it learns this lesson, it will discover the 'blender' approach of Eastern mysticism. And if a universal theory of the subjective cannot be disproven, then that theory will not feel emotionally threatened, and if it is not threatened, then it will not generate the mental hyper-agony of 'being in hell apart from God'.

However, while vague facts and 'going beyond logic' can protect religious belief from logical attack, they also prevent a religion from altering human behavior. Vague may be safe, but it doesn't get a person anywhere. Making progress on the basis of vague information is like attempting to drive through mud. Mud hinders a vehicle from making progress and it cakes the vehicle with the past. According to Buddhism, personal existence consists of endless reincarnation driven by the eternal spinning of the wheel of rebirth. Thus, according to Buddhism, the karma of previous deeds 'cakes' the individual with his personal past while the gradual accumulation of karma forces personal progress to occur slowly through the grinding mud of many lifetimes. Buddhism also says that ultimate personal salvation means losing one's personal identity and becoming reunited with a God who transcends all facts, objects, and logic. In other words, salvation means turning into mud and becoming one with infinite mud. For when one attempts to add doctrinal content to an overgeneralized theory, then one is trying to add solid Perceiver facts to a theory which cannot handle solid Perceiver facts. And that defines mud—material that acts solid but which gives way when subjected to pressure.

Concrete Thought

We have now arrived at the point in the book where we need to start examining *mental circuits*. In order to make this transition as easy as possible, we will begin by looking at the simplest mental circuit, which is *concrete thought*. This may seem like a detour, but it will eventually lead us back to our discussion about God and the three stages of learning. Except, instead of arriving back at an image of God based in Teacher overgeneralization that is incompatible with rational thought, we will end up with a concept of God that is consistent with logical thinking.

If you look at the diagram of mental symmetry, you will notice that there is a diagonal labelled 'concrete' which goes through Mercy mode and Server mode. In simple terms, this tells us that concrete thought deals with experiences and actions; the experiences are stored in Mercy mode; the actions are performed by Server mode. The experience provides the goal; the action is used to reach the goal. For instance, the experience may be an ice cream sundae with hot fudge topping and the action is eating the ice cream. Or, the experience might be seeing a waterfall out in the country and the action is driving and walking to the waterfall. Or, the experience could be getting a college degree while the action is attending classes, doing homework, and studying for exams.

So far, what we are talking about is obvious. It is also fairly obvious that a goal always has an *emotion* associated with it. I eat the hot fudge sundae because it tastes good; I go to the waterfall because it is beautiful; I get a college degree because I want a good job. Saying this in the language of mental symmetry, every Mercy experience has an emotional label.

Now let us add another element to this mental circuit. One can see on the diagram of mental symmetry that a line leads from Mercy mode to Exhorter mode. This tells us that Exhorter mode is aware of Mercy experiences. We know that Exhorter mode is the part of the mind that generates *urges* and *desires*. As I have mentioned earlier, when a Mercy experience contains a strong emotional label, then Exhorter mode will sense this Mercy emotion and use it as the basis for an urge. For instance, if I *really* like ice cream sundaes, then I will have a strong urge to eat one. However, we also know that Exhorter urges are influenced by novelty. Therefore, if I have just had an ice cream sundae, then even if I like it very much, I will not immediately sense the urge to have another one. Instead, I may feel the urge to go visit the waterfall, especially if I have not seen it for a while, or if the season has changed and it looks different, or if there has been a lot of rain and the increased water flow makes the waterfall look more exciting.

Finally, I should mention that *painful* Mercy experiences can also lead to Exhorter urges, except in this case the urge will be to *avoid* the painful Mercy experience. For instance, suppose that I am walking along the path beside the waterfall and I slip. I will feel a strong urge to avoid falling into the water.

Now let us turn our attention to the *action* side of this mental circuit. When we looked at Perceiver mode, we saw that Perceiver thought works with *facts*. Each Perceiver fact has a label of confidence. Whenever Perceiver thought notices a fact being repeated, then it will gain confidence in that fact. Similarly, Server thought works with *sequences*. Each Server sequence also has a label of confidence which can be increased by repeating that sequence. When I do an action, such as eating an ice cream sundae, or walking on the path beside the waterfall, then my physical body is performing a *sequence* of movements. The easiest way to build Server confidence in a sequence is by *repeating* an action. Some actions, like walking along a narrow, slippery path, require significant levels of Server confidence to perform successfully. Other actions, like eating an ice cream sundae, require only a modicum of Server confidence, though even here it is possible for ice cream to fail to make it to the mouth and end up landing on the shirt.

The game of golf illustrates the different roles that are played by Server mode and Mercy mode in concrete thought. When the golfer practices his swing, he is using *repetition* to program Server thought. This repetition will build Server confidence. Observing where the ball lands programs Mercy thought with emotional experiences: Landing on the fairway is a good Mercy experience, whereas slicing off into the rough is a bad Mercy experience. Effective practicing *combines* Server repetition with Mercy observation. There is no point in repeatedly swinging the club if every shot lands in the rough, for that simply perfects the art of playing badly. For such a player, making progress may mean 'unlearning' bad habits and gaining Server confidence in actions that lead to good Mercy experiences.

That brings us back to the topic of mud. It is easy to see that Server actions and Mercy experiences are involved in concrete thought. But if one looks at the diagram of mental symmetry, one notices that there is no direct connection between Server mode and Mercy mode. Instead, they are connected *indirectly* through Perceiver mode and Contributor mode. These *intermediate* modes play a key role in relating actions with experiences.

Mud illustrates what happens when Perceiver mode is not functioning. When a person is stuck in the mud his Server actions do not get him any closer to his Mercy goal. No matter what he *does*, he does not *move*. In contrast, solid ground makes movement possible. Perceiver mode plays a similar role in the mind. By organizing Mercy experiences into solid categories, Perceiver thought makes it possible to progress from one set of Mercy experiences to another. Saying this another way, Perceiver thought builds a mental map that determines how Mercy experiences are connected. In order to move from one location to another, a person must know where he is, where he wants to be, and how these two locations are connected. In terms of the golfing example, Perceiver thought compares where the ball is with where the player desires it to land.

Because one is dealing with *emotional* Mercy experiences, this type of comparing requires Perceiver *confidence*. It takes Perceiver confidence to recognize that a golf ball has landed in the rough and to admit that it should have landed on the green. This Perceiver confidence does not *remove* Mercy feelings but rather recognizes that Perceiver facts are *independent* of Mercy emotions. Perceiver mode knows that landing in the rough is *different* than landing in the green, whereas Mercy mode feels that landing in the green is *better* than landing in the rough. If the practicing golfer thinks that landing in the rough is the *same* as landing in the green, then he will lack the knowledge that is needed to improve his golfing skills. And if he does not feel that landing in the green is *better* than landing in the rough, then there will be no motivation for him to improve.

When dealing with a physical object like a golf ball and a physical boundary between rough and green, almost every person has sufficient Perceiver confidence to distinguish logically between good and bad results, which is why I chose to use this example. Determining Perceiver boundaries and acknowledging Mercy emotions becomes much more difficult when facing issues that are less physical and more psychological. However, the temptation to distort the facts for personal benefit must be present even in the game of golf, for on the back cover of the official rule book is written, "Play the ball as it lies, play the course as you find it, and if you cannot do either, do what is fair."

The actual choosing and improving is done by *Contributor* mode, for it decides how to relate Perceiver facts with Server actions. When a Perceiver fact is connected with a Server action, the mental result is a sense of *cause-and-effect*: If I *do* a certain Server action, this will lead to a specific *change* in the Perceiver facts. Connecting facts with actions is closely related to what is known as 'free will': Given the current set of Perceiver facts, which Server action will I choose? Consistent with this, the Contributor *person* has the potential to be more strong-willed than any of the other cognitive styles.

Cause-and-effect is an important concept that will come up frequently in this book. Therefore, it needs to be defined clearly. In essence, cause-and-effect is an expanded version of object recognition. Think, for instance, of a knife. It contains two elements: a blade and a handle. When these two elements are connected, the result is a knife. The images of 'blade' and 'handle' are stored within Mercy mode, while Perceiver mode notices that these two Mercy elements occur together repeatedly.

When dealing with a physical *object* such as a knife, the various elements of the object are *spatially* connected. Cause-and-effect is a type of mental object in which the various elements are *temporally* connected. Instead of being separated by space, they are separated by time. For instance, we all know that 'eating too much' is connected with 'getting fat'. But 'eating too much' does not occur at the same time as 'getting fat'. Instead, 'eating too much' is *followed* by 'getting fat'. Contributor mode generates a mental sense of cause-and-effect by connecting Perceiver facts with Server actions.

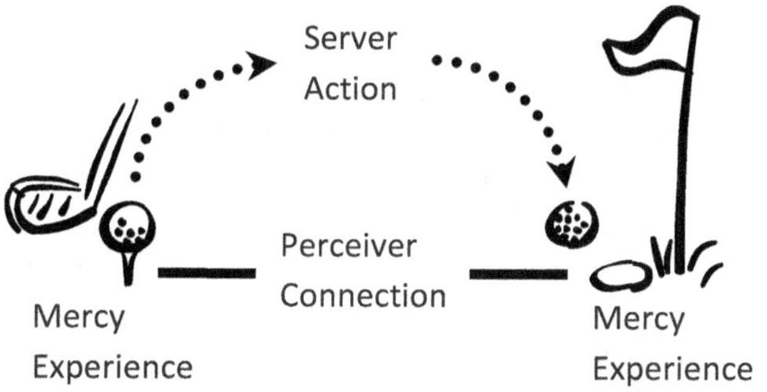

'Eating too much' leads to 'getting fat' because my physical body is *doing* something with the food. It is turning food into fat.

However, Perceiver thought still *thinks* of cause-and-effect as an object. Even though 'getting fat' occurs *after* 'eating too much', as far as Perceiver thought is concerned, 'getting fat' and 'eating too much' are simply two Mercy experiences that are connected, in the same way that 'blade' and 'handle' are two Mercy experiences that are connected.

For a more obvious example of a temporal object, thinking of playing golf. The golf ball starts in one location and ends up in another location. The ball is not in both locations at the same time. Instead, it is first in location A and then in location B. These two locations are connected by the Server action of the ball travelling through the air from location A to location B.

This book has looked at several ways in which Perceiver thought organizes Mercy experiences into categories. I suggest that self-image, ownership, common sense, and mental networks all change when Server actions are added to Perceiver facts.

Let us begin by looking at self-image. We have defined personal identity as the collection of Mercy experiences upon which Mercy thought can continue to concentrate. Perceiver thought, observing from 'next door', will notice which Mercy experiences are repeated and will come up with the mental object known as self-image. When Server actions are added to Perceiver facts, then self-image will expand to include personal *skills*—the Server actions that I am capable of doing. I mentioned this previously without explaining it. Now we see the mental mechanism by which personal skills become mentally attached to self-image. For instance, because I started violin at an early age, I used to connect the Perceiver object of a violin with my personal identity. However, I now connect the Server skill of playing a violin with my self-image.

Moving on, when we examined self-image, we looked at the difference between 'me' and 'mine', and I mentioned that ownership is determined by Perceiver mode: Perceiver thought decides which objects are connected with the mental network that represents my personal identity and which are connected with the mental networks that represent other individuals. Now that we have introduced Contributor thought, we can expand upon the concept of ownership. Ownership is rooted in Perceiver thought, but it also carries with it a strong *Server* component. When I own an object, I can choose which Server actions to perform upon this object. If I own a car, I can choose when and where it will be driven, and if I wish, I can even choose to drop the vehicle over a cliff and destroy it. When the ownership of an object changes, then the old owner loses the right to *do* things with the object, while the new owner can now choose to do as he wishes with the object.

The various roles played by Perceiver, Contributor, and Server thought in ownership could be compared to a chess board and moving the pieces on the board. Perceiver thought determines where each chess piece is currently located upon the board, Contributor thought decides which piece will be moved and where to move it, while the actual moving of the piece is done by Server mode. Similarly, *ownership* is determined by Perceiver mode, Contributor mode is responsible for *changing* ownership, while Server mode performs the *actions* that ownership makes permissible.

Moving to the next point, *common sense* also has a Server component. So far we have associated common sense with *Perceiver* facts, such as knowing that a tree consists of a trunk, root, branches, and leaves. Because we live in a physical world composed of physical objects, common sense begins with Perceiver facts about physical objects. But objects do not stay still. Instead, they move and they can be changed. As common sense observes movement and change, it will then expand to include *cause-and-effect.* Not only will common sense learn to recognize objects such as trees, but it will also learn that apples can fall from trees. And as the legend of Newton and the apple falling from the tree illustrates, when common sense starts to focus upon cause-and-effect, then science can emerge.

Finally, I have stated in vague terms that a mental network tries to 'function' or 'operate' when it is triggered. We can now see more clearly what it means for a mental network to function. A Mercy mental network is not just a collection of emotional Mercy experiences held together by Perceiver connections. It may start as that, but Server actions also get added mentally to the Perceiver facts. Thus, when I am reminded of the mental network representing father, I do not just think about experiences and facts about my father, I am also reminded of what he *does* and how he *acts*.

Economics

We have looked at how concrete thought functions. If we step back to see the bigger picture, we will notice that concrete thought operates within a framework of economic activity. Think, for instance, of the golf illustration. The land on which the game of golf is being played is owned by some person, and I must pay money to that person for the privilege of being able to swing my club and hit the ball. That owner did not build the course himself, but paid others to perform the Server actions that were needed to turn his land into a golf course. The club and the ball belong to me, but I bought them from someone else. If the ball that I hit falls on the green, then it will continue to belong to me, but if it lands in the water, then I will effectively lose ownership of it because I cannot perform the Server action of retrieving the ball. One could continue in this vein, but I think that we get the picture. The point is that in a modern world, concrete thought cannot exist apart from economic activity.

Let us look in more detail at the relationship between concrete thought and economics. Our discussion about concrete thought began with Server actions and emotional Mercy experiences. We then realized that these two are tied together by Perceiver facts and Contributor choices. Now that we know that Perceiver thought and Contributor thought play an important intermediate role in concrete thought, let us examine what they do.

We will begin by looking at the relationship between Perceiver facts and Mercy experiences. I mentioned in the previous section that this combination leads to a mental *map*: Mercy thought remembers experiences and Perceiver thought remembers how these experiences are connected. When Mercy emotions are added to a mental map, it turns into a *map* of *value*.

This is illustrated by the game of golf. The various features of the golf course are laid out physically. Perceiver thought builds a mental map of this physical layout by determining the physical relationship between these various locations: The hole is in the middle of the putting green; the sand is on the edge of the green; the water is between the green and the fairway; the rough is on either side of the fairway. Mercy thought remembers these locations and associates each one with an emotional label: The hole is obviously very good, the putting green is good, the fairway is fair, the rough is bad, and the sand and the water are very bad.

Once a map of value has been created, then personal identity is placed within this map. My *physical* location is obviously determined by the location of my physical body. Mercy thought is forced to *concentrate* upon the locations that are close to my physical body because my physical body is only capable of *sensing* locations that are close by. Similarly, my *mental* location is determined by the set of Mercy memories that continue to come to mind, such as swinging the golf club in a particular manner, slicing the ball into the rough, or attempting to sink long putts under pressure.

This combination of emotional Mercy experiences and Perceiver facts also lies at the heart of economic activity. First, economics is based upon the concept of *value.* According to Ludwig von Mises, one of the founders of the Austrian school of economics, value is synonymous with subjective Mercy emotions. In *Theory and History*, he says: "All judgments of value are personal and subjective. There are no judgments of value other than those asserting I prefer, I like better, I wish." Von Mises adds in *Human Action* that "It is vain to speak of any calculation of values. Calculation is possible only with cardinal numbers. The difference between the valuation of two states of affairs is entirely psychical and personal. It is not open to any projection into the external world. It can be sensed only by the individual. It cannot be communicated or imparted to any fellow man."

But, as Von Mises states, it is very difficult to measure or quantify a personal, private sensation. Therefore, even though economics says that value is *based* in Mercy emotions, it *represents* this value through the use of money, because money can be measured and quantified. Thus, when a person is asked the value of an item, he responds with a monetary figure and not an emotional response. Instead of saying, "I like it very much," he says "It cost $35." In the words of von Mises, "Economic calculation can only take place by means of money prices established in the market for production goods in a society resting on private property in the means of production."

If money is being used to represent emotion, then what is the relationship between money and happiness? In *Human Action*, Von Mises states that "It is ultimately always the subjective value judgments of individuals that determine the formation of prices." In other words, emotional value determines monetary value. This provides us with an answer to the age-old question of whether or not money can buy happiness. Money cannot buy happiness because money *represents* happiness. If the happiness is absent, then there is nothing for the money to represent. Similarly, if money represents happiness, then it does not make sense for a person to choose to work at a job that makes him miserable in order to make money, because then one is sacrificing value in order to gain the representation of value.

Notice that we are dealing with another version of the *objectivity* that one finds in modern science. Science attempts to avoid Mercy emotions by remaining objective. Similarly, economics attempts to avoid Mercy emotions by dealing with the representation of value rather than value itself.

Let us move on now to the Perceiver *map* that ties together emotional Mercy experiences. One sees this most clearly illustrated by the *store*, which actually creates a physical map of economic value. Items that are similar to each other are placed physically close together and each one is labeled with a price, making it easy for the shopper to compare one item with another in order to calculate value. In a store, all of the items that are for sale belong to the owner of the store; in a market, many owners come together to show their wares. In both cases, though, the result is a physical map of economic value.

That brings us to the matter of *ownership*. Von Mises says in *Civilization* that "The foundation of any and every civilization, including our own, is private ownership of the means of production. Whoever wishes to criticize modern civilization, therefore, begins with private property." Private property is based upon the concept of *ownership* which we discussed earlier when first defining personal identity.

There is a fundamental relationship between ownership and physical location. In the same way that economic value starts with Mercy emotion, so I suggest that ownership *begins* with physical location. As the expression goes, possession is nine-tenths of the law. For instance, when I visit someone's home, I assume that he owns the home because he is spending his time within that location, and I also assume that the items within the home belong to him because they are physically close to the location where he spends most of his time.

If one looks at history, one sees that physical location initially *defined* ownership. At the national level, each country had its origins in a group of people who moved to a certain physical location and decided to live there. Likewise, *Uti possidetis* (as you possessed, you shall possess henceforth) is a principle in international law that began in Roman times. According to this principle, when a peace treaty is signed after a war, then each side continues to own the property that it currently holds. This principle is also used to determine international boundaries when a colony achieves independence. Similarly, at the personal level, under homesteading, a person receives ownership of a plot of land if he physically lives for a period of time within that location.

Animals define ownership in terms of physical presence. Animals that are territorial will stay within a certain physical region and avoid physical regions that are occupied by neighboring animals. Animals may use physical scent to mark their territory. For instance, when a dog sniffs an area and then urinates, it is checking ownership and marking ownership.

We will look at ownership further, but first let us examine the relationship between concrete thought and personal identity. Remember that concrete thought uses Server actions to reach emotional Mercy goals. For instance, concrete thought may perform the Server actions of planting, cultivating, and harvesting seed in order to reach the emotional goal of harvesting a crop. Or, concrete thought may perform the Server actions of cutting down trees and assembling logs in order to reach the emotional goal of having a warm house in which to live. Now suppose that I grow some food and bandits—or government officials—show up on my doorstep and demand the food. Or suppose that some powerful neighbor likes my house better than his and decides to kick me out and move in. Under conditions such as these, I will only continue to plant crops or build houses if I am forced to do so. In other words, concrete thought will only continue to function if Mercy thought can continue to concentrate on the pleasant emotional results of performing the Server actions. Similarly, a master can only force a servant to work if the master can continue to remind the servant of the unpleasant emotional results of not performing the Server actions.

We have defined personal identity as the Mercy experiences upon which personal identity can continue to concentrate. Laws of private property make it possible for a person to enjoy the fruit of his labor, by allowing Mercy thought to *continue concentrating* on the Mercy results of concrete thought. Private property says that the land and the crops belong to me, and laws of private property ensure that some bandit or government official will not take over my house or steal my crops. As Von Mises says in *Liberalism*: "Private property creates for the individual a sphere in which he is free of the state. It sets limits to the operation of the authoritarian will. It allows other forces to arise side by side with and in opposition to political power."

However, I suggest that as with value, economics focuses upon the physical expression of personal identity and not personal identity itself. The economist asserts that Perceiver thought must be able to know with certainty which objects are 'mine', which is mentally accurate. But it is even more important for Perceiver thought to know with certainty which Mercy experiences are 'me'. And that brings us to the problem of childish identity.

In an earlier chapter, I suggested that childish identity naturally tries to *identify* with pleasant experiences and *deny* unpleasant experiences. The reason that the bandit steals the crops of the grain farmer is because he is mentally identifying with pleasant experiences: "Nice crop. I'll take it." Von Mises refers to the 'private ownership of the means of production', which says that Server actions need to be performed within the context of Perceiver ownership, but what is more basic is the *mental circuit* of concrete thought, which performs Server actions within the mental context of Perceiver self-image.

One can illustrate this concept with the example of a *steam engine*. Mercy experiences are like water, and Mercy emotions could be compared to the heat of the water. Self-image is like the boiler which holds the water, because it 'imprisons' personal identity within a 'box' of Perceiver facts. In the same way that the boiler must be made out of material that is strong enough to contain the steam, so the Perceiver facts that define personal identity need to have sufficient Perceiver confidence to handle the emotional pressure generated by personal identity. If the pressure in the boiler is too great, then the boiler will fail and the steam will escape. Similarly, identification and denial occur when Perceiver thought loses the ability to define personal identity.

The goal of a steam engine is to channel the steam into a piston so that it can produce useful work. Similarly, when the Mercy emotions of personal identity are imprisoned within the Perceiver facts of self-image, then the resulting Exhorter urge will motivate a person to perform Server actions that will lead to some Mercy goal. That describes the mental circuit of concrete thought. An economic system based in private property makes it *possible* for concrete thought to function, but only the development of Perceiver facts and Server skills, backed up by mental confidence, will actually *cause* the circuit of concrete thought to function.

Why does the economist assume that concrete thought is functioning? I suggest that the primary reason is *cognitive style.* Our research into personality suggests that most successful businessmen are Contributor persons. As one can see from the diagram of mental symmetry, Contributor mode lies at the center of the mind. Therefore, Contributor mode can only work if the circuit of concrete thought (or as we shall see later, the circuit of abstract thought) is functioning.

We have seen that ownership begins with physical location. Humans are capable of carrying out the additional step of *reassigning* ownership. As I have mentioned earlier, it appears that Contributor thought is responsible for reassigning ownership. The mental mechanism involved is simply a modified version of cause-and-effect—the basic element of Contributor thought. In normal cause-and-effect, a Server action leads from the cause to the effect. In an exchange, two people choose to perform Server actions that affect the *physical property* of each other. For instance, I may perform a Server action for you such as baking you a loaf of bread, harvesting your crops, or helping to construct your house. In return, you may perform a Server action for me such as giving me some grain, shoeing my horse, or giving me a valuable object such as a silver coin. In general terms, the Server action may involve the physical transfer of some *good* or the performance of some *service.* The point is that an exchange requires at least two people, each person performs some Server action within concrete thought, and the result of this action is that the physical property of the *other* person ends up better than it was before.

Notice the difference between an exchange and theft or servitude. In theft, one person takes a Perceiver object from another person, while in servitude, one person is forced to perform a Server action for another person. In an exchange, each person 'steals' or 'demands servitude' from the other. But because this 'stealing' and 'servitude' occurs *mutually*, Mercy thought in each person can feel *good* about the final result and Contributor mode in each person can *choose* to make the exchange instead of being forced. For instance, imagine saying to the clerk at a checkout counter, "If I give you some money, will you let me take this item from the store?" Phrased that way, the interaction sounds strange, but it describes accurately what is taking place.

However, even though an exchange may end fairly, it still may mean *giving up* one item in order to receive another. This is difficult to do when *Mercy mental networks* are involved. Think, for instance, of parting with a family heirloom, or selling the ancestral farm. The result is that an economic exchange often involves a conflict between Contributor mode wishing to give up some item in order to get a better item, and a mental network wishing to hold on to that item in order to avoid hyper-pain, especially when dealing with valuable items.

According to the saying, everything has a price, but what happens when everything has an *economic* price? When this occurs, then this means that economic exchange is occurring in the *absence* of mental networks, and *Theory of Mind* will become disabled.

Remember that Theory of Mind attempts to guess which mental networks are currently active within the mind of *another* person by being reminded of mental networks which are present within my *own* mind. If I attempt to perform an economic exchange with another person and no mental networks are triggered within my own mind, then my exchange will lack *empathy*. For instance, I will walk up to the ancestral farm with my wad of cash and feel no emotions when the owner of the farm says that the property has been in the family for generations. Or, I will buy an item for the cheapest price at the local store, even if this means that workers in another country produced this product by laboring long hours in sweatshop conditions for minimal pay.

In the extreme, I suggest that economic exchange in the absence of mental networks describes a mental condition which is clinically known as *psychopathy*. According to the general description in Wikipedia, psychopaths lack empathy, they neglect the needs of others, and they view other people as objects for their personal gratification. The psychopath feels no emotional pain when he sees another person suffer, and he suffers no remorse when he is caught. Thus, we see an *absence* of mental networks. Mental symmetry suggests that mental networks are related to the internal world of Mercy (and Teacher) thought, which is located within orbitofrontal cortex. Neurological research indicates that the brain function of psychopaths is impaired in precisely this region, as well as in the amygdala, the emotional processor of the brain.[18]

This same paper states that "A striking feature of much of the antisocial behaviour shown by individuals with psychopathy is that it is mostly instrumental in nature, i.e. goal-directed towards achieving money, sexual opportunities or increased status." In a similar vein, other researchers have found that psychopaths tend to view a crime as something that has to be done to reach a goal, and that psychopaths tend to use words such as 'because' or 'so that' which are related to cause-and-effect.[19] Thus, we see that exchange motivated by *external* benefits is functioning in the mind of the psychopath.

American law regards a corporation as a person. But while a corporation performs economic exchanges, it obviously lacks mental networks. The 2003 documentary *The Corporation*, written by Joel Bakan, analyzed corporations and concluded that the typical multinational corporation fits the clinical definition of psychopathy.

The solution, I suggest, is not to eliminate economic exchange, but rather to realize that value is based upon emotions and that economic exchange is an external expression of personal exchange. For instance, the typical Korean family spends excessive amounts of time and money upon education. There can be a tendency to emphasize the appearance of education over the actual learning itself, but the Korean infatuation with education does go beyond mere economic exchange, by using exchange to improve 'me' and not just add to what is 'mine'.

---

[18] The British Journal of Psychiatry (2003) *182: 5-7* doi: 10.1192/bjp.182.1.5

[19] http://www.livescience.com/16585-psychopaths-speech-language.html

I have mentioned that Contributor mode is responsible for performing exchange, because it thinks in terms of cause-and-effect. As I mention in the appendix on technical thought, Contributor mode is also responsible for performing *optimization*, which means letting go of what is regarded as non-essential in order to gain more of what is deemed to be essential. Combining these two points, we conclude that the Contributor person, who is conscious in Contributor mode, will naturally tend to optimize exchange by minimizing the Server actions and Perceiver facts that are being exchanged and focusing purely upon the Contributor step of changing ownership.

I suggest that this explains the *stock market* and other similar economic exchanges. In a stock market, no physical items or services change hands. Instead, what is traded is a piece of paper or a number representing ownership of some item, service, or company. And the Server action involved in performing the exchange is reduced to the raising of a hand or the clicking of a mouse button. However, it is possible to optimize even further and buy or sell merely the option to buy or sell items, services, or ownership. The end result is that Contributor thought, which began by exchanging Perceiver objects and Server actions, ends up exchanging representations that have become totally divorced from reality. We will examine this in greater detail when looking at technical thought.

Conscience

We have seen that economic activity is based upon *cause-and-effect*, and we have also seen that mentally divorcing cause-and-effect from emotions and mental networks leads to anti-social behavior. When subjective emotions are added to cause-and-effect, then I suggest that the result is *conscience*. Cause-and-effect says that 'eating too much' leads to 'getting fat'. Maintaining this connection within Perceiver thought does not require much confidence because no strong emotions are involved.

Conscience goes one step further and says that 'if I eat too much' then 'I will get fat'. Adding the personal element transforms cause-and-effect from an objective connection into one that requires Perceiver confidence. It is easy to state that 'eating too much will make me fat'. It is much more difficult to assert that 'I will get fat if I eat too much', especially if I am hungry and I enjoy eating food. And if one examines morality in general, one finds that people tend to agree about moral guidelines when they are discussed using the objective language of cause-and-effect. However, when personal emotions get involved, then it is easy for Mercy feelings to overturn Perceiver knowledge.

This principle is illustrated by an old communist joke. The party official comes to the comrade on his farm and asks, "If you had two houses, would you give one to your neighbor?" The farmer answers, "Yes." The party official continues, "If you had two horses, would you give one to your neighbor?" The farmer replies, "Of course." The party official then queries, "If you had two cows, would you give one to your neighbor?" The farmers responds, "No!" Taken aback, the party official asks why, to which the farmer replies, "Because, I *do* have two cows." That illustrates what often happens when the personal element is added to an if-then statement.

Now let us go one step further and add the effect of mental networks. Suppose that a teacher tells his students, "Anyone caught cheating on an exam will receive a mark of zero." This is a rule of conscience; it is a connection of cause-and-effect that is being applied to personal identity. But if the students have spent sufficient time with this teacher, then within the mind of each student, a mental network representing the teacher will have formed within Mercy thought, and the specific rule about cheating will become mentally attached to this mental network. Therefore, if a student thinks of cheating, then this thought will not just bring to mind the rule against cheating. It will *also* remind the student of the mental network that represents his teacher. And, like any mental network which comes to mind, that mental network will attempt to become active and function. How will it function? By mentally carrying out the Server action of writing a mark of zero on the student's exam. As long as the student thinks about cheating, the mental network that represents his teacher will continue to bring to mind the action of 'getting caught and receiving a zero'. If the student tries to think about cheating without thinking about 'receiving a zero', then the mental network that represents his teacher will feel suppressed.

Consistent with this, one of the main traits of a psychopath is a lack of conscience. Mental networks give power to the cause-and-effect statements of conscience. The psychopath who follows cause-and-effect but lacks mental networks has no conscience and shows no feelings of remorse.

Saying this in a more mathematical way, cause-and-effect is like a *function* with an input and an output. In conscience, the input comes from some *person* and some person also carries out the function that transforms the input into the output. In our illustration, a *student* does the cheating, and the *teacher* transforms the input of 'a student caught cheating' into the output of 'that student receives a zero'. A rule of conscience is emotionally backed up by the mental network representing the person who made the rule. Therefore, if a person thinks of the *input*, then the mental function will remind him of the *output*. If a person tries to think of the input *without* thinking of the output, then the mental network backing up this function will complain.

Suppose that a student does cheat and that he does *not* get caught. The experience of cheating now forms part of the student's personal identity. As a result, the student will continually be reminded of the unpleasant experience of 'receiving a zero' through a chain of two mental networks: First, because personal identity consists of experiences that continually come to mind, the student will repeatedly be reminded of his act of cheating. And because the connection between cheating and 'receiving a zero' forms part of the mental network that represents his teacher, being reminded of cheating will mentally lead to the experience of 'receiving a zero'.

Like any physical chain, this mental chain is only as strong as its weakest link. If emotional pressure plays a major role in defining personal identity, then the student will find it easy to use denial to pretend that he did not cheat. In that case, *factual* evidence will probably be required for Perceiver thought to form a solid mental connection between personal identity and cheating. The teacher may have to find cheat notes written on the student's hands, clothing, or possibly hidden in his pen. It is also possible to break the chain of guilt by focusing upon the mental network that represents the teacher. Maybe the rule of the teacher was unclear, or the student did not hear the teacher say the rule. In this case, it is the connection between the rule and the mental network representing the teacher that is being called into question. Or, in more general terms, if the student can attack the mental network that represents his teacher, then it no longer matters if that mental network threatens personal identity with unpleasant experiences. And if a person teaches school for several years as I have, then he will encounter many more creative ways in which a student can avoid guilt and deny personal responsibility.

The justice industry spends a lot of time, effort, and money on the process of establishing guilt and blame and determining punishment. However, as with science and commerce, the focus tends to be upon the objective and the physical: What does the physical evidence prove? Was the person physically present or physically absent when the crime was committed? However, the real question is a *cognitive* one: Which mental network was responsible for performing the action, and how will other mental networks respond to this event? This shows up in the question of *motive*, for when a criminal investigator is attempting to establish a motive for a crime, he is trying to determine which mental network prompted that action.

If people had sufficient Perceiver confidence to handle emotional issues, then conscience would be able to *prevent* most crimes from being committed, guilt would cause people to *confess* their crimes, and the goal of punishment would be to *restore* personal integrity and *build* mental confidence. Instead, emotional identification is used to disregard conscience, denial overrules guilt, and punishment labels the offending individual as 'bad' and quarantines him for as long as possible. This comment may seem naive and impractical, but those who are familiar with the name Friesen will recognize that I come from a Mennonite ethnic background. The Mennonite Central Committee has devoted considerable resources toward developing and applying restorative modes of justice.

Moving on to the next point, economic exchange uses the same mental circuit as conscience and guilt but focuses upon *reward* instead of punishment. For instance, suppose that I perform a job for some person. I am assuming that he will notice what I have done and that he will respond by paying me in some fashion. Putting this another way, performing the job brings to mind a mental network associated either with that person or with business in general, and one of the functions of that mental network is to 'pay for services'.

The most basic form of economic exchange occurs when two tribes meet and attempt to trade. Their interaction will be limited to the exchange of physical *objects*. That is because these groups only share in common their physical environment. When people get to know each other, then a basic form of economic exchange can emerge, which is the exchange of *favors*. The mental mechanism is precisely the same as in conscience: If I think of doing some action, then that will bring to mind the mental network representing some other person and how he will probably respond. And, just as guilt expects that the other person will respond in a certain fashion because of what I have done, so performing a favor also expects the other person to respond because of what I have done: "I did you a favor. Now you owe me one." Thus, in the same way that mental networks give power to the cause-and-effect rules of conscience, so mental networks give power to the cause-and-effect rules of economic exchange.

Moving beyond a barter economy to a money economy takes the concept of 'I did a favor; now you owe me one' and formalizes it, for money is just an IOU—a piece of paper which indicates that I did someone a favor and am 'owed one'. For instance, my grandfather owned a general store in a small town in Saskatchewan. In the 1920s he issued a series of tokens 'redeemable in merchandise at Friesen's General Store'. These coins functioned as IOUs, because a farmer who brought farm products in to the store would receive tokens in exchange, which he could redeem at some later date for merchandise at the store.

But money performs an additional useful function, one which also occurred with my grandfather's coins. Suppose that the farmer went to the barber for a haircut. He might not have any money to pay for a cut, but he did have a token from my father's store. Therefore, the barber would accept the token from my father as a substitute for money. The barber would then come in to my grandfather's store and use the token to buy something, even though my grandfather had initially given the token to the farmer.

I mentioned earlier that economic exchange occurs when two people perform Server actions that improve each other's private property. This means that economic exchange can only occur if one finds a partner with whom one can perform an economic exchange. This can be difficult, because whenever one person wants to receive a good or service from another person, then he has to find some good or service which that other person needs that he can provide. Money makes it possible to *decouple* these two Server actions. The first person can provide the second person with the good or service and the second person can reciprocate by giving the first person an IOU, which he can redeem with the second person later on, or with some *other* person.

But how does the person receiving the IOU *know* that the favor will be returned? How can he have *confidence* that he will eventually get paid? If he is given something that is universally accepted as valuable, then there is no need to know anything or place confidence in anything. That is what happens when a person is paid in gold or silver. Because gold and silver are universally valued, and because they retain their value, there is no need to trust anyone.

It is also possible to use a currency that is *backed up* by something valuable. In this case, the person receiving the IOU knows that it is worth something because it is connected by Perceiver thought to a mental network within Mercy thought. This describes the situation with my grandfather's tokens. They had no inherent value because they were made out of aluminum. But they were backed up by mental networks. Suppose that a farmer brought some butter into the store and received some of these coins in return.

First, the farmer *knew* my grandfather and how he behaved. Therefore, memories about my grandfather had formed a Mercy mental network within the mind of the farmer and this Mercy mental network predicted that my father would honor the token. Second, the store *itself* had been in existence long enough to be represented as a mental network within the mind of the farmer. And this mental network predicted that the store would function in a way that would satisfy the needs of the farmer, by turning his tokens into products that he could use.

However, it is also possible for money to be backed up by something completely *insubstantial*. That describes the situation for today's currencies, which are literally created by *fiat* out of thin air. We will see in a moment that this same 'thin air' can give power to conscience. But, before we turn to that subject, I would like to make one observation. We have seen that commerce and conscience use the *same* mental circuits. However, when dealing with conscience, the tendency is to view this mental circuit as an *impediment* to personal happiness: "Conscience is the little voice that stops me from having fun." In contrast, when applied to commerce, this mental circuit is viewed as the *key* to personal happiness. Similarly, I suggest that *guilt* and *satisfaction* also involve similar mental mechanisms, because in both cases, Perceiver thought is connecting the performance of some Server action with personal identity. And yet, we attempt to deny guilt while at the same time demanding satisfaction. If one is trying to destroy a mental circuit with the 'left hand' while at the same time attempting to build up the same circuit with the 'right hand', then obviously the mental results will be counterproductive.

Law and Teacher Mental Networks

Having said that, let us look now at the relationship between conscience, economics, and *Teacher* thought. Suppose that a school works out a consistent set of rules for its students and that it publishes these rules in a student handbook. A Teacher system of order-within-complexity has now been set up, using the Teacher language of *words*. If this Teacher system becomes sufficiently general—by applying to enough people and lasting for a long enough time—then it will form a mental network within *Teacher* thought. And this Teacher mental network will *automatically* give cognitive power to conscience: First, because the Teacher mental network is based in a *general* understanding that applies to many situations, it will *notice* infractions to the rule. Second, because a general theory feels bad when it encounters an exception to the general rule, it will *punish* infractions to the rule with emotional pain and hyper-pain.

The *strength* of this mental effect depends upon the generality of the underlying Teacher mental network. For instance, if a school is fairly small and just getting set up, then its school handbook will not be taken very seriously. On the other hand, if the school is an established institution that has been around for several decades, then its student handbook will carry much more weight. Notice that we are dealing here with a *Teacher* mental network based in order-within-complexity and not with *Mercy* mental networks associated with specific people. A Mercy mental network uses personal status and physical force to back up a rule of conscience. A Teacher mental network enforces rules through feelings of generality and universality.

This explains the difference between gold-backed currency and fiat money. Gold-backed money is supported by gold or some other specific object with desirable Mercy properties. Fiat money, in contrast, is backed up by an *institution.* It is accepted because it is an expression of an established country; the order-within-complexity of the state has formed a mental network within Teacher thought and the financial IOU which the piece of money represents is backed up by that Teacher mental network.

At the beginning of this chapter, I suggested that there is an aspect to political force that is *not* rooted in physical force. We now see what it is. The state *lives* within the mind of the average citizen as a Teacher mental network and that mental network enforces the laws of the state. Thus, government law has both a physical component and a mental component. Physically, it is enforced by the power of the state, while mentally it is enforced by the Teacher mental network formed by the institution of the state.

Natural law also has a physical component and a mental component. Physically, the laws of nature are enforced by natural cause-and-effect, which causes painful physical results when an individual *acts* in a way that violates natural law. Mentally, the laws of nature are enforced by the Teacher mental network of common sense. When a person *thinks* of acting in a way that violates natural law, this brings emotional discomfort to Teacher thought.

I stated several pages back that our digression into concrete thought would eventually lead us back to a discussion about God. We have now arrived at that point. Conscience is a principle of cause-and-effect that applies to personal identity. When a rule of conscience is backed up by a Teacher mental network, then this will lead to the concept that this rule of conscience is being enforced by God, because a Teacher mental network that applies to personal identity creates an image of God.

Notice that we are no longer dealing with a God of Teacher overgeneralization in which specific concepts are being overgeneralized in order to give the illusion of universality. Instead, we are looking at a concept of God that emerges when principles of cause-and-effect that apply to personal identity are *generalized* to form a system of law and this general system turns into a Teacher mental network.

Notice also that we have come up with two different sources for a general system of laws: First, the method of science can be used to discover general laws of natural cause-and-effect. Second, people can put together a set of laws, leading to a general system of government law.

Government law behaves quite differently than natural law. The *state* has the ability of being 'in your face'. It can publically announce its edicts and send in soldiers with guns to enforce its words. But the state is weak when it comes to enforcing its laws. Officials can be bribed, laws can be evaded, and justice can be delayed. That is because government laws, despite their initial bravado, are entirely artificial. Unless infractions are noticed and punished, government laws are nothing more than empty threats.

For *natural law*, the situation is reversed. Unlike government laws, natural laws are *always* enforced. But natural laws do not announce themselves. Therefore, a person often does not discover how implacable they are until he experiences the consequences of violating them. For instance, it may take a major accident to teach a young motorcycle driver that he must respect physical laws of momentum and energy conservation.

Because government law is artificial, it cannot *overrule* natural law. It is futile to pass legislation that violates the laws of nature. As King Canute demonstrated, a monarch cannot forbid the tide from coming in. Likewise, a government may order people at gunpoint to jump off the cliff, but eventually they will rebel.

But, the 'in your face' nature of government law means that it can *mask* natural law. If a government passes too much legislation that is *consistent* with natural law, then this will prevent people from learning about natural law. For instance, suppose that the government erects a fence in front of every potential cliff and forbids people from climbing over a fence. The *natural* boundary of a cliff has now been replaced by the *artificial* boundary of a fence. A person growing up in such an environment will not have a strong Teacher mental network of common sense, because he continually encounters the 'in your face' law of government *before* he can come into contact with the silent but inescapable law of natural cause-and-effect. He may mentally conclude that there is no such thing as natural law and may feel that all laws are artificial restrictions put in place by 'the establishment' to limit his movements.

I have suggested that an image of God forms whenever a general Teacher theory applies to personal identity. This means that both natural law and government law will lead eventually to the formation of a mental concept of God which will mentally reinforce natural law and/or government edict.

We saw this mental progression from natural law to concept of God at the end of the previous chapter when introducing the theory of evolution. People used to think that natural events demonstrated the 'ordinance of God', but objective science has replaced the concept of a 'God of Nature' with the theory of evolution, which explains personal existence through the use of a general theory that does not require the concept of some divine agent. Thus, the blasphemous apostate is no longer scared of being 'struck by lightning from heaven' for turning his back on God because the 'fear of God' has been replaced by the laws of nature.

However, we saw in the last chapter that the theory of evolution itself will inexorably acquire the traits of a divine being and end up being treated implicitly as a concept of God. Thus, it appears that if one attempts to think of nature without referring to God, then nature will eventually be treated as Nature and divine attributes will be ascribed to Nature. And if the concept of Nature turns into a mental network, then this mental network will give power to conscience. Think, for instance, of the environmental activist who preaches the message that polluting Nature is akin to committing a great crime against deity and that refusing to worship and serve Nature is a form of blasphemous apostasy. He may not use those exact words, but they do describe the meaning that is being conveyed.

The point I am trying to make is that any set of rules that govern human thought or activity which acquires sufficient Teacher generality will eventually turn into a concept of God and that concept of God will give mental power to the set of rules. Whether an actual God exists that is the source of these rules does not matter; what matters is that the mind will mentally view these rules as being enforced by a concept of God. Whether a person believes in God or claims that God does not exist is also of secondary importance. The very fact that rules of conscience are being backed up by a Teacher mental network is sufficient to give these rules divine force.

Speaking for God

We have looked at the way in which *natural* law can lead to an implicit—or explicit—concept of God. I suggest that government edict also has a natural tendency to form an image of God. In general terms, I suggest that the mental image of a Teacher-based God of conscience will emerge whenever rules that govern human behavior are stated as general laws and these laws become sufficiently universal. The government system which created these rules will then acquire religious overtones and will eventually insist that it has the right to define peoples' concept of God.

When one thinks of a God of conscience, the image that comes to mind may be that of some classic movie scene of Moses receiving the two tablets of the law from the hand of God at the top of Mount Sinai while angry clouds stab out with lightning and reverberate with thunder. But I suggest that this actually describes a rule of conscience that is being backed up by a potent *Mercy* mental network, for the God being portrayed in such a scene is not a universal Teacher-based being but rather a very powerful Mercy-based finite creature. Instead, I suggest that it is the *generality* of a rule of conscience that will lead to the formation of a Teacher mental network and result in a concept of a God of conscience.

North Korea provides a particularly striking modern example of universal government edict turning into a concept of God. The worship and obedience that North Korean citizens are expected to give to Kim Jung Il and his father Kim Il Sung goes significantly beyond anything demanded of the typical religious adherent. As far as the North Korean citizen is concerned, these two demi-gods are universal. Every person wears a pin of Kim Il Sung on his lapel, portraits of Kim Il Sung and Kim Jung Il hang in an honored location in every North Korean home, and the country contains at least 500 statues of Kim Il Sung together with over 20,000 plaster busts. In addition, it has been estimated that 40% of the school curriculum is devoted to the adoration of the two Kims.

Similar less blatant examples can be found throughout history. For instance, a transition from establishing secular law to defining an image of God occurred with Emperor

Constantine and the First Council of Nicea. The early Christian church was experiencing a religious controversy over the concept of the deity of Jesus, and so Constantine convened a council of bishops to clarify the issue, resulting in the Nicene Creed. Constantine then enforced this creed by exiling those who refused to submit.

A similar crossover occurred with the Peace of Augsburg in 1555, in which the prince of each German state chose whether his state would be Catholic or Protestant. In more general terms, the *divine right of kings* asserted that the king had absolute authority in both secular and religious issues and that to oppose the king was to oppose God. Similarly, in China, it was believed that a successful emperor was supported by the *mandate of heaven.* If an emperor was successful, then he became accepted as the official voice of God.

Moving ahead to more modern times, it was common for national governments to tell their citizens that it was their duty to God to serve their country and to fight on behalf of their leaders. In the United States today, the concept of God-and-country is still very strong. Finally, in the religion of Islam, secular law is essentially synonymous with religious doctrine.

The point is that when a person or group sets up a system of laws that govern human behavior, then it is natural for that individual or organization to claim to be the voice of God. And when a *new* group or individual achieves prominence, then it will be regarded by the average person as the new *legitimate* voice of God. For instance, as long as the Catholic Church was the main source of societal order, it was accepted by Western civilization as the messenger of God. But as Western states grew in order and structure, princes and governments began to claim the right to speak for God.

Going further, when the leadership of some authority leads to chaos, destruction, and disorder, then the regime will no longer be regarded as the voice of God. This concept is stated explicitly by the mandate of heaven, for when Chinese citizens suffered poverty or natural disaster struck, then this was regarded as a sign that the current emperor had lost the mandate of heaven. Likewise, the great human suffering and physical destruction wrought by the two World Wars caused Europeans to stop accepting their monarchs as the voice of God. But because the United States escaped this destruction, the concept of God-and-country remains intact.

God, Natural Law, and Miracles

Now that we know what it *really* means to associate an image of God with Teacher generality, let us analyze what is *actually* happening within the mind when a person uses the Teacher overgeneralization of first stage learning to form a concept of God.

In the previous chapter, we saw that a conflict will naturally arise between objective science and an image of God that is rooted in Teacher overgeneralization. Objective science develops general Teacher theories that describe the laws of nature. However, these general theories will not form an image of God because they are objective and do not apply to personal identity. But because they are based in rational thought, they will oppose existing images of God that are rooted in Teacher overgeneralization. In response, a religious attitude that is based in Teacher overgeneralization will use overgeneralization to try to 'prove' that God exists, which means looking for miraculous events which science cannot explain, because Teacher overgeneralization uses the method of 'proof by example' in which specific Mercy experiences are used to jump directly to general Teacher theories. For instance, suppose that a person is dying of cancer and is 'miraculously cured' because of praying to God. This *specific* personal example will be seen as 'proof' that the *universal* being of God exists.

It is natural for overgeneralized religion to see objective science as 'the enemy'. After all, objective science is attempting to replace a belief in God with a godless belief in natural law. However, by viewing science as the enemy of religious faith, religion may win the occasional battle but it will ultimately lose the war. That is because an image of God emerges when Teacher generality touches personal identity. And the rational thinking of science builds *true* Teacher generality, whereas Teacher overgeneralization only creates the emotional *impression* of Teacher generality. Therefore, whenever religion uses miracles to 'prove' that God exists, it is undermining the mental foundation that is required to build a mental image of God.

Let me say this again more clearly. When a religious believer asks God to violate the laws of nature in order to satisfy some personal need, then he is *indirectly* destroying his concept of God, because a violation of the laws of nature attacks Teacher thought, and an image of God is created by Teacher thought. Going further, I suggest that when a religious believer asks God for a personal exception to some moral law of conscience, then he is *directly* destroying his concept of God, because he is asking Teacher thought to violate a general Teacher theory that explains personal identity.

I suggest that this principle applies even if God exists, because a universal being who acted in an arbitrary manner would destroy the ability of the human mind to form the mental concept of a universal being. This does not mean that all divine intervention would be mentally destructive. If a real God were to cause physical events to 'work together' in a way that was statistically improbable but not physically impossible, then this *coincidence* would teach the concept of Teacher universality without violating the Teacher mental network of natural law. Or, if a real God were to influence people *psychologically* to respond in a certain manner, then this would teach the concept that personal identity was being guided by some intelligent being without encroaching upon the domain of natural law. Finally, if 'divine intervention' *restored* the ability of a person to live under natural law, then the long-term submission to natural law would make up for the short-term violation of natural law. For instance, if a person who was 'healed of cancer' was able to live for several years longer, then he would eventually associate his 'miracle' with the ability to continue living under natural law and not with the violation of natural law.

Suppose that a person did live in an environment in which natural law was continuously being violated. What would be the mental result? We answered this question in a previous chapter by referring to the accounts of those who claim to have experienced alien abductions. Whether these incidents actually occur or not, when an individual *believes* that he has been abducted by beings who are not subject to natural law, then the emotional response that he describes is invariably one of raw, gut-wrenching terror.

Notice that we have now discovered *two* ways in which the physical environment provides core content for the mind: On the *Mercy* side, being trapped within the emoting object of a physical body forces a mental network that represents the physical body to develop within Mercy thought; on the *Teacher* side, living within a natural world with its universal, unbreakable rules forces a mental network that represents natural law to form within Teacher thought. We refer to this Teacher network as *common sense* and, as we shall see later, it acts as the starting point for scientific thought.

As we all know, miraculous violations of natural law happen either never or almost never—depending upon whom one asks. This means that the mental network of common sense in Teacher thought can *always* explain events and is *never* faced with mental fragmentation. However, if a person were to live within an environment of miracles, or experienced situations that caused him to *doubt* the universality of natural law, then his Teacher mental network of common sense would become threatened. The ultimate result would be mental annihilation for Teacher thought, for just as a scientist cannot imagine working without a paradigm, so it is inconceivable for a human to imagine existing apart from natural law. Exhorter thought may find it exciting to *imagine* living outside of natural law, but if imagination ever turned into reality, then the hyper-pain felt by Teacher thought would be unbearable.

Now suppose that a person actually experienced the type of 'alien abduction' that is typically described. First, his *Teacher* mental network of common sense would be threatened by the violations to natural law. Second, his *Mercy* mental network of personal identity would be questioned by his encounter with non-corporeal beings. Obviously, such a double attack on core mental networks would lead to major hyper-pain.

This also explains why many UFO researchers attempt to analyze UFO encounters in terms of physical aliens from other planets visiting earth. A physical, natural explanation is mentally less threatening than a non-physical, supernatural one. In a similar vein, setting up a SETI program to scan the physical heavens for radio signals that indicate alien intelligence is regarded as scientifically acceptable, while proposing the existence of supernatural beings who inhabit a non-physical realm is not.

Thus, it appears that there actually is a *cognitive* limit to the occurrence of supernatural events and the existence of life after death. Even if both of these do exist, the Teacher mental network of common sense prevents a person from embracing miracles, while the Mercy mental network of physical identity drives an individual to deny the possibility of non-corporeal existence. This does not prove that neither the supernatural nor life after death exist. But it does mean that the natural world and physical body cause the human mind to develop fundamental mental networks which will use the threat of hyper-pain to force a person to insist that neither the supernatural nor non-physical life exists—regardless of whether this is the case or not.

If we combine this statement with the comment made in an earlier chapter, we conclude that the mind naturally has a schizophrenic attitude towards life after death: Because the Mercy mental network that represents personal identity acquires its initial content from the physical body, we find the idea of non-corporeal personal existence emotionally threatening, while the Teacher mental network of common sense finds it emotionally threatening to question the natural cycle of physical birth and physical death. However, the *fact* that personal identity is mentally represented by a mental network causes us to assume that it is natural for personal life to continue existing after physical death.

If one wishes to *investigate* the matter of life after death without triggering hyper-pain in either the Teacher mental network of common sense or the Mercy mental network of physical identity, then I suggest that one must extend these two core mental networks so that they are no longer limited to physical reality.

It appears that the theory of mental symmetry is capable of doing this: First, mental symmetry provides a universal Teacher theory of human existence that is based upon *mental* structure, which we will be using in this book to explain both scientific and religious thought, as well as provide a rational explanation for supernatural existence. Second, mental symmetry describes personal identity in terms of *cognitive style* and cognitive modules, a definition that goes beyond the physical human body.

Of course, none of this proves that God, the supernatural, or life after death actually exist. But it does appear that the theory of mental symmetry makes it mentally possible to *conceive* of religion and non-physical reality while remaining sane, staying in touch with reality, and holding on to scientific thinking. Putting this another way, nothing may exist on the other side of the door of physical reality. But in order to open the door and see if something *does* exist on the other side, one must first be mentally *capable* of opening the door. Until then, both Teacher and Mercy hyper-emotion will demand that one does everything in one's power to keep that door firmly shut.

However, simply *understanding* the theory of mental symmetry is not enough. Instead, core mental networks have to be *rebuilt* upon a cognitive foundation. And when one is dealing with rebuilding mental networks, then, by definition, one has entered the domain of religion, which is why the central theme of this book is a cognitive analysis of religion, focusing specifically upon the process of personal rebirth and cognitive development.

Believing in God

If one examines the two core mental networks of Teacher common sense and Mercy personal identity, one comes to the conclusion that it is mentally *natural* for a person to believe in the existence of a *real* God. Being trapped in a physical body leads to the development of a Mercy network of personal identity, while living within a physical world develops a Teacher based mental network of common sense. The combination of these two mental networks *defines* a mental image of God, while the external, *physical* source of these mental networks will lead to the belief that God exists externally within the *physical* universe.

Justin Barrett comes to a similar conclusion in his book *Why Would Anyone Believe in God.* He says that "Believing in God is a natural, almost inevitable consequence of the types of mind we have living in the sort of world we inhabit, similar to why it is that people almost universally believe in minds of humans and many animals. We have no scientific or even directly observable evidence for Gods or minds, yet belief in both is extremely common and tenaciously held. Why? Because both arise from natural workings of the human mind." In terms of mental symmetry, a belief that other people have minds and a belief in God are both the result of mental structure combined with mental networks.

If this is the case, then why doesn't *everyone* believe in God? The answer is simple. An image of God does not get along with childish personal identity. These two are like relatives who are so dissimilar that when they meet at Christmas time, they get into a big argument, storm out of the house, and spend the rest of the year pretending that they are not related. On the one hand, an image of God is based in Teacher thought, and Teacher thought wants rules to apply *everywhere*—without exception. On the other hand, childish personal identity is continually violating the rules in order to *identify* with pleasant experiences or *deny* unpleasant ones. Thus, one, by its very nature, behaves in a manner that threatens the integrity of the other. And because we are dealing with interacting mental networks, this mutual incompatibility will lead to feelings of hyper-pain. Consistent with this, in thirty years of observing marriages, we have *never* seen a Teacher person marry a Mercy person, and when these two cognitive styles are found within the same family, then the natural reaction is for them to disagree vehemently and spend much of their time acting as if they are not related. Immanuel Kant described this incompatibility as the struggle between radical evil and the categorical imperative, and we will examine this concept in more detail in a later chapter.

What does one do when one has two relatives who cannot get along with each other? One option is to visit them one at a time while making sure that they never get together. Similarly, it is natural for humans to attempt to use either Teacher thought or Mercy thought, but avoid using both at the same time. Thus, areas such as science, organization, and bureaucracy focus upon Teacher structure and general laws while suppressing Mercy feelings of individuality. In contrast, when dealing with subjective areas such as personal life, entertainment, or friendship, Mercy emotions of individuality are emphasized while downplaying organization and structure.

Summary

We began this chapter by looking at the concept of an 'act of God' and we concluded that it is our minds which connect massive events with the hand of deity. Thus, when people talk about the power of God, their comments are being driven by an image of God which is exerting *cognitive* power.

This cognitive divine power emerges when a general theory explains the subjective and this general theory turns into a mental network within Teacher thought. A concept of universal order which has *not* formed into a mental network has no real cognitive power; it can be accepted or rejected at will.

If the mind contains a *general* theory of the subjective—or image of God—that has formed into a Teacher mental network, then this mental network will have three characteristics: First, because it is a general theory, it will be triggered often. The more general it is, the more frequently it will come to mind. Second, a general theory that explains personal identity will be hard to ignore, because it explains experiences which are, by definition, difficult to ignore. Third, a general theory of the subjective tends to be unique. If such a theory falls apart, there are few, if any, alternatives to replace it.

Like any general theory that has formed a mental network, a general theory of the subjective will want to expand in generality—which it typically does by gaining more subjects. This provides the cognitive motivation for *missionary activity*. A general theory of the subjective will also attempt to explain all subjective events, especially if they are too general to be caused by a specific human agent, which explains why the mind interprets super-human events as the 'hand of God'. But when super-human events are destructive, then this will lead to the posing of the question of 'why God allows suffering in the world'. Even when an event was obviously caused by another agent, the mind may still feel that God *motivated* that other agent to act.

If a person attempts to exist apart from his mental image of God, then the Teacher mental network behind his image of God will eventually respond with the hyper-pain of fragmentation, and this mental anguish will be felt wherever the image of God mentally rules, leading to the concept that human existence apart from God is hell. Today, the average Western individual questions the existence of hell because objective science has limited his concept of God and secular technology makes it possible for him to live a secular life without thinking about God.

An image of God that is based in pure overgeneralization is difficult to disprove. Therefore, it does not lead naturally to the concept of hell. But because such a concept of God has no connection with facts, it is also incapable of influencing human existence in any substantive way, leading to the concept of karma, which says that each individual must cope through endless lifetimes with his own personal baggage.

Concrete thought combines Server mode with Mercy mode; Server mode performs actions in order to reach some emotional goal within Mercy thought. The mental urge to reach a goal or avoid a problem is provided by Exhorter mode. In order to improve some skill, one must both practice actions in order to build Server confidence *and* observe the results of these actions in order to program Mercy thought.

Mercy experiences and Server actions are connected by the *intermediate* modules of Perceiver mode and Contributor mode. Perceiver mode builds a mental map that indicates how Mercy experiences are connected. Building this mental map requires Perceiver confidence, because one is dealing with *emotional* experiences. This Perceiver confidence does not eliminate Mercy emotions but rather makes it mentally possible for a person to handle both facts and emotions, resulting in a mental map of *value.*

Contributor mode chooses how Server actions will be connected with Perceiver facts, a major aspect of *free will* and the mental basis for cause-and-effect. In addition, Contributor mode is the part of the mind that handles economic exchange and most successful entrepreneurs are Contributor *persons.*

Objective science ignores personal Mercy emotions and observes the external world in order to build general theories in Teacher thought. Similarly, economics also ignores the personal feelings that are responsible for creating value and focuses instead upon improving the external expressions of value. Thus, both modern science and modern business are *objective.* Driven by the cognitive abilities and limitations of the Contributor person, an economic marketplace will naturally optimize its economic activity to the act of buying and selling.

Cause-and-effect uses Perceiver thought to connect Mercy experiences that are separated by *time.* When experiences are separated by time, then a Server action or sequence leads from cause to effect. Because cause-and-effect involves a combination of Perceiver facts and Server actions, it is closely related to Contributor thought. When subjective emotions are added to cause-and-effect, the result is *conscience.*

Adding Server actions to Perceiver facts also gives a Mercy mental network the ability to *function.* When a Mercy network is triggered by some Mercy experience, it will attempt to function by applying a Server action to the situation. This provides the mental mechanism for conscience, for a rule of conscience is given strength by the Mercy mental network which represents the *agent* who performs the function of noticing the transgression and carrying out the punishment. A feeling of *guilt* emerges when an experience that triggers a rule of conscience becomes part of personal identity.

When Perceiver thought is functioning, then conscience will cause rules to be obeyed, guilt will cause infractions to be confessed when they are committed, and punishment will focus upon restoring personal and societal integrity. In contrast, when emotions overpower Perceiver confidence, then conscience will fail to prevent infractions, guilt will be denied, and justice will focus upon quarantining the criminal.

Economic exchange uses the same mental circuit as conscience but focuses upon reward instead of punishment. Just as guilt is the mental certainty that crime will be punished, so economic confidence is the mental certainty that economic activity will be rewarded. Money is simply an official way of stating that economic activity will be rewarded. Like any rule of conscience, money gains mental power by being backed up by a mental network that represents some valuable object or important person.

When rules of conscience are formed into a general system of laws, then this will produce a theory of order-within-complexity within Teacher thought. If this Teacher theory forms a mental network, then this mental network can provide the basis for conscience or economic activity. *Fiat* money is not backed up by any object within

Mercy thought, but instead is based upon the Teacher order-within-complexity of the modern state. Similarly, the laws of nature are not mentally backed up by any person within Mercy thought, but instead are based upon the Teacher order-within-complexity of natural law.

Natural law describes physical cause-and-effect, but it is the Teacher mental network of common sense which causes these physical laws to be mentally respected. Conversely, government laws are spread mentally, while being backed up physically by the physical might of the state. An image of God exerts only mental power, but this mental might is backed up by cognitive principles of cause-and-effect.

A God of overgeneralization attacks Perceiver thought and prefers worship to action. In contrast, when laws of conscience are used to build a concept of God, then this creates an image of God that is compatible with Perceiver thought and which requires Server actions.

Whenever rules of behavior are systematized and formed into a general structure, then this will eventually form a concept of God, and when one examines history, there is a natural tendency for institutions that define general systems of rules to become associated with the voice of God. Going the other way, whenever an existing voice of God becomes sufficiently discredited, then the natural tendency is to reject it and search for a new voice of God that is more 'user friendly'.

We saw in an earlier chapter that living within a physical body forces a mental network to form in Mercy thought which forms the core of personal identity. Similarly, living in a world of natural order forces a mental network to form in Teacher thought which forms the core of general understanding. The combination of these two mental networks leads naturally to a mental concept of God.

Because natural law forms the core Teacher mental network and because an image of God is based in Teacher thought, associating God with miracles actually ends up destroying the mental foundation for an image of God. Thus, if divine intervention is to preserve the concept of God, it must be limited to situations which bend but do not violate natural law.

The alternative is to find a more general way of defining universal law within Teacher thought and personal identity within Mercy thought. It appears that mental symmetry satisfies these requirements, because it defines personal identity in terms of cognitive style and recognizes that human thought and activity are ultimately guided by universal, inescapable laws of cognition.

✵ 8. Education

I taught high school geometry for several years at an International School in Korea. Traditionally, proving theorems forms a major aspect of this class, and I used an older textbook that assigned many proofs as homework. I have looked at some of the newer geometry textbooks, and they place much less of an emphasis upon proofs. I think that this is a shame, because theorem proving helps to develop abstract thought in the mind of the student.

When we examined personal identity, we saw that it naturally fragments into two different aspects. When personal identity deals with the physical body, then physical survival forces Perceiver thought to gain the confidence that is needed to handle emotional experiences. However, when working with non-physical aspects of personal identity, then Perceiver mode is usually overwhelmed by Mercy emotions and the mind is free to practice identification and denial. Similarly, because natural law is inescapable and universal, Teacher thought will develop a core mental network of general understanding based in common sense. However, the very nature of words makes it possible for Teacher thought to escape common sense and come up with overgeneralized theories that are only loosely based in reality.

It is these two mental splits which make education possible, for education manipulates the aspect of personal identity that is not connected with the physical body and it uses words to develop Teacher thought. This chapter will examine several aspects of education. We will then extend this discussion from education to religion by adding the personal Mercy component together with the concept of mental networks.

Motivating Education

The first question in education is that of *motivation*. The average high school freshman does *not* want to learn geometry, and he definitely does not want to be doing proofs when he could be outside enjoying the sunshine or sitting in front of a computer pretending to kill dragons. Therefore, in order to motivate the student, one has to appeal to *existing* mental networks within Mercy thought. One very powerful Mercy mental network which exists within the mind of almost every *Korean* student is known as 'The Korean Mother'—and those who have taught Korean students will confirm that I am not exaggerating. We saw in an earlier chapter that experiences with mother and father form major mental networks within the mind of the child. And we just learned in the previous chapter that Mercy mental networks can give power to conscience. Therefore, for the typical Korean student, motivation generally boils down to 'mother wants me to be here' and 'mother will make me feel bad if I do not get good marks'.

Marks also provide a strong motivation, because they place a value upon the work of the student. The process of assigning marks illustrates the interaction between Mercy emotions and Perceiver facts. A mark represents an emotion: The student feels good when he receives a high mark and he feels bad when he gets a low grade. The goal of the teacher is to try to assign marks in a way that is logical, consistent, and accurate. Mentally speaking, the teacher is attempting to apply Perceiver thought in the midst of emotional pressure. And Perceiver confidence is required because marks *will* be challenged by emotional pressure from the student: "Why did you mark this question wrong? I don't deserve this mark. You made a mistake." In moral terms, what motivates the student is *conscience*. The student is being given emotional feedback based upon his performance. And these rules of cause-and-effect have the emotional backing of mental networks within Mercy thought that represent parents, teachers, and other authority figures.

As with modern science and business, Western education generally insists that it is only evaluating the *work* of the student and not attempting to label the student *himself* good or bad. And in recent years the tendency has been to make the content simpler, the marking more lenient, or avoid giving any marks at all, motivated by a desire to make sure that the student has a 'good self-image'.

And that introduces us to the matter of mental networks. When an educator insists that a student must have a good self-image, he is saying that the mental networks which define personal identity within the mind of the student should not be faced with painful emotions. But, we know that the mind has *two* ways of generating painful emotions: Bad experiences produce emotional pain, whereas disintegrating mental networks produce emotional hyper-pain.

Suppose that the student comes from a broken home and lives on a crime-ridden street. These unpleasant experiences will form mental networks within Mercy thought, and these mental networks will be part of personal identity. For such a student, it is *difficult* to have a good self-image, for he is caught between pain and hyper-pain. Telling such a student that he *should* change will threaten the mental integrity of the mental networks that define his personal identity, whereas telling him that he does not *need* to change will leave him mentally locked within the painful experiences of his surroundings.

In general terms, whenever Mercy emotions are used to determine Perceiver facts, then I suggest that a discrepancy between emotion and hyper-emotion will emerge. Suppose that a person *identifies* with some desirable experience, such as a rock star or a sports idol. This will produce a mental network within Mercy thought that represents the hero. The result will be a combination of pleasure and hyper-pain. The pleasure comes from the pleasant experiences that are associated with the hero, while the hyper-pain results from the fact that the experiences of the hero do *not* match up with the experiences of personal identity. In addition, identification also removes the motivation for learning. For if the teacher were to allow the student to identify with his desired mark by giving him an automatic grade of A+, then the student would have no reason to learn.

Denial, in contrast, combines pain with an absence of hyper-pain. On the one hand, the reason that a set of experiences is being denied is because they are continually coming to mind and inflicting personal identity with emotional pain. On the other hand, because these experiences are being denied and not taken apart and analyzed, the hyper-pain of mental fragmentation is being avoided. Denial also aborts education, because it removes the need to learn from failure. Denial could be compared to a teacher forgetting about the subject matter and not recording the mark when the student fails a test. When this happens, the student remains ignorant in that area. That is why a teacher is expected to re-teach the topic and re-test the students when they do not grasp the material.

It is also possible for *teaching* to fall into the trap of either denial or identification. The residential schools in Canada provide an example of *denial*. From 1840 until about 1960, Native children in Canada were forced to leave their homes and attend boarding schools in which the teaching was substandard, the work was hard, they were forbidden from speaking their native languages, they were often abused, and a significant percentage suffered and died from tuberculosis. The overall goal was to 'kill the Indian in the child'. Denial treats the student as completely bad and does its best to suppress existing Mercy mental networks and replace them with new mental networks.

On the other end of the spectrum is the approach of *identification*, which tends to describe the current attitude of North American schools. Here, existing Mercy mental networks are treated as 'lifestyles' that need to be affirmed and supported. But can *every* lifestyle be celebrated as totally valid? Is the inner city experience of violence, poverty, and abuse, for instance, really a culture worth praising?

In both cases, I suggest that we are dealing with the same fundamental problem of a lack of Perceiver confidence. The bottom line is that teaching is not straightforward. Instead, it requires a great deal of intuitive psychology on the part of the instructor, in which the various mental networks that make up the personal identity of the child are teased apart and analyzed. Some of these mental networks are healthy, some are developmentally appropriate, and some are destructive and cannot be allowed to express themselves. Education is a delicate balancing act of knowing which mental networks to approve, which ones to tackle, which ones to postpone for later, and which ones to suppress. I can say from personal experience that it is this continual sorting of childish mental networks which makes the job of teaching emotionally draining.

Education realizes this dilemma when dealing with *objective* topics, for it goes to great lengths to establish a *curriculum* determining exactly which topics will be covered in what order, and what level of competence will be accepted as normal for each level of student. Teachers also spend a significant amount of time learning the skill of *classroom management*.

While *recognizing* the existence of childish mental networks and *adjusting* the method of teaching to compensate for these mental networks is a major cognitive step over the educational denial that was often practiced in the past, one is still left with the conclusion that the mind of the child contains mental networks that need to be torn apart and *reassembled.* And that goes beyond intuitive psychology to the realm of intuitive *religion*, for we have defined religion as dealing with mental integration and fragmentation.

We will finish this section on motivation by looking at the situation of the inner city school. Suppose that a teacher at an inner city school allows his students to bring their culture into the classroom. Obviously, no learning will occur. Education assumes that there is a student and a teacher and that the student will learn from the teacher. On the other hand, suppose that the teacher ignores the personal background of his students and learns nothing about their personal lives. The students will not be motivated to learn, because none of their existing mental networks are being activated: "Why should we learn from the teacher. He doesn't know anything about us or care anything about us." Instead, it appears that the successful teachers are the ones who 'care enough to make a difference'. These teachers *accept* the mental networks which exist within the minds of their students, but they also *change* these mental networks.

Going further, one often hears inner city school teachers confessing that they are only capable of helping their students in limited ways. They may be able to help their students with some aspects of personal identity but they cannot deal with the problems that these children face at home. I suggest that this is what happens when education is limited to objective matters. If one wants to transform the personal lives of students, then one must deal with core mental networks and start analyzing them, tearing them apart, and putting them back together, which, by definition, extends education into the realm of religion—which is what we are attempting to do in this book. When adding religion to education, then I suggest that the *same* principles of curriculum and classroom management apply, together with the *same* mental traps of denial and identification. But dealing with core issues obviously requires a higher level of mental confidence.

For instance, most of the residential schools in Canada were run by churches, and these churches tended to approach their religion with the same attitude of denial that they applied to their students. We have seen that Eastern mysticism falls into the mental trap of identification. For a rule-based religion, I suggest that the cognitive trap tends to be denial, and we shall see later the cognitive reason for this.

The Purpose of Education

Let us move now from the motivation of education to the *purpose* of education. We have seen that education must appeal to elements of *concrete* thought in order to function. Because the mind of the child is driven primarily by mental networks within Mercy thought that represent people, the behavior of the student must be guided through the use of conscience, Mercy emotions, and Mercy mental networks. For instance, if a math teacher tries to motivate his geometry class by telling them about the Teacher pleasure that comes from proving theorems, then most of them will respond by dozing off. But if he tells them that they will be tested on the material and that the mark will go on their permanent records, then they will pay attention.

When a student learns a *skill*, then the purpose of education matches the motivation, because both are part of concrete thought. For instance, playing golf is a skill, with Server actions and Mercy goals. Generally speaking, students are much more willing to learn when education is limited to concrete thought. The 'coach' who teaches physical education is usually well-liked by the students. That is because he is expanding *existing* Mercy mental networks by teaching practical skills that involve the physical body.

However, the primary purpose of education is not to develop concrete thought but rather to use the motivation of concrete thought to develop *abstract* thought, for the student goes to school in order to acquire information and to learn how to think. It is this crossover which makes the process of education so difficult, because one is combining elements of two distinct mental circuits. Because the motivation in education is provided by Mercy thought, the student will feel that education involves *doing*: "Teacher, what should I do if I want to get a better mark?" But the purpose of education is to learn and not to do. It is true that Server actions are involved, for the student *goes* to school, he *does* homework, he *works* on projects, and he *studies* for exams. But all of this doing is secondary to the main focus of learning. If the student does everything but does not learn, then education has failed.

The two primary components of abstract thought are Perceiver facts and Teacher theories, and we saw in an earlier chapter how Perceiver facts are used to build general Teacher theories. Education is a *shortcut* to knowledge and understanding. Adults educate children in order to pass on their knowledge and understanding to the next generation. Without education, each person would have to learn for himself.

Education can act as a shortcut to learning because it uses a mental shortcut to teach Perceiver facts as well as a mental shortcut to construct general Teacher theories. I suggest that these same two shortcuts are used when teaching either scientific facts in a secular setting or else religious doctrine within a religious setting. Secular and religious education take different paths *later on*, but they both appear to begin with the same starting point, using the same two mental shortcuts. Using a mental shortcut to develop abstract thought is risky, for it is always possible for education to get stuck at the level of the shortcut and not make the transition into abstract thought, or to conclude that the shortcut *is* the goal and that abstract thought is an unwanted aberration. And if learning is not presented in the right way and packaged in the right form, then education *will* become trapped in the shortcuts and will be unable to progress further.

The Perceiver Shortcut

Let us look now at the two shortcuts used by education, beginning with the shortcut involving the *Perceiver* module. We learned in an earlier chapter that there are two ways to program Perceiver mode with information. One way is for Perceiver mode to look for connections that are *repeated*. Obviously, a method which is based in repetition cannot function instantaneously. In addition, Perceiver thought requires confidence to function, and it takes time to build Perceiver confidence. However, it *is* possible to program Perceiver mode instantly with facts by using Mercy emotions to overwhelm Perceiver confidence.

This *second* method provides the starting point for education. The beginning student does not know facts or know how to evaluate facts. Instead, he believes facts because his *teacher* tells him that they are true. Emotional experiences associated with his instructor have formed a mental network within Mercy thought and that mental network is being used to overwhelm Perceiver thought into 'knowing' what is true, and if the emotional power of that mental network is insufficient, then it will be backed up by the mental network that represents the school principal, and if that doesn't work, then mental networks representing parents and other authorities figures will be called into play, and if that is insufficient, then the process of education will break down.

Every child acquires most of his initial Perceiver facts through this shortcut of emotionally based learning, for a child naturally accepts that 'mommy and daddy know everything and are always right'. This method of blind faith is commonly associated with *religious* learning. However, I suggest that secular education *also* begins with blind faith, and Thomas Kuhn agrees: "Science students accept theories on the authority of teacher and text, not because of evidence. What alternatives have they, or what competence? The applications given in texts are not there as evidence but because learning them is part of learning the paradigm at the base of current practice. If applications were set forth as evidence, then the very failure of texts to suggest alternative interpretations or to discuss problems for which scientists have failed to produce paradigm solutions would convict their authors of extreme bias."

This quote from Kuhn also touches upon one of the requirements which must be met if blind 'belief' is to lead to the development of Perceiver thought. The instant nature of emotionally based knowing makes it possible to impart facts quickly and efficiently. However, this also makes it possible to unlearn information or learn incompatible information just as quickly. The goal of education is not to *leave* Perceiver thought in its mesmerized state, but rather to use this as a shortcut for imparting knowledge. This means that the knowledge which is taught by using the shortcut of emotional 'knowing' must be consistent with knowledge that Perceiver thought would work out on its own. And we know that Perceiver mode looks for connections that are repeated and facts which do not change. Therefore, if education is to be successful, then the facts that it teaches must be clear, consistent, solid, and unchanging.

This means that teaching the *beginning* student with a multiplicity of facts is counterproductive, because Perceiver mode requires solid information. Once the facts have been placed within Perceiver thought, *then* it is time for the teacher to step out of the way, present the student with alternative sources of information, and encourage the student to use Perceiver mode to work out the facts for himself. For instance, when teaching high school geometry, one begins by teaching fundamental axioms which cannot be proven but must be accepted blindly. In addition, I expected my students to memorize a basic set of theorems. Korean students typically do very well at memorization, because Korean education is historically rooted in rote learning and the emotional power of 'the Korean mother' is very strong. However, my goal was not to leave Perceiver mode mesmerized but rather to give Perceiver thought the facts that are needed to do proofs. And students would often be surprised when they realized that they were now supposed to *use* the theorems which they had previously memorized.

Notice precisely what is happening. In order for the shortcut to knowledge to work, Perceiver mode must be turned *off* and facts accepted on the basis of emotional status. But once the facts have been inserted into Perceiver memory, then Perceiver mode must be turned *on* in order to digest the information. Saying this another way, rote learning is a shortcut to knowledge. During the stage of rote learning, the teacher must use his emotional status to instruct his students. But rote learning must be followed by critical thinking, in which the teacher steps out of the way and encourages the student to think for himself.

During the first stage of rote learning, it is possible for an instructor to teach his students *anything*, because Perceiver thought is turned off. If he insists that the moon is made of cheese and that little green men are living on Mars, then his students *will* believe him. But it is only possible to move *beyond* rote learning to critical thinking if the content that was acquired through rote learning is compatible with Perceiver thought—if the facts that were learned really *do* describe connections which are solid and repeatable. If the facts that were acquired through rote learning are *not* true, then these facts will only remain within Perceiver thought as long as Perceiver mode remains mesmerized and does not function, for once Perceiver mode begins to function then it will reject the facts.

At first glance, this might give the impression that all belief that remains blind must be stuck at the level of rote learning because it contains factual error. This is often the case, but there are other possibilities. It could be that the student has learned facts which are correct but which are beyond his ability—or the ability of his society—to analyze logically. Think, for instance, of a building code or an electrical code. The tradesmen applying this code generally do not fully grasp the physics and engineering principles that lie behind these rules, and so the tendency is for them to accept the rules blindly and apply them without critical thinking.

It is also possible that the person who is judging the facts as false is speaking outside of his area of expertise. In cognitive terms, he is using the emotional status that was acquired from learning how to use Perceiver thought in *one* area of expertise to make judgments about *other* topics. For instance, modern science limits its analysis to physical reality and states that religion does *not* fall within the domain of traditional science. Despite this inherent limitation, scientists are prone to making strongly derogatory statements about religious belief. For instance, when I was writing this section in May 2011, Stephen Hawking made the headlines by publicly declaring that heaven does not exist. I suggest that statements such as these are driven by *Teacher* emotion. Science may officially declare that it limits itself to physical reality, but a general Teacher theory does not like to be limited. As Kuhn points out, a scientific paradigm tends to act as if nothing exists—or has ever existed—outside of the current paradigm.

Because these two stages of rote learning and critical thinking are so different, the natural tendency is for a teacher, an educational program, or a religion system to emphasize one to the exclusion of the other. In educational circles, rote learning used to be the norm. As a result, Perceiver mode in the student was filled with information but the students did not know how to use Perceiver thought to evaluate facts. When the student who has acquired Perceiver knowledge through rote learning encounters a new set of experts, the normal tendency is for him to replace his existing facts and beliefs with a new set of facts and beliefs, because Perceiver mode is still stuck in the 'programming mode' of accepting facts blindly from instructors. Thus, students who have been taught through rote learning make good cannon fodder, for the voice of the commanding officer simply replaces the voice of the teacher.

During the latter half of the twentieth century, the educational pendulum swung from rote learning to critical thinking, and the focus was upon teaching students to think for themselves. But the results have been flawed because Perceiver mode requires both content and confidence to operate. The typical student today may know how to use Perceiver thought, but he often lacks the mental content that is required to evaluate information intelligently as well as the mental confidence that is required to deal rationally with emotional topics.

The same principle applies to religious doctrine and religious education. For instance, Islam places a high emphasis upon rote learning, but critical thinking is not encouraged. One can tell that a strong emphasis is being placed upon using emotional status to enforce belief, for in many countries, those who leave the Muslim faith are subject either officially or unofficially to the death penalty. And if winning a Nobel prize can be taken as an objective measure of critical thinking, then one notes that only six Muslims have won a Nobel prize. In contrast, critical thinking does play a major role in the Jewish religion. As David Ben Gurion observed, where there are two Jews, there are three opinions. Consistent with this, if one examines the record, then as of 2006, 165 Jews have won Nobel prizes.

Christianity tends to vacillate between rote learning and critical thinking. On the one hand, it bases its doctrines in the words of a holy book, but on the other hand, Christian doctrine teaches that simply parroting the facts does not qualify as legitimate belief, that belief should be placed in truths which are 'solid' and 'eternal', and that the believer should hold on to his beliefs even when tested by emotional opposition.

I suggest that when the primary goal of a religion is to rule over a *physical* kingdom, then there will be a strong tendency to emphasize rote learning over critical thinking. The reason for this is quite simple. Interacting with physical matter involves *concrete* thought, while the purpose of *education* is to go beyond concrete thought and develop abstract thought. Similarly, an image of God emerges when *abstract* thought is used to develop a general Teacher theory of the subjective. Putting this another way, religion and education use Perceiver truth to influence a person through conscience, reinforced by general Teacher understanding. Government, in contrast, ultimately uses Server force to control people, backed up either by the reward of pleasant Mercy experiences or the punishment of painful Mercy experiences. Thus, if 'the church' wishes to be successful, then it must not act like 'the state'. That is the conclusion which Arnold Toynbee, the British historian, came to in his analysis of the Catholic Church in *A Study of History*.

For example, the primary goal of Islam is to rule physically over existing nations and cultures through the introduction of *Sharia* law. In contrast, Jesus, when he was on trial, stated that 'my kingdom is not of this world'. Historically speaking, when the Christian Church has focused upon gaining physical property and holding on to physical kingdoms, then it has lost its ability to educate. In a similar vein, for most of its existence, the religion of Judaism has existed as a diaspora without a physical homeland, and even during the first decades of the modern Jewish state, the goal was upon turning desert and swampland into a modern society. However, the current attempt of Judaism to hold on to physical land and physical property may be provoking a shift in Jewish mentality.

The Teacher Shortcut

Let us move on now to the *second* shortcut of education. This shortcut is using *words* to program Teacher mode. Remember that Teacher emotion comes from order-within-complexity. It takes a lot of effort to create order-within-complexity using physical items, for one must gather the individual items together and then arrange them to form a structure. Words have the advantage of being insubstantial as well as inherently general, making it far easier to build order-within-complexity. For instance, saying 'cup' is much easier than constructing a cup. And when a person says 'cup', he is using a general term that describes everything from a small demitasse to a large mug. Thus, when Teacher thought works with words, the building blocks themselves already demonstrate order-within-complexity. Achieving that level of generality with real objects would mean gathering dozens of types of cups and arranging them in some fashion.

The problem with words is that they are *ephemeral.* A word is simply a vibration in the air which vanishes as soon as it is spoken. Therefore, if words are to be used to construct Teacher order-within-complexity, then they must be turned into solid form so that they can be arranged, combined, and formed into a general structure. The solution to this problem is *writing.* Writing makes words solid. Writing the word 'cup' may take a little longer than saying the word 'cup', but it is still much quicker than gathering a number of cups and arranging them. And once the word 'cup' has been recorded in written form, then it remains for other people—and even succeeding generations—to read and study.

One of the first steps in any educational program is *literacy*. For instance, if you observe a Grade One class, you will notice that two major subjects are being taught: First, the child is being schooled in paying attention to the teacher, setting up the emotional status that is required to use the Perceiver shortcut. Second, the child is being taught how to read and write, in order to enable the Teacher shortcut. Similarly, many literacy programs, both in the past and in the present, have been set up by religious missionaries as the first step in religious education.

Arithmetic forms the *third* of 'the three Rs' of Reading, 'Riting, and 'Rithmetic traditionally taught in primary school. Arithmetic is strongly related to literacy, because written symbols are being used to represent numbers and numerical operations. Saying this in more general terms, mathematics is a type of language that restricts communication to a limited set of words with very precise definitions. Similarly, formal logic takes normal speech and attempts to give it the rigor of mathematical expression. Computer languages also fall into this category, because they tell a computer what to do using a restricted vocabulary of logical and mathematical statements. We will examine math and logic further in a later chapter, and I analyze the basic elements of math in an appendix, but I introduce them now in order to point out that these are all examples of Teacher words being given stability through the use of writing.

What religious and scientific education have in common is the *book*. A book is a collection of written words, organized in a way that presents a unified message. Saying this another way, a book is an *external* example of Teacher order-within-complexity, constructed out of the Teacher building blocks of words. For scientific education, the goal of the textbook is to convey a general Teacher theory. In the words of Kuhn, "an increasing reliance on textbooks or their equivalent [is] an invariable concomitant of the emergence of a first paradigm in any field of science." Similarly, the primary purpose of the religious holy book is to teach the believer about God. As far as abstract thought is concerned, these two statements are equivalent, for a paradigm is a general Teacher theory and an image of God is based in a general Teacher theory.

The relationship between a book and a general Teacher theory is quite strong. The 'soft sciences' are not held together by integrated Teacher theories, and they do not place such a strong emphasis upon textbooks. Quoting again from Kuhn, "In music, the graphic arts, and literature, the practitioner gains his education by exposure to the works of other artists, principally earlier artists. Textbooks, except compendia of or handbooks to original creations, have only a secondary role. In history, philosophy, and the social sciences, textbook literature has a greater significance. But even in these fields the elementary college course employs parallel readings in original sources." Similarly, Judaism, the first religion based upon a holy book, was also the first religion to preach the doctrine of monotheism. Thus, it appears that if a group wants to teach its followers that everything is held together by a single theoretical system or a single Being of order-within-complexity, then it needs a book to convey this message. This era of the book now appears to be coming to an end with the advent of the computer, multimedia, and the Internet. It is not yet apparent what will emerge to take the place of the book, and school systems which have abandoned the textbook in order to embrace new technology have experienced mixed results.

The three religions of Judaism, Christianity, and Islam are sometimes referred to as the 'religions of the book' because they all base their beliefs upon the words of a holy book. And these three religions also preach as fundamental the doctrine of monotheism. Without their respective holy books, these three religions would not exist. Similarly, Thomas Kuhn says that the textbook plays an equally overwhelming role in the education of the scientist: "in the contemporary natural sciences...the student relies mainly on textbooks until, in his third or fourth year of graduate work, he begins his own research. Many science curricula do not ask even graduate students to read in works not written specially for students...Until the very last stages in the education of a scientist, textbooks are systematically substituted for the creative scientific literature that made them possible."

We have seen that books are constructed using the Teacher shortcut of words. I suggest that books play a major role in education because they embody *both* of the two shortcuts of education. Let us examine this in more detail. First, a book is written by an *expert*. Remember that the Perceiver shortcut begins by using the Mercy status of some person to mesmerize Perceiver mode into accepting information. A school textbook or religious holy book is given official backing and is authored by a Very Important Person. For a holy book, the author is usually one of the founders of the religion or else the religious believer is told that God himself penned the words.

Second, the content of a book is *consistent*. Once a book has been penned, then its content is 'written in stone' and does not change. And if the same book is given to many individuals, then the *same* Perceiver facts will be shared by many people. Remember that the Perceiver shortcut of education mesmerizes Perceiver thought into blindly accepting information. When Perceiver mode evaluates this information later on, it will look for stability and consistency, and it will reject facts that are either inconsistent or unstable. When information is presented in the form of a book, the *presentation* is consistent with Perceiver thought. Of course, the content itself could still make no sense, but at least the method by which this content is being taught is compatible with Perceiver thought.

This means that the Perceiver shortcut of education requires *exclusivity*. In blunt terms, religious education will not function properly if a society contains a multiplicity of conflicting holy books, because this will present the student with an inconsistent message. A similar exclusivity is seen in scientific education. Kuhn notes that textbooks "have to be rewritten in whole or in part whenever the language, problem-structure, or standards of normal science change. In short, they have to be rewritten in the aftermath of each Scientific Revolution, and, once rewritten, they inevitably disguise not only the role but the very existence of the revolutions that produced them."

Third, a book makes it possible to *separate* information from its emotional source. When the student is in the presence of his teacher, the emotional status of his instructor makes it difficult for Perceiver mode to function. But, if the information is contained within a book, then the student can take the book home and study the facts by himself apart from his instructor. The consistency of a book makes its information *compatible* with Perceiver thought. The portability of a book makes it easier for Perceiver mode to begin functioning so that it can *evaluate* the information contained within the book.

The ability of a student to evaluate his textbook was one of the major issues of the Protestant Reformation. Martin Luther translated the Bible into the vernacular of the German people "so that even a ploughboy could read Christ's very words." In response, the Catholic Church declared in the Council of Trent that only the clergy had the right to interpret Scripture. This remained the dominant attitude of the Catholic Church until the Second Vatican Council in the early 1960s when the laity were officially encouraged to read the Bible and permission was given to celebrate the Mass in the vernacular.

If the *content* of a holy book or textbook lacks Perceiver legitimacy, then obviously students cannot be given permission to interpret the book for themselves because they will end up rejecting the material. Plus, there is always the danger that if the instructor steps out of the way, the student will end up rejecting all sources of authority. This did happen during the Protestant Reformation, when many peasants took Luther's admonition to abandon the authority of Rome and to interpret Scripture for themselves as an excuse to reject existing political and economic authority as well.

I suggest that the solution to the problem of rebellion from authority is found in the *fourth* characteristic of a book. A book contains Teacher order-within-complexity, for it takes Teacher words and forms them into an ordered structure of sentences, paragraphs, and chapters. Thus, the very nature of a book is capable of producing positive Teacher emotions.

Enabling Abstract Thought

And that brings us back to the ultimate purpose of education: The goal of education is to enable abstract thought. This means providing information for Perceiver thought, encouraging Perceiver mode to function, providing Teacher mode with a general theory, and encouraging Teacher thought to function.

We have seen that the Perceiver shortcut of education first turns Perceiver mode off in order to impart information and then allows and encourages Perceiver mode to turn back on. Making this mental transition from 'off' to 'on' is *not* straightforward for Perceiver thought. Instead, we saw several chapters earlier that these two conditions are separated by a *threshold of confusion*, during which Perceiver thought is in a confused state of being semi-awake, operating sufficiently to begin doubting the facts taught by the instructor, but not enough to have the confidence to determine which facts are correct and which are not.

But the problem goes deeper than merely encouraging Perceiver mode to turn on. That is because the Perceiver shortcut of education has the emotional backing of strong mental networks within Mercy thought. After all, the student is being motivated to learn by emotional pressure from his teachers, his parents, and other authority figures. All of these mental networks were initially called into play in order to mesmerize Perceiver mode into being taught. But if Perceiver mode is to be able to evaluate the information that it has acquired, then it will have to learn how to function in the presence of these mental networks.

The solution to this problem is to replace *Mercy* mental networks with *Teacher* mental networks. If the material that the student learned fits together to form a Teacher system of order-within-complexity, and if this general theory forms a mental network within

Teacher thought, then this *Teacher* mental network can be used to digest the various Mercy mental networks.

This mental transition is *like* a paradigm shift but subtly different. Remember that a paradigm shift uses a *different* general Teacher theory to explain the *same* set of Perceiver facts. Repeating part of a quote from Kuhn from earlier on, a paradigm shift means "handling the same bundle of data as before, but placing them in a new system of relations with one another by giving them a different framework." In a paradigm shift, one *Teacher* mental network is being replaced by another *Teacher* mental network. When emerging from the Perceiver shortcut of education, a *Mercy* mental network is being replaced by a *Teacher* mental network.

In simple terms, this means that the student initially accepts the Perceiver facts because of the emotional respect he has for his instructor and other authority figures, but he then makes an emotional transition to accepting the Perceiver facts because of the way in which the material itself holds together.

Kuhn states that a scientist will not let go of an existing paradigm unless he is given an alternative: "Once it has achieved the status of paradigm, a scientific theory is declared invalid only if an alternate candidate is available to take its place...The decision to reject one paradigm is always simultaneously the decision to accept another." I suggest that it is possible to generalize this statement to include both Mercy and Teacher thought. Stated this way, a person will not choose to let go of one mental network unless he is provided with another mental network which can take its place. In a paradigm shift, one *Teacher* mental network is being replaced by another *Teacher* mental network. When a student discovers understanding, then a *Mercy* mental network is being replaced by a *Teacher* mental network.

This transition from Mercy mental network to Teacher mental network is also one of the hallmarks of scientific thought. Before this point, research is divided into schools of thought each led by its set of approved experts. After this point, what drives research and holds it together is a *paradigm*. When an area of research fully makes this transition, then it turns into a *hard* science. Using the field of optics as an illustration, Kuhn compares pre-science with science: "The successive transition from one paradigm to another via revolution is the usual developmental pattern of mature science. It is not, however, the pattern characteristic of the period before Newton's work, and that is the contrast that concerns us here. No period between remote antiquity and the end of the seventeenth century exhibited a single generally accepted view about the nature of light. Instead there were a number of competing schools and subschools, most of them espousing one variant or another of Epicurean, Aristotelian, or Platonic theory...Those men were scientists. Yet anyone examining a survey of physical optics before Newton may well conclude that, though the field's practitioners were scientists, the net result of their activity was something less than science."

A similar mental transition occurs within the *mind* of the student. He begins his education by submitting to some 'school of thought' in order to enable the Perceiver shortcut, and he emerges from this shortcut by gaining a paradigm within Teacher thought. The PhD program forces the student to make this transition. In order to receive a PhD, a student must do *original research*, using Perceiver mode to come up with a new set of facts and then using Teacher mode to construct a theory out of these facts which adds in some way to the existing body of knowledge. Because the doctoral student must do research that no one has done before, he is forced in some measure to become emotionally free of his instructors.

The same mental transition also occurs in *religious* education. But because religion views a general Teacher theory in personal terms, this mental transition will be stated in *personal* terms. Like any student, the religious student begins by learning truth from accepted experts teaching from an approved book, and he accepts this religious truth because of the *Mercy* status of religious experts. But if these religious facts fit together to form a system of order-within-complexity within Teacher thought, and if this general Teacher structure turns into a mental network, then this *Teacher* mental network will hold the religious message together. As a result, the religious believer will believe that his holy book is a revelation of God. Even if the words were penned by human authors, the believer will think that these authors were inspired by God to write the words.

The mental logic that is involved in reaching this conclusion is somewhat subtle, so let me try to explain the steps as clearly as possible. First, there is the *content* of the holy book. Remember that an image of God emerges when a general Teacher theory explains personal identity, and a book is a shortcut to teaching a general theory. Therefore, if a book describes a general theory of human behavior, then studying this book will lead to the formation of an image of God. If this general theory turns into a Teacher mental network, then the structure and emotions of that Teacher mental network will hold the holy book together. This book will then be viewed as a holy book in the sense that it is a revelation *about* God.

Second, there is the *source* of the holy book. When the mental Agency Detector encounters a significant incident, it attempts to associate that incident with some mental network within *Mercy* thought. We saw this several chapters back when analyzing what happens when a person hears a noise in the middle of the night. For a book, this means determining who *wrote* the book. But suppose that the content of the holy book is too clever to have been written by any human author from the time period in which it was originally penned. The Agency Detector will then fail to find any *Mercy* mental network that can be regarded as the author of this book. The Agency Detector will then conclude that the book was written by the *Teacher* mental network that the content of the holy book describes. In religious language, the holy book will be mentally viewed as having been written *by* God.

Obviously, there is a big difference between *saying* that a book is written by God and actually *knowing* what this means. The beginning religious student may state that his holy book is 'The Word of God', but he is only saying this because he was taught so by his religious teachers. In contrast, the mind will only come to the conclusion that a holy book is written by God if that holy book actually *does* contain a super-human level of order and structure. That is due to the nature of the mental Agency Detector. If some human mental network within *Mercy* thought can legitimately claim authorship, then the believer will conclude that a clever human was the author. But if the book describes significant Teacher order-within-complexity and if Perceiver thought concludes that no Mercy mental network could have penned this book, then the mind will conclude that a Teacher mental network was the author, or in theological language, that God wrote the book.

This means that a holy book which claims divine authorship must meet an exceptionally high standard of intellectual excellence. But we are dealing with *holy* books, and only a handful of volumes even attempt to claim this status. Notice that we have now come up with a *cognitive* definition for a holy book, which permits one to use rational thought to evaluate the various candidates. And a book that meets *this* definition for holiness is compatible with scientific thought and the third stage of learning and is not merely an expression of first stage overgeneralization.

For instance, Islam states that its holy book is written by God, but if some prominent individual calls into question the divine status of this book, then the tendency is to back up this claim of divine authorship with a *Mercy* mental network: "This book is the Word of God and if you reject that, then some *person* will kill you." This indicates that a cognitive transition from Mercy mental network to Teacher mental network has not occurred, for if a religious adherent really believes that his holy book is written by God, then he will support the contents of this book with the Teacher mental network of a general theory.

Consistent with this, one scholar has concluded that "the final process of collection and codification of the Quran text was guided by one over-arching principle: God's words must not in any way be distorted or sullied by human intervention. For this reason, no serious attempt, apparently, was made to edit the numerous revelations, organize them into thematic units, or present them in chronological order.... This has given rise in the past to a great deal of criticism by European and American scholars of Islam, who find the Quran disorganized, repetitive, and very difficult to read."[20] In the language of mental symmetry, the text contains no obvious order-within-complexity and one is given the strong impression that the religious student is not supposed to analyze the book. When one reads the Quran, one notices immediately that the chapters are ordered on the basis of length, with the longest at the beginning and the shortest at the end, an arrangement which is unrelated to the content. In contrast, the Jewish and Christian Scriptures are ordered thematically and/or historically. Obviously, one is dealing here with merely the surface elements of order-within-complexity, but the beginning student will notice these features and they will affect his thinking.

---

[20] *Approaches to the Asian Classics,* Irene Blomm, William Theodore De Bary, Columbia University Press,1990, p. 65

Notice that this is a twist upon the argument of *intelligent design*, for I am not trying to prove that God wrote the Bible or that God created the universe. Instead, I am attempting to show how such a belief can be made *compatible* with rational thought. In other words, I am not addressing the concept of intelligent design to the skeptic in order to convince him that God exists. Instead, I am conveying this concept to the religious adherent in order to give him the ability to approach abstract thought in a rational manner. And I am also informing the skeptic that if he wants religion to function rationally, then he must *allow* the religious adherent to believe in intelligent design. When the scientist belittles the concept of intelligent design, then he is driving the religious believer to remain at the Mercy-driven level of blind faith, turning religion into the enemy of rational thought.

Scientific Education

I have suggested that both religious and scientific education *start* with blind faith in a book, backed up by emotional respect for instructors. However, when it comes to the next step of *emerging* from the Perceiver shortcut and making the cognitive *transition* from Mercy status to Teacher structure, then science and religion take a different approach. In both cases, though, the ultimate goal is the same, which is to develop abstract thought in the mind of the student.

Objective science gains its Perceiver facts from the *external* world. The scientist observes his environment and looks for patterns that are repeated. The scientist gets very annoyed if you tell him a fact and do not back it up with data from physical experiments. He wants to know what you saw, what you observed, and what you measured. In cognitive terms, the scientist is building on to the Teacher mental network of common sense.[21] Remember that the external environment causes two major mental networks to form within the human mind: First, being trapped within a physical body causes a mental network of personal identity to form within Mercy mode. This mental network forms the basis for normal life and concrete thought. Second, living within a natural world of inescapable order causes a mental network of common sense to form within Teacher mode. This mental network forms the basis for abstract thought as well as the starting point for science.

Scientific education emerges from the Perceiver shortcut of blind 'belief' by appealing to this existing Teacher mental network of *common sense*. For instance, suppose that the middle school student studies about the water cycle. He will read in his science textbook that rain falls from clouds, gathers in rivers, and flows into the ocean. There, energy from the sun causes water to evaporate, leading to the formation of clouds, repeating the cycle. Initially, he will believe this because his instructor says that it is true. But when he observes the real world, he will see clouds forming, he will observe water flowing in a

---

[21] Scientific thought begins with common sense, but with quantum mechanics and relativity, it has now progressed to the point where it violates common sense. For instance, it does not make sense for time to slow down for an object that is moving very fast.

river, and he can visit the mouth of a river where it empties into the ocean. Because the student repeatedly observes these facts with his physical senses, Perceiver thought will eventually notice the repetition and begin to think for itself. And because the water cycle occurs throughout the world and manifests itself in varied ways, this external order-within-complexity will encourage Teacher thought to function.

In addition, by maintaining an attitude of objectivity, modern science avoids getting emotionally entangled with the Mercy mental networks of personal identity. Therefore, it does not have to *escape* these mental networks in order to build upon the Teacher mental network of common sense. However, we have seen that the *method* of education *is* propelled by Mercy emotional networks, and that provides scientific education with a dilemma.

We will introduce this dilemma with a quote from Kuhn, in which he describes the typical attitude taken by science. He refers to the "textbooks of science together with both the popularizations and the philosophical works modeled on them...All three record the stable *outcome* of past revolutions and thus display the bases of the current normal-scientific tradition. To fulfill their function they need not provide authentic information about the way in which those bases were first recognized and then embraced by the profession. In the case of textbooks, at least, there are even good reasons why, in these matters, they should be systematically misleading."

Here is the dilemma: Science is held together by the mental network of a general Teacher theory. But scientific education, like all forms of education, begins by appealing to Mercy mental networks. However, science is driven by Teacher emotion to ignore its Mercy-based parentage and to *pretend* that Teacher emotions have always been in charge. But if science *does* manage to pretend that all learning is motivated by Teacher emotions, then it will destroy the process of education, making it more difficult for the next generation to develop scientific thought.

Recent North American educational history illustrates this dilemma. For the school teacher, classroom management and student motivation are key issues, for a teacher has to know which *Mercy* 'hot buttons' to press in order to encourage his students to learn. In contrast, the typical college professor does not have to worry about motivating his students. Instead, he can assume that *Teacher*-based abstract thought is functioning. During the 20th century, educational professors in their ivory castles decided in typical paradigm-driven fashion that *all* education should be driven by Teacher emotions. They pronounced that rote learning was unacceptable, that emotional status should not be used to impose facts upon children, and that teachers should not attempt to control the behavior of their students through the use of emotional pressure. Instead, students were to be educated in a scientific manner guided by Teacher emotions of order and structure.

As a result, the school system fell apart. The *college* system survived, but it was no longer being fed with an input stream of intelligent high school graduates. Fewer students graduated from high school and the average level of the student entering college dropped dramatically. Professors found that they could no longer assume that abstract thought was functioning in their students. Instead, they had to set up remedial classes in order to teach the basics to freshmen. This decline in local students was offset by an influx of *foreign* students, who had graduated from schools that still practiced rote learning and were still using Mercy means, such as the local version of 'the Korean mother', to motivate and mold their students. Thus, the transition from Mercy mental network to Teacher mental network occurred *internationally* as foreign trained high school students from countries with strong Mercy-based cultures traveled to the United States and other Western countries to receive their college educations.

Scientific education uses the Teacher-based mental network of common sense to help the student emerge from the Mercy-based method of education. This method *assumes* the existence of common sense, and if this is lacking, then the method will fail. Common sense may have been common in the past, when children spent much of their time exploring the natural world, but the mental landscape is quite different for the child who grows up in the middle of a city, because he is surrounded by the order-within-complexity of his urban surroundings and has only limited contact with his natural environment. His water does not fall from the sky and flow into the river. Instead, it comes out of a tap and flows into a drain. Similarly, in the past, it got dark when the sun went down, and when one stepped out at night, the sky was filled with stars. However, with today's artificial illumination, some areas of the city actually appear brighter in the evening than they do during the daytime. For example, when I lived in downtown Seoul, the sky was so lit up at night that I never saw more than half a dozen stars in the sky. For a child growing up in such surroundings, it can be difficult to make the transition to scientific thought.

For instance, I recently found a science curriculum guide from the 1950s in a local thrift shop. The lesson plans in this book all assume that the school student is living in a semi-rural setting surrounded by nature, and that he can perform activities such as observing different animal tracks in the snow, or gathering leaves from different trees or shrubs. Very little from this book could be applied within today's typical urban setting.

Religious Education

Analyzing scientific education is fairly simple because one is dealing primarily with either Mercy mental networks *or* Teacher mental networks. The cognitive situation becomes more complicated when looking at religious education. That is because an image of God emerges when a general theory explains personal identity. In cognitive terms, a concept of God involves an *overlap* between the Mercy mental network of personal identity and a Teacher mental network of order-within-complexity, and this overlap introduces a number of additional cognitive mechanisms.

The scientific method of education attempts to minimize the involvement of personal identity and maximize the involvement of common sense. A religious approach to education, in contrast, takes the same cognitive steps and applies them directly to personal identity. Scientific education is mentally anchored by the natural order of the universe. This is an *external* order which is *shared* by everyone. For instance, when one person is observing part of the water cycle, he can point this out to the individual beside him and they will both see the *same* Teacher order. Willard Quine calls these common references to physical events *observation sentences*, and he says that they form the basis for scientific thought. In contrast, Mercy identity is personal and *internal.* When my physical body sends me a message of pain, this sensation is *not* felt by the individual beside me. Instead, as we saw earlier in the book, one person has to use intuitive psychology in order to guess what the other person is currently feeling, using the mental networks within his own mind to model what is happening within the mind of another individual.

Scientific education is driven by a desire to *replace* the Mercy mental networks of personal identity with the Teacher mental network of common sense. In contrast, religious education takes existing Mercy mental networks and *transmogrifies* them into a form that is compatible with Teacher thought. Thus, the religious student is taught that there is a personal God, but that God is *different* than normal humans.

Let us begin by looking at the *purpose* of education. Remember that the goal of education is to develop abstract thought in the student by using the Perceiver shortcut of revealed truth and the Teacher shortcut of words. The student may be motivated by personal Mercy feelings, but the instructor hopes that the student can be taught enough Perceiver facts and given a sufficiently general verbal explanation to turn on abstract thought in his mind so that he will discover the Teacher joy of understanding. It always gives an instructor great satisfaction when a student has an 'aha' moment and the 'light goes on inside'.

When one adds the personal element to this, one concludes that the goal of *religious* education is to know and love God. In the language of mental symmetry this means using Perceiver facts to construct a general theory of the subjective in Teacher thought, and to be motivated by the Teacher emotions produced by such a general theory.

This concept of *knowing* God needs to be explained in more detail, because it forms a key distinction between the God of overgeneralization and the image of God that we are discussing here. Remember that a God of Eastern mysticism is threatened by Perceiver mode. In contrast, we are now looking at an image of God that is constructed by *using* Perceiver thought. That may still sound somewhat vague, so I will attempt to tie this concept down by using basic definitions. Remember that we are dealing here with a method of education that *begins* with personal identity. An image of God is a Teacher theory that *explains* personal identity. Therefore, using Perceiver thought to *build* an understanding about God will begin by using Perceiver thought to *describe* personal identity. Perceiver thought looks for facts that are *stable* and do not change. Thus, using Perceiver thought to describe personal identity means being honest about myself—not using identification to pretend that pleasant experiences belong to me when they do not, and not using denial to pretend that unpleasant experiences do not belong to me when they do. In plain English, for plain English is all that a primary student can comprehend, this means telling the student 'do not lie' and backing this rule up with the appropriate authority figures. Is personal honesty exactly the same as 'do not lie'? Technically, no.

But the vast majority of lies are motivated by a desire to avoid personal honesty, and if a person cannot be honest about non-emotional issues, then he probably will not be honest about personal identity.

So, which authority figures *are* appropriate? As we saw when looking at the *motivation* for education, one has to start with existing mental networks within Mercy thought. Therefore, the teacher will tell the student, "Do not lie because I tell you so, and the principal and your parents will enforce this statement." But while Mercy mental networks provide the starting point for education, the goal is to connect personal honesty with a Teacher mental network of universal order. This means that the teacher ultimately needs to tell the student, "Do not lie because God does not want you to lie and God sees everything that you do."

By now, our discussion is starting to sound rather moralistic, which is precisely what happens when Perceiver facts get added to personal identity. But if religious education is to succeed in developing abstract thought, then the religious teacher will need to be just as insistent about applying Perceiver thought to the Mercy mental network of personal identity as the scientific teacher is about applying Perceiver thought to the Teacher mental network of common sense. The scientist is adamant about using Perceiver facts to describe his external environment and he is stubborn about using only solid Perceiver data from the natural world to build his Teacher understanding. Similarly, the religious educator has to be equally adamant about using Perceiver facts to describe internal personal identity and he must be equally stubborn about using only personal honesty to build his image of God.

There is another cognitive reason for using an image of God to enforce rules of personal honesty. Remember that emotionally based facts and beliefs are mentally unstable. But if Perceiver thought is to function, then it requires facts that do not change. One way to stop facts from changing is by writing them down in a textbook or a holy book. But how can one add stability to an *internal* rule of personal honesty? One cannot do this by appealing to *Mercy* mental networks. That is because people have limited knowledge and limited awareness. It is impossible for a teacher or a parent to monitor everything that a student is doing or saying and check it for personal honesty. However, if personal honesty is stated as a *universal* rule which forms a general theory in Teacher thought, then the resulting Teacher mental network can enforce the rule. Like any general Teacher theory, Teacher thought will attempt to apply this rule everywhere and will feel mental pain when it encounters an exception. Again, stating this in simple English that a child can understand, "God hears everything that you say or think. God demands personal honesty. When you tell a lie, you are hurting God." Notice that a religious statement such as this does not require the intervention of a *real* God to work, because it will be adequately enforced by emotional feedback from a mental image of God.

We have seen that science begins with the Teacher mental network of common sense. In a similar way, personal honesty can be encouraged by the Mercy mental network that represents *physical* identity. As I pointed out in a previous chapter, when dealing with my physical body, personal honesty is literally a matter of life and death. Personal honesty in more emotional matters can be encouraged by comparing physical identity with mental identity. For instance, Mercy identification is like trying to grab an object that is in a different city, while Mercy denial could be compared with attempting to detach a limb from my physical body.

Personal honesty takes the implicit 'God' of Nature and makes it more explicit. An image of God emerges when a general Teacher theory explains personal identity. If principles of natural cause-and-effect apply only to *physical* identity, then it is possible to avoiding dealing directly with a concept of God, because general Teacher understanding is only touching the less emotional side of personal identity. However, if principles of natural cause-and-effect are extended to apply also to the more emotional side of personal identity, then the concept of *God* becomes impossible to avoid.

In contrast, personal honesty will threaten a concept of God that is based in Teacher overgeneralization, because relating physical identity to mental identity will mentally connect God with rules of natural cause-and-effect. If these two aspects of personal identity are kept separate, then it is possible to pretend that God is 'beyond logic', because the concept of God is being connected primarily with the aspect of personal identity that ignores logic. However, if principles of natural cause-and-effect apply also to the more emotional side of personal identity, then the concept of a *rational* God becomes impossible to avoid.

If one sidesteps the question of the existence of God and focuses instead upon how an image of God affects personal identity, then one concludes that connecting physical identity with mental identity is an effective way of encouraging personal honesty—precisely because of the religious implications inherent in carrying out such a step.

Personal Honesty

Two additional points before we move on. Normally, one thinks of conscience as regulating *behavior*, because conscience is part of the circuit of *concrete* thought, where Server mode plays the active role. In religious language, the assumption is that 'salvation is by works', and that specific *actions* must be performed to gain approval with God. However, education uses the *motivation* of concrete thought to encourage the development of *abstract* thought, and when using abstract thought, Perceiver facts are used to build general Teacher theories. That is why the principle that 'God requires personal honesty' must be taught as a *fundamental* rule of conscience in religious education, for if the religious student submits to this rule, then he will learn how to use Perceiver facts to build general Teacher theories. And because he is learning how to be honest in a mental context that requires the presence of Perceiver confidence, he will tend to use this mode of thought in other less emotionally charged areas as well. Saying this more simply, if the student learns how to be honest about himself, then he will find it easy to be honest about other topics; if he gains the ability to think rationally about personal matters, then he will probably think rationally in other areas as well.

Secular education attempts to be objective and tries to reassure the student that it is only evaluating his work and not his self-image. In contrast, religious education *does* deal with personal identity, by definition, because an image of God emerges when a theory explains *personal identity*. Therefore, religious education *will* make moral statements about the individual that will affect his self-image. But because the goal of religious *education* is to enable abstract thought, the ultimate focus will be upon personal honesty as a path to understanding and not upon personal achievement or personal behavior. Of course, classroom management must also play a role, inappropriate behavior needs to be limited, and marks need to be given, but the goal of all education—religious or secular—is to develop abstract thought by programming the mind with Perceiver facts and using words to build Teacher understanding, and this is done in a religious setting by teaching that God demands personal honesty.

Because the natural tendency is to separate Perceiver facts from Mercy emotions, the concept of personal honesty as a path to understanding needs to be clarified. For instance, consider the concept of *multiculturalism.* In multiculturalism, facts about personal identity are being learned and these facts do lead to general understanding, because the student is learning about different cultures and attempting to understand them. But what is missing from this discussion is Perceiver honesty about personal Mercy feelings. All cultures do *not* lead to the same personal feelings. Instead, a culture that practices slavery or emphasizes warfare will generate a lot more personal pain than one which emphasizes freedom and pursues a policy of peace. In other words, personal honesty must include *both* feelings *and* facts in order to be honest and personal.

The second point has to do with the extent of personal honesty. Remember that the Agency Detector will only ascribe an event to the hand of God if some human agent is *not* responsible for causing that event. Thus, if religious authority figures demand that all personal details be confessed to some priest or 'accountability partner', or if teachers attempt to monitor everything that the student is doing, then this will prevent Teacher thought in the mind of the student from becoming the source of his conscience. Instead, what the instructor needs to encourage is personal honesty in the *absence* of some human authority figure, and this is something that cannot be demanded by the instructor but rather must be demonstrated by the student. Saying this another way, if the teacher is always watching, then the student will have no chance to believe that 'God is watching'.

Let us move on now to the *motivation* of the religious student. We saw earlier that identification and denial will short-circuit the motivation for education. I suggest that the same principle applies to religious education, especially when identification and denial define the interaction between personal identity and an image of God.

Obviously, religious identification occurs when a person practices Eastern mysticism and identifies with his image of God by asserting that 'I am God'. But religious identification also occurs when a person believes that 'God accepts everyone unconditionally'. As we saw earlier, an instructor who gives his students an automatic mark of 100% allows them to identify with their goal and to pretend that they have already arrived at the desired destination. A doctrine of divine unconditional acceptance goes further by turning the automatic A+ into a *universal* rule that applies to all of personal identity.

Conditional Acceptance

What is needed instead is a doctrine of *conditional* acceptance. This concept needs to be carefully defined. We have seen that personal identity has both a *physical* component and a *mental* component. It is very difficult to change both of these at the same time. Instead, if one of these is to be transformed, then the other of these must remain fixed, just as lifting up one leg means placing my weight upon the other leg. Thus, conditional acceptance will generally support one of these aspects of personal identity while encouraging the other to change: If a person is experiencing emotional growth, then his physical identity should be accepted. In contrast, if he is experiencing physical change, then he needs emotional support. We will describe this interaction in terms of parent and child, but the same principles apply to teacher and student or therapist and patient.

In the area which is *not* changing, the goal of conditional acceptance is to preserve the integrity of existing mental networks within the mind of the child. This means that the parent must protect the child from the *hyper*-pain of falling apart: "I will be there for you. You can count on me to support you. I will not abandon you. You are safe with me." But by the same token, the child must *also* preserve the integrity of these mental networks: "You must not drop out of school. You must not run away. You can only be safe with me if you stay with me." In particular, personal acceptance by the parent must not be based upon the child doing a good job. The parent must not say: "I will only accept you if you get an A+ in school." In addition, change should not be required, but acceptance should be given in the absence of change as long as minimum standards are met: "I will be happy with you even if you do not do well. You do not have to perform to receive my love and acceptance. But if we are to live together then there are certain behaviors and attitudes which are not acceptable."

In the area of personal identity that *is* changing, the goal of conditional acceptance is to encourage growth, even at the expense of hyper-pain. If existing mental networks *oppose* personal growth, then they need to be replaced with mental networks that *support* personal growth. In the language of Maslow's needs, which are analyzed in an appendix, the goal is to get the child to function at Maslow's higher level of self-esteem, which results from skill and accomplishment. In simple terms, the parent must not try to give the child a *good* self-image by giving him unwarranted positive statements, because this will encourage the identification and denial of childish identity. Instead, the parent must give the child an *accurate* self-image and then teach the child skills or knowledge that make it possible for the child to *achieve* a positive self-image as a result of skill or accomplishment.

Different cognitive styles have different natural abilities. In addition, each person has areas in which he has the potential to excel. Thus, if a person is *not* talented in some area, then reasonable growth should be expected: "I know that you are not naturally good at math. You do not have to get an A, but I do expect you to learn the material. Even if you do not do the best, you will still feel good if you accomplish something." On the other hand, if a person *is* talented in some area, then he should be expected to do his best and should be given the means to develop his skill: "You are naturally talented at art. You will take art lessons and practice your art so that you can do a good job." Notice that the goal is not to compare the student with *other* students, but rather to have the student meet his *own* standards of excellence, both in areas where he is talented and in areas where he lacks natural skills.

When one applies conditional acceptance to the child and the school system, then Piaget's stages of childhood development are especially relevant. These stages of development are analyzed in more detail in an appendix. The child *enters* school when he is in the second intuitive substage of Piaget's preoperational stage. Because his mind is held together by Mercy mental networks, it is easy for a school system to set up the Perceiver shortcut. And because Teacher mode in the child can use words and Perceiver mode can acquire basic facts, it is possible for him to learn the three R's.

Because the primary student is emotionally bound to Mercy mental networks, he must be given *emotional* acceptance. The teacher needs to act like a surrogate parent who is emotionally there for the child. This does not mean that the teacher accepts all childish emotional behavior as *good*. Inappropriate attitudes and responses need to be corrected. However, this emotional correction will be limited to punishment and displeasure. The child should not feel that he is being emotionally abandoned or rejected by his teacher. In contrast, the *physical* behavior of the child will be expected to undergo a complete transformation, for the primary student is supposed to learn how to act like a school student.

Sometime during the primary school years, the student enters Piaget's concrete operational stage. During the previous stage, the child was taught how to act like a student. During the concrete operational stage, he spends his time *as* a student, acquiring Perceiver facts and learning how to construct Teacher theories. But this mental development will have to focus upon the *physical* aspect of personal identity because the student is only capable of working rationally with concrete facts and real objects. And because the body of the primary student is growing *physically*, mental development will *have* to include the physical aspect of personal identity. This means that the primary student needs to receive emotional acceptance from his teachers and his parents. At this stage, rote learning and blind faith are both appropriate because the child is mentally incapable of anything else.

The situation changes when the student enters Piaget's formal operational stage. Physically, he stops growing and begins to experience the emotional upheaval of puberty. Mentally, he becomes capable of working with internal concepts that are independent of external reality. At this point, teachers and parents need to stop giving the student *emotional* acceptance and start giving him *physical* acceptance. He needs to know that home and school will provide for his physical needs, that his physical safety will be protected, and that he will be accepted regardless of physical appearance or physical abilities. Similarly, he needs to submit *physically* to both parental and school authority. But it is now time for him to undergo *emotional* transformation and to begin thinking and responding like an adult. This means developing critical thinking, emotionally questioning authorities, dealing with emotional issues, and emerging from rote learning and blind faith. Thus, I suggest that it is counterproductive for a high school student to receive unconditional emotional acceptance, either from teachers, parents, peers, or from his image of God.

This does not mean that physical excellence should be ignored, either in sports or in other skills. However, I suggest that at this stage in the development of the child, emotional development is more important than physical prowess. Thus, if the high school student plays sports, the primary focus should be upon the emotional aspects of the game, such as learning how to reach personal goals, cooperate with others, and deal with the emotional swings of victory and defeat. Physical ability must not be made the standard for personal acceptance, and the high school student who is not talented at sports must not be rejected by either peers or adults.

Notice the parallel between physical development and cognitive development. The *body* of the child grows physically while the body of the teenager transforms emotionally. Similarly, the child is *mentally* capable of learning concrete facts about real objects, while the teenager acquires the ability to work with internal and abstract concepts. Thus, a system of education, whether scientific or religious, will be most effective if its use of the Perceiver and Teacher shortcuts corresponds to the physical and cognitive development of the student.

Let us move on now to the relationship between religious education and unconditional acceptance. I suggest that identifying with God in worship will *non-verbally* teach a doctrine of unconditional acceptance, and when Mercy mental networks are driving the process of learning, as is the case with religious education, then non-verbal language will speak more loudly than words. Sometimes, the words of a worship song reinforce this attitude of identifying with God. For instance, there is a popular old Christian worship chorus which contains the phrase: "So forget about yourself, and concentrate on him, and worship him." Why does this describe identifying with God? Because personal identity is defined as the Mercy experiences upon which a person can continue to concentrate.

I suggest that a very potent way of non-verbally conveying a doctrine of *unconditional* acceptance is by pairing emotional Mercy experiences that express childish feelings with words that talk about focusing on God. This happens when some form of rock music is used to worship God. On the one hand, the words talk about God and religion. On the other hand, the musical style resonates with mental networks within Mercy thought that express childish and uneducated personal behavior. Combining these two will mentally associate God with childish and uneducated personal behavior, effectively imploding the process of religious education.

In contrast, religious worship will reinforce the method of religious education if words about God are paired with a musical style that reflects order and structure, and if worship emphasizes that God is *separate* from people and that it is not possible for man to identify with God. In religious terms, this means emphasizing the *holiness* of God, because the word 'holy' means separate or distinct.

Religious identification pretends that I am one with God; religious *denial* prevents God from connecting with aspects of personal identity. This will happen automatically when religion is limited to specific times, places, and events. For instance, consider the religious believer who attends a mosque on Friday, a synagogue on Saturday, or a church on Sunday. On these special days, he focuses upon God. During the rest of the week, a concept of God generally will not enter his mind. We saw in a previous chapter that this type of situation occurs naturally when the growth of objective science limits the domain of religious thought.

Religious identification associates the general Teacher theory that forms an image of God with chaotic personal content that lacks order and structure, leading to the contradiction of a God of chaos. Religious denial, in contrast, limits the extent of this general theory, leading to the contradiction of a finite God. Religious identification gives the student the impression that education is unnecessary, whereas religious denial leaves the impression that learning does not have to be applied outside of the educational setting.

Because personal identity is composed of physical identity and mental identity, both scientific education and religious education are required. Scientific education focuses upon the physical aspect of personal identity, while religious education emphasizes mental identity. When education takes a purely scientific approach, then it will downplay the essential mental foundation of blind faith and rote learning, and dismantle childish beliefs during the stage of critical learning without providing an alternative. In contrast, purely religious education will focus upon blind faith and rote learning, lose its students as a result of critical thinking, and have some of them 'return to the faith' in later years, especially when faced with the challenge of raising young children.

I should also clarify how the three stages of learning relate to what is being discussed here. Whenever a student learns a specific skill or acquires specific knowledge, then he will go through the three stages of learning with that material. Thus, these three stages apply at the *specific* level of students taking classes. In contrast, the two methods of education which we are analyzing in this chapter describe a process that takes several years and involves many classes and numerous skills.

However, the three stages of learning can also be applied to an individual in a more *general* way, by referring to the stage of learning at which that person *typically* functions. Most people reach the third stage of learning in at least some areas or skills, but it is also possible for an individual to remain mentally stuck at an earlier stage of learning and *usually* operate at that level.

Finally, the three stages of learning can be applied to *society* as a whole. That is because a society can only teach what it knows, and a student cannot learn a subject if no one will teach it to him. Thus, a student can only learn a subject to the extent that it has been worked out by his society. Once a student reaches the level of knowledge of his teachers, then he will be unable to learn further until someone within that society makes a breakthrough and that new knowledge or skill becomes part of the educational curriculum. Similarly, if a society regards a certain aspect of learning as unworthy of study, then the average student will no longer acquire knowledge or skills in that area. We will be looking at how the three stages of learning apply to society as a *whole* when examining Michel Foucault's three epistemes.

Analyzing Fundamentalism

One more point remains to be discussed in this chapter, and we will introduce this point by summarizing our look at religious education. This chapter has focused upon the process and motivation of education. I suggested that the purpose of education is to use the Perceiver shortcut of emotional 'knowing' combined with the Teacher shortcut of words to develop abstract thought in the mind of the student. We then asked how this same purpose of developing abstract thought could be achieved using religious means, and we concluded that religious education will lead to the emergence of abstract thought if religion teaches certain doctrines and practices a certain form of worship. Those who are familiar with religious thought will recognize that these doctrines *are* widely taught as religious truth and this form of worship *is* widely practiced. This is consistent with my assertion at the beginning of the book that religion is cognitive science in emotional garb. In other words, if one has an adequate cognitive model, and if one is able to see past the emotional packaging, then theology makes sense.

And that brings us to the final point of this chapter. What happens when a person uses the model of mental symmetry to come up with the *same* doctrine that is being taught as religious truth? How does the religious person respond? I have often found myself in this type of situation and have attempted to make sense of the reaction that I receive.

As far as I can tell, the response appears to depend upon whether the listener's concept of God and religion is based primarily in a *Mercy* mental network or a *Teacher* mental network. Religious education begins from a mental foundation in *Mercy* thought, because the religious adherent learns about Perceiver facts and Teacher universality from the viewpoint of holy books, religious experiences, religious experts, and personal identity. However, if the process of religious education is successful, then the believer will gradually realize that Perceiver truth is true because it is solid and repeatable and not just because it is contained within the pages of a specific holy book, he will begin to view God as a universal being of order and structure and not just as a Very Important Person, and he will start to regard his holy book as holy because of the content which it contains, and not just because of its emotional status. For such an individual, the concept of analyzing God and religion from a cognitive perspective makes sense, because that person has—at least partially—a *Teacher* concept of God, and a cognitive analysis will resonate with this Teacher mental network.

However, if a religious believer approaches God with an attitude of religious devotion and views his holy book as a 'special book' with magical words that function in some incomprehensible, mystical fashion, then a cognitive approach will 'feel wrong'. That is because such an individual has a *Mercy* concept of God and religion. For such a person, any attempt to analyze his religious faith is deeply troubling, because it threatens the integrity of the *Mercy* mental network upon which his faith is based. It is important to note that this mental sense of unease is *not* being caused by a discrepancy in content. On the contrary, it will be felt even more keenly when cognitive analysis derives the *same* Perceiver facts and portrays the *same* concept of God as is contained within the holy book and is officially taught by the religion. That is because such agreement makes it possible to *replace* the Mercy mental network upon which religion is based with a Teacher mental network, and that means dealing with the religious version of a *paradigm shift*.

And since we are dealing with a type of paradigm shift, let us turn to Kuhn for advice: "Probably the single most prevalent claim advanced by the proponents of a new paradigm is that they can solve the problems that have led the old one to a crisis. When it can legitimately be made, this claim is often the most effective one possible."

Let us look at the concept of using a holy book and the process of religious education to teach about God and truth. We have seen that this is a valid starting point. It makes sense for the religious believer to claim that his holy book contains Perceiver truth, and it is even possible that everything written in a holy book is true, for the author of a science textbook makes the same claim. But it is impossible for a single book to be the sole source of all truth, because a book is a finite object which is only capable of containing a limited amount of information. Similarly, it is possible for religious rituals, places, events, and leaders to teach about God, for the student of science also attends special lectures given on university campuses by college professors to learn about the universal laws of nature. But it is a contradiction in terms for a *universal* being to be limited solely to a religious realm.

I mention these arguments because this is the type of reasoning that a religious person must use when attempting to change a Mercy-based concept of God to one that is rooted in a Teacher mental network. The religious believer who reads this book *will* feel uneasy, and he may even feel that it is blasphemous for someone to analyze the fundamental doctrines of his religion. However, if Teacher mode realizes that a religious God is a contradiction in terms, then Teacher mode will be driven by Teacher pain to develop a more universal concept of God. Similarly, a Perceiver argument must be used to convince Perceiver mode to begin functioning: If truth describes repeated connections that *appear* in many locations, then this means that it is possible to *find* the same repeated connections in many locations. Saying this in simple language, a holy book can teach a believer about truth and it can build a mental concept of God, but limiting truth and God to the pages of a holy book will cause the mind to deny truth and worship a false God. Even if a holy book contained absolute truth penned by God himself, this would still be the case.

One final point. We have looked at the difference between Mercy-based education and Teacher-based understanding as if it were a matter of following exclusively one approach or the other. Instead, these two mindsets describe two extremes on a spectrum, and almost every individual lies somewhere in the middle, with some of his facts held together by the Teacher mental networks of rational understanding and others given stability by the emotional power of various Mercy mental networks.

Summary

Having said that, let us see if we can add to our rational understanding by reviewing the concepts presented in this chapter. The goal of education is to develop abstract thought. But the average student does not want to be in school and does not feel like learning. Therefore, education has to use the motivation of concrete thought to encourage the student to develop abstract thought, which means applying rules of conscience backed up by existing mental networks within Mercy thought.

In the West, education tries to be objective, by insisting that it is only judging the work of the student and by ensuring that the student has a good self-image. But the identification and denial that are practiced by the childish mind lead to a conflict between emotion and hyper-emotion which prevents a student from having a good self-image. On the one hand, identification combines pleasure with hyper-pain by building mental networks that cannot be sustained. On the other hand, denial combines pain with an absence of hyper-pain by leaving unpleasant mental networks intact. An educational system can also fall into the trap of denial by suppressing the existing culture of the student, or practice identification by accepting the culture of the student without question.

The solution lies in realizing that there is no easy solution, because Perceiver confidence is required to deal with emotional issues. A curriculum must be developed that determines which topics will be covered in what order, and classroom management skills are required to be able to recognize, balance, and reprogram the mental networks that exist within the minds of the students.

The purpose of education is to use the motivation of concrete thought to develop abstract thought. Because concrete thought involves *doing*, the student will think of education in terms of *Server* actions. However, the primary goal is not to perform Server actions, but rather to learn Perceiver facts.

Abstract thought uses Perceiver facts to build general Teacher theories. Education uses the shortcut of emotional 'knowing' to teach Perceiver facts and the shortcut of words to develop general Teacher theories. On the Perceiver side, the emotional status of instructors and other authority figures are used to 'turn off' Perceiver mode so that new information can be accepted. After the information has been acquired, then Perceiver mode has to be 'turned back on'. Perceiver mode is turned back on by removing the emotional pressure and encouraging the student to evaluate information for himself. Because Perceiver thought looks for connections that are solid and do not change, facts which are taught while Perceiver mode is turned off must be solid and unchanging, or else they will be rejected by Perceiver thought when Perceiver mode turns back on.

This means that education starts with rote learning which is followed by critical thinking. Because these two are so different, the tendency is to practice one to the exclusion of the other. If the student is taught only through rote learning, then he will acquire a lot of information, but he will not know how to evaluate information and he will be emotionally vulnerable to the manipulations of the demagogue. However, if the focus is purely on critical thinking, then the student will be unable to think because he has no solid information with which to work.

The *Teacher* shortcut to learning involves the use of *words*. Words are easy to produce and they are general by nature, and so it is easy to use words to construct a general theory within Teacher thought. However, a general theory that is built out of words is merely a *description* of order-within-complexity, just as the plan of a house is simply the description of a building and not the building itself.

The problem with words is that they are ephemeral. This can be solved through the use of *writing*, which leads us to the *book*. Books play a key role in both education and religion, and the three main 'higher religions' are sometimes referred to as the 'religions of the book'.

A book has several qualities which make it ideal for the purpose of education. The Perceiver shortcut can be triggered by giving emotional status to the author of a book. The facts and words of a book do not change, and these facts can be repeated by giving copies of the same book to many students. A book can be taken home and studied, allowing Perceiver mode to analyze the facts apart from the emotional status of the author. Finally, a book provides a physical example of using words to build Teacher order-within-complexity.

Education begins by using existing Mercy mental networks to mesmerize Perceiver mode into accepting information. In order to mentally escape the emotional power of these Mercy mental networks, the student must replace them with the Teacher mental network of a general understanding. A similar transition also occurs whenever a field of research turns into a science.

This transition will affect the way in which the student views the content of his textbook. Before, he sees it as facts and words told by important people. After, he views it as a description of general order and structure. For the religious student of a holy book, this mental transition will be expressed by the belief that his holy book is written by God, for that is how religion views a general theory. This provides a logical, cognitively-based method for evaluating the concept of divine authorship. If a book contains order-within-complexity which is too great to be reasonably generated by a human author, then the mind will believe that this book was 'written by God'.

Interaction between the body and the mind leads to the development of two primary mental networks: A Mercy mental network of personal identity develops that represents the physical body, and a Teacher mental network of common sense forms as a result of the order-within-complexity of the natural world. Scientific education minimizes involvement with the Mercy mental network of personal identity and builds itself around the Teacher mental network of common sense. If scientific education tries to eliminate Mercy mental networks from the process of education, then it will end up destroying the school system, and the university system will become filled with students from cultures that still practice rote learning.

Religious education is more difficult to analyze because it involves the interaction between Mercy and Teacher mental networks. It starts with the network of personal identity in Mercy thought and then creates a mental network that is compatible with Teacher mode. Because religious education begins with personal identity, it will, by definition, talk about conscience and God. The goal of education is to teach Perceiver facts and to use these facts to build a verbal Teacher understanding. When personal Mercy emotions are added, this becomes the religious doctrine that God is a God of Truth who reveals himself through words. And, since religious education begins with the Mercy mental network of personal identity, religious education will teach that God requires personal honesty. Similarly, the doctrine that 'God sees and watches everything that the student does' teaches the universal nature of Teacher thought, while the doctrine that 'personal dishonesty hurts God' teaches the principle that exceptions to the general rule produce Teacher pain.

Normally, conscience is used to regulate behavior and an image of God can give great emotional power to the voice of conscience. However, the goal of education is to use the motivation of concrete thought to develop abstract thought. Therefore, religious education will focus upon the relationship between God and personal honesty rather than the relationship between God and personal behavior.

Conditional acceptance supports some mental networks that form part of personal identity while encouraging other mental networks to be rebuilt. The primary student needs emotional acceptance as he grows physically, while the teenager needs physical acceptance as he matures emotionally.

The method of religious education will fail if the childish mechanisms of identification or denial are connected with God. A *doctrine* of unconditional acceptance will explicitly teach that childish identity is compatible with a universal God of order and structure, while a musical *style* of worship that resonates with childish identity will non-verbally convey the same message. Religious denial occurs when the God and religion are limited to specific times, events, places, and individuals, effectively limiting the domain of a being who is supposed to be universal.

Because religious education begins with the Mercy mental network of personal identity, a mental transition must eventually occur in which the concept of God and religion ceases to be a Mercy mental network that has been modified to be compatible with

Teacher thought, and turns into a bona fide Teacher mental network that is held together by Teacher emotions of order and universality. When this transition occurs, the Mercy-based pseudo-concept of God will feel like it is dying and the religious believer may feel that it is blasphemous to think about God and religion in rational terms.

In order to survive this mental transition, the religious believer must realize that if truth describes solid connections that are repeated in many situations, then it is possible to discover these connections in many situations and not just in the doctrines of a specific book or religion. Similarly, if God is a universal being, then he governs all of existence and not just religious expression. Thus, by making the transition from Mercy mode to Teacher mode, the religious believer replaces the mental simulation of an image of God with a more authentic concept of deity.

This chapter has examined the Perceiver shortcut of education and has pointed out how Teacher understanding can help the student to emerge from this Perceiver shortcut. The next chapter will examine how one escapes from the *Teacher* shortcut of using words to describe general theories. Obviously, an analysis of education applies to the setting of school and university. However, I suggest that a similar process occurs with learning in general. And because religious education applies directly to personal identity, it does not require a formal school setting to function. Thus, it is possible for the religious believer to view life itself as a 'school of learning'.

❋ 9. Math versus Science

We began the last chapter by introducing you to my geometry class. Now that we have become acquainted, let us step into the room and see what they are doing. Notice that they all have their textbooks out and are solving problems from the end of the chapter. And if we look at the top left corner of the whiteboard where the homework is written down, we see that they have been assigned more problems to do at home. This scenario summarizes the typical math lesson. First, the instructor teaches the students some new concepts, then he demonstrates these concepts by solving some problems on the board, and after that the students turn to their textbooks and start working on similar problems. Likewise, if one observes the Calculus class down the hall, the Algebra class next door, or any math course in any school, one discovers quite quickly that the emphasis is upon solving problems.

The typical science class is slightly different. A significant portion of the time is still spent working on problems, but in a science class one also performs *experiments*. However, the purpose of these experiments is not to discover new facts or to come up with new theories, for whenever a student does come up with an unexpected experimental result, then the instructor will check the work of the student carefully in order to determine what went wrong.

Only occasionally does one see either problem-solving or experiments in subjects such as English, Social Studies, or History. Instead, those classes place a far greater emphasis upon discussion, personal opinion, and the acquiring of information. The English teacher, for instance, is constantly asking students for their opinions. In contrast, the only time the math teacher asks his students for an opinion is when he is trying to see if they know how to solve a problem.

What is it about math and science that leads to such an intense focus upon working out problems? I suggest that the answer lies in the presence of a *paradigm*. Mathematics is nothing but abstract theory; the higher the math, the more abstract the theory. Science uses mathematical equations and is also paradigm driven. In the field of physics, a significant portion of a high school physics course is spent covering various aspects of Newton's laws of motion, and from there one graduates to Maxwell's equations, Einstein's theory of relativity, and the equation driven field of quantum mechanics. Chemistry uses less math, but it is held together by the paradigm of the periodic table of elements, a diagram-like general theory with its own set of equations. For biology, the situation is somewhat different, for the theories are not as universal—and one also finds that there is much less problem-solving.

This explains why the math teacher does not ask his students for their personal opinions, for math is driven by the *Teacher* mental network of a paradigm, unlike English, where much of the time is spent attempting to uncover the *Mercy* mental networks that motivated various authors as they were writing their novels.

And this also explains why we have been comparing *scientific* education with religious education, for science is driven by the general Teacher theory of a scientific paradigm while religious education is guided by the general Teacher theory behind an image of God.

Math Problem-Solving

In the previous chapter, we began with the Mercy-based mental networks of the childish mind and ended with the general Teacher understanding of a paradigm. In this chapter, we will start with the paradigm and focus upon the relationship between theory and practice. We will begin this discussion with a quote from Kuhn: "A new theory is always announced together with applications to some concrete range of natural phenomena; without them it would not be even a candidate for acceptance. After it has been accepted, those same applications or others accompany the theory in the textbooks from which the future practitioner will learn his trade. They are not there merely as embroidery or even as documentation. On the contrary, the process of learning a theory depends upon the study of applications, including practice problem-solving both with a pencil and paper and with instruments in the laboratory...That process of learning by finger exercise of doing continues throughout the process of professional initiation."

This quote from Kuhn tells us two main points: First, the student of science learns about scientific theory primarily through the process of solving problems. Second, scientific theory, application, and natural phenomena go together.

Unraveling the mental basis behind these two aspects of scientific education will entail looking at several different aspects of abstract thought: First, we will work out what is happening mentally when a person solves an *abstract problem.* Second, we will look at what happens when Server actions are *added* to Teacher words and theories. Third, we will look at the *profession*, examine the way that it combines words and actions, and notice the effect that this has upon Teacher understanding. Finally, we will inspect the typical *science* problem and see how it combines theory, application, and natural phenomena.

But, before we begin, I should mention that I will be using the term 'Teacher words' to describe *both* the words of normal speech as well as the 'words' and symbols that are used by math. Thus, 'big brown cow' is an example of Teacher words, but so is '$f = ma$' or '$y = 3x + 2$'.

We will start by looking at the process of solving a math *word problem.* Just mentioning this phrase may give some readers bad memories of high school math classes, but the process really is not that complicated. Suppose that one is given a word problem to solve. What steps are involved in solving this problem? The first step is to read the paragraph carefully and write down all of the information that is given. Then, one determines what is supposed to be worked out. After that, one looks for an equation which relates what is known with the desired answer. Next, one places the known quantities into the equation and solves for the answer. Finally, the solution is checked to see if it makes sense.

We will illustrate this with a very simple word problem which should not give us too much math anxiety: A boy goes to a candy store. The candy store sells chocolate bars for 80 cents each. The boy spends $5.60. How many chocolate bars does he buy?

Our first step is to write down what we know: Bars cost 80 cents; the total amount is $5.60. Next, we write down what we are supposed to work out: We do not know the number of bars bought, so we will represent them using the variable 'b'. Now we need an equation that relates price, quantity, and total cost, which is simply: Cost = Price x Quantity. Next, we place the known quantities into the equation giving us '5.60 = 0.80 x b'. Finally, we solve the equation, giving us 'b = 7', which tells us that the boy bought seven candy bars. Of course, with a simple word problem like this one does not have to go through all of the formal steps, but I am trying to keep the math simple in order to focus upon what is happening mentally.

Now that we have solved the problem, let us see what is occurring mentally. Remember that when *concrete* thought is being used, Perceiver mode defines locations, and Server mode is used to move from one location to another. For instance, if my current location is in Toronto and my desired location is Montreal, then I can take the train to get from Toronto to Montreal.

But we see something quite different happening here with our math problem. The starting point was not a physical location but rather a *sequence of words*, as expressed by the various sentences of the word problem. Words involve Teacher mode; sequences involve Server mode. An *equation* is also a Server sequence of Teacher words—mathematical words. In order to 'move' from the word problem to the equation, we had to determine which *facts* we knew and which we did not know, and we had to *translate* our problem from the language of English to the language of math. Facts, knowing, and translation involve Perceiver thought and Perceiver confidence. Once we arrived at the equation, we then used math to solve for the answer. I suggest that math involves more of the same sort of processing, which we will *not* be tackling here. For those who want to know those details, mathematical manipulation is analyzed in an appendix.

But how did we know *which* equation to use? Our 'movement' from word problem to equation was guided by the *general equation* of 'Cost = Price x Quantity', which is a *general* way of stating a more specific equation such as '5.60 = 0.80 x b'. Saying this another way, our Perceiver 'movement' was guided by Teacher order-within-complexity. But what *told* us that this was the appropriate general equation to use? Perceiver *meaning*. We looked at the '80 cents' and knew that this *meant* price; we saw the $5.60 and realized that this *meant* cost; we noticed the phrase 'how many' and concluded that this *meant* quantity. Once we had extricated the three elements of price, cost, and quantity from the initial word problem, then the specific word problem turned into an illustration of the general Teacher equation of 'Cost = Price x Quantity'. We then rewrote the original word problem as the equation '5.60 = 0.80 x b'.

Summarizing, abstract thought involves a strange sort of 'movement' in which the 'location' consists of Teacher words, Server thought defines 'location' by arranging Teacher words into a sequence, 'movement' is carried out by Perceiver thought, and this 'movement' is guided by a general Teacher theory.

I would like to emphasize three features from this illustration: First, notice that we are not trying to *build* a general Teacher theory. Instead, we are moving through abstract thought *guided* by a paradigm or general Teacher theory. A general theory guides the problem-solving process by causing certain elements to be *emphasized*. In our example, the emphasis was upon cost, price, and quantity. The previous chapter looked at the process of *developing* a general Teacher understanding. This chapter will focus upon the process of *using* a general Teacher theory. In religious terms, the previous chapter looked at *learning* about God, while this chapter deals with *obeying* God.

Second, notice that lurking behind this math problem is a potential Teacher mental network. Suppose that a person continues to solve problems involving price, cost, and quantity. Eventually, this collection of related problem-solving memories will gain enough Teacher order-within-complexity to turn into a Teacher mental network. When this happens, then solving this type of word problem will no longer require mental effort. Instead, any example of a price-cost-quantity problem will trigger the corresponding Teacher mental network, which will then attempt to activate itself by going through the problem-solving process. Of course, for most students this does not happen, but for the professional problem-solver, it does. And the hyper-emotion of a Teacher mental network is one of the primary mental forces which locks the scientist into his current paradigm.

Finally, notice that Server mode and Perceiver mode have *exchanged roles*. Server mode is telling us where we 'are', while Perceiver mode is doing the 'moving'. In concrete thought, Perceiver mode defines the map while Server actions move through this map. However, in abstract thought, Server mode defines the 'map' while Perceiver facts 'move' through the 'map'. In addition, Teacher emotion replaces Mercy emotion. Concrete thought is guided by the emotions associated with Mercy experiences, while abstract thought is guided by the pleasant emotions of a general Teacher theory.

This means that abstract thought and concrete thought are actually two *overlapping* circuits, because they *both* use Perceiver facts and Server sequences but they use them in *different* ways. This overlap makes it possible to go between concrete thought and abstract thought, or to modify one by including elements of the other. We saw this in the last chapter when analyzing education and 'learning about God': Concrete thought uses Perceiver facts to form a map of Mercy experiences; education uses these *same* Perceiver facts to *build* a general Teacher understanding in abstract thought. The previous chapter examined the *Perceiver* side of the overlap between concrete thought and abstract thought. This chapter will be focusing upon the *Server* side of the overlap.

The overlapping nature of abstract and concrete thought only becomes apparent when one examines *hidden, intermediate* modules. When one looks at the diagram of mental symmetry, one sees that Mercy and Server are labeled as concrete, and Teacher and Perceiver are labeled as abstract. That is the *obvious* relationship: Server actions are used to reach Mercy goals, and Perceiver facts are used to build Teacher theories. But if we look more closely at the diagram of mental symmetry, we notice that Perceiver mode and Contributor mode play a hidden, intermediate role that ties Server actions and Mercy goals together. Perceiver mode looks for repeated connections between Mercy experiences in order to place these experiences within a solid map, whereas Contributor mode makes decisions and constructs plans that determine which Server actions will be used to move throughout this map.

I suggest that the mirror image of this is occurring with *abstract* thought. So far, we have limited our discussion of abstract thought to Perceiver facts and Teacher theories, and I have suggested that Perceiver facts are used to build Teacher theories. But, just as there is no direct connection between Server actions and Mercy experiences, so there is no direct link from Perceiver facts to Teacher theories. Instead, if one examines the diagram of mental symmetry, one notices that Server mode and Contributor mode play a hidden, intermediate role.

Before we continue, it may be helpful to look at one more illustration of abstract thought: the *Internet.* When a person goes to a certain 'location' on the Internet, he is not presented with a physical location but rather a page of text—a sequence of Teacher words. (When a webpage displays a picture, it is taking a sequence of Teacher words and interpreting it as a picture.) One moves from one Internet 'location' to another by clicking on a hyper-link. For instance, if this were a web-page, then clicking on the word *Internet* in the previous sentence would lead to a page that talked about the Internet, telling more about that subject. Thus, hyper-links connect words and pages that are related by Perceiver meaning, and if they don't, then we feel that we have been misdirected.

Internet 'movement' is guided by the general Teacher theory of the *IP address*—a simple sequence of Teacher words. Every page on the Internet has an IP address. For instance, the IP address for Wikipedia is currently 208.80.152.201. Using the language of mental symmetry, one could say that each IP address is a specific example of the general Teacher theory of X.X.X.X, where X represents a number between 0 and 255. In order to carry out Internet 'movement', a name first has to be translated into an IP address. For instance, the name *www.wikipedia.org* first has to be *translated* into the number 208.80.152.201 before one can move to or from that webpage. It is *possible* to translate www.wikipedia.org into the number 208.80.152.201 because these two have the same Perceiver *meaning.*

Thus, we see that the Internet, at its most basic level, is an illustration of abstract thought and abstract 'movement'.

Words and Actions

When we described the relationship between Perceiver facts and Mercy experiences, we saw that Perceiver thought looks for connections between Mercy experiences. A Perceiver fact is simply a set of connections. When a fact is *repeated*, then Perceiver thought gains confidence in the truth of this fact. For instance, when I visited Hanoi in 2005, I noticed that two wheels, a metal frame, and one or more people sitting on that metal frame were connected. In plain English, I saw a person driving by on a motor scooter. But, I did not just see this fact once. Instead, I saw it repeated literally thousands of times, with people—or even entire families—continually zooming by on motor scooters. Thus, when I think of Hanoi, I think of the Perceiver fact of 'person on a motor scooter', and I know this fact with great certainty.

In a similar way, Server mode notices sequences, and Server mode gains confidence in a sequence when it is repeated. For instance, you are currently staring at one example of Server sequences: Sequences of letters have been arranged into words, sequences of words have been arranged into sentences, sequences of sentences have been arranged into paragraphs, and so on. Server thought knows these types of sequences with great certainty because they have been repeated so many times. Think, for instance, of how many times you have seen the word 'the'.

So, what *type* of sequences does Server mode notice? This is where is gets both complicated and interesting. Perceiver mode gets its raw material from Mercy thought. In a similar manner, it appears that Server mode gets its raw material from Teacher thought. Thus, one item that can be repeated is *Teacher words*, because words form the basic building blocks for Teacher thought.

The role that repetition plays with words becomes obvious when one is attempting to learn a new language. When one initially hears a foreign tongue, then everything that is spoken sounds like 'acoustic mud'. That is because the words have not been *repeated* enough times. However, hearing a word over and over again eventually makes it possible for the mind to recognize that word.

We can understand the role that Server thought plays in word recognition by comparing it with the role that *Perceiver* thought plays in *object* recognition. As Perceiver thought sees facts and objects being repeated, it learns how to separate them into categories of same and different: This is a cow; that is a horse; a cow is not a horse. Similarly, as words are repeated, Server thought will organize them into categories, making it possible to tell which words are the same and which words are different. Again, this is rather obvious when one is attempting to learn a new language. At the beginning, every word sounds like every other word, but gradually it becomes possible to recognize words and pick them out from the clutter of acoustic mud. Of course, simply hearing speech repeated is not enough. In the same way that Perceiver thought can be overwhelmed if it is presented with too much new information, so Server thought will find itself unable to function if it is presented with too many new words at once.

If one decomposes Teacher words into their component acoustic elements, then one comes up with another set of sequences which Server mode can notice. That is beat and rhythm. Beat is a simple repetitive pattern; rhythm is a more complicated pattern. The point is that both beat and rhythm are *repeated.* This becomes obvious when listening to the beat or rhythm of a song.

You are currently staring at another element of Teacher thought which Server mode can learn to recognize through repetition. Not letters, but rather the visual outlines out of which letters are composed. In the same way that Mercy thought can recognize the sounds of non-verbal speech, so Teacher thought can interpret the sight of visual outline. In simple terms, visual outline is a collection of lines with an orientation. Suppose that one sees a cup. Perceiver thought can recognize a cup in any orientation—whether it is right side up, upside down, or looking down at it from an angle. In contrast, letters are always viewed right side up, and as the letters 'p', 'b', 'd', and 'q' illustrate, if you rotate one letter, you end up with a *different* letter, whereas rotating a cup leads to the *same* cup.

If Perceiver mode is used to recognize letters instead of Server mode, then letters and sequences of letters that are related by rotation will be seen as the same instead of different. For instance, 'dog' will be mentally indistinguishable from 'god'. This appears to be the basic mental mechanism behind *dyslexia,* which is related most closely with damage to the left angular gyrus, a region which mental symmetry suggests handles the interaction between automatic Server thought and automatic Teacher thought.

We have now arrived at the point where our analysis starts to get both complicated and interesting. Perceiver mode and Mercy mode handle *input.* Perceiver mode can observe facts but it cannot create them. Similarly, Mercy thought can observe physical matter, but it cannot create it. Mercy mode *can* sing—it can produce a tone, and tones are the primary elements of music, which is analyzed in an appendix. But a tone is only an ephemeral sound in the air. Other than Mercy tone, it appears that Perceiver mode and Mercy mode can only perform input and not output.

The situation is totally different with Teacher mode and Server mode. Teacher mode can *talk.* Not only can it recognize words, but it can also *produce* words. This has major implications for Server repetition, because it means that a person does not have to *listen* for a word to be repeated, but he can *choose* to repeat a word by saying it again, leading to *memorization.* A word that is memorized does not gain Server confidence because it *is* repeated, but rather because a *person* repeats it.

The situation is even more striking with Server thought, because Server mode has control over the physical body. Thus, it is possible to build Server confidence simply by repeating a movement, more commonly known as *practicing.* This needs to be said once more. In order to build Server confidence, all a person has to do is repeatedly move his body in the same way. This repeated Server action does not have to make sense or have any purpose. Mere repetition is sufficient. If an illustration of repetitive, senseless, purposeless movement is desired, one simply has to observe the dancing of a typical teenager.

Even when Server action is being driven by some Mercy goal, it is easy for the Server actions to become mentally disconnected from this goal and for Server thought to continue doing a sequence of actions simply because it has been done that way before. As a musician, I often notice this when an amateur music group rehearses. The group may practice a song for hours, repeating it countless times, but the performance never improves, because each run through is merely a repetition of the previous one. This type of practicing is actually counterproductive, because the resulting Server confidence mentally locks in the inadequate performance, making it *more* difficult to fix mistakes. I notice this when attempting to play violin pieces which I first learned as a child. The natural tendency is for my fingers to fall into old, clumsy patterns, and it is sometimes easier to perfect a piece that I have not played before.

If we examine the mental effects of these various methods of building Server confidence, then I suggest that we end up with an obvious mental split and a less obvious one. We will start by looking at the obvious one.

When we looked at the relationship between Perceiver facts and Mercy experiences, we saw that there is a natural tendency for one to function without the other. On the one hand, emotional Mercy experiences can overwhelm Perceiver mode and impose 'facts' upon Mercy thought. On the other hand, Perceiver thought can try to protect itself from being overwhelmed by avoiding Mercy emotions. As I mentioned earlier, 'Mercy controlling Perceiver' corresponds to the MBTI® category of Feeling, while 'Perceiver ignoring Mercy' corresponds to the MBTI® category of Thinking.

When we examine the relationship between Teacher mode and Server mode, we see that each has its own way of producing output: Teacher thought can generate words, and Server thought can produce actions. Thus, the natural tendency is for Teacher thought to function *independently* of Server thought, with Teacher thought focusing upon words and Server thought upon actions. This separation between words and actions is fundamental to the development of the mind, and it appears to be one of the main reasons for the difference between abstract thought and concrete thought. Abstract thought develops because a person can *talk*, and concrete thought develops because a person can *do*. Of course, the mind does contain two different mental circuits, but one main reason that they develop in the way that they do is because abstract thought can talk and concrete thought can do.

And there is no built-in connection between talking and doing. This is demonstrated by the fact that each language has its own way of connecting words with actions. For instance, the action of pumping one's legs back and forth connects with the word 'aller' in French, 'gehen' in German, 'walking' in English, and 'halicha' in Hebrew. In order to connect words with actions, Perceiver mode is required, because Perceiver thought knows that 'aller', 'gehen', 'walking', and 'halicha' all have the same *meaning* of moving one's legs back and forth.

It is not entirely accurate to associate words with *only* Teacher thought and actions with *only* Server thought. Instead, what happens is that one of these will play the dominant role while the other acts as an assistant. When the emphasis is upon Teacher words, then Server confidence will be gained through memorization, and words will be connected with the Server action of *writing*. But, here again, we see the requirement for Perceiver meaning. After all, not only is the action of walking associated with a different sequence of sounds in different languages, but this verb may be written down using a different alphabet. For instance, in Hebrew one writes 'הליכה' and not 'halicha'. Or, this verb may be written without an alphabet, such as '步' in simplified Chinese characters. Or, if one goes back to ancient Egyptian hieroglyphics, one finds that the written symbol for 'walking' actually matches the physical action: '𓂻'. My goal is not to analyze the details of how the mind handles the various aspects of speech. Instead, I am simply pointing out that in the literate person, speaking and writing form a mental unit, with Teacher words playing the dominant role and Server thought acting in a supporting manner. In order to emphasize the dominant role of Teacher words, I will refer in this book to a 'sequence of Teacher words', even though it is Server thought which is giving mental stability to this sequence.

When the focus is upon *Server actions*, then as we have seen, the repetition of *actions* will lead to the development of a *skill*, such as driving a car, or playing a violin. Because a skill is a collection of similar Server actions, it will lead indirectly to Teacher feelings of order-within-complexity. I suggest that this Teacher emotion is one of the main motivations for *art*. The artist is not just trying to perform the Server actions of some skill. Rather, he is attempting to use these Server actions to convey the 'universal message' of some 'general' Teacher theory. For instance, he is not merely 'painting a pile of soup cans', but rather he may be attempting to convey the more general Teacher message of 'portraying the consumer society'.

Physical movement requires the coordination of many different muscles. When the various aspects of physical movement are performed in a smooth manner, this leads to feelings of physical *elegance*. Action that is elegant appears easy because there is order to the complexity of movement, but it takes a lot of practicing to achieve elegance that appears effortless. Anyone who has tried to play Mozart will know what this means, because when the music of Mozart is played very well, then it sounds easy and simple. Similarly, one sees this in the movements of a skilled backhoe or excavator operator. In order to control an excavator, one must manipulate two joysticks along with numerous pedals and levers. A skilled operator combines these manipulations in a way that makes the entire operation appear smooth and easy.[22] Note that art refers more to the skill in

---

[22] Server thought does not observe movement directly. Instead, the mental processing used to *observe* movement is like the processing that is used to *produce* movement. In both cases, Perceiver

general, whereas physical elegance focuses specifically upon the physical movement itself.

Summarizing, the ability of the human body to say words and do actions causes the human mind to develop in two independent ways: First, there is an abstract realm in which Teacher words are dominant. Teacher words acquire Server stability through memorization and can become associated with the Server actions of writing or typing. Second, there is a concrete realm in which Server actions are dominant. These Server actions lead indirectly to Teacher emotions of elegance and artistry. I suggest that the realm of words and writing describes the MBTI® category of iNtuition (with a capital 'N'), while the realm of actions corresponds to the MBTI® category of Sensing.

Let us turn our attention now to the less obvious mental split. Perceiver thought gains confidence by observing connections that are repeated, while Server thought gains confidence by observing sequences that are repeated. However, Server thought has an *additional* way of gaining confidence which does *not* require observation. It is also possible to build Server confidence by repeating words or repeating actions. Thus, when Server thought in the mind of some person gains confidence in some sequence, this could mean that the person *observed* this sequence being repeated, or that the person *himself* repeated this sequence.

For instance, consider the typical artist. He performs his actions with great certainty, and he may feel that his Server actions convey the message of a general Teacher theory. But, what is the *source* of this certainty? Did the artist *observe* Server sequences being repeated? Probably not. Rather, the artist himself repeated Server sequences and this practicing is the source of his Server confidence. Similarly, what is producing the artist's Teacher feelings of order-within-complexity? Did the artist *observe* many similar Server sequences? Probably not. Instead, the artist himself has performed many similar Server sequences, resulting in Teacher feelings of order-within-complexity, and because the artist spends such a large *proportion* of his time performing these actions, the Teacher theory that explains the actions of the artist *feels* universal.

Before we examine science in more detail, there is one related subject that should be addressed, which is the concept of *close* and *distant*. We will start with Perceiver thought, because it is the easiest to visualize. Determining which objects are *physically* close is obvious, because our minds work this out hundreds, if not thousands, of times a day. For instance, the car may be parked next to the tree while the truck is parked on the opposite side of the street. Mentally speaking, Perceiver thought is forming a map of

---

thought is recognizing objects and facts, and Server thought is coming up with sequences based upon the *changes* in Perceiver facts. This is backed up by the discovery of *mirror neurons*, which fire both when a person is performing an action and when a person observes another person carry out that action. Teacher mode will then generate an emotion based upon the order-within-complexity of the action. If the various movements fit together smoothly, then Teacher thought will produce feelings of elegance.

reality and Mercy thought is placing specific items, such as the car and the truck, within this map.

However, it is also possible to build a mental map based upon *shared Perceiver connections.* For instance, a car is 'close' to a truck because they both have a body, wheels, and a motor. A tree is 'distant' from a truck because one has a motor and the other does not, one moves and the other does not, one has a trunk, branches, and leaves while the other has a trunk, frame, and wheels, and so on. Concrete thought focuses upon using action to move through a *physical* map. If one wishes to develop abstract thought, then part of the process is for Perceiver thought to stop thinking merely in terms of physical location and start thinking about shared connections and mental 'distance'.

A similar situation exists with Server thought. Server sequences can also be related or unrelated. For instance, baking cookies is related to baking bread because they both share the common Server steps of mixing edible ingredients, placing them in the oven, and eating the results. In contrast, baking cookies is not related to changing the oil in a car, because none of the Server steps are similar.

Suppose that I learn a certain set of Server skills, and that I meet another person with a similar set of skills. I will feel 'close' to that person because of our shared Server skills. In general terms, people who share a similar set of Server skills will feel that they are related to each other. One sees this sort of camaraderie through shared skills with the members of a profession. I sense this, for instance, when meeting an engineer, because studying engineering taught me a set of skills, and I find that this same mindset is present in other engineers. This kinship through shared skills is formalized with professional associations, in which individuals are only permitted to become members and practice certain skills if they have gone through the proper process of acquiring these skills and if they demonstrate that they can perform these skills in the accepted manner. However, this type of relationship can also exist *informally* as epitomized by the phrase 'that is how we do things around here'.

Notice that people are feeling connected because they have gained Server confidence in similar sequences by *doing* actions that are similar. For instance, one baker feels connected with another baker because they both *do* similar Server actions involving baking bread. In the case of bread-baking, the common Server actions have a strong connection with reality, but this does not have to be the case. Consider, for example, secret societies or fraternities whose members recognize each other through common hand signals, gestures, and rituals. For instance, the members of a certain group may all perform a 'secret handshake', in which a person places his fingers or thumb in a particular position. Server actions such as these are completely *arbitrary.* But if many people perform the same set of arbitrary Server actions, then these people will feel 'close' together. That is what happens when Server closeness is based upon Server actions that a person *does. Any* action which is physically doable can be repeated and can form the basis for 'camaraderie through shared skill'.

However, it is also possible to base Server 'closeness' upon Server actions that one observes *Nature* 'doing'. For instance, whenever a person lets go of an object, then Nature performs the 'action' of making it 'fall to the ground'. As a result, Server thought will regard one act of 'falling to the ground' as *close* to another act of 'falling to the ground'. This Server similarity lies at the heart of the legend of Galileo dropping a small ball and a large ball from the top of the leaning tower of Pisa. In that story, the small ball performed the same action of 'falling to the ground' as the large ball. These two Server actions were similar not because some *person* or group of people performed the same actions, but rather because *Nature* 'acted' upon the balls in a similar manner.

Unlike the actions which *people* do, the 'actions' of Nature are *not* arbitrary. Instead, they are annoyingly repeatable, consistent, and inescapable. An object will fall to the ground *every* time that it is dropped, it will always fall to the ground in the *same* way, and there is no way to *stop* it from falling to the ground.

Defining Science

I suggest that this distinction between Server confidence and Server similarity based upon sequences that people *do* versus Server confidence and Server similarity based upon sequences that people *observe* Nature 'doing' allows one to come up with a simple definition of science: Science is abstract thought that is based upon Server sequences that are *observed* in Nature. Notice that this simple definition involves both of the mental splits that we have described. First, science *observes Nature.* It tries not be sidetracked by Server sequences that I or some other person have performed either through doing or writing, and attempts to focus instead upon the Server 'actions' that it observes being 'performed' by Nature. Second, science uses abstract thought to describe the 'actions' of Nature. Thus, science combines Teacher words with Server actions, by using the abstract Teacher words of math to analyze the concrete Server 'actions' of Nature.[23]

This also allows us to expand our definition of common sense. I have stated earlier that science grows out of common sense. Common sense is not static, but rather develops mentally. It begins by gathering Perceiver facts about the natural world, such as facts about trees, which we discussed earlier. However, when the mind learns about cause-and-effect, then Perceiver facts will acquire a sense of time. Common sense will learn that while objects are solid, they can change and be changed. This will extend the focus of common sense from Perceiver facts to Server sequences. Common sense will then discover that what is *really* solid is Server sequences and not Perceiver facts. We saw this

---

[23] Thus, science acts as a major counterexample for the fundamental categories of MBTI®, because it bridges Sensing with iNtuition. This may be one reason why MBTI® has not been accepted as a mainstream scientific theory. However, we already know that bridging Thinking and Feeling is very difficult, and we shall see that bridging Sensing and iNtuition also takes significant mental effort. In general terms, I suggest that the MBTI® categories describe major *software* splits in the mind that result from the influence which the physical body has upon the human mind.

illustrated by our example of the water cycle, because the water cycle is not a Perceiver object but rather a Server sequence. When common sense finds out that the invisible Server sequences of Nature are unchangeable while the visible Perceiver objects of Nature can be altered through human action or Natural 'action', then common sense is on the verge of turning into science and a mental transition has also been made from concrete thought to abstract thought, because in abstract thought Server mode defines 'location' while Perceiver thought 'moves'.[24]

With this in mind, let us revisit the passage from Kuhn that we quoted at the beginning of this chapter: "A new theory is always announced together with applications to some concrete range of natural phenomena; without them it would not be even a candidate for acceptance. After it has been accepted, those same applications or others accompany the theory in the textbooks from which the future practitioner will learn his trade. They are not there merely as embroidery or even as documentation. On the contrary, the process of learning a theory depends upon the study of applications, including practice problem-solving both with a pencil and paper and with instruments in the laboratory...That process of learning by finger exercise of doing continues throughout the process of professional initiation."

Note first the intimate relationship between Teacher theory and Server application: "A new theory is always announced together with applications"; "these same applications...accompany the theory in the textbooks"; "the process of learning a theory depends upon the study of applications." Notice also that a 'concrete range of *natural* phenomena' is the ultimate *source* of these applications.

However, Kuhn appears to be saying something quite different in the *postscript* to his book: "A paradigm is what the members of a scientific community share, and, conversely, a scientific community consists of men who share a paradigm." Here, he is clearly stating that scientific theory is based in common Server sequences that *people do.* But if this is the definition of a scientific paradigm, then how does one distinguish a scientific theory from a shared secret handshake?

I suggest that this mental transition often occurs when science is *taught.* When a scientific theory is *first* developed, then it comes from observing *Nature* 'act' in ways that are similar. As Kuhn says, "A *new* theory is always announced together with applications to some concrete range of natural phenomena." But the *next generation* of scientists

---

24 Similarly, the mind does not directly *observe* the 'actions' of Nature. Instead, Perceiver thought recognizes physical objects and notices that these objects are moving. Server thought then works out a sequence based upon the movement of these objects. This is similar to the way that a movie works because, technically speaking, a movie also does not show movement. Instead, it portrays a succession of images one after another with each image being slightly different than the previous one. Server thought then works out a sequence of actions based upon the *differences* between each of these individual images. However, it is much easier to talk about *observing* the 'actions' of Nature, just as it is easier to refer to a movie instead of a 'rapid succession of slowly changing still pictures'.

acquires its scientific theory in a quite different manner. In Kuhn's words, "A scientific community consists, on this view, of the practitioners of a scientific specialty. To an extent unparalleled in most other fields, they have undergone similar educations and professional initiations; in the process they have absorbed the same technical literature and drawn many of the same lessons from it." Thus, science *starts* by observing the similar Server 'actions' of Nature, but a scientific community emerges as scientists *do* similar Server actions.

And once science turns into a group of people who *do* similar Server actions, then it is possible for science to forget, or even deny, that it began by *observing* the similar Server 'actions' of Nature. For instance, Kuhn says that the common perception is that "A scientific theory is usually felt to be better than its predecessors...because it is somehow a better presentation of what nature is really like." But Kuhn concludes that "There is, I think, no theory-independent way to reconstruct phrases like 'really there'; the notion of a match between the ontology of a theory and its 'real' counterpart in nature now seems to me illusive in principle."

Thus, we conclude that science contains an inherent contradiction. It begins by observing the Server 'actions' of Nature, but the very act of *doing* science together with other scientists tends to replace Server confidence in the similar 'actions' of Nature with Server confidence in the similar actions of 'me and my group of scientists'. Thus, when science insists that it is based in *empirical* data taken strictly from observation, then this may describe how a branch of science *begins* but it does not necessarily describe how a branch of science *functions.*

Mental symmetry suggests that it is *inevitable* for Server confidence in my personal actions to mentally infiltrate Server confidence based in observation. At the level of *specific* actions, science recognizes this weakness and goes to great lengths to ensure that the actions of the experimenter do not 'contaminate' the results of his experiment. However, mental symmetry suggests that the same sort of 'contamination' is often happening at a more global level: The corporate actions of a *community* of scientists are contaminating the very *concept* of scientific observation.

If Server confidence in actions that *I* perform can cause even a scientist to ignore Server sequences that *Nature* is performing, then I suggest that the only solution is to make sure that the actions which I perform are *consistent* with the actions that Nature performs. One can illustrate this with an example from teaching school. The ultimate goal of education is to teach—to cover a set of subjects and topics in a certain order. The *curriculum* of a school contains a summary of what that school teaches and the order in which this material will be taught. In other words, the curriculum describes the overall Server *sequence* of education; it describes what a *school 'does'.* However, when teachers teach, then they are all doing similar actions, such as studying the material, planning lessons, assigning homework, coordinating their activities, attending staff meetings, performing discipline, preparing and marking exams, and so on. It is easy for the common Server actions which school teachers are *doing* to take precedence over the Server sequence of the curriculum. In the end, the typical teacher has so many things to *do* that he has little time or energy left over to teach. A similar principle applies to any organization, because 'that is the way we do things around here' has a tendency to replace 'this is what our organization is supposed to be doing'. The solution is to continually evaluate what the *members* of an organization are doing and to stop doing it if it is counterproductive to what the *organization* is supposed to be doing.

However, buried within this obvious solution is a deeper problem which we will mention now and discuss in a later chapter. When Server thought contains many Server sequences that are similar, Teacher thought will notice the order-within-complexity and interpret this Server similarity as a general Teacher theory. In the case of science, this Teacher theory comes from similar actions which a person observes *Nature* 'doing'. Thus, we are not just dealing with Server similarity, but also a general *Teacher* theory that is the result of this Server similarity.

In addition, when we examined the concept of the *Agency Detector*, we saw that the mind naturally assumes that all actions are performed by some *agent*. But when Nature 'acts', then who or what is 'doing' that action? Is Nature some gigantic invisible person who 'acts' everywhere in a way that is repeatable, consistent, and inescapable? Obviously, we have returned to a concept of God, because we are again looking at a situation of a general Teacher theory impinging upon personal identity.

But in this case we have an image of God that is based in Server confidence and Server similarity. Unlike a God of Teacher overgeneralization that *attacks* scientific thought, this concept of a 'universal divine agent' appears to be necessary for *preserving* science and preventing it from turning into a social organization based merely in similar personal Server skills.

In other words, if the scientist is to remain a scientist, then he must believe that *Nature* 'acts' in ways that are repeatable, consistent, and inescapable. But this implies that Nature is a supernatural agent who is acting in a way that demonstrates Teacher order-within-complexity, which the Agency Detector will naturally turn into a belief that Nature *is* God. In simple cognitive terms, belief in a God of Nature is a mental defense mechanism which the scientist can use to help prevent scientific thought from turning into 'skills shared by the members of a scientific community'.

Of course, this does not prove that a God of Nature actually *exists*. Rather, it suggests that a *belief* in a God of Nature may be a *mental* requirement for continuing to practice science—whether such a God really exists or not. In the words of Johannes Kepler, the scientist should regard science as "thinking God's thoughts after Him." Obviously, we have just opened a very large can of metaphysical worms, which we shall now proceed to ignore until a later chapter. Until then, we will treat this can of worms like Schrödinger's cat, for we will talk about the 'actions' of Nature, but we will place the word 'action' in quotes, effectively leaving the can of worms in an ambiguously opened state.

Science versus Philosophy

We began this chapter by analyzing how abstract thought solves a simple math problem. We saw that abstract thought involves a strange form of 'movement' in which Perceiver facts and meanings are used to lead from one Teacher sequence of words to another, and we noticed that this 'movement' is being guided by a general Teacher theory. We then spent some time looking at the relationship between Server thought and Teacher thought, emphasizing the impact that the physical body has upon the mind, and leading us to propose a simple definition of science. We will now examine the relationship between abstract thought and science.

We saw earlier that abstract thought is *guided* by a general Teacher theory. This concept of *guiding* allows us to come up with a more technical definition for a general theory. In the same way that we defined *personal identity* as the set of experiences upon which *Mercy* thought can continue to concentrate, so we can define a *general theory* as the set of symbols upon which *Teacher* thought can continue to concentrate. For instance, when we were solving our simple math word problem, abstract thought was being guided by the general equation of 'Cost = Price x Quantity'. In other words, as this problem was being solved, Teacher thought was *concentrating* on this general equation and using it to bring order to the complexity of the problem-solving process.

This means that both personal identity and general theory are directly related to the idea of *concentration*. Briefly pursuing this idea of concentration, if one examines the *behavior* of the seven cognitive styles, one notices that only three of them have a natural ability to concentrate: *Mercy* mode can concentrate upon experiences, *Teacher* mode can concentrate upon a theory, and *Contributor* mode can concentrate upon a plan. In keeping with this, the brain appears to contain three corresponding concentration *circuits* that use acetylcholine, one in the right hemisphere controlled by Mercy mode, another in the left hemisphere controlled by Teacher mode, and a third in the interneurons of the basal ganglia, the location for Contributor processing.[25]

I should clarify that when Mercy thought is concentrating on an experience or Teacher thought is concentrating upon a theory, this does not mean that these cognitive modules are thinking about *just* that memory. Instead, Mercy and Teacher concentration could be compared to the anchoring of a boat. (As we shall see later, Contributor concentration functions more like a fence.) The boat can move around, but it is anchored to a certain point and moves around that point. Similarly, concentration continues to think about many memories, but they will all be viewed in the light of the mental anchor. That also

---

[25] The wiring of the first two concentration circuits is suggestive, because the right hemisphere acetylcholine circuit receives projections from restricted regions of the Mercy module in the brain, but sends projections back to the entire Mercy module as well as the Perceiver module. Similarly, the left hemisphere circuit is controlled by Teacher mode but projects to both Teacher and Server modes. *Brain (1984) 107 (1): 253-274. doi: 10.1093/brain/107.1.253.*

explains why Teacher emotion is described as order-within-complexity. The 'order' is the anchor; the 'complexity' describes the memories which are viewed in the light of this mental anchor.

Why does concentration cause Mercy mode to focus upon *specific* experiences and Teacher mode to focus upon *general* theories? It appears that the mind itself is not responsible for this discrepancy. Instead, Mercy thought focuses upon specific emotional experiences because the physical body both *provides* it with specific emotional experiences and because it *forces* it to pay attention to these emotional experiences. Similarly, Teacher thought focuses upon general theories because the physical body does *not* sense Teacher emotion, whereas the natural world *does* exhibit Teacher order-within-complexity. We will examine this in more detail in the final chapter when we discuss the topic of aliens.

The idea of abstract thought being *guided* by a general theory also makes it possible to understand more clearly the relationship between abstract thought and science. In science, the general Teacher theory that guides abstract thought is based in the Server sequences which one observes *Nature 'doing'*. This statement may sound confusing, so let us try to clarify it starting with a quote from Kuhn. In the postscript to his book, he struggles to define more carefully how Server sequence affects scientific theory and comes up with the concept of the *exemplar*, which he defines in the following way: "By it I mean, initially, the concrete problem-solutions that students encounter from the start of their scientific education, whether in laboratories, on examinations, or at the ends of chapters in science texts...All physicists, for example, begin by learning the same exemplars: problems such as the inclined plane, the conical pendulum, and Keplerian orbits."

Kuhn's exemplar has several key features: First, it is not just a problem to solve, but a *concrete* problem-solution. Look at the examples that Kuhn gives: An *inclined plane* describes moving up or down an incline; a *pendulum* is a weight that swings back and forth; the path which the earth takes on its way around the sun is a *Keplerian orbit.* In each case, a concrete sequence is happening—and *Server* thought deals with concrete sequences.

Second, all physicists begin by learning the same exemplars. *Why* are they all solving similar science problems? Because, wherever one goes and whoever one is, one finds Nature performing similar concrete Server sequences: *Every* pendulum swings in a similar manner; *all* orbits are like each other. Thus, we have a combination of concrete Server sequences and general Teacher theory, because the *repetition* of countless *similar* concrete Server sequences is producing Teacher feelings of order-within-complexity.

Notice the subtle difference between art and science. The general Teacher theory within the mind of the artist is the result of many similar concrete Server sequences which *he* does, while the general Teacher theory of science is the result of many similar concrete Server sequences which a person observes *Nature* 'doing'. However, when a technician or specialist spends a lot of time *doing* a repetitive set of actions, then it is easy for that person's understanding of natural processes to become warped by his own personal skills. As Abraham Maslow put it, "When the only tool you have is a hammer, every problem begins to resemble a nail."

And because so many students of science are *doing* similar problem-solving, it is easy to conclude that the Server similarity lies in all of the similar problems which *people* are solving, leading to a camaraderie of shared skills. But the more fundamental similarity lies in the shared 'actions' of Nature. The ultimate reason that all science students are performing similar science problems is because Nature consistently *'acts'* in a similar manner wherever and whenever.

I suggest that this idea of starting by observing the Server 'actions' of Nature is one of the key features which distinguishes science from philosophy. Kuhn puts it this way: "The paradigm as shared example is the central element of what I now take to be the most novel and least understood aspect of this book...Philosophers of science have not ordinarily discussed the problems encountered by a student in laboratories or in science texts, for these are thought to supply only practice in the application of what the student already knows. He cannot, it is said, solve problems at all unless he has first learned the theory and some rules for applying it. Scientific knowledge is embedded in theory and rules; problems are supplied to gain facility in their application. I have tried to argue, however, that this localization of the cognitive content of science is wrong."

In other words, philosophy tends to regard science as something that *begins* with abstract thought, theory, and rules, and it thinks that scientific applications are then 'bolted on' to this theoretical structure. Kuhn, in contrast, argues that application plays a much more fundamental role in scientific thought. Philosophy regards an example as simply an illustration of a paradigm, whereas Kuhn regards the example as *the* paradigm, precisely because it is *shared.* The swinging of a pendulum, for instance, is not an illustration of a paradigm. Instead, the swinging of the pendulum *is* the paradigm because all pendulums swing in a similar manner; one discovers Teacher order-within-complexity by observing the swinging of many pendulums and noticing this similar behavior.[26]

A philosophical bias against action can be found back in the writings of Aristotle, one of the founders of Western philosophy. The Greek word 'schole', from which we get the English word school, means leisure spent in the pursuit of knowledge. Aristotle stated that the goal of education is to free the mind from material constraints so that it has time to contemplate, and he concluded that vocational training should *not* form a part of any educational system.

When one compares the fruit of philosophy with the fruit of science, one observes an interesting contrast. Philosophy has given birth to many intellectual children, for most

---

26 This does not apply to all philosophy. In the final chapter, we will examine the philosophy of Martin Heidegger, which starts with personal action. However, Heidegger based his philosophy upon actions that *he* performed, and not upon actions which he observed *Nature* 'performing'.

branches of science began as an aspect of natural philosophy. But history also tells us that these intellectual children have had to leave their home in order to prosper, leaving philosophy effectively barren. Compare that with technology, the fruit of science, which has been transforming the world for two centuries, beginning with the Industrial Revolution in the 19th century.

Kuhn describes this family squabble between philosophy and its offspring: "When, in the development of a natural science, an individual or group first produces a synthesis able to attract most of the next generation's practitioners, the older schools gradually disappear...The new paradigm implies a new and more rigid definition of the field. Those unwilling or unable to accommodate their work to it must proceed in isolation or attach themselves to some other group. Historically they often simply stayed in the departments of philosophy from which so many of the special sciences have been spawned."

So, *why* does philosophy give birth to children, why do these children leave, and why are they successful? Mental symmetry suggests a possible answer. Philosophy gives birth to children because philosophy develops abstract thought, and abstract thought—especially the *technical* version of abstract thought that we will examine in a later chapter—is a very powerful tool.

I suggest that the children of philosophy 'leave the nest' because of a form of *paradigm shift.* Remember that a paradigm guides the problem-solving process; it is the Teacher statement upon which Teacher thought continues to concentrate as a problem is being solved. When philosophy uses abstract thought, it is usually acquiring its general Teacher theory from the realm of *words.* Science, in contrast, takes its general Teacher theory from *concrete Server sequences* that it observes in the external world. Thus, even though logic, math, philosophy, and science all use abstract thought, what abstract math, abstract logic, and philosophy find interesting is *different* than what science finds interesting.

For instance, think of René Descartes' famous statement: "I think, therefore I am." Descartes was trying to find some foundation for all knowledge, some concept that would guide him as he set out on his path of philosophy. Because he was capable of expressing self-doubt, he concluded that his mind must exist. Compare this with the legend of Galileo dropping two balls from the top of the tower of Pisa, or the story of Newton being hit on the head by an apple. These accounts may not be true, but they illustrate a completely different focus in which repeated concrete Server sequences are guiding abstract thought.

Finally, I suggest that science is *successful* because it builds its paradigms upon what *Nature* 'does'. If one understands how the *world* works, then it becomes possible to improve the world by using logic to *manipulate* how the world works. In other words, one can take the strange 'movement' of abstract thought and apply it to the physical world.

The contrast between philosophy and science suggests that, contrary to what Aristotle said, abstract thought based in Teacher words is not enough. Instead, the success of science and technology shows us that if one wants to transform the world, then abstract thought must base its general Teacher theories upon the Server 'actions' of Nature. Notice that this is the *mirror image* of the conclusion that we reached when examining the right hemisphere. Childish identity, with its Mercy-driven identification and denial, is also not sufficient. Instead, if one wants to progress as an individual, then one needs to combine Perceiver facts with Mercy feelings.

This does not mean that words are meaningless, or that philosophy is worthless, even though that appears to be the conclusion which Wittgenstein the philosopher reached in his *Tractatus*. After all, the goal of education is to develop abstract thought, and philosophy is a carefully constructed expression of abstract thought. However, I suggest that philosophy is insufficient because it remains within the Teacher shortcut of using words. If one wishes to make further progress, then one must emerge from this shortcut by combining Server actions with Teacher words.

Because the relationship between Perceiver and Mercy is the mirror image of the relationship between Server and Teacher, one can state the two shortcuts of education more elegantly: The Perceiver shortcut of education uses Mercy emotions to overwhelm Perceiver mode, while the Teacher shortcut uses Teacher words to form emotional structures which do not require Server actions. The Perceiver shortcut can be escaped by replacing Mercy mental networks that mesmerize Perceiver mode with Teacher mental networks which use Perceiver thought. Similarly, I suggest that the Teacher shortcut can be escaped by replacing Teacher mental networks of verbal understanding with more general mental networks that include the use of Server actions.

By now, I may have confused the reader and so we will try to summarize these various stages with the help of a table:

	Perceiver Shortcut	Teacher shortcut
Based in Emotions	Mercy overwhelms Perceiver	Teacher ignores Server
Inherently Unstable	Experts can change Opinions	Words are Ephemeral
Needs Artificial Stability	All Facts from a Single Source	Writing and Memorization
Needed to Transfer	Perceiver Facts	Server Actions
Direction of Transfer	From Mercy to Teacher	From Teacher to Mercy
Result of Transfer	Teacher-based Paradigm	Mercy-based Technology

The first row in the table describes how one *begins* to use the shortcut. The second row states the inherent *limitations* of the shortcut, while the third row describes how this limitation can be *overcome*. The fourth row lists the mental content that is required to *exit* the shortcut. The fifth row describes the shift in mental networks that occurs as one exits the shortcut, while the final row describes the *benefit* of exiting the shortcut.

This final row needs clarifying. In the previous chapter we saw that education *begins* by using Mercy emotions to motivate the student, but it *results* in a general Teacher understanding that is driven by Teacher emotions. Similarly, *designing* and *building* technology is motivated by abstract thought and Teacher emotions of order-within-complexity, but the consumer *uses* technology as a tool to generate good experiences for Mercy thought.

We have spent some time examining how abstract scientific thought is guided by a general Teacher theory that is based in the Server 'actions' of Nature. We will now examine how abstract thought itself functions when solving a scientific problem. But attempting to describe abstract thought involves, by definition, an abstract explanation. Therefore, we will begin by looking at a concrete illustration of abstract thought which emerged as a result of science. Saying this once more in simple English, I just mentioned that science leads to technology. Technology produces *machines*. A machine is a real object which illustrates scientific-like thought. Let us analyze the machine.

Remember that in abstract thought, Server sequence describes 'location' and Perceiver thought 'moves' from one 'location' to another, guided by a general Teacher theory. When this form of thought is applied externally, it leads to the *machine*. First, a machine is constructed out of parts. Concrete thought views parts as Perceiver objects: This is a pedal; that is a wheel; there is a chain. Abstract thought, in contrast, looks at the *function* of each part, the concrete Server sequence which it carries out: A pedal pushes; a wheel goes around; a chain loops. Second, these parts are then *assembled*: The pedals are connected to the chain; the chain is connected to the wheel; the wheel is attached to the frame, and so on. In concrete thought, Perceiver mode plays the *passive* role of constructing a mental map. With abstract thought, Perceiver thought takes the *active* role of assembling the parts of a machine.

A machine is a device with a *general function*. In our illustration, assembling the various parts builds a bicycle, a machine that has the general function of transporting a person from one location to another. In a machine, all of the individual parts *work together* to produce this general function, and this 'working together' generates Teacher emotions of order-within-complexity, because the complexity of parts is producing the order of a general function. Notice the guiding role played by a general Teacher theory: During the design process, Teacher thought is concentrating upon the general Teacher theory of 'transporting a person', while during the manufacturing process, Teacher thought is concentrating upon the general Teacher theory of 'building a bicycle'.

Now that we have looked at a physical illustration of abstract scientific thought, let us see if we can decipher abstract scientific thought itself.

Explaining Scientific Thought

We began this chapter by looking at a simple math word problem. In this section, we will analyze a typical *science* problem. These next few pages are somewhat technical, but not excessively so.

We will start by looking at the guiding general Teacher theory, making use of an example which Kuhn uses in his book: $f = ma$. This is one of Newton's three laws of motion, which says that force is mass times acceleration. In the language of mental symmetry, Newton's law is a Teacher theory constructed out of words. If one limits oneself to normal speech, then this simple equation remains largely devoid of meaning. As Kuhn puts it, "the sociologist, say, or the linguist who discovers the corresponding expressions is unproblematically uttered and received by the members of a given community will not, without much additional investigation, have learned a great deal about what either the expression or the terms in it mean, about how the scientists of the community attach the expression to nature." In simple terms, if you say "force = mass times acceleration" to the average man on the street, he will hear the words, but will not comprehend what they mean.

The scientist *comprehends* these words by *replacing* pieces of the equation with their equivalent and then *comparing* these modified equations with Server sequences. Kuhn's quote does contain some math, but I have eliminated the longest equation: "It is not quite the case that logical and mathematical manipulation are applied directly to $f = ma$. That expression proves on examination to be a law-sketch or a law-schema. As the student or the practicing scientist moves from one problem situation to the next, the symbolic generalization to which such manipulations apply changes. For the case of free fall, $f = ma$ becomes $mg = m\frac{d^2s}{dt^2}$; for the simple pendulum it is transformed to $mg\ sin\Theta = -ml\frac{d^2\Theta}{dt^2}$...for other more complex situations, such as the gyroscope, it takes still other forms, the family resemblance of which to $f = ma$ is still harder to discover. Yet, while learning to identify forces, masses, and accelerations in a variety of physical situations not previously encountered, the student has also learned to design the appropriate version of $f = ma$ through which to interrelate them, often a version for which he has encountered no literal equivalent before."

Let us see if we can analyze this quote without stepping too deeply into the math or getting too complicated. We have a mathematical equation, in this case $f = ma$. Teacher mode—in the mind of the scientist—regards this simple equation as a general theory. That is because the scientist uses this *one* equation to describe the dropping of an object, the swinging of a pendulum, and the spinning of a gyroscope, in addition to numerous other situations. Notice that all three applications in this example involve *physical movement*: the *falling* of an object, the *swinging* of a pendulum, and the *spinning* of a gyroscope, illustrating the emphasis that science places upon Server actions, which we have already discussed.

But we are also seeing something new. As mentioned before, the scientist is viewing the Server 'actions' of Nature as a general Teacher theory. But he is also taking actions that don't obviously act the same and managing to tie them together: A falling object traces out an arc; a swinging pendulum goes back and forth; a spinning gyroscope moves in circles. As far as Server thought is concerned, moving in an arc is not the same as going back and forth or moving in a circle. But the scientist ties these various Server movements together using a single equation of $f = ma$, an equation that looks suspiciously like abstract math.

In order to apply the equation $f = ma$ to these various physical movements, pieces of that equation have to be *replaced* by mathematical equivalents which have the same *meaning*. When solving a free fall problem, for instance, the 'a' in 'ma', which stands for acceleration, is replaced by $\frac{d^2s}{dt^2}$, which represents the change in the velocity of the object. Thus, we are dealing again with *abstract thought*, in which the basic elements are sequences of Teacher words and Perceiver meaning is being used to 'move' from one sequence to another.

However, this time we will add one more detail to our explanation: While Perceiver thought uses meaning and logic to perform *large* intellectual 'movements', Server thought is capable of rearranging and manipulating symbols in order to generate *small* intellectual 'movements', which could be compared to rearranging and manipulating the cars of a train at a railroad switching yard. For instance, $\frac{d^2s}{dt^2}$ is another way of writing $\frac{d}{dt}\left(\frac{ds}{dt}\right)$. In order to get from one to the other, one only needs to know how to manipulate mathematical symbols. Thus, this is only a small intellectual 'movement'. However, no amount of symbolic manipulation will lead from the symbol 'a' to the sequence of symbols $\frac{d^2s}{dt^2}$. That connection has to be made by Perceiver thought, which is capable of taking the *larger* abstract 'step' of connecting words that have the same Perceiver *meanings*.

Similarly, Server thought will notice that the swinging of one pendulum is like the swinging of another pendulum, because both pendulums act in a similar manner. But Perceiver thought is needed to recognize that the swinging of a pendulum is like the spinning of a top or the dropping of a ball.

When we looked at the role which Perceiver mode plays in *concrete* thought, we saw that there are two types of Perceiver facts: There are *spatial* facts, which connect experiences that are spatially related, and there are *temporal* facts, which connect experiences separated by time. A knife is an example of a spatial fact because it contains a blade and a handle that are spatially connected together. 'Smoking causes cancer' is an example of a temporal fact, because while smoking is connected with cancer, the smoking occurs first and then the cancer. Perceiver thought, by itself, will only discover spatial facts; it learns about temporal facts of cause-of-effect as Contributor mode modifies Perceiver facts by adding Server sequences.

Likewise, when one is dealing with abstract thought, there also appear to be two types of Server similarities: similarities of *sequence* and similarities of *meaning.* For instance, in English one can turn the present into the past by adding '-ed' to the verb. Thus, 'I cook dinner' becomes 'I cooked dinner'. This is a similarity of sequence which involves *only* Server thought, because one is simply adding two letters to a sequence of letters—in essence attaching two more cars to the end of the train. However, one does not get from 'buy' to 'bought' by adding, subtracting, or rearranging letters. Instead, one must use *Perceiver* thought to realize that 'bought' has the same *meaning* as 'buyed'. Here too, Contributor thought plays an enabling role. Server thought, by itself, is capable of noticing similarity of sequence. However, similarity of meaning only emerges when Contributor thought assigns Perceiver meanings to Server sequences.

Applying these two type of Server similarity to our science problem, the two symbolic expressions of $\frac{d^2s}{dt^2}$ and $\frac{d}{dt}\left(\frac{ds}{dt}\right)$ are related by similarity of sequence. In contrast, 'a' is related to $\frac{d^2s}{dt^2}$ by similarity of meaning, because no amount of symbolic manipulation will lead from one to the other. Likewise, the movements of various pendulums are all related by similarity of sequence, while the movements of pendulums and gyroscopes are related by similarity of meaning.

Notice that similarity of sequence allows a certain region of problems to be explored, whereas similarity of meaning makes it possible to connect one region of problems with another. In other words, Server mode organizes abstract problems into similar families, while Perceiver thought builds connections of meaning between these various families of problems.

This distinction became clear to me when teaching mathematics in Korea. Generally speaking, Korean students are excellent at learning and performing Server sequences, but they find it much more difficult to use Perceiver thought to compare one family of Server sequences with another. Thus, my students found it easy to solve math problems or physics problems, as long as these problems fell into the same *family* of problems as they had solved in class. However, if the problems contained some sort of mathematical twist, or if verbal descriptions had to be translated into mathematical equations, then they found it much more difficult, because this went beyond similarity of sequence to similarity of meaning.[27] A similar statement can be made of all math students, but with Korean students, the contrast between expertise and inability is especially noticeable.

Because Perceiver thought is binding together 'families' of word and action, one can say in general terms that Perceiver facts are being used to *construct* general Teacher theories. Previously, we looked at the way in which Perceiver facts *limit* the extent of Teacher generalization, which may have left the impression that Perceiver thought plays

---

[27] After spending eight years in South Korea and observing carefully from the viewpoint of a Perceiver person, I have come to the conclusion that this description applies to Korean society in general.

primarily a *negative* role in forming general Teacher theories. However, we see here that Perceiver thought also plays a *positive* role in constructing a theory by building bridges of *meaning* between various sub-theories. In terms of what we discussed in an earlier chapter, Perceiver thought is *translating* between one sub-theory and another.

Kuhn describes this process of looking for families of science problems that can be solved in similar ways by using the same general Teacher theory: "The student discovers...his problem is *like* a problem he has already encountered. Having seen the resemblance, grasped the analogy between two or more distinct problems, he can interrelate symbols and attach them to nature in the ways that have proved effective before. The law-sketch, say $f = ma$, has functioned as a tool, informing the student what similarities to look for, signalling the gestalt in which the situation is to be seen. The resultant ability to see a variety of situations as like each other, as subjects for $f = ma$ or some other symbolic generalization, is, I think, the main thing a student acquires by doing exemplary problems, whether with a pencil and paper or in a well-designed laboratory."

The end result is that Teacher thought can concentrate upon a general equation such as $f = ma$, and can interpret many families of problems in the light of this single equation. Thus, this simple equation brings Teacher order-within-complexity to all of the various problems that are being solved.

Notice how a science problem looks rather like an abstract math problem: Perceiver thought is 'moving' from one sequence of Teacher words to another, guided by a general Teacher theory. The primary new concept that we have come across is the idea of families of problems, resulting from the difference between similarity of sequence and similarity of meaning.

However, one phrase in Kuhn's last quote tells us that we are dealing with something *more* than just math, which is the phrase, 'attach them to nature'. The sequence of writing $mg = m\frac{d^2s}{dt^2}$ on a piece of paper has nothing in common with the action of dropping a ball and watching it fall to the ground. That is because the equation involves the *abstract* realm of Teacher words, whereas the situation inhabits the *concrete* realm of Server actions. But by using Perceiver meaning, it is possible to relate one to the other: 'm' is the mass of the object being dropped, 'g' is the force which gravity exerts on the object, and $\frac{d^2s}{dt^2}$ describes the acceleration of the object as it plummets to the floor. In each case Perceiver thought is connecting a set of mathematical symbols with their physical equivalent; it is using Perceiver meaning to 'attach the equation to nature'.

But we are still using Teacher words to *describe* the Server 'actions' of Nature. We are not actually observing Nature 'act'. Thus, it is possible to teach science as a series of mathematical word problems, in which verbal descriptions of how Nature 'acts' are attached to mathematical equations, much like the way that our word problem about the boy buying candy was translated into the language of math. Similarly, the typical math textbook contain numerous 'science problems' which are analyzed strictly from the viewpoint of abstract thought.

When we first looked at Server confidence, we saw that Server thought can gain confidence in sequences by *observing* them repeatedly. But we saw that Server thought can also gain confidence either by repeating sequences of words or by repeating sequences of actions. This additional ability creates two mental splits. The first involves a distinction between placing confidence in Server sequences that I *observe* and Server actions that I *do*. This mental split has been discussed at length. We saw that science is *officially* defined as Server sequences that I observe Nature 'doing', but once a branch of science has been established, it is possible to redefine science as the Server actions that are performed by a group of scientists.

We now see the *second* mental split appearing. Mathematics is limited to the abstract realm of *words* and *writing*, while science is officially based in the Server 'actions' of Nature. Perceiver meaning makes it *possible* to connect the words of math with the actions of science. But if these Server actions are only described using words and never observed directly, then science has ceased to be science and has turned into a form of applied math. Instead of bridging words and actions, it remains within the realm of words.

This adds additional meaning to a quote from Kuhn which we presented in an earlier chapter: "No process yet disclosed by the historical study of scientific development at all resembles the methodological stereotype of falsification by direct comparison with nature. That remark does not mean that scientists do not reject scientific theories, or that experience and experiment are not essential to the process in which they do so. But it does mean—what will ultimately be a central point—that the act of judgment that leads scientists to reject a previously accepted theory is always based upon more than a comparison of that theory with the world."

Previously, we looked at the role that Teacher mental networks play in locking the mind into a paradigm and we saw that Perceiver confidence is needed to acknowledge facts which have the potential of contradicting general Teacher theories. Here we see that two *more* factors are at play: Science says that it is based in the 'actions' of Nature. But if science is treated as applied math, then a paradigm cannot be *falsified* 'by direct comparison with Nature', because that paradigm is not being *compared* with Nature. In addition, how can a paradigm be falsified by direct comparison with Nature if a scientist *defines* a paradigm as 'what the members of a scientific community share' and ignores what *Nature* is 'doing'?

The solution is to make sure that scientific education includes observing Nature and doing experiments. The purpose of observing Nature is not to discover new facts, because most of the easily observed facts of science have already been discovered. Instead, the goal of observation is to teach the student that Nature really *does* function in ways that are repeatable, consistent, and inescapable. And the experiment expands the mathematical word problem into a science problem, because instead of starting the math problem with a verbal description of how Nature 'acts', the experiment begins the math problem by allowing Nature to 'act'. This is easy to do when living in the countryside surrounded by the 'actions' of Nature. It is much more difficult when living in an urban setting surrounded by the actions of humans.

'Works' versus 'Righteousness'

Now let us take what we have learned from analyzing math and science and apply it to religion, starting with a little review. We saw in the last chapter that the *first* stage of education uses Perceiver facts to build a general Teacher understanding. *Scientific* education uses facts from the external world to program Perceiver thought with reliable information, leading to a Teacher understanding about natural law, while *religious* education uses conscience to enforce personal honesty, leading to a mental concept of God. In both cases, the goal is to wean the student from his emotional dependence upon the Mercy mental networks of authority figures and have his knowledge be held together by the Teacher mental network of a general theory.

However, such a student is still locked into the Teacher shortcut of words. The scientific student may know facts about the world and be able to analyze his textbook rationally, but he only possesses a verbal understanding. Likewise, the religious student may know how to use Perceiver thought to analyze the concepts of his holy book and be able to compare religious facts with secular information, but he still thinks in terms of written doctrine and verbal truth. In order to escape from this *Teacher* shortcut of words and verbal understanding, the student must enter the second stage of education in which he combines Teacher words with Server actions.

The default is for personal behavior to be motivated by *Mercy* mental networks. That is because the childish mind contains numerous Mercy mental networks, and as we have seen, these mental networks provide the starting point for education. If the *first* stage of education is completed, then the result will be a general Teacher understanding backed up by one or more Teacher mental networks. The goal of the *second* stage of education is to use these Teacher mental networks to guide Server actions, instead of having Server actions be motivated by the Mercy mental networks of childish identity.

This *indirect* path to action forms a key aspect of both modern education and Christian doctrine. In modern society, the child does not enter the work force immediately. Instead, he takes the detour of *leaving* the workforce in order to attend school, acquire Perceiver facts, and build Teacher understanding. After he graduates from school, he *then* enters the workplace in order to work. However, his Server actions will now be guided by the knowledge and understanding that he gained going through school.

In terms of religious doctrine, behavior that is motivated by Mercy mental networks can be defined as 'works', while action that is motivated by the Teacher mental network behind an image of God can be defined as righteousness. In simple terms, righteousness is action that is consistent with a person's mental image of God.

Christian doctrine makes the statement that 'salvation is not by works'. This makes sense from a cognitive perspective if one interprets it as describing an *indirect* path to action: First, personal honesty is used to construct an image of God. Then, Teacher emotion from this concept of God is used to guide Server actions, resulting in righteousness. Consistent with this interpretation, one finds described in the first part of the Lord's Prayer the concept of a verbal understanding of God 'in heaven' being applied through action 'on earth' that is consistent with this verbal understanding: "Our Father in heaven, hallowed be Your name. Your kingdom come. Your will be done on earth as it is in heaven" (Matt. 6:9-10).

I suggest that the *Industrial Revolution* provides an illustration of the contrast between 'works' and righteousness. Manufacturing before the Industrial Revolution was 'by works' because objects were individually crafted by skilled workers. Each item was unique, a personal expression of the Server skills and Mercy emotions of a specific craftsman. The Industrial Revolution introduced the assembly line and the replaceable part. No longer was manufacturing driven by the personal Mercy emotions of the craftsman, but instead it was guided by the Teacher emotions produced by the *structure* of the assembly line and the *repeatability* of the replaceable part. The focus changed from finding the right *person* to construct the object to putting together a manufacturing *process* of order-within-complexity. In religious terms, manufacturing by 'works' gave way to manufacturing by righteousness.

The *Industrial* Revolution was made possible by the *Scientific* Revolution that occurred several centuries earlier, led by Newton, Galileo, and other scientists. The Scientific Revolution developed paradigms that explained the natural world; the Industrial Revolution used these paradigms to change the world. The Scientific Revolution used the Teacher mental network of a scientific theory to escape the Mercy mental networks of alchemy and astrology; the Industrial Revolution used actions guided by the verbal theories of scientific theory to transform the Mercy mental networks of culture and craftsmanship.

When objective science coexists with images of God that are based in Teacher *overgeneralization*, then righteousness will be interpreted as abandoning scientific thought and allowing one's behavior to be dictated by irrational religious devotion, possibly by leaving the comforts of modern civilization and living in a grass hut among the natives, or by living in a monastery in a small village in Tibet.

However, when an image of God is based in a general Teacher theory, then a rather different picture emerges, for righteousness simply means acting in a manner that is consistent with general Teacher understanding. This may give the impression that it is easy to be righteous, but I suggest that there are three major factors which have to be considered.

The first factor is the problem of *pre-existing* Server content. Remember that Server thought can gain confidence in sequences of Teacher words either by saying the words repeatedly or by writing them down. Server thought can also gain confidence in sequences of Server actions by simply repeating these actions. In addition, there is no inherent connection between words and actions. Instead, words and actions only become mentally connected when Perceiver thought decides that they have the same meanings.

Because both repeating words and repeating actions builds Server confidence in Server sequences, Server mode will contain content that was placed there by talking and doing. And because words and actions do not naturally connect with one another, mental content within Server thought that is based in words may be quite different than mental content that is based in actions. This explains why it is often necessary to tell a person 'do what I say and not what I do'. The goal of the second stage of education is to *combine* words with actions. However, if a person tries to do this, he will find that he is extending Server sequences that are associated with verbal Teacher theory into an area of Server thought which *already* contains content that was placed there by Server actions.

But what *prompted* most of these Server actions? Childish Mercy mental networks with their identification and denial. As anyone who has observed little children knows, Server actions that are driven by childish Mercy mental networks are *chaotic*. Thus, when one attempts to extend verbal theories into the realm of actions, then Teacher thought will encounter not nothing, but chaos, and not just chaos, but rather chaos backed up by Server confidence and Mercy emotions.

We can illustrate what this means through the use of a contrived, but accurate, illustration. Suppose that I wish to talk about the subject of bananas, but whenever I mention the words 'bananas' I have to say 'spoon banana three'. This restriction is going to make it very difficult to talk coherently about the subject of bananas, for if I attempt to say something like 'I like bananas that are ripe', what will come out instead is 'I like spoon banana three that are ripe'. In fact, nothing that I say about bananas will make sense, because every statement about bananas will include a phrase that makes no sense. In order to talk about bananas and make sense, I will have to learn how to say *other* phrases, such as 'yellow bananas' or 'ripe bunch of bananas'.

That describes the problem which occurs mentally when one attempts to take a verbal Teacher theory and apply it using Server actions. Server thought is not a *tabula rasa*, for it already contains sequences that were placed there through Server actions. But remember that *any* sequence of Server actions that is repeated will gain in Server confidence, whether this sequence of Server actions makes sense to Teacher thought or not.

In practical terms, this means that attempting to apply theory in action can actually lead to mental *confusion*, because Teacher thought is having to contend with implicit, non-verbally induced, chaotic thinking. And if this mental chaos continues, then it will threaten the Teacher mental network with hyper-pain. As the old saying goes, 'Your actions are speaking so loudly that I cannot hear what you are saying'. Putting this more simply, the person who chooses to act in a way that violates rational understanding will eventually lose the ability to think rationally in that area. The way to restore clarity to

Teacher thought is by *doing* an action which *is* consistent with Teacher understanding, in essence making it possible to say 'yellow bananas' and not just 'spoon banana three' when the topic of bananas comes up.

Before we move on to the second factor, let us translate this first problem into religious language. Remember that when personal identity is added, then a general Teacher theory turns into an image of God, action that violates Teacher order will be sensed as 'displeasing to God', and verbal information from Teacher thought will be mentally interpreted as the 'voice of God'. Suppose that I realize that I have acted in a way that is 'not pleasing to God'. I will sense the voice of God telling me to act in a different manner. If I do not respond by acting in a way that is 'pleasing to God', I will sense that my disobedience is deeply displeasing to God, and I will find that I can no longer clearly discern the 'voice of God'. However, once I do act in 'obedience to God', then I will no longer feel 'disapproval from God' and the 'voice of God' will again become clear and certain. All of this will occur merely as a result of building a *mental concept* of God.

The second factor results from the fact that religious education involves both Teacher mental networks and Mercy mental networks. When we first looked at an image of God, we saw that the mind will only attribute some event to the Teacher mental network that represents an image of God if it concludes that no Mercy mental network could have caused the event. I suggest that a similar mental principle applies when attempting to become righteous. If a person performs a Server action and is rewarded by some human individual for performing that action, then that action will become mentally connected with the *Mercy* mental network which represents that human person, and it will *not* become mentally connected with the Teacher mental network in which the image of God is based.

This is an important distinction, because the reason that a person 'obeys God' is to combine Server actions with Teacher words in order to become righteous, and this mental 'gluing' will not happen if the action that one does is rewarded by some human agent, even if that action *is* an expression of general Teacher understanding.

In other words, 'obeying God' will only lead to righteousness if an action is done out of *altruistic* motives. But the reason for performing this altruistic action is not to deny self or to receive religious approval from people, but rather to combine Teacher words with Server actions. If one *does* receive religious kudos from others for performing 'selfless acts for God', then this will negate the altruism, because the act will become mentally connected with some Mercy mental network and not with the Teacher mental network of an image of God. However, even though the purpose of altruism is to mentally connect Teacher words with Server actions, this is ultimately a *selfish* goal because, as science and technology illustrate, a *combination* of Server actions and Teacher words is capable of transforming society, whereas Teacher words by themselves remain 'castles in the air', able to educate others and to transform the mind, but unable to change the physical world.

Stating this in religious terms, when a person 'obeys God' in a way that receives 'approval from God' rather than 'approval from man', he has then acted in a righteous manner. One finds this concept described in the introduction to the Lord's Prayer that was quoted a few paragraphs earlier: "Take heed that you do not do your charitable deeds before men, to be seen by them. Otherwise you have no reward from your Father in heaven. Therefore, when you do a charitable deed, do not sound a trumpet before you as the hypocrites do in the synagogues and in the streets, that they may have glory from men. Assuredly, I say to you, they have their reward. But when you do a charitable deed, do not let your left hand know what your right hand is doing, that your charitable deed may be in secret; and your Father who sees in secret will Himself reward you openly" (Matt. 6:1-4).

Because the purpose of acting in an altruistic manner is to 'glue' Teacher words and Server actions together, it is possible to *reintroduce* Mercy feelings and personal reward once this 'gluing' has occurred. In religious language, this process is called 'offering the first fruits of labor to God'.

One can tell that altruism is no longer required when doing the action provides its *own* emotional reward, which will happen when the Server action generates *Teacher* emotions of order-within-complexity by being *consistent* with Teacher understanding. Notice that when Server actions are motivated by *Mercy* mental networks, then emotions will be viewed as a reward which one achieves by *reaching* a goal. For instance, I may work hard in order to make enough money to go on a vacation. The work that is needed to reach this goal may be unpleasant, but the final reward of the vacation feels good. However, when Teacher emotions guide Server action, then the *doing* of an action will feel good, regardless of whether this action ends with a Mercy reward or not.

Even though it is only necessary to apply a theory altruistically for a few times within a given context, this process will probably have to be repeated within *each* major context. That is because one is attempting to add specific Server actions to a *general* theory which applies to *many* different situations. Saying this another way, if one 'obeys God' by acting in an altruistic manner, then I suggest that the mind will automatically apply this mental connection to situations that have similarity of sequence and fall into the same *family* of problems. However, if one wishes to extend this mental connection to a different family of problems, then it will probably be necessary to perform another set of altruistic actions within the new context.

Immanuel Kant

Immanuel Kant the philosopher lived after the Scientific Revolution, but before the Industrial Revolution. In his moral philosophy, one finds the religious equivalent of the Scientific Revolution, but only the first phase of the Industrial Revolution. Kant tried to build a rational foundation for religion, in keeping with what we are attempting to do in this book. When I first started to read about the ideas of Kant in detail in 2010, I was surprised at the consistency between his concepts and the theory of mental symmetry, and I keep stumbling across additional similarities. Looking at Kant from the viewpoint of cognitive science, it is amazing that Kant came up with what he did considering the age in which he was living. However, while Kant developed a cognitive explanation for many religious concepts, I suggest that it is possible to use mental symmetry to tackle theological concepts that Kant was unable to analyze.

We will begin with Kant's idea of the *categorical imperative*, Kant's most famous moral concept. Kant formulated this idea in several ways, but his first formulation fits in best with the theory of mental symmetry. The simplest way to explain the categorical imperative is through the use of an example. Suppose that I want to determine whether lying is morally right or morally wrong. I ask myself what would happen if *everyone* were to lie. If everyone lied, then no one would believe anything that anyone said, and it would no longer be possible to lie. Thus, lying is morally wrong because it is not possible for everyone to lie—the action of lying cannot be stated as a universal law.

In an earlier chapter, I suggested that an image of God can give mental power to the voice of conscience. We looked there at the relationship between a rule of conscience and a Teacher mental network. Here we see that Kant is saying how an image of God can be formed out of conscience: Conscience is a rule of cause-and-effect that applies to personal identity. The categorical imperative takes a rule of conscience and turns it into a universal Teacher theory that governs personal behavior—which is, by definition, a mental concept of God. If every rule of conscience is stated in terms of Kant's categorical imperative, then this is cognitively equivalent to saying that conscience is ultimately based in God. That is because the Teacher mental network that was formed by generalizing rules of conscience will claim ownership of these rules of conscience.

Kant also talks about another form of conscience, which he refers to as the *hypothetical imperative*. This is a moral rule that a person follows because he is motivated by some personal reward or punishment. For instance, a person may choose not to lie because he knows that if he is caught, then he will be reprimanded. When a person follows the categorical imperative, then the moral rule is being reinforced by the *Teacher* mental network behind a mental image of God, whereas with the hypothetical imperative, some *Mercy* feeling, usually backed up by the *Mercy* mental network associated with some person or group, is providing the motivation.

Thus, if we compare these two types of imperative, then the categorical imperative corresponds to action that is *righteous*, whereas the hypothetical imperative describes 'works'. Kant argued that the highest form of conscience is driven solely by duty to the categorical imperative and not by any personal motives related to the hypothetical imperative. Thus, Kant agrees that action should be an expression of righteousness and not 'works'.

Looking back at Kant from the other side of the Industrial Revolution, we can now come up with a rationale for Kant's statements and take them to the next step. Kant is describing a cognitive shift from Mercy mental networks to Teacher mental networks, and if this shift is to be complete, then the Mercy mental networks that guide behavior through conscience must fall apart and be replaced by the Teacher mental network of a general understanding. In religious language, an individual must act altruistically—he must obey God even when there is no personal reward for doing so. For Kant, this is the end of the story. However, we now know that when actions are added to the words of a general theory in the realm of the *objective*, then this leads eventually to the *Mercy* benefits of modern technology, which Kant would not have known because he lived before the Industrial Revolution. This leads one to hypothesize that adding actions to the words of a general theory in the realm of the *subjective* should have similar *personal* Mercy benefits.

The Basis for a Concept of God

Let us move on now to the *third* factor that makes it difficult to apply understanding. The first factor resulted from the mental split which naturally develops between words and actions. The third factor results from the distinction between sequences that I *observe* and sequences that I *say* or *do.* Integrating words and actions is a significant and necessary step, but words are still spoken by *people* and actions are done by *people.* And people can basically say anything and do almost anything. Thus, integrating words and actions ultimately boils down to integrating one *artificial* mental structure with another *artificial* mental structure.

The solution is to place Server confidence in sequences that one *observes* being repeated, rather than merely gaining Server confidence by *repeating* sequences. Science—at least officially—is based upon *observing* the Server 'actions' of Nature, actions which are repeatable, consistent, and inescapable.

Suppose that I observe millions of people saying, memorizing, and reading the *same* sequence of Teacher words. That describes the situation when millions of people use and revere the same holy book. Does this solve the problem of observing versus doing? I suggest that it only moves it back a step. As far as *I* am concerned, I may be observing a sequence of words that is fairly repeatable, rather consistent, and somewhat inescapable. But the reason that so many copies of this holy book exist is because *people* repeated the *action* of printing this book and distributing it. And the reason that this book exists in the first place is because some person or group of people *wrote down* words that were *spoken* by some religious expert. Thus, we are still dealing with people repeating sequences. The same principle applies when millions of students use the same science textbook. A science textbook may describe observations of Nature, but that book was still written by people, printed by people, and distributed by people.

This is a significant issue, so let us state it once more using religious language. If an image of God forms when a general Teacher theory applies to personal identity, then how can one form a *science*-like image of God? Note that an image of God that is rooted in a holy book is capable of being math-like, but it is incapable of being science-like because it is based, by definition, in words that were spoken by people. One may be able to use rational thought to *understand* such a concept of God, and one might use Server actions to *apply* this Teacher understanding, but the final source is still the *words* of some book.

In order to escape this mental predicament of basing Server confidence upon Server sequences that were generated by people, one must find a source of Server 'actions' which each person can himself observe that 'acts' upon the mind in a way that is repeatable, consistent, and inescapable.

Science is made possible by the fact that something external to the mind is 'acting' in a way that is predictable, repeatable, and unalterable. For instance, when I drop an object, it will *always* fall down, it will always fall down in a *similar* way, and I cannot *prevent* it from falling down. And, I *myself* can observe the object falling to the ground. Science studies these repeated falls and comes to the conclusion that they can all be described by the single general Teacher theory of $f = ma$.[28]

Mental symmetry suggests that a similar principle applies to the mind, which one can understand by comparing the mind with a computer. A computer can be programmed to perform many different tasks, but the software of a computer is ultimately limited by its hardware. One cannot take an application for a smart phone, for instance, and expect it to run on a PC, because the *hardware* is different. Most current smart phones use ARM processors while most PCs use Intel-compatible processors. Likewise, if the hardware of my computer does not contain a DVD drive, then software that requires a DVD drive will not work. Again we see that software is limited by hardware.

In a similar manner, mental symmetry suggests that human 'software' is limited by the mental 'hardware' of cognitive modules. Like computer CPUs, these modules are amazingly general-purpose, but they still have their limitations.

Thus, in the same way that the consistent, repeatable, inescapable behavior of Nature makes it possible to come up with scientific general Teacher theories, so it appears that the consistent, repeatable, inescapable behavior of cognitive modules makes it possible to come up with a science-like theory of the mind. But because personal identity resides within the mind, this science-like general Teacher theory will lead to a science-like concept of God. Saying this another way, we are taking Kant's transcendental argument and using it as the basis for forming an image of God. Notice that I use the term science-*like* rather than scientific.

As I pointed out in the introduction to this book, the cognitive modules that mental symmetry uses do correspond to major brain regions and they can be identified and observed using the empirical methods of science. This describes scientific observation. But a general theory of the mind and an image of God will only form if one *extends* this

---

[28] When science gets too complicated, then it becomes difficult for an individual person to actually *observe* science. But if a person does not observe Nature 'acting', then Server thought will no longer base its Server confidence in Server sequences that are being *observed.* And if Server confidence is not rooted in observed Server sequences, then what a person is practicing no longer falls within the official definition of science, for science claims that it is based purely in physical evidence. In addition, we will see in a later chapter that science also has a tendency to enter the mental realm of technical thought, which is, by definition, partially disconnected from observation.

observation from the external to the internal. And when one is mentally observing the behavior of cognitive modules, then one is being science-like but not necessarily scientific.

Obviously, this book also contains only a verbal description of the theory of mental symmetry. Even if the words of this book are faithfully applied, the very fact that one is applying words means that one remains within the Teacher shortcut of words. Thus, the reader who wishes to escape the Teacher shortcut will have to convince himself that cognitive modules really do exist, and he will have to base his understanding of mental symmetry in the behavior of cognitive modules that he himself observes, just as the student of science who wishes to escape the Teacher shortcut of textbooks and written problems will have to observe Nature himself for long enough to be convinced that Nature really does function in ways that are repeatable, consistent, and inescapable.

Does studying religion from a cognitive perspective lead to a *new* religion and a *novel* concept of God? As we shall see increasingly throughout the rest of this book, the answer appears to be no. Instead, when one uses cognitive modules to analyze religious concepts, one ends up deriving *existing* religious doctrine. This suggests that religious thought really *is* guided by mental architecture, even if a religious person or group does not recognize that its religious doctrine is being shaped by mental architecture and can be analyzed using cognitive principles.

Thus, one must make a distinction between mentally behaving in a predictable manner and *acknowledging* that one is being mentally predictable, just as it is possible to be subject to scientific law without understanding scientific law. After all, objects did not start falling to the ground when Newton formulated the law of gravity. Objects have *always* fallen to the ground; Newton's discovery simply came up with a mathematical way of analyzing the law of gravity. Likewise, human thought has *always* been guided by mental architecture; mental software has *always* been constrained by mental hardware. But it is possible to be unaware of this mental restriction or refuse to acknowledge its presence.

However, if one wishes to construct a science-like image of God, then it appears that one can only do this by acknowledging and understanding mental hardware and by basing one's concept of God *upon* this mental hardware. And, if one *bases* theology in cognitive structure, then it becomes mentally possible for religious education to escape the Teacher shortcut of words.

But basing theology in cognitive structure goes even further, because it makes it possible for a person or group to go beyond worshipping and obeying a concept of God that was created in their *own image*. Server sequences that come from repeated actions or words are *artificial*; they have no ultimate basis in reality because they are based in words and actions which *people* have decided to repeat. Any resulting image of God will be similarly artificial with no direct basis in reality. However, cognitive structure is both unchanging and common to everyone. Thus, a mental concept of God that is based in cognitive structure can actually claim to be a universal concept of God which applies to all people from all cultures.

This does not mean that an image of God which is based in a holy book is *wrong*. It simply means that there is no inherent way of *telling* whether it is right or wrong, just as there is no inherent way of telling whether the words of a science textbook are right or wrong. One can search for internal consistency, but is that enough? Of course, a concept of God that is based in cognitive modules could also be wrong. That is because there is no way of knowing for *certain* that cognitive modules exist, let alone the specific cognitive modules described in this book. But every scientist will tell you that general theories which are based in observation are never 100% certain. As Willard Quine points out in *The Web of Belief*, scientific theory is the result of hypothesis which is built upon observation. Hypothesis is always uncertain. But by increasing observation and by formulating hypothesis more carefully, it is possible to become increasingly certain about scientific theory. Similarly, by observing cognitive modules in more areas of thought and by formulating the hypothesis of cognitive modules more carefully, it is possible to become increasingly certain about the theory of mental symmetry.

This also does not mean that *words* and *actions* are wrong. It is impossible to exist as a human without talking and doing. The first stage of education uses words to build general Teacher theories, the second stage of education uses actions to apply Teacher understanding, and the third stage of education uses actions to transform experiences. But the ultimate *basis* for words and actions needs to be cognitive structure, for the simple reason that the ultimate limitation for words and actions *is* cognitive structure.

Notice the precise relationship between words, actions, and observation. Our starting point is a general Teacher theory of personality taught by the words of some person. This theory may describe the behavior of cognitive modules, but this behavior is still being *described* and not observed. In order to go beyond words, one must personally *observe* the behavior of cognitive modules.

But even when one observes behavior, one is still using words to describe what one observes. In order to go further, one must use Server actions to apply these Teacher words; in religious terms, one must become righteous. But when one attempts to extend verbal theory into the realm of Server actions, one will discover that one has *already* done Server actions that *violate* theory. Thus, in order to *think* clearly when attempting to apply theory, one must form Server sequences which are *consistent* with that theory by *doing* actions that *apply* the theory.

It is interesting that these two issues of words versus actions and doing versus observing appear to be described in the Gospel of John. As usual, what concerns us here is the cognitive principles that are being discussed. This book opens with the phrase, "In the beginning was the Word, and the Word was with God, and the Word was God." Thus, we are dealing with a concept of God based in words. A few verses later it says, "And the Word became flesh and dwelt among us", indicating that Teacher words about God are being applied in Server actions. A few chapters later, Jesus says, "Most assuredly, I say to you, the Son can do nothing of Himself, but what He sees the Father do; for whatever He does, the Son also does in like manner" (John 5:19). We see here that Jesus is saying that he only *does* Server actions which are consistent with the Server actions that he *observes* God 'doing'.

Finally, I should mention that it is often possible for mental software to be *temporarily* inconsistent with mental hardware. That is because the restrictions of mental hardware typically take *time* to show up. We can illustrate this by looking at computer hardware. Suppose that I continue filling the hard drive of my computer with information. Eventually, the hard drive will fill up and the computer will stop running properly, but it will take time for the hard drive to fill up; the software will not immediately encounter the limits that are placed upon it by the hardware. However, when my hard drive *does* become full, then I will have no choice but to immediately stop saving files and start deleting information.

But stopping what one is currently doing and starting to do something else is precisely what the human mind does not *naturally* do, because *any* words or actions that are repeated will build Server confidence, leading to the mental certainty that 'the way we do things around here' is the way that one should always continue to do things. As the current debate over global warming or peak oil demonstrates, it can be very difficult to get a group of people to even consider the possibility that they might have to change the way that they behave.

We will finish this chapter with two examples, starting with one based in personal experience. Suppose that I am learning how to play the violin. Obviously, reading books about playing the violin is not enough. But simply picking up the instrument is also dangerous, because it will lead to the development of bad habits. Instead, theory must be combined with practice. However, hidden within the obvious need to combine words with actions is a more subtle factor. A violin is not just a passive object. Instead, when it is played, it acts like a collection of springs that vibrate at certain natural frequencies. Think, for instance, of the bouncing of a violin bow. Thus, playing a violin well includes observing how the instrument responds and basing one's actions upon the natural responses of the violin. If one plays in a manner that acknowledges and respects how the instrument reacts, then the playing will sound natural and effortless. However, remember that any action which is repeated builds Server confidence. Thus, when one practices, then the tendency is to impose learned Server sequences upon the instrument. Such playing will sound forced and will also be more tiring, for one is constantly fighting the instrument instead of cooperating with it.

Now let us turn our attention from art to warfare. A modern professional army combines Teacher words with Server actions through chain of command and specialized skills in a way that illustrates Teacher order-within-complexity. But the bottom line for an army is neither the physical environment nor the social environment. Instead, an army imposes the artificial words and actions of a group of people upon both its physical environment and its social environment.

One could focus upon the human cost of the military, but instead we shall limit ourselves to the fairly benign matter of air conditioning military tents in the middle of the Afghanistan desert in the heat of the summer. The temperature outside is fifty degrees Celsius. The tents have no insulation. Every gallon of fuel has to be shipped into the country and then driven by fuel convoy over several hundred miles of barely existent road. And fuel conveys are a prime target for insurgent attack. In just the one year of 2007, almost ninety million gallons of fuel were transported by convoy in Afghanistan, as well as over half a million gallons in Iraq, at a human cost to Americans of 170 casualties. That definitely is a case of using human will to impose structure upon both the physical and social environment.

Does this imposed structure acknowledge how the environment behaves? Looking merely at the case of air conditioning, tests were done in which tents were treated with polyurethane foam. The insulation cut energy use by 92%, but army commanders responded to these improvements with comments such as "It's not my lane. We don't need to tie the operational commanders' hands." In other words, observation from the physical environment should not hamper the ability of the military system to impose its artificial structure of human words and human actions upon the environment. But the physical—and mental—environment will *always* hamper the ability of a human system to impose its artificial structure of words and actions. One can choose to ignore natural law, but one cannot escape it. But, if one chooses to *continue* ignoring natural law, then it will take effort to do so and one will eventually become exhausted and run out of resources.[29]

Summary

Let us summarize. We began this chapter by looking at how a paradigm guides abstract problem solving. We saw that abstract thought involves a strange sort of 'movement' in which Teacher words form the basic elements, Server thought defines 'location', and Perceiver thought is used to 'move' between abstract 'locations', guided by a general Teacher theory.

Because abstract thought uses a general Teacher theory to *guide* abstract 'movement', we can define a general Teacher theory as a *verbal* or *symbolic* sequence upon which Teacher thought can continue to concentrate, just as personal identity is defined as the set of *experiences* upon which Mercy thought can continue to concentrate. This premise is consistent with data from personality and neurology, which suggest that only the three modules of Teacher, Mercy, and Contributor are capable of concentration.

We then looked at the relationship between words and actions. Server thought places confidence in sequences that it observes being repeated. These sequences may be composed of words, musical rhythm, or visual outline. However it is also possible to build Server confidence by *repeating* words or actions. Because the human body is capable of saying any sequence of words and performing a wide range of actions, Server

---

[29] *Among The Costs of War: Billions a Year in A.C.?*, npr.org, June 25, 2011. And, *Casualty Costs of Fuel and Water Resupply Convoys in Afghanistan and Iraq*, army-technology.com, February 26, 2010.

thought can gain confidence in sequences that have no connection with reality. Thus, one must make a mental distinction between Server sequences that a person *observes* repeatedly versus Server sequences that a person *chooses* to repeat through words or actions.

In addition, there is no inherent connection between words and actions, and each language connects words with actions (and objects and experiences) in a different way. This leads to a natural split between Teacher thought and Server thought. On the one side, Teacher thought uses words to build general theories. Sequences of Teacher words gain Server confidence through memorization or through the Server action of writing. On the other hand, learning a skill programs Server thought with many similar Server sequences, leading indirectly to the formation of a general Teacher theory. This split between words and actions corresponds to the MBTI® division between iNtuition and Sensing. Perceiver mode is needed to bridge this split, because Perceiver thought connects words and actions that have the same *meaning*.

Physical location is represented within Perceiver thought as a mental map, but Perceiver thought can also base distance upon shared Perceiver connections. Similarly, Server thought can construct a form of mental 'map' based upon shared skills and sequences. When 'closeness' is based upon common skills, then people who share skills will feel 'close' together. This type of 'closeness' is reflected formally in professional societies and informally in 'the way that things are done around here'. Server 'closeness' can also be based upon similarities between sequences that are *observed*. Thus, the swinging of one pendulum is 'close' to the swinging of another pendulum because they act in similar ways.

Science places Server confidence in similar sequences that it observes Nature 'doing', and uses abstract problem-solving to analyze these Server sequences. Thus, science is officially rooted in *natural phenomena* and *empirical observation*. But once a system of science become established, then it is possible for scientists to view science as a set of common skills shared by scientists, replacing Server confidence based in sequences that are *observed* with confidence based in sequences that are *performed*. Addressing this issue means analyzing a mental concept of God, because the Agency Detector will naturally ascribe divine attributes to Nature.

Science bases its general Teacher theories in the 'actions' of Nature, leading to what Kuhn calls the *exemplar*, or a set of common concrete problem-solutions. Philosophy, in contrast, tends to view action as something that is added to verbal theory. Because science bases itself upon the repeated Server 'actions' of Nature, it is able to transform the natural environment through the use of technology. When abstract scientific thought is used with physical objects, then this leads to the development of machines.

A scientific problem looks much like an abstract math problem, because in both cases Perceiver thought is moving between sequences of Teacher words guided by a general Teacher theory. But a science problem also uses Perceiver meaning to connect sequences of Teacher words with the 'actions' of Nature, and it uses Perceiver thought to tie together families of similar sequences being 'performed' by Nature, increasing the generality of the verbal Teacher theories that guide abstract 'movement'.

If one merely *describes* the 'movement' of Nature instead of actually observing it, then science turns into a form of applied math, and math textbooks contain many 'science problems' which start with verbal descriptions of how Nature behaves. And if one defines a scientific paradigm as a set of skills shared by a group of scientists, then science ceases to be science because it is no longer based in *natural* law.

Education leads to Server action through an *indirect* path. The *direct* path to action uses Mercy goals to motivate Server actions. This combination defines concrete thought and corresponds to the religious path of 'salvation by works'. In contrast, education uses conscience to encourage the development of abstract thought, and the resulting general Teacher understanding is then used to guide Server action. When this general theory produces an image of God, then the combination of Teacher understanding and Server action describes *righteousness*. In the language of Kant, *'salvation by works'* is guided by the hypothetical imperative, whereas *righteousness* is guided by duty to the categorical imperative.

The religious student has to contend with both Mercy and Teacher content. Therefore, becoming righteous requires the performance of altruistic action, because altruism will ensure that Server actions become mentally connected with a Teacher mental network and not with a Mercy mental network. The Industrial Revolution introduced a form of righteousness to manufacturing, because the craftsman with his personal Server skills was replaced by the assembly line that is guided by the process of a general Teacher theory.

In addition, childish Mercy mental networks will motivate Server mode to perform actions that are chaotic and inconsistent, leading to the development of childish habits. When a verbal Teacher understanding is applied in action, these chaotic Server sequences will be encountered, leading to confusion for abstract thought. In order to clear up this mental confusion, Server actions will have to be performed that *are* consistent with general Teacher understanding.

Summarizing all of this in simplest terms, the ultimate purpose of building a general Teacher theory is to use this theory to transform the world of Mercy experiences. But in order to *change* Mercy experiences, one must use Server actions, which means taking a verbal theory and extending it into the realm of Server actions. If one does not use actions to apply verbal theory, then the actions that one *does* do will either twist verbal theory or lock it within the realm of words.

If one uses Server actions to transform the world of Mercy experiences, then the world will only *stay* transformed if the Server actions that one performs are consistent with the natural Server sequences of the environment. The greater the inconsistency between what *I* do and what my *environment* does, the more effort and energy it will take to maintain this inconsistency, and the quicker the transformation will revert back to the original state when that effort and energy is removed. However, if Mercy experiences are transformed by taking *existing* natural processes and combining them in novel ways, then maintaining this transformation will take the least effort and energy. Ideally, the transformation will actually become *self*-sustaining.

✵ 10. Applying Theory

When I introduce people to the theory of mental symmetry, they often ask me if it has any practical applications. When I attempt to answer this question, I typically find that people regard my reply as inadequate. As far as I can tell, this is because the average person views science and psychology as a source of *tools* which can be used to achieve existing Mercy goals more effectively. For instance, e-mail is a physical tool that allows people to contact each other more quickly, while MBTI® is a psychological tool which makes it easier to assign jobs to people. Therefore, people typically want me to show how mental symmetry can provide them with some new psychological tools that can be learned in a few hours and then added to their existing toolkit. To some extent, this can be done, by breaking off concepts and teaching them as isolated principles.

However, mental symmetry is a *general* theory of human personality, and not just a specialized tool of psychology. Therefore, in order to truly apply this theory, I suggest that one must take an *indirect* approach to action similar to the one that is taken by scientific and religious education. And because the theory of mental symmetry can be used to analyze both scientific and religious thought, I suggest that applying the theory of mental symmetry will involve elements of *both* secular and religious education.

Remember that the goal of the *first* stage of education is to acquire Perceiver facts that are held together by general Teacher theories. Scientific education bases its Teacher understanding upon the behavior of Nature but avoids personal identity; religious education includes personal identity, which causes the Teacher understanding that is acquired to form an image of God. Mental symmetry combines these two approaches. On the one hand, the theory of mental symmetry is ultimately based in the behavior of cognitive modules; on the other hand, analyzing cognitive modules includes personal identity which means that developing a general Teacher theory will cause an image of God to emerge.

Learning Mental Symmetry

If one wishes to build a general Teacher theory upon the behavior of cognitive modules, then obviously one has to *observe* cognitive modules. Thankfully, this is very easy to do, because we are all surrounded by people with different cognitive styles. If one wishes to observe the behavior of the Perceiver module, for instance, then one only has to observe the behavior of the typical Perceiver person. Determining a person's cognitive style is not always easy, but one can begin by observing the behavior of friends, family members, and colleagues whose cognitive style *is* obvious. In this book, we have only touched upon this behavioral data, but one can find more information on the mentalsymmetry website. Of course, every individual is unique and a person's behavior is not determined solely by the cognitive module that is conscious, but it is amazing how predictable the average person is and how much information one can gain from observing cognitive style.

Most of us already use what cognitive science calls Theory of Mind to observe and analyze the behavior of others. Thus, I am not proposing anything new. But by using the concept of cognitive modules, it is possible to develop a more *rigorous* form of Theory of Mind.

The next step is to observe one's *own* behavior. This will start to happen automatically if one observes others for long enough, because emotional memories associated with the typical behavior of each cognitive style will form a mental network, and this mental network will be triggered when subconscious thought in one's own mind behaves in a similar manner. Because mental networks form out of *emotional* memories that are related, these mental networks will probably form first around the behavior of family members and colleagues that is particularly annoying and predictable: "You are just like my dad. He is always telling corny jokes. I wish that he would stop."

Notice that this process of cognitive self-analysis can be carried out whether one is thinking or acting, performing normal activity, practicing religion, or studying science. As long as the mind is being used—and it always is, it is possible to determine which modules within the mind are currently guiding behavior. The important thing is not to get cognitive modules confused with mental networks. When culture is strong, then it can be difficult to look past the behavior that is being motivated by the mental networks of culture to determine the behavior of the cognitive modules themselves. In fact, when culture is sufficiently strong, then it may be difficult even to determine a person's cognitive style.

I should emphasize that I am not suggesting either exhaustive or exhausting self-analysis. In most situations, simply determining which of the seven cognitive modules is currently the most active is sufficient. Likewise, there is no point in trying to construct a comprehensive catalog of mental networks. When a mental network is triggered, it will make its presence known through the appearance of potent feelings and stubborn habits. All one has to do is recognize a mental network when it shows up on the scene. The important thing is to perform this simple self-analysis over a period of time and in a number of different contexts. It is this repetition and variety that will turn the theory of mental symmetry into a general Teacher understanding of human behavior.

Because one is using a general Teacher theory to explain personal identity, the mental result will be an image of God. Whether this mental concept of God corresponds to a real deity or not, the general Teacher theory of human behavior that emerges will come into mental contact with other existing general Teacher theories and this mental interaction will induce religious feelings. That is why we spent so much time describing what happens when Teacher theories interact, and why I am attempting in this book to use the theory of mental symmetry to analyze such a wide range of topics—both religious and scientific, subjective and objective. My goal is to minimize the inevitable Teacher conflict that will arise from attempting to learn the theory of mental symmetry.

Building a potent image of God means taking the most general Teacher theory and applying it as much as possible to Mercy personal identity. Therefore, the concept of God that emerges from learning the theory of mental symmetry will be the most powerful if one is following a path of education that includes *both* a scientific *and* a religious component. Analyzing scientific thought will increase the *Teacher* generality of the theory of mental symmetry, while analyzing religious activity will increase the extent to which the theory of mental symmetry applies to personal *Mercy* experiences.

The result of this first stage will be a Teacher mental network related to the theory of mental symmetry, and this Teacher mental network will start to drive the process of self-analysis. As I mentioned earlier, self-analysis may feel at first like a chore, but when the theory of mental symmetry 'turns on', then it will start 'eating up' the mind, and one will have to choose *not* to analyze thoughts, people, and situations. Notice that this general theory of mental symmetry goes *beyond* merely learning to recognize the behavior of different cognitive styles and different cognitive modules, just as the general equation of $f = ma$ goes beyond noticing that all pendulums swing back and forth in a similar manner. Recognizing cognitive modules leads to the development of *Mercy* mental networks which will become activated when distinctive personal behavior is encountered. The theory of mental symmetry will cause a *Teacher* mental network to form that explains this behavior and ties together these various Mercy mental networks.

I should mention that it is possible to skip this initial phase of observing behavior and approach mental symmetry purely as an abstract theory of personality that is based in words, just as it is possible to ignore the fact that science is based in observation and treat science purely as a form of applied math. However, if one does this, then I suggest that it will not be possible to use the theory of mental symmetry to escape the Teacher shortcut of words. In order to base the theory of mental symmetry in the behavior of cognitive modules, one must observe cognitive modules long enough to generate Teacher emotions of order-within-complexity. One must not just *observe* cognitive behavior; one must observe this behavior *generally* in many places, many people, and many contexts.

When this mental threshold is crossed and the theory of mental symmetry forms a Teacher mental network, then the natural tendency will be to shrink back and attempt to drop the subject. That is because the average Western individual does not know what it means to have a theory 'eat up the mind'. Therefore, he associates this sort of emotional fervor with fanaticism, cults, and brainwashing. However, I suggest that a distinction needs to be made between the *content* of a theory and the *feeling* that it produces. There is no reason to regard with suspicion a general theory of human behavior that explains *normal* behavior and includes major aspects of *existing* thought and activity. But the Teacher emotion that results when one takes these various puzzle pieces of human behavior and puts them together to produce a general Teacher theory will produce an emotional response that feels 'abnormal', and this 'abnormal feeling' will either cause a mental image of God to start forming or else call into question one's existing concept of God. Again, I suggest that a distinction needs to be made between feeling 'typical' and feeling 'normal'. Within Western society, it is *typical* for the mind to function in a semi-fragmented mental state. But it is *normal* for the mind to be emotionally integrated.

I suggest that the emergence of these sorts of questions signals the beginning of the *second* stage, in which Server actions need to be added to Teacher understanding. In religious terms, the image of God that results from understanding mental symmetry will begin to affect personal behavior through the voice of *conscience.* In order to comprehend what this means, we will need to examine the system of conscience that emerges when mental symmetry 'eats up the mind'.

Universal Conscience

This transition from the first stage of *analyzing* the mind to the second stage of *applying* a system of conscience brings us to the 'is-ought' problem raised by the philosopher David Hume. In simple terms, how can one go from a description of how the mind *is* working to a prescription of how the mind *ought* to work? I suggest that the answer can be found in the difference between mental *software* and mental *hardware.* If one uses the theory of mental symmetry to analyze how the mind *is* operating, then one will conclude that a large gap exists between how the mind *is* functioning and how it *could* function. All seven cognitive modules of the mind *could* function effectively and cooperatively. That describes the potential made possible by mental hardware. But all seven cognitive modules are *not* functioning effectively and cooperatively. That is because living in a physical body in a physical world alongside other human beings causes mental networks to form which use only *some* of the mental hardware.

But how can one learn how the mental hardware *could* function if everyone is subject to the same set of systemic biases—if everyone within the neighborhood has the same type of mind within the same world within the same culture? Because, cognitive *style* will cause each person to emphasize the cognitive module in which he is conscious.[30] The Contributor person, for instance, is naturally governed by childish Mercy mental networks just like every other individual, but he tries to express these Mercy mental networks in a manner which ensures that Contributor mode is functioning. Similarly, the Perceiver person expresses his childish Mercy mental networks in a way that tries to keep Perceiver mode functioning, and so on. Thus, as long as people have the mental and physical freedom to develop conscious thought, then it is possible to put together a *composite* picture of how the human mind *could* function, even if the average person is only using part of his mind.

---

[30] Living for a while in a different neighborhood with a different culture definitely makes it easier to see how the mind could function. However, it is important to remember that the main goal is not to learn about different mental networks, but rather about different cognitive modules.

I suggest that this cognitive discrepancy between how cognitive modules *are* functioning and how they *could* function makes it possible to come up with a *Teacher*-based moral code rooted in the theory of mental symmetry, or in the language of Kant, to describe morality in terms of a categorical imperative. Teacher thought appreciates the order-within-complexity that results when many individual situations can be explained by a simple theory. When cognitive modules are fighting one another, functioning in a fragmented manner, or pursuing different strategies in different contexts, the result is mental *complexity*. But when cognitive modules operate in an integrated, consistent manner, this produces order-within-complexity. How can the mind achieve the *greatest* level of order-within-complexity? By functioning in a way that is consistent with mental hardware, which one could also describe as 'reaching mental wholeness'. In contrast, any other type of mental functioning will end up being more complicated, just as using a hammer to dig holes and a shovel to hammer nails is more complicated than using a shovel to dig holes and a hammer to drive in nails.

If one follows this chain of thought, then I suggest that one ends up with a more rigorous version of the *golden rule*, which is generally phrased as, "Do unto your neighbor as you would have them do unto you." In 1993, 143 religious leaders from all of the world's major religions declared at a Parliament of the World's Religions in Chicago that the golden rule forms a fundamental principle of human morality. Thus, one can regard this rule as a universal moral standard of existing religions.

In brief, cognitive style combined with cognitive modules makes the golden rule equivalent to reaching mental wholeness. That is because one of the deepest personal needs is for an individual to have the freedom and ability to use conscious thought. In the language of Maslow's hierarchy of needs, which is analyzed in an appendix, using the cognitive module that is conscious is the most basic form of self-actualization. But that same cognitive module also exists within all other cognitive styles, though in subconscious form. Therefore, if I want to reach mental wholeness by using all seven cognitive modules within my own mind, then this is mentally equivalent to respecting the conscious operation of all seven cognitive styles. If I find Exhorter persons bothersome, for instance, then Exhorter mode within my *own* mind is probably functioning inadequately. Likewise, if I shut down Mercy mode within my mind, then I will probably treat Mercy persons in a similar manner.

Going further, in order to treat my neighbor *as* myself, I must use Perceiver and Server thought to *compare* my behavior and my situations with the behavior and situations of my neighbor. When this Perceiver and Server comparing is done within the context of cognitive modules, it will discover that similar mental behavior shows up repeatedly, consistently, and in many different contexts, leading to the formation of a *general theory* of human behavior within Teacher thought, which, by definition, will create an image of God, because it is a general Teacher theory of *human* behavior.

Therefore, not only do cognitive style and cognitive modules make practicing the golden rule equivalent to reaching mental wholeness, but this will also create an image of God that is consistent with mental hardware—the only type of image of God that a mind is capable of holding over the long term. Any other concept of God will lead to mental complexity, bringing emotional pain to Teacher thought, and it will end up fighting the built-in structure of the human mind, bringing hyper-pain to Teacher thought.

It is interesting that the formulation of the golden rule which one finds in the Gospels combines these two factors, and Jesus also adds that this version of the golden rule brings order to the entire complexity of Jewish religious law: "'You shall love the LORD your God with all your heart, with all your soul, and with all your mind.' This is the first and great commandment. And the second is like it: 'You shall love your neighbor as yourself.' On these two commandments hang all the Law and the Prophets." (Matt. 22:38-40)

Let us go through the main points once more, this time from a more practical perspective. I suggest that mental symmetry creates a more *rigorous* version of the golden rule by defining 'me' and 'my neighbor' more precisely. If one does not know how the mind functions, or how one mind differs from another, then I suggest that one will end up applying the golden rule inadequately. For instance, suppose that I really love receiving gifts of chocolate. My natural reaction will be to 'do unto others' by giving them chocolate. But what if the other person hates chocolate, or is allergic to it? By giving him chocolate, I am not really treating him the way that I would like him to treat me, because what I *really* want is for others to know and meet my personal needs. In order to treat another person in that fashion, I must first know what his personal needs are and how to meet them, which means knowing how his mind functions and not just extrapolating from my own personal experiences. Thus, if the golden rule is to function adequately, it must be placed within the larger context of a general understanding of human personality—it must be guided by a *trained* Theory of Mind.

Cognitive Mode	Needs Freedom to...
Mercy	Work with emotional experiences guided by emotional absolutes.
Perceiver	Build and evaluate facts guided by factual absolutes.
Teacher	Use words to form general theories and be guided by theories.
Server	Construct and follow sequences guided by fundamental sequences.
Exhorter	Have novelty and excitement, without boredom or frustration.
Contributor	Build, modify, and implement plans within an area of expertise.
Facilitator	Adjust and experiment, within a framework of solid facts and procedures.

The theory of mental symmetry trains Theory of Mind in four major ways: First, it forces me to *acknowledge* 'neighbors' whom I would normally try to ignore. For instance, it is easy for a Perceiver person to treat other Perceiver persons as 'neighbors' and to apply the golden rule to them. But when the Perceiver person and the Exhorter person meet, then the natural tendency is for one to suppress the thinking of the other, because the typical Exhorter person exaggerates too much for the Perceiver person, while most Exhorter persons regard Perceiver persons as technical and boring. However, if one knows which cognitive modules exist, and if one attempts within one's own mind to get them all to function in an integrated manner, then one will acknowledge the existence of these cognitive modules when one encounters them in other cognitive styles. If I as a Perceiver person give Exhorter *mode* within my own mind the freedom to function, then I will also give an Exhorter *person* the freedom to be himself.

Second, a *theory* of mental symmetry replaces a *personal* Mercy viewpoint with a *universal* Teacher viewpoint. Instead of regarding others as modified versions of myself, I can see both others and myself as specific expressions of a universal theory of human personality. Thus, rather than starting with the idea that I like chocolate and then trying to modify this by remembering that other people may not share my tastes, I can begin with the idea that people exist who actually like raw seafood and that they are not just pretending to like raw seafood while suppressing a hidden desire for chocolate.

Third, mental symmetry makes it possible for me to understand more *clearly* what another person truly wishes. It is easy for one Perceiver person to understand the personal needs of another Perceiver person. It is much harder for the Perceiver person and the Exhorter person to comprehend each other's needs. Understanding precisely how each cognitive module functions makes it possible for me to mentally 'put myself in the shoes of another person'. Thus, not only can I realize that some people like raw seafood, but I can also understand—to some extent—what it *means* to like raw seafood.

Finally, mental symmetry gives me a *reason* to apply the golden rule. Suppose that I as a Perceiver person wish to develop Exhorter thought within my own mind. The easiest way to do this is by spending time with an Exhorter *person*. If I respect his way of thinking and meet his personal needs, then this will end up programming my own Exhorter module, and I will experience the personal benefits of a more integrated mind.

Let us turn our attention now to the task of building the Perceiver and Server structure that makes it possible to treat my neighbor *as* myself. I mentioned earlier that a rule of conscience is formed when a Contributor connection of cause-and-effect is applied to personal identity. For instance, mother may tell me that if I do not eat my broccoli, then I will not get any dessert.

When one is constructing a building, then the primary limitation is the strength of the building material. If the load-bearing members cannot handle the stress, then the building will collapse. Similarly, I suggest that the extent to which one can build mentally will ultimately be limited by the level of Perceiver confidence and Server confidence. This leads us to formulate the following basic principles of mental cause-and-effect: If I *think* in an emotional situation either by blindly accepting the facts, or by suppressing my emotions, then I will become less able to handle stress. However, if I respond to an emotional situation by holding on to the facts while also acknowledging the feelings, then I will become more able to handle stress. Similarly, if I *act* in an emotional situation either by blindly following instructions, or else by 'doing my own thing' and ignoring what is happening around me, then I will become less able to handle stress. However, if I carry out my own actions while at the same time acknowledging and responding to my environment, then I will become more able to handle stress.

Learning how to apply the golden rule may sound complicated, but in practice it is usually rather obvious what needs to be done. Most children already spend the formative years of their lives enduring the process of education, and so we are looking here at modifying an existing process rather than creating one from scratch. And most of this modification involves changing the *way* in which one thinks and acts, and not changing the thoughts and actions themselves. For instance, suppose that I am attending school. I can either treat the classes as unpleasant Mercy experiences to endure, or I can see them as opportunities to develop a Teacher understanding. Similarly, I have learned that performing in a musical concert can be seen as an emotional crisis to get through or as an opportunity to learn how to function under stress.

Unfortunately, there are disciplines and industries which are based upon the assumption of mental fragmentation, where the prime purpose is to gain personal advantage by preying upon the mental or physical weaknesses of other individuals. Acting in such a manner violates the golden rule, and no amount of rationalization will alter this conclusion.

That brings us to the matter of *mental networks*. If one has reached the second stage of applying the theory of mental symmetry, then this theory will have turned into a Teacher mental network, and like all mental networks, it will wish to be 'fed' with compatible information and it will generate hyper-pain if it is forced to endure incompatible information.

I suggest that this Teacher mental network will *automatically* drive most of the process of applying the theory of mental symmetry. When a situation arises where the theory of mental symmetry could be applied in a way that develops the mind and leads to greater mental integration, then, like any mental network, the theory of mental symmetry will make its presence known and will suggest the appropriate course of action.

The key is knowing how to respond when the Teacher mental network of mental symmetry is triggered at the same time as some *other* mental network. If this other network is a *Mercy* mental network which is suggesting a course of action that *attacks* mental integrity and is *opposed* to mental wholeness, then one will have to choose between one hyper-pain and another. Either one decides to build up the mind or else one chooses to destroy the mind. In religious terms, one must choose between 'obeying God' and 'obeying man'. Stated that way, the choice appears obvious, but unless one can view a situation in such stark terms, I suggest that it will be very difficult to choose mental integrity when one is caught in the middle of the dilemma and exposed to all of the emotional pressures. That is why it is better not to perform jobs or enter occupations which require, create, or assume a lack of mental integrity. Achieving mental wholeness is already a difficult task. Why make it harder?

Another possibility is for the Mercy mental network to be *consistent* with mental integrity and mental wholeness. This will happen when one performs a job or enters an occupation that *requires* mental content and mental integrity. In this case, the principle of *altruistic* action applies. If one simply obeys orders or 'goes with the flow', then one will be doing the right action for the wrong reason. In order to mentally connect Teacher understanding with Server action, one must choose to perform the action guided *solely* by the Teacher mental network and not by any Mercy mental network. In other words, one must mentally turn the hypothetical imperative into a categorical imperative. This altruistic action needs to be continued until the action provides its own emotional reward. Once that point has been reached, then Mercy mental networks, such as receiving approval or getting paid, can and should be added. As was mentioned previously, this step of altruism only needs to be carried out *once* within each mental context, because all related situations will be regarded as Server similar because they mentally fall within the same *family* of problems.

The final possibility is for the Teacher mental network of mental symmetry to come into contact with some other *Teacher* mental network. In this case, the first step is to work out the relationship between these two general Teacher theories, by attempting to translate one theory into the language of the other. Once this has been done successfully, then it will probably be necessary to carry out a set of altruistic actions in order to apply the theory of mental symmetry to this new mental context. In this case, the related situations will be regarded as Perceiver similar because a new *family* of problems has been uncovered.

We can illustrate what it means to apply mental symmetry with a brief description of the mental process which occurred within my *own* mind. When I started studying human personality, my brother and I began by using a system of cognitive styles to divide people into the seven different categories of Perceiver person, Mercy person, and so on. The end result was a collection of Perceiver facts tied together by a general Teacher theory. Instead of viewing people as mental networks within Mercy thought, we began to see them as specific illustrations of a general theory within Teacher thought: "There goes John, a typical example of a Perceiver person. His wife is Mary, a Mercy person. It is very common for the Perceiver person to marry the Mercy person." Because our general Teacher theory of human personality had formed into a Teacher mental network within my mind, I was able to approach people more rationally on the basis of Perceiver facts, and I was less susceptible to the emotional tricks used by fields such as marketing and religion, which appeal to mental networks within Mercy thought. However, I still had a *verbal* theory and was locked within the Teacher shortcut of words.

Over time, I gradually began to realize that the theory of mental symmetry is not *just* a set of seven Perceiver categories into which one can sort human beings. Instead, it also describes a *process* by which the mind develops. In order to understand this process, I had to acquire certain mental skills. First, like the scientist modifying his equation of $f =$

ma, I had to learn how to translate the diagram of mental symmetry to fit the particular situation. For instance, what function was Perceiver mode playing in economics, in education, in religion, or in my Mercy mother when she could not remember where she had stored something for safekeeping?

Second, I realized that simply observing human behavior was insufficient. Instead, I had to combine theory with practice. Thus, as I learned more clearly how each cognitive module functioned, I attempted to develop that mode of thought within my own mind. This personal practical application added Server stability to my verbal Teacher theories. Finally, just as the student of science learns his craft through endless problem-solving, so I found that my understanding of mental symmetry developed through years of analyzing, translating, and applying. Eventually, this skill became second nature, just as the trained scientist instinctively applies the scientific method to situations that he encounters.

Third, it gradually became apparent that I was not just attempting to use Server actions to *apply* a verbal Teacher theory, but the Teacher theory *itself* was based in the inherent behavior of cognitive modules. This realization tended to occur in cycles. Whenever I wrote about mental symmetry, the theory would become more math-like, turning into a *verbal* theory held together by internal logic. Similarly, when I took steps to apply the theory, then my focus would turn to personal reward. But when my verbal understanding came into question or my practical application was thwarted, then I would step back, look at the evidence, and decide again that people really *do* seem to behave in a predictable manner—which is not too hard to do when one is continually being faced with examples of people behaving in a predictable manner. But each episode of verbal theorizing or practical application made it possible for me to observe this behavior with greater depth and accuracy.

Before we move on, I would like to make some final comments about escaping the Teacher shortcut. Remember that education uses two shortcuts. The Perceiver shortcut uses Mercy status to mesmerize Perceiver mode in accepting 'truth' from experts, while the Teacher shortcut uses words to build general theories within Teacher thought. Escaping the Perceiver shortcut is fairly straightforward. Critical thinking helps Perceiver thought to 'wake up', while the Teacher emotions produced by a general theory replace the Mercy feelings of status that are associated with the expert. The tricky part lies in conveying the right facts and teaching the right general theory. If Perceiver thought is taught facts that are not really true, then critical thinking cannot be permitted, because this would cause Perceiver thought to reject the facts that were taught. And if the facts really do not fit together, then Teacher thought will not acquire the Teacher emotions of order-within-complexity. When Perceiver truth and Teacher theory is lacking, then one will eventually find oneself back at square one: talking to students and using Mercy emotions to keep them submissive and mentally pliable.

On the surface, escaping the Teacher shortcut also appears straightforward. If a person is doing, then it is obvious that he is no longer merely talking. And once a person starts doing, then he can take his mind off words and start to focus upon experiences. But what if the actions are unnatural or difficult? Words of exhortation and instruction will then be required to keep the actions happening. This means that one has not *really* escaped the Teacher shortcut, because the actions will only continue as long the words continue. However, if the actions are *natural*—if they flow, then a continual stream of words will not be necessary. And, what is *natural* action? Action that is consistent with how the environment itself functions.

This principle is easy to grasp when dealing with *physical* action and *natural* law, but I suggest that it also applies to a theory of the mind. Suppose that I develop some grand new theory of human personality. I will feel that I need to get the message out, spread the word, and gather an audience. But if the theory describes how the mind *really* functions, then endless talking is not required. Instead, one simply has to point out processes which are already occurring within the mind. And even if words cannot be used, it is still possible to build the structure of a Teacher understanding by juxtaposing mental processes in non-verbal ways. When this realization sinks in, then one becomes emotionally free of the mental tyranny of Teacher words—one *truly* escapes the Teacher shortcut. This does not mean that one stops speaking altogether. Instead, one attempts to say the right words at the right time, in order to make people aware of what is *already happening* within their minds.

A similar principle applies to religious proselytizing. The religious believer who feels that he must *preach* about his religion and continually *tell* others about God is caught within the Teacher shortcut of words. He is convinced that *words* hold together his concept of God and that *words* are needed to spread his concept of God. But if an image of God is ultimately based in how the *mind* functions, then endless preaching is not necessary. In fact, excessive preaching is counterproductive, because it distracts a person from paying attention to what is happening within his mind. Instead, what is needed is to say the right words at the right time, in order to point out to a person how he can reach mental wholeness by harnessing *existing* mental processes.

But one still needs something that can *replace* the abstract realm of Teacher words, which means re-entering the concrete world of Mercy experiences. However, the goal is not to *return* to existing Mercy experiences, but rather to use Teacher words and Teacher understanding to *transform* Mercy experiences. That brings us to our next major topic.

Platonic Forms

The second stage of education focuses upon the relationship between Teacher words and Server actions. We will now turn our attention to the *Mercy* benefits that result from combining words with actions, which describes what occurs during the *third* stage of education. However, in order to understand how words, facts, and actions affect Mercy thought, we will have to go back to the first stage of education and analyze what is happening within Mercy thought as the process of education is unfolding, beginning with Plato's concept of *Forms.*

We know that Perceiver mode looks for connections between Mercy experiences that are *repeated*. At the most basic level, this leads to object recognition. For instance, all Mercy experiences about chairs have in common the features of four legs supporting a horizontal flat surface that is connected to a vertical flat surface. Perceiver mode notices these repeated connections and comes up with the fact of a chair. That much we already know. However, when a person thinks of a chair, what comes to mind is not just a generic chair with four legs, a seat, and a back, but rather a stylized, simplified, regularized version of a generic chair. Plato referred to this *idealized* generic version of a chair as the *Form* of a chair, which I will refer to by capitalizing the word, in order to distinguish between a Platonic Form and using 'form' as a normal verb or noun.

This tells us that Perceiver facts are being *modified* by Teacher mode. Teacher thought is turning the Perceiver facts about a chair into a general theory about a chair by getting rid of all of the details and focusing upon the essentials of 'chairness'. This is a miniature version of the same process that occurs during the first stage of education, because Mercy experiences are leading to Perceiver facts which are being formed into general Teacher theories. But when Perceiver facts are modified by Teacher mode, then this has an indirect effect upon Mercy memories. Thus, when a person hears the word 'chair', what Mercy mode recalls is the image of an imaginary, idealized chair which does not exist in real life.

This Teacher-driven idealizing process can continue further. For instance, suppose that I refer to a *triangle*. Chairs exist in real life. Thus, the Form of a chair describes the idealized image of a *real* object. Triangles, though, do not exist. Instead, a triangle is a *general* description that applies to *many* types of specific objects, indicating again the presence of Teacher thought. However, when one thinks of a triangle, what comes to mind is not any triangular shape, but rather the mental image of an *equilateral* triangle, one which has been simplified and regularized so that all of the sides are the same length. According to Plato, there are six levels of Forms, beginning at the lowest level with the mental image of an object, with each level of Form being a generalization of the level below it. At the highest level is the Form of Good.

Here is the progression in more technical detail: Perceiver mode begins by looking for solid connections between Mercy experiences, a step which involves *concrete* thought. Then, Teacher mode comes up with words that describe these various Perceiver categories, a step which crosses over from concrete thought to *abstract* thought. For instance, suppose that Perceiver mode notices the repeated occurrence of horizontal and vertical surfaces attached to four legs. This repetition will convince Perceiver thought that this is a stable category. Teacher mode will then come up with the word 'chair' for this Perceiver category, and the Perceiver category will become the *meaning* of the Teacher word 'chair'. Can this process work without words? Possibly, but words form the normal basic building blocks for Teacher thought.

Once the basic Teacher words and Perceiver meanings have been established, then Teacher emotion will guide the process further. Perceiver categories will be adjusted so that Teacher thought can focus upon a verbal description that is simple and elegant, because this produces the greatest Teacher feelings of order-within-complexity. For instance, when observing chairs, Perceiver mode may notice that the seat and the back are usually shaped to fit the contours of the human form. But there is no simple way for Teacher thought to *describe* this shape. It is much simpler for Teacher thought to describe a chair seat as a flat trapezoidal shape with rounded corners. Likewise, the simplest way to describe a chair leg is as a tube or a cylinder. These adjusted Perceiver facts about chair parts will then lead to the modified, idealized Form of a chair within Mercy thought.

The development of *equal-tempered pitch* in music provides an illustration of this simplifying and idealizing process, and I will try to describe this in a way that makes sense to those who are not familiar with music. The primary intervals in the musical scale are the octave, the perfect fifth, and the perfect fourth. These musical intervals feel good because the frequencies of the notes are related by simple ratios. For instance, if one begins the song *Twinkle Twinkle Little Star* with the A that is just below middle C, then the first note has a frequency of 220 Hz and the second has a frequency of 330 Hz. 330/220 = 3:2, which is a simple ratio, known musically as a perfect fifth. According to legend, Pythagoras, the Greek mathematician, was the first to discover that perfect intervals are related by simple ratios.

If one tunes a piano so that all of the perfect intervals are in-tune, then one discovers that the instrument will only sound in-tune in the key in which it was tuned, and that it will sound distinctly *out*-of-tune when one plays in unrelated keys. However, if the intervals on a piano are slightly *mistuned* so that every adjacent piano key is related by the *same* ratio, then it becomes possible to play in any key. This slight mistuning is known as *equal-tempered pitch*. Johann Sebastian Bach was the first Western composer to popularize the use of a version of equal-tempered pitch, a concept initially developed in China.

Translating this into the language of mental symmetry, Mercy mode handles *non-verbal* speech, including musical tones. When tones with similar frequencies are played together, Mercy thought feels good. Perceiver mode notices that this occurs repeatedly, and comes up with a set of facts regarding musical intervals. These Perceiver facts are then adjusted to produce greater Teacher generality and simplicity, for equal-tempered pitch makes it possible to play in any key, and it allows all musical intervals to be described using the single ratio of approximately 1.059:1. But using the principles of equal-tempered pitch to mistune musical intervals also has an indirect impact upon Mercy thought, because all music will now sound slightly out-of-tune. For the ear that is accustomed to tempered pitch, true pitch can actually end up sounding slightly 'wrong'. For those who wish to follow this reasoning further, I have included an analysis of music in an appendix.

Changing Perception

Let us move on to the next point. We have seen how Perceiver facts are being modified to increase Teacher feelings of generality. And we know that Perceiver facts provide the meanings for Teacher words. One of the results is that it will become difficult to *translate* one theory into the language of another, or to *explain* one paradigm to those who follow a different paradigm. For even if these two theories use the same Teacher words, the Perceiver meanings that are applied to these words will be subtly different. As Kuhn puts it: "Since new paradigms are born from old ones, they ordinarily incorporate much of the vocabulary and apparatus, both conceptual and manipulative, that the traditional paradigm had previously employed. But they seldom employ these borrowed elements in quite the traditional way. Within the new paradigm, old terms, concepts, and experiments fall into relationships one with the other. The inevitable result is what we must call, though the term is not quite right, a misunderstanding between the two competing schools."

And when Perceiver categories are shifted, this not only alters the meanings of words, but it also adjusts the Perceiver categories that the mind uses to observe its environment. Kuhn describes this effect as well: "These examples point to the third and most fundamental aspect of the incommensurability of competing paradigms. In a sense that I am unable to explicate further, the proponents of competing paradigms practice their trades in different worlds...The two groups of scientists see different things when they look from the same point in the same direction. Again, that is not to say that they can see anything they please. Both are looking at the world, and what they look at has not changed. But in some areas they see different things, and they see them in different relations one to the other."

Kuhn's quote contains a perceptive remark which leads us to our next point: "The proponents of competing paradigms practice their trades in different worlds." A general Teacher theory ties together many separate elements through order-within-complexity. When this integrating effect reflects back upon Mercy thought, then Mercy experiences will also become interconnected. Think, for instance, of Plato's hierarchy of Forms culminating in the Form of Good. When a person accepts a new paradigm, then his mental hierarchy of Forms will change as well, leading internally to the formation of a new and different world within Mercy thought. The experiences may be all the same, but the way in which these experiences are connected has changed, together with the Forms that express the ideal versions of these experiences.

When the focus is upon science and objective thought, then the natural tendency will be for students to use these idealized facts to build general theories within Teacher thought. For instance, geometry takes the Forms of Plato, such as triangles, line, circles, and planes, and uses them to construct a general Teacher theory of logical manipulation. Geometry was invented by Euclid, a Greek who lived about a century later than Plato.

The Holy Spirit and Heaven

So far we have looked at what happens when dealing with *objective* Mercy experiences. When subjective Mercy emotions are added to the equation, then a paradigm turns into a mental image of God, and Plato's hierarchy of Forms becomes a *Mercy* concept of universality which is an expression of a person's image of God but also distinct from it. Let me say this one more time: An image of God is produced when a general Teacher theory explains personal Mercy experiences. When an image of God is combined with solid Perceiver facts, then this will cause a system of Forms to emerge within Mercy thought, leading to the Mercy image of universal, interrelated, Platonic Forms. In religious language, this Mercy image is a *Holy Spirit* of *Truth*. It is holy because it is connected with a mental image of God and is distinct from and more perfect than normal experiences; it is a spirit because it is an invisible image that resides within Mercy thought; it is an expression of Truth because it is formed when Perceiver facts that describe repeated connections rearrange Mercy experiences.

Compare this with the fragmented nature of the childish mind, in which each emotional experience within Mercy thought defines its own local version of Perceiver 'truth' and external input from the environment determines which mental fragment will currently be active.

Because this Mercy sense of universal spirit is the indirect result of a general Teacher theory, it will not be grasped by those who follow a competing paradigm. Instead, as Kuhn states, each paradigm will build its own unique way of viewing the world. And because we are now dealing with a general theory which *includes* subjective emotions, this means that each image of God will build a unique concept of *Holy* Spirit, a concept that is not shared by those who have a different concept of God.

Related to the Holy Spirit of Truth is the concept of *heaven*. I suggest that the convergence of several cognitive factors will to lead naturally to a belief in heaven. First, Plato felt that the world of Forms is more real than the physical world because Forms are perfect, unchanging, and exist outside of space and time. We see in Plato's description several characteristics of Teacher thought: We already know that Teacher generalization and simplification causes Forms to be more perfect than the objects from which they are formed. And when we first discussed how the mind forms an image of God, we saw that Mercy thought will view a general Teacher theory as existing outside of space and time. Finally, because a Form is based upon Perceiver *repetition* held together by a timeless, universal theory, it will remain mentally fixed even as physical objects come and go.

Second, an aspect of personal identity will *live* within the internal Mercy 'environment' that is provided by the Holy Spirit of Truth. Here is the logic: An image of God forms when Teacher understanding explains personal identity. When this same Teacher understanding creates a system of Forms within Mercy thought, it makes sense that these Forms will also be related to personal identity. But they will relate to the *non-physical* aspect of personal identity, because Forms are by their very nature, non-physical. In contrast, the aspect of personal identity that relates to the physical body will be mentally connected with the physical objects which acted as the original source of these Forms.

Putting this together, every person knows that his physical body will eventually die. But suppose that the *non-physical* aspect of personal identity is mentally living within the idealized Mercy environment of the Holy Spirit of Truth. If the non-physical aspect of personal identity is already inhabiting a system of Forms which is permanent, unchanging, and more perfect than physical reality, the natural belief will be that a non-physical part of personal identity will continue to live after death in a non-physical realm which is more permanent and more perfect than physical existence, peopled by individuals who are purer and less flawed than their physical expressions. In essence, one could say that people in heaven are living in a sort of Euclidian geometry where everything is pure and simple, and all personal interaction is guided by Platonic love.

Notice that a belief in heaven goes *further* than what was mentioned in previous chapters. Because the Mercy mental networks that represent other people within Mercy thought will try to continue existing even when those other people die physically, this will lead to a general sense that current human personal existence continues unaltered after death. This cognitive effect occurs in *all* individuals. In contrast, the mental concept of a heaven of idealized perfection only emerges when a general Teacher theory based in Perceiver facts is used to describe personal identity.

The *non-physical* nature of Forms combined with the *physical* nature of human existence faces the religious believer with an internal conflict. On the one hand, only the non-physical aspect of his personal identity can relate directly to his concept of the Holy Spirit, because this concept is being generated by Forms which are perfected, idealized versions of physical reality. On the other hand, the physical needs of the physical body force an individual to turn his back on imaginary Forms and live within the imperfect, real world. If the religious believer ignores his physical body, then he will die. But if his personal existence ignores the internal world of Forms, then he fears that he will not be able to live in heaven when he dies. Notice that, unlike the previous similar mental effects which we have described, this mental effect will not happen to everyone. Instead, this effect will only occur when a concept of God leads indirectly to the emergence of a system of interconnected Forms.

Religious Self-denial

For the religious student who is still functioning within the Perceiver shortcut of emotional 'knowing', there is the additional factor of *religious self-denial.* Several chapters back, we compared the attitude of the child with that of the teenager. For the child, adults loom large and have emotional status that is much greater than the status of personal identity. As a result, the child will accept every Perceiver fact which an adult says as 'gospel truth'. However, when the child turns into a teenager, then he no longer regards adults as more important than he, and as a result he will no longer blindly swallow truth when it is spoken by an adult.

A holy book or textbook uses the emotional method of the child to implant Perceiver 'truth' into the mind of the student. If this Perceiver 'truth' is used to build a general theory and if this general theory turns into a Teacher mental network, then this Teacher mental network will only continue to exist as long as personal identity remains emotionally insignificant, for if personal identity gains sufficient emotional status, then this will bring into doubt the Perceiver 'truths' that were used to build the Teacher mental network. This combination of Mercy status and an image of God will generate potent feelings of religious self-denial, for if personal identity gains emotional status, then the image of God will feel personally threatened. In religious terms, the believer will feel that any display of self-worth exhibits the sin of pride and he will sense that pride hurts God deeply.

Notice that this religious self-denial is functioning, at least partially, at the level of *hyper*-emotion. Thus, the religious believer who bases his concept of God in blind 'belief' will actually feel that his personal *existence* is an affront to God; deep down, he will be troubled by the conviction that he has no *right* to exist.

For the religious believer who practices blind 'belief', Perceiver thought is seldom *totally* mesmerized. Instead, Perceiver mode is usually caught in a religious version of intuitive psychology, for Perceiver thought has sufficient confidence to manipulate religious concepts, but not enough confidence to analyze the doctrines themselves. Such an individual will talk about God and theology, but his religious facts will still be ultimately based in religious experts and holy books.

The desire to live in the utopia of heaven acts as the 'carrot', religious self-denial functions as the 'stick'. These two working together propel the religious student to the monastery and, to a lesser extent, the secular student to the 'ivory tower of academia'. Religious self-denial motivates the religious student to turn his back on personal prestige, suppress personal desire, and adopt an attitude of personal humility. The Form of Good replaces this with a life of order, purity, simplicity, and contemplation upon God. Thus, the monastery or some version of 'full-time service' is an attempt to live in heaven here on earth, by turning one's back upon personal and physical need and identifying as fully as possible with the non-physical heavenly realm of Forms.

I suggest that a *scientific* mindset will also lead to a confused view of heaven. On the one hand, scientific thought will cause Platonic Forms to emerge within Mercy thought, because the scientist is building general Teacher theories and these theories will lead to simplified and idealized Perceiver facts. Think, for instance, of the idealized facts and Forms of geometry. On the other hand, science bases its Perceiver facts upon physical evidence and insists that nothing 'exists' apart from physical reality. Thus, the Forms of science will only be idealized versions of physical objects and the Teacher theories of science will explain only the physical aspect of personal identity. As a result, science will verbally insist that physical death is the end for human existence and will declare that a non-physical heaven cannot exist.

However, when the scientist practices science, a non-physical aspect of his personal identity *is* living within an internal Mercy world of idealized physical objects. Therefore, the scientist will *act* as if some aspect of personal identity will survive physical death: He may try to do something of lasting significance in order to make a name for himself; he may attempt to save the physical environment from long-term catastrophe; he may work on a project which will not be finished during his lifetime. But what is the point of attempting to 'leave a personal legacy' if a person is not around to enjoy that personal legacy? That is logically inconsistent. And yet, the *Mercy* Forms that result from working with logically based Teacher theory will mentally drive a person to *act* as if part of personal existence will live forever, even if the *Teacher* theory which created these Mercy Forms explicitly *states* that personal existence does not continue forever.

So far, our discussion has looked at what happens when Perceiver mode is used but *not* Server mode. This type of education builds verbal theories and leads to imaginary images of perfection. These Platonic images remain castles in the air, utopias that exist only within the minds of thinkers, a heaven that can only be experienced after death 'by and by up in the sky', and which can only partially be realized here on earth by denying both physical reality and physical desire.

Turning dreams into reality requires the addition of *Server* mode. That is because Perceiver mode can create a mental image of perfection, but Server mode steps out and realizes this image. This principle is illustrated by the *Benedictine Order*, a family of monasteries which played a major role in civilizing medieval Europe. The primary motto of this order was *ora et labora*, or pray and work. Words were combined with actions, and all Benedictine monks were expected to study theology as well as perform manual labor. For many centuries the Benedictines ran most of the schools, preserved the ancient Greek writings, demonstrated efficient farming techniques, provided shelter to travelers, and helped reduce poverty. Thus, to a substantial degree, they did manage to turn vision into reality.

In a similar vein, it is interesting to note that the Biblical book of Revelation portrays heaven at the beginning of the book as a *passive* realm of endless religious self-denial in which everyone focuses upon the perfection of God. This is followed later in the book by a new group of religious believers who perform *active* service instead of passive worship. By the end of the book, the heaven of endless adoration has been replaced by an eternal city filled with the *bustle* of industry and commerce which descends out of heaven onto earth.

In general terms, if one wants to affect the external world, then one must use concrete thought, because we live in a concrete world. This means using Server actions to reach Mercy goals guided by a Perceiver map. Going further, if one wishes to *change* the way that one affects the external world, then one must develop new Server actions, new Mercy goals, and new Perceiver maps. Objective education develops new Perceiver maps by introducing Platonic Forms into the mind. But if this is the extent of education, then the result will be general theories that use words and symbols to manipulate Forms. This type of education will probably escape the Perceiver shortcut, but it will remain locked within the Teacher shortcut as well as leaving personal identity unchanged.

Religious education has the potential of moving further, because it adds the Mercy emotions of personal identity to the Platonic Forms of objective education. This will create the mental image of a better personal existence within Mercy thought, together with an Exhorter urge to live within this more perfect version of reality. However, the lack of Server actions will mean that this vision remains 'pie in the sky', while the presence of Mercy emotions will make it more difficult for Perceiver mode to function, leading to an image of God which requires an attitude of religious self-denial to remain intact. The religious student who is in this mental state will want to live in heaven, but he will not know how to make heaven real, and if he does get the opportunity to live in heaven, then he will feel that it is his duty to God to continue practicing self-denial. For such an individual, heaven means bowing before the throne of God in endless worship.

Scientific education will also move further, but in a different direction. Because science is objective, it will find it fairly easy to develop a Perceiver map of logical facts. And because science bases its Server sequences in the Server 'actions' of Nature, science will gain an understanding of natural processes. And because science uses abstract thought to manipulate these Server sequences, it will also learn how to use abstract thought to manipulate natural processes. And if science combines Teacher words with Server actions, then it will learn how to build machines that can harness natural processes, which people will use to transform the physical world. However, because Mercy identity is being ignored and because scientific facts and understanding deal primarily with physical reality, this will lead to a transformation of only the *physical* environment, leaving personal identity unaltered. That describes our present world. We beam soap operas into peoples' homes using geosynchronous satellites, and we build an international computer network in order to watch videos of cute cats. The solution is to combine the strengths of religious education and scientific education—to have God live with humans in the middle of a city that is heaven on earth.

Making Application Easier

Adding actions retroactively to an *existing* theory is not easy. When we examined the relationship between Perceiver mode and Mercy mode, we saw that the presence of Mercy emotions makes it difficult for Perceiver thought to function. That is because the human mind is bombarded with Mercy emotions. Teacher emotions, in contrast, take longer to form. However, if a student remains locked within the Teacher shortcut for a long enough time, then the strong *Teacher* emotions generated by his *verbal* theories will make it difficult for Server thought to function.

One sees this, for instance, in the *absent-minded professor*. His mind is focused so fully upon the Teacher emotions of his general theories that he literally loses the ability to perform the Server actions of everyday life. To a lesser extent, every academic faces a similar struggle.

I suggest that there are two main reasons why it is difficult to move beyond theory to application. The first problem is that actions are *specific*. It feels good to live within generality and to use words and symbols to address universal problems. Adding Server action to this general theory means stepping down from the clouds of generality and walking on the solid earth one physical step at a time. Because applying a theory means doing *specific* actions guided by a *general* understanding, Server confidence is required, for one must continue to act in the presence of Teacher emotion without allowing the mind to focus upon this Teacher emotion.

The second problem is that action is *messy*. Working with Platonic lines, planes, triangles, and other Forms is clean and neat, and Teacher thought appreciates such elegance and simplicity. Physical action messes up this perfection with the complexities of real life. One sees this contrast in the relationship between physics and engineering. When solving physics problems, one usually works with perfect objects moving within a simplified, idealized world. In this sort of environment, equations work well and solutions are elegant. Engineering, in contrast, must deal with real objects moving within a complicated, actual world. As a result, simple equations have to be modified to deal with real world situations, and 'fudge factors' have to be added to the results to account for possible inaccuracies. When equations have to be modified and results have to be fudged, then the result is a drop in Teacher pleasure.

Technology bridges both of these gaps—in the *external* world. First, the *specific* nature of Server actions is changed through the use of *machines*. Using a shovel and muscle power, a single worker can only move a small amount of dirt. However, that same worker can dig an entire foundation in a few hours using an earthmoving machine. Thus, the machine increases the generality of Server actions, lessening significantly the emotional gap between theory and action.

Second, technology transforms the world into a form that is more regular and more consistent. For instance, several years ago I visited a museum in Israel on the Sea of Galilee which contains the shell of a fishing boat dating from the Roman era. The boat is completely irregular without a single square edge or straight line. Instead of being constructed out of rectangular planks, each piece of wood was individually shaped as it was added to the existing uneven structure. In contrast, the modern framework holding this ancient relic is formed out of metal tubing that is gleaming, precise, and visually flawless. Even the scale model which shows how the boat once appeared was built using miniature rectangular planks with square edges and uniform sizes. Comparing the frame with the artifact, it feels as if reality is being held by a Platonic Form. Teacher thought finds far more pleasure in a world that is regular and smooth than one which is messy and misshapen.

And, looking forward to the next chapter, I suggest that when sufficient Perceiver facts and Server sequences are acquired, then it becomes possible for the mind *itself* to begin functioning in a *technical* manner which is more regular and consistent than normal thought. And one of the main features of technical thought is that it is capable of integrating the specific actions of concrete thought with the general theories of abstract thought.

False Gods

Science and technology have produced a world that is far more clean and structured, but this regularity and simplicity is limited to the external world of objects. Thus, buying an item at the store is smooth and simple, while personal relationships remain messy, misshapen, and disordered. Probing deeper, the *absence* of subjective Mercy emotions has created a world that is mechanistic and inhuman, in which humans are treated either as objects or machines. Looking even deeper, these inhuman, object-oriented social systems have then been used to meet personal human needs, creating false images of God that pretend to deal with personal identity, but which only address peoples' physical, social, and occasionally psychological needs.

For instance, consider the typical large corporation. Its official purpose is to deliver financial value for its stockholders. In other words, it is driven by money, an *external* symbol of subjective Mercy emotions. Each company is ruled by a system of general procedures. The employee who spends years working within a corporation learns how to combine the written regulations of his company with the actions of 'working the system'. In return, the corporation provides the worker with employment, housing, medical coverage, and other fringe benefits, addressing all of the physical needs of the employee. As a result, the company mentally functions as God for its workers by creating a system of Teacher order within which they exist.

A monotheistic image of God is universal and extends beyond space and time. However, if a system of Teacher order applies to all of an individual's *personal* experiences, both past and future, then as far as that person is concerned, the image of God that is produced *is* universal. In many Asian companies, lifetime employment at a single corporation is the norm, and the employee is expected to spend most of his waking hours at the company. In addition, the personal services that an Asian company provides for its employees are extensive, including entertainment, holidays, and even matchmaking. Thus, cognitively speaking, the Asian corporation takes the place of a monotheistic God for its employees.

The United States has followed a slightly different path. Instead of taking the place of God, the American corporation has officially displaced the human individual, for according to American law, the corporation is legally regarded as a person with all of the rights of a human individual. As a result, most current American legislation protects the 'personal' rights of the corporation while ignoring the rights of the human individual. But what type of 'person' is the corporation? It is a superhuman entity with much greater power than any individual human, it does not have a limited lifespan, it is not restricted to a specific physical location, and it is untroubled by normal human emotions of conscience or guilt. In other words, it possesses many of the attributes of a divine being. Thus, while the American corporation may be a person in the eyes of the law, for the average citizen it acts as a god.

And the corporation is not the only example of modern, massive inhumanity. There is also big government and big labor, together with the numerous international professional societies and accreditation boards which govern personal activity. All of these have filled the emotional gap left by objective science and technology and have created mental images of God.

Notice how this concept of God relates to the one discussed in a previous chapter. Earlier on, we saw that a concept of God can form when some group becomes a source of Perceiver rules for society. Here, we are seeing that a system of Server procedures can also lead to a concept of God. Looking at this historically, *countries* used to claim the right to *speak* for God. However, today it is more common for the *corporation* to *act* as God.

Summary

Applying the theory of mental symmetry is an indirect process. During the first stage, the primary goal is to observe the behavior of cognitive modules and mental networks in order to construct a general Teacher theory of human thought. The easiest way to start is by analyzing the behavior of friends, family members, and colleagues whose cognitive styles are easy to determine. This will lead to the development of Mercy mental networks which represent the typical behavior of each cognitive style. In essence, one is attempting to educate Theory of Mind to look beyond the obvious behavior that is being produced by the mental networks of other people to the less obvious, but more pervasive, behavior that is being driven by cognitive modules. These same Mercy mental networks will make it possible to analyze *subconscious* thought. For instance, if I learn how the typical Mercy person behaves, I will be able to recognize Mercy mode when it is functioning within my own mind.

The diagram of mental symmetry makes it possible to integrate these various observations through the help of a simple Teacher theory. Thus, the Mercy mental networks that were acquired from observing others and self will eventually become held together by the Teacher mental network of a general understanding, and because this general understanding explains personal identity, it will form an image of God. This image of God will be the most potent if mental symmetry is used to analyze both scientific and religious thought. When this Teacher mental network emerges, it will feel as if the theory is 'eating up the mind', but that is to be expected.

The contrast between mental 'hardware' and mental 'software' provides a solution to the 'is-ought' problem posed by David Hume. The mental hardware of cognitive modules describes how the mind could function, while the mental software of mental networks controls how the mind does function. The discrepancy between 'is' and 'ought' leads to a system of morality which takes the form of a categorical imperative, because mental functioning that is compatible with mental hardware is elegant and structured, whereas mental functioning that violates mental hardware is complicated. One could describe this system of morality as 'reaching mental wholeness'.

Cognitive style combined with cognitive modules makes practicing the golden rule equivalent to reaching mental wholeness, because the way that I treat a certain cognitive style will correspond to the way that I treat that cognitive module within my own mind.

During the second stage of applying the theory of mental symmetry, the Teacher mental network of mental symmetry will motivate a person to reach his mental potential by using the 'hardware' of cognitive modules more effectively, instead of being limited by the 'software' of mental programming. If this guidance *conflicts* with Mercy mental networks, then a person will have to choose which mental network to follow. If it is *consistent* with Mercy mental networks, then altruistic behavior is required to become righteous. If other *Teacher* mental networks are triggered, then they will need to be translated into the language of mental symmetry.

Perceiver mode organizes Mercy experiences into objects. These Perceiver facts can be mentally modified to increase Teacher feelings of generality, which will have the indirect effect of creating imaginary images in Mercy thought that are purer, simpler, and more elegant than the original Mercy memories which were the source of the Perceiver facts. By continuing this process, the mind can generate increasingly idealized images within Mercy thought, leading to Plato's hierarchy of Forms.

When Perceiver facts are adjusted to increase Teacher emotions, then this will affect both Teacher words and Mercy experiences. On the Teacher side, the meanings of words will subtly change, making it difficult to translate one paradigm into the language of another paradigm. On the Mercy side, the categories used in object and fact recognition will shift. As a result, people with different paradigms will actually view the physical world in slightly different ways.

Because a general Teacher theory ties together many related items, a paradigm has the indirect effect of bringing unity to Mercy thought. When this general theory explains subjective experiences, then the resulting Mercy unity will be viewed as a Holy Spirit of Truth. This will lead to a split in personal identity. Part of identity will relate to the physical body and the external world of real objects, while another aspect of personal identity will relate to the internal, idealistic, unchanging realm of Forms, leading naturally to the belief that the aspect of personal identity that relates to the realm of Forms will survive physical death and live with God in an eternal realm that is purer, simpler, and flawless.

The emotional perfection associated with the internal realm of Forms will also create an Exhorter urge to live in this realm by adopting a life of simplicity that focuses upon God and ignores physical reality. This drive can be mentally reinforced by the feeling of religious self-denial that results from building a concept of God upon a factual foundation of emotional 'knowing'.

The mental tension between reality and Forms can be relieved by using Server actions that are guided by Teacher understanding to change reality so that it matches the Form more closely. In general terms, this means using abstract thought to transform concrete thought.

Adding Server action to a general Teacher understanding is not easy. Because actions are *specific*, applying theory stops Teacher thought from focusing upon the pleasure of generality. And because the world is *messy*, applying theory faces Teacher thought with experiences that do not fit the general rule. In the *physical* world, technology has minimized both of these tensions. Machines allow humans to perform Server actions which are far more general than the specific actions of manual labor, while modern manufacturing has created a world of objects which are more regular and Form-like than the natural environment.

Science and technology have transformed the physical environment, but personal identity remains unaltered. This subjective vacuum has been filled by corporations, governments, and organized labor. By catering to the personal needs of individuals, these various general entities have implicitly formed mental images of God. And when an individual spends most of his lifetime working within one of these entities, then, as far as that person is concerned, the institution functions as a monotheistic God.

✷ 11. Technical Thought

We have stepped into the geometry classroom to watch for a few minutes as well as taking some time to examine the science student as he learns his craft. We will now drive across town to the university in order to observe the scientist at work. While we are on the way, let us see if we can predict what we will find. We should see scientists discovering new Perceiver facts, building novel general Teacher theories, and coming up with experiments to test their hypotheses. After all, this describes the scientific method, and it is obvious that scientists practice the scientific method.

This does describe a large aspect of what I have been doing, for I have spent over two decades gathering evidence from various sources about human personality and using this data to develop, check, and test the general theory of mental symmetry. And I continually find myself in situations where I either have to translate the theory of mental symmetry into the language of another paradigm in order to communicate with others or else translate another paradigm into the language of mental symmetry in order to evaluate that paradigm.

However, when I interact with scientists, I generally find that they are doing something quite different. This contrast between what scientists *supposedly* do and what they *usually* do forms the core of Thomas Kuhn's theory of scientific thought.

According to Kuhn, "Mopping-up operations are what engage most scientists throughout their careers. They constitute what I am here calling normal science. Closely examined, whether historically or in the contemporary laboratory, that enterprise seems an attempt to force nature into the preformed and relatively inflexible box that the paradigm supplies. No part of the aim of normal science is to call forth new sorts of phenomena; indeed those that will not fit the box are often not seen at all. Nor do scientists normally aim to invent new theories, and they are often intolerant of those invented by others. Instead, normal-scientific research is directed to the articulation of those phenomena and theories that the paradigm already supplies."

This blunt diagnosis bears repeating. The typical scientist does *not* discover new Perceiver facts or build general theories. On the contrary, "no part of the aim of normal science is to call forth new sorts of phenomena," and when the scientist does encounter new facts, he tends to ignore them. Similarly, the average scientist does *not* build novel general theories, and is "often intolerant of those invented by others."

So, when *does* the scientist discover new facts and develop novel theories? When his existing paradigm crumbles. In Kuhn's words: "All crises begin with the blurring of a paradigm and the consequent loosening of the rules for normal research. In this respect research during crisis very much resembles research during the pre-paradigm period, except that in the former the locus of difference is both smaller and more clearly defined." "By proliferating versions of the paradigm, crisis loosens the rules of normal puzzle-solving in ways that ultimately permit a new paradigm to emerge."

Kuhn refers to the type of thinking that occurs during intellectual crisis as *revolutionary science*, while what the scientist normally does he calls *normal science.* When we compared math with science, we saw that there can be a discrepancy between how science *officially* functions and how it *actually* functions, and we noted some of the mental reasons for this discrepancy. In this chapter we will pursue this topic further, guided by Kuhn's study of normal science and revolutionary science.

Normal Science versus Revolutionary Science

What then is the relationship between normal science and revolutionary science? In simplest terms, normal science is a *tighter* version of revolutionary science. Revolutionary science develops and evaluates paradigms; normal science works within an *existing* paradigm. In Kuhn's words, "Men whose research is based on shared paradigms are committed to the same rules and standards for scientific practice. That commitment and the apparent consensus it produces are prerequisites for normal science." When a paradigm breaks down, then normal science gives way to the looser form of revolutionary science.

But normal science is not just a concentrated version of revolutionary science. Instead, I suggest that normal science is under the control of a *different* mental module than revolutionary science—the module of Contributor thought, a mental module which until now we have largely ignored.

One can see by looking at the diagram of mental symmetry that Contributor mode connects Perceiver memories with Server memories. When the mind is being programmed, then Contributor mode plays largely a passive role, either connecting Server actions with Perceiver facts or else connecting words with Perceiver meanings. However, if *enough* Perceiver and Server content becomes interconnected, then Contributor mode can start taking a more active role.

Kuhn compares normal science to the solving of puzzles: "Turn now to another, more difficult, and more revealing aspect of the parallelism between puzzles and the problems of normal science. If it is to classify as a puzzle, a problem must be characterized by more than an assured solution. There must also be rules that limit both the nature of acceptable solutions and the steps by which they are to be obtained."

Translating this into the language of mental symmetry, doing normal science requires three things: First, there is a set of *Server* guidelines which establish the 'nature of acceptable solutions' or the type of sequences that can be used. For instance, when playing chess, all acceptable solutions involve moving the pieces on the board in an approved manner. Body checking the opponent or moving a rook diagonally is not an 'acceptable solution'. Second, there is a set of *Perceiver* rules that guide the steps that may be taken. For instance, the game of chess starts with a certain layout, players alternate taking turns, and each player can decide which piece he will move next. Third, this network of approved Server sequences and Perceiver rules must be sufficiently complex to make it interesting for Contributor thought.

As long as the basic 'rules of the game' do not change, then Contributor thought can function within this structure and choose different ways of combining the various approved elements. For instance, when playing chess, each turn consists of a player deciding which one of his pieces he will move an approved manner.

The average scientist spends most of his time solving intellectual problems guided by the 'rules of the game'. Seldom does he either question these rules or come up with a new game. In Kuhn's words, "The scientific enterprise as a whole does from time to time prove useful, open up new territory, display order, and test long-accepted belief. Nevertheless, *the individual* engaged on a normal research problem *is almost never doing any one of these things.* Once engaged, his motivation is of a rather different sort. What then challenges him is the conviction that, if only he is skilful enough, he will succeed in solving a puzzle that no one before has solved or solved so well."

In a previous chapter, we looked at abstract thought, and we saw how abstract thought can be used to solve math problems or science problems. Here we are seeing the same cognitive elements show up in normal science: Server sequences define the 'locations', Perceiver thought is used to move from one 'location' to another, and this 'movement' is being guided by a paradigm or general Teacher theory. Thus, one can say that Kuhn's normal science is simply another version of abstract thought.

However, there is an additional factor. What is being used is a *restricted* version of abstract thought: Only a limited set of Server 'locations' are being considered, and only a limited number of Perceiver operations are being permitted. This restricted 'playing field' is one of the hallmarks of normal science, and is one of the main features that distinguishes normal science from abstract thought. Because normal science is actually a restricted form of abstract thought, we will be referring to it as *technical thought.*

The person who is solving a math problem or a science problem is probably using the limited 'playing field' of technical thought, but not necessarily. One of the goals of a math teacher is to develop technical thought in his students by instructing them in the accepted techniques of mathematical problem-solving, in essence teaching them the 'rules of the game'. For instance, before we analyzed the math problem of the boy buying candy, we outlined a set of officially accepted steps for solving a word problem. But the best mathematicians and scientists are the ones who are able to transcend this carefully defined, restricted 'playing field' and pursue unorthodox solutions, in essence going beyond the mental bounds of Kuhn's normal science. That is why we looked at abstract thought *before* mentioning technical thought. Technical thought is a limited version of abstract thought which goes *beyond* abstract thought, but is still based *upon* abstract thought.

Summarizing, when one is gathering Perceiver facts to build a general Teacher theory, then this is *always* an expression of *normal* thought. When one chooses to work within an *existing* paradigm, then one is *using* abstract thought *guided* by a general Teacher theory. However, if one chooses to work within an existing paradigm *and* limit Server actions and Perceiver facts to a restricted playing field, then one has entered technical thought.

Technical Thought

A *formal* language, such as logic, mathematics, or computer programming, exhibits the type of thinking that is applied during normal science, because only a specific set of statements are permitted and strict rules govern the ways in which these statements may be manipulated. For those who want the mathematical details, the relationship between math and abstract technical thought is described in an appendix. Everyday speech, in contrast, is far too vague to be an expression of normal science. However, everyday speech *is* an expression of human thought, and if one understands the various ways in which cognitive modules can interact, then it is possible to make sense of everyday communication with its various assumptions, inconsistencies, and irrationalities.

This provides us with several different ways of looking at a paradigm. For Teacher mode, a paradigm is a general theory that is a source of pleasant emotions. For Perceiver mode, it is 'the big picture' which ties various facts together. For Mercy mode, it creates Platonic Forms as well as an image of God. For Server mode, it is a guide for actions which adds elegance to movement. Contributor mode, in contrast, views a paradigm as the 'rules of a game'.

Each paradigm creates its own set of rules, and the rules of one game do not apply to other games. This means that *formal* languages, such as logic or math, cannot be used to prove a paradigm. This is one of Kuhn's primary points: "Like the choice between competing political institutions, that between competing paradigms proves to be a choice between incompatible modes of community life. Because it has that character, the choice is not and cannot be determined merely by the evaluative procedures characteristic of normal science, for these depend in part upon a particular paradigm, and that paradigm is at issue. When paradigms enter, as they must, into a debate about paradigm choice, their role is necessarily circular. Each group uses its own paradigm to argue in that paradigm's defense."

One result is that the Contributor person will view changing paradigms as a *loss of control.* As long as the rules of the game are clear, Contributor mode can play the game. But, when a paradigm falls apart, then there are no clear rules and Contributor mode falls apart. Obviously, this loss of control will be felt most keenly by the Contributor *person,* but it will also be experienced to a lesser extent by other cognitive styles, especially the Facilitator person, who functions 'downstream' from Contributor mode.

The way out of this dilemma is to do as Kuhn did and come up with a general theory which states that general theories will occasionally fall apart. This may sound like a logical contradiction, but it is not because we are dealing with two different mental circuits. The Contributor-controlled circuit of formal languages and normal science may periodically come unglued, but it is possible to describe this mental ungluing and regluing as a general Teacher theory, and this Teacher theory can form a Teacher mental network which will survive even when the Contributor circuit of normal science falls apart.

Kuhn examines the relationship between normal *science* and revolutionary *science*. I suggest that it is possible to *extend* his findings to practical thought as well as the realm of religion, and that this extension leads to some significant conclusions.

The Mental Circuits of Cp and Ci

We have introduced the technical version of abstract thought and I have suggested that it is under the control of Contributor mode. Contributor mode is actually involved in *both* abstract and concrete thought, and it functions in *both* of these realms in a way that is more technical and more rigorous than normal thought. I will refer to these two mental circuits as *intellectual* Contributor thought and *practical* Contributor thought, which I will abbreviate as *Ci* and *Cp*. Lane Friesen discovered these two modes of Contributor thought when studying the biographies of Contributor persons in the early 1980s. During periods of revolutionary science, the mind is using *abstract* thought to collect Perceiver facts and build Teacher theories. Normal science, in contrast, corresponds to Ci, a mental circuit controlled by Contributor mode which limits its thinking to 'puzzle solving' within some existing paradigm. I should clarify that what Kuhn calls *normal* science, I will be referring to as *technical* thought, and I will refer to non-technical thought as normal thought. However, whenever I use the phrase 'normal science', I will be using *Kuhn's* definition. Similarly, everyday existence is guided by *concrete* thought, in which Server actions are used to reach Mercy goals. However, it is also possible to live within a limited, more formal subset of reality guided by the mental circuit of Cp, which is also under the control of Contributor mode.

We can illustrate the *concrete* technical circuit of Cp by comparing the game of soccer with real life. Soccer is a physical game which involves physical movement. Each player performs Server actions that are designed to achieve the Mercy goal of placing a ball within the net of the opposing team. But, a soccer game is a very *limited* version of reality, restricted to moving the ball within the confines of the playing field. And this limited form of reality is also clearly *defined*, for the rules of the game determine precisely which Server actions are permissible and which ones are forbidden.

Let me say this again more carefully. Normal existence uses concrete thought to maneuver through the physical world. Mercy mode remembers experiences along with the associated emotions; Perceiver mode organizes these experiences in order to build a mental map; Server mode then performs the actions that are required to move through this map. But in normal concrete thought, all of these various elements are open-ended and only partially defined. When the average person goes through the day, he does not know exactly what he will experience, where he will go, or what he will do. He may have worked out a partial plan, but it will change throughout the day as it comes into contact with reality.

The technical circuit of Cp, in contrast, works within a world which is strictly defined. In a game of soccer, for instance, Perceiver facts such as the size of the field, the placement of the goals, and the number of men allowed on the playing field are all strictly controlled. Any deviation from these official Perceiver facts is flagged and leads to some sort of penalty. In addition, each player is only allowed to carry out a specific list of permissible Server actions. For instance, in soccer only the goalie is permitted to touch the ball with his hands. The practical circuit of Cp then uses Contributor thought to function within this *limited* and *strictly defined* world.

Similarly, the world of business attempts to transform normal reality into a version that is more technical, more limited, and more clearly defined. Business interactions are guided by contracts, which determine the 'rules of the game'. One of the key aspects of the corporation is the idea of *limited liability*, which ensures that the 'game' remains restricted to the 'playing field'. And, just as the goal of a game is clearly defined—often as 'the goal', so the goal of most business ventures is monetary profit, something which is also easy to measure.

We spent considerable time in previous chapters examining *cause-and-effect*. A connection of cause-and-effect combines Server thought with Perceiver thought; Perceiver thought decides that two Mercy experiences are connected because a Server action leads from one Mercy experience to the other. But Contributor thought is responsible for forming connections between Server sequences and Perceiver facts, and technical thought is under the control of Contributor thought. Thus, in the same way that experiences are the basic building blocks for Mercy thought and words are the building blocks for Teacher thought, so I suggest that cause-and-effect forms the foundation for the technical circuit of Cp. In fact, I suggest that Cp can only function when cause-and-effect is clearly defined. For instance, when government raises taxes too high and eliminates the connection between investment and profit, then business stops working. In general terms, business can only function within the context of the 'American Dream': If I pursue opportunity and work hard, then I will prosper.

For Ci, I suggest that the basic building block is the *definition*, because Ci works with words and not actions. A definition combines a Server sequence of words or letters with a Perceiver meaning. Again, we see the role played by Contributor mode in connecting Server sequences with Perceiver facts. In simple terms, if Ci is to function, then words must have clear meanings.

When one examines fields such as normal science, professional sports, and business ventures, one finds that the Contributor *person* naturally excels in these areas. Earlier in this book, we looked at the relationship between Contributor thought, the Contributor person, and the market exchange. I suggest that we have now explained the cognitive reason for this relationship.

We can also see more clearly the third aspect to mental *concentration*: Mercy mode can concentrate upon an experience; personal identity is defined as the set of experiences upon which Mercy mode can continue to concentrate. Teacher mode can concentrate upon symbols and words; a general theory can be defined as a set of symbols or words upon which Teacher mode can continue to concentrate. Contributor mode can concentrate upon a *plan*. When Contributor mode is concentrating upon a plan, then either the circuit of Ci or the circuit of Cp is functioning. When normal science is being practiced, then Contributor mode is concentrating upon a plan using Ci. Mercy concentration and Teacher concentration could be compared to a *stake* set into the ground, because the concentration occurs *around* a specific memory. In contrast, Contributor concentration is more like a *fence*, because it limits thinking to the restricted bounds of some limited 'playing field'.

I should emphasize that when I am referring to a mental circuit which is *controlled* by Contributor mode, I do not mean that *only* Contributor mode is functioning. Instead, both Cp and Ci can involve the cooperation of *all* seven modes of thought with Contributor mode playing the coordinating role. It *is* possible to operate these two circuits in a restricted manner which *does* shut down much of the mind and which does give freedom only to the Contributor module. The Contributor *person* who is functioning this way will behave in a manner that is very *controlled*. However, Cp and Ci normally function in a manner that gives *some* freedom to other cognitive modules, allowing them to function within limited parameters, effectively putting them 'on a leash'.

Finally, I should mention that Contributor confidence functions in a slightly different manner than Perceiver and Server confidence. Perceiver and Server confidence is defined as the ability to handle emotional pressure without being overwhelmed. Contributor confidence, in contrast, is the ability to channel Exhorter drive while continuing to hold on to a plan. Thus, Contributor confidence has a more *functional* definition than either Perceiver or Server confidence, and could be compared to the ability to ride a horse without being thrown off.

Let us turn now to the technical *abstract* circuit of Ci. This operates the same way that Cp functions, except that the roles played by Perceiver mode and Server mode are reversed. With Cp, Perceiver mode builds the map and Server mode moves through the map; with Ci, Server mode constructs the 'map' and Perceiver mode performs the 'movement'. As I mentioned in a previous paragraph, the same basic elements are present in both abstract thought and Ci: Server sequences are being used to form the 'map' and Perceiver mode is building connections between sequences within this 'map' guided by a general Teacher theory. But Ci is a technical version of abstract thought which *limits* and *strictly defines* the Server sequences and Perceiver steps that may be taken.

We can illustrate this with an example from *Boolean logic*, which we will take a few paragraphs to discuss. Consider the statement "If it is raining and I am walking to work, then I will take an umbrella." One sees here the familiar elements of abstract thought. The 'locations' are sequences of Teacher words: 'It is raining', 'I am walking to work', and 'I will take an umbrella'. The 'movement' occurs as Perceiver thought assigns labels of certainty to facts: If one knows that it is 'raining', and if one knows that one is 'walking to work', then one can also know that one will 'take an umbrella'. The 'movement' is being guided by a general Teacher theory, because every if-then statement of this type can be written in the form 'If A and B then C'.

In addition, we see the characteristics of *technical* thought: The elements of this statement must occur in a certain order. One is not permitted to say something like "Then I will take an umbrella, and I am walking to work, if it is raining." *Some* rearranging may be permitted, but this too is strictly defined. For instance, in our example it is possible to exchange 'A' with 'B', leading to the equivalent statement: If 'B' and 'A' then 'C'. Also, only a limited list of acceptable logic words may be used. For instance, "Before it is raining and after I am walking to work, then I prefer to take an umbrella" violates this principle. Finally, the statements that are inserted for 'A', 'B', and 'C' must also be grammatically clear. Therefore, just as Cp limits the Perceiver map to an accepted playing field in a game of soccer, so in Boolean logic, Ci limits the Server sequences to an 'accepted playing field' of allowable order, permitted rearranging, permitted operations, and clear expressions.

Analog Certainty versus Digital Certainty

If one writes the statement 'If it is raining and I am walking to work, then I will take an umbrella' as a *truth table*, then another characteristic of technical thought becomes apparent.

Raining	Walking to Work	Take Umbrella
False	False	False
False	True	False
True	False	False
True	True	True

This version of logic statement is familiar to anyone who has worked with electronics. Each row in the table describes a different possibility. For instance, looking at the second row, if 'Raining' is False and 'Walking to Work' is True, then 'Take Umbrella' will be False.

We know that Perceiver mode adds a label of *confidence* or *belief* to facts, and that this label can vary all the way from 'totally correct' to 'possibly valid' to 'maybe wrong' to 'definitely wrong'. However, Boolean logic uses only the two labels of 'totally correct' and 'definitely wrong', or True and False. Nothing else is considered. Any information that is used by Boolean logic must be either 'totally correct' or 'definitely wrong'; facts in Boolean logic are not permitted to be 'possibly valid' or 'maybe wrong'. Similarly, any answer is also stated with total certainty, and if it is not possible to achieve total certainty, then Boolean logic shrugs its shoulders and states that no answer exists.

Saying this more generally, Perceiver mode is capable of working with *analog* certainty; Perceiver facts may be partially certain and somewhat known. Boolean logic, in contrast, works only with *digital* certainty. Either a fact is *known* to be true or else it is *known* to be false. It cannot be both true and false, and it cannot be neither true nor false. The first principle is known in logic as the 'law of noncontradiction' and the second is known as the 'law of the excluded middle'.

Both Ci and Cp share the same two basic features of restricting thought to a limited set of Perceiver facts and Server sequences as well as working with *digital* certainty. For instance, in a game of soccer, the list of permissible Server actions is precisely defined and one knows with digital certainty when the Mercy goal of 'scoring a goal' has been accomplished. Similarly, in Boolean logic, the list of permissible statements and operations is precisely defined and one knows with digital certainty whether the final answer is True or False.

This contrast between analog certainty and digital certainty first became apparent to me back in the 1980s when Lane Friesen and I were studying personality. When we examined the behavior of people who carry out plans that seem foolhardy to other individuals, such as jumping across a canyon on a motorcycle, or climbing a sheer cliff without any ropes for support, we noticed that they usually had the cognitive style of Contributor person. As a Perceiver person with my *analog* sense of certainty, I look at such an activity and think of all the possible ways in which I could get killed. However, the Contributor person performing the activity seems to radiate an aura of confidence, totally certain that he can accomplish his goal without failing. When asked to explain his confidence, the Contributor person typically replies that he is not taking a risk because he has considered everything that could go wrong and has a solution for every possible disaster. And even if some finite chance of disaster still remains, the Contributor person will talk about 'acceptable risk', as if he possesses the mental ability to ignore a small level of risk and act as if it does not exist.

Eventually, I concluded that the Contributor person really is mentally blind and functions with a digital sense of certainty. Saying this more clearly, if the confidence level of a Perceiver fact or Server sequence is above a certain threshold, then Contributor mode will believe this information with complete certainty. Similarly, if the Perceiver confidence that a fact is false or the Server confidence that a sequence will not occur is above a certain threshold, then Contributor mode will also believe this with total certainty.

My natural reaction as a Perceiver person is to view this mental blindness as a handicap, but I gradually came to the realization that it also has its advantages, for it permits the Contributor person to step forward and blaze the way for others. For instance, the only reason that the average person can get on an airplane and fly across the ocean is because Contributor persons 'took the acceptable risk' of flying and testing airplanes when they were first being developed. *The Right Stuff*, a book about test pilots written in 1979 by Tom Wolfe and later made into a movie, describes the thinking and behavior that typifies this type of Contributor person.

I have also repeatedly experienced this principle at work within my own mind. As a Perceiver person, my natural tendency is to gather data endlessly in an attempt to raise my mental level of certainty. But I kept discovering that it was impossible to achieve 100% certainty. Instead, a point would eventually come when I had to stop gathering data and start implementing a plan—despite the fact that I was not totally certain. If I wanted to make progress, then I had to stop using Perceiver thought to control my mind and I had to allow subconscious Contributor mode to take control.

This led me to the following chain of reasoning. When I studied engineering, I was taught in great detail about the contrast between the digital certainty of mathematics and the analog approximations that one must make when dealing with real life. Similarly, when I studied personality, I kept reading about the digital certainty which the Contributor person placed in his plans and how these plans would shatter when the Contributor person encountered real life problems that he had not considered. Eventually, I came to the conclusion that these two behaviors are related. When the mind is using the technical circuits of Ci and Cp, it is under the control of Contributor mode, and it is being guided by a digital sense of certainty. Similarly, when the Contributor person uses conscious thought to control his mind, then he also has a natural tendency to work with digital certainty.

In summary, we conclude that the mental circuits of Ci and Cp have the following characteristics: First, they are under the control of Contributor mode. Second, they use Contributor concentration to limit thought to a specific context. Third, they use only a limited repertoire of carefully defined Perceiver facts and Server sequences. Fourth, they function on the basis of digital certainty. This provides us with a more technical definition of technical thought.

When concrete thought and abstract thought function normally, they work with open-ended plans, partially defined information, and uncertain results. However, when the Contributor driven circuits of Ci and Cp take over, then plans become limited, information becomes well defined, the mind assumes that information has absolute certainty, and thinking comes up with results which are also treated as absolutely certain.

Now let us apply this principle of analog versus digital certainty to the development of science, the thinking of engineering, the method of philosophy, and the task of constructing a cognitive model of the mind. Science begins by observing the real world. But every experimental measurement carries with it an uncertainty. In the real world, a distance is not 2.3 meters. Instead, it is 2.3 meters plus or minus 0.2 meters. Similarly, the time is not five seconds. Instead, it is 5.0 seconds to an accuracy of 1/10 of a second.

Technical thought can make *allowance* for analog uncertainty by adding details based in digital certainty. For instance, when using the 'digital' categories of whole numbers to measure quantities, then any measurement between 4.5 and 5.5 will be *rounded* to the whole number of 5, which is a fairly crude approximation. However, it is possible to make allowance for analog certainty by adding more digits. Thus, 5.000 represents a value between 4.9995 and 5.0005. However, 5.000 is still a 'digital' category in which analog certainty has been replaced by digital certainty. But because it is a smaller, more detailed category, less information is lost in the transition from analog to digital certainty. Saying this another way, one of the reasons that technical thought becomes so preoccupied with details is so that the risk that is introduced by functioning with digital certainty can be reduced to an acceptable level.

When one moves from the real world of measurement to the theoretical world of mathematics, then partial certainty turns into total certainty. For instance, when I taught high school physics, the textbook that I used devoted a whole chapter to the uncertainty of measurement. But when I taught high school mathematics, then the textbook acted as if all numbers were certain and it completely ignored the possibility of uncertainty. This difference in approach existed even when the *same* problem occurred within both the math textbook and the physics textbook. In math, the answer was given in exact terms, while in physics the student was required to give an approximate answer. For math, the answer was 5 seconds, while for physics it was 5.00 plus or minus 0.005 seconds.

Science makes allowances for uncertain *measurements*, thus acknowledging the *analog* nature of real life. However, science is still using math to solve its problems, and math is an expression of the technical circuit of Ci with its limited and clearly defined set of tools. Thus, whenever a physicist uses math to solve a real world problem, he is always solving an *idealized* version of the problem, a caricature of the situation in which all of the shades of gray have been replaced by clear lines and sharp distinctions. Before the physicist starts to solve a problem, he will make a set of *assumptions* which transform the messy real world situation into one that fits neatly into the idealized technical world of Ci. Part of challenge of being an engineer is to know which factors can be ignored and which factors must be included when moving from real life to mathematics.

Going the other way, when one moves from mathematics back to real life, then one has to reintroduce a sense of uncertainty. For instance, when an engineer is designing a building, he will use mathematical equations to work out levels of mechanical stress in order to determine how strong each structural member has to be. But after he has come up with a mathematical solution, then he will add 50% to his solution or even double the answer in order to provide a margin of safety. That is because he knows that the real world is mathematically messy and that one can only know about the real world with partial certainty. He hopes that the addition of this 'fudge factor' will make up for the conditions which he ignored when moving from real life to mathematics. And I suggest that 'hope' is the right word, because absolute certainty is not possible when dealing with the real world.

While absolute certainty is not achievable in engineering, it is possible to *increase* the level of certainty. One way is through the use of *redundancy*. The most obvious form of redundancy is *physical* redundancy. For instance, one may install a backup generator to produce electricity in case the power fails. There can also be *intellectual* redundancy. If one can come up with the same answer using two totally different methods of calculation, then this increases the probability that the mathematical incursion through technical thought did not introduce any fatal flaws.

Redundancy also plays a major role in the theory of mental symmetry. For instance, if one can examine religion from a cognitive perspective and come up with the *same* answers as are being taught using blind faith, then this increases the probability of being correct. Similarly, if mental symmetry independently comes up with the same mental mechanisms that are being described by the philosophy of science, then this also increases the level of certainty.

Another common technique used by engineering to increase certainty is *reasonableness*. I was taught in Engineering school that using only mathematics to calculate an answer is never sufficient. Instead, one should also use crude methods to come up with an *approximate* answer. This 'ballpark figure' can then be used to determine whether the technically calculated solution makes sense or not. For instance, how much power is required by a city of one million people? One can use mathematics to work out a detailed answer, but the 'rule of thumb' states that each person in a modern Western city uses about one thousand watts of power. Thus, the answer should be about a Gigawatt of power. Obviously, this is only a crude answer, but a lot of engineering starts with crude answers. And if the technically calculated mathematical solution comes out to 4,352,000 Watts, then one can know that a mistake was made somewhere, because the answer should be at least one hundred times larger.

It is interesting to note that there is a form of logic that deals with analog values, known as *fuzzy logic*, which is widely used to control electronic devices, such as washing machines and digital cameras. In typical engineering fashion, fuzzy logic systems are usually designed using a sort of systematic trial and error approach, and not through the application of formal logic. Thus, fuzzy logic works well in the real world of partial certainty but it does not fit cleanly into the rigorous realm of technical thought with its digital certainty.

Notice that math and abstract thought *are* being used when calculating approximations. But *technical* thought is not being used. The information used is only approximate and the answer is not certain; the methods of calculation are not clearly defined and one is probably using shortcuts that step outside of the bounds of the officially sanctioned 'playing field' of mathematics. But even though the method is not rigorous, an answer that is calculated using both technical thought and approximation is more reliable than one which was calculated using only technical thought. That is because the approximate answer provides a mental context for Perceiver thought, and this mental context can be used to evaluate the reasonableness of the technically derived solution. And one needs to emphasize that there is a big difference between an approximate answer and a wild guess. Anyone can make a wild guess. An approximation, in contrast, requires a rational understanding of the subject. It may be a guess, but it is an *educated* guess; it may not be rigorous, but it is *semi*-rigorous.

This explains why it is important to illustrate mental symmetry using examples from everyday life. Even though these examples are not rigorous, they serve as more than just examples, because they indicate whether the theory makes sense or not by providing a mental context within which the facts of the theory can be evaluated.

Officially, science and engineering are similar, because both deal with the real, messy world of partially certain information. In practice, though, once science enters the neat, clearly defined, digitally certain realm of technical thought, it tends to remain there, while still paying lip service to the uncertainty of the real world. Thus, when Kuhn observes the typical scientist at work, he sees the technical thought of normal science, and not normal abstract thought. Engineering, in contrast, does not have the luxury of remaining within the digital certainty and limited playing field of technical thought, for when it does, it tends to get rudely awakened by collapsing bridges and crashing airplanes.

Notice that we have now come up with *three* reasons why the scientist becomes mentally locked within his paradigm. First, we saw that general Teacher theories can turn into Teacher mental networks which will use hyper-emotion to protect their integrity. Second, we saw that once a group of scientists start to use a paradigm, then the definition of a paradigm can change from a general description of how the environment behaves to a general description of how scientists behave when they are working with a paradigm. Here, we see that technical thought can also lock a person into a paradigm. When a person enters technical thought, then he assumes that information is accurate and he limits his thinking to the current rules of the game. Information that does not fit into the current paradigm is ignored because it lies outside of the accepted 'playing field', while information that is too vague is rejected because technical thought deals only with information which is certain. In addition, we will see in a later chapter that Facilitator thought naturally filters out information which falls too far outside of the current school of thought. However, science is still officially rooted in real data from the physical world. The end result is the tension between what science claims and what science usually does that Kuhn describes in his portrayal of normal science.

In practice, these four factors do not usually stop science from happening, but rather *limit* the range of its effectiveness. As long as a scientist is working with physical data within his area of specialization, he will probably search for physical evidence, acknowledge physical evidence, and respect physical evidence. However, when a scientist encounters data that violates the current paradigm, when he spends more time talking about science than doing science, when he focuses upon the math behind the science, and when he becomes a respected member of a school of thought, then the scientist will find it increasingly difficult to practice science. As Arthur C. Clarke put it, "When a distinguished but elderly scientist states that something is possible, he is almost certainly right. When he states that something is impossible, he is very probably wrong."

We can also see why *philosophy* (especially analytical philosophy) often runs into difficulties. That is because the *method* of philosophy uses the *technical* circuit of Ci. Thus, it attempts to use rigorous logic to prove results with absolute certainty. But the *topic* of philosophy is the human mind, a computing device that jumps to partially certain conclusions based upon incomplete information and which only operates in a mode of absolute certainty when using the technical circuits of Ci and Cp.

Therefore, when the philosopher Kant pointed out that the mind is jumping to conclusions because of the way that it is constructed, the philosopher with his *digital* sense of knowing concluded that it is *impossible* to know anything about the external world, because the philosopher has defined knowing as being 100% certain. But absolute certainty applies only to Ci and Cp. The human mind is capable of functioning quite well with incomplete certainty when using normal thought.[31]

Similarly, the philosopher with his digital sense of knowing looks at Kuhn's concept of incommensurability and concludes that it is impossible to compare one paradigm with another. But rigorous logic only applies to a specific context, because it only develops when the technical circuit of Ci is used, and Ci always limits its activity to a specific context. Thus, using a system of rigorous logic outside of its defined context is like trying to apply the rules of soccer to another game or to real life. It doesn't work.

When one is comparing one paradigm with another paradigm, then one *is* going outside of a specific context, which means that one can no longer use the rigorous logic of any specific context. However, when one leaves a realm of rigorous logic, one does not abandon logic altogether. Instead, one enters the normal realm of partially certain information and partially certain conclusions.[32] Thus, it is *difficult* to compare one paradigm with another, but it is not impossible. One cannot prove for certain that one paradigm is better than another, but one can become *reasonably* certain. And it is possible

---

[31] Is the human mind able to conceive of a physical reality that is inconsistent with mental architecture? I suggest that the development of *quantum mechanics* provides an answer. As far as concrete thought is concerned, quantum mechanics does not make sense. But because quantum mechanics can be defined using mathematics and abstract thought, concrete thought can get a *partial* grasp of what quantum mechanics might look like through the use of incomplete analogies. Thus, by playing one cognitive module against another, it is possible to partially violate Kant's transcendental argument.

In addition, I suggest that it is possible for one cognitive module to *emulate* functioning that it does not find natural, similarly to the way in which one computer chip can be used to run or develop software for another chip. The emulating chip will run software which makes it act as if it is the other chip. Emulation is always *slower* than normal processing. Similarly, when one mode of thought is attempting to model a way of thought that is inconsistent with its normal functioning, then there will be hesitation, reflection, and second-guessing.

[32] In this book, I am treating a *paradigm* as equivalent to a general theory. I have defined a general Teacher theory as a set of symbols upon which Teacher thought can continue to concentrate. If technical thought is functioning within a specific context guided by a defined set of rules and parameters, then this will also define a region of thought within which Teacher thought can continue to concentrate upon a general theory. For instance, I live in Canada, subject to the rules and procedures of Canadian law. This defines my legal context. But I can also view Canada as a region over which the Queen of England rules as a 'general theory'.

to become *more* skilled at comparing paradigms and *increase* the confidence of one's conclusions.

Similarly, because the theory of mental symmetry is a theory of *all* human thought, and not just a theory of *rigorous* human thought, it cannot be stated using the rigorous language of Ci. And if it is 'tightened up' by using language that is too rigorous, then it will lose its ability to stand outside of paradigms and translate between paradigms.

When philosophy insists upon digital certainty, then I suggest that it is setting itself up for an epistemological crisis. The sequence is as follows: First, the technical thinking of Ci will emerge within some region of thought. When the mind makes the transition from normal abstract thought to technical abstract thought, then it will make a logical leap from partial certainty to certain certainty. However, a person will not *notice* that he is making this leap because he is applying the standards of normal thought, which always jumps to conclusions based upon partial information. Second, as Ci continues to function, definitions will become formalized and proofs will become more rigorous. Third, as Ci encounters the limits of its intellectual domain it will eventually realize *retroactively* that its rigorous thought is built upon an uncertain foundation.

This will trigger an epistemological crisis in which Ci questions the basis for its existence. When philosophy faces this existential question, then philosophical knowledge tends to implode, because rigorous logic has come to the conclusion that rigorous logic cannot come to any conclusions. Like the young Wittgenstein, philosophy may literally conclude that philosophy is meaningless. As Wittgenstein put it, "*Wovon man nicht sprechen kann, darüber muß man schweigen.*" Or in English, "What we cannot speak about we must pass over in silence."

Then, like the later Wittgenstein, it may limit itself to the cataloguing of semi-rigorous normal speech, or like the philosopher Willard Quine, it may focus upon the realm of empirical science with its partially known data and its uncertain hypotheses. For those who want to read further, an analysis of Quine's *Web of Belief* can be found in an appendix. I should mention in passing that I first read the *Web of Belief* after I had finished writing this book and was editing the manuscript. Quine's language is clear and concise, and his comments correspond in detail with the theory of mental symmetry.

In a similar way, I suggest that modern technological society has set up the *concrete* circuit of Cp for a potentially devastating crisis of knowing. This vulnerability is portrayed quite effectively in the opening episode of James Burke's *Connections* series. I mentioned previously that the machine is a physical example of technical thought, and that the consumer uses the machine as a tool. We also know that technical thought becomes possible when there is a network of Perceiver facts and Server sequences. The modern city dweller lives in a physical analog to the mental circuit of Cp in which his actions, words, and objects are funneled through limited, technically defined channels of travel and communication. The average consumer has no understanding of how this network functions, but he places *digital* certainty in the assumption that his grocery stores will stock food, his trains and subways will be on time, there will be gas for his car, electricity will be provided, and so on. If this physical network were to collapse, the resulting crisis of knowing would be both overwhelming and deadly.

Before we continue, let us step back and make some general conclusions: In its normal mode of operation, the mind uses abstract thought and concrete thought. These work with open-ended plans, incomplete knowledge, and uncertain goals, such as "I need to study for this test" or "Let's go out and have a bite to eat." But the uncertain nature of normal thought makes it difficult to build further. If a person or society wants to develop some region of thought or activity, then it needs to use the technical circuits of Cp and Ci. However, these technical circuits can only emerge when the mind acquires a network of related Perceiver facts and Server sequences.

In the *concrete* world, living in a physical body provides the mind with enough Perceiver facts and Server sequences to jumpstart the circuit of Cp. Thus, practical expertise will emerge even in a primitive tribal society, as the technical circuit of Cp is used to gain mastery over the natural environment in a specific area. However, history shows us that living in a world of natural order does *not* provide abstract thought with sufficient Perceiver and Server content to jumpstart the circuit of Ci, except perhaps in limited domains such as astronomy and legal practice. As a result, it is necessary to *seed* abstract thought with a collection of Perceiver facts and Server sequences which will cause the circuit of Ci to emerge. This is known as *education*, which forms one of the main themes of this book. But seeding abstract thought with a collection of Perceiver facts and Server sequences means using the method of *revealed truth*, which forces us to contend with the topics of fundamentalism, scholasticism, and theology.

In a previous chapter, we described the process of *using* a general Teacher theory. At first glance one may think that using a Teacher theory automatically causes the mind to enter the technical circuit of Ci. This is often the case, but not necessarily. I suggest that it depends upon the stage of learning of the individual combined with the nature of the environment. If a person is in the first stage of learning, then he will lack the Perceiver knowledge and Server skills that are required to enter technical thought. Therefore, he will simply plunge in and attempt to cope with problems as they arise. The individual in the second stage of learning is most prone to using technical thought when he commits to a theory or plan. This type of approach attempts to 'go by the book' and 'play by the rules of the game', by following 'established procedures' and ignoring thinking that is 'outside of the box'. This form of thinking is easy to recognize when encountered because one feels as if one has entered a small, limited world in which everything is carefully defined—which describes what is happening mentally.

The person in the third stage of learning is capable of committing to a plan or theory without becoming locked in by technical thought. When the mind enters technical thought, Contributor mode is taking control of the mind. If Contributor mode is willing to 'lose control', then it becomes possible for the mind to move between normal thought and technical thought without becoming stuck within technical thought. This type of mindset is also is easy to recognize because one sees a combination of expertise and spontaneity. Plans and theories may still be used, but they will be adapted as conditions change, and there is an overall atmosphere of flexibility.

When a person who is in the third stage of learning comes up with educated guesses, they are usually fairly close to the solution which a person would derive using more rigorous methods. For instance, the story is told that Murray Gell-Mann, a Nobel prize winner, was asked how Richard Feynman, another Nobel prize winner, solved problems in physics. Gell-Mann responded: "'Here is Feynman's method. First, you write down the problem.' Squeezing his eyes closed and holding his fists against his forehead, he continued: 'Second, you think *really* hard.' Opening his eyes, he concluded: 'Third, you write down the answer.'"

Environment also plays a major role in determining whether committing to a theory or plan implies entering technical thought. For instance, consider what happens when one flies on an airplane. By entering the plane, one is implicitly making a mental leap from analog to digital certainty, because one is assuming that the flight will arrive safely. And when one is on an airplane, then one physically occupies a very restricted world in which the options are limited and clearly defined: A passenger can sit in his seat, try to sleep in his seat, or walk for a few minutes along a narrow aisle.

In contrast, I discovered that it is difficult to remain within technical thought when living in South Korea, because plans keep changing *after* one commits to all of the technical details. To the Korean mind, a signed contract is not 'set in stone', but rather is regarded as a starting point which may be altered if conditions change. In order to avoid mental frustration, I had to learn to let go of technical thought with its carefully defined structure and allow myself to 'go with the flow'. And things usually ended up working out in the end.

Obviously, cognitive style also plays a role. The Exhorter person, for instance, generally tries to avoid technical thought, while the Contributor person or the Facilitator person often demands technical thought, develops it if it does not exist, and then imposes it upon those who are around him.

The Bottom Line

Even though technical thought may not appear emotional, emotions still play a major role. We have already seen the *overall* role which emotions play. Both abstract thought and technical abstract thought are guided by a general Teacher theory, and each additional application of a general theory will increase the generality of that theory, adding to its Teacher feelings of order-within-complexity. In addition, Ci can become locked into its current paradigm by the hyper-emotions of a Teacher mental network, while Cp can also become imprisoned within a practical plan by the hyper-emotions of a Mercy mental network. Think, for instance, of the professional sports player. Playing the game often defines his personal existence; if he had to leave the game he would no longer know who he was.

But emotions also play a more *local* role in technical thought by providing the *bottom line.* The soccer player, for instance, does not play the game merely for the purpose of moving the ball around. Instead, he wants to win the game by scoring more goals than the opposing team. Similarly, the aspiring businessman who opens up a hotdog stand does not do so for the pleasure of preparing thousands of hot dogs. Instead, he limits himself to the restricted world of standing behind a counter and frying wieners in order to make money.

Using technical thought for any length of time leads almost inevitably to the formation of a mental network. That is because the bottom-line focus of technical thought will create emotional memories, while the limited playing field will ensure that similar emotional memories are continually being encountered. Mental networks form when there are emotional memories that are similar.

Thus, when the practical technical circuit of Cp is being used, emotions show up in primarily two forms. There is the hyper-emotion produced by the Mercy mental network associated with the overall plan, and there are the specific Mercy emotions that result from pursuing a bottom line within the confines of this plan. The various methods which Cp uses to pursue its bottom line are described in more detail in an appendix.

Similarly, the abstract technical thinking of Ci occurs within the general context of a general Teacher theory, and as we have seen, when technical thought uses a paradigm for sufficient time, then this general Teacher theory will form into a Teacher mental network. But Ci is not just being driven by the hyper-emotion associated with a Teacher mental network, or even the Teacher emotion that results from applying a general Teacher theory. Instead, the main focus of Ci is usually upon increasing Teacher emotions in a more specific way. Think, for instance, of the person solving a difficult math problem. As anyone staring at a page of mathematical manipulations can tell, there is complexity. But the goal is to end up with a simple solution, something along the lines of 'The answer is 42'. This simple answer adds order to the complexity of the problem, and it is the order-within-complexity of finding a simple answer to a complicated problem that provides the emotional bottom line for Ci. Likewise, when a person derives a complete system of logic from a simple set of axioms, he is also creating order-within-complexity, but in this case he is starting with the order and adding the complexity.

In addition, Mercy emotions may also play an indirect role in motivating Ci, for a person may wish to solve a problem which no one else has yet solved, or come up with a better solution to a problem than anyone else, or maybe even win a Nobel Prize.

Notice that Ci and Cp are *hybrid* circuits that combine emotion and logic. The bottom line is *emotional*, and the ultimate goal is to increase the feelings associated with the bottom line. But rational thought is being used to *compare* one emotional option with another. Cp uses Perceiver facts to compare one emotional Mercy experience with another, leading to the map of value which was discussed earlier. Similarly, Ci uses

Server confidence to give stability to Teacher sequences, making it possible to define sequences clearly and compare one sequence with another. Think, for instance, of the carefully defined sequences of words which one finds in formal logic, or the precisely formulated equations of mathematics. That is what it means to use Server thought to define sequences of words.

Rational thought is then used to *improve* the bottom line. For Cp, this means using Server actions to reach a carefully defined goal. For Ci, this means using Perceiver facts, meanings, and rules to arrange the sequences of words in a way that is most elegant.

We can use the construction of a high rise tower to illustrate how these three stages work in Cp. Obviously, a high rise tower is more valuable than an empty building lot. The goal of turning the empty lot into a high rise provides the emotional bottom line. Various types of building plans, construction methods, and building materials will then be compared and the best alternative will be chosen. This illustrates how Contributor mode works with a map of value, using Perceiver facts to compare the various alternatives and then choosing the best one. Once the best alternative has been chosen, then the construction begins. The Server actions used for constructing a high rise are not haphazard, but rather require trained skills, complicated tools, and clearly defined sequences of action. The end result is a valuable building which can survive intact for decades.

We could look at logic or math as an illustration of Ci, but in order to introduce another side of technical abstract thought, we will look at the example of the *mystery novel*. The writing of a mystery novel illustrates how these three stages function in Ci. The emotional bottom line of a mystery novel is provided by Teacher emotions of problem-solving: Who did it? How can the order of a simple explanation be brought to the complexity of the story? The writing process begins by searching for the plot line—the sequence of events, described in Teacher words—which contains the greatest drama. Once the plot has been chosen, then the plot of the story has to be turned into the text of a book, just as in our previous illustration Cp turned the plot of land into a high rise tower. But writing a mystery novel is not simply a matter of writing a sequence of words. Rather, the reader needs to be given the right facts at the right time, setting up the context of the story but not including facts which are irrelevant, leaving a trail of clues that can be followed, dropping hints that will end up being significant later on, giving the reader inside knowledge which the characters in the story do not possess, and so on. The end result is a 'book which cannot be put down', because there is always the possibility that the crime might be solved but never the certainty of a solution, and always the threat of the investigation being thwarted but never total failure.

I have mentioned that cause-and-effect is the basic building block for Cp and that definitions are the basic building blocks for Ci. Because Cp and Ci are hybrid circuits which use rational thought but are driven by emotions, the basic building blocks for Cp and Ci also tend to acquire emotional overtones. Thus, even though Cp focuses upon cause-and-effect, what really drives Cp is *conscience*, which is cause-and-effect with the addition of subjective Mercy emotions. For instance, the story is told that one

Vancouver business tycoon who began his career owning car dealerships would automatically fire the lowest performing sales person each month. Such a method is very effective at motivating the Contributor person, but it also strikes 'below the belt'. Because conscience plays such a fundamental role in Cp, the practical Contributor *person* often finds it very difficult to apologize or admit wrong-doing, for such an admission faces him with the failure of guilt. In a similar manner, definitions of words also tend to occur within the larger context of a problem or theory. This is illustrated by the *crossword puzzle*, which the typical Contributor person enjoys. A crossword puzzle focuses upon the basic building block of Ci, because the goal is to determine words based upon cryptic definitions. However, these words are placed within the restricted 'playing field' of the crossword grid, and they intersect with each other, leading to Teacher feelings of order-within-complexity.

Notice how the technical circuits of Cp and Ci differ from normal concrete and abstract behavior. Everyone tries to pursue goals and solve problems. But the difference between normal thought and technical thought is like the difference between a dog that barks at trespassers and one that lunges at an intruder, fastens on to him with its teeth, and refuses to let go. First, technical thought does not just choose some goal. Instead, it uses rational thought to find a *worthwhile* goal to pursue. Second, it does not simply attempt to follow a goal. Rather, it systematically carries out careful steps in order to reach this goal. Third, it does not just try hard and hope for the best. Instead, it uses concentration to keep focusing upon the task until the goal is actually achieved. Finally, it does not simply decide to follow some plan. Instead, it places total confidence in its plan, committing all the resources that are needed to arrive at the desired destination.

It is this 'killer instinct' which distinguishes technical thought from normal thought, and this 'killer instinct' is found in its purest form in the Contributor *person*. Everyone wants to be successful; the Contributor person is capable of using conscious thought to add the extra edge which ensures that success is achieved—even if people or institutions are destroyed as 'collateral damage'.

Much more could be said about the details of these two circuits of Cp and Ci. Practical Contributor thought is responsible for discovering opportunities, doing cost/benefit analysis, planning for contingencies, and optimization, and Ci generates similar thought processes in the realm of abstract thought. For those who want to delve deeper, I have described these two circuits in more detail in an appendix. In the main text, we will be treating Cp and Ci simply as technical versions of concrete and abstract thought, and we will not be looking at any of the secondary ways in which Contributor thought can manipulate a network of Perceiver facts and Server sequences.

The Reality Distortion Field

Once the technical circuits of Ci and Cp begin to function, then they will have a naturally tendency to continue functioning for several reasons: First, Mercy feelings will drive those who use Cp to continue improving and developing their current bottom line, while Teacher feelings will drive those who use Ci to continue improving and extending their current paradigm. Second, the digital confidence that is assumed by technical thought will cause those who are using Ci or Cp to disregard uncertainty about knowledge or process. Third, Contributor concentration will cause those who are pursuing Ci or Cp to ignore anything that lies outside of the current context. Finally, the formation of mental networks will emotionally lock the mind into the current mental context.

These factors will occur in any technical field, but they are demonstrated most strongly by a Contributor *person* who is using Ci or Cp. When this type of Contributor person encounters someone who is pursuing a *different* plan, then there is a tendency for the Contributor person to project the sense that the other person is a worthless individual who is pursuing a useless goal that is devoid of value or meaning. Those who have experienced this type of projected aura will know that I am not exaggerating.

Because technical thought is a *hybrid* circuit, the aura will contain a combination of emotions and rational thought. The purpose of the aura is emotional; it is meant to overwhelm the opponent emotionally so that he has no way of responding. But this emotional assault will be couched in rational terms, because technical thought uses rational means to achieve its emotional bottom line. This makes it especially difficult to know how to respond to an aura. If one responds emotionally, then this will be taken as a sign by the Contributor person that he has won, because he is using rational thought while the other person has 'lost control' and succumbed to emotional pressure. But if one responds rationally, then the Contributor person will use emotional tricks to avoid facing the logic or to undermine his opponent. This often comes out as some form of *sarcasm*, in which an emotional attack is veiled in rational language.

The mental circuit of Ci develops technical thought within some area of expertise. But it is also possible for the Contributor *person* to become an expert in *several* fields, and the breadth and depth of knowledge shown by such individuals can be intimidating. However, the aura that accompanies this encyclopaedic knowledge can be equally intimidating, and the sarcasm that is used to dismiss those who are deemed to be unworthy can be withering. For such an individual, the challenge of learning about a field or successfully defending a paradigm in debate may be more important than the subject matter that is contained within that paradigm.

I should emphasize that, to a large extent, the aura and the ability go together. Entering technical thought means taking a mental leap from analog to digital certainty. But it is precisely the total commitment which this change in labeling implies that makes it *possible* for technical thought to perform its amazing feats, leading to major advances in terms of rigor and professionalism. And this change in labeling also makes it *necessary* for technical thought to perform its amazing feats, because technical thought must compensate for its lack of analog certainty by obsessing with details and formulating precise definitions. However, these technical advances will only occur in the specific areas upon which technical thought is focusing its efforts, leaving other regions with the aura but not the expertise.

The end result is a confusing combination of aura and ability. For instance, those who knew Steve Jobs, the wunderkind head of Apple Computers, talked about him 'projecting a reality distortion field'. Evidence from personality strongly suggests that Steve Jobs was a Contributor person. The mental mechanism behind the 'reality distortion field' is as follows: Entering technical thought leads to an attitude of digital confidence. Technical thought makes it possible to make major improvements—in specific areas. These technical improvements are then used to justify the attitude of digital confidence in areas which have not been improved. In crude terms, the technical Contributor person uses his brilliance in certain areas to 'prove' that he is right in other areas, and he uses his ability to use technical thought to 'prove' that the thinking of others is unworthy of evaluation. Everyone is capable of doing this, but it is the technically oriented Contributor person who is most capable of using a 'reality distortion field' to overwhelm his opponent.

Because technical thought insists upon doggedly pursuing its current goal, and because it combines professionalism with the self-deception of digital certainty, it will eventually reach a dead end, often by digging itself into some hole from which it cannot escape. It will then turn to normal thought for help. In the language of Kuhn, normal science grinds to a halt and is followed by an episode of revolutionary science, which leads to the development of the next paradigm.

The global financial crisis of 2008 provides a recent example involving the concrete circuit of Cp. Financial 'experts', mainly Contributor persons, pursued grand financial schemes with an attitude of digital certainty, using a combination of financial expertise, complicated concepts, and aura to convince everyone that they knew what they were doing, insisting with great confidence that nothing could go wrong. However, when the underlying structure fell apart, these various schemes collapsed, and the *real* financial world of mortgages, taxes, and the middle class was then called upon to bail out the 'game' world of Contributor-based financial self-delusion. The engineer has learned how to combine technical thought with real life. The financier, it appears, has forgotten the lessons that were learned at great cost during the Great Depression of the 1930s.

When one is using or analyzing technical thought, then the concept of mental networks will seldom, if ever, come up. That is because technical thought uses logic and pragmatism, and it tends to view emotional attachments as character flaws which need to be overcome. In more colloquial terms, the businessman believes that 'everyone has his price' and he would be willing to 'sell his grandmother if the price is right'. Similarly, the technical thinker insists that everything should be a valid topic of rational analysis and that there should be no 'sacred cows'.

However, if one looks behind the technical thought, one notices that mental networks do play a prominent—though unacknowledged—role. First, as I have already suggested, mental networks set the *context* for technical thought. As Kuhn mentions, a scientist is highly reluctant to let go of his current paradigm and cannot imagine functioning without a paradigm, which tells us that the paradigm has formed into a Teacher mental network. Similarly, the Western businessman who is willing to 'sell his grandmother' is usually far more reluctant to abandon the 'game of high finance', for this Mercy mental network defines his personal identity. But such a Mercy mental network does *not* have to define business activity. Living for several years in Korea exposed me to a form of business in which the bottom line is *not* money but rather a combination of money and honor for oneself, one's group, and one's country.

A mental network wants to be 'fed' with data that is compatible with its structure, and it responds with hyper-pain if it repeatedly encounters incompatible information. If continuing to use technical thought within some region of thought leads naturally to the development of a mental network, and if technical thought is driven by an emotional bottom line, then this may help to explain the ultimate motivation behind the aura so often displayed by the Contributor person. On the one hand, the positive hyper-emotion that comes from 'feeding' a mental network will motivate the Contributor person to use his aura to convince others to value his area of expertise. On the other hand, the hyper-pain that comes from 'feeding' a mental network with incompatible information will drive the Contributor person to use his aura to belittle those who pursue a different set of values.

Second, Teacher and Mercy mental networks can lead to undiscussable '*elephants*' which 'stand in the middle of the room' but are never acknowledged. The individual who works within a specific field knows instinctively what these 'elephants' are and can avoid them effortlessly, giving the impression that they do not exist. That is because his mind has acquired the mental networks of his field, and he uses intuitive psychology to mentally maneuver around them. When someone from a *different* area of expertise attempts to enter the field, then he will learn very quickly what these 'elephants' are, for when he mentally bumps into one, those who are in the field will let him know through a combination of expertise and aura that only a fool or an idiot would question the presence or necessity of that mental network. If the newcomer does insist upon analyzing the 'elephant in the room', then he runs the risk of being ostracized by the rest of the group for being 'incapable of rational thought'.

Finally, a mental network can provide the *foundation* for technical thought. This will happen if a person has analyzed a mental network and has come to the conclusion that it is essential for the existence of technical thought. Those who lack this personal knowledge may *assume* the presence of the mental network but not realize why its presence is critical. For instance, business requires a stable currency, as well as laws of private property. But this lesson is usually only grasped by the individual who has experienced an unstable currency or the expropriation of private property. Similarly, scientific research requires intellectual integrity. Quine, in *The Web of Belief*, assumes that this will always be present in the scientific community. However, today's politicized scientific atmosphere is teaching us that intellectual integrity is a precious commodity which cannot be taken for granted—even among scientists. As the tired but accurate cliché goes, eternal vigilance is the price of liberty.

Before continuing, I should emphasize that I am not trying to belittle technical thought, question the validity of rigorous logic, or suggest that the scientist or businessman is being irrational. Technical thought describes the mind functioning in its most rigorous, rational manner. However, I am attempting to point out that technical thought occurs within a larger mental context which is less rigorous and more emotionally aware, and that pretending that this larger context does not exist is both mentally and societally counterproductive.

Foucault's Epistemes

Now that we have the big picture, let us add a historical context, guided by the concept of *epistemes* which Michel Foucault presents in his book *The Order of Things: An Archaeology of the Human Sciences.* In order to preserve our continuity of thought, I will only present the highlights of Foucault's model here. A more extended analysis can be found in an appendix.

Foucault proposes that Western knowledge has gone through three distinct intellectual periods, which he refers to as the Renaissance episteme, the Classical episteme, and the Modern episteme, and he suggests that each of these periods is characterized by a unique mode of thought.

Foucault's Renaissance episteme describes a form of thought which mental symmetry calls *overgeneralization*, in which Teacher thought forms general theories guided by Perceiver associations within automatic thought, unrestricted by Perceiver logic or Perceiver facts. Thus, what matters is *surface* similarity together with *Mercy* feelings.

Earlier on, I suggested that learning goes through three distinct stages. Foucault is telling us that the overgeneralization of the first stage of learning was practiced by Western society *as a whole* during the time of the Renaissance. I would agree with this conclusion but add one additional factor. Medieval thinkers were capable of using abstract technical thought, but they used Ci to evaluate the revealed texts of the Church fathers and the Greek philosophers.

Foucault's Classical episteme describes a society in which Ci functions within an overall context of abstract thought, based upon the assumptions of scholasticism. Saying this another way, revealed truth had jumpstarted Ci during the Renaissance episteme, but this logical thinking was limited to the realm of revealed texts. During the Classical episteme, this method of technical thinking was extended to the natural realm, leading to a discovery of the universal laws of nature. In the language of Kuhn, the Classical episteme was characterized by a *balance* between normal science and revolutionary science. Scientists were using Ci to perform technical analysis within restricted contexts, but the *overall* goal was to use Perceiver logic to build general Teacher theories. In other words, to a large extent, science was doing what science claims to do: using the scientific method to gather data and come up with general theories.

Foucault's Modern episteme could be described as the triumph of normal science over revolutionary science, or the suppression of abstract thought by the technical circuit of Ci. That is because today's intellectual world is characterized by *hyper-specialization*—technical expertise driven by Ci within some small field of knowledge governed by its own paradigm. As I have learned from personal experience, each specialization is like a tiny fiefdom, with its own set of accepted experts, its own technical vocabulary, its own list of approved procedures, and its own collection of professional hurdles by which it keeps out the 'unwashed' and the 'unlearned'.

Foucault says that Modern intellectual thought is characterized by *self-questioning.* In other words, most modern fields of thought have experienced the *epistemological* crisis which was described a few paragraphs earlier. During the Classical period, scientists *assumed* that they could know and they observed the *natural* world for facts and order. During the *Modern* period, scientists came to the realization that they cannot know and therefore they study the process of observation in order to learn more about the knowing process.

I suggest that *Perceiver* thought is the main casualty of self-questioning. When an epistemological crisis occurs within a specific field, then all of the Perceiver facts and Server sequences within that field will fall into doubt. However, whenever a person repeats an action, then he is building Server confidence in that action. Therefore, carrying out the *process* of self-questioning will restore Server confidence—in the process of self-questioning. The result is that the Perceiver and Server content which *used* to be accepted and taught by that field will be replaced by the process of acquiring content, practiced in a highly technical manner.

We saw this transition when comparing math with science. Science originally defines a paradigm as a general description of how Nature 'acts'. However, when a scientific field becomes established, it tends to redefine a paradigm as a general description of what a community of scientists does. An epistemological crisis often motivates this change in definition, because it calls into question the very concept that one can know anything about the external world and replaces it with self-questioning.

For instance, philosophy used to be a search for knowledge using rigorous thought. It is now primarily a highly technical analysis of *how* one searches for knowledge. Similarily, the theologian used to study the Bible in order to discover what it says. Now, the primary focus is upon analyzing in a technical manner *how* one studies the Bible. In more general terms, the focus of the graduate thesis has shifted from making new discoveries to learning the process of doing technical research. As we shall see in the final chapter, the philosophy of Martin Heidegger illustrates what happens when self-questioning replaces existing Perceiver and Server content with Server confidence that is the result of physical action.

This does not mean that the process of technical research is wrong, or that self-questioning should be avoided. Rather, I suggest that technical thought is a useful tool and self-questioning helps to improve this tool. But a tool is meant to be used. In simple terms, the specialized, technical, self-questioning of the Modern episteme could be compared to the car mechanic who spends all of his time tinkering in the garage with his vehicle but never uses his automobile to drive anywhere—because he is no longer convinced that 'anywhere' exists.

And that is where the theory of mental symmetry becomes relevant. In the *physical* realm, science has learned—at least partially—how to reconcile incomplete knowledge of the physical world with the assumed confidence of mathematical analysis. But the *metaphysical* realm of human thought and the *social* realm of human interaction are still reverberating with the repercussions of epistemological crises. I suggest that the theory of mental symmetry provides a possible way out. First, it uses the modern *method* of self-questioning, describing the mental *mechanisms* for human thought. Second, it is based upon the concept of cognitive *modules*. If the *same* cognitive modules are being used in many different fields of thought, then this repetition makes it possible to place Perceiver confidence in the existence of these cognitive modules, replacing the Perceiver facts that fell into doubt during the epistemological crisis. And if the same modules show up in *different* specializations, then one can also use this commonality to build a general *interdisciplinary* theory of knowledge, escaping the mental prison of hyper-specialization. Theoretically, this should make it possible to achieve, once again, a *balance* between the technical thinking of Ci and the rational thinking of normal abstract thought, while still speaking the modern language of self-questioning.[33]

Three Stages of Learning

Before we continue with our main discussion, I would like to take a few pages to clarify the three stages of learning that were introduced several chapters earlier, which we will now relate to the interaction between normal thought and technical thought as well as the three epistemes of Foucault. A few pages back, we touched briefly on the relationship between technical thought and the three stages of learning. This discussion will add more details.

When I first mentioned these three stages, I suggested that the first stage is characterized by overgeneralized Teacher theories, the second stage by Perceiver facts, Server sequences, and a lack of general theories, and the third stage by the building of general Teacher theories that incorporate Perceiver facts and Server sequences. That is an overview of how the three stages of learning appear when one is acquiring knowledge and developing *abstract* thought. However, I suggest that the three stages of learning also apply to the acquisition of a *practical* skill. Therefore, we will look at both the abstract and the concrete version, which I will refer to as *abstract* learning and *concrete* learning.

The first stage of *abstract* learning is characterized by Teacher overgeneralization. What *seeds* this overgeneralization is usually emotional 'truth': The emotions of some Mercy experience mesmerize Perceiver thought into accepting the specific arrangements of that experience as universal 'truth'. Teacher thought observes this strong Mercy

[33] Quine's *Web of Belief* describes in detail how Perceiver thought functions when using normal thought, and modern science often stresses the need for interdisciplinary research, but when one actually uses normal thought to do interdisciplinary research, one finds that the modern bias toward hyper-specialized technical thought can be overwhelming.

emotion, interprets it as Teacher generality, and builds a general theory upon the specific situation. The end result is 'proof by example'. What makes this overgeneralization *possible* is Perceiver and Server *vagueness*: On the one hand, Perceiver thought is not functioning. Instead, most Perceiver content is being provided by mental associations within *automatic* Perceiver mode—hearsay information which a person overheard, or connections which are based upon *surface* similarities. On the other hand, Server mode also lacks solid content and is being guided primarily by mental associations within automatic *Server* thought. Such Server vagueness occurs when a person does not know how things *work*. Either he has not *done* anything related to the topic or else he has not *observed* carefully the sequence of events.

The result is like trying to assemble a cheaply made picture puzzle in which all of the pieces have similar shapes and are cut out of flimsy cardboard. Starting from some 'gut feeling', a person takes pieces which look like they should match and jams them together. This describes Foucault's *Renaissance* episteme, in which all sort of dissimilar mental pieces were being jammed together in order to produce overgeneralized theories.

A similar situation occurs during the first stage of *concrete* learning, except here the vagueness of mental content results in *clumsy* actions, in which all sorts of mismatched actions are being 'jammed together' in order to attempt to reach the desired Mercy goal.

Exaggeration is prominent in the first stage of learning: Theories are exaggerated and movement is exaggerated. That is because *Exhorter* mode is being attracted to emotional memories, and this Exhorter attraction is not being limited or channeled by any solid Perceiver or Server content. One could compare this mental situation to a big room filled with piles of candy. Set a child loose and he will run directly from one pile of candy to another. Solid Perceiver and Server content fills this big room with walls, doors, and hallways, forcing the child to take detours, explore rooms, and take a less direct route to his goal of finding chocolate treasures.

Let us move on now to the *second* stage of learning. I said previously that the second stage of *abstract* learning is characterized by the acquisition of Perceiver facts and Server sequences combined with a lack of general Teacher theories. In simple terms, this signifies the emergence of technical thought. In order to *enter* this stage, the mind requires a network of interconnected Perceiver facts and Server sequences. This means that one must first acquire some mental content before one is capable of performing technical thought.

This principle applies to both abstract learning as well as concrete learning—both Ci and Cp. For instance, when I taught in a high school, I often got frustrated when teaching the *first* chapter of a textbook, because the content seemed contrived. This is because the beginning student does not know enough to start the technical process of learning. Therefore, when an author writes the first chapter, he has to find some way of jumpstarting the process of learning while still appearing rigorous.

A similar situation arises when teaching a concrete skill. Consider, for example, the challenge of teaching someone to play the violin. Before the actual teaching can begin, the student has to learn how to stand properly, how to hold the violin, and how to grasp his bow, along with other preliminary basic skills. Only then is it possible to begin the technical task of formal instruction.

All technical instruction, whether abstract or concrete, has similar features. First, it concentrates on specific *aspects* of learning. For instance, in geometry, a specific class might focus upon learning the five ways of proving that two lines are parallel, or when teaching violin, a lesson may focus upon learning how to apply equal pressure to both strings when playing double notes by using the correct bow angle. The beginning abstract student wants to *overgeneralize* and learn the whole book—right now. Similarly, the beginning violin student wants muddle his way *clumsily* through the entire piece of music without stopping. In both cases, technical instruction takes the attention of the student away from the *entire* content and forces the student to focus upon one *specific* aspect. Thus, we see the imposition of Contributor *concentration*, accompanied by a focus upon technical *details*.

Second, technical instruction focuses upon troubleshooting, improving, optimizing, and perfecting—within the 'rules of the game'. For instance, suppose that one is teaching in school. Technical instruction does not walk into the classroom and 'wing it'. Instead, the curriculum determines what topics will be covered in the course, while the lesson plan sets out what will be done in each specific class period. A lesson plan may include contingencies that cover what will be done if students get confused or if they finish their work early, but there is no unstructured time in technical instruction.

The Contributor *person* who teaches typically uses a combination of expertise and aura to control his students. Spontaneity is discouraged, as is questioning of authority. Instead, teaching is like a game of chess, in which the instructor views his students as chess pieces which he 'moves' in response to the current situation. And these 'chess pieces' are not supposed to develop a life of their own or move independently.

However, as Helmuth Karl Bernhard Graf von Moltke, the German Field Marshal, observed: "No battle plan survives contact with the enemy." In the language of mental symmetry, technical thought may come up with plans that are certain, but reality is messy. Therefore, implementing a plan means interfacing between internal certainty and external uncertainty. The Contributor *person* typically deals with this problem in several ways. First, he may use force of personality to impose his plan upon the messy world, denouncing followers whose abilities or skills fall below his threshold of assumed perfection. For instance, professional symphony conductors have historically been infamous for the absolute perfection and discipline which they demand from musicians. Second, he may subdivide his plan into details and use rigorous logic to work out precisely how knowledge or skill can be conveyed in a step-by-step fashion, what errors a student could make, and what should be done to correct each possible misconception or failure. Thus, by making the digital steps sufficiently detailed and by exploring enough of the possibilities, the analog task of learning is turned into a digital 'game' with fixed moves and countermoves. Third, if a Contributor person cannot deal with a situation in a sufficiently digital manner, then he may decide to ignore it completely and move on to something else which can be successfully 'tamed'. Finally, students or followers may be subjected to a Contributor plan for a period of time and then permitted to leave for a while in order to recover mentally. Similarly, a person may find that he can only use technical thought for a while before his own mind rebels and demands some recovery time.

Again, I need to reiterate that all cognitive styles are capable of technical thought. But for the Contributor *person*, Ci and Cp emerge when *conscious* thought controls the mind. Therefore, the characteristics of technical thought are usually seen most clearly in the behavior of the Contributor person. And when technical thought becomes the norm, as occurs in Foucault's Modern episteme, then the Contributor person naturally excels, and he uses his combination of technical expertise and aura to 'prove' that he should be in charge, and because technical thought is accepted as the norm, others accept this 'proof' as valid.

I should also mention that entering the second stage of learning is like establishing a *beachhead*, for technical thought begins within one specific area of thought or action and then spreads from there to other topics and abilities. For instance, the intermediate geometry student may know how use technical thought to prove that two lines are parallel, but when it comes to proving that a quadrilateral is a parallelogram, then he may still use wishful thinking and overgeneralization. Similarly, the theologian may be a technical expert at the rational analysis of *peripheral* theological issues, but when it comes to analyzing core doctrines, then he too may be reduced to the analogies and surface similarities of Teacher overgeneralization.

Let us move now to the *third* stage of learning. When examining *abstract* learning, I described this as the building of general Teacher theories that incorporate Perceiver facts and Server sequences. For *concrete* learning, one could define this as the reaching of emotional *Mercy* goals which incorporate Perceiver facts and Server sequences.

Music provides a good illustration of the contrast between the second and third stages of learning. The second stage technical student may play every note perfectly and perform flawlessly, but hearing him play is like listening to a computer synthesizer because the notes are present, but the music is not.

What happens mentally in the third stage of learning is that technical thought *releases control* of the mind. One might think that this would cause a regression back to the first stage of learning with its overgeneralized theories, but the content that was acquired during the second stage of learning prevents this from happening. In the first stage of learning, mental associations are being channeled by the *surface* similarities and *clumsy* movements of automatic thought. The second stage of learning uses technical thought to replace this vague mental content with solid Perceiver facts and Server skills, but technical thought also restricts and controls mental associations, leading to the clinical perfection of the technician. The third stage of learning restores *freedom* to Exhorter-driven mental associations, which will now be *channeled* by the solid Perceiver facts and trained Server skills that were acquired during the second stage. And instead of using information from automatic thought to *build* theories and *guide* actions, Facilitator mode uses information from automatic thought to *smooth out* solid facts and trained skills.

The musician who enters this third stage of learning transcends the notes and makes music. He retains the technical expertise that was acquired during the second stage but adds to it expression, phrasing, and emotion. Similarly, when a school instructor enters the third stage of learning, the curriculum and the lesson plan are still there, but they no longer control the situation. The students are learning, but they do not just sit there 'on task'. Instead, there is a *flow* to the class. The ebb and flow of teaching and response may leave the lesson plan temporarily, but the instructor still manages to convey the required information to the student. And because the students are emotionally involved, they remember what they are taught, they find the class interesting, and they stop looking at the clock to see when the class will be over.

For Contributor mode, the third stage of learning produces a feeling of confidence which goes beyond normal confidence. The Contributor person may feel that he has 'lost control' of the situation, but somehow his mental content prevents order and structure from falling apart and the end result is even better than what he would have achieved if he had attempted to remain in control of his mind by using technical thought.

The Inner Game of Tennis, along with similar books written by Timothy Gallwey, attempts to describe this third stage of learning in which Contributor mode is 'out of control' and yet still functioning successfully. Gallwey describes how this type of thinking can emerge with *physical* movement. In this book, we are attempting to analyze how this level of functioning can be achieved in *all* areas of thought.

I suggest that this is what it *really* means to 'go beyond logic'. When rational thought is limited to the objective, then one can only go 'beyond logic' by abandoning logic and embracing emotionally driven irrationality. In contrast, the third stage of learning allows emotions to travel along mental paths which were constructed using logic and rational thought. Saying this more precisely, Exhorter mode is given the freedom to be attracted to emotional Teacher and Mercy memories. But Exhorter mode will travel along the mental connections which were formed using rational, logical, and technical thought.

In more general terms, the third stage of *abstract* learning represents a *balance* between abstract thought and Ci, and the third stage of *concrete* learning represents a balance between concrete thought and Cp. The technical circuits of Ci and/or Cp are used to *perfect* learning in some area, and then normal abstract and/or concrete thought is used to *broaden* this learning to related areas. Technical thought goes *deeper*, normal thought goes *wider*. Using the two together combines expertise with integration.[34] Saying this

---

[34] It appears that the male mind emphasizes the three cognitive modes that use confidence, while the female mind emphasizes the three cognitive modes that use emotion. This effect is independent of cognitive style and describes a tendency for certain cognitive modes to function, whether they are conscious or subconscious. In terms of the three stages of learning, the female

another way, during the third stage of learning, the mind is able to move *between* normal thought and technical thought because the one becomes similar to the other. On the one hand, technical thought recognizes that it is a hybrid circuit driven by an emotional bottom line and it stops trying to use rational thought and control to clamp down on emotions and pretend that they do not exist. On the other hand, when technical thought gives freedom to emotions, the behavior that results is sufficiently rational to be compatible with technical thought.

Now let us tie in Foucault's epistemes. During the Classical episteme, there *was* a balance between abstract thought and Ci, because the search to develop technical paradigms occurred within the greater context of building general Teacher theories. In the language of Kuhn, there was a balance between normal science and revolutionary science. Similarly, the *practical* professional skills that were developed by Cp during this period were not divorced mentally from the personal experiences of concrete thought. Think, for instance, of the movie cliché of the Victorian scientist and inventor, which represents the epitome of this type of thinking. There was technology, but the pieces of a machine were large enough for its operation to be viewed by the individual, simple enough to be understood by the individual, and clumsy enough to be manufactured by an individual. Compare that with today's typical computer. It functions invisibly and is far too complicated for any person to be able to grasp or manufacture.

The Modern episteme has both improved and destroyed this balance. On the one hand, the *self-questioning* of the Modern episteme makes it possible for modern man to analyze the assumptions of blind faith that were developed during the Middle Ages and used during the Classical period. On the other hand, the *objectivity* of modern science combined with the *specialization* of modern learning makes it difficult for the modern technocrat to *escape* technical thought and enter the third stage of learning. That is because the third stage of learning is guided by emotions, and objectivity removes Mercy feelings while specialization limits Teacher emotions. Thus, the most that the average modern man can achieve is third stage learning *within* an area of expertise. The modern individual is capable of reaching the third stage of 'going beyond logic' when he is teaching a specific topic, doing research within a paradigm, playing a game, or performing a piece of music. As was illustrated by a previous quote, Richard Feynman, the famous physicist, is an example of someone who functioned at this third stage of learning at the level of scientific thought in general. But it is difficult for modern man to reach the third stage of learning as a *person.* Thus, we could say that in the Modern episteme, normal abstract and concrete thought have become the *servants* of technical thought.

---

mind operates naturally at the first stage, the male mind tends to function at the second stage, while the third stage could be described as a sort of 'mental marriage' between male and female thought.

Comparing Cp and Ci

Let us continue now with our main discussion. When attempting to analyze religion from a cognitive perspective, then I suggest that there are two questions regarding technical thought which play a critical role. First, what is the *difference* between Ci and Cp. Second, why are there *two* mental circuits?

The first question is easy to answer but harder to explain. As far as Contributor mode is concerned, there is *no* difference between Ci and Cp, because both involve rearranging elements within an existing network of Perceiver facts and Server sequences; in both cases, Contributor mode is restricting thought to the 'rules of some game'.

This is a fairly abstract statement, so let me explain it with the help of an example. Suppose that I am working with a machine such as a car engine. An engine contain *parts* that *work*. Perceiver mode thinks in terms of *parts* and objects; Server mode deals with *work*, sequences, and actions. Thus, an engine physically expresses a network of Perceiver facts and Server sequences.

It is possible to approach an engine using *concrete* thought. In this case, the engine performs a Server action that helps to reach a Mercy goal. For instance, the goal may be to drive the car from point A to point B as fast as possible, or using as little fuel as possible. Cp will then approach this goal in a *technical* manner, doing things such as adjusting timings, replacing parts, or fine-tuning settings. All of these steps involve rearranging elements within an *existing* network of facts and sequences. None of them question or change the overall plan of driving a car from point A to point B. The overall goal or bottom line is being provided by *Mercy* emotions and a technical, restricted version of concrete thought is being used.

However, it is also possible to deal with the same engine using *abstract* thought. Here, the engine will be viewed as a collection of functions which cooperate to generate the order-within-complexity of a general Teacher theory. In this case, the purpose is not to reach some goal in Mercy thought, but rather to create Teacher pleasure by having the various parts work together more effectively or more efficiently, or to avoid the Teacher displeasure that occurs when the engine breaks down and the parts cease to function in a unified manner.

The abstract viewpoint is usually taken by the person who *designs* or *builds* a machine, while the concrete viewpoint is typically taken by the consumer who uses the machine as a *tool*. However, both viewpoints involve the same machine, and it is possible to switch between one viewpoint and the other.

Similarly, suppose that I am practicing a musical instrument. I can adjust my playing in order to pursue *Teacher* goals such as eliminating mistakes or increasing efficiency of movement. Or I can focus upon *Mercy* goals such as improving my tone or optimizing my musical expression.

Both Cp and Ci involve a network of Perceiver facts and Server sequences, and in both cases Contributor mode is performing the *same* task of rearranging items within this network. Thus, as far as *Contributor* mode is concerned, there is no difference between Cp and Ci. However, Cp is being guided by a *Mercy* goal whereas Ci is being driven by *Teacher* emotion.

Let us turn our attention now to the second significant question. If Contributor mode can be guided by either Teacher emotions or Mercy emotions, then why does Contributor mode separate into the two distinct circuits of Cp and Ci? Before I address this question, I should mention that our study into personality backs up this mental division. Most Contributor persons use *either* Cp *or* Ci. The practical Contributor person who is good at business or sports is generally not very skilled at abstract thought. Instead, his abstract thinking is limited to a small collection of facts, slogans, proverbs, and stories. In contrast, the intellectual Contributor person can have an encyclopaedic knowledge within his area of expertise but is often lacking in practical skills. Hence, the absent-minded professor.

I suggest that the human mind contains the two distinct circuits of Cp and Ci because the human body can express itself either through *speech* or through *action*. Let us begin by reminding ourselves of how a *language* is learned. Suppose that I say 'awantweet' to someone who does not speak English. That may not be what I said, but that probably describes what was heard. The listener must then separate this string of sounds into distinct syllables and words, either by having me repeat what I said more slowly and clearly, or else by having me write it down. Eventually he will realize that what he initially heard as 'awantweet' is actually 'I want to eat'. This separating and clarifying of speech is done by Server mode as it divides the Teacher sounds of speech into sequences that are repeated. Given enough repetition, the listener will learn to recognize words like 'want' and 'eat' even when they occur in the middle of a sentence. And, once the sounds of speech are divided into the distinct chunks of words, then Perceiver mode can assign meanings to each of these words.

Contributor mode lies in the middle of this process of recognizing words and assigning them meanings. During the initial process of learning, Contributor mode simply connects words with their meanings, a process which involves a minimum of Contributor thought. However, when abstract thought acquires a sufficiently large vocabulary, then the mental *circuit* of Ci can begin to function. As this process of developing technical thought repeats itself, the operation of Ci becomes increasingly sophisticated. However, it all starts with words and their meanings, and it starts there because Teacher mode is capable of expressing itself by wagging the tongue and making verbal noises.

Action develops in a similar manner. The child discovers that he can move his body and he learns that this movement has physical consequences. All physical movement is initially unskilled and unintelligent. However, as a person *repeats* movements, then this practicing builds Server confidence and teaches skills. Similarly, if a person uses Perceiver mode to observe the results of his actions, then he can adjust his actions in order to produce pleasant Mercy results and avoid painful ones. Again, Contributor mode is in the middle of all of this *adjusting*, and when sufficient Server skills and

Perceiver facts are acquired, then the mental circuit of Cp will start to function and a person will limit his actions to some set of skills and focus his energy upon improving these skills.

The problem arises with the next step of *combining* words and actions. There is no natural reason for the sound 'ou-awk' to be connected with the physical action of standing up and pumping one's legs and arms back and forth. Instead, these two will only become connected if Perceiver thought decides that they have the same *meaning*. And that describes how words initially acquire their meanings. The speaker points at an object and says 'budderfula'. The listener asks him to repeat more slowly and he says 'but-ter-fly'. The listener then makes a connection within Perceiver thought between the *object* being pointed at and the *meaning* of the word. Hopefully, the speaker was pointing at the butterfly and not at the flower on which the butterfly was resting.

This means that attaching *accurate* meanings to words requires Perceiver thought. If Perceiver mode is not functioning, then words will have vague meanings that depend upon the emotional context. Similarly, the *meaning* of a word is only as reliable as the level of Perceiver confidence. When emotions overwhelm Perceiver confidence, then words lose their meanings. A person may still say the same words, but they no longer have any connection with reality.

I suggest that this is why it is not possible for philosophy to use logical speech to analyze normal human activity. Logical speech belongs to the technical circuit of Ci with its precise definitions. Human activity, in contrast, is an expression of non-technical concrete thought with its Mercy emotions. In order to bring these two together, one must first turn concrete thought into Cp by limiting practical activity to the technical rules of some 'game'. Only then can one use Perceiver thought to come up with technical definitions of words.

Education in Terms of Cp and Ci

Now let us take what we have learned about technical thought and walk through the process of education, beginning with the child entering school. He thinks that school is simply another way to spend a normal day. But it is actually a carefully crafted version of abstract thought masquerading as concrete thought, for the school curriculum determines which topics will be covered as well as the manner in which they will be taught. Thus, the instructor is being limited in what he can teach, while the student is being limited in what he can do. The instructor is expected to limit his words to the technical requirements of the curriculum, indicating that he is functioning within Ci. The student is expected to submit to the rules and structure of the school environment, demonstrating that he is functioning within Cp. Because both abstract thought and concrete thought are being limited and defined, it is possible to bring these two together, and to use the *Mercy* emotions of concrete thought to motivate the student into developing abstract thought with its general *Teacher* theories.[35]

The first stage of school sets up the method of education by putting into place the two shortcuts. On the Perceiver side, the primary student is taught to obey his teacher and to accept what the teacher says as true. On the Teacher side, the primary student is taught the 'three verbal Rs' of literacy and basic math. As the student continues through his primary years, he learns how to play by the rules of the 'game' of school: If he *attends* school and *works* hard, then he will receive good marks. As far as his mind is concerned, school is simply a version of Cp set up by the adult world.

Sometime during the learning process, the student will make the shift to abstract thought. Instead of being driven by Mercy emotions of approval and disapproval, he will start to be guided by Teacher feelings of generality and understanding. For some students, this shift happens in high school, for others it does not occur until graduate school, for some it never occurs. Remember that several related factors are involved in this mental shift: First, Perceiver mode is 'waking up' and testing the facts that it was taught. Second, as Perceiver mode compares one situation with another, then this helps Teacher mode to develop general theories. Third, when Teacher mode integrates Perceiver facts, then these facts will be modified to fit together more simply, and these modified Perceiver facts will form an integrated collection of imaginary Forms within Mercy mode that are better and purer than real life.

As far as *Contributor* mode is concerned, this mental shift is the first step in the process of integrating Cp and Ci. Remember that Contributor ties together Perceiver and Server. Thus, when the student shifts from concrete to abstract thought and Perceiver thought 'wakes up', then the *Perceiver* side of Perceiver-plus-Server starts to come together.

Notice that this is as far as *verbal* education can go. It can develop abstract thought using words to build general theories, and it can turn this abstract thinking into the *technical* circuit of Ci. This describes what happens in fields such as logic and mathematics. However, when education stops at this stage, then there is a tendency for Ci to become disconnected from Cp and to begin operating autonomously.

For instance, what is the Perceiver meaning of 'x' and 'y' in the equation $y = 3x + 2$? These letters have no meanings because they are *variables* which can take on *any* meaning. 'x' could represent watermelons while 'y' could be the price of having watermelons delivered to your house. In essence, a variable could be described as a Perceiver object of a Perceiver object. Thus, what began in primary school as adding watermelons turned in middle school into a math equation involving watermelons and in high school into an abstract math equation that has nothing to do with watermelons or with any other specific Perceiver object.

---

[35] A structured learning environment makes it possible to use Cp and Ci to bridge abstract thought and concrete thought. But normal life is not structured, and abstract thought is not limited purely to Ci. Therefore, education requires structure but must also go beyond structure.

In the language of mental symmetry, math starts with Perceiver objects in Cp, these Perceiver objects give meanings to mathematical symbols in Ci, and these Perceiver meanings eventually become disconnected from the objects from which they initially acquired their meanings. This pedagogical transition is good for teaching abstract thought, but it also makes it possible for the theoretician to live within a Ci that is completely divorced from the real world of Cp.

Let us move on to the next step. Once the student has a general understanding in Teacher thought, then he can use this understanding to guide his Server actions. Saying this another way, the scientific method of education which we discussed in a previous chapter can only begin *after* the student knows how to work with general theories. Saying this yet another way, in order to use math to solve science problems, the student has to know how to do math. Obviously, this is when the *Server* side of Perceiver-plus-Server comes together. And, as Kuhn indicates, this is a long and drawn out process which involves the solving of countless problems.

Once the student has acquired the skill of combining words with actions, then it is time for him to graduate from school and re-enter the world. He now faces a choice. He can either continue to live in the physical world the way that he *used* to live, or else he can use the skills that he has acquired to *change* the way that he lives. In technical language, Ci has been developed and it has been expanded to include Cp. It can now replace the existing Cp. For instance, think of the graduate who has learned new methods of farming who returns to his home village. He can either farm the way that everyone else does in the village or else he can apply the new agricultural principles that he has learned in school.

As the Industrial Revolution demonstrates, replacing traditional methods with scientific methods will result in major societal upheaval, for in order to introduce new ways, the old ways will have to die. The type of upheaval that is experienced will depend upon the nature of the education. Scientific education is by nature *objective*; it ignores subjective Mercy emotions. Therefore, when science changes the world, it will replace *human* Mercy-based culture with *inhuman* industrial methods, while leaving the core Mercy mental networks of humanity untouched.

Religious education, in contrast, is by nature *blind*; it uses Mercy emotions to define Perceiver truth. Thus, when religious education sends out missionaries to transform a society, the tendency is to *replace* the existing tribal society with the imported religious variety. This describes what typically happened when the Catholic countries colonized America, or when the Protestant missionaries of the 19th century took Christianity to non-Western societies. The 'natives' were expected to abandon their existing culture and embrace the Western way of life.

However, as scientific education includes more of the subjective, and as religious education discovers the rational principles that lie behind religious doctrine, then societal transformation will attempt to modify *existing* elements of society instead of simply ignoring the old or throwing out the old and replacing it with the new. For instance, this might mean teaching basic medical principles to traditional healers or having tribal leaders organize the digging of wells.

Summarizing, the objective approach tends to *ignore* the subjective, the religious approach tends to *suppress* the subjective, whereas a truly rational approach will *digest* the subjective. Whatever the method, the old is being replaced with the new. Society is still experiencing the practical equivalent of a paradigm shift in which traditional Mercy mental networks are being replaced by mental networks that are held together by Teacher words and Teacher understanding.

However, one must not forget that a society will only *remain* transformed if the new methods are compatible with natural law. Otherwise, it will only be possible to maintain the transformation through continual human effort. One could compare this to building a city in the middle of a jungle. As ancient ruins demonstrate, keeping the jungle at bay is a continual struggle, for as soon as one stops fighting the trees and the vines, they will start to reclaim their original territory. On the other hand, one can also find irrigation systems that are thousands of years old which still function—because they take advantage of natural processes instead of attempting to fight Nature.

Let us move on to the next step. When a society experiences a type of 'Industrial Revolution', then a new avenue of employment opens up for technical Contributor thought, known as *research and development* or R&D. R&D lives within abstract thought, but it comes up with applications that improve concrete thought. During the previous stage, traditional ways of making a living became obsolete and were replaced by new scientific ways of living; the existing technical plans of Cp came to an end and were replaced by technical plans which combined Cp with Ci. R&D becomes possible when a *combination* of Cp and Ci becomes accepted by society.

The result of combining Cp with Ci through R&D is to turn Forms into reality. For instance, think of geometry with its lines, planes, right angles, and logical theorems. The computer that sits on a desk is a physical manifestation of lines, planes, right angles, and logical theorems. It comes from the Platonic world of Forms, but it is not just a mental concept locked within the mind. Instead, it is a real object that exists within the physical world that is more Form-like than anything which Plato ever conceived.

Religious Education, Technical Thought & Mental Networks

Objective science has transformed the world through the Industrial Revolution and it continues to make the physical world more Form-like through R&D. But because objective science *avoids* Mercy emotions, our modern Form-like world is also impersonal and inhuman. The solution is to add the personal element to the path of education, which leads to *religious* education. But when one adds the personal element, then *Mercy* mental networks become involved, which means that the path of education will now lead to a struggle between Mercy mental networks and Teacher mental networks, a struggle which objective science largely avoids by building Teacher mental networks in areas where Mercy mental networks are *not* present.

We have seen that education leads to the development of Teacher mental networks. We have also analyzed education from the viewpoint of the two technical circuits of Cp and Ci. Let us now see what happens when one adds the influence of Mercy mental networks.

As we know, education begins with a major misconception upon the part of the student. He thinks that attending school is just like another physical activity, when it is actually a carefully planned expression of general Teacher understanding. This translation from abstract to concrete is being coordinated by *Contributor* mode, because Ci is being used to develop a plan for building a general Teacher understanding and this plan is being presented to the student as a series of goals and activities which involve Cp.

If we add the personal element, then I suggest that the overlap between Cp and Ci provides a cognitive explanation for the religious concept of *incarnation.* When we examined Eastern mysticism, we saw that it is possible to form an *emotional* bond between personal identity and an image of God by combining overgeneralization with identification. However, such an emotional connection with the divine can only be maintained by suppressing Perceiver facts and avoiding Server sequences.

Now we see that it is possible to connect a general Teacher theory with a plan for personal identity via Contributor mode. In religious terms, Contributor mode can act as an *intermediary* between God and man. Unlike the religion of first stage learning, this type of mental connection *demands* Perceiver and Server content and it is an expression of the *second* and *third* stages of learning. What is also being connected is subtly different. In Eastern mysticism, the individual believes that personal identity *is* God, whereas a Contributor incarnation acts as a cognitive intermediary between personal identity and the mental image of God.

Let us relate the concept of incarnation to the process of education. The mind of the child is built around Mercy mental networks that practice identification and denial, which by their very nature oppose the Perceiver facts that are required to tie Cp and Ci together. Thus, it is not possible to mentally construct an incarnation by *starting* from personal identity. However, if one *begins* with a general Teacher understanding, then one can use the Perceiver and Teacher shortcuts of education to teach this Teacher understanding to students *despite* their childish Mercy mental networks. In religious terms, sin prevents man from knowing God accurately; thus, God must reveal himself to man through incarnation, and because this revelation is occurring in *verbal* form, the incarnation will be seen as a human expression of words.

Notice precisely what is occurring with incarnation. The Contributor circuit of Ci works within an existing Teacher paradigm using a network of abstract Server sequences and Perceiver meanings. If this Teacher paradigm explains personal identity, then in religious terms, Ci 'lives with God'. The Contributor circuit of Cp works with a personal plan that uses Server actions guided by Perceiver facts to improve Mercy experiences. If this Contributor plan involves personal identity, then in religious terms, Cp is 'bringing salvation to personal identity'. Because Cp and Ci both involve a network of Perceiver and Server content, it is possible to bring Cp and Ci together, resulting in a Contributor incarnation that simultaneously 'lives with God' and 'brings salvation to personal identity'. In the external world, this overlap is epitomized by R&D, which uses technical Contributor thought *both* to improve the general Teacher understanding of science *and* to produce 'new and improved' gadgets for the individual consumer.

Now let us return to the school situation. The first step of education is to set up the two shortcuts of education by using people with emotional status to implant Perceiver 'truth' and by using words to build general Teacher theories. In religious language, the instructor will tell his students, "This book teaches you about God and it is special because important people say that it is special." However, notice that the instructor is actually using his *own* Mercy status to program the mind of the primary student with facts and rules, and *he* is either rewarding or punishing the student with emotional Mercy experiences. Therefore, the teacher may be telling his students to obey God, but it is the Mercy mental networks which represent teachers and parents that motivate the behavior of the students.

So far, we are on familiar ground. But, how will *technical* thought respond to this situation? I suggest that the technical circuit of Cp will emerge, guided by the 'rules of the game' which are being provided by the *Mercy* mental networks of school authority figures. Cp will then pursue the Mercy goal of gaining the greatest amount of personal approval from authority figures. A similar result occurs whenever an organization sets up a system of Perceiver rules and Server procedures to guide personal behavior.

The next stage of education involves 'weaning' the religious student from Mercy mental networks and the approval and disapproval that they provide. *Scientific* education does this by *replacing* the Mercy emotions of personal approval with the Teacher emotions of a general understanding. *Religious* education takes a different approach, for instead of *suppressing* Mercy feelings, it first alters them to be *consistent* with Teacher thought and then it ensures that Teacher feelings take *precedence* over Mercy emotions.

As we saw in a previous chapter, Mercy mental networks that drive personal behavior can be made *compatible* with Teacher thought by telling students that "These rules come from an unusual person called God. God is an invisible person who sees everything that you do and say. He feels bad whenever you break a rule. He lives in words and you can interact with him by talking to him through prayer."

The result is that personal behavior will be driven by Mercy mental networks *masquerading* as Teacher mental networks. It is possible to develop abstract thought by starting from such an emotional foundation. In essence, such a student will be doing the *right* thing for the *wrong* reason. He will be developing abstract thought, which is the right thing. But he will still be motivated by Mercy mental networks, which is the wrong reason. However, if the instructors shape their personal approval to be *compatible* with Teacher mode and abstract thought, then the learning student will acquire both the Mercy feelings of personal approval and the Teacher feelings of gaining understanding.

In religious terms, such a student will grow in favor in both the sight of God and the sight of man.

Notice that it is only possible for a student to receive emotional support *simultaneously* from Mercy approval and Teacher understanding if the school system and the instructors act as a sort of incarnation to their students, because they are using Perceiver rules and Server procedures to *translate* the needs of abstract thought into language of Mercy approval and disapproval. For instance, the instructor may give the student a good mark if he reads a story carefully, takes factual notes, and writes an essay focusing upon some aspect of the story. The student is using abstract thought in a manner which builds general Teacher understanding, but he is receiving Mercy approval for doing this.

This *Mercy* support of growing Teacher understanding needs to continue until Forms emerge within the mind of the student, because this is a sign that Teacher understanding has become sufficiently developed to replace Mercy approval, for Forms can act as a Mercy *substitute* for the Mercy-based approval of the instructor. Obedience to approval means doing something because some *person* will reward or punish me, whereas obedience to Forms means doing something because I want to meet my own *internal* standards of perfection. In religious language, when this step is reached, then the Holy Spirit becomes connected with incarnation.

At this point, it is *possible* for a student to stop being motivated by Mercy networks of approval and start being motivated by Teacher mental networks of understanding. However, the student will only *make* this mental transition if he passes certain mental tests. In particular, I suggest that the motivation of the student will have to be tested in three basic ways which correspond to fundamental principles that have been discussed previously. We will describe these three tests both in terms of mental networks and from the viewpoint of technical thought.

First, Teacher emotion must *replace* Mercy emotion. This was discussed previously as using Teacher understanding to escape the Mercy shortcut. Mercy emotion is driven by *specific* experiences, whereas Teacher emotion comes from *general* understanding. A student who is driven by Mercy feelings of approval will only learn what is required to get approval from his instructor. In contrast, Teacher emotions lead to *curiosity* which will motivate the student to learn *more* about a subject, even if this is not required by the instructor. For technical thought, this indicates that Cp is turning into Ci. Cp is driven by a specific Mercy bottom line such as getting an A+; Ci takes the *same* content and attempts to gain a *deeper* understanding. When a student learns more, even when it is not required, this indicates that Teacher mental networks of understanding are taking *precedence* over Mercy mental networks of approval.

Second, Mercy feelings of approval must be replaced by *Forms*. The previous point deals with the emergence of Ci, which will lead to a greater *depth* of scholarship. This second step involves a change in Cp, which will affect the *quality* of work. Cp is driven by a Mercy bottom line. When Cp is guided by Mercy mental networks of approval and disapproval, then a person will try to gain *external* status and importance. Forms, in contrast, are by their very nature *internal*. Pursuing Forms means meeting internal Mercy standards of perfection rather than external standards of approval. For Cp this means being motivated by the bottom line of doing a good job, even if this does not result in a better mark or lead to the best mark. Notice that the goal is not to abandon Cp, but rather to alter the *nature* of Cp. When a student follows internal standards of perfection, then this indicates that Teacher mental networks of understanding are *changing* Mercy mental networks of approval.

Third, Mercy mental networks of personal approval must not be allowed to *override* Teacher mental networks of understanding. When Teacher mental networks can survive intact in the face of potential disapproval, then this indicates that Perceiver thought has 'woken up' from its attitude of blind faith. That is because approval uses emotional pressure to overwhelm Perceiver thought, whereas understanding uses Perceiver thought to build Teacher theories. As far as technical thought is concerned, this principle involves *optimization*. As is mentioned in the appendix on technical thought, optimization drops elements which are regarded as non-essential in order to emphasize those which are deemed to be essential. When Cp and Ci are used together, then one will tend to run better than the other. When a student makes the mental transition from concrete thought to abstract thought, then he will ensure that Ci continues to function well, even if this means that Cp does not run as well.

Finally, these three mental transitions need to be tested in the *absence* of emotional support from existing Mercy mental networks. In other words, the student must make these choices when the instructor is *not* peering over his shoulder. Notice that this is different than the avoidance of Mercy mental networks that occurs when doing altruistic behavior. Altruism means *doing* actions guided solely by Teacher understanding and not by any rewards from Mercy mental networks. In contrast, we are looking here at an earlier stage of *studying* and *learning* in the absence of Mercy mental networks.

Scientific education sidesteps this epistemological crisis by avoiding Mercy emotions, but it forms a major personal crisis in religious education because Mercy mental networks are being included as a core component. Those who go through this crisis of knowing often describe it as a sort of 'wilderness experience' devoid of Mercy feelings during which they had to think issues through for themselves guided solely by the 'internal voice of God'.

For instance, the current cheating fiasco involving the 'No Child Left Behind' educational program in the United States illustrates what happens when these three principles are *not* followed and educational motivation does not shift from Mercy emotions to Teacher emotions. In 2001, the No Child Left Behind Act was passed which mandated that all students in certain grades would be given a set of standardized tests and that schools whose students did poorly on these tests would receive less federal funding than schools whose students did well. Thus, education, which is supposed to develop Teacher thought and the abstract circuit of Ci, was forced to follow a Mercy-based bottom line driving the practical circuit of Cp.

As a result, instead of teaching a broad range of subjects, schools cut programs in order to focus more attention upon core subjects, violating the first principle of extending learning beyond the box imposed by Cp. Second, teachers taught students how to pass the tests and not how to acquire and analyze information, violating the second principle of following Forms rather than approval. Finally, systemic cheating broke out, with entire school districts eventually being indicted. For instance, one New York Times article describes how 44 schools and at least 178 teachers and principals were caught cheating in Atlanta, with the school administration altering records, hiding information, and punishing whistle-blowers. This is what it means for Mercy mental networks of personal approval to override Teacher mental networks of understanding.[36] Finally, there was no 'wilderness experience' devoid of Mercy emotions. Instead, Mercy emotions were continually present in the form of government inspectors together with the carrot-and-stick of federal funding.

Religious Application, Technical Thought & Mental Networks

Let us move on to the next stage of adding Server actions to Teacher understanding. We saw previously how altruism can be used to mentally attach 'families' of Server sequences to general Teacher theory. We will look here at the influence played by mental networks and technical thought. Remember that we are dealing with a situation in which abstract thought is being developed in the presence of Mercy mental networks.

When technical thought makes the transition from concrete thought to abstract thought, then the natural tendency will be to *abandon* Mercy mental networks and focus totally upon using Ci to develop abstract understanding. As mentioned previously, the Contributor person who follows this path will turn into the 'absent minded professor' whose logical powers and knowledge are impressive but who lacks practical skills and social graces. The presence of Platonic Forms will reinforce this tendency to abandon Mercy mental networks because a person will want to embrace the Teacher based perfection of Platonic forms and turn his back upon the Mercy mental networks which are based in the imperfect real world.

However, abandoning concrete thought will *not* add Server actions to Teacher understanding but rather will leave the mind trapped in the Teacher shortcut of words. In religious language, I suggest that abandoning the 'sinful world' and focusing upon 'worshipping God' and studying theology will abort the process of personal transformation.

The solution is to remain connected with the Mercy mental networks of real life while using technical thought to prevent these Mercy mental networks from corrupting the Teacher mental networks of understanding. This is an application of technical thought which we have not yet discussed, but which forms a critical aspect of modern

---

36 *Systemic Cheating Is Found in Atlanta's School System*, Kim Severson, New York Times, July 5, 2011.

capitalism. Before we start, I should mention that the altruism which we discussed earlier mentally 'glues' a Server action to a Teacher mental network, while the principle which we are introducing here preserves the integrity of a Teacher mental network *after* a Server action has become mentally attached to it through an episode of altruism.

Technical thought limits itself to a restricted 'playing field' with carefully defined Perceiver rules and Server procedures. This defining and restricting makes it possible to predict and control the mental effects of personal interaction. For instance, suppose that I take my car to a mechanic to have the brakes fixed. Before he starts to work on my car, we both commit to a plan defining precisely the 'playing field' within which the mechanic will work together with his final goal: He may work on the brakes but not the rest of the car; he must limit himself to using parts within a certain price range and quality; and the final result must be functioning brakes. Of course, things do not always work out as planned, but if one performs a technical skill, then one can usually determine with considerable confidence what will happen. In addition, by paying for the work, the plan will end with neither party owing anything to the other party. Therefore, there will be no lasting emotions of guilt or obligation attached to any Mercy mental networks. This defines the typical method by which one purchases and delivers goods and services in a modern economy. Each transaction is a *contract*; a contract is a plan to which both parties agree; by committing to a formal plan, the mind enters technical thought with its limited options and clearly defined goals.

The contract makes it possible to add actions to Teacher understanding without having Mercy mental networks damage Teacher mental networks. By encapsulating each application of theory within a contract, that episode can be evaluated before it is performed to see if it is consistent or inconsistent with Teacher understanding. If it is consistent, then one can commit to that specific plan knowing with considerable confidence that it will not harm Teacher understanding.

For instance, suppose that a musician joins some group and agrees to play with them wherever they play and whatever they play. Such an *open*-ended commitment places the Mercy mental network of the group above the Teacher mental network of understanding. The result is that Server actions will end up *warping* Teacher understanding instead of *applying* Teacher understanding. However, suppose that a musician commits as a freelance player, evaluating each set of musical gigs to determine if they are consistent with Teacher understanding before committing to playing. Interacting on a *contract* basis makes it possible to include Mercy mental networks while still ensuring that Teacher mental networks of understanding take precedence over Mercy mental networks.

Of course, there is always a price to pay when one does not commit totally to any group or organization. Saying this another way, when one is using both Cp and Ci, then one will function better than the other. Interacting with others on a contract basis ensures that Ci will continue to function—at the cost of making Cp less effective. However, if one wishes to follow the second stage of religious education, then I suggest that this is the price that must be paid.

In religious terms, following such a path will lead to a growth in the mental concept of the Holy Spirit. Remember that Perceiver facts combined with Teacher understanding lead to the emergence of Platonic Forms. When Server actions are added to this mixture, then the mental Mercy picture of how experiences could *be* expands to become an internal vision of how people could *act*. And when Mercy emotions are included, then what also becomes mentally apparent is what could *motivate* people. In this manner, Forms turn into an alternative mental reality—a new way of living and existing that is guided by Teacher understanding. The end result is a new *Mercy* mental network which could be real but is not. It *could* be real because it is constructed out of the raw material of existing Mercy experiences. But it *is* not real because the Perceiver facts and Server connections that tie these Mercy experiences together all come from Teacher understanding and internal mental structure.

Eventually, this internal vision of how one *could* live will become sufficiently developed to make it possible to enter the *third* stage of religious education. That is the stage of *personal rebirth*, in which one starts living in what could be and turns it into reality, which is the subject of the next chapter.

When society in general follows a path of *objective* science and technology, then I suggest that application through contract will have to be adopted by those who wish to follow the second stage of religious education. That is because subjective thought in the average person is being driven by childish Mercy mental networks, and open-ended commitments will allow these Mercy mental networks to corrupt the Teacher understanding which one gains by following the first stage of religious education.

Objective science and technology make it both easy and difficult to interact through contract. On the one hand, because technical thought is dominant, contract will be the dominant *official* way of conducting business, making it easy. On the other hand, because the subjective is not guided by rational thought, there will often be a *hidden* emotional commitment which one will be expected to make in order to gain the privilege of making contracts. For instance, as a professional musician, I play musical gigs on the basis of contract, agreeing to play specific musical pieces in specific venues on specific dates. However, in order to have the *privilege* of making most contracts, a professional musician must be a member of the American Federation of Musicians, a closed-shop union founded in 1896, which controls all major live music throughout North America. An individual who is not a member of the musician's union is automatically disqualified from playing in any major orchestra in North America, especially if the program is being broadcast or televised.

When faced with such a situation, the individual who wishes to follow the path of religious education will have to choose which takes precedence, his Teacher understanding of God, or the Mercy mental network of some group, because one will mentally shape the other. I suggest that a similar principle applies when working with any religious group, denomination, organization, or company. Either the mental commitment to the Teacher understanding of God will be more solid, or the personal commitment to the Mercy group will be more solid. One will take precedence over the other. For example, over the years, I have discovered that my decision not to join the musician's union has made it much easier for me to give mental preference to Teacher mental networks of understanding, though the personal cost in terms of missed opportunity and lost income has been and continues to be significant.

When scientific thought is limited to the objective, then the *technical* nature of society will lead to the formation of groups whose purpose is to ensure that technical excellence is maintained and physical safety is protected. Joining such a group will help to promote rational thought and will build Teacher understanding. But because subjective thought is still being guided by *childish* Mercy mental networks, groups will also form whose primary purpose is to enhance the Mercy experiences of some set of individuals at the expense of other individuals—regardless of skill, ability, cost, or efficiency. Obviously, joining this type of group will preserve childish Mercy networks at the expense of rational thought and Teacher understanding.

In practice, every group will tend to be a mixture of these two extremes. In addition, each person begins the path of religious education by starting from a unique set of Mercy mental networks, and cognitive style also plays a major role. Therefore, each individual will have to decide for himself which groups are mentally safe to join and which ones are not. Going further, if a group of which one is a member abandons rational thought and embraces childish emotions, then one may have to protect Teacher understanding by playing the role of whistleblower or conscientious objector.

These decisions will usually be *triggered* by mental networks but need to be *supported* by logic. If the behavior of a certain group is inconsistent with Teacher understanding, then the corresponding Teacher mental network will complain—because it is being 'fed' with incompatible data. However, because the path of religious education begins by modifying Mercy mental networks to make them consistent with Teacher thought, these 'gut feelings' may be mistaken. Therefore, it is important to double-check an emotional reaction by examining the situation as logically and rationally as possible.

Obviously, in order to interact with others on the basis of technical skills, one must first acquire a technical skill. But if a person is following a path of *education*, then this should not be a problem. I suggest that the best way to ensure that Teacher understanding takes precedence over the Mercy mental network of any specific group or organization is to gain technical proficiency in more than one area of specialization and to divide one's time between these two or more areas. This continual crossing from one technical area to another will force Teacher thought to develop a general understanding. On the *abstract* side, this will ensure that normal thought is combined with the technical thinking of Ci, because a person is not limiting his thinking to one paradigm but is moving between paradigms, which will help a person to escape from the mindset of Foucault's Modern episteme. On the *concrete* side, the perspective that this gives will make a person feel like an outsider to any specific plan in Cp, making it easier to avoid becoming emotionally trapped by Mercy mental networks. This could be compared to the bilingual individual who lives in two cultures. It is much easier for him to step back from emotional involvement and understand what is happening around him, which is precisely what one is attempting to achieve when adding Server actions to Teacher understanding.

From the viewpoint of technical thought, when theory continues to be applied, then Ci will gradually expand and become compatible with Cp. As I have already mentioned, this will happen if one does Server actions that are guided by *Teacher* emotion, but not if one does actions which are guided by *Mercy* emotions or studies *words* guided by Teacher emotion. For instance, think of the research farm. Like surrounding farms, it plants and harvests crops, and to the untrained eye, it looks like just another farm. That is because the average person sees only the 'tip of the iceberg' which consists of the visible growing plants. However, the purpose of the research farm is not to pursue the Mercy bottom line of growing food but rather to explore Teacher theories about growing crops. The agricultural researcher 'sees' in his mind's eye the 'entire iceberg' with its Perceiver facts, Server sequences, Teacher understanding, and Mercy possibilities. For him, the visible plants are only a small part of the big picture.

Notice finally the relationship between the previous transition and this one. Contributor mode ties together Perceiver mode and Server mode. Making the transition from Mercy-based approval to Teacher-based Forms will bridge the *Perceiver* side of this pair, whereas applying theory in action ties together the *Server* side. Both Perceiver mode and Server mode work with *confidence.* Perceiver confidence grows as facts are tested under emotional pressure. Server actions, in contrast, take *time* to perform, therefore building Server confidence at this stage will mean repeatedly choosing to act in a way that is consistent with Teacher understanding.

Summary

We will continue this discussion in the next chapter, but first let us review. We began the chapter by examining the job description of the scientist. The typical science textbook tells us that science gathers new Perceiver facts in order to build general Teacher theories. And we have taken considerable time in this book to analyze abstract thought and its relationship to science. However, Kuhn tells us that the typical scientist spends most of his time doing what Kuhn calls *normal* science, which is solving technical problems using an *existing* paradigm. Very seldom does science do what Kuhn calls *revolutionary* science and gather facts in order to construct *new* paradigms.

Mental symmetry suggests that both concrete thought and abstract thought can function in a normal mode and a technical mode. During normal, everyday life, concrete thought uses Server actions to reach Mercy goals, guided by a map of Perceiver facts. But when enough Perceiver facts and Server skills are acquired, then the mind can function in a *technical* manner, in which activity will be limited to a restricted 'playing field' and guided by the 'rules of the game'. Similarly, during typical speech, abstract thought uses Perceiver meanings to build Teacher understanding, guided by a repertoire of Server words and phrases. But when enough Perceiver meanings and Server sequences are acquired, then abstract thought can function in a *technical* manner, during which reasoning will be limited to the acceptable solutions of an existing paradigm.

Both forms of technical thought are under the control of Contributor mode, which uses concentration to limit thought to an existing plan, and manipulates Perceiver facts and Server sequences within this plan guided by a digital sense of confidence. When moving from normal thought to technical thought, the mind makes a 'leap of faith' from the analog certainty of normal thought to the digital certainty of technical thought, which can be minimized by adding details to technical thought. Going the other way, the structure developed by technical thought has a better chance of surviving contact with the real world if a 'safety margin' is added.

Ci refers to the mental circuit of intellectual Contributor thought, in which abstract thought functions in a technical manner. Similarly, Cp describes the mental circuit of practical Contributor thought, the technical form of concrete thought. What mental symmetry calls Ci, Kuhn refers to as *normal* science, because it describes how the scientist normally thinks, but the scientist is *not* a normal person, and formal language or mathematics does *not* describe normal conversation. Thus, it is better to describe this as technical thought.

As far as Contributor mode is concerned, there is no difference between Cp and Ci, because they both involve rearranging Perceiver facts and Server sequences within a grid of fixed Perceiver and Server content. It is possible to approach most technical situations either from the Mercy perspective of improving some bottom line or from the Teacher perspective of improving order-within-complexity. Technical Contributor thought separates into the two distinct circuits of Ci and Cp because of the distinction between talking and doing. Talking leads to words and meanings, which provides the foundation for Ci. Doing creates physical consequences, which leads to the circuit of Cp. Perceiver thought integrates what is *said* with what is *done* by connecting the *meanings* of Teacher words with the *facts* that describe Mercy experiences.

Michel Foucault divided Western history into three periods or *epistemes*. During the Renaissance episteme, Ci was limited to scholasticism and 'scientific' thought was characterized by Teacher overgeneralization. During the Classical episteme, Ci functioned within the overall context of normal thought, while in the Modern episteme, the norm is to use Ci to specialize within some specific context and focus upon the process of learning.

The first stage of learning uses normal thought and lacks Perceiver knowledge and Server skills. The second stage of learning develops technical thought by focusing upon details, while the third stage of learning combines technical thought with normal thought. The learning of the individual is limited by the knowledge and skills of his society.

The two technical circuits of Cp and Ci play a major role in the path of education. Because of the *Perceiver* shortcut, Cp in the primary student will learn to play the 'rules of the game' by obeying the teacher and working hard. When Perceiver mode in the student emerges from this shortcut and the student discovers Teacher understanding, then Cp will turn into Ci, driven now by the Teacher goal of gaining verbal understanding in some subject. This transition will bridge the *Perceiver* side of Perceiver plus Server.

If the student follows the scientific path of combining words with actions, then he will escape the Teacher shortcut of words. This transition will bridge the *Server* side of Perceiver plus Server. When the student makes it through this second transition, then he is ready to graduate, because the mental circuit of Ci operates and it has been extended to provide a new alternative for Cp.

The graduate faces a major choice, for he can either continue to be guided by childish mental networks within Mercy thought, or else he can choose to follow the technical circuit of Cp plus Ci which he acquired through education. The graduate who chooses to follow Cp plus Ci will experience a type of 'Industrial Revolution' in which the existing Mercy mental networks 'die' and are replaced by new Mercy mental networks. This will lead to the emergence of a form of R&D, in which Contributor mode uses Cp plus Ci to come up with 'new and improved' experiences for Mercy thought. Saying this another way, R&D turns the external world into one which is more Form-like.

Ci works with a general theory in Teacher thought. When a general theory explains personal identity, then this creates a mental image of God. Cp improves experiences in Mercy thought. When personal identity is improved, then this becomes personal salvation. Combining Cp with Ci provides a cognitive explanation for the religious doctrine of *incarnation*, because the Ci side of this unified mental structure 'lives with God' while the Cp side of this same mental structure 'saves humans'.

Religious education makes the transition from Mercy driven blind faith to Teacher driven understanding by first *modifying* the childish image of God which comes from Mercy status to be compatible with Teacher thought, and then *testing* this modified image of God to ensure that it is based in a Teacher mental network. Religious application ensures that Teacher understanding is not corrupted by Mercy mental networks by interacting with concrete thought on a *contract* basis. When rational thought in a society is limited to the realm of the objective, then following contract will be *officially* easy, but in *practice* one may have to avoid joining organizations that protect Mercy feelings at the expense of rational thought.

✵ 12. Personal Rebirth

Many years ago, I encountered a book called *Stutter No More*, written by Martin Schwartz. He discovered that people who stutter are tensing their vocal cords just before they speak and that stuttering will be eliminated if the vocal cords are in a relaxed state when a person starts to talk.

What struck me was his description of the effect which this cure has upon *self-image*. When a person stutters, this speech impediment defines part of his identity; he becomes known both to himself and others as a stutterer. When a person suddenly stops stuttering, then his self-image becomes disoriented and he no longer knows who he is. Dr. Schwartz relates that such an individual may feel a deep sense of dread or experience anxiety attacks. He will feel an urge to start stuttering again, and if he does resume stuttering, then his feeling of dread will go away. However, if a person refuses to stutter for about two weeks, then this sense of angst will dissipate. Dr. Schwartz found that these crises of self-image occur only in patients who suffer from moderate to severe stuttering who become fluently quickly, but at least 1/3 of such patients experience crises of identity.

When a person recovers from stuttering, he is experiencing a minor form of personal rebirth. But *two* forms of rebirth are actually occurring. First, he is experiencing *physical* rebirth as he learns to control his vocal cords. That is the obvious change. But this physical rebirth is being accompanied by a *mental* rebirth as the Mercy mental network which represents his personal behavior of stuttering is being reborn. Remember that a mental network needs to be 'fed' with compatible information. The Mercy mental network that represents the behavior of stuttering is continually being 'fed' by the behavior of stuttering, and because this mental network cannot be ignored, it forms part of personal identity. When the stuttering stops, then this mental network will start to fragment, and it will respond by producing the hyper-pain of anxiety and dread. The solution is either to 'feed' the mental network by resuming the stuttering or to endure the hyper-pain of allowing the mental network to die, leading to the formation of a new personal identity. This tells us that *physical* rebirth must be accompanied by *mental* rebirth, for the mind that does not experience mental rebirth will reject physical rebirth.

The idea of being 'born again' or 'resurrected from the dead' plays a central role in religious belief. The main focus is generally upon the *physical* rebirth of receiving a new physical body. However, the example of stuttering tells us that behind the obvious topic of physical rebirth lies the hidden matter of *mental* rebirth. How can a person construct a new *mental* identity? How can he rebuild the mental networks that represent personal identity?

At the beginning of this book I suggested that one could postpone dealing with the question of whether God actually exists or not and focus instead upon analyzing a mental image of God. Similarly, I suggest that one can defer the question of whether or not physical personal rebirth exists and look instead at the rebirth of *mental* personal life. That is because, whether physical rebirth exists or not, mental rebirth appears to be a precondition for physical rebirth. For, if self-image is such a major stumbling block when dealing with the relatively minor issue of stuttering, one can imagine that it would play a defining role if one experienced physical rebirth in any significant way.

With this in mind, let us continue with our discussion of the path of education, focusing now upon the third stage of *personal rebirth*. The first stage of education uses Perceiver facts to build a general Teacher understanding. In religious terms, this is *learning about God*. The second stage combines Server actions with Teacher understanding. In religious language, this is *obeying God*. During the third stage the Mercy mental networks that represent personal identity are rebuilt.

Opposing Mercy Mental Networks

When an individual continues to follow a path of combining words with actions, then conflict with existing culture will become inevitable. As was mentioned in the previous chapter, this is the type of conflict that occurs when the college graduate returns to his childhood village and tries to replace traditional ways with the new scientific methods that he learned while at university, or when the researcher at the experimental farm tells other farmers to adopt his new methods of agriculture. And even when the content does not change there will still be conflict, for the *assumptions* are radically different: Traditional culture kowtows to personal status whereas theory applies equally to everyone regardless of personal status. When science becomes applied in technology, then this turmoil will be limited primarily to the external environment. However, because religious education deals directly with personal identity, the turmoil that is produced will also affect the core of personal identity. The science graduate tells people that they need to change what they *do*; the religious graduate will tell people that they must transform who they *are*. Because the message is more personal, the backlash that is experienced will also tend to be more personal.

In terms of mental networks, Mercy thought now contains two *incompatible* sets of mental networks. On the one side are the existing Mercy mental networks which first developed in childhood. On the other side are the new Mercy mental networks that have been formed by building and applying general Teacher understanding. As we saw earlier in the book, childish Mercy mental networks practice identification and denial, and they were initially formed around emotional experiences from authority figures and cultural icons. In contrast, the new Mercy mental networks are guided by general understanding, logical thinking, and rational application, and they do not give any special status to people or icons.

Obviously, these two types of Mercy mental networks will oppose one another. Therefore, one of these two will have to fragment and be replaced by the other. In terms of our experimental farm analogy, either the farmers forsake their traditional ways and embrace the newfangled methods of the experimental farm, or else they expel the experimental farmer and close down the experimental farm. Both of these responses occurred during the Industrial Revolution, when the machine replaced the artisan and the cottage industry gave way to the factory. But even though groups like the Luddites tried their best to destroy the new methods, eventually the old way of life died and was replaced by a new form of personal existence.

The precise form of rebirth that occurs will depend upon the extent of the general Teacher theory. The Scientific Revolution used physical data to build a general Teacher understanding of the natural universe. Therefore, the Industrial Revolution that followed was limited to the physical and the objective; the physical *environment* was transformed and the physical aspect of personal identity was *affected*, while the mental aspect of personal identity was left unchanged.

The theory of mental symmetry, in contrast, presents a general Teacher theory of human thought based upon cognitive principles. Applying such a theory makes it possible to construct a new form of *mental* identity—the part of personal identity which does *not* relate to the physical body.

We saw earlier that adding personal Mercy emotions to the process of building a general Teacher understanding will lead to the formation of a mental image of God. Going further, obeying this image of God by doing actions that are consistent with Teacher understanding will lead to the personal character trait of righteousness. If this process is continued, then what will eventually emerge is a new personal identity based in rational understanding that is capable of *replacing* childish identity with its identification and denial. In religious terms, the new 'me' is pleasing to God whereas the old 'me' is opposed to God; God demands that the old 'me' die in order to be replaced by the new 'me'; if a person allows the old 'me' to fragment and die, then God will replace it with the new 'me'.

Notice that all of this is happening to the *mental* part of personal identity, and is being driven by cognitive principles and a mental image of God. None of this mental process requires a real God to function. But for the person undergoing this process of rebirth, it will feel as is personal identity is dying and being brought back to life by God, because this describes how Mercy thought will view what is happening to the emotional part of personal identity. In addition, I suggest that at this stage personal identity will be emotionally *forced* to go through rebirth because it is outnumbered. On the one side are the fragmented Mercy mental networks which make up childish identity. On the other side is the *Teacher* mental network behind the mental image of God, reinforced by the *Mercy* mental network of the new potential identity, which is backed up by the more general Mercy mental network of the 'Holy Spirit of Truth'.

Obviously, if a Teacher paradigm becomes *redefined* as the methods and views of a community of experts, then there will be no rebirth, because the new 'me' is made out of the same stuff as the old 'me'—both are rooted in the opinions of experts. There may be a paradigm shift as the old experts are dethroned and replaced by a new set of experts, but the underlying mental foundation will not change.

Describing Personal Rebirth

Because personal rebirth is such an intensely emotional process, it is important for us to look in detail at exactly what is and is not expected to die. We will look here at what happens when the theory of mental symmetry is followed to the point of personal rebirth. First, I suggest that any form of emotional identification, emotional denial, or blind faith will be expected to die. That includes political correctness, emotional escapism, rationalizing of personal faults, fundamentalism, hero worship, irrational religious rituals, adherence to schools of thought, blind faith in holy books or religious experts, the idolizing of parents and other authority figures, and the worship of tribe, country, or culture.

However, the goal is not to *destroy* Mercy thought, eliminate personal emotions, or eradicate personal identity. Mercy thought is essential, Mercy feelings are healthy, and personal identity is necessary. The problem is not with Mercy experiences or Mercy emotions but rather with the connections *between* these experiences. Unfortunately, childish identity will not grasp this distinction between experiences and facts, because it uses emotional Mercy experiences to mesmerize Perceiver thought into defining the 'facts' which connect these experiences. But if the Form-based mental image of the Holy Spirit has been developed sufficiently, then Mercy thought will be able to 'see' mentally that it *is* possible to 'live' and feel within a new type of personal identity which no longer contains any of the traits that were mentioned in the previous paragraph.

In addition, the new personal identity that emerges will be *more* compatible with the physical body and physical emotions. We saw at the beginning of this book that the physical body forces the physical aspect of personal identity to learn how to combine Perceiver facts with Mercy emotions. When personal identity is transformed as a result of applying the theory of mental symmetry, this *extends* the cooperation of facts and feelings from the physical aspect of personal identity to the *mental* aspect of personal identity, making the two compatible with one another and leading to the formation of an *integrated* personal identity. Personal identity will then become emotionally driven by hyper-emotion to *maintain* this integrity, causing a person to satisfy physical desires in ways that preserve the integrity of both the physical body and personal identity.

Next, there is the *moral* aspect. If one uses the theory of mental symmetry to construct a new personal identity, then obviously this personal identity will find it emotionally difficult to violate the theory of mental symmetry. But if the theory of mental symmetry is based in cognitive modules which actually exist within the mind, then this new personal identity will be compatible with mental wholeness, an individual will feel personally driven to apply the golden rule, and he will feel personally fulfilled when his mind reaches its full potential.

In addition, there is the matter of *scientific* thought. If the new personal identity is based upon a Teacher general theory that is *compatible* with scientific thought and was constructed through a mental process that is an *extension* of scientific education, then the resulting personal identity will naturally be attracted to scientific thought. Such a person will not find personal pleasure in pretending to violate natural law by either calling on irrational miracles from God or by identifying with the irrational miracles portrayed by Hollywood.

Finally, there is the aspect of *religion.* We have been using a lot of religious terminology, and when one talks about submitting one's personal identity to an image of God that results from the theory of mental symmetry, then this implies that one is promoting a new religion. However, those who are familiar with Christian theology will recognize that the path of religious education which we have been outlining corresponds to the Biblical description of the life of Jesus. Saying this another way, the story of the birth, childhood, temptation, ministry, death, and resurrection of Jesus makes sense from a cognitive perspective. It is an accurate *allegory* of the process of religious education, whether it is historically true or not. And if one analyzes the portrayal of Jesus as presented in the Gospels from a psychological perspective, it describes the behavior of a Contributor person, which is mentally consistent with the Christian assertion that Jesus is an incarnation of God.

I have summarized these parallels in the following table:

Educational Stage	Characteristics	Religious Equivalent
School Curriculum	Ci masquerading as Cp	God in human form
Obedient Student	Setting up shortcuts of education	Approved by God and man
Idealistic Student	Following theory and Forms	Filled with Spirit and tempted
Scientific Student	Adding actions to theories	Doing what God does
Humble Graduate	Losing status to effect change	Death and Resurrection
R&D	Using theory to improve life	Living with God to send Spirit

Thus, rather than starting a new religion, it appears, in contrast, that all we are managing to do with the theory of mental symmetry is to explain *existing* religion. For whenever we come up with a religious concept, we find that it is already being taught as theology by some religion. In other words, religion really *does* appear to be cognitive science in emotional garb.

But we have managed to separate the *doctrine* of religion from the *attitude* of fundamentalism, and that is significant. For the person who applies mental symmetry to the point of personal rebirth will feel personally driven to hold on to the doctrine while rejecting the attitude.

We have defined personal identity as the set of emotional experiences upon which Mercy thought can continue to concentrate. When personal identity is reborn, it does not immediately start focusing upon a new set of experiences. Instead, what changes is the mental response to these experiences. One can see this continuity by comparing daily life today with life before the Industrial Revolution. Citizens today still eat, work, play, sleep, converse, and travel. As far as these basic elements are concerned, nothing has changed. But the way in which we do these various activities, as well as the thinking behind these activities, has changed dramatically.

We will end this section by exploring what it means in practical terms to go through personal rebirth, beginning with our illustration of the college graduate returning back to his childhood village with new methods of farming.

Suppose that the college graduate returns home and attempts to alter traditional ways by playing village politics. In order to impose his new methods upon the village, he will have to learn or re-learn the ways of the village so that he can play the political game of using existing Cp to improve his personal status. The end result is that his *new* mental structure of Cp + Ci will become subservient to the old village structure of Cp. Instead of using rational understanding to *transform* childish identity, his rational understanding will be *corrupted* by childish identity. By winning the battle of gaining influence, he will lose the war of transforming his village. Notice that the person who defines a paradigm as a school of thought which is practiced by a community of scholars will naturally choose the political option, because he has *already* defined his general Teacher theory in political terms.

However, if the college graduate returns home and chooses *not* to play the political game, then he will experience two mental benefits. First, any remaining childish Mercy mental networks based upon approval that still exist within his own mind will be forced to fragment and die, because they will not be satisfied. Second, he will be driven by Teacher emotion to comprehend the predicament in which he finds himself and come up with a rational solution. Thus, by being willing to lose the battle, he will eventually win the war. In religious terms, if the old identity is willing to die, then it will eventually be brought back to life by God.

When personal identity is reborn, then I suggest that this will trigger a type of Industrial Revolution which will replace traditional culture with rational culture. This will open up a new area of technical expertise for Contributor thought, because Cp and Ci have become integrated and they are now being accepted as a source of new development by society. In the objective, this leads to R&D. Research is Ci guided by Cp, while development is Cp guided by Ci. R&D takes the imaginary world of Forms and uses machines to turn them into real objects. Forms were first encountered *internally* when making the transition from Mercy-based approval to Teacher-based Forms. Now, *everyone* experiences the benefits of living in a world that is increasingly Form-like. In religious language, incarnation is first filled with the Holy Spirit. Now, everyone who submits to the plan of incarnation experiences the Holy Spirit.

R&D is a sort of hybrid between theory and real life, for it lives in a technical realm of theory, surrounded by equipment and equations, but it uses this environment to create new gadgets for the average person to enjoy. When one adds the personal element to this, one comes up with the concept of Contributor incarnation living within the heavenly realm of Forms and developing new items for personal identity.

The Minimally Counterintuitive Concept

I have suggested that religion is cognitive science in *emotional* garb. But why the emotional garb? Why does *allegory* play such a major role in religion? Why describe the process of religion education in *anthropomorphic* terms? Why not simply present a theory as a logical structure supported by scientific thought? I suggest that the cognitive science of religion provides an answer for this question. I will first present the concept as Justin Barrett describes it, then explain this concept using mental symmetry, and finally apply it to our current analysis.[37]

Religion, according to Justin Barrett, is *minimally counterintuitive*. Our mind naturally accepts information that is intuitive, because it makes sense. For instance, when a person sees a horse, then this is accepted as intuitively reasonable, because horses are common. In contrast, the concept of an alien from outer space will be rejected as counterintuitive, because one does not see such beings walking down the street. A *minimally* counterintuitive concept is one that is normal except for one or two unusual elements. Thus, a Pegasus or winged horse is minimally counterintuitive because it is a normal horse with the addition of wings. Likewise, a giant is minimally counterintuitive because it is like a normal human being in every respect except size, as is a Cyclops because it is a normal human—but with only one eye. The point is that the mind will instinctively reject information that is counterintuitive but it *will* accept that which is *minimally* counterintuitive.

We saw earlier in the book that Perceiver mode provides the mental context for Facilitator thought. One of the functions which Facilitator mode carries out is to act as the *input filter* for the mind. When Perceiver mode sets a context for Facilitator thought, then Facilitator mode will use this context as a guideline for evaluating information from the external world, accepting it as *intuitive* if it matches and rejecting it as *counterintuitive* if it does not. Thus, Perceiver mode *sets* the current context, while Facilitator mode *uses* the current context. For instance, suppose that the current context is horses. Perceiver mode will bring to mind all of the facts that it knows about horses.

---

[37] In most cases, the research of others has confirmed or clarified findings that I discovered independently. However, the minimally counterintuitive concept was developed by Justin Barrett. It fits well into the theory of mental symmetry, but I did not come up with it, and there is a logical reason why a Perceiver person like myself would not discover this idea.

Facilitator mode will then use these facts to evaluate whatever it encounters about horses as either intuitive, counterintuitive, or minimally counterintuitive.

A fact is most likely to be regarded as minimally counterintuitive if it can be made intuitive through a simple application of Facilitator thought. Facilitator thought can *adjust* the level of a memory and it can *mix* portions of memories together. In mathematical terms, this is known as a *linear combination*. For instance, a giant is a normal human in which the 'level' of size has been adjusted, whereas a Pegasus is a horse which has been mixed with the wings of a bird.

When one observes the behavior of the Facilitator *person*, one notices that he usually rejects information which lies outside of the norm. That is because subconscious Perceiver mode within his mind is setting the context for conscious filtering. In contrast, the Perceiver person is quite willing to accept unusual information from unorthodox sources—if he can connect it in some way to what he thinks is correct. For if conscious thought in the Perceiver person finds a valid context for new information, then his subconscious Facilitator filter will automatically accept it as intuitive. Because the mental definition of what is and is not minimally counterintuitive is continually being altered by conscious thought in the Perceiver *person*, he will not come up with the *concept* of being minimally counterintuitive.

Now let us apply this concept to the topic of religion. During the Roman Era when Christianity was founded, almost all religious thought was anthropomorphic. One can see this by examining the pantheon of Greco-roman gods and the temples in which they were worshipped. Science did not exist. This intellectual milieu set the mental context for the Facilitator filter within the mind of the average person. Describing the path of education in theoretical cognitive terms would have been like trying to explain quantum mechanics to a person living in the Middle Ages. Both would have been rejected as counterintuitive. But if these same principles could be conveyed in anthropomorphic terms, then they would be accepted as minimally counterintuitive. Thus, portraying the process of education using the anthropomorphic allegory of an unusual human being would have made sense to a Greco-roman audience, whereas presenting the theory in cognitive terms would have been rejected.

Today, the situation is reversed, for theory that is portrayed in anthropomorphic terms is instinctively rejected, whereas cognitive theory is regarded as intuitively acceptable. That is because the modern mind associates anthropomorphic analogies with subjective Mercy emotions and non-scientific thought, while it connects rational thinking with technical descriptions and mathematical equations.

This brings us to a further question. If it is possible to use the cognitive theory of mental symmetry to make sense of Christian theology, then why isn't the theory of mental symmetry contained within the Bible? Actually, the core of it is—in anthropomorphic terms.

Here is the original Biblical quote: "I beseech you therefore, brethren, by the mercies of God, that you present your bodies a living sacrifice, holy, acceptable to God, which is your reasonable service. And do not be conformed to this world, but be transformed by the renewing of your mind, that you may prove what is that good and acceptable and perfect will of God. For I say, through the grace given to me, to everyone who is among you, not to think of himself more highly than he ought to think, but to think soberly, as God has dealt to each one a measure of faith. For as we have many members in one body, but all the members do not have the same function, so we, being many, are one body in Christ, and individually members of one another. Having then gifts differing according to the grace that is given to us, let us use them: if prophecy, let us prophesy in proportion to our faith; or ministry, let us use it in our ministering; he who teaches, in teaching; he who exhorts, in exhortation; he who gives, with liberality; he who leads, with diligence; he who shows mercy, with cheerfulness" (Romans 12: 1-8).

Some of the specific terms that are used in this passage for the seven cognitive styles are different, but that is simply a matter of translation because the New Testament was originally written in Greek. Notice that the passage refers to mental development and that it presents the concept of interacting cognitive modules, using the anthropomorphic language of the parts of a physical body. And it also suggests that personal transformation is a *mental* process guided by submission to an image of God, as opposed to permitting personal identity to be determined primarily by sensory input from the *physical* body.[38]

Radical Evil

Before we continue, let us remind ourselves of the underlying problem. Since Immanuel Kant described this problem so clearly, we will use his terms. In a previous chapter, we examined Kant's concept of the *categorical imperative*, which defines rules of morality in terms of general theory. In simple terms, if it is possible for *everyone* to *continue* carrying out a certain pattern of behavior, then that behavior is morally correct. Otherwise, it is morally wrong.

Related to the categorical imperative is Kant's idea of *radical evil*, which he viewed as a rational substitution for the Christian doctrine of *original sin*. We can explain radical evil by using the illustration of lying. Why do people lie? In order to gain a personal advantage. In the language of mental symmetry, childish identity uses identification

---

[38] Scientific research wants sources to be acknowledged. As far as I can tell, Bill Gothard in the early 1970s was the first to suggest that the Biblical list in Romans 12 describes personal motivation, but most of the original research in this area was done by Don Pickerill. What we (Lane Friesen and myself) inherited from these two was about four pages of information consisting primarily of seven labels along with a list of about a dozen character traits for each 'motivational gift'. Bill Gothard was briefly aware of our work in the 1980s but he broke off the relationship fairly quickly because he felt that our research was 'too secular'. Looking at this from a cognitive perspective, an Exhorter person such as Bill Gothard has the natural ability to develop overgeneralized theories and add some technical content (and attractive packaging) to these theories. In contrast, a Perceiver person such as myself can take a partially developed theory and make it more rigorous, which is what I have attempted to do.

and/or denial to overrule Perceiver facts in order to make personal identity within Mercy thought feel better. Why does lying work? Because, the person telling a lie does so within a social environment where it is expected that everyone will tell the truth. A lie only works when the person who is listening does not expect to hear a lie. In Kant's terms, radical evil describes an attitude of choosing to violate a categorical imperative for personal advantage. In the language of mental symmetry, radical evil results from a conflict between Teacher mode and Mercy mode. Teacher mode wants rules to be applied universally without exception, whereas Mercy mode is driven by childish personal identity to continue seeking exceptions to the rule. In religious terms, there is a natural conflict between personal identity and a mental image of God. That defines the underlying problem.

We have just seen that applying the theory of mental symmetry results in a *long-term* solution to the problem of radical evil. If the path of religious education is followed to its conclusion, then the childish identity which practices radical evil will die and be replaced by a new personal identity which is consistent with the categorical imperative.

But applying this long-term solution leads to a chicken-and-egg sort of problem. If one follows a plan of programming Cp and Ci with rational content, then one will ultimately escape radical evil. But as long as personal identity is still governed by radical evil, any long-term attempt to program Cp and Ci will be derailed by radical evil. Saying this another way, childish identity practices identification and denial. But in order to transform childish identity, one must pursue a rational path of education which is based upon personal honesty and not upon identification and denial.

What typically happens in practice is that instead of Cp and Ci *transforming* childish identity, childish identity ends up *corrupting* Cp and Ci. Thus, radical evil spreads from childish identity to the technical circuits of Cp and Ci.

Here is the process: Remember that when the mind is using either Cp or Ci, then Contributor mode is manipulating Perceiver facts and Server sequences within an existing grid of Perceiver facts and Server sequences. This means that *some* Perceiver facts and Server sequences must *not* be tampered with because they either define the rules of the game for Cp or define the paradigm for Ci, while *other* Perceiver and Server content is 'fair game' and may be modified by Contributor thought. When Contributor thought tampers with the rules of the game while pretending to play the game, then the result is *cheating*. Cheating is an easy way to 'win the game', but it is also mentally self-destructive, because it destroys the mental foundation upon which the circuits of Cp and Ci are based. Cheating is a form of radical evil, because it only works if some people cheat while everyone else obeys the rules of the game; the person who cheats must pretend that he is still 'playing by the rules', and he must prevent others from discovering that he is cheating.

For instance, consider the 'game' of business. One of the fundamental rules of business is that money represents value. Thus, in order to gain money, one must give up something of value. Counterfeiting money breaks this rule—while assuming that others still apply the rule. One concludes that when a 'central bank' which is owned by private bankers creates money out of nothing, then the owners of this bank are practicing radical evil, for they can only continue to print money as long as no one else knows what they are doing and no else practices what they are doing. And, as the global economic crisis of 2008 demonstrated, when the entire world is playing the same economic 'game', then this type of cheating has the potential to destroy the global economy.[39]

The Mental 'Trick' of the Christian 'Prayer of Salvation'

As I have mentioned, the path of education *solves* the conflict between Mercy mode and Teacher mode by altering these two to become compatible with one another. On the Mercy side, the practical circuit of Cp is modified to teach Perceiver facts, leading to Teacher understanding, whereas on the Teacher side, the intellectual circuit of Ci is modified to include Server actions, resulting in better Mercy experiences. When the path of education is applied in the objective, then the end result is R&D, which uses a combination of Cp and Ci to simultaneously build general understanding and improve personal experiences. In religious terms, following the path of education to completion reconciles man with God, but it does so in a way that *preserves* mental content and is *compatible* with technical thought.

That is the *long-term* solution. But actually putting this plan into practice is another matter. For how can one pursue a path of education that *starts* with personal honesty when it only becomes possible to practice personal honesty at the *end* of this path? What is needed is a mental 'trick' that can be applied at the *beginning* of the process which can be used to *jumpstart* an attitude of personal honesty.

This mental 'trick' will have to take account of several mental factors. First, the main reason that childish identity avoids personal honesty is because it 'makes me feel bad'. Therefore, the 'trick' will have to provide an emotional reward for personal honesty that will *balance* the emotional pain of making me feel bad. Second, because the path of education uses the technical circuits of Cp and Ci, this 'trick' will need to be defined in terms of *Contributor* thought. Finally, because the ultimate goal is to become rational, then this 'trick' will also need to be based ultimately in *rational* thought. However, because it is being applied by *childish* identity, it must also make sense to childish identity.

I suggest that the solution involves taking advantage of the different way in which Ci and Cp handle functions. This concept of approaching a function in two different ways

---

[39] Lane Friesen noted in his study of biographies that *dictators* tend to be Contributor persons who have experienced some form of major rejection in their childhood. Because the 'rules of the game' labels them as losers, they are emotionally driven to become 'winners' by manipulating these rules. Thus, they practice the radical evil of secretly breaking fundamental rules of society while simultaneously presenting the public persona of being the guardian of these rules.

is described in more detail in the appendix on math, and it can also be used to throw light on some unsolved philosophical problems.

Let us begin by examining the function. For the *concrete* circuit of Cp, a function is a connection between cause and effect. These two are separated by *time*, with the cause occurring first, followed by the effect. For instance, an object hits the ground *after* it is dropped from my hand. As I have mentioned before, the connection of cause-and-effect is the basic building block of Cp.

Now, remember that as far as Contributor mode is concerned, Cp and Ci are simply two different ways of looking at the same collection of Perceiver facts and Server sequences. Therefore, as one can see when analyzing math, the abstract circuit of Ci will take the functions that were developed by Cp and view them from the vantage point of abstract thought. However, abstract thought works with *generality* and views sequences as *building blocks*. For Ci, a function does not connect incidents that are separated by time, but rather it is a symbolic sequence which can be combined to form logical structures.

Written music provides an illustration of this difference in viewpoint. When a song is played or one listens to a piece of music, then one hears a sequence of notes that are separated by *time*. It is impossible to hear all of the notes of a song at the same time. That is because a song is a sequence of musical tones that has been constructed by the concrete circuit of Cp. However, when a song is written down on paper, then it is possible to view the entire song at once, because it has been written down using the abstract symbols of Ci.

Suppose that one takes the entire path of religious education and represents it as a Contributor function. A function has an *input* which it *processes* to produce an *output*. In a typical school, the child enters the institution as a primary student, time passes as the process of education occurs, and then the graduate emerges at the other end. For the path of religious education, the process takes somewhat longer and requires additional intermediate steps: The childish mind with its self-destructive, chaos-spreading pursuit of radical evil enters the process. Much time passes. Finally, the transformed mind with its self-preserving, order-producing, personal embrace of the categorical imperative emerges. If one were to put a label on this process, one might call it *salvation-through-rebirth*, because it leads to mental integration through a journey which involves extensive tearing down and rebuilding of mental networks. Obviously, an image of God that is based in general Teacher understanding will find the chaotic creature who enters the process emotionally repulsive but will appreciate the specimen that emerges at the other end as an illustration of Teacher order-within-complexity.

However, suppose that personal identity within Mercy thought is not viewed *directly* by Teacher thought but rather is viewed *indirectly* through the Contributor lens of the function of salvation-through-rebirth. Now, the sequence of the childish mind turning into the adult mind becomes an illustration of the Contributor function of salvation-through-rebirth, and Teacher thought will view this entire process *all at once*. Instead of being jarred by the disharmony at the beginning of the song, Teacher thought will 'see' the whole sheet of music, and will view the *entire* piece as an illustration of cacophony-to-harmony.

Let us run through this one more time, using the illustration of enrolling in a school. As far as Teacher thought is concerned, childish identity is chaos personified, akin to the screaming three-year old brat who spills food on the carpet, pulls his sister's hair, makes rude noises, and continually tries to climb on a person's lap while that person is attempting to have a serious intellectual discussion. That is what it feels like when a Teacher-based image of God comes face-to-face with childish identity. However, suppose that this bundle of chaos is enrolled in school and placed within a school uniform. Teacher thought will now see the child through the lens of the school system as an illustration of the general process of acquiring an education. In simple language, "Oh look at Johnny in his cute little school uniform playing with all of the other schoolchildren. Doesn't he look so grown up getting educated?" Johnny may still be the same little brat, but in the view of Teacher thought, he has turned into an example of Teacher order. Even though he has only started the process of learning, his personal status has changed from 'childish pest' to 'learning student'.

Similarly, when an individual mentally 'enrolls' in the 'school' of religious education, then Teacher thought will view personal identity as an *illustration* of the Contributor function of salvation-through-rebirth. This will radically alter the way that Teacher thought regards personal identity. On the one hand, Teacher thought hates exceptions to the rule, because they produce Teacher pain. On the other hand, Teacher thought loves illustrations of a theory, because they make the theory more general. If Teacher thought feels good about the childish student *enrolling* in the 'school' of religious education, then obviously Mercy identity will sense this Teacher emotion and feel good about *attending* school, leading to a major upward shift in the overall emotional level of the mind, because childish identity has gone from being a cause of Teacher pain to being a source of Teacher pleasure. In religious language, the individual will go from being an enemy of God to being at peace with God. This positive Teacher emotion will balance the Mercy pain that results from adopting a path of personal honesty.

But simply enrolling in *any* school is not enough to jumpstart a path of personal honesty. Instead, one must enroll in a school of *personal honesty*. In other words, personal honesty must be made an 'entrance requirement' for attending the 'school' of religious education. That is because the path of religious education that leads from childish identity to adult identity requires personal honesty to work.

Once this mental 'trick' based upon the Contributor function of salvation-through-rebirth has been put into place, then a person will be driven by Teacher emotion to *continue* practicing a policy of 'personal honesty before God'. Obviously, personal honesty leads to Mercy pain, because it uses Perceiver thought to connect unpleasant Mercy experiences with personal identity. But if this personal honesty occurs within the mental context of the Contributor function of salvation-through-rebirth, then this *same* Perceiver thought will also connect this unpleasant aspect of personal identity with the Contributor function of salvation-through-rebirth, making this function feel more *general* to Teacher thought, leading to further positive Teacher emotions about personal identity from the mental image of God. In terms of our school analogy, *setting up* the mental 'trick' enrolls a person in school, while *further* steps of personal honesty sign him up for additional classes within the school. A school will not feel general if it has many students enrolled but none of these students are signed up for any courses.

Personal honesty plays an essential role in this entire process for the simple reason that personal honesty 'wakes up' Perceiver thought in an area of strong subjective emotions. In order to attend a school, a person must be physically capable of showing up and he must be able to register for classes. Similarly, childish identity can only submit mentally to the Contributor function of salvation-through-rebirth if Perceiver thought is able to *define* personal identity and *attach* personal identity to the Contributor function of salvation-through-rebirth. And that will only happen if Perceiver thought 'wakes up' and stops being mesmerized by Mercy emotion.

Perceiver confidence cannot be acquired instantly. Instead, it is developed gradually, one emotional area at a time. In practical terms, this means that a person will *think* that he has enrolled his entire person in the total range of courses offered by the 'school' of religious education, while in actual fact only a *fragment* of his personal identity has been enrolled in *some* of the classes. However, each additional step of personal honesty will enroll another aspect of personal identity in school and sign up for another class, increasing the Teacher generality of the Contributor function of salvation-through-rebirth, which will encourage further personal honesty. If this process is followed for long enough, then it will turn into a Teacher mental network, which will respond with hyper-pain if a person does *not* continue applying a policy of personal honesty. At this stage, the individual has become a 'professional student' who is emotionally driven to continue attending school and signing up for courses.

Now that we understand the process, let us turn our attention to some of the technical details. Several mental factors must be in place in order to *set up* the Contributor function of salvation-through-rebirth. Remember that we are examining the path of religious education which includes *both* Mercy mental networks and Teacher mental networks. Therefore, a person must first acknowledge *simultaneously* the emotional demands of both Teacher thought and Mercy thought: Teacher thought demands the categorical imperative; Mercy thought practices radical evil. Teacher thought hates the chaos produced by childish identity; Mercy thought rebels from the structure imposed by Teacher thought. Thus, each threatens the other with the hyper-pain of mental fragmentation. And because we are looking at an *overlap* of Teacher generality and Mercy identity, this acknowledgement will involve an image of God: God is perfect while childish identity is a sinner; God hates sin but childish identity naturally sins.

The next step is to set up the Contributor function. This will happen if one believes that a function of salvation-through-rebirth exists within Cp which is capable of transforming personal identity. And because Mercy thought thinks in terms of people and agents, Mercy thought will have to believe that this Contributor function of salvation-through-rebirth is actually an imaginary 'person' who can save personal identity. This concrete Cp function then needs to be translated into the abstract language of Ci and connected with Teacher generality. That is done by believing that this imaginary person is an incarnation who also exists in the realm of Teacher words and who also co-exists with the mental image of God.

Once the various mental elements have been established, the emotional conflict can then be resolved by inserting the Contributor function between the Teacher image of God and childish Mercy identity. This is done on the Mercy side by submitting personal identity to the imaginary 'person' of the Contributor function, and it is done on the Teacher side by verbally requesting Teacher thought to regard childish identity as a subset of the Contributor function of salvation-through-rebirth.

Notice also that *all* of this is based in the mental interaction between cognitive modules. Thus, it will *work* whether a real God exists or not, and if one wishes to practice personal honesty, then I suggest that it will also be *necessary*—whether a real God exists or not. And if this mental 'trick' seems far too complicated to be of any practical use, I should point out that it corresponds verbatim to the 'prayer of salvation' which a person says in order to 'become a Christian'. But the vast majority of individuals who are applying this mental 'trick' to 'become a Christian' are accepting it as a magical formula stated in anthropomorphic terms. And I suggest that that is how childish identity will naturally view this 'trick', because childish identity is defined by people and it practices the 'magical thinking' of identification and denial. However, because this 'trick' is based in cognitive principles, it will still work even when it is treated as a magic formula, and the person who blindly mouths these words will feel as if his 'sins are forgiven' and that he is 'at peace with God'. He will also gain the emotional motivation to follow a path of personal honesty. And that is a significant result, whether God exists or not, and whether this mental 'trick' is understood or not. The bottom line is that it both works and is necessary.

When we looked at Eastern mysticism, we saw that 'mystical union with God' only works if the process is *not* analyzed. In contrast, I suggest that analyzing and understanding the Christian 'prayer of salvation' actually makes it mentally more potent. That is because a mental concept of God appears when a general Teacher *theory* explains personal identity. Therefore, it makes sense that a method of reconciling childish personal identity with an image of God will work best if it is described in terms of a general Teacher *theory*. Saying this another way, if I can make friends with a foreign individual when speaking through a translator, it should be *easier* for us to become friends if I learn to speak his language.

As was mentioned in a previous chapter, it is essential that this personal honesty occurs *internally* before an image of God and that the resulting sense of forgiveness also comes from a mental concept of God. Personal confessions to other people should be limited to situations that involve those other people. As we saw earlier, it is easy for an influential group to claim to speak for God, and *all* religious education starts with people and books claiming to deliver messages from God. However, if a group really does speak for God, then it will do its best to build an internal concept of God in its followers and transfer the emotional allegiance of its students to that internal image of God. Notice that religious allegiance which is transferred over to an internal concept of God will only continue to survive if the message that is being taught is *consistent* with mental functioning. In other words, if the religious doctrine that is being taught really *is* cognitive science in emotional garb, then the religious leaders can let go of the emotional garb and permit adherents to encounter the cognitive science directly.

Mentally speaking, it is *easier* to confess one's sins to a human priest or to practice honesty with a human 'accountability partner' than it is to be honest with the internal image of an imaginary person. However, if one wishes to become mentally integrated, then I suggest that confessing one's deepest thoughts and shortcomings to another human is counterproductive. If a person finds that he must confess to other people, then this is probably a sign that his mental concept of God is inadequate—a common problem in today's world of objective science, and one which I am attempting to redress by writing this book.

If the student continues to practice personal honesty and follows the path of religious education, then he will eventually *become* 'righteous' and think and act in ways that are consistent with general Teacher understanding, and he will ultimately *achieve* personal salvation through rebirth. However, the beginning student is obviously not at that stage. He has enrolled in the school, but the school has not yet transformed the way that he functions. But as long as he wears his school uniform and continues to attend school and take classes, then Teacher thought will continue to view him as an illustration of the function of salvation-through-rebirth.

In theological terms, a distinction must be made between 'being righteous' and being 'verbally declared as righteous'. The graduate of the school *is* righteous, for his actions are consistent with Teacher understanding. The student, in contrast, is *declared* as righteous, because he has acquired the verbal label of 'student enrolled in the path of education'. And as long as the student continues to progress along the path of education, Teacher thought will continue to *declare* him as righteous. However, if the student repeatedly rebels against school authority or else drops out of school, then he will no longer receive a verbal declaration of righteousness. This relates to the concept of 'conditional acceptance' that was described earlier.

In mathematical terms, personal identity is being transferred to the domain of the Contributor function of salvation-through-rebirth; in political language, personal identity acquires a new citizenship. The beginning religious student will not understand this concept because he is using Mercy mode to interpret Teacher mode. As we just saw, Mercy mode thinks in terms of *events* that are separated by time. Teacher mode, in contrast, combines *processes* in order to build general order. Religious education starts with a strong focus upon Mercy thought and personal identity. As a result, the beginning religious student will tend to think that being *declared* righteous means that he *is* righteous. But these two are not the same.

This distinction can be clarified with an example. Suppose that a person is waiting in the departure lounge to fly from New York to Paris. Because he has cleared customs and gone through security, he is officially 'on the way to Paris'. According to Teacher thought, Paris is the declared destination which he is in the process of reaching. But as far as Mercy thought is concerned, he is still on the ground in New York. However, if he continues the process of 'flying to Paris', then eventually he will reach the state of 'being in Paris'.[40]

If the distinction between 'being righteous' and 'being declared righteous' is not sufficiently understood, then the mental 'trick' will substitute for the learning process. In essence, the path of religious education will turn into a 'diploma mill' in which one simply has to enroll in the school in order to receive a diploma. Childish identity will naturally fall for this fallacy, because the mental sensation of 'having moral violations overlooked by God' and 'finding peace with God' feels akin to the sense of mental relief that childish identity achieves when it manages successfully to *deny* its shortcomings and *identify* with its heroes. However, one approach enables personal honesty while the other is the antithesis of personal honesty. This fallacy will become entrenched if the 'instructors of the school' themselves do not understand that they are supposed to teach. Their goal will then be to enroll as many people as possible into the 'school of religious education' by having them 'say the prayer of salvation', while at the same time ignoring what is actually being taught by the school and what the students are learning.

I should emphasize that personal honesty *by itself* is insufficient. It is possible to describe personal behavior with great accuracy without applying the mental 'trick' of the Contributor function, as long as this behavior is treated as something inherent which cannot be changed. The Facilitator person, who is conscious in the mode of thought which observes and balances the rest of thought, is naturally talented at observing personal behavior, but he finds it more difficult than anyone else to *change* this behavior. In addition, *understanding* personal behavior will produce positive Teacher emotions, which will encourage further self-analysis. However, if one is to jumpstart the path of religious education, then personal honesty must be combined with an emotional labeling of personal behavior, together with an acknowledgement that the Mercy mental networks which drive childish behavior need to be torn apart and reassembled. That is why the mental 'trick' of a Contributor *function* is required, because Contributor mode takes personal identity *from* one location *to* another location.

I should also explain why I am using the term *mental 'trick'*. It is a mental trick, because Contributor thought is taking advantage of the difference between concrete thought and abstract thought to get Teacher mode to focus upon the elegance of the journey instead of the state of the passengers. But it is a 'trick' because if a passenger completes the

---

[40] The pre-Socratic philosophers struggled with the concept of movement because, like the typical religious believer, they too were attempting to define everything in terms of *objects* and *states.*

journey, then it will *become* possible for Teacher mode to focus upon the state of that passenger. Saying this another way, when a person is 'declared righteous', what actually *is* righteous is the Contributor function of salvation-through-rebirth. By submitting to that function, childish identity acquires a verbal label of righteousness, and by following that function, childish identity adds to the Teacher generality of that function. However, if the function is followed long enough, then childish identity will *itself* turn into an adult identity that is righteous.

Substitutionary Punishment

Theologians have come up with a number of different ways of interpreting what is called the 'doctrine of atonement', and there is considerable discussion over which of these interpretations is the correct one. A number of these explanations fall under the category of *substitutionary punishment*, a concept which also takes mental advantage of the difference between Cp and Ci. Because this is an important theological topic, we will take a few paragraphs to analyze it. We will look at two different ways of interpreting the concept of substitutionary punishment, beginning with the more popular one.

For Cp, the basic building block is the connection of cause-and-effect. For instance, "Eating too much food leads to body fat." Conscience takes a connection of cause-and-effect and applies it to personal identity: "If *I* eat too much food, then *I* will get fat." The abstract thinking of Ci replaces the specific objects of concrete thought with *variables*: "If *someone* eats too much food, then *someone* will get fat." One version of substitutionary punishment keeps the function intact while replacing the specific person to whom the variable refers, thus changing "If someone eats too much food, then *that person* will get fat" to "If someone eats too much food, then *someone else* will get fat." As long as the *function* is carried out, then Ci will be satisfied, and as long as someone *else* gets punished, then personal identity will be content. In religious terms, God demands that divine rules apply without exception. Therefore, any violation of a divine rule must be punished. Substitutionary punishment satisfies God by carrying out the punishment, but saves me by punishing someone else.

Now that we understand the basic mechanism, let us look at the details. Cognitively speaking, what is the appropriate *punishment* for 'violating a law of God'? Remember that we are dealing with two fundamentally incompatible mental networks: The Teacher mental network upon which the image of God is based cannot handle violations to the rule, while the Mercy mental networks of childish identity practice identification and denial regardless of the rules. If these two sets of mental networks attempt to coexist, then one or the other will fragment. And it is natural for these two mental networks to have to coexist, because a universal theory applies everywhere and personal identity continually comes to mind. This means that the Teacher mental network of universal law will only remain intact if the Mercy mental networks of childish identity fall apart; in religious language, the person who sins against God must die.

Therefore, if substitutionary punishment is to be cognitively adequate, then we conclude that some living creature must die instead of me. That brings us to the next question.

Who is the appropriate substitutionary *victim*? I suggest that the answer depends upon the mind's ability to create Forms. When Perceiver facts that affect personal identity come from *physical* events, then the substitutionary victim will also have to be a *physical* living entity, which leads us to the concept of *animal sacrifice.* (Human sacrifice is not an option because we are trying to find a *substitute* for human death.) In religious terms, God accepts the death of an animal as a punishment for my moral infraction. The problem is that this type of mental solution is both bloody and inefficient: Animals have to be slaughtered and each new infraction requires another animal sacrifice.

When the mind becomes capable of constructing Forms, then the death of an *imaginary* person can substitute for animal sacrifice. Remember that a Form is an imaginary Mercy image that emerges when Teacher thought adjusts and idealizes Perceiver facts. The Form of a *person* will emerge when Teacher thought takes Perceiver facts about people and simplifies them, leading to the *Form* of an ideal, perfect person. Suppose that one believes that the Form of a person was killed as a substitute for personal moral infractions. Because Forms extend beyond specific incidents, it is possible for a single substitutionary punishment to cover *all* moral infractions. In mathematical terms, instead of punishing a *specific* person, the *variable* of a person is being punished.

I suggest that there are two ways of interpreting this concept of having one divine punishment *represent* all other punishments. One way is to look at the substitution in *specific* terms as we did a few paragraphs back and assert that one person is being punished for the crime committed by another person. In terms of our example, *I* eat and someone *else* gets fat. This type of *specific* interpretation will have several flaws. First, it can only be applied to punishment that comes from *people*, because only a *person* can decide to punish someone else instead of me. In contrast, specific substitution does not work with natural law; I cannot ask for someone else to fall to his death when I step over the cliff. Obviously, if I eat too much food, then *I* will get fat and not some other person. Second, it mentally weakens the concept of cause-and-effect because it gives people the idea that they can transgress rules without suffering the consequences. Therefore, instead of developing scientific thought with its emphasis upon natural cause-and-effect, specific substitutionary punishment will oppose scientific thinking.

Third, specific substitutionary punishment deals with the *symptom* while ignoring the underlying problem. The symptom is the specific infraction that childish Mercy identity has committed against universal moral law. Substitutionary punishment removes the feeling of 'guilt against God' by saying that the crime has been punished. But the underlying problem still remains; childish identity still needs to be torn apart and rebuilt. Mentally speaking, a personal identity which 'sins against God' really *must* die, and trying to avoid this conclusion makes as much sense as thinking that someone else can get fat when I overeat.

Specific substitutionary punishment provides a *partial* solution to this problem through the mental mechanism of 'I owe you one', which we described when examining commerce. Suppose that someone does me a big favor. I will feel morally indebted to that person. Similarly, if I believe that the Form of a person was punished for my crime, then I will feel indebted to that imaginary person. And because the Form of a person is by definition more perfect than any other person, I will feel a moral obligation to a person with high moral standards. In religious terms, if I believe that 'Jesus died in my place', then I will feel that 'I owe my life to Jesus'.

However, it is also possible to approach substitutionary punishment from a *general* perspective. Explaining this will take a few paragraphs. Think of the person who follows the path of religious education in some new region of thought or behavior. In essence, he is attempting to answer questions that no one else is asking, by pursuing personal honesty in areas where others are oblivious. Such an individual will receive disapproval from *others*, because the Perceiver facts that he discovers will make it more difficult for them to practice the identification and denial of childish identity. In addition, he will feel disapproval from his *own* mental concept of God, because he is extending Teacher understanding into areas where the personal behavior of his culture is chaotic.

Going further, suppose that this individual then attempts to act in a way that is *consistent* with his expanded image of God. Others will not share his concept of God because they lack his Teacher understanding. Instead, they will actually think that he is disobeying God, because he is acting in a way that is inconsistent with *their* concept of deity. In addition, he will have to protect his own concept of God by avoiding groups that are driven by childish Mercy mental networks, which will make it difficult for him to achieve personal success. And the tendency will be for others to interpret his lack of success as punishment from God for disobeying God.

Finally, suppose that this individual attempts to realize the mental image of possible existence which forms within his mind. On the one hand, others will not take too kindly to his visions of utopia. On the other hand, his mental image of God, backed up by his mental concept of the Holy Spirit, will insist that he live within this utopia.

Many of the inventions and societal advancements that we currently enjoy were originally developed by individuals who blazed the way by pursuing this type of lonely path.

For instance, consider the story of Dr. Ignaz Semmelweis. Today, he is known as the 'savior of mothers', but that does not describe what happened during his lifetime. In 1847, he was working in Vienna as an assistant within a maternity clinic. He noticed that 13% of the women giving birth at his hospital were dying and he attempted to answer a question which no one else seemed to be asking: *Why* are so many mothers dying? He noticed that doctors were going directly from doing autopsies to delivering babies without washing their hands. When he told doctors to wash their hands after doing autopsies, the mortality rate dropped from 13% to 2%. But the local doctors turned upon Semmelweis because they felt that he was undermining their authority.

So, Semmelweis went to a primitive hospital in his home country of Hungary in order to apply his understanding, and he managed to cut the mortality rate in this hospital down to 1%. In 1861 he wrote a book describing his methods, which was largely ignored by the medical establishment. Unfortunately, at this point Semmelweis started to play the political game, writing polemic diatribes in which he accused his fellow physicians of murder, and in 1865, he suffered a mental breakdown and died of an infection. However, his findings were starting to have an impact, and if he had simply continued with his pioneering work, it is quite possible that he would have achieved the breakthrough which he desired.

Analyzing this path from a cognitive perspective, one could view it as a general form of substitutionary punishment, because the person going through the path is experiencing divine condemnation and punishment which others are not receiving—both internally from his concept of God and externally as a result of other peoples' concepts of God. But by following this journey, the pioneer makes it possible for others to avoid the 'divine punishment' that comes from violating universal principles of cause-and-effect. And this is a *general* form of substitutionary punishment, because *one* person is enduring punishment so that *many* other individuals can avoid punishment.

In essence, this form of substitutionary punishment brings us to the idea of *setting* up a school. As we saw when looking at the three stages of learning, a student can only learn what his teacher has already worked out. The individual who originally works out the principles endures condemnation so that those who follow him can go to a school and learn these principles. Saying this in more religious language, the pioneer acts as a type of incarnation who develops a new method of reconciling universal Teacher laws with personal human needs, and he endures the punishment of God so that others do not have to be punished.

Notice that the person who *founds* the school must discover the curriculum without the benefit of *attending* a school. Thus, we are still left with our original dilemma of asking how a person can pursue a path of personal honesty if he must finish the path before being able to practice personal honesty, except that now we have moved the problem back one step. Before, we asked how the average person can practice personal honesty, and we came up with the solution of a school system. Now, we are facing the question of how the *founder* of this school can learn to practice personal honesty.

When dealing with obvious physical issues like learning to wash one's hands, then the breakthrough can be ascribed to some unusual combination of personality and events. But when addressing the core issue of personal honesty, then I suggest that we are still left with a paradox. Some person has to discover and practice personal honesty without the benefit of any school system or mental 'trick'.

Cognitively speaking, it appears that the only way out of this paradox is to postulate that some unusual person existed who was able to go through the process of religious education because he was not subject to the normal human conditions of childish identity and radical evil, and that this person worked out the curriculum and set up the school. Christian theology addresses this problem by stating that the process of religious education was pioneered by a Contributor incarnation, and that this Contributor incarnation then became the Contributor function that enabled the mental 'trick' of the 'prayer of salvation'. Obviously, something unusual must have happened, because a book *exists* that describes a person following the path of religious education, and people are *using* the mental 'trick' to achieve 'peace with God'.

Salvation-through-Rebirth as a Paradigm

We have seen that the Contributor function of salvation-through-rebirth makes it possible to follow a mental path of personal honesty. But if this path is to work, then this Contributor function must be given the Teacher status of a general theory.

That is because the mental 'trick' works by balancing the Mercy pain of personal honesty with the Teacher pleasure produced by personally submitting to the Contributor function of salvation-through-rebirth. But Teacher pleasure comes from *generality*, therefore the mental 'trick' will only work if the Contributor function of salvation-through-rebirth is a *general* function. One option is to use worship to *artificially* produce feelings of Teacher generality. Therefore, if the religious believer *worships* the name of the Contributor function of salvation-through-rebirth and treats this imaginary individual as a Very Important Person, then this will give Teacher thought the illusion that the Contributor function has generality. I suggest that this describes what is happening mentally when the typical Christian believer 'worships the name of Jesus'.

However, if the mental 'trick' is to be *compatible* with rational understanding, then the function of salvation-through-rebirth must *truly* have generality, which means that the function must be ubiquitous.

Before we continue, I need to warn the reader that our discussion will take a number of pages, span several sections, and involve the opening of more than one 'can of worms'.

According to Kuhn, *rebirth* is a general process: "To the extent that the book portrays scientific development as a succession of tradition-bound periods punctuated by non-cumulative breaks, its theses are undoubtedly of wide applicability. But they should be, for they are borrowed from other fields. Historians of literature, of music, of the arts, of political development, and of many other human activities have long described their subjects in the same way. Periodization in terms of revolutionary breaks in style, taste, and institutional structure have been among their standard tools. If I have been original with respect to concepts like these, it has mainly been by applying them to the sciences, fields which had widely thought to develop in a different way."

In this book, we have *generalized* Kuhn's concept of paradigm shifts in two major ways: First, we have suggested that Kuhn was only describing the abstract half of the picture. Kuhn's normal science corresponds to a mind that is using the *abstract* technical circuit of Ci. However, it is also possible for *concrete* thought to function in a technical manner by using the circuit of Cp. These two technical circuits are *both* under the control of Contributor mode. When a paradigm shift occurs, then this is a sign that the *abstract* side of Contributor thought has mentally lost control, but the concrete side of Contributor thought can also lose control and experience a form of 'paradigm shift'.

Second, we have generalized Kuhn's model by placing the paradigm shift within the larger context of a process of *education*. Kuhn, along with most scientists and logicians, regards technical thought as 'normal' and 'revolutionary science' as the aberration. That is because, as Kuhn states, the scientist spends most of his time delving *deeper* within the context of some field of expertise. However, it is more normal for the mind to *broaden* knowledge by using the cognitive modules of Mercy, Perceiver, Teacher, and Server to build connections *between* one mental context and another. If one follows the path of education, this will lead eventually to mental integration and mental wholeness, with *all* cognitive modules functioning together in a cooperative manner.

As far as the *mind* is concerned, I suggest that salvation-through-rebirth is the most general Contributor function. On the one hand, it applies to the mind as a *whole* as Ci and Cp go through the 'rebirths' of various forms of 'paradigm shifts' in order to reach the 'salvation' of mental wholeness. On the other hand, it describes how Ci and Cp *themselves* affect the rest of the mind as Contributor thought tinkers in various ways with existing networks of Perceiver facts and Server sequences in order to achieve either improved Mercy results or a superior Teacher theory. Think, for instance, of the process of cleaning a room. Before the room becomes cleaner, it will temporarily become quite a bit messier.

And that brings us to our first 'can of worms', a 'can of worms' which we partially opened in a previous chapter but then decided to leave in a semi-opened state. Science tries to avoid using words such as 'salvation' because they imply *teleology*—they suggest that the mind or the universe is either heading toward or being guided toward some ultimate purpose.

This scientific reluctance is illustrated by Kuhn's struggle with the idea of scientific *progress*. Obviously, if one paradigm is being replaced by another paradigm, then this suggests that the new paradigm is *better* than the old one and that scientific *progress* has been made. Kuhn admits that scientific progress *does* happen: "The nature of such [scientific] communities provides a virtual guarantee that both the list of problems solved by science and the precision of individual problem-solutions will grow and grow...a sort of progress will inevitably characterize the scientific enterprise so long as such an enterprise survives."

But it bothers him that this implies that scientific progress is bringing society *closer* to some absolute standard of truth: "We may, to be more precise, have to relinquish the notion, explicit or implicit, that changes of paradigm carry scientists and those who learn from them closer and closer to the truth."

He 'solves' this problem by suggesting that it is permissible to look *back* and see progress, but one must not look *forward* and see progress: "Does it really help to imagine that there is some one full, objective, true account of nature and that the proper measure of scientific achievement is the extent to which it brings us closer to that ultimate goal? If we can learn to substitute evolution from-what-we-do know for evolution-toward-what-we-wish-to know, a number of vexing problems may vanish in the process."

The basic problem is that—whether a scientist likes it or not—the mind appears to function teleologically. It is driven by *purpose*. And the two aspects of human thought which are most *purely* purpose-driven are the two technical circuits of Cp and Ci. The concrete circuit of Ci is motivated by the Mercy *goal* of improving personal experiences, while the abstract circuit of Ci is driven by the Teacher *goal* of extending order-within-complexity. The primary reason that technical thought makes such dramatic progress is because it is so intensely driven to form goals and reach them.

As we have seen, science uses these two technical circuits. First, it uses the practical circuit of Cp to observe or experiment with a limited and carefully controlled subset of the real world in order to discover connections of cause-and-effect. Normally, Cp uses these connections of cause-and-effect to go from cause to effect in order to reach some *goal*, and it uses knowledge of cause-and-effect to formulate plans which make it possible to achieve a *better* final effect. This is teleological thinking, for it is driven by a desire to reach some experiential goal.

But instead of using a function of cause-and-effect to reach some Mercy goal, objective science *ignores* the input and output of cause-and-effect and focuses instead upon the Server action that leads from input to output. This Server sequence then becomes the raw material for the abstract circuit of Ci. As we saw when looking at Kuhn's analysis of $f = ma$, Ci uses Server and Perceiver thought to compare one connection of natural cause-and-effect with another in order to find *common* Server sequences and general Teacher laws. Thus, science attempts to work out the *functions* of natural mechanisms, but it avoids suggesting that these functions have the purpose of reaching some Mercy goal. A similar mental transition occurs in the mathematical treatment of functions—and this change in view also makes possible the 'Christian prayer of salvation'.

For instance, think of the story of Galileo dropping the big ball and the small ball from the top of the Tower of Pisa. This describes a natural connection of cause-and-effect, because the cause of dropping the ball was followed by the effect of the ball hitting the ground. The concrete circuit of Cp uses this information to achieve a better Mercy result, which might be making a bigger hole in the ground, or strengthening the object on the ground so that it is not destroyed by a falling ball. However, Galileo used the abstract thinking of Ci to compare the cause-and-effect of the big ball with that of the small ball, leading to the general *Teacher* theory that all objects, whether big or small, take the same time to fall to the ground if they are dropped from the same height.

The abstract circuit of Ci also pursues a goal—the Teacher goal of solving intellectual problems in a way that demonstrates order-within-complexity. But normal science does not come up with *new* paradigms. Instead, it uses and improves *existing* general theories. Thus, by focusing upon the 'trees' which define technical solutions to technical problems, Ci can ignore the fact that these trees lie within the 'forest' of a general Teacher theory. This makes it possible for normal science to ignore the fact that it too is functioning teleologically and pursuing a goal. But when Kuhn talks about replacing one paradigm with a better one, then the idea of making intellectual progress and reaching a goal becomes impossible to avoid, which explains why Kuhn is forced to address the issue.

We have now reached the point in our analysis where the metaphorical worms are about to crawl out of the opened can. *Why* is modern science so adamant of avoiding teleological thinking, especially when goals and purpose form such an integral part of the technical mental circuits which science is using? Historically, this was not always the case. During Foucault's Renaissance episteme, teleological thinking was the *norm*. For instance, why does the giraffe have such a long neck? To the medieval mind, the purpose of the giraffe's long neck is to eat leaves from tall trees. However, in today's Modern episteme, teleological thinking has become taboo in scientific circles. Metaphorically speaking, teleology is an 'elephant in the middle of the room' which must not be discussed.

But *why* has it become taboo to think in teleological terms? First of all, one needs to point out that the scientific taboo against teleology is not universal. When the scientist studies science or applies for a position at a university, he is pursuing the Mercy goal of being respected and having a good job and a nice home. Similarly, when the scientific student takes a course in science, he is pursuing the Teacher goal of gaining a better Teacher understanding. Thus, as long as he or some other human agent is involved, the scientist is fully willing to embrace teleology.

And that, I suggest, tells us why the scientist avoids teleology when dealing with science. Teleology implies the existence of some divine agent who has *designed* the universe, humans, and other living organisms for a purpose. In fact, the teleological argument is one of the main 'proofs' for the existence of God.

But *why* does the typical scientist try to avoid a belief in God? I suggest that the framework of Foucault's epistemes provides an answer for that as well. During the Renaissance episteme, God was referred to as the final cause. Thus, the medieval mind reasoned that the giraffe has a long neck because God designed it that way so that it could eat leaves from tall trees. But medieval thinking was governed by the *first* stage of learning with its Teacher overgeneralization, and it is natural for Teacher overgeneralization to come up with an image of God. However, as we saw when first looking at the three stages of learning, the natural impulse of scientific thinking with its technical circuits of Cp and Ci is to *dismantle* Teacher overgeneralization together with any associated concepts of God. Thus, when the Modern episteme with its dominant technical thinking emerged, God 'died'.

Therefore, I suggest that the *real* problem is that science does not want to believe in God. And who can blame it. When believing in God means adhering to blind faith, rejecting logical thought, jumping to conclusions, believing in miracles, practicing self-delusion, ignoring the real world, submitting to arbitrary decrees, denying physical pleasure, abandoning rigorous thought, and taking existential leaps into ecstatic mysticism, then it is mentally understandable for science to attempt to become free of a belief in God.

However, if one examines the matter from a cognitive perspective, one concludes that denying a belief in God is actually a futile quest. First, as Justin Barrett argues, the presence of the mental Agency Detector makes it mentally *natural* for a person to believe in God. For in the same way that Mercy mental networks cause a person to ascribe events to the hand of some human or animal agent, so Teacher mental networks will attempt to claim responsibility for any universal mechanisms, general laws, or other examples of Teacher order-within-complexity which apply to personal identity, leading to the formation of a concept of God.

Second, it may be natural for technical thought to question a concept of God that is based in Teacher overgeneralization, but when one combines the two technical circuits of Cp and Ci, then I suggest that one is actually constructing a *more stable* mental image of God. On the one hand, the main goal of Cp is to improve the emotional Mercy experiences of *personal identity*. On the other hand, the main purpose of Ci is to improve *general theories* in Teacher thought. If one integrates the two circuits of Cp and Ci, then this will indirectly bring personal identity in Mercy thought into contact with general theory in Teacher thought, resulting in a mental concept of God. In religious terms, combining Cp and Ci builds the mental concept of an *incarnation.*

This explains why the scientific mind tries to avoid the emotional implications of using the technical circuits of Cp and Ci. It must do so in order to avoid constructing a mental concept of God. Consistent with this, when science deals with *general* concepts and adds the *personal* dimension, then the topic of God seems to come up rather often, either as a concept to be cautiously embraced, a topic to be vigorously shunned, or a particle to be discovered.

So, if forming an image of God is mentally natural as well as a by-product of scientific reasoning, then why fight mental architecture? Why pit one part of the mind against another? As the mechanical science fiction monster asserts, 'resistance is futile'. If a mental concept of God is a natural result of cognitive functioning, then why not *embrace* the inevitable and attempt to construct an image of God that is *compatible* with scientific thought—which describes what we have attempted to do in this book. But doesn't a belief in God imply adhering to blind faith, rejecting logical thought, jumping to conclusions, believing in miracles, practicing self-delusion, ignoring the real world, submitting to arbitrary decrees, denying physical pleasure, abandoning rigorous thought, and taking existential leaps into ecstatic mysticism?

I suggest that these undesirable qualities are all the result of an *attitude* of fundamentalism, in which Perceiver thought is being mesmerized by Mercy emotions. Faith becomes blind when Perceiver thought is emotionally overwhelmed, and logical thought will be rejected when Perceiver thought is not functioning. A person jumps to conclusions when he constructs his Teacher theories upon 'facts' that are based in defining experiences, and he believes in miracles when these overgeneralized theories form his image of God. He practices self-delusion because emotional Mercy experiences define personal identity, and he ignores the real world because the resulting personal identity is incompatible with common sense. He submits to arbitrary decrees because his 'truth' is defined by people and books with emotional status, and he denies physical pleasure because physical pleasure raises the emotional status of personal identity and causes him to doubt 'truth'. Finally, he takes existential leaps into ecstatic mysticism because he uses emotional Mercy experiences to define his religion.

So, what the scientist really, really does not like is *fundamentalism.* However, we have seen that it is possible to separate the *content* of religion from the *attitude* of fundamentalism by using a paradigm to describe the content. And when we use the theory of mental symmetry to analyze religion, we discover to our surprise that we keep encountering *existing* religious doctrine. Therefore, we can go further and suggest that it is possible to separate the content of *existing* religion from the attitude of fundamentalism by using the paradigm of mental symmetry. And if religious doctrine is actually based in cognitive structure, then we can go even further and suggest that the *proper* way to analyze religion is by using cognitive science and not by applying the blind faith of fundamentalism.

Now let us see if we can start working our way back to the original question, which was the matter of teleology and the Contributor function of salvation-through-rebirth. Science rejects teleology because it implies the presence of a divine agent, and it avoids believing in God because a belief in God implies fundamentalism and science is opposed to fundamentalism. But if it is possible to analyze religion and an image of God without invoking fundamentalism, then we can examine the concept of teleology without the fear of triggering some irrational mental monster.

Teleology is divided into *intrinsic* finality and *extrinsic* finality. Intrinsic finality says that the purpose of an organism is to perform according to its *own* potential. In the words of Thomas Aquinas, "By the form which gives it its specific perfection, everything in nature has an inclination to its own operations and to its own end, which it reaches through these operations. Just as everything is, such also are its operations and its tendency to what is suitable to itself." Extrinsic finality says that the purpose of an organism is to meet the needs of *another* organism. For instance, Aristotle argued that animals exist for the sake of man.

The theory of mental symmetry suggests a technical version of *intrinsic* finality: The purpose of human existence is to function in a manner that is consistent with the cognitive modules of the mind. However, because the human mind does not *naturally* function in such an integrated manner, it is possible to define a system of morality based upon the *discrepancy* between the purpose of the mind and its present state. Religion involves the process of taking the mind from its present state to the state of functioning in an integrated manner, while theology describes the mental beliefs that are required to reach the goal of operating the mind in an integrated manner. And because forming a mental concept of God is an inevitable cognitive by-product of reaching mental integration, it is possible to acknowledge the implications of a teleological approach without flinching.

Notice that all of this is based in *mental mechanism.* There is no need either to postulate the existence of some external God who demands that one behave in a certain way and reach a certain goal, or in contrast to insist that such a God does not exist. Developing the mind *will* cause an image of God to form, and that image of God *will* demand that a person reach the goal of functioning in an integrated manner. That is sufficient. Thus teleology, together with the implication that God might exist, both become aspects of mental mechanism.

Now that we have addressed the issue of teleology, let us remind ourselves of *why* we originally tackled the question of determining the Teacher generality of the Contributor function of salvation-through-rebirth: If the human mind wishes to function in an integrated manner, then it must follow the path of religious education. But following that path requires personal honesty. However, personal honesty is only possible if one applies the mental 'trick' of inserting the Contributor function of salvation-and-rebirth between personal identity and Teacher generality. That mental 'trick' balances the Mercy pain of personal honesty with the Teacher pleasure of order-within-complexity. But because Teacher emotion comes from *generality*, this mental 'trick' will only continue to function if the Contributor function of salvation-through-rebirth truly is a general Teacher theory, which means that it must be more general than *competing* theories.

The Theory of Evolution

So far, we have assumed that the goal is to *integrate* Teacher thought with Mercy thought. In the *long*-term, this is done by following the path of religious education, while in the *short*-term, the Contributor function of salvation-through-rebirth can be inserted between personal identity in Mercy thought and an image of God in Teacher thought.

There are two other options. One option is to allow the mental image of God to *suppress* personal identity. This happens when blind 'belief' leads to an attitude of religious self-denial. If truth is acquired by using the emotional significance of important people to mesmerize Perceiver thought, then the Perceiver module will only remain in its mesmerized state if personal identity stays emotionally insignificant compared to the source of 'truth'. Going further, if this Perceiver 'truth' is used to construct an image of God and this image of God turns into a Teacher mental network, then the integrity of that image of God will depend upon personal identity remaining insignificant. In religious language, I will feel that it is my religious duty to God to remain personally insignificant, and in the extreme, I will fear that the 'sin of pride' will 'send me to hell'. We have discussed this option earlier and will not examine it further.

The other option is to find a way of mentally existing *without* an image of God. This is the option that we will now examine, and this analysis will lead us to our *second* 'can of worms'. *Why* would a person attempt to free himself mentally from his image of God? When objective science is combined with images of God that are based in Teacher overgeneralization, then I suggest that this is a *natural* outcome.

Suppose that a person goes to university and learns to think rigorously by studying topics such as math, science, and philosophy. These various topics use logic to program Teacher thought with general theories. The overgeneralized theories and blind 'belief' of traditional religion will feel juvenile when compared with the elegant and sophisticated theories of secular education. As a result, the student of objective science will feel *ashamed* of having a personal connection with religious faith, because this personal connection will face personal identity with Teacher feelings of intellectual inadequacy. But when a person mentally divorces personal identity from Teacher theories, then, by definition, he is denying his belief in God, because an image of God emerges from Teacher theories that apply to personal identity.

In addition, religious belief will be rejected as *unreasonable*. In order to understand this, we need to look at the *left hemisphere* version of the counterintuitive concept. In the *right* hemisphere, Facilitator thought evaluates facts and experiences guided by the current *Perceiver* context. As I have mentioned, facts and situations which fall outside of the current context will be filtered out as unreasonable or *counterintuitive*. I suggest that a similar mechanism is at work in the *left* hemisphere, in which Facilitator thought evaluates sequences and theories guided by the current *Server* context. The Server context of science is established by the endless problem-solving of the scientific learning process, during which the general Teacher laws of nature are being used to guide Server steps. Seen in this light, traditional religion, with its invisible Gods and irrational miracles, will be rejected as highly counterintuitive.

Thus, the student of science will experience two desires. First, he will be *emotionally* driven by Teacher emotion to find a replacement for his image of God. In order to *stop* creating an image of God, one must avoid triggering the *Agency Detector*, especially when dealing with *universal* explanations for *personal* existence, because it is this combination that leads to an image of God. This means coming up with a universal explanation for personal existence which does not *require* the presence of some agent, and which does not *imply* the activity of some agent by using teleological concepts such as plan, goal, design, or intelligence.

Second, this replacement for a concept of God will have to be one which the *Facilitator* reasonableness filter can regard as either scientifically intuitive or at least scientifically minimally counterintuitive. This means coming up with a replacement for God that is objective, physical, and natural, because science is *objective*, it observes *physical* processes, and it comes up with *natural* laws.

A mental mechanism *does* exist which is capable of making progress in the *absence* of any intelligent agent, a mechanism that does not require any overall understanding. This mechanism is provided by the Facilitator module, which stands *apart* from the rest of thought and which observes and mixes the activity of other cognitive modules. Normally, Facilitator mixing is guided by information from the *rest* of the mind. But suppose that other modes of thought fail to provide any guidance. Facilitator thought will then make *random* changes in the hope that one of these will lead to a beneficial result.

For instance, evidence suggests that Thomas Edison was a Facilitator person. In his search to find the right material to use for the filament of a light bulb, he filled 40,000 pages with notes and tested over 1600 different possibilities, including hair from a friend's beard, before finally settling upon carbonized bamboo.

If one combines random change with objective, physical, natural processes, one comes up with the theory of *evolution.* The theory of evolution is left hemisphere *minimally counterintuitive*, because it explains the universe by using Facilitator mixing to *extend* current natural, objective, physical processes into the distant past and distant future. Just as a Cyclops is a normal human being except for the presence of only one eye, so evolution is a normal scientific theory except for the extension of time. This relates to four of the five reasons for believing in the theory of evolution that were given earlier in the book: Evolution is natural, it is objective, it is scientifically minimally counterintuitive, and it is superior to a belief in a God of overgeneralization. As for the final reason for believing in evolution, we have now examined technical thought sufficiently to understand why normal science would denigrate any theory that falls outside of the current paradigm, especially if such a theory questioned the fundamental operating assumptions of objective, natural science.

Evolution explains personal existence by appealing to mechanisms that are used by *Facilitator* thought, which operates *apart* from mental networks and thus does not require the presence of any intelligent agent. Facilitator mode uses *mixing* to decide which mental streams will be emphasized and which ones will be filtered out. This corresponds to *natural selection*, which 'chooses' which organisms will survive and which will not. In the absence of intelligent guidance, Facilitator mode can make *random* changes in the hope that this will produce beneficial results, which corresponds to the random changes of *mutation.* However, as the research of Edison shows, random experimentation is highly inefficient, corresponding to the concept that most evolutionary mutations are harmful. Facilitator thought is limited to making incremental changes within the current context and can only go beyond the current context through extrapolation. Similarly, macroevolution is regarded as the outcome of long periods of microevolution. When mental content is lacking, then the context for Facilitator thought will be provided by the external environment. Likewise, evolution says that *adaptation* causes organisms to lose old features or develop new ones. Facilitator thought acquires its knowledge of external context *indirectly*, because Perceiver and Server thought identify the facts and sequences that are present externally and this Perceiver and Server processing sets the context for Facilitator thought. This indirect acquisition of context can cause the mental context of Facilitator thought to *lag* behind the external context. In a similar manner, an evolutionary *exaptation* is a feature which was originally adapted for one function but coincidentally has benefits within another context. In the right hemisphere, Facilitator thought adjusts facts and experiences, while in the left hemisphere it adjust symbols and sequences. Similarly, the theory of evolution was originally defined in terms of the mutation and adaptation of physical features, but it is now viewed as the mutation and adaptation of genetic code.

Thus, if the goal is to replace a juvenile concept of God with a scientifically acceptable, minimally counterintuitive explanation for human existence which does not require the existence of some divine agent, then the theory of evolution appears to be the best candidate for the job. But we have just seen that the real problem is not a mental image of God, nor is it the concept of a divine agent or the use of teleological thinking. Instead, the real enemy of science is the *attitude* of fundamentalism. Going further, we now know that divine agents, images of God, and other fundamental theological concepts can all be explained logically and rationally through the use of mental mechanisms which function in a manner that is independent of the existence of any external divine agent. Saying this in plain English, I suggest that the theory of mental symmetry removes the psychological need to believe in the theory of evolution.

As I mentioned earlier in the book, the theory of evolution is highly unusual in that it has no personal physical consequences. If a person stopped believing in the theory of gravity and acted as if it were not true, then it would only be a matter of time before he stepped over some precipice and plummeted to his death. But if a person stopped believing in the theory of evolution and acted as if it were not true, then nothing would happen to him. He would experience no negative physical consequences. However, he would receive substantial approval or disapproval from various segments of society. Thus, one concludes that the theory of evolution meets primarily a *psychological* need.

In this book, we have been attempting to replace a juvenile concept of God with one that is compatible with science by using a *cognitive* model to *extend* the *method* of science into the realm of the subjective and the internal. We have discovered that this approach makes it possible to explain *existing* religious doctrine in terms of cognitive mechanisms. The theory of evolution differs from this approach in three major ways: Instead of starting from a cognitive model, evolution is based upon *physical* mechanisms; rather than applying the method of science, evolution adopts the *assumptions* of science; instead of extending science to include the internal and the subjective, evolution *avoids* the internal and the subjective.

I suggest that the end result is that the theory of evolution cannot meet the psychological need for which it was initially formulated. We will illustrate this conclusion by referring to the account of 'the fleeing jungle native', the story mentioned earlier that forms the starting point for the cognitive science of religion, which I will refer to as 'the story'.

Science is based upon empirical data; the *assumption* of science is that only data acquired by observing the physical world is worthy of analysis. Thus, evolution uses the *physical* mechanism of genetic adaptation to explain *mental* behavior. This replaces mental software, which an individual *can* change, with mental hardware, which a person *cannot* change. We have learned that irrational thought in the area of the subjective is driven by childish mental networks and that these childish mental networks need to be reprogrammed. Evolution takes attention away from these mental networks and focuses instead upon a person's genetic background. For instance, the story says that natives who were fearful of wild animals survived and passed on their genes, while those who did not were eaten, causing the Agency Detector to become part of the human gene pool.

The theory of evolution avoids the concept of an *agent* by following chains of cause-and-effect only *back* in time and not *forward* in time. This has several mental consequences: First, if current personal behavior is determined solely by *past* chains of cause-and-effect, then this adds to the sense of *fatalism* that is caused by focusing upon hardware instead of software, because it is impossible to change the past. For instance, the story explains present religious belief in terms of the behavior of jungle natives in the distant past. Second, this replaces a good role model with a poor one, because present mental activity is being explained by *less* intelligent behavior from the past rather than *more* intelligent behavior from the future. For instance, the story attributes religious thought to the behavior of primitive, smelly, dirty, jungle natives eking out an existence on the edge of starvation.

Evolution avoids the idea of an *intelligent* agent by attributing human existence to *random* mutation. This also has mental consequences: First, this replaces intelligence with ignorance. We have seen that childish identity is governed by the semi-random effects of emotional Mercy experiences and that education replaces this with the order and structure of a general Teacher understanding. A random mutation is, by definition, a *breakdown* of genetic order and structure, just as a miracle is a *violation* of universal natural law. For instance, in the story, it was the native who happened by chance to develop an Agency Detector who survived to pass on his traits. Second, this replaces hope with *hopelessness*. The vast majority of mutations are harmful. Offering a solution which usually fails does not lead to hope. Saying this in more personal terms, irrational thought clings to its emotional crutches because it does not want to feel bad. Like a scared rabbit, it needs to be coaxed out of its emotional cocoon. Evolution responds to this emotional vulnerability by painting a picture of rabbits being eaten by predators and proto-rabbits being tossed on the garbage-heap of history as evolutionary failures. For instance, in the story, most natives ended up being torn to shreds and eaten by wild animals because they did not possess a fully functioning Agency Detector.

Evolution *extrapolates* from existing mechanics of adaptation, saying that major change can be achieved by performing sufficient minor adjustments. However, one cannot turn a childish Mercy mental network into an adult Mercy mental network by making minor adjustments. Instead, it has to be torn apart and reassembled. That is because the emotional 'knowing' which glues a childish Mercy mental network together is separated by a Perceiver 'threshold of confusion' from the rational facts which hold together an adult Mercy mental network. For instance, the story views the thinking of the modern human as a modification of the thinking of the jungle native, glossing over the numerous paradigm shifts which lie between the thinking of the one and the thinking of the other.

Finally, evolution encourages the same type of Teacher *overgeneralization* that generates a juvenile concept of God. Overgeneralization begins with some specific Mercy incident and then follows implausible mental channels to come up with a general Teacher theory. Similarly, evolution starts with the experience of some mutation and then follows implausible channels which *might* have occurred in order to come up with a general

Teacher theory. For instance, the story begins with the specific situation of the fleeing jungle native and then generalizes from there to a general description of the Agency Detector by following unlikely steps that could have happened. The end result is to *perpetuate* the underlying intellectual problem of Teacher overgeneralization.

Thus, if the goal of believing in evolution is to replace a juvenile belief in God with something more scientific, then we conclude that the theory of evolution is not doing its job, because it ignores the problem and focuses upon what cannot be changed, it attacks order and exalts ignorance, and it downplays the necessity for mental transformation while perpetuating the type of thinking which it is supposed to replace.

In contrast, I suggest that the theory of mental symmetry actually *solves* the underlying problem of irrational thought in the realm of the subjective, because it focuses upon *reprogramming* mental software, it *extends* the order and structure of scientific thought, and it provides the positive role model of an *integrated* mind in which childish identity has been transformed and Teacher overgeneralization has been superseded.

Summing up, if the theory of evolution meets primarily a psychological need, if the theory of mental symmetry removes this psychological need and solves the underlying problem, if believing in the theory of evolution perpetuates the underlying problem, and if not believing in the theory of evolution has no physical consequences, then why believe in evolution? If the answer is 'because important scientists believe in evolution', then I suggest that one is dealing with precisely the type of blind 'belief' which the theory of evolution was originally supposed to avoid.

Evolution versus Revolution

Does this mean that the theory of evolution is *wrong*? No, the *physical* mechanisms that evolution describes do exist. For instance, genes do have an effect on behavior. This is illustrated by a fascinating study which was done in Russia on breeding foxes, which is described in the March 2011 issue of *National Geographic*. It began in the 1950s when Dmitry Belyaev starting breeding foxes based upon their behavior. Those that reacted in a friendly manner to humans were bred further. It only took a decade of breeding for the foxes to start behaving like pets, wagging their tails like dogs, jumping into peoples' arms, licking peoples' faces, and clamouring for human attention. And the physical appearance of these friendly foxes also changed. For instance, their fur was no longer just a single color but often had white spots. Genetic analysis of these foxes has shown that breeding for domestication leads to a cluster of genetic changes.

In addition, we have seen that evolution describes a valid mode of *thought* which is practiced by the Facilitator module. But in the same way that the secretary of a company can only adjust the flow of information that passes by his desk if the rest of the company *provides* information to pass by his desk, so the Facilitator module can only adjust the flow of mental information if mental information is being *provided* by other modes of thought. Thus, I suggest that both the theory of evolution and Facilitator thought work best when they take a *secondary* role.

This conclusion is backed up by observations of the Facilitator *person.* Our research indicates that the Facilitator person does the most effective job when he is in the number two position, facilitating the decisions and projects of other individuals—often Contributor persons. If he is placed in charge, then his natural tendency will be to replace progress with constant incremental change that uses up resources but ends up going nowhere. However, if subconscious cognitive modules are sufficiently programmed within the mind of the Facilitator person, then he can be placed in charge and still be mentally capable of making major progress.

In essence, I suggest that the issue boils down to the matter of *evolution* versus *revolution.* Which of these two is more universal? Does revolution occur within a context of evolution, or is evolution the subset which occurs within the more general context of revolution?

Kuhn makes it clear that these two are interrelated. Repeating part of an earlier quote: "Historians of literature, of music, of the arts, of political development, and of many other human activities have long described their subjects in the same way. Periodization in terms of revolutionary breaks in style, taste, and institutional structure have been among their standard tools. If I have been original with respect to concepts like these, it has mainly been by applying them to the sciences, fields which had widely thought to develop in a different way." Similarly, our examination of mental development has included both a description of evolutionary mental programming and an analysis of revolutionary mental reprogramming.

In the last three pages of his book, Kuhn attempted to reconcile his general theory of scientific *revolution* with a universal theory of *evolution* by suggesting that scientific evolution is the *primary* process while scientific *revolution* corresponds merely to a *secondary* struggle between competing paradigms during which the 'fittest struggles to survive': "The analogy that relates the evolution of organisms to the evolution of scientific ideas can easily be pushed too far. But with respect to the issues of this closing section it is very nearly perfect...The resolution of revolutions is the selection by conflict within the scientific community of the fittest way to practice future science. The net result of a sequence of such revolutionary selections, separated by periods of normal research, is the wonderfully adapted set of instruments we call modern scientific knowledge."

But Kuhn also says that there is a strong tendency for the scientific mind to act as if evolution is more general than revolution and to rewrite history so that revolution appears to be merely a footnote in the overall flow of evolution: "Textbooks, however, being pedagogic vehicles for the perpetuation of normal science, have to be rewritten in whole or in part whenever the language, problem-structure, or standards of normal science change. In short, they have to be rewritten in the aftermath of each scientific revolution, and, once rewritten, they inevitably disguise not only the role but the very existence of the revolutions that produced them. Unless he has personally experienced a revolution in his own lifetime, the historical sense either of the working scientist or of the lay reader of textbook literature extends only to the outcome of the most recent revolutions in the field."

And, as we saw earlier, Kuhn tells us that science will actually pretend that evolution is universal and that revolution never occurs: "However, science textbooks...refer only to that part of the work of past scientists that can easily be viewed as contributions to the statement and solution of the texts' paradigm problems. Partly by selection and partly by distortion, the scientists of earlier ages are implicitly represented as having worked upon the same set of fixed problems and in accordance with the same set of fixed canons that the most recent revolution in scientific theory and method has made seem scientific."

That leaves us with a conundrum. Does Kuhn conclude in the final pages of his book that evolution is more general than revolution because it really *is* more general, or because he himself has fallen into the cognitive trap which he describes in his book?

Let us explore this cognitive trap with the help of a few historical examples. One of the classic military examples of evolution versus revolution is the Battle of Agincourt in 1415, in which an army of French knights who represented the evolutionary pinnacle of armored development was wiped out by the revolutionary new weapon of the English longbow. Similarly, the French lost to the Germans in the Blitzkrieg of 1940 because the French defended their country with the Maginot Line, an evolutionary development of First World War trench warfare, while the Germans adopted the revolutionary new tactic of tank warfare. What principle can we draw from these illustrations? In a nutshell, evolution leads to extinction, while those who embrace revolution survive.

The recent example of the Eastman Kodak Company brings out this conclusion rather vividly: In 1888, George Eastman invented roll film, and by the 1960s, Kodak was a household name known worldwide with Kodak film available in almost every village throughout the world. Amazingly, Kodak actually *invented* the digital camera in 1975, but it responded by taking the *evolutionary* step of continuing to sell and develop photographic film. As a result, Kodak has become eclipsed by other companies that adopted the *revolutionary* new product which Kodak itself invented, and Kodak has recently declared bankruptcy. Thus, even if a company comes up with a revolutionary new invention, it still has to adopt an *attitude* of revolution in order to succeed.

So, why do we keep thinking that *evolution* is the key to development, when history is littered with so many examples of evolution being made extinct by revolution? Why do we keep fighting the *previous* battle, like the French in the Second World War; why do we assume that customers will *always* use our product, like Kodak and photography film; and why are we so confident, like the French knights at Agincourt, that evolutionary improvements will always *triumph*? And, turning to what Kuhn tells us, why does scientific thought continually try to rewrite history in order to make it look like all scientific progress is evolutionary and that revolutionary change never occurs? Finally, why do most scientists ridicule anyone who might suggest that evolution is not the universal theory of human existence, even though innumerable books have been written and countless seminars delivered upon 'thinking outside of the box' and 'pursuing revolutionary change'?

I suggest that the answer ultimately boils down to *mental networks.* Revolution occurs when mental networks are torn apart and reassembled: Political revolution occurs when political regimes are overthrown and replaced with new regimes; scientific revolution happens when paradigms fall apart and are replaced with new paradigms; social revolution occurs when cultural norms fall apart and new cultural norms emerge.

But we only partially comprehend mental networks. For instance, Quine describes normal thought quite accurately, but mentions the concept of mental networks only *peripherally.* Kuhn goes one step further and describes the effect that a Teacher mental network has upon the mind of the scientist, but he views it as a mental *snare* from which the individual scientist cannot escape. The cognitive science of religion goes yet further and describes the function of *Mercy* mental networks with its Agency Detector, but does not realize that its explanations are being biased by *Teacher* mental networks based in objective science. Religion *uses* mental networks, but treats its mental procedures as magical formulae revealed by God. Psychology *analyzes* mental networks, but only has limited success in manipulating them.

In the Middle East, *Mercy* mental networks rule supreme. Western countries discover the power of these mental networks whenever they attempt to intervene in Middle Eastern politics. Western thought, in contrast, tends to be ruled by *Teacher* mental networks. That is because the *objective,* rational thinking of Western society *avoids* Mercy networks. But when a person embraces scientific thought and professionalism, then he becomes mentally trapped by *Teacher* mental networks. According to Kuhn, the typical scientist is just as incapable of changing his paradigm as the average person in the Middle East is of questioning his religion or his culture.

Technical thought gives the mind the ability to *modify* mental networks, but it is incapable of *transforming* mental networks. That is because technical thought, by its very nature, functions within a limited 'playing field'. It optimizes an *existing* plan; it performs its logic within an *existing* paradigm. Thus, what technical thought generates is *evolutionary* change. In order to produce *revolutionary* change, in order to experience the paradigm change of 'revolutionary science', existing mental networks must be torn down and replaced with new ones.

As Kuhn tells us, evolution alternates with revolution. But Western society with its technical expertise only understands the *evolutionary* half of this cycle. As far as we are concerned, progress occurs in the following manner: Technical thought makes great strides in some limited area of thought. Technical thought eventually reaches an impasse because it is pursuing evolutionary change. A mysterious form of thought then emerges which leads to some revolutionary breakthrough. This breakthrough then makes it possible to resume evolutionary growth in this new area and these new developments make existing methods and products obsolete.

This repeated cycle of normal, technically driven, evolutionary change punctuated by mysterious, emotionally driven revolution, has become accepted as the norm by the Facilitator filter in the *right* hemisphere. Thus, not only is the *process* of evolution accepted as minimally counterintuitive in the *left* hemisphere, but the *cycle* of evolution is viewed as minimally counterintuitive by the *right* hemisphere.

However, we have seen that one *can* analyze what is happening during a revolution when mental networks are being reborn. In addition, gaining sufficient Perceiver and Server confidence makes it possible to *manipulate* mental networks, while overlapping one mental network with another allows one to play one mental network *against* another, or to change the *form* of one mental network so that it can 'give birth' to another. And when one gains the ability to manipulate and transform mental networks, then one realizes that the greatest change occurs through the *revolution* of manipulating mental networks and not through the *evolution* of technical thought. When one views technical thought within this larger mental framework, then one concludes that evolution is a subset within revolution, because evolution improves *existing* mental networks while revolution *transforms* mental networks.

However, simply *saying* this is not enough. What is needed is a method of escaping evolutionary change that is potent enough to overcome the mental networks of entrenched thought, established behavior, and institutional kingdoms. And that, by definition, requires a *religious* solution, because religion deals with the disassembling and reassembling of mental networks. This brings us back finally to the Contributor function of salvation-through-rebirth, which we first introduced within a *religious* context. For what a Contributor function of salvation-through-rebirth essentially does is recognize the supremacy of revolution over evolution—using the language of Contributor thought at the level of mental networks.[41]

But we still have Foucault's Modern episteme to contend with: *Physically* speaking, the complex modern world of objective science and technology that came into existence at the end of the 19th century can only continue to exist through the use of Contributor-controlled technical thought. *Personally* speaking, the typical modern individual who wants to make a decent living must become technically proficient in some objective specialization. And *mentally* speaking, self-questioning has reduced most fields of knowledge to technical skill in specialized process. Thus, not only do mental networks trap us into evolutionary development, but so does a worldview which is sufficiently universal to form a mental concept of God.

Thus, not only do we need a religious solution, but the Contributor function of salvation-through-rebirth must acquire sufficient Teacher generality to alter a mental

---

[41] Notice that salvation-through-rebirth involves Contributor mode whereas evolution involves Facilitator mode. When Contributor mode restricts thought to some limited, objective, scientific, technical 'playing field', then this automatically sets a general mental context for Facilitator thought, which will then regard evolution as minimally counterintuitive.

concept of God. And that brings us back to the same conclusion that we reached when looking at the Contributor function of salvation-through-rebirth in the context of *personal* change: If the function of salvation-through-rebirth is to provide the Teacher emotions that are needed to balance the Mercy pain of both describing and transforming personal identity, then it must be mentally accepted as a general Teacher theory, for Teacher emotions come from generality. And in both cases we also came to the conclusion that a universal theory of evolution acts as a major stumbling block: We saw previously that believing in the theory of evolution perpetuates juvenile thinking in the realm of the subjective, and we see now that it gives people the illusion that revolutionary goals can be achieved using evolutionary methods.

If the function of salvation-through-rebirth is given *insufficient* Teacher generality, then it will lack the Teacher feelings that are needed to force the core of personal identity to change. The result will be personal salvation that is limited to the periphery of personal identity. Current society illustrates what it means to experience limited, peripheral, personal salvation. Science and technology have improved the physical world, but not people. Medicine saves the body, but not the person. Business seeks the external symbols of value but not personal value itself. Organized labor can improve working conditions, but not the mindset of the worker. Psychology can modify mental networks, but it cannot tear them apart and rebuild them. All of these may be aspects of personal salvation, but they are also incomplete because they deal with the periphery and not the core.

Turning from the person to the *group*, if the function of salvation-through-rebirth is given insufficient Teacher generality, then, employing the tired but true language of well-worn cliché, technical thought with its evolutionary growth will continually try to prevent revolutionary thinking from 'rocking the boat', but by limiting itself to the evolutionary change of 'rearranging the chairs on the deck of the Titanic', it will guarantee that the 'unsinkable ship' of the current paradigm or institution eventually plunges to the bottom of the ocean when it plows full steam into the hidden 'iceberg' of revolutionary change.

Looking at this relationship from the other side, I suggest that the cognitive science of religion illustrates two problems that arise when the theory of evolution is given too *much* Teacher generality. We have just seen that the theory of evolution provides an explanation for existence that avoids the concept of purpose and does not require the intervention of any divine agent. Quine, in *The Web of Belief*, summarizes this scientific mindset: "One proposed solution has been to assume Someone whose purpose was at work at the beginning of all causal chains. Here is a grand hypothesis, calculated to personalize the impersonal teleological explanations and so to accommodate them under the head of efficient cause after all. It is one of the classical arguments for the existence of God, and is known as the *argument from design*...Charles Darwin, then, to the rescue, with his abundantly documented hypothesis of natural selection. The seeing eye can evolve in the vertebrate, and hydrotropism in the willow, with never the intervention of purpose human or divine...[This] reduces the teleological explanations of biology sweepingly to explanations in the proper causal sense. Easy answers like 'To see with' and 'So that their seeds will float away' become, thanks to Darwin, interpretable as shorthand allusions to long causal chains of natural selection."

However, we have seen that the mind naturally forms a concept of God. Saying this more technically, if a Teacher theory that describes personal identity is made *sufficiently general*, then it *will* form a mental concept of God. Thus, when evolution is elevated to the level of a *universal* theory of *human* existence, then it is only a matter of time before this theory forms a mental image of God—even if evolution itself explicitly denies the existence of both design and God. As Justin Barrett points out in *Why Would Anyone Believe in God*, "One of the embarrassing realities for evolutionary theorists is the difficulty of consistently thinking or talking about natural selection without using mental-states language. At an implicit level, natural selection amounts to a sanitized and scientifically sanctioned 'God' that may displace God." Consistent with this, if I counted correctly, Tremlin uses the word 'design' 48 times to describe the work of evolution in his book *Minds and Gods.*

Moving on to the second problem, if the mind naturally forms a concept of God, then when cognitive science studies the mind, it will discover—as the cognitive science of religion has done—that the mind naturally forms a concept of God. If evolution is elevated to the level of a *universal* theory of human existence, then the theory of evolution will be used to explain *why* the mind naturally thinks in terms of agents and why it forms a concept of God. Thus, the theory of evolution, which was originally formulated to *avoid* concepts such as agents and God, will be asked to *explain* concepts such as agents and God.

In Tremlin's words, "Gods matter largely for reasons that are biological rather than theological in origin. Due to the shaping work of selective forces in our evolutionary past, human beings have minds that easily and quite naturally entertain religious concepts. And for equally natural reasons, religious concepts can easily become personally compelling. The ordinary properties that structure representations of gods activate the brain's most powerful inference systems, while the extraordinary properties of god concepts make them seem highly relevant to human life. These mental responses are governed by cognitive processes that are automatic, nonconscious, and shared by people everywhere—a claim supported by the ubiquity and similarity of god concepts the world over."

Quoting once more from Tremlin's book *Minds and Gods*: "The human brain is endowed with an array of tools for organizing and interpreting the world. Given our natural environment, the presence of agents is much more relevant than objects. Agents can injure and agents can nurture. Agents can attack and agents can protect. Agents can be good to eat and agents can be good at eating. So evolution has designed a mental mechanism, ADD [Agency Detector Device], to quickly detect and respond to agents." In this quote, we see *both* problems being illustrated. First, Tremlin is treating a theory that denies the existence of supernatural agents as a supernatural agent; second, he is using a theory that abhors agents to explain the concept of agents.

My goal is not to pick on Tremlin. Rather, I am attempting to illustrate the cognitive futility of viewing the theory of evolution as a universal theory of human existence. Even if the theory of evolution *is* a universal theory of human existence, it appears that the mind is incapable of *regarding* the theory of evolution as a universal theory of human existence: First, a general theory that explains personal identity will turn into an image of God, even if the core essence of that general theory denies the existence of God. Second, a universal theory of human thought will be called upon to explain the mental concept of God, even if that theory explicitly avoids dealing with the concept of God.

Notice that the mind is capable of *temporarily* regarding evolution as a universal theory of human existence, just as human effort can be used to *temporarily* cut back the jungle and build a city in the midst of a tropical rain forest. But both are unnatural; both can only be maintained through continual attention and effort or else they will revert back to their original state.

If even a respected expert in the field of the cognitive science of religion cannot escape these cognitive effects, then it seems that we have no choice but to come to terms with the mental concepts of God and divine purpose. And that means developing a general theory of human thought which can both *explain* a concept of God and handle the religious implications of being used to *form* an image of God.

The Ten Commandments Revisited

When we first introduced the concept of mental networks, we looked at the second half of the Ten Commandments and concluded that they all involve mental networks. It appears that the first half of these Ten Commandments address the path of religious education.

The First Commandment defines the image of God: "I am the LORD your God, who brought you out of the land of Egypt, out of the house of slavery." Notice that God is being defined in terms of *salvation* for the Jewish people. And if one reads the Biblical stories of the Ten Plagues of Egypt, the death of the Firstborn, and the crossing of the Red Sea, one sees that the *method* of salvation involved a form of *rebirth*. As usual, my goal is not to determine whether this describes actual history or not. Instead, what matters cognitively is that the Jewish God is being defined in terms of *salvation-through-rebirth*.

The First Commandment continues, "You shall have no other gods before Me." Translating the original Hebrew more literally, this says that 'different gods should not be before my face'. We see here an expression of Teacher emotion. Contradiction brings emotional pain to Teacher thought. As we saw when looking at competing theories, a general Teacher theory is threatened when it is forced to coexist with contradictory general theories.

The Second Commandment is a prohibition against idolatry: "You shall not make for yourself an idol, or any likeness of what is in heaven above or on the earth beneath or in the water under the earth. You shall not worship them or serve them, for I, the LORD your God, am a jealous God." Three cognitive principles are described here: First, general Teacher theories are supposed to be *independent* of Mercy experiences. Second, we notice that Teacher thought functions *emotionally*. Third, we see here a version of Kant's radical evil, because Mercy-based idolatry is leading to thought and behavior that contradicts the general Teacher understanding of God.

The Third Commandment addresses the concept of Teacher generality: "You shall not take the name of the LORD your God in vain, for the LORD will not leave him unpunished who takes His name in vain." The word 'vain' literally means *empty* or *void of content*. When a general Teacher theory becomes restricted in domain and loses its generality, then it becomes empty. The phrase 'leave him unpunished' can also be translated 'acquit' or 'hold innocent'. Thus, the original Hebrew states that the method of using the name of God to remove feelings of guilt will not work if the name of God loses its Teacher generality, which matches the conclusion that we reached a few pages back.

The Fourth Commandment talks about a day of rest: "Remember the sabbath day, to keep it holy. Six days you shall labor and do all your work, but the seventh day is a sabbath of the LORD your God." In essence, this prohibits the use of concrete thought for one day in seven. If concrete thought is not allowed, then the only alternative is to use abstract thought. This is like the mother telling her child to 'go sit in the corner, face the wall, and think'.

Finally, there is the Fifth Commandment, which was also mentioned earlier: "Honor your father and your mother, that your days may be prolonged in the land which the LORD your God gives you." We know that parents create the strongest Mercy mental networks within the mind of the child. Honoring parents ensures that abstract thought includes the subjective and does not block it off. If the subjective is included, then the final stage of R&D, when general Teacher understanding produces Mercy results, will last much longer. Otherwise, the undigested emotional core of childish identity will eventually bring technological society to a halt, which describes what is happening in today's society.

Thus, we conclude that the writer of the Ten Commandments had a deep awareness of cognitive principles, because the first five summarize the essence of the path of religious education. Notice that this is a *cognitive* conclusion which is valid regardless of whether a real God exists or not. As Voltaire put it, *Si Dieu n'existait pas, il faudrait l'inventer*. Or, in English, if God did not exist, it would be necessary to invent him.

Summary

Following the path of education will eventually lead to a conflict between existing culture and the new culture that is made possible by extending Ci to include Cp. Replacing the existing culture with the new culture will lead to a form of rebirth as Mercy mental networks are torn apart and reassembled. The precise region and extent of rebirth will depend upon the form of the preceding education. The goal of rebirth is not to destroy personal identity, but rather to rebuild it upon a more stable and satisfying foundation.

When one examines the Biblical story of the life, death, resurrection, and ascension of Jesus from a cognitive perspective, then it corresponds to the 'path' that Contributor mode takes during the process of religious education. And these same principles are contained within the first five of the Jewish Ten Commandments. Thus, when one uses the theory of mental symmetry to analyze religion, one ends up with *existing* religious doctrine.

Facilitator mode acts as the mental filter, using the current Perceiver context to evaluate facts in the right hemisphere and the current Server context to evaluate sequences in the left hemisphere. Teacher theories only became emotionally independent of Mercy mental networks during the Scientific Revolution. Before this time, Teacher theories had to be described in anthropomorphic terms in order to be accepted by the Facilitator filter as minimally counterintuitive. After the Scientific Revolution, Immanuel Kant attempted to recast Christian doctrine in theoretical terms and came up with a number of significant moral concepts, such as the categorical imperative and radical evil.

The path of religious education contains a chicken-and-egg type of problem which prevents it from being followed, because the path begins with personal honesty but total personal honesty only becomes possible when the path is finished. This problem can be solved by the mental 'trick' of representing the path of religious education as a Contributor function, which we could call salvation-through-rebirth, and taking advantage of the different way that Cp and Ci view functions. For Cp, the function of salvation-through-rebirth is a sequence that leads *from* the childish mind *to* the integrated mind. Ci, in contrast, views the *entire* function all at once. If personal identity mentally submits to the Contributor function of salvation-through-rebirth, then childish identity will be seen by Teacher thought as an example of order rather than chaos, and each further step of personal honesty will increase the Teacher feeling of order-within-complexity that is produced by the Contributor function of salvation-through-rebirth. The difference between applying the mental 'trick' and following the path of religious education could be compared to the difference between enrolling in school and graduating from school. In Christian circles, this mental 'trick' is known as the 'prayer of salvation'. It is more effective when the process is understood but it will also work when applied as a magical formula.

If this mental 'trick' is to work, then the Contributor function of salvation-through-rebirth must acquire strong positive Teacher emotion, which means that it must be a *general* theory. Salvation-through-rebirth is a general mental Contributor function because Contributor thought functions by taking other cognitive modes through a form of rebirth in order to achieve the 'salvation' of an improved bottom line, and Contributor mode itself must go through rebirth several times in order to reach the salvation of an integrated mind. Treating evolution as a subset of revolution is mentally equivalent to regarding the Contributor function of salvation-through-rebirth as a general Teacher theory.

According to Kuhn, *rebirth* is a general theory. However, science in general does not like the concept of *salvation*-through-rebirth because this implies the concept of *design*, and design implies the existence of a *designer*, and a concept of God reminds science of fundamentalism and Teacher overgeneralization. The problem is that technical thought is by nature *purpose*-driven and will lead naturally to the formation of a concept of God. Science ignores the purpose-driven nature of Cp either by focusing solely upon the connection of cause-and-effect while ignoring where these connections lead, or by following chains of cause-and-effect into the past but not into the future. And specialization makes it possible for science to use Ci while ignoring the purpose of Ci, which is to improve a general Teacher theory.

Thus, in order to avoid forming a concept of God, science, which strives to build technical thought, must deny the implications of using technical thought. Mental symmetry suggests that both purpose and a concept of God can be defined in terms of mental mechanisms, allowing science to acknowledge these concepts while sidestepping the question of cosmic purpose and the existence of a real God.

Science is based upon *physical* phenomena, but evolution is an unusual theory because believing it or disbelieving has no physical repercussions. However, the theory of evolution does satisfy the mental need of providing a scientifically minimally counterintuitive explanation for existence which does not require either purpose or a designer. The theory of evolution also corresponds to the behavior of Facilitator thought when mental content is lacking. But mental symmetry suggests that the underlying problem is not the idea of purpose or a concept of God, but rather the attitude of fundamentalism. And if one examines the mental side effects of believing in evolution, one comes to the conclusion that it encourages the continued use of irrational thought in the realm of the subjective. In contrast, following the path of religious education as described by mental symmetry actually *solves* the underlying problem of fundamentalism.

Treating evolution as a universal theory of human existence will lead to two mental contradictions: Because a mental image of God forms when a general Teacher theory explains personal identity, the theory of evolution will be treated as a divine agent, even though it explicitly denies the existence of divine agents. And when researchers discover that the mind naturally forms an image of God, they will use the theory of evolution to explain this finding, even though evolution expressly avoids the concept of a divine agent.

✵ 13. Jews, Aliens, and Martin Heidegger

It may seem incongruous—or even offensive—to mention these three in the same phrase, but I suggest that they all share similar cognitive elements. This chapter will begin by examining the philosophy of Martin Heidegger, we will then take a look at Judaism, and we will end with an analysis of aliens. I should mention that all three of these are somewhat alien to me, because they all emphasize a mode of thought which is most deeply subconscious for me as a Perceiver person. Therefore, writing this chapter is like 'flying on instruments' for me.

The philosopher may feel that my attempt to tackle Heidegger lacks intellectual rigor, and one of the signs of a true philosopher is the ability to navigate the arcane terms and concepts of Heidegger. However, my primary goal is not to immerse myself within the world of Heidegger, but rather to attempt to decipher what Heidegger says about the mind and how it functions. I have tried to summarize the concepts of Heidegger clearly and accurately, but I will be translating them into the language of mental symmetry. And when one is attempting to construct a paradigm of human personality or trying to translate one paradigm into the language of another, then as Kuhn tells is, it is not possible to strictly enforce the rules of formal logic.

Let us begin with the negative side of Martin Heidegger. As most Jews know, he lived in Germany during the Second World War and was a member of the Nazi party. Thus, he belonged to a group which tried to implement a 'final solution' that would rid the physical world of an entire race of people. However, if one examines Heidegger's philosophy from the viewpoint of mental symmetry, then one concludes that his philosophy describes a *mental* 'final solution' that rids the *internal* world of an entire cognitive module—the Perceiver module. As a Perceiver person, I find it disconcerting when one of the most popular philosophers of the 20th century attempted to come up with a paradigm of human thought that defines me out of existence. It may seem incongruous to link a mental final solution to a physical one, but Hitler wrote *Mein Kampf* before he implemented it. So, if I can manage to analyze Perceiver-hating Heidegger, then I suggest that the Jew who is reading this book should be able to manage reading my analysis of Jew-hating Heidegger.

Calling Heidegger a Perceiver-hater may seem like an overreaction, so let us begin by counting the ways that Heidegger hates me: Perceiver mode organizes Mercy experiences into categories, leading to the concept of *objects*. Heidegger tries to avoid using the word 'object'. Perceiver mode looks for repeated connections in order to determine truth. Heidegger rejects this method of determining truth. Perceiver mode notices which Mercy experiences are repeated and uses this to define self-image.

Heidegger insists that neither object nor subject exist and comes up with a different way of defining personal identity. Perceiver mode rearranges Mercy memories guided by Teacher understanding in order to create an inner world of Forms. Heidegger says that a mindset that separates the internal world from the external world is fundamentally flawed. Perceiver mode uses Forms to create the mental concept of eternal existence. Heidegger builds his philosophy upon the personal annihilation of death. Perceiver mode views existence as a succession of mental snapshots. Heidegger insists that this is invalid. Perceiver mode connects cause with effect in order to come up with conscience. Heidegger redefines conscience to remove any sense of cause-and-effect. Perceiver thought comes up with meanings which translate the concepts of one language into another. Heidegger deconstructed all philosophy that came before him and developed his own philosophical language. Perceiver mode thinks in terms of space. Heidegger interprets everything in terms of time. Thus, we see that Heidegger's rejection of Perceiver mode is quite thorough. Like the Jew-hating Nazi, he has systematically searched every mental village in order to identify and destroy the offending mental module.

But *why* would a philosopher who attempts to systematically eliminate an entire cognitive module be so popular? I suggest that the answer can be found in Foucault's *Modern* episteme. Foucault says that modern thinking is characterized by self-questioning, in which one stops searching for facts and sequences, and instead analyzes the method by which one searches for facts and sequences. I suggest that Heidegger's approach matches this mindset, because it analyzes the Server *process* of living human life and then redefines all Perceiver facts and Server sequences in terms of this Server sequence of personal existence. This book takes a similar approach but concludes that the results are *consistent* with Perceiver thought and do not require the *elimination* of Perceiver mode. Thus, what Heidegger calls the *only* way of interpreting reality, mental symmetry views as an *alternate* way of viewing the world.

Time and Everydayness

Now that we have dealt with the *negative* side of Heidegger, let us focus upon the positive. I suggest that Heidegger provides important insights into an *alternate* way of viewing reality, one which is based upon *Server* mode instead of *Perceiver* mode. One can know that Heidegger is using Server mode because he says that human existence is based upon *time* and *average everydayness.* In the language of mental symmetry, Heidegger is using a mode of thought that is sequential and concrete, which defines Server mode. If one translates the concepts of Heidegger into the language of mental symmetry, then they appear to make sense. In other words, Heidegger's philosophy describes a possible method of programming the human mind. Obviously, approaching Heidegger from such a mental programming perspective would be viewed as heretical by Heidegger, because I am *translating concepts*—and both translation and concepts are functions of Perceiver mode which Heidegger says do not exist.

I also suggest that Heidegger's model is *incomplete*. But it suffers from a rather strange sort of *universal* incompleteness. On the one hand, one can explain Heidegger's concepts if one includes modes of thought which Heidegger says do not exist. Thus, his model is incomplete. But Heidegger's method of becoming authentic requires the Teacher emotions of a universal theory, which will only be produced if one assumes that Heidegger's incomplete model *is* complete.

One can tell that Heidegger is treating an incomplete mental model as complete because of his response to the Jewish holocaust. Even though Heidegger played an implicit role in killing six million Jews, he could not acknowledge this atrocity because it did not fit into his model of human behavior. One can find a good summary of Heidegger's inadequate response to the holocaust on Wikipedia. At the beginning of this book, I suggested that a universal Teacher theory of human personality has the mental power to build and destroy civilizations. In Heidegger's case, the formal logic of his personal philosophy gave him both the mental ability and the mental motivation to ignore the deaths of millions of innocent victims.

We will begin with *self-image*, which Heidegger calls *Dasein*, or 'there-being'. Perceiver mode defines personal identity as the set of Mercy experiences that continue to be repeated. However, it is also possible to define self as the set of Server skills that I possess, or the Server sequences which I am capable of repeating. For instance, a plumber can repeat the sequence of installing water pipes, and a doctor can repeat the sequence of diagnosing and curing physical ailments. This is a valid way of defining self, but because humans live in a physical world of objects and experiences, it is not the *natural* way.

Heidegger insists that the very concept of self-image is invalid, for the word 'image' implies an *internal* realm of facts and objects, which Heidegger says do not exist. In addition, Heidegger says that it is incorrect to talk about living in a world, for that implies an *external* realm of facts and objects. Instead, Heidegger tells us that Dasein finds itself immersed in a condition of Being-in-the-world in which one cannot distinguish the world from personal identity.

If one uses *Server* mode to define identity, then Heidegger's statements about self-image make sense. This became clear to me many years ago when my brother and I were attempting to decipher the personality of the Server *person*. By observing the Server person, one can conclude that this cognitive style exists, because the Server person behaves in a way that is quite distinctive. However, when one *asks* a typical Server person to describe or explain his personality, one discovers that he cannot do so, because he does not have a mental image of self. In general terms, if my 'self-image' is based in Server mode, then I will know what I can and cannot do and I will be able to compare my abilities with those of other individuals, but I will not be able to step back and observe myself.

Notice, by the way, that Heidegger *is* stepping back and observing himself. This suggests that Heidegger had the cognitive style of Facilitator person, and that he developed left hemisphere subconscious thought but not right hemisphere thought. Consistent with this, Heidegger's father was the sexton of the local Catholic church. Catholicism tends to focus upon ritual and the sexton is the religious official who performs all of the Server actions in a church, such as physical maintenance, logistics, and grave-digging. Thus, Heidegger's family life strongly emphasized *Server* thought. On the *Perceiver* side of the equation, Heidegger published his groundbreaking *Sein und Zeit* in 1927, a decade after Germany had experienced the historic defeat of the First World War which called into question established *political* Perceiver beliefs, and four years after a hyperinflation which destroyed existing *economic* Perceiver beliefs.

The Facilitator person is conscious in the cognitive module which *observes* and *balances* mental processing. It appears that the Facilitator person shares the Contributor person's *digital* sense of confidence. Thus, when a Facilitator person experiences the epistemological crisis that characterizes Foucault's Modern episteme, mental content that previously was assumed will fall into doubt. However, the extended self-questioning that follows will re-establish *Server* confidence in the *method* of self-analysis, while the repeated physical action that accompanies living average everydayness will build Server confidence in *physical existence.* Therefore, I suggest that one can explain Heidegger's philosophy as a combination of cognitive style, personal upbringing, German postwar uncertainty, and Foucault's Modern episteme.

Perceiver mode views the physical world from an *exocentric* perspective. It constructs a mental map of reality, and then places objects and personal identity within this map. Like drawing an X and a Y axis on a piece of graph paper and then placing items on the graph, every item can be identified by its X and Y distance from the origin.

Heidegger, in contrast, takes an *egocentric* approach to space which corresponds to the way that Server mode represents reality. Egocentric space is defined in terms of direction and distance. Instead of pointing to a location on the map, it tells the person to "walk in the direction of the big tower for ten minutes until you come to a big intersection, then turn left and walk two blocks." Except, Heidegger describes distance also in terms of personal Server action. Movement 'makes farness vanish' and 'brings things close'. Heidegger also organizes physical locations into functional *regions.* Thus, the kitchen is a place-for-cooking which contains tools-for-cooking, while the office is a place-for-doing-paperwork. In other words, each location is defined by its Server context—the set of Server skills that this location brings to mind.

It is possible to approach the world either exocentrically or egocentrically. Both are valid methods, and the Perceiver *person* usually thinks exocentrically whereas the Server *person* functions egocentrically. But which of these two methods is more fundamental? When dealing with the physical world, I suggest that egocentric thought is a *secondary* method of representing objects which *assumes* the existence of an underlying exocentric spatial framework.

We saw in an earlier chapter that concrete thought uses Server actions to reach Mercy goals and that these two are tied together by a hidden, *assumed* mental map which is constructed by Perceiver thought. This tells us that the spatial Perceiver approach is more fundamental and that the functional Server approach builds upon the spatial Perceiver approach. But it is possible to ignore Perceiver mode, as Heidegger does, and to approach physical reality from a purely functional Server perspective. However, when Perceiver mode is not functioning, then the *external* world must provide a substitute for a mental map.

This is illustrated by the behavior of the typical Server person. Because Perceiver mode in his mind is deeply subconscious, it is usually underdeveloped.[42] Thus, the Server person prefers a physical environment in which everything 'lives' in a specific place: The scissors 'live' here, the newspapers 'live' there, and so on. Moving to a new house or a new city is mentally traumatic for the Server person, and so he typically spends most of his life living in the same home. This indicates that the Server person's egocentric approach cannot exist without the presence of some type of spatial map, which must be provided externally if it does not exist internally. Consistent with this, it is interesting to note that Heidegger spent most of his career teaching at the university where he received his initial training, even though he received lucrative offers from other universities.

Heidegger describes objects by their *function*. Thus, a chair is a-thing-for-sitting, and a pen is a thing-for-writing. This is how *Server* mode interprets objects, for instead of seeing them as objects, it views them as tools which can be used to perform Server sequences. According to Heidegger, a tool that is available for use is ready-to-hand or *Zuhanden*. Ready-to-hand includes another aspect as well. When a hammer is used as a tool, then Server mode does not consider the hammer to be distinct from the human arm holding that hammer. Instead, the hammer is mentally treated as an extension of the physical body. Mental symmetry suggests that Perceiver mode is responsible for making this mental adjustment, by temporarily modifying the mental object that represents the physical body to include the hammer as part of the body.

For instance, suppose that I am learning to drive a car. Initially, the car and I will feel like separate objects. However, if I continue to drive this car, then I will no longer think about me and the car as distinct objects, but instead I will simply drive around, acting as if the car is part of my identity. Mentally speaking, Perceiver mode has temporarily adopted a different body image—that of the car. Thus, I feel as if I am sitting on wheels and that I have a width of two meters and a length of four meters. This Perceiver object then becomes the 'vehicle' which Server mode moves around in order to reach its Mercy goals. Heidegger looks at this mental identification and concludes that one must not distinguish between the object of the car and the object of my physical body. And he is partially correct, for when one is driving in a car, then movement occurs most

---

[42] I say *deeply* subconscious because Server mode is the *opposite* of Perceiver mode and all interaction between Server mode and Perceiver mode occurs indirectly *through* another mental mode. In more concrete terms, after thirty years of observing people in terms of cognitive styles, I have yet to see a marriage between a Server person and a Perceiver person.

smoothly if one does not use Perceiver thought to discriminate between car and driver. But, when one steps out of the car and starts to walk, then it is important once again to make a mental distinction between the object of the car and the object of my physical body. If Perceiver thought did not exist as an intelligent strategy, then I suggest that it would not be possible to make a mental shift between car-and-me and 'car as opposed to me'.

Heidegger also *evaluates* tools according to their functionality. Thus, if some condition prevents a tool from being used, then it becomes *unready-to-hand* because Server mode is being prevented from using that tool. But hidden within this Server unreadiness is an underlying Perceiver problem. This is illustrated by the three types of unready-to-hand which Heidegger describes: For instance, if a lamp has a broken wire, then Heidegger says that it has a *conspicuous* problem. However, a broken wire is a Perceiver disconnection in physical matter which prevents the Server sequence of the flow of electricity from happening. If the lamp is missing a bulb, then this qualifies as an *obtrusive* problem. In this case, some Perceiver object is missing, which is preventing the lamp from functioning in an integrated manner. Finally, an *obstinate* problem occurs when some other object blocks me from interacting with a device in a functional manner, such as when the lamp blocks my view of the computer screen. Again, the simplest way to interpret this is in terms of one Perceiver object getting in the way of another. Notice that in each of these three situations, one *can* view the problem as a loss of Server functionality, but the *underlying* cause still involves some Perceiver object, indicating that when dealing with the physical world, objects are more basic than functions, and functions assume the existence of objects. In order to ignore these underlying objects, as Heidegger does, one must adopt the use of convoluted terminology, which Heidegger also does.

Moving on to the next point, when the external world provides the Perceiver map that ties Server mode and Mercy mode together, then it is not possible to separate personal identity from the external world, because the external world is providing the mental glue which personal identity requires to function.

Consistent with this, the average Server person lives in the present and focuses upon using Server actions to solve the immediate emotional need. For instance, when someone spills food on the floor, then the Server person is usually the first to find a rag and clean up the mess. In a similar vein, Heidegger says that living is associated with *mood.* According to Heidegger, mood is neither internal nor external but rather an integral part of human existence, and if one turns away from one mood, then one simply encounters another mood. As we saw several chapters earlier, this type of mindset describes childish identity, in which personal identity automatically identifies with any emotional experience that it encounters. Perceiver thought can prevent the current environment from determining mood by asserting that the present situation is *not* part of personal identity. Perceiver thought can also provide an emotional alternative to the current environment by constructing internal *Forms* which feel *different* than the current environment. But when Perceiver mode is suppressed, then all that remains is the mood of Heidegger.

Authenticity

Unlike the typical Server *person*, Heidegger is not just living in concrete thought using Server mode, because he is constructing a *general theory* based upon Server mode. General theories are built by abstract thought, which is a *different* mental circuit than concrete thought. However, because Heidegger is trying to build everything upon Server thought, he describes abstract thought as a type of stepping back from action, which he calls present-at-hand, or *Vorhanden*. Thus, abstract thought becomes something like concrete thought, only less intense and more distant. And when one builds a universal Teacher theory upon Server actions as Heidegger does, then abstract thought *will* turn into a sort of distant replica of doing.

When we looked at self-image, we saw that childish identity is composed of a collection of Mercy mental networks formed through identification and denial, because Perceiver mode in the childish mind lacks the confidence that is needed to operate in the presence of these strong Mercy emotions. One of the main purposes of the path of religious education is to gain sufficient Perceiver confidence to be able to rebuild these childish mental networks into something that is more stable and long-lasting.

Heidegger attempts to redefine this personal struggle in terms of Server mode by making a distinction between *authentic* and *inauthentic* existence. According to Heidegger, the authentic individual chooses what he will do, whereas the inauthentic person has no real personal identity but instead simply goes with the flow and does what 'they' do, mindlessly following the dictates of *Das Man*. This is a valid distinction, and it does relate to Server confidence. For instance, think of the little child who says to his parents, "Don't help me or show me how to do it; I want to do it all by myself." That is a sign of Server confidence. When Server mode is copying the actions of some other person, being guided by some example, or being propelled by some strong emotion, then Server confidence is not required. However, when Server mode goes against the flow in some way, then Server confidence is needed. Thus, learning to tie my own shoes requires Server confidence, as does singing harmony when everyone else is singing melody, or carrying out a complicated set of actions. Walking across a narrow bridge takes Server confidence, as does applying a theory instead of just talking about it. In each case, Server mode is attempting to carry out a sequence in the presence of emotional pressure that threatens to tear this sequence apart.

But I do not think that Heidegger would label 'tying my own shoes' or 'walking across a bridge' as authentic existence, because *everyone* ties their shoes and *everyone* walks across bridges. Instead, Heideggerian authenticity seems to include the additional component of *being unique*. Thus, the jazz player is authentic because he is 'doing his own thing', whereas the soldier is inauthentic because he is 'going with the flow' and following orders. However, as a professional violinist who is fairly talented at improvising, I can assure you that a major part of playing jazz is 'going with the flow'. In order to improvise, one must immerse oneself in what is happening musically and then perform a sequence that conforms to this flow. And I have played in enough professional orchestras to realize that even though the orchestra musician is only playing the notes that are written on the page and even though he must coordinate his activities with the musicians around him, true music emerges when each musician makes the music his own and plays in an authentic way. And while playing jazz does require Server confidence, I find that improvising is usually less stressful for Server mode than playing a difficult classical piece. I am also convinced that it takes much more Server confidence for a soldier to obey orders under fire than it does for a jazz musician to play a musical solo.

Thus, while Heidegger's distinction between authentic and inauthentic appears to be significant, it cannot be explained adequately using Heidegger's limited mental vocabulary of time and action. Instead, one must also include the effect of Mercy mental networks. The unauthentic person is being driven by the Mercy mental networks of his environment. Mother, father, teachers, policemen, as well as numerous authority figures, all 'live' within Mercy thought as mental networks and these mental networks are driving personal behavior. Escaping this emotional pressure does require Server confidence, but it requires *more* than just Server confidence.

Why then is Heidegger's *Das Man* so vague and anonymous? Why isn't this social pressure separated mentally into father, mother, teacher, and so on? Because, *organizing* Mercy mental networks and mentally *assigning* feelings of approval or disapproval to different mental networks requires Perceiver thought. When Perceiver thought is functioning, then Heidegger's vague *Das Man* becomes separated into distinct mental categories such as mother, uncle George, Europeans, and scientists, resulting in the intuitive psychology and Theory of Mind which we discussed many chapters earlier. For instance, I may try to avoid the subject of religion around uncle George because I know that he hates talking about religion. However, when Perceiver mode is not functioning, then all that remains is a vague sense in Mercy thought that someone dislikes talking about religion. Thus, the inauthentic person will attempt to avoid the subject of religion for fear that someone might get offended, because Mercy thought encountered an emotional situation in which someone did get offended. But exactly who got offended and why he was offended will not be remembered, because that type of mental connecting requires Perceiver thought. Intuitive psychology helps to free Mercy identity from a *general* fear of disapproval, because knowing the likes and dislikes of individuals and groups indicates which behavior is 'safe' within each environment. The path of religious education then takes this one step further by using Perceiver thought to *digest* childish Mercy mental networks.

Embracing Angst

Heidegger describes the process of becoming authentic, and I suggest that mental symmetry can be used to analyze this description. According to Heidegger, the inauthentic person feels that his world is *heimlich*, or comfortable and home-like, and he has the sensation of being fully involved in his *Umwelt* or social environment. In the language of mental symmetry, behavior is being guided by childish Mercy mental networks. Because these mental networks are being formed by emotional experiences from the external world, the world feels *heimlich*. But because these externally formed mental networks are guiding personal behavior, personal behavior is inauthentic, emotionally ruled by the vague approval conscience of *Das Man*.

When core mental networks fall apart, then this will lead to the hyper-pain of *angst*. Heidegger says that angst makes the familiar world feel *unheimlich*, or distant and foreboding. But Heidegger also says that angst leads to personal freedom and authenticity. Based upon Heidegger's statements, we can make several conclusions: First, because angst makes the *Umwelt* feel uncanny or foreboding, we know that *Mercy* mental networks are falling apart—because these were the mental networks which previously made the environment feel *heimlich* or comfortable. Second, Heidegger says that this angst frees a person from the demands of *Das Man*, which also indicates that the Mercy mental networks that used to drive behavior have fragmented. Third, angst is normally viewed as a feeling of dread which must be avoided at all costs. Heidegger, in contrast, is embracing his angst and saying that angst leads to personal freedom and authenticity. This tells us that his childish Mercy mental networks are being *replaced* by other mental networks and that these new mental networks are related to Server actions. Finally, Heidegger says that the feeling of being immersed in the world changes to a sensation of feeling *distant* from the world. Earlier on, we concluded that Heidegger defines Teacher thought as present-at-hand, because abstract thought makes the world appears more distant. Thus, Heidegger is describing a process by which Mercy mental networks that are based in identification and denial are falling apart and being replaced by Teacher mental networks that are supported by Server actions, which corresponds to the stage of rebirth in the path of education.

What makes it possible for a person to handle the Mercy hyper-pain of angst? The Teacher emotion of a general theory. If I *understand* what is happening to me, then the situation does not feel as bad. But because Teacher emotion comes from generality, then only a Teacher theory of personal existence that is *universal* will provide enough Teacher pleasure to counteract the Mercy pain that is felt when the core of childish personal identity falls apart. We learned this in the previous chapter.

The Teacher pleasure of a universal theory of the subjective makes it *possible* to handle the pain of 'dying to self'. But this 'dying' will only happen if the Teacher theory *demands* that the Mercy mental networks of childish personal identity be extinguished. In the path of religious education, this demand comes from the struggle between the categorical imperative and radical evil, for a general Teacher theory that is based in universal order cannot handle the lawlessness of childish identity.

Heidegger creates his Teacher emotion by building a universal theory of time and personal existence. That is the fundamental thesis of his book *Sein und Zeit*: Being can only be understood in terms of time. Heidegger then shoehorns all of personal existence into this 'universal' theory. One can tell that Heidegger is *forcing* everything to fit within his universal theory because he comes up with a new set of words—the basic building blocks for Teacher thought—which refer only to time and never to space. If Heidegger's theory really were universal, then he could *translate* the words of others into his own language, as I am attempting to do with the theory of mental symmetry. But by using his own terminology and rejecting the words of others, Heidegger eliminates from Teacher thought any verbal building blocks that contradict his 'universal' understanding. The end result is a Teacher theory that *feels* universal, and it is this Teacher *feeling* of universality which makes it possible to endure the Mercy pain that occurs when personal identity falls apart.

The drive for 'dying to self' comes from Heidegger's view of *death*. According to Heidegger, what defines human existence is its finite duration. Each person is 'thrown' into the world, he lives, and then experiences the personal annihilation of death. Heidegger says that authenticity comes from embracing the inevitability of death through an attitude of being-toward-death. Being-in-the-world programs childish Mercy mental networks. Obviously, physical death will bring this mode of existence to an abrupt and total end, and the uncertainty of life means that the grim reaper could strike at any moment. But the inauthentic person ignores the evidence of death that surrounds him and continues to live as if his childish Mercy mental networks will never die. By making finite personal existence a fundamental part of his universal Teacher theory of being, the resulting Teacher pleasure gives Heidegger the ability to emotionally *face* his impending demise, and because death forms a fundamental part of his Teacher understanding he is *forced* to face his coming death.

When one experiences a Heideggerian type of mental rebirth, then it leads to a rather strange form of conscience. Heidegger does not have a Perceiver based conscience, for he insists that good and evil do not exist—even when faced with the evil of the holocaust. But his method of building a universal Teacher theory upon personal Server actions and then submitting to this theory through the angst of facing death does create a sort of *Server* conscience. This is shown in two ways: First, we know that Server sequences give stability to Teacher words. Heidegger says that the mind of the inauthentic person is filled with mental *chatter*. This describes what happens when Teacher words *lack* Server stability. Teacher thought babbles. When Heidegger's 'conscience' emerges, then Teacher thought stops talking, and it silently focuses mental attention upon the current action. Why is Teacher thought focusing upon what I am doing right now? Because it contains a universal theory that is based upon the action which I am currently performing. Why is it silent? Because what I am doing right now *defines* the universal theory.

Second, we know that Teacher thought builds *general* theories, whereas Server mode performs *specific* actions. Thus, even though Heidegger's conscience says nothing, it conveys a constant sense of *guilt*. When personal identity is based upon Server actions and when Server actions are generalized to form a universal Teacher theory, then personal identity will *always* fall short of Teacher understanding simply because a person is *finite*. For instance, whenever I choose to eat pancakes for breakfast, then I am choosing *not* to eat cereal or toast. If Server mode performs the action of eating pancakes, then Teacher thought will think of all the foods that could have been eaten and will conclude that my choice falls short of this personal potentiality. That is the mental price of building a *universal* Teacher theory upon *finite* personal actions.

And that seems to describe Heidegger's concept of God. On the one hand, Heidegger appears to be an atheist. I have suggested that an image of God emerges when a general Teacher theory explains personal identity in Mercy thought. Heidegger has a general theory that explains personal identity, but his personal identity does not reside within Mercy thought. Thus, like the objective scientist, Heidegger does not believe in God. But, unlike the objective scientist, Heidegger acts and talks as if he is making theological statements and these statements seem to indicate that each person is his own God, which is what happens when one builds a general Teacher theory upon personal identity.

Before we turn from Heidegger to Judaism, I would like to make a few closing remarks. First, as I have mentioned earlier, society is currently going through a rare period during which 'God is Dead'. Because the Western world has no monolithic concept of God, it is possible to follow the example of Heidegger by constructing a universal theory of personal existence and submitting one's identity to this 'universal' theory. But not all universal theories are equivalent. If one applies Heidegger's definitions, then the Nazi regime was authentic because it pursued a 'final solution' which embraced the angst of genocide and broke free of *Das Man* of traditional Western Judeo-Christian morality. But does one *want* to worship and serve such a God? I hope not. It makes more sense to worship and serve a concept of God which saves the individual human by removing radical evil.

Second, even though Heidegger's model is incomplete, it does describe part of a mental process. The path of religious education that this book describes begins with morality, goes through understanding, and then adds authenticity. Heidegger rejected the moral part, twisted the understanding, and went straight to the authenticity. Being authentic is *good*, in the same way that the driver of a car must be able to control where he goes, especially when surrounded by the gullies, cliffs, and swamps of *Das Man.* However, there is no point in being able to control a car if one does not know where one is going or where one wants to go. Similarly, there is no point in being authentic if one lacks a moral compass.

Judaism

We will now turn our attention to Judaism. I cannot claim to be an expert on the subject, but I have thought about the matter in some depth, I have checked my conclusions with those who have more experience with Judaism than I do, and I have tried to back up my statements with evidence. Because this book is examining the concept of God from a cognitive perspective, it is only proper to discuss the religion which taught the world about monotheism.

We have seen that Heidegger constructed a model of human existence which defines everything in terms of Server mode and which denies the existence of Perceiver mode. I suggest that a similar cognitive bias exists within Judaism, though in a less extreme form than that taken by Heidegger. In other words, it appears that Judaism *emphasizes* Server mode while *downplaying* Perceiver mode.

The origins for this mindset can be found in the Torah, which is the first five books of both the Jewish and the Christian Bible. The Ten Commandments which we analyzed earlier come from the Torah. About half of the Torah contains a list of detailed rituals, practices, procedures, and rules given to the Jews by God. What concerns us here is not the validity of these rituals, but rather the cognitive result: The Jews follow a written set of *Server instructions* that are connected in their minds with the voice of God. Thus, the Server actions of the Jews are guided by the Teacher words associated with a mental concept of God. As I mentioned earlier, Heidegger came from a similar religious background, for his father was sexton of the local Catholic church.

This emphasis upon Server actions is reinforced by the *history* of the Jewish people. Judaism is a very old religion. Abraham, its founder, was a member of the Sumerian civilization. Much of the Jewish Tanach, which Christians call the 'Old Testament', outlines the history of the Jewish people and the Jewish nation and portrays how God has guided the actions of the Jews. The typical modern Jew has a strong sense of *ethnic history* and views himself as being part of a long historical sequence of faith and tradition. For instance, Tisha B'Av is an annual Jewish fast day on which Jews mourn the destruction of the first temple in 586 BC, the destruction of the second temple in 70 AD, and the expulsion of the Jews from Spain in 1492.

Thus, the typical Jewish mind shares with Heidegger a focus upon Server actions, sequence, and time as well as a direct mental connection between Server actions and Teacher understanding. But Heidegger bases his Teacher theory upon the Server actions of an *individual* and takes as his starting point the birth, life, and death of a single human being. For Heidegger, personal Server action *is* the general Teacher theory. The Jew, in contrast, places his personal actions within the larger context of the Jewish nation. Instead of basing his Teacher theory upon the actions of *one* person, he builds his Teacher understanding upon the combined actions of a group of people over several millennia. While Heidegger forces specific Server action and general Teacher theory together, Judaism says that Teacher understanding extends *past* the actions of one individual to include his descendents, and that it extends *beyond* one individual to include all of his relatives, thus permitting Teacher thought to be more *general* than Server actions.

An Eternal Covenant

This is described in the Torah as a covenant between God and the descendents of Abraham: "And I will establish My covenant between Me and you and your descendants after you in their generations, for an everlasting covenant, to be God to you and your descendants after you. Also I give to you and your descendants after you the land in which you are a stranger, all the land of Canaan, as an everlasting possession; and I will be their God." (Genesis 17: 7-8) Notice that an *eternal* covenant with a person and his descendents takes the specific Server actions of one individual and makes them *universal* in the direction of *time*. Again, my goal here is not to debate the validity of this covenant, but rather to notice the cognitive results. Whether this is covenant is real or not, it *has* shaped the mindset of a world religion, and that is what concerns us here.

This covenant is being made between God and a *group* of people who are being promised a *region* of land. Perceiver mode distinguishes between one individual and another, and between one object and another. When a concept of God is being connected with a group and a region, then this will have the mental effect of downplaying Perceiver thought. In contrast, we saw at the beginning of this book that the Ten Commandments *are* described in terms of the individual, because they repeatedly talk about a person and his *neighbor*.

Thus, one finds a fundamental ambiguity in Judaism. We know that the childish mind identifies with emotional experiences in Mercy thought. Obviously, it is pleasant for the childish mind to imagine that The Eternal God has chosen my ethnic group, because it connects the emotions of a universal Teacher theory with personal identity. For the childish mind, the natural tendency will be to equate 'God has chosen us' with 'God has chosen *me*'. This type of emotional identification also occurs with the sports fan, for when his favorite team wins, then he feels that he *personally* is a winner. It also occurs with the theory of evolution, because Mercy thought is finding pleasure in the concept that the human species is continually evolving, even though the *individual* human within this species is governed by the far harsher rule of survival of the fittest. However, when one examines the last five of the Ten Commandments, one notices that they place severe limitations upon Mercy identification: Don't steal your neighbor's possessions; don't have sex with your neighbor's wife; don't tell lies about your neighbor. In fact, the tenth Commandment is actually a general prohibition against Mercy identification: Don't covet anything that belongs to your neighbor.

Christianity was founded in Roman times, in a culture which viewed gods and religion in anthropomorphic terms. Judaism, in contrast, came to birth in an era of tribalism, in which each tribe had its own god and its own ancestral land, and individuals regarded themselves as members of a tribe and not as individuals. Because this defined the norm, the Facilitator filter of that time would have rejected any non-tribal religion as counterintuitive.

Jewish Angst

Heidegger states that individuation is achieved through the angst of coming face to face with one's death. If one examines Jewish history, one notices that the Jewish people have experienced several episodes of tribal angst, in which Jewish existence itself was threatened. However, these periods of angst have not destroyed Judaism but rather have caused it to become more authentic.

The first major episode of Jewish angst occurred during the Babylonian Exile, when most of the Jews were expelled from their tribal homeland for a period of seventy years. There are several parallels between this transitional period of Jewish history and Heidegger's process of becoming authentic.

Jewish thinking before this period was tribal. Tribalism is inauthentic: First, tribalism uses Mercy identification to identify with the tribal *homeland*. Like the typical Server person who finds it mentally difficult to move to a new home, the tribal land provides an external substitute for a mental Perceiver map. Tribal land feels *heimlich*, and the tribal person is in the mental condition of being-in-the-world. Second, tribalism uses Mercy identification to identify with its tribal *group*. Thus, the tribal person does not choose his actions. Instead, his behavior is largely governed by *Das Man* of the tribal group. Third, the tribal individual does not have an internal source of feelings. Instead, his emotions are subject to the *mood* of his environment.

During the Babylonian Exile, tribal Judaism was transformed into something more authentic. Instead of being mentally bound to the land, Jews became a *diaspora*—a term first used to describe the Jews of the Babylonian Exile—able to maintain their way of life even when distant from the tribal homeland. And instead of being driven by the mood of the moment and passively following the dictates of the tribe, the Jewish people learned how to continue performing their rituals even when those around them acted in a radically different manner.

What made this mental shift *possible* was a combination of Teacher understanding and Server actions. During the Babylonian Exile, Jews began to *study* the Torah and they started to *practice* the Torah. Each Jewish male was expected to study the Jewish scriptures and to practice a trade. And the Jewish Talmud began to take shape, in which Jewish scholars attempted build a systematic understanding of what it means to live as a Jew.

What *forced* this mental shift to occur was the tribal angst caused by the Babylonian conquest. The Jewish nation was conquered, the city of Jerusalem was destroyed, the holy temple was burned to the ground, and most of the Jewish leaders were killed or taken into exile. Like Heidegger, the Jewish prophets told the Jewish people to *embrace* this angst and promised that the nation, the people, and the religion would re-emerge in stronger form.

Before we continue, let us step back and examine the bigger picture. In this chapter, we are seeing a form of mental rebirth that is somewhat different than the path of education described in previous chapters. What exactly is the relationship between these two? In simple terms, I suggest that the Jewish version of rebirth skips the *first* step of the path of education. The path of education begins with Perceiver facts and personal identity. It then moves to Teacher understanding and Server actions. This leads through the angst of rebirth to a new way of functioning which combines abstract and concrete thought. The Jewish path, in contrast, does not use Perceiver facts to define personal identity. Instead, it starts with the tribe and the land. It then adds Teacher understanding and Server actions to the tribe by carrying out the divinely ordained daily rituals of Jewish life. As one Jew described it to me, Jewish ritual takes care of the personal emotional problems which the normal person faces, allowing the Jew to get on with the task of living. When provoked by the angst of ethnic destruction, this becomes transformed into a more authentic mode of existence. Similarly, Heidegger ignores Perceiver thought, begins by combining Server actions with Teacher understanding, and then goes through angst to authentic existence.

Judaism and the Group

Thus, what is missing from the Jewish path of rebirth is the first step of becoming an individual and acquiring an internal voice of conscience. The Jewish scriptures say the same thing. Jeremiah, a Jewish prophet who preached during the start of the Babylonian Exile, the first episode of Jewish angst, writes: "In those days they shall say no more: 'The fathers have eaten sour grapes, and the children's teeth are set on edge.' But every one shall die for his own iniquity; every man who eats the sour grapes, his teeth shall be set on edge. Behold, the days are coming, says the LORD, when I will make a new covenant with the house of Israel and with the house of Judah—not according to the covenant that I made with their fathers in the day that I took them by the hand to lead them out of the land of Egypt, My covenant which they broke, though I was a husband to them, says the LORD. But this is the covenant that I will make with the house of Israel after those days, says the LORD: I will put My law in their minds, and write it on their hearts; and I will be their God, and they shall be My people" (Jeremiah 31: 29-33). Jeremiah says that the group-think of inauthenticity will be replaced by individual accountability and that a new form of Jewish religion will emerge that includes the internal voice of conscience. In a similar vein, Ezekiel, another Jewish prophet who lived during the same time as Jeremiah, quotes the same proverb and devotes a whole chapter to describing the mental transition from corporate responsibility to individual accountability.

One reaches a similar conclusion when one compares Jewish theology with Christian theology. Remember that a mental image of God emerges when a general Teacher theory explains personal identity in Mercy thought. Going further, when Perceiver facts are used to reconnect Mercy experiences and Teacher thought is used to simplify these Perceiver facts, then Forms emerge within Mercy thought, and when Teacher thought integrates these Forms, then this leads to a hierarchy of Forms, and when Teacher thought explains emotional experiences, then this creates a concept of the *Holy Spirit.* And when Contributor mode is used to bridge general Teacher understanding with personal identity, then this leads to the concept of an *incarnation* which is both God and man.

For the Jewish mind, the fundamental religious connection is between God, the Jewish people, and the land of Israel; for the Jew, the people and the land are the divinely ordained Perceiver categories. Thus, the Jewish diaspora has historically been driven mentally by the Form of *L'Shanah Ha'Ba'ah B'Yrushalayim*, or 'Next year in Jerusalem'.

The internal vision that motivated the Jew was a mental image of a future Israel in which the Jewish people lived at peace in the Jewish homeland.

As Plato tells us, a Form is mentally seen as more *permanent* than external objects, for Forms are rooted in Perceiver facts that do not change, backed up by a general Teacher theory which transcends space and time. In keeping with this, Christianity views the Holy Spirit as an imaginary person who takes up *permanent* residence within the mind of the believer. Reading Jewish literature gives one the impression that the tribal Form of 'Next year in Jerusalem' did take up permanent residence within the mind of the Jewish diaspora. However, Jewish scriptures and Jewish theology do not contain the concept of a Holy Spirit of God living permanently within the mind of the individual. Instead, they talk about the spirit of God temporarily coming on a person so that he can perform a task associated with national survival. Thus, Judaism connects the Spirit of God with the land and the group, and the individual only experiences this as he performs Server actions which are directly related to this land and this group. In the language of Jeremiah, this is what happens when one mentally associates God with 'bringing Israel out of the land of Egypt' instead of with 'writing law on the heart'.

Jewish Scripture also talks about the *Shekhinah* or 'presence of God' appearing within the temple of God. In most tribal religions, the idol is displayed prominently for everyone to see. In Judaism, the holy relic of the Ark of the Covenant was hidden from sight within the temple. Thus, the presence of God, which took the form of a shapeless cloud, was associated with a holy relic that no one could see. This is cognitively similar to the concept of a Form, but again it was associated with the national religion and not with the individual Jew.

Judaism does not ascribe to the Christian concept of *incarnation*. I suggest that this also is a cognitive result of connecting God with the *group* of Israel rather than with the *individual* person. Incarnation uses Contributor mode to connect a general concept of God with the specific experiences of personal identity. Mentally speaking, the Jewish nation takes the place of an incarnation, because it is seen as the intermediary between God and man which reveals God to the rest of mankind.

What one does find in some streams of Judaism is the concept of *Chokhmah*, or divine wisdom, which states that wisdom is personifed and is co-eternal with God. Wisdom combines Teacher understanding with Server actions. It is theory put into practice; it is behavior that is guided by understanding. This concept of divinity would emerge when Server actions are combined with a Teacher theory of God.

Moving on to the next theological contrast, Judaism has a different concept of *conscience* than Christianity. For the Jewish mind, religious law gives the Jewish adherent a set of instructions that tells him what to *do*. The collection of Jewish law is referred to as *halakha*, a Hebrew word that is derived from the verb for *walking*. This is quite different than the Christian view of religious law, which equates rules with Perceiver categories of right and wrong and Mercy labels of good and evil. Law for the typical Christian defines a set of walls which must not be breached and the one who violates these restrictions is labeled as evil. In contrast, when the Jew sins, his rabbi typically tells him to *do* better next time.

In a related vein, Judaism also does not include the Christian concept of *original sin*. Christianity views people as being born in a *state* of sin, a doctrine which can be explained by Kant's concept of radical evil, because Mercy identification and denial will naturally motivate childish identity to behave in ways that violate the Teacher order of the categorical imperative. Judaism says instead that sin is an *action* and that the individual is born with a *yetzer ha-tov* or tendency to *do* good and a *yetzer hara* or tendency to *do* evil. Similarly, the commands of the Torah, traditionally collated into a list of 613 *mitzvot* or commands, are viewed as a list of *actions* which should be done together with a list of *actions* which should be avoided.

The problem with defining sin as an *action* is that this is cognitively incomplete. This is because Mercy experiences are organized through a *two-step* process. First, Perceiver facts divide Mercy experiences into categories. Then, Server actions are used to go from one Perceiver category to another. When dealing with personal identity, Perceiver facts are more basic than Server actions. Therefore, changing my Server actions will alter my behavior but it will not affect the personal feelings that motivate this behavior. In contrast, changing the Perceiver facts that define personal identity will alter the emotional landscape which drives personal behavior, making it possible to permanently change my behavior. That is why the path of religious education begins with Perceiver facts and then adds Server actions.

Saying this another way, when morality is defined in terms of Server actions, then Perceiver facts that define personal identity will not be mentally digested. Two of the major Perceiver facts which define Jewish identity are the ethnic *group* and the ancestral *land*. As long as these Perceiver categories play a defining role in Jewish identity, then, by definition, one is skipping the first step of the path of religious education in two fundamental areas.

Earlier on, when looking at the concept of a holy book, we asked whether it was possible to define a holy book in a way that is compatible with rational thought. We then came up with a cognitive definition for a holy book: If a holy book contains an unreasonable amount of Teacher order and structure, then the Agency Detector within the mind will conclude that this book could not have been written by any normal person within Mercy thought, but must have been authored by an invisible general 'person' within Teacher thought—otherwise known as God. Obviously, it is only possible to define a holy book in this manner if the holy book satisfies the requirement of unreasonable Teacher order and if the content of this book is taught as a general Teacher theory.

In a similar fashion, I suggest that it is possible to come up with a cognitive definition for 'chosen race'. If an ethnic group behaves in a way that exhibits an unreasonable level of Teacher order and understanding, then the Agency Detector within the mind will conclude that this group is not connected with the normal Mercy emotions of a tribe, but instead is connected with an invisible general 'person' within Teacher thought—otherwise known as God. When one examines the Jewish people, one notices, for instance, that, as of 2010, 22% of the Nobel prizes have been awarded either to Jews or to those with two or more Jewish grandparents. However, Jews only form 0.2% of the world's population. This describes an unreasonable ethnic relationship between Judaism and general Teacher understanding.

I need to emphasize that I am not attempting to *prove* that the Jews are a chosen race. Instead, I am describing a cognitive mechanism by which a group of people can believe that God has chosen their ethnic group *without* mentally descending into the Mercy-driven attitude of racial superiority. For one does occasionally read of Jewish rabbis saying that Jews are *racially* closer to God than non-Jews. For instance, Rabbi Abraham Isaac Kook, the first chief Rabbi of British Mandate Palestine, wrote that "The difference between the Jewish soul, in all its independence, inner desires, longings, character and standing, and the soul of all the Gentiles, on all of their levels, is greater and deeper than the difference between the soul of a man and the soul of an animal, for the difference in the latter case is one of quantity, while the difference in the first case is one of essential quality."[43] When 'chosen race' is approached from a Mercy viewpoint, then Jews will see themselves as members of a divinely ordained club and they will exclude non-Jews from participating in this club. In response, other ethnic groups will also view Jews as members of a special club and they will respond with anti-Semitic behavior. However, when 'chosen race' is seen from the vantage point of *Teacher* understanding, then the success of the Jewish people becomes an exemplar—an illustration of a general process which can be emulated by anyone, regardless of race or ethnicity. In religious terms, the Jews then become a 'light to the nations'.

Judaism versus Christianity

That brings us to the next question. *Why* are Jews so over-represented in the Nobel prizes? *Why* is Israel such a hotbed of high-tech industry? I suggest that this is because the Jewish path follows the *second* part of the path of religious education.

The path of religious education has three main components: The first stage uses Perceiver facts to go from experience to theory. Perceiver facts are used to describe personal identity and these Perceiver facts are used to build a general theory in Teacher thought. In religious terms, conscience is used to construct a mental image of God which leads indirectly to Forms and the concept of the Holy Spirit. The second stage uses Server actions to go from theory to experience. Server thought applies Teacher understanding and this is used to come up with a new way of acting within the physical world. In religious language, righteousness leads to a kingdom of God.

The third stage involves a struggle between the Teacher-based rational culture that was developed in the first two stages and the surrounding traditional Mercy-based culture. In

---

[43] In the book *Orot Yisrael*, chapter 5, article 10.

religious terms, there is a conflict between the kingdom of God and the kingdom of man. The kingdom of God focuses upon understanding, example, and possibility, while the kingdom of man fights this with force, control, and the status quo. If the new way adopts the methods of the old way, then the path of religious education will be stillborn. But if the new way focuses upon example and possibility and embraces the angst of letting go of the status quo, then society will eventually become reborn.

Christianity focuses upon the *first* stage and then applies the third stage *personally*. Christian doctrine emphasizes using conscience and belief to change the Mercy 'heart' of the individual, leading to the concept of the Holy Spirit. That describes the first stage. However, Christianity gets stuck attempting to enter the second stage of understanding because Christian doctrine has not been formulated as a general Teacher theory. The first stage begins with personal identity. Because Christianity focuses upon the first stage, it is capable of transforming *personal* identity. As a result, *individual* Christians go through the mental rebirth of the third stage, and the societal transformation that is produced focuses upon the personal. Thus, Christian organizations have played a major role in helping the 'down and out', spreading literacy, building hospitals, and civilizing traditional culture. In educational terms, Christianity emphasizes the *elementary* level of learning which takes the childish mind and turns it into a good, moral, obedient student.

This does not mean that Christians are only involved in elementary education or that Christianity has not played a role in setting up institutions of higher learning. However, I suggest that the Christian influence on higher learning was felt most strongly during Foucault's *Classical* episteme, a time during which learning as a whole was less esoteric and less technical. Similarly, I suggest that current Christianity has its greatest influence at lower levels of education and more personal aspects of human need.

In contrast, Judaism focuses upon the *second* stage and then applies the third stage *corporately*. It skips the first step of using Perceiver thought to change the individual and begins with the second stage of combining Teacher understanding with Server actions. Because Judaism starts with the group and does not address the individual, it experiences transformation as a group. This *group* transformation is triggered when Jews go through a period of tribal angst which threatens the existence of the Jewish group. When a group goes through rebirth, then only some of the individuals in the group will survive the process, and the transformation that occurs in those who do survive usually will not include the core of personal identity. This concept of a remnant being saved through a time of troubles is a major theme in Jewish scriptures.

In educational terms, Judaism emphasizes the *secondary*, *scientific* stage of learning and living, which explains why so many Jews win Nobel prizes and why Israeli R&D does so well. And when one examines the last Jewish cycle of Jewish rebirth, one sees that the angst of the holocaust provoked the rebirth of the state of Israel, in which Jewish pioneers transformed a desert wasteland into a thriving economy.

Saying this more simply, Jews take the abstract and make it concrete, whereas Gentiles take the concrete and make it abstract. This is how a friend of mine who has lived in Israel for many years describes it.

If Christianity focuses upon the first step and Judaism emphasizes the second step of the path of religious education, then one would think that the solution lies in getting these two to work together.

I suggest that this can be done in one of two ways. The *constructive* way is to bridge Christianity and Judaism through *Teacher* understanding. If the goal of the first stage is to build a general Teacher theory of personality and if the second stage begins with a general Teacher theory, then obviously one must complete the first stage in order to prepare for the second stage. This means placing Christian doctrine within a general Teacher theory of human personality that is compatible with scientific thought—which we are attempting to do in this book. The *destructive* way is to bridge Christianity and Judaism through *Mercy*-based tribalism. This occurs when Christians give unwavering support to the land and people of Israel, regardless of how the people within this land behave. What this does for the Christian mind is replace conscience with idolatry. Conscience uses Perceiver facts to describe personal behavior, even when these facts make personal identity feel bad. Idolatry goes the other way and uses emotional Mercy experiences to define Perceiver 'facts' and Perceiver 'beliefs'. When a group is regarded as *always* right and *always* good, no matter how it behaves, then that group has become a mental idol which defines 'truth' and overrules conscience, and the core of the Christian message of personal honesty has been negated.

A similar principle applies to the Jew who 'accepts Jesus as his Messiah'. If the Christian concept of 'revealed truth' is added to the Jewish concept of being a 'chosen race', then I suggest that the mental result is a mindset which is doubly bigoted, for it regards other races as inferior and other systems of truth as wrong. Ironically, while this type of mindset thinks that it is doubly chosen by God, it is in fact doubly bound by the two mental traps of tribalism and blind 'belief'. The fundamentalist Christian who believes that his country is 'chosen by God' practices a similar form of double bigotry, for he is adding the Jewish concept of 'chosen race' to the Christian concept of 'revealed truth'.

This combination of tribalism and blind 'belief' tends to characterize the religion of Islam. A person who is born into a Muslim family or a country that is officially Islamic is not permitted to convert away from Islam, and those who do can suffer major repercussions. Thus, political control of a group of people and an area of land is strongly associated with belief in God. In addition, Islam emphasizes rote learning and discourages critical thinking, leading to blind 'belief'. However, there are some initial signs that the 'Arab Spring' of 2011 may lead to a more open form of Islam. Only time will tell what eventually happens.

In general terms, I suggest that the solution for all three religions involves going past blind 'belief' to rational understanding and beyond childish Mercy networks to internal content. And part of that transition means submitting to a cognitive definition of holy books and holy people.

Aliens

Let us turn our attention now to the third example of using Server mode without Perceiver mode, which is *aliens*. It may seem strange to discuss beings which may not exist, but that has not stopped us before, so it does not need to stop us now. If one approaches this topic from a cognitive perspective, then I suggest that it is possible to come up with a number of interesting conclusions and predictions.

In order to decipher what it means to be *alien*, we must first describe in basic terms what it means to be *human*. We learned several chapters back that personal identity begins with the Mercy mental network that represents my physical body. Let us see if we can follow this chain of reasoning further.

We know that the mind contains two mental circuits, which we have called concrete thought and abstract thought. Concrete thought uses Server sequences to change Mercy experiences, and these Server sequences and Mercy experiences are held together by Perceiver facts. Perceiver facts provide the stability, Server sequences produce the change, while Mercy experiences contain the emotions. Similarly, abstract thought uses Perceiver facts to change Teacher theories, and these Perceiver facts and Teacher theories are held together by Server sequences. Server sequences provide the stability, Perceiver facts produce the change, while Teacher theories contain the emotions. Those are the two primary mental circuits, which we could call the Mercy circuit and the Teacher circuit. Describing concrete thought and abstract thought in these theoretical terms allows us to look purely at what is happening within the mind as a result of mental structure.

But what makes concrete thought concrete, and abstract thought abstract? In order to answer that question, we have to turn our attention to the effect that the physical body and the physical world have upon the mind. Let us look first at the physical body.

First, each human is trapped within a physical body for the duration of his life. This physical body is a Perceiver object which senses Mercy emotions and can perform various Server actions. Thus, the physical body functions in a manner that is an expression of the *Mercy* circuit. And because human life is literally defined as existing within such a body, personal identity becomes associated with the Mercy circuit.

Second, a physical body *occupies* a specific physical location, it can only *sense* sights and sounds from that specific location, it can only use Server actions to *influence* that specific location, and it can only move from that specific location to locations that are *nearby*. For instance, when I am sitting at my kitchen table, I can only see, taste, and eat the food that is on that table. I cannot see or take the food that is on any other table. Thus, personal identity within the Mercy circuit becomes associated with *specifics*, because the physical body can only interact with specifics at a specific location.

Putting this together, the physical body forces the human mind to associate the Mercy circuit and Mercy emotions with specifics and personal identity.

Now let us look at the physical environment. As science has taught us, the 'actions' of Nature are repeatable, consistent, and inescapable; wherever we look in Nature, we see the same Server sequences. This consistency and repeatability leads to Teacher feelings of order-within-complexity. And, while the Server sequences of Nature are inescapable, by using Perceiver thought to combine and recombine matter, it is possible to get the 'actions' of Nature to cooperate.

For instance, certain atoms have the inherent property of being radioactive. By placing many radioactive particles together, it is possible to create an atomic explosion. Assembling all of these radioactive particles into a Perceiver object does not change the natural behavior of the radioactive atoms, but rather leads to a situation in which the natural 'actions' of the radioactive atoms *cooperate* to produce an atomic reaction. An atomic bomb can be assembled by humans, like any other machine, but evidence indicates that atomic reactions have also occurred naturally when natural forces have brought sufficient radioactive atoms in close proximity.

Putting this together, we notice that Nature 'acts' in a way which reflects the *Teacher* circuit. Because the forces of Nature exist *throughout* the universe, we associate the Teacher circuit with generality. And because the *same* natural forces exist throughout the universe, this leads to Teacher emotions of order-within-complexity. Finally, because this Teacher circuit functions whether humans are present or not, the mind does not associate the Teacher circuit with personal identity.[44]

Let us run through this one more time, from a different perspective. I suggest that a finite person can experience Server and Perceiver repetition in one of three ways: First, he can find that the same Server sequences and the same Perceiver facts *occur* wherever he goes. Second, he can hold on to a specific set of Server sequences and Perceiver facts and take them *with* him wherever he goes. Third, he can gain the ability to *produce* a consistent set of Server sequences and Perceiver facts.

For instance, consider the *tourist.* Suppose that a person wants to stick with familiar facts and sequences as he travels. One way is for him to limit his traveling to within his own country. If he does this, then wherever he goes, he will still be in a familiar culture where people accept similar Perceiver facts and perform similar Server actions. Another option is for him to travel on a tour bus with fellow citizens, which will allow him to take a piece of his culture with him. The third option is for him to learn how to reproduce elements of his culture using local ingredients. This describes the expatriate who lives in a foreign country but performs a job using skills and knowledge which are familiar to him. The first possibility of finding that similar Perceiver facts and Server

---

44 While the nature of the physical world provides the *raw material* for abstract thought, the human ability to comprehend and produce words makes it possible for the mind to construct an *internal* representation of abstract thought.

sequences are *repeated* corresponds to abstract thought and generality; the second possibility of *taking* along a specific set of Perceiver facts and Server sequences occurs with concrete thought and specifics.

Summarizing, if one wants to create an external environment that is compatible with Perceiver repetition and Server repetition, then the two alternatives are to place the mind within a natural environment of *repeatable* Perceiver facts and Server sequences or to house Perceiver and Server thought within a specific container with *consistent* Perceiver facts and Server sequences. Going beyond these two possibilities requires the development of *internal* Perceiver and Server structure.

But why does the human mind associate the *Mercy* circuit with a specific *container* possessing Perceiver and Server content and the *Teacher* circuit with a general *environment* of Perceiver and Server content? Because, in the human container, Perceiver facts are *input* and Server actions are *output*. The human body has a shape and lives among shapes; that is input. And the human body is capable of producing action; that is output. When Perceiver is input and Server is output, that describes the Mercy circuit. Moving to the human environment, Server sequences are *input* and Perceiver facts are *output*. The Server 'actions' of Nature can be observed, but they cannot be changed; that is input. But the Perceiver objects of Nature can be altered; that is output. In the Teacher circuit, Server is input and Perceiver is output.

For those who find this logic hard to follow, I am simply saying that there appears to be no fundamental *mental* difference between abstract thought and concrete thought. Rather, it is the nature of the physical *body* which makes concrete thought act concrete, and the nature of the physical *world* which makes abstract thought function in an abstract manner. The physical body and the physical environment are responsible for associating Mercy emotions with specific concrete experiences and Teacher emotions with general abstract theories. The mind itself is capable of functioning in a different manner, and if the environment and the physical body were changed, then it *would* function in a different manner.

Exchanging Concrete Thought with Abstract Thought

Now let us take a closer look at concrete thought. Suppose that I want to build an autonomous robot. What are the most basic programming requirements? How does such a machine have to *think* in order to become autonomous? First, the machine must be *aware* of its environment. Second, it must *know* where it is. Third, it must have a way of *changing* where it is. Of these two, *knowing* location is more basic than *changing* location. Fourth, it must have a way of *choosing* how it will change its location based upon the knowledge of where it currently is. Fifth, it must have a sense of self-preservation so that it does not damage or destroy itself. Sixth, it must have a reason to explore and move. Obviously, a lot more detail could be added, but that describes the basic outline.

In the human mind, each of these requirements corresponds to a cognitive module. Mercy mode makes me aware of my environment. Perceiver mode determines where I am; Server mode allows me to change my location. Connecting these two is Contributor mode, which chooses the Server action that will be used to change my Perceiver location. The sense of self-preservation is provided by mental networks within Mercy thought, while the motivation to explore and move comes from Exhorter mode.

Notice that the module that provides the *output* is preceded by three modules which analyze *input*. Mercy mode is aware of experiences but cannot create experiences; Perceiver mode, the next in the chain, can know location but cannot create location; Contributor mode can choose actions but cannot control outcomes. It is only Server mode, the fourth module in this chain, which can actually change location.

What would happen if one of the three preceding modules could generate output? I suggest that the chain of mental processing would stop at that point and go no further. For instance, as a Perceiver person, I am conscious in the second stage of concrete thought. I have often wished that I could create facts and not just observe them. But if I had that ability, then I would never learn how to *do* anything, and Server thought in my mind would remain stillborn. This principle is illustrated by the Server *person*, who *is* conscious in a cognitive module which can generate output. Even though concrete information has to pass through *three* other modules before it finally makes it to Server mode, our observations of personality suggest that the Server person tends to have the least developed mind of all of the cognitive styles, because he can substitute doing for thinking.

Now let us extend this concept. The human mind contains *two* mental circuits which we refer to as concrete thought and abstract thought. We just saw that concrete thought is concrete because it is hooked up to the 'autonomous robot' of the human body. But suppose that *abstract* thought were hooked up to the 'autonomous robot' of a 'body'. For such a mind, abstract thought would become concrete thought and concrete thought would be regarded as abstract thought. Such an individual would have precisely the same mind as a human being and yet it would be utterly alien.

This cognitive exercise is useful for a number of reasons: First, it is fascinating to explore the possibilities of an alien way of existence that would be regarded by the mind as totally 'normal'. Second, it is possible for humans to alter their environment into a form that treats abstract thought as concrete, and when they do, then they begin functioning in a manner which 'normal' humans regard as alien. Third, the relationship between living in concrete thought and living in abstract thought appears to correspond to the symmetry between matter and energy which one finds in physics. Fourth, if one explores what it would mean to live as an alien within an abstract 'body' and an abstract 'world', then the results appear remarkably similar to religious descriptions about angels and popular stories about UFOs. Fifth, religion deals with topics such as the supernatural and life after death. If one is to present religion as a general theory of cognition, then this theory must also include a rational explanation for the supernatural as well as for life after death. Thus, I present the following as a hypothesis which may or may not be true, but cognitively speaking, it is a viable possibility that needs to be explored.

I should emphasize that while the mode of existence which I am hypothesizing is compatible with the human mind, it is *not* compatible with the Mercy mental network that represents the physical body *nor* is it compatible with the Teacher mental network of common sense. That is because we are looking at a situation in which the human mind is being placed within a *different* body and a *different* world.[45]

For a human whose personal identity is built around his physical body, encountering such an alien being would be terrifying, because such a creature would not live within a human *body*, even though the alien creature would have the same *mind* as humans. As I mentioned in a previous chapter, when one reads about human encounters with angels or UFOs, one notices that the human usually has an emotional reaction of utter terror. Therefore, in order to interact with such a being without experiencing personal hyper-terror, a human would have to define his personal existence in Mercy thought in a way that did not require the presence of a physical body, and this internal definition of personal identity would have to form a stable Mercy mental network.

Similarly, if one bases science solely upon the Teacher mental network of common sense from the physical world, then one can only protect the integrity of scientific thought by debunking the existence of non-physical alien realms. This describes how most of the scientific community responds to accounts of supernatural encounters. However, if one extends objective scientific thought to include the internal and the emotional, then this cognitive *extension* of science would be compatible with our hypothetical alien existence. It is interesting to note that science now contains two major areas—quantum physics and relativity—that are *not* consistent with common sense and which can only be observed indirectly through the use of scientific instruments. And to my semi-rigorous engineering trained mind, the weirdness of quantum mechanics sounds very much like the cognitive weirdness which we are about to explore.

Am I suggesting that angels, spirits, and UFOs are *real*? No. That is because the word *real* describes something material which exists in the physical world. Instead, my hypothesis is that aliens inhabit a realm which is entirely unreal, and that the only commonality between here and 'there' lies in a common mental structure. In addition, I am suggesting that this external difference causes the *same* type of mind to develop *incompatible* fundamental mental networks. Finally, I am suggesting that at extreme scales and conditions, these two external environments begin to resemble one another, and that it might be able to cross over from one to the other.

I should also emphasize that this chapter is attempting to describe alien life as a *human* would view it. In other words, we are trying to *translate* alien existence into human terms. We are not looking at alien existence the way that an alien would perceive it, for that

---

[45] After writing this book, I came to the conclusion that spirits and demons interact with humans by empowering mental networks, as illustrated by 'demon possession' or being 'filled by the Holy Spirit'. This suggests that there is also a spiritual realm in addition to the supernatural realm of angels and aliens being discussed in this chapter. Developing healthy mental networks would be a prerequisite for beneficial interaction with spiritual beings.

would probably be incomprehensible to the human mind, because we are dealing with a situation in which the theory of the one is literally the reality of the other. That is what it means for abstract thought and concrete thought to switch places. In essence, we are like the Western tourist visiting the 'inscrutable East' who returns to the West and relates his experiences to a Western audience. Simply describing the journey is difficult enough; entering into the mindset of the local inhabitants would be nigh impossible.

Because we are looking here at a situation in which abstract and concrete are flipped, we will have to adjust the way that we refer to these two. In order to minimize confusion, whenever I am using a term such as *abstract* or *concrete*, I will use the word *without* quotes when defining it the way a human would, and put the word *in* 'quotes' when using the alien definition. Thus, a human uses abstract thought, but an alien would live in abstract thought, which he would define as 'concrete' thought. Similarly, an alien would live in a 'body', but this 'body' would not appear like a body to a human.

An alien would associate Teacher thought with 'concrete' specifics, because his mind would occupy a Teacher-based 'body'. In human terms, this combination describes a *name*. But we are not looking here at the human situation in which a verbal label is slapped on to a specific personal identity. Instead, we are dealing with a name that defines the personal essence of an individual—a Teacher label which traps the alien mind as thoroughly as the body does for the human mind. A human *profession* comes close to doing this. Consider, for instance, the medical doctor. This label defines someone who is almost regarded as a different species of human being, for in order to become a medical doctor, one must take years of postgraduate studies and pass numerous difficult exams, and the medical doctor is given a label which the average individual is forbidden to use, and is both permitted and expected to perform numerous activities which are banned to the normal human. Now imagine a person who was only a medical doctor, who was always a medical doctor, and who could not perform anything outside of his medical profession. That is what it would mean to live within a specific Teacher name. Consistent with this, it is interesting to note that the word *angel* means *messenger*. A message is a specific arrangement of Teacher words. Thus, the term messenger conveys the concept of a being who lives within a name.

That brings up an interesting question. We have seen that one mental circuit is concrete while the other mental circuit is abstract. But, if either mental circuit could be concrete, then why couldn't humans be equipped with *two* concrete modes of thought? Why not place the human mind in a container that is a combination of a human body and an alien 'body'? As we discussed a few paragraphs back, I suggest that such a combination would shortcut the process of developing mental content by providing the mind with too much *output*. The human circuit permits Server mode to generate actions, while the alien circuit would allow Perceiver mode to generate facts. How much mental content would a child acquire if he could generate an object simply by snapping his fingers, clasping his arms, wriggling his nose, or waving his wand? One can answer that question by examining the rich child who 'generates' objects by waving money around.

It is interesting to note that the Jewish Torah appears to describe such a situation in the sixth chapter of Genesis, where it talks about the 'sons of God' interbreeding with the 'daughters of men'. According to this account, the resulting offspring were *physically* superhuman, but *mentally* they were driven by Kant's radical evil. The story in the Torah continues by saying that God responded by 'pressing the reset button' through the flood of Noah. Whether this story is physically true or not, it definitely is valid from a cognitive perspective.

In addition, if both modes of thought were concrete, then abstract thought would not develop, because the mind would focus so much upon specifics—and have such complete control over specifics—that it would be incapable of discovering generality. Because an image of God emerges when generality touches personal specifics, such a mind would be godless. In keeping with this, it is interesting to count the number of times that the word 'ungodly' occurs in the following Biblical passage spoken by a person who supposedly living during this period of human-alien interbreeding: "Now Enoch, the seventh from Adam, prophesied about these men also, saying, 'Behold, the Lord comes with ten thousands of His saints, to execute judgment on all, to convict all who are ungodly among them of all their ungodly deeds which they have committed in an ungodly way, and of all the harsh things which ungodly sinners have spoken against Him'" (Jude 14-15).

However, one also notes that both Jewish and Christian Scriptures talk about new bodies *and* new names being given to those who demonstrate sufficient internal content, conveying the belief that a mature mind would be able to handle powers and abilities that would overwhelm a childish mind.

Flipping Concrete Thought and Abstract Thought

Before we continue, let us pause to catch our breath. We have discovered that the human mind is symmetrical, for it contains two equivalent mental circuits. One of these two circuits is hooked up to a body, leading to concrete thought involving specifics, while the other circuit must observe the environment from a distance, leading to abstract thought and generality. We have also concluded that *either* mental circuit could be hooked up to a body and become concrete. However, for the undeveloped mind, it is imperative that only *one* mental circuit is concrete while the other one remain abstract.

In the human mind, Mercy mode deals with concrete specifics while Teacher mode handles abstract generality. In contrast, the alien mind would associate Teacher mode with 'concrete specifics' and Mercy mode with 'abstract generality'. Thus, in order to comprehend alien feelings, we need to come up with a more general definition of emotion, for until now we have associated Mercy emotions with specific experiences and Teacher emotions with general theories.

Teacher emotion comes from order-within-complexity. Teacher mode feels good when many items can be placed within a single package. In order to increase Teacher feelings, one can either add items to the package or else decrease the size of the package. For instance, a country such as the United States produces strong Teacher emotions because of the size of its economy and the power of its military. That is an example of Teacher generality. In contrast, a country such as Singapore produces Teacher emotions because so much structure is contained within the tiny package of a single city state. Similarly, electronic devices feel good to Teacher thought because they take a lot of complexity and place this complexity within the container of a small consumer device.

Moving on, I suggest that Mercy generality produces good emotions through *mutually beneficial interaction*, a feeling more commonly known as *love*. When many Mercy items interact in a way that is harmonious and peaceful, then this generates positive Mercy feelings that are associated with generality.

The human mind *is* capable of sensing emotions associated with Teacher specifics and Mercy generality, but these emotions are not provided directly in obvious form by either the physical body or the physical environment. However, it is possible to *artificially* alter the environment so that they can be sensed externally.

That brings us to the following general principle: When one tries to imagine what it would be like to live as an alien within abstract thought, it *is* possible to come up with examples from the human world, because the human mind can function in an alien mode. But because the physical body and the natural world are compatible with *human* thought, the human examples of alien thought which one finds in the human world generally come from either artificial environments or manufactured objects. In this chapter, our examples will come from the government, the military, and technology.

Let us look now in more detail at what it would be like if abstract and concrete were reversed. Remember that the human circuit of concrete thought has four stages: First, emotional experiences enter Mercy mode. Second, Perceiver mode organizes these experiences into categories, building a mental map. Third, Contributor mode chooses which Server actions will be added to the Perceiver facts. Fourth, Server mode implements physical actions which can move through this map. These actions alter the external environment, which then leads to a new set of emotional experiences for Mercy mode.[46]

The best way to describe the alien version is through the example of the *Internet*. In order to access the Internet, one requires a computer. The physical body interprets specific Mercy experiences; a computer interprets the specific Teacher words of a computer program. In the physical realm, each individual is mentally represented as a specific set of Mercy experiences; on the Internet, each 'individual' is represented by the specific words of a *home page*. A physical body is a Perceiver object; a home page contains a Server sequence of words. The physical body uses Server actions to move from one physical location to another; the Perceiver connection of the *hyper-link* allows one to travel from one 'location' on the Internet to another. Moving through the

---

[46] This mental cycle is quite similar to the OODA loop of Observe, Orient, Decide, and Act proposed by Colonel John Boyd.

physical world means choosing which action will be done in each situation; browsing the web is done by choosing which hyperlink will be clicked on each home page.

I hope that it is starting to become clear why I am including a discussion about aliens in a chapter that talks about using Server mode without Perceiver mode. Humans live within the Perceiver object of a physical body which occupies a physical realm of Perceiver objects. For the human mind, Server sequences are not real, for the human mind cannot directly see movement, but it must infer movement from the way in which physical objects move over time. In contrast, an alien would live within the Server sequence of a name which would occupy a non-physical realm of Server sequences. The alien mind would not see Perceiver objects, but instead it would have to infer their existence from the way in which Server sequences changed over time.

This description may sound somewhat strange, but it describes the process by which pictures are produced on the old bulky television sets with their Cathode Ray Tubes or CRTs. When you see a picture of a person on a television screen, that person is not really there. Instead, the CRT is drawing the picture of a person one line at a time, the same way that an inkjet printer prints a document or a person reads the words on a page. On a North American television screen, the CRT heads back to the top of the screen every 525 lines and starts redrawing the picture. But because this line-drawing process is happening 15750 lines per second, the picture of the person appears solid to the eye. When watching a moving picture on a television screen, one is mentally inferring this picture from the way in which the Server sequences of drawn lines change over time.

When Heidegger attempted to redefine human existence in terms of Server sequences, he was describing a way of thinking that would appear natural and obvious to an alien mind. Heidegger had to begin his Server based system of thought by deconstructing traditional philosophy with its emphasis upon Perceiver objects, facts, truth, and Forms. In contrast, the alien individual could discover Server mode simply by using his 'body' to interact with his 'world'.

Living in Abstract Thought

Let us move on to the next question. I refer to the alien 'world' as a non-physical realm of Server sequences. What would this be like? The human world is composed of atomic *particles*, the raw material for Mercy experiences. In contrast, the basic building block for Teacher mode is the word, which is a sound *wave*. The normal person regards particles and waves as entirely different, for one sits somewhere while the other wiggles over time. However, according to physics, every particle is also a wave, and modern electronics are based upon the general principle that small particles can act like waves.

This leads us to the hypothesis that the alien 'world' would be composed of waves. But we are not talking about the ephemeral acoustic waves of human speech. Instead, we are referring to waves which are in some way 'solid'. In keeping with this, it is interesting to note that accounts of supernatural beings consistently associate these beings with electromagnetic waves of light and energy. UFO stories talk about 'creatures of energy' using devices of 'solid light'. The Christian Bible talks about Satan 'disguising himself as an angel of light', but the Bible also associates light with 'enlightened' humans, suggesting that the human mind might be compatible with alien existence. For instance, the Jewish book of Daniel says that "Those who are wise shall shine like the brightness of the firmament, and those who turn many to righteousness like the stars forever and ever" (Daniel 12:3). And in the New Testament there is the well-known story of the transfiguration which says that Jesus "was transfigured before them. His face shone like the sun, and His clothes became as white as the light. And behold, Moses and Elijah appeared to them, talking with Him" (Matthew 17:2-3).

The human mind uses *Perceiver* thought to determine location and *Server* actions to change location. An alien 'body', in contrast, would use *Server* thought to locate itself and would affect its environment through *Perceiver* power. This idea of associating Server sequences with 'location' and Perceiver facts with 'movement' is difficult to grasp, but it does make sense of the strange behavior attributed to angels and UFOs. One notices in these accounts that these creatures never seem to sit around and do nothing. Instead, they appear suddenly, perform a task, and then disappear just as suddenly. Human medical doctors function in a similar manner, for they also seldom sit around and chat. Instead, they walk in the door, do their job, and then disappear out the door. For the medical doctor, the examination is regarded as an 'event', and 'movement' involves going from one examination to another. Similarly, the alien would only remain in a single physical location for the duration of a task because the *task* would define 'location'. For such a creature, 'location' would have nothing to do with physical space. To the human observing the incident, it would appear as if the alien being was teleporting in and out, whereas the alien would simply regard this as 'moving' to the next 'event'.

The Internet provides an illustration of how this works. When I click on a hyperlink, I am 'moving' from one home page to another. The website to which I 'move' could be hosted on a computer which is next door, or I could be accessing information on a computer located on the other side of the world. When I am browsing the web, the physical location of the computer is irrelevant. Instead, what defines closeness on the Internet is the presence or absence of a hyperlink. But if a person were to sit beside one of these computers and observe my visit, he would see me teleporting in, browsing, and then teleporting out. Thus, we see a concept of 'space' and 'distance' that would make far more sense to Heidegger than it would to the average human.

Heidegger attempted to define all of human existence in terms of *time* rather than *space*. Similarly, it appears that in an alien 'universe', time and space would actually change places, an idea which is almost impossible to visualize. However, one does find in popular UFO literature precisely this concept that humans live in space-time while aliens live in time-space. According to the *Law of One*, which was supposedly dictated to humans by aliens, in space-time a person can manipulate objects but he has only a limited awareness of time. In contrast, time-space permits an individual to observe and compare personal sequences, but he loses the ability to manipulate objects and events. Similarly, both Jewish and Christian Scriptures associate angels with *prophecy*—an ability to *see* through time and predict what will happen.

Before we continue, let us step back again for a brief moment. Newton's three laws of motion regard time and space as absolute. Einstein's theory of relativity stood this notion on its head by suggesting that time and space are not absolute. Instead, Einstein suggested that time and space can shrink and stretch and that the real absolute is the speed of light in a vacuum.[47] In a similar way, the objective scientist regards the physical universe as absolute and regards mental content as secondary. I am suggesting that it may be possible to explain more by turning this relationship around and *beginning* with the structure of the mind. On the surface, this may appear similar to the Eastern mystical concept that 'God is within you', but instead of using Teacher overgeneralization to attack facts and suppress sequences, I am presenting a cognitive model that makes room for both scientific and religious thought.

Aliens and Religion

So far, we have examined the concept of alien existence from a theoretical perspective. Let us now add the religious dimension. Notice that we are already dealing with topics which are implicitly religious, for when one theorizes about the *same* mind living within a *different* body, then one is making a distinction between the mind and the physical body. And when one distinguishes between the mind and the body, then one is dealing with the topic of life after death, because that simply describes the mind continuing to exist without the body. Consistent with this, it is interesting to note that one often finds dead humans showing up in accounts of both UFOs and angels. For instance, the Biblical story of the transfiguration talks about a shining Jesus conversing with the dead figures of Moses and Elijah.

Suppose that life does continue after death and that the mind does survive the demise of the physical body. Would this alter what we have discussed in the rest of this book? I suggest not. Instead, it would only add intensity to the existing concepts. I have suggested that the goal of religion and education is to gain internal content and to develop and integrate cognitive modules. If this conclusion is valid when the mind is living inside of a physical body, then it would be even more critical if the mind continued to exist after the body ceased functioning. And if it is important to extend scientific thought into the realm of the internal and subjective when one is living in a physical world, then it would be even more necessary to do this if there were no external world to hold the internal together and no physical body to give structure to the subjective. Finally, if mental networks play such a major role in determining personal behavior when they are hidden within a physical body and are counterbalanced by a

---

47 Notice that this is an example of Teacher thought, which is taking a seemingly specific principle—the speed of light in a vacuum—and treating it as a universal law.

physical world, one could imagine that mental networks would play the defining role if the body and the world were not present. And if one can only transform mental networks with great difficulty when one is living within a body and inhabiting a world, then one can postulate that it would be essentially impossible to rebuild existing mental networks after death.[48] And that brings us back to one of the major themes of this book, which is choosing to build a concept of God that is compatible with human happiness and personal salvation while this option is still mentally possible.

Let us turn now to the topic of aliens and religion. Suppose that an alien who lived in abstract thought appeared on earth. Would human religion apply to such an individual? If the mind of the alien is the same as the mind of the human, and if religion is defined in cognitive terms, then one can conclude that the *same* religious system would apply to both human and alien.

However, I suggest that this religious equivalence would only become apparent at the *end* of the path of religious education. That is because humans and aliens would *begin* this path from radically different starting points. The human student begins with a mind that is governed by childish Mercy mental networks. As far as he is concerned, Teacher mode does not even exist. Similarly, the alien student would begin with Teacher mental networks, oblivious to the existence of Mercy mode.

School uses the *technical* thought of a controlled environment and carefully defined curriculum to integrate the two mental circuits of Cp and Ci. Technical thought belongs to the *second* stage of learning. When the student does not develop technical thought, then the *first* stage of learning is free to flourish, which leads to the overgeneralized Teacher theories of the instant expert.

When one examines Eastern mystical religions which are based in Teacher overgeneralization, one finds that they contain extensive descriptions of contacts with supernatural creatures and supernatural powers. But most of these supernatural creatures are described as malevolent beings with destructive powers. If one assumes that these descriptions are valid, then I suggest that one can make three conclusions: First, what Eastern religion claims to be discovering is not *consistent* with what Eastern religion is preaching, because it is searching for the all-in-one vagueness of nirvana and then encountering distinct supernatural beings. Second, the method that Eastern religion is using is not *conducive* to good relations, because the supernatural creatures are responding to human probing in a generally negative fashion.

Third, the method of Teacher overgeneralization appears to *work*. Gurus of Eastern mysticism often claim to have gained supernatural powers, and those who write about UFO encounters often suggest that the meditation of Eastern mysticism is an effective

---

[48] Saying this another way, the disembodied mind would be irresistibly drawn by its core mental networks to a spiritual environment that resonated with these core mental networks, where the disembodied mind would interact with other beings whose minds were governed by similar core mental networks.

way of contacting 'them'. Theory suggests that the method of Eastern Mysticism would work for two reasons: First, it associates Teacher thought with personal identity. Second, it removes the human mental networks that prevent the human mind from acknowledging the possibility of supernatural existence: When a person believes that the physical world is illusion and that All is One, he is mentally letting go of the Teacher mental network of common sense. And when a person stops physical movement and mentally identifies with this Oneness, then he is letting go of the Mercy mental network that represents his physical body.

But in the same way that some images of God are more beneficial than other concepts of deity, so mental symmetry tells us that all paths of supernatural contact would not be equally helpful. When the recommended way to contact another country is by pretending that I and my country do not exist, then one concludes that this is not a good starting point. Similarly, if I enter a foreign country and insist that 'they all look like each other' and that 'there is no substance to their ways of doing things', then this also does not make for good relations. Instead, one needs diplomats and traders who are capable of bridging the two cultures and translating one culture into the other.

If humans live in concrete thought and aliens lived in abstract thought, then the best way to bridge these two would be by integrating them in a manner that respects the content of both. And that would be done by following the path of religious education through rebirth to the very end, for the final end of this path is a mindset and a culture that combines Ci and Cp.

Modern R&D provides a partial illustration of this integrating process. When society goes through the rebirth of an Industrial Revolution, then a new way of living emerges which combines abstract thought with concrete thought: First, research is being guided by the *general* Teacher laws of nature. Second, development produces machines that are *specific* examples of Teacher order-within-complexity. Third, development comes up with *specific* consumer gadgets which bring Mercy pleasure to the human individual. Fourth, technology creates a new *general* Mercy infrastructure which ties humans together in a web of trade, travel, and communication. Notice how all *four* elements are present simultaneously: Teacher generality, Teacher specifics, Mercy specifics, and Mercy generality. Thus, in the *objective*, R&D has created a world that combines both human and alien existence. That explains why it is possible to find illustrations of alien thought in the realm of modern technology.

But it is also possible to partially bridge alien thought and human thought in ways that are destructive and not constructive. Think, for instance, of the military-industrial complex. It uses R&D which is driven by the general Teacher laws of nature to come up with machines that are specific illustrations of Teacher order-within-complexity. But it does not produce consumer gadgets that bring Mercy joy to the individual. Instead, it manufactures high-tech bombs and bullets that destroy Perceiver objects and inflict the hyper-pain of mental anguish, physical dismemberment, and death upon human individuals.

In other words, the military-industrial complex is actually an example of alien existence *without* human existence—carried out by beings who are physically human. But how can a human soldier function in an environment which is inhuman? By *thinking* and *acting* like an alien. A professional soldier is not treated as a human individual. Instead, he is defined by his professional skills and his rank. His skills determine which Server actions he can perform, while his rank determines whose orders he must obey and to whom he may give orders. For the soldier, the Server sequence of carrying out an order is more important than physical life itself.

Thus, I suggest that it is no accident that Heidegger was a proud member of the Nazi party, with its inhuman, warmongering combination of military and industrial, for that is what happens when one defines identity in Server terms and suppresses Perceiver thought. And if abstract aliens really exist, then it makes sense that these aliens would be in contact with the human military, because they would share a common mindset.

In general terms, I suggest that there is a tendency for humans to turn alien whenever personal identity is defined in Server terms. I suggest that this is an inevitable by-product of *specialization* and *regulation*. Theorists tell us that specialization is a hallmark of civilization. The reason for specialization is obvious: It takes time to develop Server skills, and a person with Server skills can perform a job much faster and much more efficiently than someone who lacks these skills. Thus, it makes sense for each person to focus upon learning and performing a unique set of Server skills. But this leads to people being defined by their Server skills and not by their physical identities. As a result, John becomes known as John the basket weaver.

As we saw a few pages back, a human being lives within the Perceiver object of a physical body, while an alien would be trapped within the name of a Server profession.

Once government steps into to *regulate* skills, then humans also become trapped within their Server professions by the force of government law. In today's Modern episteme, humans are severely restricted in the Server actions which they can do. If a person wishes to practice a certain skill, then he must take official courses, pass official exams, and become officially certified. The end result is that humans become like aliens.

Now let us add the *religious* element to our discussion about integrating alien thought with human thought. When we suggest that the final stage of the path of religious education unifies alien and human thought, then in Christian terms, we have just concluded that personal salvation is possible for angels, demons, and UFOs through a generalization of the Christian doctrine of incarnation and the Christian message of salvation. If one says this to the average Bible-believing Christian, then he will question it, for he is convinced that angelic beings 'cannot be saved'. And I suggest that the *Bible-believing* Christian is right, because he is basing his religious doctrine in the Mercy status of a holy book and does not understand it as a Teacher-based general theory. Obviously, if one wanted to 'save' beings who lived in abstract thought, then one would have to translate the Christian message of salvation into the language of abstract thought.

Curiously, the Christian scriptures appear to agree with me and not with the typical Christian: "For by Him all things were created that are in heaven and that are on earth, visible and invisible, whether thrones or dominions or principalities or powers. All things were created through Him and for Him...For it pleased the Father that in Him all the fullness should dwell, and by Him to reconcile all things to Himself, by Him, whether things on earth or things in heaven, having made peace through the blood of His cross" (Colossians 1:16,19-20). When one reads this passage from the viewpoint of mental symmetry, one notices two significant points: First, beings are being referred to as 'thrones or dominions or rulers or authorities'. This sounds like Teacher-based creatures who live in abstract thought, because all four of these terms describe a Teacher theory with a limited domain. Second, 'reconciling all things to Himself' and 'making peace through the blood of the cross' describes the Christian message of salvation-through-rebirth in anthropomorphic language.

We saw that the Ten Commandments are aimed at a mindset which practices *Mercy* identification. Because humans live in a physical body, there is a natural mental conflict between Teacher universality and Mercy specifics. On the one hand, Teacher mode wants rules of conscience to be applied universally. On the other hand, Mercy thought pursues personal goals even when this violates universal moral standards. Kant describes this conflict as radical evil.

Obviously, a being which lived in abstract thought would not be subject to such human temptations. However, if one uses the *mirror image* of Kant's concept of radical evil, then I suggest that one can work out how a 'childish' alien would behave. That is because abstract thought is the mirror image of concrete thought. Thus, for an alien mind, the 'childish' conflict would be between Teacher specifics and Mercy generality. On the one hand, the 'childish' alien would want to carry out the functions of its specific Teacher name. On the other hand, Mercy generality would define universal standards of mutually beneficial interaction—otherwise known as love. In simple human terms, this would lead to a conflict between *personal agenda* and the physical or social *environment.*

For instance, think of a mine that extracts ore in a manner that sends poisonous waste into the local river. On the one hand, the mine is carrying out a specific agenda; it is performing the specific Teacher function of removing-ore-from-the-ground. On the other hand, it is doing this in a way which harms the Mercy experiences for everyone in the neighborhood because they can no longer drink the water or eat the fish. Because it is not possible for everyone to continue behaving in such an irresponsible manner, we are looking at a violation of Kant's categorical imperative, but this is an alien-type violation which combines Teacher specifics with Mercy generality.

Now let us apply this definition to the typical alien abduction scenario, which begins with the alien floating in through the wall or ceiling. Does the alien in this story have a personal agenda? Yes, it is attempting to kidnap a human. Does this personal agenda respect the *physical* Mercy environment? No. Instead, the alien is ignoring surrounding physical objects such as walls, ceilings and other impediments. Does this personal agenda respect the *social* Mercy environment? No. That is because kidnapping a human violates general Mercy standards of love. Thus, we conclude that an alien behaving in this manner would be violating the alien version of the categorical imperative and would need to be 'saved' by the alien version of the path of religious education.

A human soldier behaves in precisely the same way. He has a personal agenda in the form of the specific orders which he is supposed to follow. Any thing or person in the environment that stands in the way of him carrying out his personal agenda is killed or destroyed. Thus, we conclude that if aliens existed, then the human military would naturally associate with 'childish' aliens. Similarly, if one examines the Christian charismatic religious meeting where the preacher marches up and down the stage 'casting out demons' and 'slaying people in the spirit', then one concludes that if there is any spiritual validity to this exercise, then it too is an example of pursuing a personal agenda in an unloving manner, and any aliens that were involved in this exercise would also require personal salvation. In simple religious terms, one could say that the Holy Spirit is a gentleman.

This last phrase requires some explanation. We have seen that an Industrial Revolution has the potential of integrating general Teacher, finite Teacher, finite Mercy, and general Mercy. When the personal element is added, then one concludes that not only do personal experiences acquire both a human and an alien aspect, but the human concept of God becomes combined with the alien concept of God. For a human mind, an image of God emerges when Teacher generality explains Mercy personal identity. For an alien mind, an image of God would form when Mercy generality encompassed Teacher 'personal identity'. Thus, the human concept of God would be viewed by an alien mind as the 'Holy Spirit', while the alien view of 'God' would be viewed by humans as the Holy Spirit. These two concepts of Deity would converge into the form of a Trinity at the end of the path of religious education.

Aliens and Science

We have spent some time looking at the religious implications of alien existence. How would the *scientific* mind view alien activity? I suggest that the answer can be found by extending the concept of intelligent intervention. As usual, the Industrial Revolution provides a good partial illustration. Before the Industrial Revolution, everything was handmade. After, items became divided into the two categories of made-by-a-human and made-by-a-machine. As I have mentioned before, a machine is a specific physical example of Teacher order-within-complexity. It can also be viewed from the human perspective as a black box which takes some input, performs a set of functions, and then produces an output. Like the hypothetical alien, it transforms one object into another. To the uninitiated eye, the machine looks like it is performing alien magic, but it is actually subject to a system of natural laws.

Alien intervention would become an extension of this, for an alien creature would appear to humans like a machine that was alive. To the uninitiated mind, it would appear as if this 'living machine' was performing magic, but in fact the transformations produced by these 'living machines' would be subject to a form of 'natural law' that was related through symmetry to the natural laws of science. And, scientists *love* symmetry, because it is a very effective way of adding elegance to a general Teacher theory.

In other words, we are looking here at another extension of the mental Agency Detector introduced at the beginning of the book. Currently, the cognitive science of religion uses the concept of an Agency Detector to distinguish between the two categories of 'human' and 'other', and anything which cannot be explained in human terms, such as God, aliens, or angels, is placed within the category of 'other'. Earlier on, I suggested that the concept of Agency Detector should be expanded to include the category of *Teacher generality* and that this can explain how a mental concept of God emerges. Now, I am suggesting a further mental category of *Teacher specific.* The *machine* is an example of a Teacher specific, because it expresses Teacher order-within-complexity within a specific finite package. Thus, if a natural law were 'violated' within some situation, then this would not necessarily mean that the generality of natural law had been overturned. Instead, it would indicate that an alien had intervened. Because an alien is a finite creature, this intervention would always be limited to specific incidents, and because an alien is personally subject to Teacher emotions of order-within-complexity, then this intervention would appear to human minds like the actions of a living, intelligent machine.

Thus, the *disclosure* of aliens living within 'abstract' thought would have a similar effect upon human society to the effect which the coming *singularity* will have upon human society when machines begin to exceed humans in intelligence, for both would appear to humans as intelligent machines.

Summary

That brings us to the end of both this chapter and this book. This final chapter covered three related subjects: the philosophy of Martin Heidegger, the religion of Judaism, and the alien mindset. All three of these share the common trait of focusing upon Server mode while downplaying Perceiver mode.

Heidegger took this to the extreme, because he developed a universal theory of human thought and behavior which literally defines Perceiver mode out of existence. According to Heidegger, there are no objects, no subjects, no facts, no Forms, and space does not exist. Instead, Heidegger defined all of these Perceiver concepts in terms of Server actions. One can make this conclusion because Heidegger begins his analysis with *time* and *average everydayness*, which corresponds to Server mode, and Server mode combines analytical (or time-oriented) and concrete.

Heidegger's Server-centered system does describe a valid *alternate* way of defining human existence, but because humans inhabit the *object* of a physical body and live within a world of *objects*, this is a secondary form of definition. And in order to explain Heidegger's system, one must introduce modes of thought which Heidegger says do not exist. Thus, this book analyzes Heidegger from the viewpoint of cognitive science: If one examines the path of Heidegger and analyzes what is happening within the various cognitive modules, then one concludes that this programming method will produce the results that Heidegger claims.

Heidegger defines self-image in terms of Server skills—a valid definition. And he also defines objects in terms of their Server functions. Thus, a telephone is a tool-for-talking-with-other-people, a light is a tool-for-making-it-easier-to-see, and so on. Heidegger says that in normal existence there is no distinction between me and my environment, but rather a person finds himself immersed within his world—doing. One finds this combination of doing without self-observing in the typical Server *person*, who uses Server mode but tends to use physical location as a substitute for a map in Perceiver thought. Heidegger defines physical space in an egocentric manner, based upon personal physical movement. When one moves, one is 'making farness vanish' and 'bringing items close'. Physical location is organized into functional regions. Each tool—for everything in Heidegger's 'world' is a tool—is contained within a functional region. Thus the device-for-brushing-teeth is contained within the functional region of the bathroom, and so on.

When Perceiver mode is parasitic upon physical location for its facts, then personal feelings will be governed by the immediate emotions of the current situation, which Heidegger refers to as *mood*, and the immediate environment will feel *heimlich* or comfortable. But Heidegger is not just using Server mode to move through his personal world, he is also using Teacher mode to build a universal theory of Server actions—he is using abstract thought to observe concrete thought. Since Heidegger's universal theory explains everything in terms of Server actions, he defines abstract thought as present-at-hand, or in other words, a more distant form of potential action.

Because Heidegger has a *universal* Teacher theory of personal behavior, he can use the Teacher emotions generated by this theory to free himself from the emotional pressure of childish Mercy mental networks. Heidegger defines these childish mental networks by the Server behavior that they provoke: They cause a person to follow the crowd and do what everyone else does, which Heidegger calls inauthenticity.

Heidegger frees himself from this Mercy pressure by basing his Teacher theory upon the personal Server sequence of birth-life-death. Embracing this being-toward-death brings joy to Teacher thought because it adds generality to Heidegger's 'universal' theory of personal Server action. But personal death signifies the cessation of all personal action, which implies the end of all personal Mercy mental networks. When these Mercy mental networks die, Heidegger feels angst, and the world feels distant and uncanny. But because Heidegger's mind is now based upon a universal theory guided by personal Server actions, Heidegger becomes an authentic person who can choose what he will do, instead of being driven by the emotional demands of his community. However, when a *universal* Teacher theory is built directly upon my own *specific* Server actions, then I will always feel guilty for the simple reason that I am finite and must choose between various possibilities.

Like Heidegger, Judaism also builds a universal Teacher theory upon Server actions. But, unlike Heidegger, Judaism does not base its universal Teacher understanding upon the Server actions of the *individual* and *deny* the existence of Perceiver thought. Instead, it relates its universal Teacher theory to the Server actions of the *group*, and this focus upon the group *indirectly* prevents Perceiver facts from being applied to the individual. In religious terms, Judaism believes that a monotheistic God dictated to the Jews a detailed set of instructions telling them how they should behave, and that God chose the Jewish people to carry out a specific function in history.

Reinforcing this mental connection between the Server actions of the group and a universal Teacher theory of God is the Jewish sense of ethnic history, which sees God guiding the Server actions of the Jewish people throughout their long existence, starting with an 'eternal covenant' made almost four millennia ago between God, the descendants of Abraham, and the land of Israel. Thus, while both Heidegger and Judaism base their universal Teacher understanding upon Server actions and time, Heidegger shortens his Teacher theory to fit the finite lifespan of a single individual, whereas Judaism extends the actions of the individual through his descendents to fit the eternal 'lifespan' of a universal being.

Childish identity *identifies* with experiences that are pleasant, even if they do not apply directly to me. The idea that God has chosen my ethnic group is a pleasant one, therefore the tendency is for childish identity to make a mental leap from 'God has chosen my group' to 'God has chosen me'. It is interesting to note that Jewish scriptures attempt to forestall this Mercy identification by stating repeatedly that God's promises do *not* apply to every individual Jew but instead apply only to a 'believing remnant' of individuals within that group.

Heidegger says that the behavior of a person becomes authentic when he experiences and embraces the angst of his impending personal demise. Similarly, one notices that the Jewish people have gone through periods of angst several times in which they faced the impending demise of their ethnic group. Each time, the individuals who survived this trauma ended up transforming Jewish society into a form that was more authentic. For instance, the Jews of the Babylonian Exile provided the initial definition for the term *diaspora*, for they were able to continue their unique Jewish ways even when surrounded by *Das Man* of the surrounding culture. In the same way that Heidegger's authentic individual becomes distant from his world and holds on to the universal Teacher theory of his Server actions, so the Jewish diaspora became distant from their social environment and focused upon synagogue activity and the writing of the Talmud with its study of how the Jew should interpret and apply divine law.

In terms of the path of religious education, both Heidegger and Judaism perform the *second* major step of combining Server actions with general Teacher understanding and then go through the rebirth that is triggered by the angst of dying to traditional ways. However, what is missing is the *first* step of using Perceiver facts to define personal identity.

It is interesting to note that one of the major Jewish prophets during the first major episode of Jewish angst predicted that a new form of Jewish religion would emerge that would be based upon the individual instead of the group and which would apply Perceiver facts to subjective Mercy emotions.

Because Judaism applies Perceiver truth associated with God primarily to the group and not to the individual, this modifies the mental concept of the Holy Spirit. Instead of having a mental image of a Holy Spirit, the Jewish Diaspora has been motivated over the centuries by the internal vision of a renewed state of Israel. Similarly, Judaism refers to a spirit of God being connected with the *national* symbol of the religious temple. And rather than God becoming mentally connected with an internal *Mercy* image, the Jewish mindset connects God with a set of Server actions, leading to the concept of divine wisdom.

Likewise, instead of having a concept of incarnation, in which an image of God connects with the individual through Contributor mode, the group of Israel takes the place of incarnation, because it reveals God to other ethnic groups through the actions of the Jewish people.

And just as Heidegger replaces a Perceiver-based conscience with one rooted in Server actions, so the typical Jew views laws through the Server lens of doing and not in Perceiver terms of being. Thus, childish identity is not seen as being in a *state* of sin but rather having a tendency to *do* evil, and the person who sins is expected to *do* better next time.

The concept of 'divinely chosen group' can be made compatible with rational thought *if* the members of this group exhibit behavior that demonstrates an unusual level of Teacher order and understanding. This does not prove that this group *is* chosen by God or prove that God *exists*, but it does give this group the mental tools that are needed to replace Mercy mental networks of tribalism with Teacher mental networks of rational understanding while continuing to hold on to the concept of being 'chosen by God'.

If one looks at Judaism and Christianity in the light of the path of religious education, one notes that Christianity emphasizes the *first* step of applying Perceiver facts to personal identity, but it can only partially enter the second step of combining Server actions with Teacher understanding because Christian doctrine has not been described as a general Teacher theory. In contrast, Judaism emphasizes the *second* step of combining Server actions with Teacher understanding but it partially skips the first step because the concept of God choosing a group of people to inhabit a plot of land has not been fully digested mentally. Thus, Christians experience the third stage of rebirth as *individuals*, whereas Judaism goes through the third stage of rebirth as a *group*.

These two subsets of religion can be integrated in one of two ways. The *constructive* way combines the personal element of Christianity as a rational theory with the group element of Jewish research and application. The *destructive* way combines the Christian mindset of revealed 'truth' with the Jewish attitude of chosen race.

Moving on to the final topic of aliens, humans use *concrete* thought to live in a world of Mercy matter and Perceiver objects. However, it is possible for the human mind to live in an abstract world composed of Teacher waves and Server sequences. Mentally speaking, concrete and abstract thought are symmetrical; one mental circuit is the mirror image of the other. But concrete thought is concrete because it is hooked up to a physical body, whereas abstract thought functions in an abstract manner because of the nature of the physical environment. External repeatability occurs either when the same facts and sequences *accompany* a person wherever he goes, leading to concrete specifics, or when the same facts and sequences are *encountered* wherever a person goes, resulting in abstract generality.

The human circuit of concrete thought begins with the three input stages of Mercy experiences, Perceiver facts, and Contributor choices, which leads to the output stage of Server actions. However, it is possible to hypothesize the existence of an alien circuit of 'concrete' thought which would begin with the three input stages of Teacher waves, Server sequences, and Contributor choices, and lead to the output stage of Perceiver power. This type of mental container is like a *name*, and this type of personal existence is partially illustrated by the *profession*. When humans cooperate to develop civilization, then specialization combined with government regulation causes them to create artificial modes of existence which illustrate abstract alien modes of existence.

If the childish mind had both a human body and an alien name, then output from one mental circuit would shortcut mental development of the other circuit, leading to a juxtaposition of physical super-powers with mental infancy. Additionally, the absence of general thought would prevent the mind from forming a concept of God.

Both science and personal identity would find an alien mode of existence emotionally threatening. Science bases itself upon the Teacher mental network of common sense that comes from observing the external world. Alien existence would not share this Teacher mental network, and so science must protect itself from the possibility of hyper-pain by insisting that supernatural existence has no theoretical validity. Personal identity is based upon the Mercy mental network that represents the physical body. An alien being would not possess such a body, therefore encountering an alien creature would face the typical human with the Mercy hyper-pain of angst.

A human mind lives within a Perceiver world of objects, experiences specific Mercy emotions, and acquires Teacher feelings through order-within-complexity. An alien mind would live within a Server 'world' of sequences, experience the specific Teacher feelings of order within a *small* package, together with the general Mercy emotion of mutual beneficial interaction—otherwise known as love. A human exists within a specific Perceiver-defined *location*. He then uses Server actions to *move* from one location to another. For the alien 'body', a Server task would define 'location', while 'movement' would involve using Perceiver mode to teleport from one task to another.

If humans and aliens have the same minds, and if religion can be defined in terms of the mind, then this means that humans and aliens would share the same religion. But this religious convergence would only be apparent at the end of the path of religious education, because that is when abstract thought and concrete thought become mentally integrated. And a single incarnation could act as intermediary for both human and alien because Contributor mode can integrate the *four* elements of specific Mercy, general Mercy, specific Teacher, and general Teacher. In religious terms, the initial alien concept of 'God' would correspond to the human concept of the Holy Spirit and vice versa, and these would eventually converge to the concept of a divine Trinity held together by a Contributor incarnation.

If human and alien thought were integrated *internally* through the path of religious education, then this could lead to an external environment which combined these two modes of existence. However, if external means were used to bridge these two, then the mind probably would not be able to handle this dichotomy and would split into isolated mental networks, each triggered by the corresponding external environment.

Objective science is not compatible with alien intervention, because objective science insists that natural laws are never violated. However, science can handle the concept of God by extending the mental Agency Detector to include *general* Teacher thought, and it could incorporate the concept of aliens by extending the mental Agency Detector to include *specific* Teacher thought.

Bibliography

Barrett, J. L. (2004). *Why Would Anyone Believe in God?* Lanhan, MD: Altamira Press.

Fieser, J. (2011). Retrieved from Internet Encyclopedia of Philosophy: http://www.iep.utm.edu/

Foucault, M. (1970). *The Order of Things: An Archaeology of the Human Sciences.* Pantheon Books.

Friesen, L. (2006). *All Sorts of People: Ordered Complexity.* Victoria, BC: Trafford Publishing.

Gallwey, W. T. (1974). *The Inner Game of Tennis.* New York: Random House.

Heidegger, M. (1996). *Being and Time.* Albany: State University of New York Press.

Kuhn, T. S. (1996). *The Structure of Scientific Revolutions, Third Edition.* Chicago: The University of Chicago Press.

Quine, W. V. (1978). *The Web of Belief.* McGraw-Hill.

Tremlin, T. (2006). *Minds and Gods: The Cognitive Foundations of Religion.* Oxford: Oxford University Press.

Zalta, E. N. (2011). Retrieved from The Stanford Encyclopedia of Philosophy: http://plato.stanford.edu/

❋ Cp and Ci Explained

In the main text, the mental circuits of Cp and Ci are treated as black boxes that work with networks of Perceiver content and Server content. For those who want more details, here is a description of what is happening within the black boxes. Remember that both Cp and Ci are mental circuits which can potentially involve the participation of all seven cognitive modules. However, these mental circuits are being controlled by Contributor mode and limited by Contributor concentration. We will look first at the circuit of Cp, which works with concrete thought.

Cp

Bottom Line: The bottom line is the specific emotional Mercy experience that Contributor mode is attempting to achieve, acquire, improve, or avoid. It could also be referred to as the *goal* which Contributor mode is attempting to reach. When the Contributor person is pursuing a bottom line, he may specialize, ignore unrelated fields, and even modify his personal character in order to gain better results in this particular area.

A bottom line exists within a map of *value*, which is constructed by using Perceiver facts to compare emotional Mercy experiences. Cp requires a map of value to function, but this map of value is constructed by cognitive modules which function *before* Contributor mode and *independently* of Contributor mode. If Perceiver thought is able to function in the presence of personal Mercy feelings, then the bottom line will be related to personal identity. The result will be enlightened *selfishness*, in which the ultimate goal is to bring lasting improvements to personal identity.

When Perceiver thought has sufficient confidence to evaluate emotional experiences, then it becomes possible to work out the emotional pleasure that is *inherent* in each specific situation. For instance, this means choosing to eat an apple because it tastes good and is nourishing, not because it looks good, is recommended by others, is popular, is cheap, or is regarded as a luxury item. Pursuing a goal for its *inherent* emotions is positive-sum, because the pleasure of one person is not diminished when other people also acquire the same goal.

However, it is difficult for Perceiver thought to operate in the presence of strong emotions. Therefore, in most cases, Cp pursues a lesser bottom line. If the core of personal identity is defined by mental networks that must not be altered, then Cp will improve *peripheral* aspects of personal identity which can be changed while leaving the core of personal identity untouched. This could be compared to buying expensive art while neglecting the eyes that are needed to enjoy art.

If Perceiver mode cannot function in the presence of Mercy emotions, then Contributor mode will take an *existing* set of Perceiver facts and treat it *as* a map of value. One option is to take the Perceiver 'truth' that is defined by people with emotional status and view this as a mental map. Cp will then pursue the bottom line of acquiring and increasing personal status. In this case, success will be defined primarily by the opinions of people. Because people can only judge what they observe, what will really matter is the *appearance* of success. Treating personal status as a bottom line is zero-sum and leads to personal competition, because people are finite beings with a limited amount of attention. If one person receives more personal status, then this means that another person must receive less.

Another option is to take some objective area where Perceiver thought can function and *add* Mercy emotions. For instance, think of the runner who is trying to set a new world record. There is minimal inherent pleasure in running around a track for a few minutes. But because this bottom line relates to the physical body, it easy to compare, measure, and quantify. Therefore, the athlete who is using Cp will give up valuable experiences and items in order to shave a few seconds off his time. Emotional status can be used to increase the level of Mercy emotions when improving objective areas. For instance, if a runner sets a new world record, then he will become famous. But this leads to zero-sum competition, because in order for one person to win a race, others must lose the race. In order to avoid zero-sum competition, an athlete will often 'compete against himself' by defining success as 'achieving a personal best'.

Emotions can also be added to objective Perceiver facts through the use of *Forms*. This generally happens with *money*. Money serves primarily the *Perceiver* function of making it possible to *compare* the value of one item with another; value itself is indicated by the emotional label that is attached to each specific item in Mercy thought. The problem arises when business attempts to remain objective by *ignoring* these Mercy emotions of value, because emotion will then be *added* to economic thought via the *Form* of money. Remember that a Form is an imaginary Mercy image that emerges when a general Teacher theory modifies Perceiver facts. The Teacher order-within-complexity of an economic system will lead to Perceiver facts about money which will generate the Form of money within Mercy thought—a sort of idealized coin or bill that does not correspond to any physical coin or bill. Think, for instance, of the typical caricature of the businessman with dollar signs in his eyes; that portrays the Form of money. The emotion produced by the *Form* of money will then turn into a bottom line; what began as a way for *Perceiver* thought to compare value has now become a goal within *Mercy* thought.

For example, suppose that it were possible to gather 'kilometers'. While most people would be using kilometers to measure distance, others would be attempting to acquire kilometers. Obviously, this would end up distorting physical measurement, because those who had all of the 'kilometers' could disregard physical distance and use their surplus 'kilometers' to buy up the 'kilometers' of others, effectively shortening distance for them and lengthening distance for others. With physical distance, this makes no sense, but with money this describes the norm, because those who treat money as a *Mercy* bottom line will distort its use as a *Perceiver* comparison.

Now that we have looked at the map of value that provides the *assumed foundation* for Cp, let us look at the actual operation of Cp itself.

Opportunity: The circuit of Cp compares all Mercy experiences with the current bottom line. If a specific Mercy situation has the potential of increasing this bottom line, then it becomes an *opportunity*.

Seeing an opportunity usually occurs automatically and subconsciously in the Contributor *person* as subconscious Exhorter mode finds excitement in the emotions of some Mercy opportunity. The Contributor person often looks at a situation and responds, "Someone should do something here. There is an opportunity waiting to be pursued."

Cost-Benefit Analysis: Once an opportunity has been spotted, then the next step is *cost-benefit analysis*: personal identity is currently 'here'; the opportunity is 'there'. Reaching 'there' has an emotional payoff; letting go of 'here' has an emotional cost. Getting from 'here' to 'there' also has a cost—in this case the cost of performing the Server steps necessary to complete the journey. If the benefit is greater than the cost, then Cp may choose to pursue the opportunity.

Opportunity spotting is driven primarily by Exhorter mode and Exhorter imagination. Cost-benefit, in contrast, uses Contributor mode to *evaluate* an opportunity that was uncovered by Exhorter imagination, by examining the Perceiver facts and Server skills that are involved in *reaching* this opportunity. Thus, the typical Exhorter *person* finds it easy to discover opportunities, but his natural tendency is to plunge in without performing detailed cost-benefit analysis, and then to move on to the next opportunity when problems arise.

Contingency Planning: Once an opportunity has been checked out using cost-benefit analysis, then the *path* that leads to this opportunity needs to be explored for possible unwanted consequences or dead ends. Therefore, the Contributor person who is constructing a plan will use conscious thought to mentally 'walk' through all the aspects of the plan in order to see if subconscious Exhorter mode is attracted to any potential problems. For each possible Mercy disaster, Contributor mode will then work out a Server step that can put the plan back on track. Similarly, other cognitive styles will use conscious thought, sensory input, or advice from other individuals to 'jostle' their minds into exploring the various side roads and byways of a potential plan.

Optimization: The final aspect of practical Contributor thought is *optimization*. This takes an operating plan and replaces elements of it with equivalent parts that perform the same function but improve the Mercy bottom line. This method is illustrated by the *simplex method*, a popular computer algorithm.

Optimization has a cost associated with it. The benefits of optimization are only worth this cost if a specific plan is going to be repeated enough times. If a plan will only be carried out a few times, then a quick-and-dirty solution may be more cost effective. In contrast, a plan that is repeated many times may warrant extensive optimization.

Optimization can have major consequences because it involves *replacing* subsections of a plan with their equivalent. For instance, suppose that a car manufacturer decides to replace the gasoline engine in its cars with electric motors. One is equivalent to the other because both provide motive force for a car. However, if gasoline engines stop being manufactured, then this will have major implications for all of the sub-industries that gain their livelihood from making engine parts.

Optimization can be mentally damaging when Cp is only functioning in *peripheral* areas. Suppose that the core of personal identity is governed by Mercy mental networks which are not allowed to be changed. Cp will then function in less emotional areas. Now suppose that either the success of Cp causes new mental networks to emerge, or that personal failure causes core mental networks to fall into doubt. Optimization may then decide to radically alter or even sacrifice core aspects of personal identity in order to optimize peripheral areas. One thinks, for instance, of the entertainer or politician who fabricates an official life history in order to increase his popularity, or the businessman who changes his personality or abandons his moral standards in order to optimize his ability to make money.

Optimization improves the bottom line by removing sub-elements that are deemed to be non-critical, but this often has the unintended side-effect of making it more difficult to *leave* the current plan of Cp and adopt *another* plan. That is because elements which are unneeded in one plan may play an essential role in another plan. One often reads of companies going bankrupt because they ignored processes or technologies which later became critical when the market shifted.

Facilitator thought also optimizes; however, Facilitator optimization functions in an *analog* manner by emphasizing certain elements and downplaying other elements; Facilitator optimization will only remove elements if they violate the norm in a major way. Because Facilitator mode operates 'downstream' from Contributor mode, Facilitator processing can restore smoothness to the digital decisions made by Contributor mode, and the Contributor *person* who is a manager often has an executive secretary who is a Facilitator *person*. In this type of situation, if the Contributor person tells the Facilitator person to eliminate some major subcomponent in the interest of optimization, then the Facilitator person may use *Facilitator* optimization to implement this decision, emphasizing the new while still preserving critical elements of the old. This Facilitator subordination can lead to institutional foot-dragging when major change is required, but it can also save an institution by making it possible to follow 'plan B' when 'plan A' fails or when the market shifts.

One can summarize the various elements of Cp by using the analogy of a trip: Opportunity spots an attractive location on the horizon; cost-benefit checks the wallet along with the price of gas in order to see if it is worth going there; contingency planning examines the route for potential potholes, filling stations, restaurants, and bandits. Finally, once the trip has been taken several times, then optimization searches for a better route or a more economical vehicle.

Because the Contributor *person* is conscious at the center of this mental circuit, he is naturally better at performing these various technical steps, but his analysis also tends to be 'narrow-minded', getting all of the details right, but unaware of the larger picture. When Contributor persons set the standard for society, then personal success becomes defined as the ability to achieve technical excellence within some restricted area. Thus, for instance, the Olympic athlete is celebrated because he can run a fifty yard dash a few milliseconds faster than his opponent.

Ci

We divided Cp into the stages of opportunity, cost/benefit, contingency planning, and optimization. It appears that Ci also goes through similar stages. We will take a few paragraphs to look at the 'mental map' that guides Ci before examining the function of Ci itself.

Intellectual Bottom Line: Server sequences make it possible to *compare* one general Teacher theory with another. Cp has to deal with the problem of *too much* data: The physical body fills Mercy thought with emotional experiences, while physical appearance either suggests or imposes facts upon Perceiver thought. Ci, in contrast, has to work with *insufficient* information: Teacher words have no inherent emotion and Server sequences and procedures must be constructed.

One option is to use the Mercy emotions of personal approval to substitute for Teacher emotions. This happens, for instance, in a debate, a political campaign, or a trial, in which Ci uses words to convince people to give personal approval to arguments. By setting up formal Server procedures, it becomes possible to determine winners and losers more clearly. Obviously, this type of intellectual thought is zero-sum, because each speaker is attempting to convert listeners to his point of view.

Another option is to build Teacher generality by having more *people* use certain words or theories. This is the method used by *teaching*, which increases Teacher generality by spreading a theory to more people. For instance, everyone regards Benjamin Franklin to be a significant individual, because everyone learned about Franklin in school. Similarly, a religion can increase the feelings of Teacher generality that are associated with its theology by gaining more converts who use these words. *Broadcasting* is an effective way of spreading a message to many different people at the same time. Thus, if something or someone appears on television or goes viral on the Internet, then it will acquire Teacher emotions of generality.

It is easy for teaching to confuse speech with understanding. If many people say certain words, then this will give the impression that these words have Teacher generality. However, this does not mean that people understand what they are saying. For instance, most people can say $E = mc^2$ and associate these words with Einstein, but few people understand the meaning behind this equation.

Teaching tends to be zero-sum because spending more time on one topic invariably means spending less time on another. A *curriculum* makes it possible to compare the relative generality of each Teacher theory by quantifying how much time will be devoted to teaching each theory.

Finally, it is possible to look for Server sequences that are repeated and use these to build general Teacher theories. This is the method that science uses to build its general Teacher theories, because it searches for *natural* sequences which occur repeatedly in the *external* world. Similarly, mental symmetry looks for *cognitive* sequences which occur repeatedly in different areas of human thought. Scientific research is positive-sum because each person can independently build Teacher understanding by searching for Server sequences.

Approval and teaching are *artificial* ways of creating Teacher generality; research, in contrast, looks for *inherent* generality. The theory of mental symmetry illustrates the contrast between approval, teaching, and research. Because mental symmetry is a new theory, not many people use it, and because it deals with topics that tend to be avoided, it does not naturally receive approval. Thus, when viewed from the vantage point of 'audience share', it currently has low Teacher generality. However, because mental symmetry appears to describe generality which is *inherent* in mental processing, it has significant Teacher generality from a research perspective.

Now that we have described the mental foundation upon which Ci can be built, let us look at how Ci itself functions.

Intellectual Opportunity: First, there is the intellectual *opportunity*. This emerges when Exhorter mode is attracted to the strong emotions associated with some general Teacher concept. Because Perceiver facts tend to limit Teacher theories, Exhorter mode is often attracted to Teacher theories that contain the most uncertain Perceiver facts, because this gives Teacher thought the freedom to overgeneralize, which inflates the Teacher emotion of a general theory, making it more exciting for Exhorter mode.

However, if Perceiver thought is being used to *build connections* between theories, then the presence of clearly defined Perceiver facts makes it possible to increase Teacher generality by *translating* one theory into the language of another, leading to a combined theory with greater order-within-complexity.

Intellectual Cost/Benefit: Next, there is the intellectual equivalent of *cost/benefit* analysis. The *benefit* of building a Teacher theory is the Teacher emotion produced by a general theory. The *cost* is the emotional price of letting go of the current explanation combined with the cost of learning a new set of facts. As Kuhn mentions, going through a paradigm change is mentally costly, because it involves rebuilding emotional structures. That is why graduate students tend to be the most open to learning new theories. They have the skills that are needed to build general understanding, while they have not yet invested major time and effort in any specific theory. As Thomas Kuhn states, professors are often close-minded to new paradigms, because the cost that they would have to pay to learn a new Teacher theory is usually too great.

In a similar vein, most religious conversions occur at an earlier age before a person has developed a complete worldview. Likewise, computer users often find it easier to stay with an existing computer program rather than install a new program and learn how to use it. This also explains why bureaucratic methods tend to become entrenched.

Intellectual Contingency Planning: Intellectual *contingency planning* examines a theory for potential holes and logical contradictions. This describes what one does when preparing for a debate or argument: "If he says this, then how will I respond?" or "What is my counterargument to his argument?" As with Cp, Ci gives Exhorter mode the freedom to explore the various mental pathways for potential problems, to which Contributor mode responds by coming up with Perceiver facts that will bring the discussion back on track. The Contributor *person* can excel at debate and may do almost anything to avoid losing an argument. Unfortunately, when Perceiver thought is mesmerized and Mercy emotions determine Perceiver 'facts' and Perceiver 'beliefs', then winning a debate turns into using Mercy emotions to establish the Perceiver 'facts' that back up the Teacher theory which is being defended. Therefore, the 'successful' debater will make frequent references to 'sacred cows' such as God, country, apple pie, and The American Way—or whatever describes the local version of this combination.

The development of the machine and the computer program has expanded the application of contingency planning. Ci will be used to test machines to see how they could break or malfunction and then come up with ways of either avoiding or recovering from these situations. Similarly, contingency planning will search for bugs in computer programs and either fix the bugs or else develop workarounds.

Intellectual optimization: Intellectual *optimization* occurs when theories or systems of order are well established. For instance, this is the type of thinking that is used when setting up a process for assembly line operation. The goal here is not to achieve some Mercy bottom line, but rather to increase Teacher order-within-complexity by eliminating unnecessary steps, reducing periods of inactivity, shortening movement, or using new processes.

For instance, optimizing a machine will either modify parts in order to reduce unnecessary material or else replace one part with another one which does the same function in a more efficient way. Similar, optimizing a computer program will focus upon speeding up portions of code which are run frequently or else replace one subroutine with an equivalent program that is more efficient.

Notice that the same process can be subjected to both intellectual and practical optimization. Intellectual optimization tries to increase *Teacher* feelings of efficiency and avoid the Teacher pain of unreliability; practical optimization attempts to increase the *Mercy* pleasure of benefit and reduce the Mercy pain of cost. These two methods often come to similar goals, but not always. There is an old engineering proverb that says: "Good, cheap, fast. Pick any two."

✵ Piaget, Maslow, and Kohlberg

Jean Piaget is famous for his theory of cognitive development. I first read about Piaget's research back in the late 1980s, and so my early thinking was probably influenced by his work. Abraham Maslow is known for his hierarchy of needs. Like most people, I am familiar with this hierarchy, but I only thought about it in detail when writing this section. Lawrence Kohlberg extended Piaget's development stages to the area of morality, and I only encountered his model in 2011. Thus, I would like to take a few pages to examine these models in the light of the theory of mental symmetry. I suggest that it is possible to explain them in terms of cognitive modules and mental networks. Information about these two models was taken primarily from Wikipedia and then checked by 'googling' the topic.

Jean Piaget

Let us begin with Piaget's four stages of development:

1) **Sensorimotor stage:** Piaget says that this stage lasts from birth to the development of language, which occurs at about the age of two. During this period, interaction with the physical body leads to the development of *concrete* thought (not to be confused with Piaget's use of the word concrete).

Let us look at this in more detail. As we have mentioned elsewhere, emotional experiences from the physical body program Mercy mode in the newborn infant. A baby also learns how to control his physical body, leading to the development of Server mode. In addition, the baby repeats actions that lead to pleasurable results, combining Server actions with emotional Mercy goals.

Around one year of age, hand-eye coordination begins to emerge, indicating that Perceiver mode is starting to tie together the 'means' of Server actions with 'end' of Mercy goals. This leads to goal-oriented behavior, in which the child plans and executes steps in order to meet a goal, which shows that Contributor thought is starting to 'wake up'. The infant then begins to work out *new* ways of reaching goals and meeting challenges, which tells us that the circuit of Cp is starting to function.

Notice that this mental development is occurring entirely as a result of existing within a physical body and is limited to the use of the physical body. By the end of this period, the core of *physical* identity has formed. According to Piaget, this stage ends with the development of object permanence, in which the child realizes that an object continues to exist even when it cannot be physically sensed, leading us to conclude that Perceiver thought has developed to the point where it can form lasting facts about real objects.

2) **Preoperational Stage:** This stage lasts between the ages of two and seven. During this stage, language develops and the child learns how to represent and utilize objects through the use of images, words, and drawings. The development of language tells us that *abstract* thought is starting to function—at the basic level of speech. Teacher thought learns how to work with words, and these words are being assigned Perceiver meanings based upon the Perceiver facts about real objects that were learned at the end of the previous stage.

Notice that Teacher thought acquires its basic mental building blocks of words directly from the external environment *independently* of other cognitive modules. However, all of the meanings that are assigned to words, as well as the theories which are constructed out of words, depend upon content which is provided by *other* cognitive modules.

During the first *symbolic function* substage, mental networks develop within Mercy thought, and these mental networks control thinking. The child play acts, pretending to be people he encounters, such as 'mommy' or 'a fireman'. The child also practices animism, treating inanimate objects as living beings with feelings. In essence, one could say that thought is being controlled by a Mercy-based Agency Detector. However, the concept of self-image is not yet present, because the thinking of the child is still egocentric. In other words, the child can use mental networks within Mercy thought, but he lacks the ability to use Perceiver thought to observe these mental networks from 'next door'.

The *intuitive thought* substage occurs between about four and seven. Perceiver mode begins to operate independently during this stage, as the child collects mental facts. However, these facts remain isolated, and they do not mentally connect together. The child will 'centrate', focusing upon one Perceiver fact to the exclusion of another, and not realizing that one fact is related to another fact, even if they are obviously connected. Thus, we conclude that Perceiver thought is now functioning at the level of facts, but Teacher thought has not yet started to use Perceiver facts to build general theories.

3) **Concrete Operational Stage:** This stage occurs between the ages of seven and eleven. During this stage, the child learns how to use logic, which tells us that *abstract* thought is now functioning at a level that goes beyond words and speech. However, the child can only use abstract thought to work with concrete information. Abstract thought cannot yet function independently of concrete thought.

The child learns how to examine situations from another person's viewpoint, indicating the emergence of self-image. This describes intuitive psychology, in which Perceiver thought learns how to describe and compare existing mental networks within Mercy thought. The child stops thinking magically, and no longer treats inanimate objects as alive, telling us that Perceiver thought is now able to function independently of Mercy mental networks, and that Teacher-driven mental networks based in common sense are starting to interpret information. And the child learns that objects that appear different can actually be similar, indicating that Perceiver facts are becoming internally connected.

Finally, the child learns how to bring order to physical objects by arranging them or classifying them, indicating that Perceiver objects are being used to construct Teacher order-within-complexity. Thus, the child can construct general Teacher theories as long as these theories involve concrete facts and real objects.

4) **Formal Operational Stage:** This final stage starts at about the age of eleven. The teenager is capable of abstract thinking and can work with hypothetical situations, telling us that abstract thought is now able to function independently of concrete thought. In addition, the ability to do logical proofs indicates that the circuit of Ci can now start to function. Platonic Forms also start to exist within the mind of the teenager, because he can now mentally envision how things could be and can understand imaginary 'objects' such as love and justice.

Summarizing the previous paragraphs:

Sensorimotor Stage: Concrete thought develops using the physical body.

Preoperational Stage: Abstract thought develops using words. Mercy mental networks guide thought.

Concrete Operational Stage: Perceiver thought becomes independent of Mercy mental networks. Abstract thought builds Teacher theories using concrete Perceiver facts.

Formal Operational Stage: Abstract thought becomes independent of concrete thought. As abstract thought builds general Teacher theories, Perceiver facts become independent of Mercy experiences, leading to the formation of imaginary images within Mercy thought.

Abraham Maslow

Most people are familiar with Maslow's hierarchy of needs. Maslow said that fundamental human needs must be satisfied before dealing with higher needs, and that higher needs emerge when more basic needs are sufficiently satisfied.

Physiological Needs: The most basic human need is physical survival. This is the result of being trapped within a vulnerable physical body for the duration of human life. Since mental programming *starts* with sensory input from the physical body, this is obviously the most basic need. In order to become free of physiological need, a person would have to mentally construct a personal identity that was independent of the physical body and then acquire the ability to exist as a disembodied mind/spirit.

Safety Needs: The next need is personal safety. Maslow defines this primarily in terms of physical safety: Is the physical body safe; is physical health protected; are physical possessions safe. Maslow is referring here to anything that is related to *physical* identity. Using the language of mental symmetry, the Mercy mental network that represents my physical body must not be threatened by impeding fragmentation. *Physiological* need refers to the physical body itself, while *safety* need involves the mental network within Mercy thought that represents the physical body.

Love and Belonging: Maslow then turns his attention to *mental* identity—the aspect of personal identity that goes beyond the physical body: Does a person feel a sense of belonging and acceptance; does he have friendship, intimacy, and family. Again we are dealing with protecting a Mercy mental network from fragmentation, but in this case it is the mental network which represents the *emotional* side of personal identity.

Note that mental identity is being defined in terms of its relationship to other Mercy mental networks. This is because mental identity begins its existence held together by 'facts': People and groups with emotional status are mesmerizing Perceiver thought into 'knowing' what is true, and this 'knowledge' is holding mental identity together.

Esteem: Maslow says the next level of personal need is respect, self-esteem, and self-respect. Maslow divides this into a lower and a higher need. The lower need is for status, recognition, attention, or fame from *others*, whereas the higher need is for self-respect based in freedom, independence, and an internal sense of competence gained through experience.

The first three needs dealt with *integrity*: the integrity of the physical body, the integrity of physical identity, and the integrity of mental identity. Thus, they all involve some form of *hyper*-emotion. The need for esteem deals with *normal* emotion. Once physical identity and mental identity hold together, then it is possible to improve how they feel. In essence, Maslow is affirming that hyper-emotion takes precedence over normal emotion.

Maslow's lower need makes personal identity feel better by using positive emotions from people who are respected. Thus, if my father says 'well done', or my teacher gives me an A+, then my self-esteem goes up. This is a 'lower need' because it uses *external* input from *other* people to make mental identity feel better. Because the facts about mental identity are being determined by emotional 'knowing' based in people whom I respect, it is easy to make personal identity feel better by using positive statements from people whom I respect to change these 'facts'. Thus, a verbal pat on the back from someone whom I respect is a shortcut to feeling good about myself. But by a similar token, a verbal attack from someone whom I respect is also a shortcut to feeling bad about myself.

Maslow's 'higher need' builds self-esteem through *internal* mechanisms of competence, skills, mastery, and accomplishment. In the language of mental symmetry, when a person becomes capable of *repeatedly* and *reliably* producing good Mercy results, then Perceiver thought gains the confidence to believe that these good Mercy experiences are part of personal identity. Because this good self-image is based upon repetition, it is stable; because it is based in confidence, it leads to self-confidence; because it does not require positive statements from others, it leads to freedom; and because it is independent of the opinions of others, it leads to independence.

Maslow says that these two forms of self-esteem are related, and that an internal definition of self-esteem will take precedence over external approval or disapproval. Mental symmetry goes further and suggests that it is possible to replace the 'lower' method with the 'higher' method by going through a process of personal rebirth. In addition, this process of rebirth can be made easier by keeping one aspect of personal identity stable while rebuilding the other aspect. Thus, protecting physical identity makes it possible to endure the mental pain of rebuilding mental identity, and vice versa.

Self-actualization: Maslow's highest need is that of self-actualization, defined as 'what a man can be, he must be'. Mental symmetry would interpret this as mental functioning which is *consistent* with the Mercy mental network that represents personal identity and/or the Teacher mental network that represents personal skills. (Teacher thought is included because personal identity begins in Mercy thought with personal experiences, but expands to include Server skills, and these Server skills can lead to the formation of mental networks within Teacher thought.) In simple terms, every mental network feels satisfaction when it experiences mental activity that is consistent with its structure. A person feels self-actualized when the mental network that represents personal identity experiences mental activity that is consistent with its structure.

Mental symmetry suggests that the most basic form of self-actualization is the ability to express conscious thought. For instance, the Exhorter person will only feel self-actualized if he is able to function in a way that uses and satisfies the Exhorter module. When the mind is fragmented, then a person will often express conscious thought at the expense of disabling or frustrating subconscious cognitive modules. However, it is also possible to use conscious thought in a way that both permits and encourages other cognitive modules to operate. Thus, there is a *hardware* side to self-actualization based in cognitive style which is more fundamental than the *software* side to self-actualization which is rooted in the mental networks of personal identity.

Expressing a personal mental network enhances the *integrity* of that mental network. Reaching one's potential goes one step further and expresses personal mental networks in a way that leads to *good* emotions. For Mercy thought, this means producing pleasant results; for Teacher thought it means performing professionally, elegantly, and error-free.

According to Maslow, people who have reached self-actualization embrace reality and facts instead of denying truth. This implies that Perceiver facts are being used to define personal identity, for the mental network that represents personal identity will only *resonate* with reality and the facts if its structure is *consistent* with reality and the facts. Self-actualized people are also spontaneous, telling us that the mind is naturally functioning in a self-consistent manner, and that one cognitive module is not trying to censor or inhibit another cognitive module. Such a person is 'focused upon problems outside of himself' because the more basic issues of defining self and being true to self have been solved. One could say that the focus is upon using the car to drive places rather than upon continually stopping to tinker with the car or attempting to fix the car when it breaks down. Finally, a self-actualized person accepts his own human nature and tends to accept others, telling us explicitly that the mind is functioning in a manner which allows the mental network that represents personal identity to express itself without inhibition.

One criticism which has been made of Maslow's scheme is that it regards sex as an aspect of the lowest physiological level of the hierarchy. I suggest that this confusion arises because sex has both a physical and an emotional component. The physical component involves an interaction between two *physical* bodies, which is at the lowest level of Maslow's hierarchy. But the emotional component involves an interaction between two mental networks that represent the *emotional* side of personal identity. In order to interact at this emotional level, one must first *define* these mental networks, which means building a stable internal concept of mental identity, which describes the higher level of Maslow's Esteem level.

Summarizing:

Physiological help preserves the integrity of the physical body.

Safety preserves the integrity of physical identity—the mental network that represents the physical body.

Love and Belonging preserves the integrity of mental identity—the mental network that represents the emotional part of personal identity.

Esteem uses a lower and/or a higher method to improve the feelings associated with the mental networks that represent personal identity.

Self-actualization uses the mind in a way that is consistent with cognitive style and personal identity, and it attempts to function in a manner that produces the best Mercy and Teacher feelings for personal identity.

Lawrence Kohlberg

Kohlberg extended the work of Piaget to come up with six stages of moral development. Mental symmetry defines conscience as a Perceiver connection between cause and effect which applies to personal identity within Mercy thought. A rule of conscience can be given emotional strength either by a Mercy mental network representing some person, or by a Teacher mental network representing God or some social or governmental institution.

Kohlberg states that a child's sense of morality shifts when he enters Piaget's formal operational stage. Before this, moral judgment is based upon *external* consequences, indicating that Perceiver facts are being determined by concrete facts and physical objects. After this age, the teenager takes *motive* into account, telling us that Perceiver thought is now able to work with internal facts that are *independent* of physical reality. In addition, younger children regard rules as fixed and unchangeable, indicating that mental functioning is under the control of existing Mercy mental networks.

Now let us look at Kohlberg's six stages of morality, which he organizes into the three levels of pre-conventional, conventional, and post-conventional.

1) **Obedience and Punishment Orientation:** Here, the individual focuses upon the consequences of actions. An action is bad simply because it is punished. Rules must be

obeyed, they cannot be changed, and they are handed down by those who are in authority.

Mental symmetry says that a rule of conscience forms when a Perceiver connection of cause-and-effect applies to personal identity within Mercy thought, and that a rule of conscience can be given cognitive power by being connected with a Mercy mental network. In the child, Mercy mental networks come from parents and other authority figures. For the child who is in Piaget's preoperational stage, Mercy mental networks determine thought and cannot be questioned. Therefore, any rule of conscience which is connected with a Mercy mental network will be viewed as fixed and immutable. However, because Perceiver thought is still fragmented, rules of conscience will be dependent upon Mercy mental networks and a rule of conscience will only be mentally triggered when the appropriate Mercy mental network is active. Thus, conscience will be viewed purely as the possibility of being punished by a powerful person.

2) **Self-interest Driven:** This type of conscience is based upon 'you scratch my back, I'll scratch yours'. In other words, it is guided by a type of barter system in which mutual favors are exchanged, expressed by the phrase 'I owe you one'.

Commerce and conscience appear to use the same mental combination of cause-and-effect applied to personal identity. In conscience, doing something bad is expected to lead to a negative payback from some significant person, while in commerce, doing something good is expected to lead to a positive payback from some significant person. This type of barter system, which is marked by an exchange of favors, describes the first stage in commerce, and corresponds to Kohlberg's self-interest driven conscience.

Such thinking emerges when practical Contributor mode (which is rooted in personal cause-and-effect) attempts to function in a mental environment composed of Mercy mental networks by pursuing 'opportunities' of receiving approval and by using 'contingency planning' to avoid disapproval.

3) **Interpersonal Accord and Conformity Driven:** At this stage, morality is driven by a desire to fulfil social roles. A person may try to be a 'good boy' or a 'good girl'. This tells us that the child is functioning at the level of intuitive psychology and that Perceiver thought is being used to compare and organize Mercy mental networks, because what is being followed is an ideal internalized image of what a person should be, rather than the commands of any specific Mercy mental network. One can also tell that Platonic Forms are emerging because the person now relates conscience to internal motives such as love, empathy, trust, and concern.

Platonic Forms develop when Perceiver facts are modified by general Teacher theories. The development of Teacher theories makes it possible for the emotional focus to shift from Mercy thought to Teacher thought. Thus, conscience is no longer determined solely by *Mercy* mental networks of powerful people but also by *Teacher* mental networks based in general concepts of social roles.

4) **Authority and Social Order Obedience Driven:** In the previous stage, there was a balance between Mercy mental networks and Teacher mental networks. Here, the balance shifts to Teacher mental networks, because the goal is no longer to acquire approval from individuals, but rather to transcend the requirements of the individual and focus upon society as a whole. Saying this another way, the emphasis is upon *law and order* as an abstract entity and not upon specific people and specific infractions. This tells us that the Teacher mental network of a general system of morality is now more important than the Mercy mental network associated with any specific individual within that system of morality.

Kohlberg says that in this stage of morality, rules are often determined by a central set of ideals, and that fundamentalism operates at this level of morality. Kohlberg's system avoids dealing explicitly with religion, but mental symmetry suggests that an image of God emerges when a general Teacher theory explains personal identity, and a 'central set of ideals' definitely refers to a general Teacher theory.

We have seen that the path of religious education *starts* with Mercy mental networks, and that it *modifies* the structure of these Mercy mental networks to make them compatible with Teacher thought. Reviewing this process, the parent, teacher, or priest starts by using his emotional status to teach the child moral rules; he then tells the child that these rules actually come from an invisible 'person' who lives everywhere, never sleeps, never dies, sees everything that the child does or thinks, and feels bad when the child violates the rules. This strange sort of 'person' describes how Mercy thought would view a universal Teacher theory. If this universal Teacher theory turns into a Teacher mental network, then a person will feel as if such a 'person' is living within his mind, leading to the mental concept of a universal God who is the source of moral rules.

Notice the difference between Kolberg's previous stage and this stage. During the social convention stage, Mercy mental networks representing people have been generalized to form internal concepts of interpersonal norms, such as 'being a good boy', but the focus is still upon producing *external behavior* that fulfils these idealized interpersonal norms. During the law and order stage, the rules themselves have combined to form a Teacher mental network of understanding that functions *independently* of people, and this Teacher structure *internally* generates negative Teacher emotions when it encounters thought or behavior that violates the general structure of law and order. Punishment is then viewed as an external reinforcement of this internal standard of law and order.

However, at the law and order stage, this *Teacher* system of morality is still seen as ultimately being revealed or set up by some special book, person, or group of people. For instance, the constitution may be accepted as a general source of morality, but this constitution was initially established by a set of 'founding fathers'.

5) **Social Contract Driven:** This stage confused me for a while, and I found it interesting to note that Kohlberg also found the transition from stage four to stage five perplexing. I finally concluded that one is actually dealing with three different

mechanisms that appear similar on the surface but which end up having different results. Kohlberg's description of stage five includes elements of all three of these mechanisms and does not distinguish between them. Therefore, my explanation for this stage will be rather extensive.

Stage four contains two incompatible components. On the one hand, there is the Teacher mental network of universal law. On the other hand, there is the Mercy mental network representing the person or group that is the ultimate source of this universal law. Thus, we have universal law based upon a specific source. As a result, one can emerge from stage four either by focusing upon the specific source or upon the universal law. Two of the mental mechanisms that we will discuss focus upon the *source* of law, while the other mental mechanism focuses upon the law *itself*.

If one focuses upon the personal source of law, then one will come to the conclusion that moral law comes from *people* and that some group or person is imposing its standards upon the rest of society. If the emotional status of this group or person is called into question, then moral reform will be seen as stopping this group or person from making others feel bad by imposing its standard of morality upon them. The result will be Kohlberg's stage 4+ in which the moral legitimacy of society as a whole is called into question. As Kohlberg observes, one finds many college students at this level, because they are learning how to question what they were taught in childhood by 'the establishment'.

If this situation continues, then the rebellion against established authority will eventually be formulated as a universal moral principle something like "Do not make people feel bad. Any group that judges others and makes them feel bad should be removed from authority."

Moving on, a focus upon the *source* of truth can also arise when different societies with different systems of law and order have to coexist. For instance, suppose that Muslims who follow the Quran live amongst Christians who believe in the Bible. Now there are two holy books, with each holy book fighting for emotional status and being regarded as inadequate by the followers of the other holy book.

When there is a multiplicity of established experts, then the tendency is to use Facilitator thought to find 'truth' through *consensus* or compromise.[49] For instance, the holy days of all major religions may be recognized, or each religion may be given the freedom to teach its own religious classes at school. This type of statistical approach has two aspects: Data points that are in the middle will be averaged to come up with an answer, while data points which are extreme will be eliminated as outliers. Similarly, moral compromise will include all 'moderate' views while ignoring 'extreme' positions. The problem is that those who believe in universal principles of morality will also be

---

[49] I suggest that the mental flaw does not lie in using Facilitator mode, but rather in focusing upon the finite human source of morality. When Facilitator mode is used to search for universal principles of moral cause-and-effect, then the result is moral *proverbs*.

regarded as extreme, because they refuse to alter their principles in the face of societal pressure.

This too will lead to the formulation of a universal principle along the lines of "Do not preach absolute truth. Any group which holds dogmatically to its moral principles should be disregarded and silenced."

Now let us look at the third group that focuses upon formulating moral *principles*. This situation tends to arise when some group or individual is faced with a violation of a moral principle for so long and in so many circumstances that it eventually concludes that a universal moral principle exists which needs to be followed. This is similar to how Hegel himself originally defined the process of what his followers later called thesis-antithesis-synthesis.

The mental mechanism behind this is interesting. I have defined a general theory as a set of words upon which Teacher thought can continue to concentrate. If the social environment forces a group or individual to continue focusing on a single issue, then this effectively turns that issue into a 'universal theory', because it is one which that group or individual finds itself continually being forced to face. This repeated exposure will gradually give that group or individual the mental ability to call into question the Teacher mental network of established morality—when discussing this particular issue.

For instance, this occurred during the civil rights movement in the United States. Wherever blacks went in the South, they were continually being reminded of the fact that they were being excluded purely on the basis of their skin color. This continual exposure to racial prejudice eventually led individuals to the conclusion that racial equality is a universal moral principle.

Notice that losing emotional status, consensus, and universal morality all lead to the questioning of existing morality and the formulation of universal principles. Therefore, they appear on the surface to be the same. However, the nature of the 'universal' laws that are being promoted is quite different.

Rebellion from authority focuses purely upon *emotional state*, and assumes that people cause emotional states. Therefore, if some person or group is feeling bad, then the assumption is that some other person or group is causing them to feel bad. In particular, any person or group which makes moral statements about the person or group that is feeling bad will be blamed for making them feel bad and will be morally denounced as a source of emotional pain. For instance, if some group is living in poverty, then this means that they are being exploited by those who are rich. The proposed solution will be to take money from the rich and give it to the poor. Underlying principles of moral cause-and-effect will be ignored.

Consensus focuses upon *dogmatism*. This who are willing to compromise are invited to the table of moral consensus, while those with extreme positions will be asked to leave. Because consensus focuses upon the attitude of the *source* of a moral rule and does not examine the rule *itself*, both fundamentalists—who use emotional pressure to mesmerize

Perceiver thought, and those with moral principles—who have discovered a universal moral principle and have gained the Perceiver confidence to hold on to this principle despite emotional pressure, will be lumped into the same category and rejected as extreme.

Moral principle, in contrast, focuses upon *cause-and-effect*. The goal is to identify behavior that produces painful results and to change that behavior. Because this method is actually *searching* for universal rules of morality, it can lead to stage six morality. In contrast, the other two methods will tend to regress to earlier stages of morality.

Notice that all three methods focus upon personal rights, but rebellion from authority promotes *fairness* in which everyone is given an equal 'slice of the pie', consensus leads to *political correctness*, while moral principle promotes *justice* and *equal opportunity*.

6) **Universal Ethics Principles Driven:** During this stage, moral reasoning is guided by abstract reasoning based upon universal ethical principles, which describes how the mind constructs a universal Teacher theory. Kohlberg relates this sixth level to the categorical imperative of Kant, in which morality is based purely upon a rational search for universal principles.

Kohlberg associates this level with the willingness to endorse *civil disobedience*. I suggest that a person will be willing to take a step of civil disobedience if his moral understanding has formed a Teacher mental network within his mind and if the emotional power exerted by this Teacher mental network is stronger than the influence of existing Teacher and Mercy mental networks.

Kohlberg was unable to find enough people who functioned consistently at this level of morality to be able to define it clearly, and he eventually stopped assigning anyone to this level. Similarly, I have also discovered in my research that few people connect morality and personal growth with a rational universal theory. They may say that they do, and they may know about Kant's categorical imperative, but in practice one discovers that there are many 'ifs' and 'buts' which restrict the application of rational moral thought.

Obviously, building a truly *universal* understanding of morality means finding a Teacher theory of morality which is *independent* of the *specific* people and groups that promote religious and societal ethical codes. This book proposes a universal Teacher theory of morality that is based upon the interaction of cognitive modules. Mental symmetry defines that which causes cognitive modules to function and interact better as morally good, and that which pits one cognitive module against another or shuts down cognitive modules as morally bad.

7) **Transcendental Morality:** Kohlberg postulated a seventh stage of morality that linked religion with moral reasoning, but emphasized that this was purely speculative. I suggest that this *seventh* level is the topic of this book, because it presents religion as a universal Teacher theory based upon reaching and following the moral goal of having all cognitive modules function in an integrated manner.

Summarizing Kohlberg's seven stages of morality:

1) Rules of conscience are backed up by Mercy mental networks.

2) Contributor thought pursues personal advantage by working with existing Mercy mental networks.

3) Teacher thought looks for common patterns between Mercy mental networks, resulting in rules of conscience that express idealized Mercy mental networks.

4) Rules of conscience are based in a Teacher mental network that has its source in some person, book, or group with Mercy status.

5) Existing Teacher mental networks of morality are called into question. This may be the result of rebellion against authority, multiculturalism and consensus, or discovery of universal moral principles.

6) Rules of conscience are based upon a Teacher mental network that is constructed out of universal moral principles which are independent of Mercy mental networks.

7) A Teacher mental network based upon universal principles is used both to define moral principles and to derive a system of religion.

❋ Michel Foucault's Epistemes

Foucault writes with a French philosophical style that somehow manages to be both clear and obtuse at the same time. His book *The Order of Things: An Archaeology of the Human Sciences* separates the recent history of Western thought into the three main periods of what he calls the Renaissance episteme, the Classical episteme, and the Modern episteme. He looks at the shift in thinking that occurred in the three fields of linguistics, biology, and economics. In this section, I will attempt to do a brief analysis of his model focusing primarily upon his comments with respect to the history of scientific thought. I should mention that I found John Protevi's summary of Foucault's book to be quite helpful.[50]

The Renaissance Episteme

Let us start with the Renaissance episteme, which Foucault says ended about 1650. Foucault uses four main adjectives to describe thinking during this period, which we will describe in terms of mental symmetry. I suggest that these adjectives describe a type of thinking which we have referred to as Teacher overgeneralization. This type of thinking is *seeded* by Mercy mental networks, and it is *guided* by Perceiver facts and associations that are based primarily in *physical appearance*—the type of information that *automatic* Perceiver thought acquires from categorizing sensory input. Saying this another way, Perceiver facts and Server sequences are being used to describe and compare Mercy mental networks, but no Teacher mental network of rational understanding exists that would allow the mind to analyze and dissect Mercy mental networks.

First, there is *spatial arrangement*, in which Teacher thought is ordering elements on the basis of physical characteristics such as size, shape, and similarity, similar to the way that a person might take a pile of blocks and arrange them from smallest to largest. Foucault illustrates this with the quote: "As with respect to its vegetation the plant stands convenient to the brute beast, so through feeling does the brutish animal to man, who is conformable to the rest of the stars by his intelligence; these links proceed so strictly that they appear as a rope stretched from the first cause as far as the lowest and smallest of things." Notice that this quote also describes a type of thinking in which *Mercy mental networks* that represent living organisms are being arranged into a Teacher sequence.

Second, there is *emulation*, which builds Teacher understanding by using Perceiver mode to tie together elements which appear to imitate one another based upon surface appearance. For instance, Foucault quotes from one medieval book: "The stars are the

---

[50] http://www.protevi.com/john/Foucault/PDF/OT_I.pdf

matrix of all the plants and every star in the sky is only the spiritual prefiguration of a plant, such that it represents that the order of things plant, and just as each herb or plant is a terrestrial star looking up at the sky, so also each star is a celestial plant in spiritual form, which differs from the terrestrial plants in matter alone."

Third, there is *analogy*. Here, one thing which appears to function like another is said to be like another. Again we have Perceiver thought working at a surface level. Quoting from Foucault's example: "A plant is an upright animal, whose nutritive principles rise from the base up to the summit, channelled along a stem that stretches upwards like a body and is topped by a head – spreading flowers and leaves: a relation that inverts but does not contradict the initial analogy, since it places 'the root in the lower part of the plant and the stem in the upper part, for the venous network in animals also begins in the lower part of the belly, and the principal vein rises up to the heart and head.'"

Finally, there is *sympathy*. We see here the mental Agency Detector running wild, with personal Mercy feelings being ascribed to inanimate objects. Quoting from one of Foucault's examples: "It is fairly widely known that the plants have hatreds between themselves. . . it is said that the olive and the vine hate the cabbage; the cucumber flies from the olive . . . Since they grow by means of the sun's warmth and the earth's humour, it is inevitable that any thick and opaque tree should be pernicious to the others, and also the tree that has several roots."

What Foucault does not mention is that technical thought *did* exist during the Renaissance time, but it was limited to restricted realms. On the practical side, there was the *craftsman*, who used Cp to develop physical skills. On the intellectual side, Ci existed primarily in the church and the university. Medieval philosophy used logical technical thought, but this thinking was being applied primarily to Christian books and Greek texts, resulting in *scholasticism*. As far as Contributor thought was concerned, these books provided the mental 'playing field' for the 'game' of intellectual activity. Acceptable Server sequences were limited to the sentences written in approved texts, while Perceiver mode was permitted to come up with theoretical conclusions by comparing one quoted passage with another.

It is important to note that scholasticism can emerge even when Perceiver thought is *mesmerized*. As I mentioned earlier, revealed truth uses the emotional status of some *source* of 'truth' to mesmerize Perceiver thought into 'believing' what is true. But if this 'truth' is revealed in *written* form, then it acquires both stability and digital confidence. The Server sequences do not change because they have been written down on paper. And the Perceiver facts do not change because Perceiver thought 'believes' that the sentences which are written down on paper are true. This makes it possible for the technical circuit of Ci to begin functioning, even when Perceiver mode is still 'asleep'. Perceiver thought will then begin to 'wake up' when *analyzing* revealed texts, while still remaining 'asleep' when considering the *source* of these revealed texts.

This describes the type of transitional thinking that emerges during the process of education, and explains how the blind 'belief' of revealed truth can lay a mental foundation for the critical thinking of science.

The Classical Episteme

Let us move on now to Foucault's second stage of the *Classical episteme*. Foucault says that this lasted from about 1650 to 1880. The first date corresponds to the time of the Scientific Revolution, while the second date corresponds to the beginning of the consumer society, when the Industrial Revolution began to transform life for the average individual. This is when the use of the railroad became widespread, and when society-changing devices such as the automobile, the telephone, and the machine gun were invented.

Foucault's analysis of classical thought is rather complicated, but it is possible to make some general observations. First, he says that there is an emphasis upon *order*. In his words, "This relation to Order is as essential to the Classical age as the relation to Interpretation was to the Renaissance." In the language of mental symmetry, instead of assuming that interaction is being driven by *Mercy* emotions of love and hate, there is a *Teacher* driven search for order and structure.

Second, instead of viewing Perceiver truth as a sort of divinely written revelation, Perceiver thought is being used actively to look for solid connections. As Foucault puts it: "[Before], its task was to uncover a language which God had previously distributed across the face of the earth; it is in this sense that it was the divination of an essential implication, and that the object of its divination was divine. From now on, however, it is within knowledge representing itself that the sign is to perform its signifying function; it is from knowledge that it will borrow its certainty or its probability. And though God still employs signs to speak to us through nature, he is making use of our knowledge, and of the relations that are set up between our impressions, in order to establish in our minds a relation of signification."

Third, the Perceiver connections that are being discovered are being used to build rational Teacher understanding: "It is no longer the task of knowledge to dig out the ancient Word from the unknown places where it may be hidden; its job now is to fabricate a language, and to fabricate it well – so that, as an instrument of analysis and combination, it will really be the language of calculation."

Fourth, Perceiver thought is being used to find similarities between abstract concepts and not just between surface appearances. In Foucault's words, "The relation of the sign to the signified now resides in a space in which there is no longer any intermediary figure to connect them: what connects them is a bond established, inside knowledge, between the idea of one thing and the idea of another."

Finally, Teacher thought is building general theories based upon these abstract Perceiver connections: "The signifying idea becomes double, since superimposed upon the idea that is replacing another there is also the idea of its representative power. This appears to give us three terms: the idea signified, the idea signifying, and, within this second term, the idea of its role as representation."

Summarizing, Perceiver thought is being used to build general Teacher theories. If possible, these theories are described using the language of mathematics, or if the material is too complicated, then the Teacher theory is presented in the form of a table, such as the periodic table of elements, or a taxonomy, such as Linnaeus' system of taxonomy. As Foucault puts it, "What makes the totality of the Classical episteme possible is primarily the relation to a knowledge of order. When dealing with the ordering of simple natures, one has recourse to a mathesis, of which the universal method is algebra. When dealing with the ordering of complex natures (representations in general, as they are given in experience), one has to constitute a taxinomia, and to do that one has to establish a representing system of signs. These signs are to the order of composite natures what algebra is to the order of simple natures."

Foucault's comments make sense in the light of mental symmetry, though he seems to be missing the emphasis upon Server sequence and Contributor cause-and-effect which also played a major role in the emergence of scientific thought. However, Foucault does acknowledge that it is traditional among historians to recognize the intellectual breakthrough that occurred when rational thought was used to analyze *movement*: "since it had proved possible, by means of experimentation and theory, to analyse the laws of movement or those governing the reflection of light beams, was it not normal to seek, by means of experiments, observations, or calculations, the laws that might govern the more complex but adjacent realm of living beings?"

In general terms, Foucault's description of the classical period describes a form of thought in which the technical circuit of Ci functioned within an overall context of abstract thought, a period of time in which there was a balance of power between Kuhn's revolutionary science and Kuhn's normal science. Scientists were building paradigms and they were using Ci to perform technical analysis within these paradigms. However, the overall purpose of intellectual thought was to use Perceiver thought to build *general* Teacher theories and the technical circuit of Ci was being used as a mental tool to achieve this overall purpose.

The Modern Episteme

Foucault uses a lot of words to present his concepts. In describing the modern way of thinking, he seems to be saying the same thing in many different ways. Therefore, in order to present a feeling of what he appears to be describing, I will quote some of the ways in which he presents his point.

In general terms, Foucault views the modern era as the age of the overthrow of Platonism. Representation is no longer seen as the basis for human thought. Instead, facts must be explained in terms of some deeper mechanism. Instead of basing understanding upon unchanging Perceiver truth, truth is seen as something that changes over time through a historical process. In the language of mental symmetry, Perceiver facts are no longer seen as the foundation for Teacher understanding. Instead, there is a shift in focus from Perceiver facts to Server sequence.

One sees this change in focus from Perceiver fact to Server sequence in the attitude of business. Foucault says that the classical view of business is to think in terms of commodities, goods, and wealth, and to see business as an exchange of objects. In contrast, he says that the modern view of business views the Server actions of *labor* as the ultimate source of economic value.

According to Foucault, Kant played a critical role in the transition to modern thought, because Kant stated that it was not possible to know Perceiver facts about the external world with absolute certainty. Instead, Kant looked at the conditions for knowledge, trying to work out how the *functioning* of the mind determined the way that it viewed Perceiver facts.

Today, the emphasis is not upon gaining Perceiver facts or building general Teacher theories, but rather upon trying to decipher *how* one acquires facts or builds theories. And here I will quote at some length from Foucault: "For the threshold of our modernity is situated not by the attempt to apply objective methods to the study of man, but rather by the constitution of an empirico-transcendental doublet which was called man. Two kinds of analysis then came into being. There are those that operate within the space of the body, and—by studying perception, sensorial mechanisms, neuro-motor diagrams, and the articulation common to things and to the organism-function as a sort of transcendental aesthetic; these led to the discovery that knowledge has anatomo-physiological conditions, that it is formed gradually within the structures of the body, that it may have a privileged place within it, but that its forms cannot be dissociated from its peculiar functioning; in short, that there is a nature of human knowledge that determines its forms and that can at the same time be made manifest to it in its own empirical contents. There were also analyses that—by studying humanity's more or less ancient, more or less easily vanquished illusions—functioned as a sort of transcendental dialectic; by this means it was shown that knowledge had historical, social, or economic conditions, that it was formed within the relations that are woven between men, and that it was not independent of the particular form they might take here or there; in short, that there was a history of human knowledge which could both be given to empirical knowledge and prescribe its forms."

Similarly, Foucault says that language becomes detached from meaning, and the focus instead is upon attempting to decipher language itself. In terms of mental symmetry, Perceiver meaning loses its importance, while the Server process of arranging words and speech comes to the fore. In the words of Foucault: "At the beginning of the nineteenth century, the law of discourse having been detached from representation, the being of language itself became, as it were, fragmented; but they became inevitable when, with Nietzsche, and Mallarme, thought was brought back, and violently so, towards language itself, towards its unique and difficult being. The whole curiosity of our thought now resides in the question: 'What is language, how can we find a way round it in order to make it appear in itself, in all its plenitude? In a sense, this question takes up from those other questions that, in the nineteenth century, were concerned with life or labour.'"

And he describes the human sciences in a similar way: "The human sciences, when dealing with what is representation (in either conscious or unconscious form), find themselves treating as their object what is in fact their condition of possibility. They are always animated, therefore, by a sort of transcendental mobility. They never cease to exercise a critical examination of themselves. They proceed from that which is given to representation to that which renders representation possible, but which is still representation. So that, unlike other sciences, they seek not so much to generalize themselves or make themselves more precise as to be constantly demystifying themselves: to make the transition from an immediate and non-controlled evidence to less transparent but more fundamental forms. This quasi-transcendental process is always given in the form of an unveiling."

Now let us see if we can translate this mental transition into the language of mental symmetry. In simple terms, I suggest that the technical circuit of Ci is 'eating up' abstract thought. Saying this another way, the circuit of Ci is a mental tool for developing abstract thought. But the modern focus tends to be upon improving and analyzing the tool itself rather than using the tool to achieve results. This is like the computer owner who spends his time and money benchmarking his computer and trying to make it run faster, but who doesn't actually use his computer to perform useful work, or like the car enthusiast who tinkers endlessly with his vehicle but doesn't use it to travel anywhere. If one were to sum this all up in a single word, that word would be *self-questioning*.

The point Foucault is trying to make, with which I agree, is that these are not isolated incidents. Instead, one sees similar situations everywhere one looks. Thus, we are dealing with a general worldview or in Foucault's words, a Modern *episteme*.

Jean Piaget, in his book *Structuralism*, compares Foucault's episteme with Thomas Kuhn's paradigm, and there is some validity to this comparison, because we are looking at a form of order-within-complexity. Teacher thought will notice this commonality of approach and the result will be positive Teacher emotions. However, I would refer to Foucault's episteme more as an implicit monotheistic 'God of an Age'. It is implicit because it describes a mindset within which one finds oneself immersed, it is monotheistic because one finds this mindset occurring universally, it is an image of God because it is a universal mindset that affects human behavior, and it is a God of an Age because it governs a historical time period.

However, when one is discussing Ci, then a paradigm normally refers to the Teacher theory that summarizes the mental context within which a specific set of technical rules apply. For instance, the field of chemistry would be summarized by the periodic table of elements. In contrast, Foucault's Modern episteme is more like a paradigm of paradigms, an implicit worldview which guides people as they use Ci to function within their various paradigms.

Now that we have some grasp of the nature of modern thought, we will conclude by attempting to use mental symmetry to explain why this occurs. I suggest that it is the result of a number of interrelated cognitive factors.

The first factors lead to the societal domination of the technical circuit of Ci:

1) **The Triumph of Technology:** Foucault's Modern episteme took over about the same time that gadgets become technical. A mechanical, electrical, or electronic gadget is an external example of technical abstract thought. In order to invent, build, or fix such a machine, one has to use the technical circuit of Ci. Today, even the *user* of a gadget or machine is forced to develop technical abstract thought to some extent.

2) **Specialization:** Developing the technical circuit of Ci within some area of technology takes training, which requires time, effort, and money. This makes it difficult to enter a profession, and gives a person an incentive to stay within a profession once he is trained. Acquiring skills in more than one profession is even more difficult. The result is specialization.

3) **Legislation:** The untrained person lacks the technical knowledge of the professional. Therefore, he is unable to distinguish the real expert from the fake. As a result, government steps in and legislates the training and approval of official experts in order to protect the untrained person from fraud. The end result is that the might of government enforces specialization.

4) **Explosion of Knowledge:** The Contributor driven technical circuit of Ci improves, explores, and optimizes. When Ci can express itself externally through technology, then this leads to a positive feedback loop in which knowledge breeds technology which leads to a further growth of knowledge. The result is an explosion of knowledge, fragmented into different specializations, each with its own experts, paradigms, and technical vocabulary.

5) **Arrogance:** Expertise has a tendency to lead to arrogance, which will appear in three main forms, corresponding to the three modes of concentration. First, there will be a Teacher arrogance produced by professionalism. Second, there will be a Mercy arrogance based upon status. Third, there will be a Contributor arrogance related to competition. For instance, think of the college professor. First, working at a college provides an environment of technical expertise that makes Teacher thought feel good. If the professor had to live with 'normal people', then he would be surrounded by intellectual mediocrity. Second, being a professor at a respected university gives a person Mercy status which one does not have when working at a 'normal job'. Third, the professor is motivated to solve intellectual problems better than his peers and to come up with intellectual advancements within his field of specialization.

The next factors lead to a questioning of Perceiver truth and the demise of Platonic Forms, making it harder to escape the technical mindset of Ci and more difficult to tie various fields of specialization together.

5) **Progress:** In a traditional society, Perceiver facts and Perceiver objects do not change quickly. Instead, there is a sense of Perceiver permanence as knowledge and possessions are handed down from parents to children. In contrast, both Perceiver facts and Perceiver objects change at a rapid rate in a technological driven society. For instance, when I lived in Korea, it felt as if even concrete was not a solid object, because houses, buildings, and sometimes entire city blocks were continually being torn down and rebuilt. What replaces Perceiver thought as a source of mental stability is the Server sequence of continual progress driven by technical thought.

6) **Objectivity:** Perceiver confidence is required to think logically in the presence of strong emotions. When a person becomes a specialist in an objective field of knowledge, he can avoid the struggle of building Perceiver confidence. But this lack of Perceiver confidence also makes it more difficult for him to question the Teacher emotions that result from thinking within a paradigm.

7) **Specialized Vocabulary:** Teacher thought feels good when complicated concepts can be described efficiently through the use of carefully defined technical vocabulary. As a result, each specialization will be driven by Teacher emotions to come up with its own vocabulary of technical terms. This adds a further barrier to crossing the gap of specialization. For before one can use Perceiver thought to compare one field of knowledge with another, one must first learn the technical vocabulary of both fields.

8) **Epistemology:** When the mind makes a transition from abstract thought to the technical circuit of Ci, it makes a logical leap from analog certainty to digital certainty. This logical leap will not be noticed when *entering* the circuit of Ci because normal abstract thought has no problem with jumping to conclusions based upon incomplete data, for it does this all the time. However, when Ci starts to function within a field of thought, then the standards for proof become more rigorous, because Ci is a *technical* circuit that uses rigorous thought. This leads to the mental contradiction of Ci using rigorous logic to work within a field while *assuming* that its basis for knowledge is certain. However, eventually Ci will realize *retroactively* that it is built upon an uncertain logical foundation, leading to an 'unveiling of knowledge' in which the field enters a stage of self-questioning.

When this realization occurs, Ci will come to the conclusion that because digital certainty cannot be achieved, it is not possible to know anything about either Perceiver facts or Server sequences, leading to a massive loss of Perceiver and Server confidence. However, while Perceiver thought gains confidence by *observing*, Server confidence can be increased by *doing*—and the researcher continues to *do* the action of research. Therefore, Server confidence will be *restored* by applying the Server skill of using technical thought to perform technical analysis. And because Ci functions by using Perceiver thought to work with Server sequences, Perceiver thought will gain confidence in the logic that is used by the technical field to perform its technical analysis. The end result is that the circuit of Ci will continue to function, but it will become disconnected both from reality and from other fields of thought. Instead of using Ci to analyze Perceiver facts and Server sequences, Ci will be used to analyze in great technical detail the Server sequences involved in performing technical thought in that specific field of research. In simple terms, research has turned into self-questioning.

9) **Questioning Revelation:** When looking at the Renaissance episteme, I suggested that Ci was functioning during the Middle Ages, but it was being used to analyze the revealed texts of Christianity and Greek philosophers. During the Classical episteme, this technical method of thought continued to function, but the *topic* of study turned from ancient books to the natural world. As I have described elsewhere in this book, this gradually caused Perceiver thought to 'wake from its slumber' and begin to *doubt* the opinions of the old experts. However, it was the development of modern technology which caused people to *throw out* the old tomes, for who needs a God of miracles and descriptions of fantastic realms when technology, driven by Ci, can be used to deliver daily wonders.

Originally, the revealed texts provided the Perceiver *foundation* for logical thought. But as scholars lost their emotional respect for the sources of this revelation, the revealed texts themselves ended up being analyzed using the Ci technical method of textual analysis and higher criticism. Thus, the self-questioning of the Modern episteme ended up questioning the *method* of scholasticism which had made the Classical episteme possible. Putting this another way, once people no longer believed in the existence of absolute truth, then they no longer had any reason to search for Perceiver truth.

10) **Flipping Modes:** This final concept is discussed in greater detail in the last chapter of the main text. Normally, the mind associates Mercy emotions with specific experiences and Teacher emotions with general theories. That is because living in a physical body provides Mercy mode with specific emotional experiences, while living in the physical world teaches Teacher thought common sense related to general principles of natural order.

However, we have just seen that the Modern episteme causes the mind to associate Teacher emotion with technical expertise within a *specific* field, while the demise of Perceiver thought makes it more difficult to construct *general* Teacher theories.[51] Looking at the Mercy side, technology also leads to the breakdown of physical distance, allowing a person to get quickly from here to there and to communicate instantly between here and there, making it possible to view Mercy experiences in much more general terms. This concept of Mercy generality is reinforced by the fact that most technical progress requires the combined efforts of a team of individuals.

---

[51] Thomas Kuhn mentions that one reader accused him of assigning twenty-two different meanings to the word *paradigm*. Since writing this book, I have decided to use the word paradigm to refer to the Teacher theory, either implicit or explicit, that lies behind some technical specialization, consistent with Kuhn's analysis. I suggest that using technical thought to define a paradigm too precisely is a category mistake because a paradigm is a Teacher structure of order-within-complexity that provides an emotional framework for some system of technical thought. I refer to other theories as Teacher theories or general theories and use the term meta-theory to refer to a general theory that ties together other theories.

This will cause the human mind to 'flip modes' and enter a stable mode of operation that regards Teacher thought in finite terms and Mercy thought in general terms. As we see elsewhere, this mode of thought is mentally stable, but it is not compatible with human existence within the natural world.

Notice again the role that technology plays in this process. Normally a tool is seen as an aid for reaching some Mercy goal. For instance, I use my car to drive to work. If I learn the skill of driving a vehicle, then I am using the concrete technical circuit of Cp. But as we have seen, the order-within-complexity inherent within modern technology forces the professional to interact with tools using the abstract circuit of Ci. Cp uses a tool to reach a Mercy goal. Ci, in contrast, focuses upon designing, maintaining, and repairing a tool so that it continues to function without falling apart.

One final point. Technical thought consists of both the *abstract* circuit of Ci and the *concrete* circuit of Cp. This section has been describing the Modern episteme as the triumph of Ci over normal thought. Where does Cp fit into the picture? It appears that two factors are at play: The first is a shift from normal thought to technical thought. But within technical thought one also sees the abstract thinking of Ci becoming increasingly emphasized rather than the concrete thinking of Cp.

One notices this first in the expansion of *higher learning*. Attending university used to be rare. Now it is difficult to get a good job without a college degree. Second, most manual labor in Western countries is done by *machine*, and as machines become increasingly sophisticated, they require more training and abstract thought to use and maintain. Third, in countries and industries where manual labor is still prevalent, the skilled laborer is being replaced by the factory worker, who is *treated* as a machine. Fourth, with the advent of the computer, the Internet, and modern telecommunications, a whole new class of job has emerged in which a person *interacts* with machines using abstract thought. Fifth, the objective nature of science and technology tends to discourage the use of Cp with its bottom line of *Mercy* emotions. Finally, the growth of government regulations together with corporate procedures and union restrictions means that even when a person does perform physical action, he has effectively *'flipped modes'* and is actually being guided by Ci rather than Cp.

<u>In Conclusion</u>

As I mentioned in the introduction to this book, it is not possible to use the technical circuit of Ci to analyze the entire mind, because technical thought only forms a *subset* of human thought. Instead, if one wants to understand the mind, one must acknowledge the existence of all modes of thought, which means going beyond the technical realm of Ci. But the Modern episteme is highly biased toward the exclusive use of Ci.

This means that any attempt to present a comprehensive theory of human thought will end up fighting the Modern episteme. And if an episteme actually forms an implicit mental image of a universal God, then constructing and presenting a *comprehensive* model of human thought turns into a religious struggle in which one must attempt to dethrone the implicit image of the modern monotheistic God and replace it with an alternative mental image of God that is based in mental *wholeness*. In practical terms, this means using a comprehensive model of human thought to explain an unreasonably broad range of specializations at a level that is sufficiently rigorous to be acceptable to the experts in each field while being sufficiently vague to avoid the trap of succumbing to technical thought. That describes what this book is attempting to do.

In order to recover from the Modern episteme, one must find a source of solid Perceiver truth that can *replace* the truth which modern self-questioning has discredited. And this Perceiver truth must apply to the *realm* of self-questioning to which the Modern episteme finds itself drawn. Mental symmetry suggests that this Perceiver truth can be found in *cognitive modules*, because they are solid and do not change. And a theory of cognitive modules applies to the realm of self-questioning, which by its very nature is subject to the structure of the mind. In addition, using Perceiver thought to *compare* the self-questioning that is occurring within one specialization with the self-questioning that is occurring within another specialization builds Perceiver confidence, because the same Perceiver facts are being *repeated* in many fields. These Perceiver facts construct internal connections which can be used to mentally reintegrate the fragmented modern world of specialization.

The end result is that abstract thought can once again be viewed as the *partner* of Ci, leading hopefully to the formation of a new episteme which combines elements of all three previous epistemes. For when learning transforms the structure of the *entire* mind, then even the overgeneralization of the Renaissance episteme becomes useful, because the mind is now free-associating within an *educated* mental structure. Saying this another way, when a person becomes enough of an expert, then he can start to trust even his intuition.

✵ Mathematics

I should begin this section by saying that I am only competent in mathematics. I have a Master's Degree in Engineering, and in Engineering school one studies as far as partial differential equations. In addition, I have taught Geometry, Algebra, Precalculus, and AP Calculus at the honors level for several years at an American curriculum high school. All of the math that we will be discussing in this section can be found in the curriculum of these high school courses. The goal of this section is not to *derive* mathematics using rigorous logic. That task was partially done by Alfred North Whitehead and Bertrand Russell in the *Principia Mathematica.* I say 'partially' because the authors ran out of energy after finishing three volumes and they never wrote their fourth planned volume on geometry.

Instead, I have a far more modest goal. In the main text, I suggest that mathematics is an expression of technical abstract thought, which I call Ci. In this section, we will be addressing two main topics: First, we will look at the relationship between math and the technical circuit of Ci. Second, we will look at the process by which math is taught and relate it to the process of starting with the practical circuit of Cp and then translating this into the technical circuit of Ci.

Let us begin by reviewing the mental circuit of Ci, a formal, restricted version of abstract thought. We will first describe the circuit, then illustrate it using math. If this description is confusing, then please refer to the diagram of mental symmetry. Teacher words provide the basic building blocks for abstract thought. In math, these Teacher words take the form of math symbols. These Teacher symbols can acquire Server stability through repetition and writing. Server thought arranges these symbols into sequences as well as rearranges symbols within existing sequences. Because abstract thought is driven by Teacher emotions, the emotional goal of this arranging and rearranging will usually be to produce order-within-complexity.

The next stage of abstract thought is for Contributor mode to assign Perceiver meanings to Server sequences. Going further, using Perceiver thought to connect Server sequences with similar meanings allows one to construct Teacher theories which are more general than those that could be achieved through the use of Server thought alone.

The circuit of Ci is a technical form of abstract thought which differs from normal abstract thought in three ways: First, it works within an existing general Teacher theory. Second, it uses a limited set of carefully defined Server sequences and Perceiver operations. Third, while normal abstract thought deals with uncertain information, technical thought requires absolute certainty.

Now let us look at how these various elements show up in math. The basic building block of math is the symbol, such as 'x', '+', or ')'. Looking briefly at basic mental processing, Mercy mode handles primarily *vision* while Teacher mode interprets *sound.* But Mercy thought is capable of interpreting non-verbal sounds such as music, while Teacher thought appears to be able to decipher visual input which consists of *lines* at a specific *orientation.* Letters of the alphabet and mathematical symbols are both examples of lines at a specific orientation, which one could refer to as *visual outlines.* Consistent with the limited nature of Ci, math uses a limited set of symbols which are all carefully defined.

Math symbols are arranged to form Server sequences, called *expressions.* A math expression consists of a sequence of written symbols, such as 'x + (2 – y)'. Expressions are also permitted to be written in only a limited number of carefully defined ways. In mathematical language, a clearly defined math sequence is called a *well formed* expression. For instance, 'x + (2 – y)' is well formed, whereas 'x +) – (y' is not.

Elements within a math Server sequence can be rearranged, duplicated, and combined by applying an official set of Server rules. These *Server* rules can be applied without having any knowledge of Perceiver meaning. Because one is dealing with *technical* thought, these Server rules are also limited and clearly defined. These Server rules are:

Reflexive property	A = A
Commutative property	A + B = B + A
Associative property	A + (B + C) = (A + B) + C
Distributive property	A (B + C) = AB + AC

The equal sign tells us that these Server manipulations leave the Perceiver meaning unchanged. However, Perceiver thought is not required to carry out these manipulations.

The purpose of performing mathematical manipulations is usually to *simplify* an expression. When a complicated expression is turned into a simple expression, this creates Teacher feelings of order-within-complexity. For example, the expression '3x + 4(2x – 3) – 2x' can be simplified by using the rules above, along with basic facts about numbers, to produce '9x – 12'.

Math also simplifies expressions by using shorthand or abbreviations. For instance, x^4 is shorthand for x•x•x•x. (I am using '•' to represent multiply in order to distinguish it from the variable 'x'.) Notice that a simple abbreviation such as a power sign can be interpreted through the use of Server rearranging.

However, consider the more complicated expression '[sec(x) $\sin^2$(x)]/[1 + sec(x)]', which can be simplified to '1 – cos(x)'. In order to simplify this expression, one must know that 'sec(x) = 1/cos(x)' and that '$\sin^2$x + $\cos^2$x = 1'. Knowing these subsidiary relationships means going beyond merely manipulating Server sequences to working with the *Perceiver* meanings of these Server sequences; 'sec(x)' uses different Teacher symbols than 'cos(x)'; therefore, it is not possible to use only Server thought to turn one into the other. However, Perceiver thought can know that these two Server sequences are connected because 'sec(x)' is *defined* as '1/cos(x)' and definitions involve Perceiver thought.

Going further, the relationship '$\sin^2 x + \cos^2 x = 1$' can be proven by combining the Perceiver definitions of trigonometric functions with Pythagoras' theorem about the hypotenuse of a right triangle. Here we see that Perceiver thought is getting some of its definitions from *concrete* thought. A right triangle is a form of *object*, and objects are defined when Perceiver thought uses concrete thought to organize Mercy experiences. Similarly, the relationship between trigonometric functions and the various sides of a right triangle is also defined *spatially*, indicating a combination of abstract thought and concrete thought.

Finally, notice also that all of these manipulations come up with answers that are *certain*. As long as no mistakes have been made, one can *know* with absolute certainty what the answer is. This digital certainty is consistent with the demands of technical thought.

Transforming Cp into Ci

So far, we have seen that the manipulations of math are consistent with the way in which Ci operates. Going further, I suggest that a major portion of the math which a student learns in high school can be intepreted in terms of the concrete circuit of Cp being transformed into the abstract circuit of Ci.

Let us begin with some review. Contributor thought connects Server sequences with Perceiver facts. We have just seen that in *abstract* thought, the Server sequences are formed using Teacher symbols while Perceiver thought assigns meanings to these sequences of symbols. In *concrete* thought, Perceiver facts are used to describe the *locations* of Mercy experiences while the Server sequences describe *actions* which can be used to get from one location to another.

I have mentioned that *cause-and-effect,* or the *if-then* statement, is the fundamental building block for Cp. Both are examples of *temporal* facts. A fact is a Perceiver connection that ties together Mercy experiences. A *temporal* fact is a Perceiver connection which ties together Mercy experiences that are separated by time. Cause-and-effect says that two Mercy experiences which are separated by time are connected because a Server sequence leads from one experience to the other. Similarly, if-then says that if the first Mercy experience occurs, then it will be followed by the second Mercy experience, implying that the two are connected by a Server sequence.

In math, the if-then statement is represented by the *function.* A function has an input, an output, and some sort of mechanism that turns the input into the output. For instance, one could consider a steering wheel as an input, the angle of the front wheels as the output, and the steering mechanism as the function that transforms the input into the output.

Math takes the *concrete* elements of cause-and-effect and represents them using *abstract* symbols:

First, the *Mercy* experiences which are the starting point and the finishing point for cause-and-effect are turned into *Teacher* symbols through the use of the *variable*. In order to make this clear, we will represent our Mercy experience by the non-verbal picture of a pencil: ✎. The practical circuit of Cp works with non-verbal items, such as a ✎. It then attempts to get more pencils, bigger pencils, brighter pencils, or longer-lasting pencils. Math says, let ✎ be represented by the letter 'x'; instead of writing ✎, we will use 'x' to represent ✎.

Replacing ✎ with a variable produces positive Teacher emotions. That is because ✎ is a *specific* item. A variable, in contrast, is *general* because it can represent many different types of items and not only markers. When one symbol can represent many items, then this produces Teacher feelings of order-within-complexity. Notice that both ✎ and 'x' have a Perceiver meaning, but the variable has a more *general* Perceiver meaning because it can be used to *represent* many different specific items. Thus, a variable is a kind of Platonic Form.

Second, the mechanism that leads from input to output is represented mathematically by the *function*. The math student is taught that a valid function must pass the 'vertical line test'; in simple English, each possible input must lead to one and only one output. We see here the insistence which technical thought places upon *certainty*. The output of a function must be known with certainty; there can be no ambiguity. Technical thought also limits its activity to a restricted 'playing field'. In a math function, this limited 'playing field' is described by the *domain* and *range* of a function. The domain describes the set of accepted inputs, while the range describes all possible outputs.

A function requires *two* variables, one for the input and the other for the output. In the typical high school math problem, 'x' is used to represent the input and 'y' is used to represent the output. In mathematical language, 'x' is the *independent* variable because it describes the input, while 'y' is the *dependent* value because it represents the output, which depends upon the input.

It is possible to represent the relationship between input and output *spatially* by drawing an x-y graph, something which every math student learns how to do. Notice that a graph is still a form of *concrete* thought, because the concrete relationship between input and output is being represented using non-verbal lines and points.

In a math function, the connection between input and output is indicated by an '=' sign. When a mathematical equation is used to represent a function of Cp, the '=' sign implies a sense of *direction* in which input *leads* to output. That is because concrete thought uses Server *actions* to lead from input to output.

For instance, suppose that a serviceman charges $25 an hour for labor plus $30 for making a house call. How much will it cost if the worker spends 2 hours on a job? First, one must define the input and output variables. One could use 'x' to represent the number of hours worked and 'y' to represent the total cost. The relationship between input and output would then be written as '$y = 25x + 30$'.

Notice that the concrete relationship between cause and effect has been transformed into an abstract sequence of symbols. Earlier on, we saw how Ci is used to manipulate math expressions. A function is translated from the 'language' of Cp to the 'language' of Ci by replacing each concrete element in a cause-and-effect relationship by its abstract equivalent.

Notice also that the symbolic representation is more *general* than the initial situation. The initial question asked about the specific situation of working for two hours. In contrast, the math function allows one to calculate the total cost for a job lasting *any* time duration. Again, we see the implicit presence of Teacher emotion.

Adding the '=' sign turns the expression into an *equation* in which one expression is made equal to another. We now have to modify the Server rearranging rules which were described earlier in order to make allowance for the '=' sign. This is done by introducing *properties of equality*, which state that one side of an equation can be modified using any acceptable method, as long as the same modification is also applied to the *other* side of the equation. For instance, one might wish to subtract 30 from both sides of the previous equation giving '$y - 30 = 25x + 30 - 30$'. One can also continue to apply the original Server rearrangements to *one* side of an equation as long as the Perceiver meaning is left unchanged. Thus, '$25x + 30 - 30$' can be simplified to '$25x$'.

When one makes a transition from Cp to Ci, then fundamental definitions become altered to reflect the thinking of Ci. In addition, Ci will begin to apply its *own* form of processing leading to expressions that can no longer be translated from Ci back to Cp.

First, the definition of *input* can be expanded to reflect the symbolic processing of Ci. In a concrete function, the input is a value such as '$x = 2$', representing a *Mercy* experience. In contrast, function notation allows the input to be a *Teacher* symbolic sequence as well as a *Mercy* experience. For instance, function notation writes '$y = 25x + 30$' as '$f(x) = 25x + 30$'. As before, it is possible to let '$x = 2$', but it is also possible to use an expression such as '$2t - 1$' for 'x'. This leads to the result '$f(2t - 1) = 25(2t - 1) + 30$' which evaluates to '$50t + 5$'. Thus, the function which initially led from one concrete experience to another now leads from one abstract symbolic sequence to another.

Second, it is also possible to replace the *output* with a symbolic sequence. For instance, instead of merely writing math equations of the form '$y = 25x + 30$', one can also write '$3y - 2 = 25x + 30$' or '$3x - 5 = 25x + 30$'. This makes it possible to write equations that are not functions. Remember that the function was initially defined using Cp and then translated into the language of Ci. But Ci is now using its own processing to come up with equations that Ci regards as valid but which Cp no longer regards as meaningful functions.

Third, the definition of *domain* alters. Cp regards domain as the set of possible inputs. For instance, in our labor example, 'x' could vary between zero and eight. The serviceman might ring the doorbell, find no one home and leave right away, charging $30 for his travel time. Or, he might look at his watch, realize that he had worked eight hours and then declare that it was time for him to go home.

But when Ci is used, then domain becomes defined as the set of possible values where the equation is *defined*, because Ci works with precise definitions. In our example, the equation works everywhere because any possible value of 'x' can be used. In contrast, the equation 'y = 10/(3 – x)' becomes undefined when 'x = 3' because this leads to the forbidden condition of dividing by zero. Saying this another way, Teacher thought views domain as the area within which a general Teacher theory applies, like the domain of a ruler or the domain of a set of laws.

These two definitions of domain often collide. For example, it is possible to plug in a negative value for time into the equation 'y = 25x + 30'. Ci domain would regard this as acceptable, while Cp domain would reject this as meaningless.

Fourth, the '=' sign acquires a different meaning. Cp views '=' as a one-way arrow leading from input to output. That is because '=' represents a *Server* connection and Server thought deals with time. However, Ci views '=' as a way of indicating that two mathematical expressions are equivalent, which represents a *Perceiver* connection. For Ci, evaluating an equation means performing a *Perceiver* connection followed by *Teacher* simplification. In other words, if Perceiver thought joins two expressions together to form an equation, then how can this symbolic statement be simplified.

For instance, consider the equation 'x + 3 = 2x – 5'. The properties of equality say that equality will be preserved as long as the same operation is done to both sides of an equation. Thus, this equation can be changed to read 'x – x + 3 + 5 = 2x – x – 5 + 5'. This can be simplified to '8 = x', which can be rewritten as 'x = 8'. Cp would view this as 'the correct answer'. Ci, in contrast, would see 'x = 8' as the *simplest* way to write the sequence of symbols 'x + 3 = 2x – 5'.

In some computer languages, different symbols are used to represent these two meanings of the '=' sign. For instance, in Pascal, when a value is being assigned to an output variable based upon the evaluation of some input equation, then ':=' is used. In contrast, '=' is reserved for determining if two expressions are equivalent.

Finally, a different definition is used for Perceiver *truth*. For Cp, a math function is a tool for predicting the relationship between input and output. Given a certain input, what will be the output. Or, what type of input should be chosen in order to reach a desired output. Checking a result usually means either looking in the back of the textbook for the 'right answer', or else comparing the predicted value with the actual value. Saying this more formally, truth is usually viewed as being based in either *correspondence* with reality or *revelation* from a 'special book'.

Ci, in contrast, looks for *coherence*. Ci does not see any need to check its answers with some outside source. Instead, what matters is internal consistency. In other words, have mathematical operations been applied correctly and is the solution free of internal contradiction. Of course, this assumes that Perceiver thought is functioning adequately. It is also possible for Ci to base its functioning upon a Perceiver foundation of revealed truth. When this is the case, then the student of math will probably compare his answers with what is written in the back of the textbook.

Even if Perceiver thought is functioning, Perceiver knowledge cannot be gained instantly, and Server skills of manipulating symbolic expressions cannot be acquired effortlessly. Therefore, the more advanced student may still ensure that he did everything right by checking with the textbook. If the beginning student finds a discrepancy, then he will assume that the textbook is correct. If the advanced student finds that his answer disagrees with the textbook, then he will check his work for mistakes, and if he finds none, then he will *also* check the textbook answer for errors. Similarly, the math expert will check his solutions with his peers when doing advanced calculations in order to uncover possible mistakes.

The Number System

Turning to more basic math elements, let us look now at the development of the number system. Suppose that I have ✎✎, ✎, and ✎✎✎✎. Teacher thought will find this inelegant because there is complexity but not order. It is possible to increase feelings of Teacher order by arranging the items in *sequence* and by making each step in this sequence the *same*. In our example, rearranging the items gives us ✎, ✎✎, and ✎✎✎✎, while making the steps the same size prompts us to *add* an intermediate quantity, giving us ✎, ✎✎, ✎✎✎, and ✎✎✎✎. (I should mention that this same technique is used to derive rules of musical harmony.) Notice that we have taken a collection of *Perceiver* objects and have arranged them into a *Server* sequence. Then we have increased *Teacher* feelings of order-within-complexity by ensuring that the items in this sequence are separated by *equal* steps. This increases Teacher order by allowing a *number* of steps to be described by a *single* statement.

So far, we have used abstract thought to bring order to concrete elements. The next step is to replace the concrete objects with abstract symbols. The simplest way to do this is by representing each object with a slash, so that ✎ = 'I', ✎✎ = 'II', ✎✎✎ = 'III', ✎✎✎✎ = 'IIII', and so on. In this way, a Perceiver group of objects is represented by a collection of symbols. But this is inelegant, and inelegance makes Teacher thought feel bad, so the most obvious way of producing Teacher order-within-complexity is by organizing the slashes into groups. Therefore, 'IIIII' might be replaced by '𝍸'. A better way of bringing order to complexity is by using a *single* symbol to replace the complexity of a *collection* of symbols. This brings us to Roman numerals, which replaces 'IIIII' with 'V', 'VV' with 'X', 'XXXXX' with 'L', and so on. Notice that the Roman method is superior because it can handle both small groups and large groups. Because a larger range of numbers can be represented using a smaller number of symbols, this leads to greater Teacher feelings of order-within-complexity.

The Western number system takes this system several steps further. First, it separates the groups by equal steps. In Roman numbers, 'V' is five times as big as 'I', while 'X' is only twice the size of 'V'. In Western numbers, each group is ten times the size of the previous group. A similar comparison can be made between imperial measurements and metric measurements. A yard is three feet, while a foot is twelve inches. In contrast, a meter is ten decimeters, a decimeter is ten centimeters, and so on.

Second, the *Perceiver* concept of the group is replaced by the *Contributor* concept of the *function*, because one can step up from one group to the next larger group by performing the function of multiplying-by-ten. On the one hand, Roman numerals are all defined with respect to a *single* item. For instance, 'L' describes 50 items while 'M' is 1000 items. The Western number system, in contrast, defines each group with respect to the *previous* group, with each group ten times larger than the previous group. Because a *single* function can lead from one group size to the next, this leads to greater Teacher feelings of order-within-complexity.

Finally, this Contributor *function* of multiplying by ten is then represented by the *Server* step of rearranging symbols within a sequence. Thus, '100' is ten times as large as '10' because the '1' in '100' has moved one place to the left. The position of a number in the sequence is indicated by using '0' as a place holder, giving '0' a *Server* definition of defining order in a sequence and not just a *Perceiver* definition of representing 'nothing'.

Of course, we all learned this back in elementary school. But what I am pointing out here is the mental processing that is being used. Perceiver thought is organizing Mercy experiences, Cp is turning these Perceiver groups into Contributor functions, and Ci is representing these functions as symbolic manipulation. And all of this manipulation is ultimately being guided by Teacher feelings of order-within-complexity.

And just as Ci takes the translated concept of the Cp function and generalizes it to form numerous types of equations, so Ci has taken the translated concept of the Cp Western number system and generalized it to form additional kinds of numbers. So far, we have come up with an efficient way of representing *whole* numbers, which start from 0 and count in the positive direction. But, we are still viewing numbers as a way of representing a group of objects. Thus, we can have 0✎, 3✎, 20✎, 28✎, and so on. It is possible to generalize numbers further by again replacing the object with a sequence.

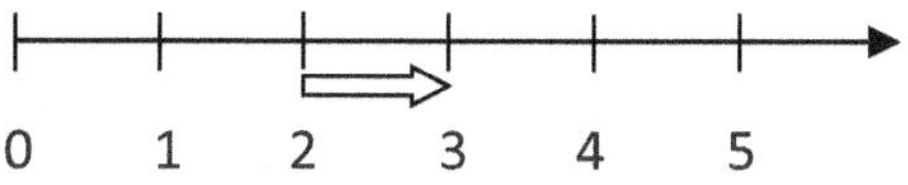

This is done by representing counting as *movement* along a number line. Instead of viewing counting as repeatedly adding one more item to a group, counting turns into the Server action of moving one step to the right. Similarly, organizing items into a group that is ten times as large becomes taking a step along the number line that is ten times as large. By viewing counting as taking a sequence of Server steps along a line, two generalizations are possible—and Teacher thought feels good when ideas can be generalized.

First, it is possible to move *left* as well as right on the number line, leading to the concept of *negative* numbers. Second, if one can represent numbers which are ten times as large by moving ten times as far, then by moving 1/10 as far, it should be possible to represent numbers which are ten times as small. And if a number that is ten times as large is represented symbolically by moving one place to the *left* in a Server sequence of symbols, then a number that is ten times as small can be represented by moving one place to the *right* in the sequence of symbols, leading to the *decimal system.*

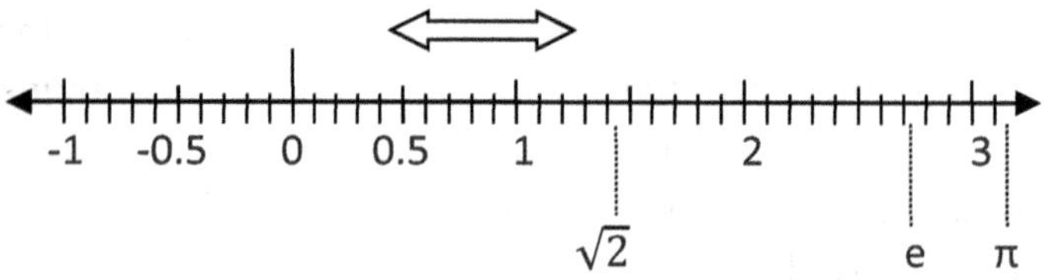

The number line together with the decimal system solves two problems that are related to abstract technical thought. First, remember that the technical circuit of Ci works with a limited number of clearly defined elements. The decimal system allows any number to be represented through the use of ten symbols and a decimal place.

Second, Ci wants to know with certainty. It wants clear categories and precise numbers. But the real world is messy and not precise. A mathematical line may be precisely two units long, but a real line is always two inches plus or minus a bit, and it is that 'bit' which annoys technical thought with its precise categories. However, by dividing quantities into smaller and smaller groups, it is possible to represent a real, messy quantity by a sequence of clean, numerical digits. For instance, 2 inches and a bit turns into 2.136 inches, or possibly 2.136432903257 inches. Of course, as every physics teacher will tell you, the extra digits in the second number are probably meaningless, because it is physically impossible to measure an item with that much precision, but in theory, the decimal system can represent any quantity to any desired level of accuracy using the clean notation that is preferred by technical thought.

What decimal notation cannot solve is the problem of *irrational* numbers, such as those shown in the number line above. Some of these, such as e and π, are imposed upon math by the messy real world, and math has no choice but to use the kludge of representing each irrational number with a special symbol. With other irrational numbers, such as $\sqrt{2}$, it is possible to take the more general step of representing them as a combination of a function and a symbol.

Turning Synthetic into Analytic

I have suggested in the main text that, in the human mind, concrete thought develops first and abstract thought emerges from concrete thought. We have just seen that this occurs through a standard process which can be explained using the diagram of mental symmetry: First, Cp takes normal concrete thought and describes it in terms of technical functions. Then, Contributor thought takes these functions and translates them into the symbolic language of Ci. Finally, Ci uses its own form of processing to extend these now-abstract functions in ways that extend beyond concrete thought.

I suggest that this clarifies the argument between the philosophers Carnap and Quine over the existence of *analytic* statements. Rudolf Carnap suggested that the truth of a *synthetic* statement is based in experience, whereas the truth of an *analytic* statement is based purely in meaning and theory. Quine argued that pure analytic statements do not exist because every abstract statement ultimately has its source in concrete experiences.

In the language of mental symmetry, Carnap said that Ci and Cp are independent, whereas Quine insisted that Ci is ultimately dependent upon Cp.

I suggest that they are both right. Except for the basic Teacher elements of words, symbols, and visual outlines, all of analytic thought appears to be seeded by concrete thought, as Quine stated. However, we have just seen that even though Ci is initially seeded by Cp, it is possible for Ci to redefine abstract thought to exclude any elements of Cp and then to extend abstract thought in ways that do not apply directly to Cp. In other words, even though Cp is the 'trunk' and Ci is the 'branch', Ci can 'saw off the branch on which it is sitting', disconnect itself from the trunk of Cp, be 'held up' purely by the emotional force of Teacher emotion, and then proceed to build entire 'castles in the air'. When Ci reaches this final stage of *disconnection* and *extension*, then I suggest that it does make sense to distinguish between synthetic and analytic statements as Carnap did.

Saying this another way, the mental circuit of Ci is a self-contained mental jurisdiction which applies its own private rules of analysis. Ci uses internal logic to generate analytic statements, it uses an internal method to error-check its results, and it works with absolute certainty. Synthetic statements are generated through the assistance of other mental circuits which use others means of testing information. Therefore, it is important to make a distinction between analytic statements and synthetic statements. However, as the field of engineering demonstrates, it is possible to enter and exit the realm of Ci, and to move between the analytic statement and the synthetic statement, if one takes the proper care.

Finally, I should point out that while the word 'analytic' being used here is related to the term 'analytical' on the diagram of mental symmetry, they are not the same. An analytic statement is the counterpart to a synthetic statement, whereas analytical thought is the opposite of associative thought.

Calculus

Calculus is based upon the concept of the *limit*, which says that one can get as close as one wishes to a desired number, but can never reach the actual number itself. A limit is cognitively interesting, because it violates the absolute certainty that is demanded by technical thought. Instead, a limit resembles the type of confidence that is associated with Perceiver and Server confidence. For Perceiver thought, a fact is never totally certain. Instead, it always carries with it a level of uncertainty. Perceiver thought can use various methods to increase the certainty of a fact, but absolute certainty can never be achieved.

When the mind enters technical thought, it makes a logical jump from partial certainty to absolute certainty. This logical leap is especially apparent to the Perceiver *person*, for when he implements a concrete plan, then he must choose to hand mental control over to subconscious Contributor thought, even though he is not totally certain of the facts and even though he can never become totally certain of the facts.

As technical thought develops, it will eventually realize that its sense of absolute certainty is built upon an uncertain foundation. Technical thought will then have an epistemological crisis and enter a period of self-questioning. This is described in greater detail in the main text as well as in the section on Foucault's three epistemes. In order for technical thought to continue functioning, it must accept that it is *based* upon a foundation of partial certainty, that it is possible to *increase* this sense of certainty, but that it still must ultimately take a logical *leap* to reach an answer. I suggest that the same sort of mental transition occurs when working with a limit.

It is interesting to examine the formal definition of a limit in the light of mental symmetry. Suppose that a person wishes to find the *answer* with a certain level of certainty. In math terms, suppose that one wants to know the answer to an accuracy of $+/- \varepsilon$. Mathematically, the limit exists if it is possible to reach any possible ε that one desires by controlling the input to an accuracy of $+/- \delta$. In the language of mental symmetry, the limit is being defined in terms of Contributor choice using the circuit of Cp. In simple terms, Contributor thought says, "Even though I am no longer certain, I still have not lost control, because I can achieve any level of certainty that I wish as long as I choose to control the input with sufficient care."

Let us look briefly at the derivative and the integral from a cognitive perspective, asking why the mathematician is interested in calculus and what mental mechanisms are at play. The use of the limit gives us a cognitive clue. I have suggested that the technical circuits of Ci and Cp work with total certainty, whereas Perceiver thought and Server thought use partial certainty. A limit is a mathematical version of partial certainty. This suggests that we are looking at the involvement of Perceiver and Server thought.

Now let us turn to the basic definition of the derivative and the integral. The starting point is the *function*: $y = f(x)$. There is an input variable 'x', an output variable 'y', and some function $f(x)$ which connects these two. Based upon what we have discussed so far, we can make two conclusions: First, we are dealing with *Cp*, because the basic building block for Cp is the function. Second, we are using the *language* of Ci, for we are stating everything using equations written with symbolic terms. Thus, I suggest that the purpose of the derivative and the integral is to meet the needs of Cp using the language of Ci.

When Cp is given some function or plan to implement, it is concerned primarily with two elements. We can see what these are by examining the behavior of the Contributor *person*, who is conscious in Contributor mode. First, there is a focus upon *choice*. That is because Contributor mode is the part of the mind which chooses; it chooses how to connect Perceiver facts with Server sequences, and it controls technical thought. Second, there is an emphasis upon '*the bottom line*'. That is because Contributor planning is guided by the emotional result that is the end product of following a certain plan. With Cp, this emotional result is provided by the Mercy emotions of 'the bottom line'. The Contributor person finds the 'butterfly effect' fascinating because it brings these two factors together; it describes a situation in which a single choice has a major impact upon the bottom line.

Now let us look at the mental circuit of Cp, in which Contributor mode ties together Server actions and Perceiver facts. In concrete thought, Perceiver facts define the map and Server actions are used to get from one location to another within this map. Contributor mode *chooses* by examining the current Perceiver location and then deciding which Server action to implement. A physical action has two characteristics: First, it occurs only in the present moment; second, it produces change. Thus, when Contributor mode chooses to perform a Server action, then it is activating a mental strategy which produces *instantaneous change*. That defines the derivative.

There is also the role played by Perceiver thought. Whenever Contributor mode implements a step in some plan, this changes the Perceiver location. As the plan continues to be carried out, these changes add up, leading to an accumulative result. Perceiver thought does this *accumulating* by keeping a mental record of what is 'me' or what is 'mine'. That defines the integral.

Saying this in simple cognitive terms, the function is the basic building block for Cp, a concrete circuit that is controlled by Contributor mode. When Cp is operating, then the interaction between Contributor mode and Server mode defines the derivative, while the interaction between Contributor mode and Perceiver mode defines the integral. Thus, these two mathematical concepts appear to have matching cognitive components.

Starting from this mental foundation, it is then possible for Ci to extend the concept of the derivative and the integral in various ways, including those which make no sense to Cp. But it appears that the basic ideas of the derivative and the integral are rooted solidly in the cognitive structure of Cp.

Logic

Logic is not math, but it is related to math. Therefore, I would like to add a few paragraphs about logic here as an appendix to the appendix on math. I should emphasize that I will not attempt to analyze logic rigorously or use rigorous terminology, but rather I will limit myself to discussing some general concepts of logic in the light of mental symmetry. My primary source of information is Wikipedia; in areas where Wikipedia is inadequate, I have 'googled' the subject until it became clear.

If-Then

Let us begin by looking at the *if-then* statement. Logic assigns several distinct meanings to this statement, and I suggest that these meanings can be analyzed in terms of mental circuits. First, there is the meaning of *causality*, which describes how Cp interprets if-then. As I have mentioned several times, the connection of cause-and-effect forms a basic building block for Cp. Cp views cause-and-effect in terms of *time*, with the cause leading through some Server action to the effect. This Server action may be performed by an agent, or it may be a Server 'action' that is performed by Nature. In math, this interpretation of if-then leads to the *function*, which has an input, typically represented by 'x', and an output, typically written as 'y'.

Second, there is the *material conditional*, which defines if-then by means of a *truth table*. The truth table for 'If A then B' is below. Notice that the statement 'If A then B' is True unless 'A' is True and 'B' is False.

Using this definition of if-then, the statement 'If it is Saturday, then 1 + 1 =2' would evaluate to True because the 'B' statement of '1 + 1 = 2' is always True. Obviously, this type of if-then statement does not make *sense*, because sense is based in how Cp defines an if-then statement. This contrast in meaning is discussed further in the appendix on problems in philosophy.

A	B	A -> B
True	True	True
True	False	False
False	True	True
False	False	True

What concerns us here is how this interpretation of an if-then statement relates to the mind. I have suggested in the main text that the truth table is an expression of the technical abstract circuit of Ci.

Let us elaborate. First, abstract thought 'moves' from one sequence of Teacher words to another. In our example, the 'movement' is from the statements 'It is Saturday' and '1 + 1 = 2' to the statement 'If it is Saturday, then 1 + 1 = 2'. Second, abstract 'movement' is guided by a general Teacher theory, which in this case is 'If A then B', because that is the most *general* way of writing an if-then statement. Third, Ci defines terms precisely and limits operations. Similarly, each expression in a logical if-then statement must be *well formed*, and logic only allows certain operations to be carried out. Fourth, Ci works with digital certainty. Similarly, in a truth table, only certainty labels of True or False are permitted. Finally, Perceiver thought performs the *'movement'*. We know that Perceiver thought builds connections between facts and that it labels new facts on the basis of labels that are applied to existing related facts. This describes what happens when a truth table is applied. The fact 'A' has a label of either True or False, and the fact 'B' also has a label of True or False. When these two facts are combined, then this leads to a new fact which is given a label of True or False based upon the labels possessed by the facts 'A' and 'B' and the rules of the logical formula.

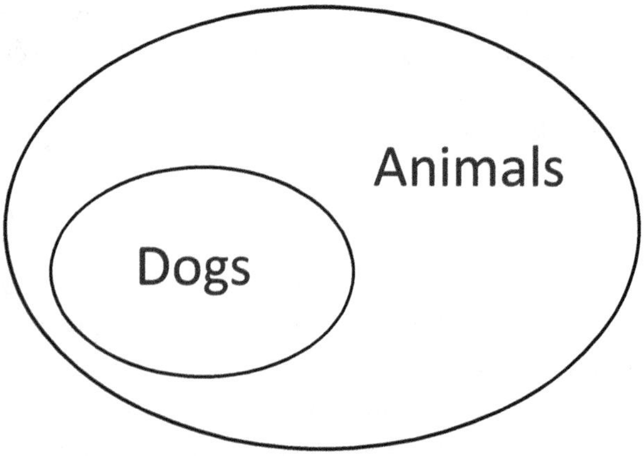

The third definition of the if-then statement is an expression of *normal abstract* thought. I have mentioned in the main text that Teacher thought makes general statements while Perceiver facts limit the generalization of these statements. An if-then statement can be used to indicate that one set of items is a *subset* of another. For instance, the statement 'If it is a dog, then it is an animal' can be shown using an *Euler diagram*. Because the circle of Dogs lies *within* the circle of Animals, this indicates that Dogs are a subset of Animals.

Dogs are a subset of animals because all dogs are animals, but it is possible to find animals, such as cats, which are not dogs. Notice how this thinking relates to *normal* abstract thought. First, Teacher thought would like to make the statement Dogs as general as possible, but Perceiver thought restricts the generality of this statement by coming up with *counter-examples*, such as Cats, which restrict the generality of Dogs. Second, Teacher thought comes up with a general statement by taking a Teacher memory and attempting to *concentrate* on it. When Teacher thought concentrates on a specific set of words or symbols, then other Teacher words and symbols will be viewed in the light of this focus of concentration, thus turning it into a general theory. For instance, Teacher thought will find that it can concentrate on the term Animals as long as the topic includes Dogs, Cats, and similar living creatures. However, if Teacher thought attempts to concentrate on Animals when the topic of computers comes up, then Perceiver thought will come up with a counter-example that will limit the generality of Animals: "A computer is not alive. It is not an animal."

Syllogism

The syllogism was invented by Aristotle and defines the main type of logic used before modern times. A syllogism contains a major premise, a minor premise, and a conclusion. The classical example is: All men are human; all humans are mortal; therefore all men are mortal. Each statement in a syllogism can be one of four types: 'All are' is a type A, 'Some are' is a type I, 'Some are not' is a type O, and 'None are' is a type E. When one makes a syllogism, one states the major premise, the minor premise, and the conclusion, and then one determines whether the conclusion follows from the major and minor premises. For instance, the following is a syllogism with a valid conclusion: Some dogs have no tails; all dogs are animals; therefore some animals have no tails.

Syllogisms can be evaluated through the use of *Venn diagrams*. What interests us here is how this relates to what we have discussed about if-then statements. We will look first at how a Venn diagram is used to solve type A and type E syllogisms that use *universal* statements, such as *all* dogs are animals, or *no* computers are alive.

In simplest terms, a universal syllogism is valid if the overlapping Venn diagram can be turned into a non-overlapping Euler diagram. For instance, borrowing a picture from Wikipedia, the statement 'No P is M' is shown on the top right by excluding the overlap between M and P, while the statement 'All S are M' is shown on the top left by excluding the part of S that does not include M. Putting those two together produces the three overlapping circles in the middle. The conclusion of 'No S is P' is shown on the bottom by eliminating the area of overlap between S and P. The *validity* of the conclusion is checked by comparing the middle circles with the bottom circles. If everything which is eliminated in the bottom circles is *also* eliminated in the middle circles, then the 'if', which is represented by the white part in the middle circles, is a *subset* of the 'then', which is represented by the white part in the bottom circles. In other

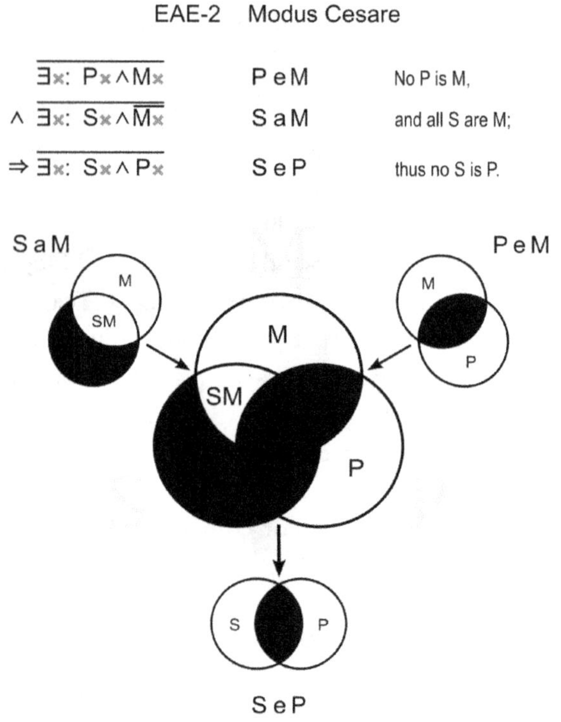

words, the syllogism is valid because the overlapping Venn diagram can be turned into a non-overlapping Euler diagram.

Now let us relate this to the mind. Normal abstract thought works by using Perceiver facts to restrict the generality of Teacher theories. Notice how each set of circles was generated by using the Perceiver meanings of a statement to restrict the Teacher generality of that statement. Notice also that we ended up with an if-then statement which is like the if-then statement that was generated earlier by using Perceiver thought to restrict the generality of Teacher theories. Thus, we conclude that universal syllogisms do *not* represent technical thought in its purest form, but rather are a technical version of *normal* abstract thought.

When a syllogism contains *particular* statements, such as 'some dogs have no tails', or 'some computers are not portable', then an extra step is required. First, universal statements are used to limit Teacher generality, as before. But the particular statements are then evaluated by asking whether a Perceiver connection can be made. If a solid connection does exist, then the statement is valid; if a solid connection does not exist, then the statement is not valid. Obviously, when Perceiver thought is looking for connections, then it will assume that something *exists* which can be connected. Thus, the statement 'Some are' or 'Some are not' assumes the existence of at least one item.

The evaluation of a syllogism that contains a particular statement can be explained in terms of *normal concrete* thought. A particular statement involves *specific* items; in normal concrete thought, Perceiver mode observes specific Mercy experiences to look for *connections* that are *repeated*. A set of connections that are repeated is defined as a Perceiver fact. Perceiver belief in a fact indicates the certainty which Perceiver thought has in that connection. Normally, Perceiver confidence in a connection increases as Perceiver thought continues to observe that connection being repeated. For instance, a knife is a blade connected with a handle. The more that Perceiver thought observes blades connected with handles, the more confident it becomes in the fact of knives. In a syllogism, logical statements are being used to determine whether connections exist or not and technical thought is demanding absolute certainty, but Perceiver thought is still using the presence of a solid connection to define truth.

Logic and Foucault's Epistemes

Modern logic uses a form of thinking that is not based upon the syllogism. Instead, modern logic can be explained in terms of truth tables. This means that modern logic uses a *different* mental circuit than the syllogism. We have just seen that syllogisms can be explained in terms of *normal* abstract thought, which uses Perceiver facts to limit the generalizing of Teacher theories; this is the type of thinking which the mind uses when *building* general Teacher theories. Syllogism takes the *construction* of a general Teacher theory and makes it technical by limiting the 'playing field', defining terms carefully, and looking for answers that are certain.

If one attempts to explain syllogism in terms of a simple general Teacher theory, one discovers that the results are inelegant. There are 256 types of syllogisms, but only 24 of these are valid, and these valid forms are usually remembered through the use of Mercy-based mnemonic names, such as Barbara, Cesare, Datisi, and so on, rather than as expressions of a general Teacher theory. This is because syllogisms do not come *from* a general Teacher theory but rather are a technical version of the thinking that normal abstract thought uses when it tries to *build* a general Teacher theory.

In contrast, modern truth table based logic corresponds to how the technical circuit of Ci *uses* a general Teacher theory. The technical thinking of Ci does not build general Teacher theories. Instead, it works *within* a general Teacher theory. Mentally speaking, when one constructs a system of modern logic, one begins with the technical constraints of Ci and then formulates a general Teacher theory within which technical thought can be performed.

The start of modern logic can be traced back to the publication of Gottlob Frege's *Begriffsschrift*. Frege's goal was to show that math is identical to logic, and his system of logic went much further than his predecessors in terms of rigor and formality. It is interesting to note that Frege's groundbreaking volume was published in 1879, precisely when Foucault said that the Modern episteme began. I have suggested that the Classical episteme represents a balance between normal thought and technical thought. A syllogism is a technical version of normal abstract thought. In contrast, technical thought has become the dominant mode of mental operation in the Modern episteme. Similarly, modern logic describes a way of thinking which represents pure technical thought.

Thus, it appears that the theory of mental symmetry can be used to explain the mental mechanisms behind syllogism and modern logic, while the transition from syllogism to modern logic can be explained by Foucault's epistemes, which themselves can be explained in terms of mental symmetry.

✵ Music

Countries that are part of the British Commonwealth have a conservatory system for studying music. As part of my violin training, I wrote a number of conservatory exams on music theory, so I am familiar with musical concepts such as perfect and plagal cadences, German, French, and Italian sixths, and the taboo against parallel fourths, fifths, and octaves. However, it was when I played in the Canadian National Youth Orchestra and took a class in music harmony that I realized for the first time that the rules of harmony are not just arbitrary but instead reflect a deep, underlying structure.

While I was writing this section, I stumbled across an essay by Robert Fink which uses overtones to explain the origins of the chord and the musical scale (Robert Fink, Greenwich Publishing). I mention him because I have incorporated a few of his concepts into my explanation.

__The Physics of Music__

Music is deeply rooted in physics, therefore in order to understand music, we need to start with some basic physics. When a string vibrates, then this vibration contains a fundamental frequency as well as a number of overtones. The fundamental vibration of a string, together with the first six overtones, are shown in a diagram. Similar principles apply when playing a pipe, but only some of these overtones will be present. On a violin, if a finger is placed lightly on one of the dots shown on the diagram, then the resulting sound will be a harmonic or overtone and not the basic frequency. It is visually striking when one places a finger on the dot marked '1/3' and can actually see where the string is not vibrating at the other node.

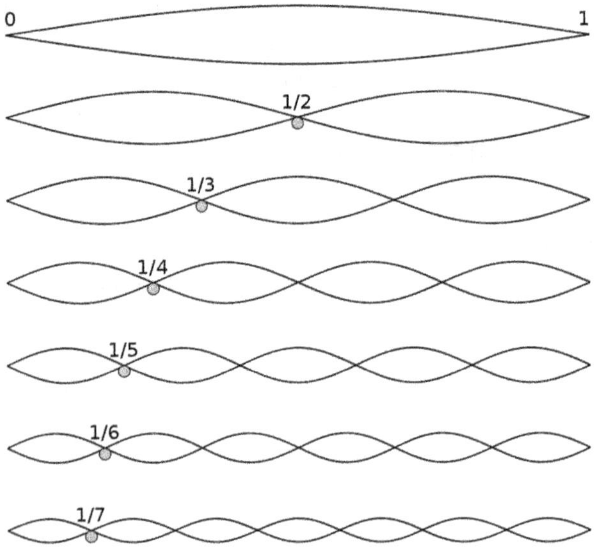

The human mind senses pitch *logarithmically* and not linearly. A note that vibrates at twice the frequency is sensed as an *octave* higher; one that vibrates at four times the frequency is noticed as *two* octaves higher. When two notes are separated by exact octaves, then the mind views them as higher or lower versions of the same note. That is why the musical scale goes from A to G and then returns back to A. The second A is one octave higher than the first A and is mentally seen as a higher version of the first A.

Whenever two notes are played together, then their frequencies will be related by *ratios* such as 2:1, 3:2, 115:23, and so on. When two notes are related by a *simple* ratio, then the mind regards this interval as pleasant, pure, and unified. For instance, the octave ratio of 2:1 feels essentially identical. The next two simple ratios of 3:2 and 4:3 also feel mentally *pure*. These three ratios are known in music as the *perfect* intervals, consisting of the octave, the perfect fifth, and the perfect fourth. The next two ratios feel pleasant but not as pleasant: The ratio of 5:4 defines the major third, while the ratio of 6:5 defines the minor third.

If one moves the bottom note up an octave by multiplying its frequency by two, then one ends up with other ratios which also feel pleasant. The perfect fifth ratio of 3:2 turns into 3:4 which is the perfect fourth, the major third ratio of 5:4 becomes the minor sixth interval of 5:8, while the minor third ratio of 6:5 becomes the major sixth interval of 6:10 or 3:5. In musical terms, both 3:5 and 5:3 refer to the interval of a major sixth. One is called the interval *below* a given note, while the other describes the interval *above* a note.

Notice that these relationships can also be stated in terms of the overtones that are shown on the diagram of string vibrations. The interval between the fundamental and the first overtone is an octave; the interval between the first and second overtones is a perfect fifth; the second and third overtones are related by a perfect fourth; the third and fourth overtones are related by a major third; and the fourth and fifth overtones are related by a minor third. This is known as the *harmonic series* and was originally discovered by Pythagoras.

Now let us put together the ratios that we have described, choosing the ones in which the smaller number is four or less and the larger number is five or less, starting with C as the fundamental note. We end up with C = 1:1; E = 5:4; F = 4:3; G = 3:2; A = 5:3; C = 2:1. This describes all except two notes of the major scale. The missing D can be added if we stack the two most pleasing perfect intervals, leading to a perfect fifth of a perfect fifth, which is 3:2 of 3:2 moved down an octave, which is 9:8. All that remains missing from the major scale is the *leading note*, and that is a strange beast which we will discuss later. It is possible to come up with the leading note by stacking a major third on top of a perfect fifth, but that is a less than perfect method which leads us to conclude that the leading note is acoustically a strange beast.

A scale is a Server *sequence* of notes. Server sequences are sensed by Teacher thought, which appreciates order-within-complexity. The complexity of the natural scale of C E F G A C can be made more ordered by filling in the gaps in the scale with regular sized steps. This explains why a D is added between the C and the E, and why a leading note of B is inserted between the A and the high C. In musical terms, this 'regular step' is referred to as a *whole tone*. Notice the *balance* between Mercy emotions and Teacher emotions. Mercy thought wants to use notes that are *related* to the home note, while

Teacher thought wants the scale to contain *regular* steps which avoid gaps. When dealing with the major scale, Mercy feelings produced by simple ratios take *precedence* over Teacher feelings produced by regular steps. Teacher thought can demand that the gaps in the scale be filled in, but the size of the steps of the scale still remain irregular.

Now let us do this ratio analysis once more, except this time instead of looking for the simplest ratios we will take the first four overtones of a *fundamental* frequency. That gives us 2:1, 3:1, 4:1, and 5:1. If we set C as the bottom note and write the higher notes of the ratio, we end up with C G C E. These three notes of C E G define the *chord* of C major. If we go further and add the two additional overtones of 6:1 and 7:1, this gives us C G C E G and a note that is close to Bb. This combination of 'C E G Bb' is known as the dominant seventh or V^7 chord of C major.

So far, I have not said anything new. Others have made similar observations. But I want to emphasize two points. First, both the musical scale and the musical chord are *not* arbitrary. Instead, they are based in simple mathematical principles of physics: When one takes all the frequencies that are related to a fundamental frequency by simple ratios and fills in the gaps, one comes up with the musical scale of that fundamental frequency, and when one takes the first four overtones of some note, one produces the major chord of that note. Second, music is evaluated emotionally. Simple musical ratios feel good, whereas complicated ones do not. For instance, the augmented fourth interval was historically known as the *devil's interval* because the ratio of frequencies is $\sqrt{2}$:1. Because music combines physics with emotions, one could refer to it as emotional mathematics.

It is this combination of emotion and physics which makes it difficult to discuss the topic of music. When the mind makes a mental separation between objective and subjective, then it will assume that emotions and logic are mutually exclusive. Music produces an emotional response. That is what makes music appealing. Because music produces a *subjective* response, the average listener assumes that it is not possible to analyze music rationally, and he will protest vigorously if someone does attempt to use logical thought to analyze musical taste. However, the emotional response that is produced by music is *not* arbitrary, but instead is ultimately determined by rational laws of physics.

Normally, when one violates the laws of physics, one experiences *physical* consequences from the natural world. In contrast, violating the laws of physics that apply to music leads to *emotional* consequences: It *feels* unpleasant. Thus, composers will often *temporarily* violate these rules in order to create emotional tension.

Now that we have introduced the physics behind music, let us turn our attention to the theory of mental symmetry. Neurology tells us that the left temporal lobe, which is associated with Teacher mode, interprets *verbal* speech, while the right temporal lobe, which is associated with Mercy mode, interprets *non-verbal* speech. Stating this another way, Teacher mode focuses upon sound that changes, whereas Mercy mode focuses upon sound that stays the same, because verbal speech is full of consonants and sounds that change, while non-verbal speech comes from the underlying tone of voice.

Saying this once more in a more technical manner, any frequency that is below about 20 Hz is handled by *Teacher* mode, because every individual cycle will be noticed as a change in sound by Teacher thought. Above 20 Hz, the mind is too slow to notice individual changes and starts to hear the repeated pattern as a steady tone, which is interpreted by Mercy thought as a musical note with a certain pitch. Going further, if this tone changes quickly, then Teacher mode will interpret this change as a consonant or transient.

This leads us to make the following conclusions, which are backed up by observations of personality. *Mercy* thought handles musical notes as well as musical tone. Note refers to the *fundamental* frequency; tone refers to the *harmonics* as well as the fundamental frequency. A musical note can have a tone which is harsh, sweet, clear, or muddy, and so on. These various tones all produce Mercy emotions. For instance, compare the soothing tone of a flute with the announcing tone of a trumpet. *Teacher* thought interprets beat and rhythm. Beat refers to the overall pulse, like the regular banging on a drum or the tapping of the foot; rhythm, in contrast, describes a repeated pattern of transient noises.

Notice that both Mercy thought and Teacher thought deal with simple elements as well as complicated elements. A Teacher beat is merely a sound that repeats at a low frequency; a Mercy note is simply a sound that repeats at a high frequency. A Teacher rhythm, in contrast, contains order-within-complexity. For instance, compare a rock beat with a Latin rhythm. The rhythm is far more complicated than the beat. Similarly, Mercy tone results from the interaction between fundamental frequencies and overtones. For instance, the tone of a flute sounds pure because it contains primarily the fundamental frequency. The pitch of a note can be measured with a frequency meter, the tone of a note cannot.

The most fundamental aspect of music is the *note*. The main difference between normal speech and song is the emphasis upon notes. When a person talks, his speech has a fundamental pitch but the mind ignores this as irrelevant (except in tonal languages). When a person sings, his words are the same but he now controls and emphasizes the pitch at which he is talking. Because music is based upon the *Mercy* experience of the note, it is an example of *concrete* thought, in which Server sequences are used to go from one Mercy experience to another, guided by a Perceiver map.

Before we continue, I would like to point out the relationship between math and music. The fundamental element of math is the *Teacher* symbol, while the fundamental element of music is the *Mercy* note. Math begins with the technical circuit of Cp and then transforms the concrete elements of Cp into the abstract elements of Ci, leading to a final structure which is a purely abstract combination of Teacher symbols. As we shall see, classical music also begins with the technical circuit of Cp. But because music is guided by *Mercy* emotions, it remains within Cp. However, in Western classical music, the abstract circuit of Ci has expanded the musical elements of Cp, leading to a form of music which is able to produce a far greater *range* of personal Mercy emotions.

Saying this another way, the primary element of Cp is the *function*, a chain of cause-and-effect in which the cause leads to the effect through a Server sequence which occurs over *time*. In math, the abstract thinking of Ci removes this Server sense of time and replaces it with a Perceiver sense of equivalence. In music, the sense of time remains, because a musical piece is defined as a collection of musical notes which occur over *time*, with one set of notes *leading* to another set of notes.

Personal identity is represented within the human mind as a set of emotional Mercy experiences. As a person moves physically through the world, his physical surroundings bring emotional Mercy experiences to mind. Similarly, as a musical song is played, the succession of notes will also bring emotional Mercy experiences to mind. Thus, a musical song feels to Mercy thought like a personal journey. This, I suggest, describes the core of how music affects the mind.

Now let us turn to the roles that are played by Perceiver mode and Server mode in music. Perceiver mode looks for Mercy experiences that are similar and organizes them into groups. With music, the basic Mercy experience is the *note*. Our look at physics has already described two types of similarity that Perceiver thought will notice: First, there is the Perceiver similarity of the *chord*, which ties together notes that have frequencies that are *closely* related. As a Perceiver *person*, I am sensitive to the chord structure of a musical piece, and when I play by ear, I mentally fit my notes into an internal 'roadmap' that represents the chords and how they change through the song. Second, there is the Perceiver similarity of the *scale*, which ties together notes that have frequencies that are *less* closely related. Thus, Perceiver thought will mentally connect the note C with the chord of C major and the scale of C major. Because the chord of C major and scale of C major are tied together by the note of C, music speaks of the *key* of C major.

Server mode works with *sequences*. In concrete thought, Server mode *moves* from one Mercy experience to another. In music, the *note* provides the Mercy experience. Thus, Server thought generates *sequences* of notes which move from one note to another. In music, this sequence of notes is called a *melody*.

Note the relationship between these various elements: Perceiver thought works with *spatial* facts, connecting Mercy items that occur together at the same time; a chord is a collection of *related* notes which are played *simultaneously*. Server thought naturally works with *sequences*, connecting Mercy items that are separated by time; a melody is a *sequence* of notes which occur one at a time, and the notes of a scale are also played one at a time. But we know that Perceiver thought first constructs a mental map by tying together Mercy experiences, and then Server actions are used to lead from one location to another within this map. Similarly, the scale is a Server sequence that connects notes which Perceiver thought regards as related.

Melody

In the key of C major, the scale is the white notes on the keyboard: C D E F G A B C. A melody that is written in a certain key will limit itself to using primarily the notes of that key. Consider, for example, the simple melody of 'Twinkle, Twinkle, Little Star' in the key of C. We will be using this tune to illustrate various musical principles, so if you cannot sing it in your head, then it may be helpful to play the notes on a keyboard or piano. The first half of this melody is C C G G A A G. F F E E D D C. All of these notes belong to the *scale* of C major. In addition, both phrases end on a note that belongs to the *chord* of C major: The first phrase ends on a G; the second phrase ends on a C.

Personal identity is defined as the set of emotional experiences upon which Mercy thought can continue to concentrate. Mercy thought can journey away from the 'home' of personal identity, but eventually it has no choice but to return back to 'home'. Similarly, a musical piece is written in a specific *key*. Each key defines a 'home' note, (known musically as the *tonic*), a chord, and a scale. A musical song is a 'journey' *away* from the musical elements of 'home' to related musical elements followed by a *return* to 'home'.

For instance, in the song, 'Twinkle, Twinkle, Little Star', the first phrase ends with a G. G is part of the home chord of C, but it is not the home note of C. Therefore, it will feel as if this phrase returns close to home but not to home itself. The second phrase does end on the home note of C, therefore, it does feel like returning to home. In contrast, the third phrase of G G F F E E D ends on a D, which, while part of the scale of C major, is related to the note of C major through the fairly distant ratio of 9:8. Therefore, this phrase will feel like traveling to a location that is *away* from home. *Repeating* this phrase intensifies the sensation of being away from home. However, this journey away from home is followed by a repeat of the first phrase which leads to the closure of arriving back at home, and the song ends on the home note of C.

Thus, even in a simple song like this, there is a variety of evoked emotions, defined by the distance of a note from the home note of C. For instance, consider again the first phrase of C C G G A A G. It begins at the home of C, moves to G which is close to home, moves further away to A, and then returns to G which is close to home. This movement away from home creates a sense of emotional tension which leads to a feeling of emotional resolution as musical movement returns closer to home. I stated previously that a melody restricts itself to the notes of the home scale. It is possible to increase emotional tension by using notes that are not part of the home scale. However, this must be done sparingly, because if too many unrelated notes are used, then the sense of home will be lost, just as experiencing too many unrelated emotional experiences can fragment an individual's sense of personal identity.

In general terms, the creation of musical tension, followed by the resolution of musical tension, plays a major role in music. The greatest tension is formed by notes that are *almost* correct, which can be resolved by following them with notes that *are* correct. For instance, when we looked at the musical scale, we were able to use simple ratios to come up with all except two of the notes: C...E F G A...C. And we were able to fill in the gap between the C and the E by *stacking* two simple ratios. What is missing is the note between A and C. This gap can be filled in by adding the *leading note* of B. It is called a leading note because it *leads* back to the primary note of C. If one plays a musical scale and stops with the leading note, then this will create a strong sense of musical tension, which is resolved by playing the final C. Try playing C D E F G A B on a piano and notice the strong urge to finish the scale by playing the final C. Thus, while most of the notes in the major scale are *closely* related to the key, the leading note is only somewhat related, and it helps to define the key primarily because it creates a sense of desire to *return* to the fundamental note of the key.

If one examines *non*-Western music, one finds that it does not make a distinction between the chord and the scale. Instead, some version of the *pentatonic* scale is usually used, which is halfway between a chord and a scale. Several types of pentatonic scale exist, but one of the most common is C D E G A C. This scale can be generated by continually moving up by perfect fifths, the simplest non-octave ratio, musically known as moving through the 'circle of fifths'. If one starts with the note of C, the first five notes of this sequence of fifths are C G D A E. Placing all of these notes within the same octave generates a pentatonic scale. Another form of pentatonic scale is C D F G A C, which contains the basic ratios of C:G = 2:3, C:F = 3:4, C:A = 3:5 as well as D, which is 3:2 of 3:2 (divided by 2). This form of pentatonic scale is used in Asian music.

Turning to another emotional aspect of music, raising the pitch of a note sounds happy and bright, while lowering the pitch sounds sad and dark. Over the centuries, tuning has risen in frequency in order to make music sound brighter. One can use this relationship between lowered pitch and sadness to explain the *minor* scale. A scale is composed of all the notes that are related to a home note that are separated by regular steps. A minor scale lowers all the notes of a scale which *can* be lowered without destroying the sense of relationship to the home note. For instance, in the scale of C, the notes of F and G cannot be lowered, because they are so closely related to the home note. In addition, the D cannot be lowered because it already is barely related to the home note, and lowering it would make it completely unrelated. Therefore, only the E, the A, and the B will be lowered. Lowering E to Eb changes its frequency ratio from 5:4 to 6:5 which is still a fairly simple ratio, lowering the A changes its ratio from 5:3 to 8:5 which is acceptable, while flattening the leading note improves its ratio from 15:8 to 9:5. That defines what is musically known as the *natural* minor scale.

However, as was mentioned before, there is still the matter of the leading note. The urge to 'return home' that is created by the leading note is very strong, but Teacher thought wants a scale to be constructed out of regular steps. One solution is to follow Mercy emotion at the expense of Teacher emotion, leading to the *harmonic* minor scale in which the A is flattened while the B is not, resulting in an unnaturally large step between the Ab and B. The term 'harmonic' tells us that Mercy feelings produced by harmony are being followed. The other solution is that of the *melodic* minor, which keeps both the A and the B unflattened on the way *up*, thus preserving the effect of the leading note leading to the home note, while flattening them both on the way down, preserving the minor feeling. The label of 'melodic' tells us that the Teacher-driven rule of avoiding excessive step size is being preserved.

Simple Harmony

Separating the chord from the scale makes it possible to play notes that belong to the scale but are not part of the chord. As we saw in our look at melody, playing too many of these notes leads to a feeling of being distant from home. That is why methods of elementary music education often start by teaching the pentatonic scale, because a student can play any combination of notes and they will feel right—they will feel 'close to home'. But separating the chord from the scale also makes it possible to stay within the scale while changing the chord, leading to musical *harmony*.

Thus, when the Western ear listens to pentatonic music, it sounds pure, because it only uses notes that are related to the key, but it also feels monotonous, because it is not able to move harmonically from one chord to another. And because harmonic movement is not possible, the concept of *harmony* does not exist when using a pentatonic scale.

We can illustrate the basic rules of harmony by returning to our sample song. We have seen that the *perfect* intervals of 3:2 and 4:3 define the notes which are most closely related to the home note. In a similar way, the two major *chords* which are most closely related to the home note are the two chords that start on one of these perfect intervals. In other words, if C is the home note, then 'C E G' is the home chord, 'G B D' is the chord which starts with G which is a perfect fifth above C, and 'F A C' is the chord which starts with F which is a perfect fourth above C. These three chords are commonly denoted musically by using the Roman numerals of I, V, and IV, and many simple songs are harmonized using only these three chords.

For instance, let us look again at Twinkle. The first phrase is C C G G A A G. The first four notes, along with the last note, belong to the chord of I and therefore will be harmonized using the home chord. The A in the middle, in contrast, is part of the chord of IV and so that chord will be used, leading to the *chord progression* of I IV I. If we look at the second phrase of F F E E D D C, one would think that the chord progression will be IV I V I, and this is possible. However, there is another musical choice, and in order to understand this, we have to look at the difference between *Perceiver* closeness and *Server* closeness.

When a person takes a personal journey, he uses Server actions to get from one Mercy location to another. We know that a melody represents this sequence of Server actions. Server thought defines closeness in terms of *distance*. When a person walks, he takes one step at a time with each step moving to a location that is near by. If we examine the melody of Twinkle, we see that most of it is composed of steps; there are very few jumps. A melody which has too many jumps will sound fragmented.

In contrast, chords are defined by *Perceiver* mode. Perceiver thought defines closeness in terms of *similarity*. For Server thought, D is closest to C because it is only one step away on the scale. For Perceiver thought, G is closest to C because the frequencies are most similar; they are related by the simple ratio of 3:2. The difference between Server similarity and Perceiver similarity can be seen by comparing the *melody* of a song with the *bass* line. The melody is guided by the *scale*, the bass reflects the *chords*. A melody *walks*; a bass *jumps*. It feels strange when a melody jumps too much or a bass walks too much.

Music creates emotional tension and then resolves this tension. The strongest way of resolving musical tension is by *returning home*. However, Server mode and Perceiver mode define 'returning home' in different ways. *Server* mode 'walks' from one Mercy note to another using the notes of the scale, therefore 'almost home' is a note that is one step away from the home note on the scale. The last phrase of Twinkle indicates one Server way of returning home. The phrase F F E E D D C walks its way back to the home note of C from the top down. A lot of melodies end this way, but a very effective way of arriving home is by playing the leading note followed by the home note. As we saw when introducing the leading note, it creates a strong emotional desire to lead to the home note.

Perceiver mode works with chords and defines musical closeness in terms of related frequencies. Therefore, returning home means playing the chord most closely related to the home chord followed by the home chord. In the key of C, this means playing the V chord of G followed by the I chord of C. This is in known in musical circles as a *perfect cadence*, because it is usually used to signify the end of a phrase or piece of music.

Notice that the song of Twinkle ends with both Server and Perceiver versions of 'returning home'. The melody finishes with F F E E D D C, indicating that the melody is taking Server steps to return home. And the penultimate note of D is part of the V chord while the home note of C is obviously part of the I (or home) chord of C.

Two additional musical features are often added to a perfect cadence in order to heighten the musical sensation of returning home, which we will illustrate using the key of C. First, notice that the leading note of B is a note within the chord of V. Therefore, even if the melody does not end with the leading note being followed by the home note, this sequence of notes is still embedded within the chord sequence of V I and can be emphasized. Second, V^7 is often used instead of V. In the key of C, this means using 'G B D F' instead of 'G B D'. Adding the F produces the 'devil's interval' between B and F, increasing the emotional tension of the 'almost home' chord, while the tension introduced by the F is released by 'returning home' to the E which is part of the home chord.

That brings us finally to the alternative way of harmonizing the second phrase of F F E E D D C in Twinkle. Instead of using IV to harmonize the F, V^7 may be chosen because the following E can be harmonized by the home chord of I. Thus, if we indicate the end of each phrase by a comma, the harmony for the whole song becomes: I IV I, V^7 I V I, I V I V, I V I V, I IV I, V^7 I V I. In other words, almost the whole song can be chorded as a series of perfect cadences. The chord sequence of IV I is another common cadence known as a *plagal cadence* and it shows up commonly in the 'Amen' to a hymn. And if one plays I V instead of V I, then this is called an *imperfect* cadence, which is used to indicate musical arrival at some point which is *not* home.

The difference between chord and scale allows us to define *two* kinds of musical movement to and from home. Changing chords is like moving from one 'house' to another within the 'neighborhood' of the key, while changing the note of the melody while staying with the same chord is like moving from one room to another within the same house. For instance, in the song 'Mary Had a Little Lamb', the home chord of I is usually used with the first seven notes of E D C D E E E. The D is not part of the home chord of C, but it forms part of the Server sequence of 'walking' between E and C. This is known musically as a *passing note*, and can be likened to moving from one room to another. If we analyze the harmony of the entire song of 'Mary Had a Little Lamb', it is composed of I V I, I V I. Notice, however, that the first phrase ends with E G G, while the song ends with E D C. Thus, the first phrase ends with the *chord* returning home but not the melody, while the song ends with *both* the chord and the melody returning home.

Abstract Thought and Foucault's Epistemes

We have looked at the type of simple harmony which chord and scale make possible. However, this harmony is limited to *one* key. It is possible to extend this by introducing the *chromatic* scale of twelve notes. The key of C uses only the white keys on the keyboard. A chromatic scale fills in the blanks by adding the *black* keys. The idea of the chromatic scale was known back in Greek times, and it was constructed by moving along the 'chain of fifths' by starting with some note and then continuing to go up by the ratio of 3:2 until arriving back at the original note. Except, one does not *quite* arrive back at the original note, which we will discuss in a moment.

What emerged at the end of the Renaissance era was the idea of using the chromatic scale as a way of forming twelve different keys and *modulating* from one key to another, and I suggest that this matches up cognitively with Foucault's transition from the Renaissance to the Classical episteme. Scientific theory emerged during the Classical episteme as researchers used abstract thought to come up with general Teacher theories based upon facts and sequences from the natural *world*. Likewise, the idea of keys and modulation emerged as composers used abstract thought to come up with a general musical structure based upon the chords and scales of natural *music*.

Two factors about the chromatic scale tell us that thinking is being guided by *Teacher* emotion. First, there is increased *order-within-complexity*. The seven uneven steps of the major scale are being replaced by twelve even steps. Making all the steps of the scale *equal* brings increased order to the complexity of the scale. Second, there is greater Teacher *generality*. Instead of remaining in only one key, each note of the chromatic scale can act as a home note that defines a key and a song can move from one key to another, known musically as *modulation*. Modulation also generalizes the concept of harmonic *closeness*. In the same way that the V chord is considered to be 'close to home' because it starts with a note that is an interval of 3:2 above the home note, so the *key* which is based on the note that is 3:2 above the home note is 'close' to the home key.

If moving from the home chord to a related chord is like walking to the house next door, then moving from the home key to a related key is like traveling to the next neighborhood. Thus, modulation can be used by composers to increase the emotional tension of 'leaving home' and 'returning home'.

Perfect pitch is the ability to hear a note and know what it is. I have perfect pitch and can tell by ear, for instance, whether a song is written in the key of C or the key of C#. Perfect pitch is uncommon; however, it seems to me that most people must have some subconscious form of perfect pitch, or else every musical key would sound the same. Going further, it appears that the average Western person has heard the 'white keys' so often that the key of C sounds normal to his mind, while the key of C# does not. Therefore, because raising pitch is associated with happiness and lowering pitch with sadness, this explains why songs that are written in keys with several sharps sound more cheerful than songs written in keys with many flats.

If a chromatic scale is tuned using the natural intervals of the key of C, then a musical piece will sound in-tune in the key of C, but it will sound out-of-tune if one plays in keys which have many sharps or flats. This is because moving along the 'chain of fifths' does not quite return back to the home note. Over the years, many different solutions have been proposed, but they all involve some method of adjusting the tuning so that it is possible to play in a wider selection of keys. The most common modern method is known as *equal tempered pitch*, in which each semi-tone is tuned to be $\sqrt[12]{2} \approx 1{:}1.059$. By making each interval the same, the mistuning is spread out over the keys, and it becomes possible to play in any key without sounding abnormally out-of-tune.

Cognitively speaking, equal-tempered pitch demonstrates a mental shift in which abstract thought takes precedence over concrete thought, which leads mentally to the formation of Platonic Forms. In normal tuning, Perceiver categories of pitch are determined by *Mercy* feelings of chord and dischord. In contrast, equal-tempered tuning is guided by *Teacher* emotions of structure and order, because all of the intervals are made *exactly* the same, even if this makes them sound slightly out-of-tune. In concrete thought, Perceiver facts provide a solid map, based upon facts that do not move. Abstract thought, in contrast, 'moves' Perceiver facts in order to increase Teacher emotions. In equal-tempered tuning, the Perceiver categories of pitch *are* being moved in order to increase Teacher emotions.

When society made a shift from Foucault's Classical episteme to his Modern episteme, then not only did abstract thought take *precedence* over concrete thought, but the technical abstract circuit of Ci *replaced* normal thought. In music, this was when *modern classical* music emerged. Over the years, I have had the 'privilege' of playing many modern works in orchestras. During the Classical episteme, technical thought occurred within an overall context of normal thought, because the goal was to use technical thought to build general Teacher theories and improve Mercy experiences. In music, this meant attempting to communicate emotionally with the listener by writing technically within the overall structure of musical harmony. The music of Johannes Brahms illustrates the ultimate expression of classical music, because it is harmonically complicated but still obeys the structure of harmony and contains melodious tunes.

The Modern episteme is characterized by technical science, specialization, and self-questioning. Because science is objective, Mercy emotions are suppressed. Similarly, specialization allows Teacher emotion to be disregarded, while self-questioning causes Perceiver facts to fall into doubt. What remains is technical thought based upon the Server *process* of thinking. Modern classical music exhibits all of these elements: First, the average listener does not appreciate it. That is because the core element of music is the 'personal journey' of the melody and the subjective Mercy emotions which this triggers, and when this is removed from music, then it no longer communicates. Second, most modern music is fragmented; it lacks order-within-complexity. Third, modern music breaks the Perceiver rules of harmony, coming up with new scales, new chords, new harmonies, new rhythms, and even new systems of tonality. What remains is technical expertise based upon Server sequences and Server skills: Modern musicologists are technically competent at analyzing music, modern composers are technically trained in the process of writing music, and modern players are technically proficient at playing music.

Music and Technical Thought

Music begins with the emotional Mercy experience of the note, and music is an expression of concrete thought. Folk music remains largely at this mental stage and is guided by the instinctive emotions provided by dissonance and harmony. As we saw with our simple examples, folk harmony generally sticks with one key and uses primarily the basic chords of I IV and V. But it is possible for Cp to formalize the structure of music and make it more technical, which it does by limiting the 'playing field' to clearly defined rules of permissible behavior.

We can notice the mental influence of technical thought by examining how Cp deals with the basic musical element of the *note*. A musical note can be any frequency. But technical music says that only notes which belong to the officially sanctioned scale may be used. Any other frequency is not allowed, and if one is playing a piano, then it is not *possible* to play any other frequencies. The technical circuit of Cp then both *assumes* that all notes fall into this *discrete* categories and uses expertise to make sure that all notes *do* fall into these discrete categories. For instance, in most countries, A is defined as the frequency of 440 Hz. If a person plays a frequency of 435 Hz, then the mind will *interpret* this frequency as an out-of-tune version of the note of A, thus making a logical jump from the analog thinking of concrete thought to the digital thinking of Cp. But the professional musician will also go to great lengths to ensure that whenever he attempts to play an A, the frequency that he produces is not 435 Hz, but rather a frequency which is much closer to the target frequency of 440 Hz. Saying this more simply, out-of-tune notes are mentally interpreted as being out-of-tune versions of correct notes, but the ultimate goal is to play in-tune and not out-of-tune.

Similarly, the *duration* of a musical note could conceivably be any length, but written music restricts the allowable durations of a note to the discrete categories of whole notes, half notes, quarter notes, and so on. When one plays in a professional orchestra, then one is expected to start and finish every note precisely as it is written. In addition, one does not simply guess how long a note should last or when to come in. Instead, every player is supposed to have an internal metronome going to which he aligns his notes. The point is that professional music uses the technical circuit of Cp and this is demonstrated by the insistence upon discrete categories in both pitch and timing.

We saw in our analysis of math that when math moves from concrete to abstract thought, Ci can extend the concepts of Cp to form new structures which no longer make sense to Cp. In music, the prime example of this is found in the *chord.* The major chord was initially defined in terms of a fundamental note and its harmonics—a Mercy based acoustic definition. But a chord can also be defined as a sequence of Server steps: Start with a note of the scale; move two notes up the scale; add that note; repeat the previous two steps. It is possible to apply this simple algorithm to any note of the scale, leading to the chords of I, II, III, IV, V, VI, and VII. And why stop at only two extra notes? Why not repeat the loop more times and add more notes? Thus one can speak of a V^7 or a V^9, or even a V^{13} or a IV^{11}. As we saw earlier, the V^7 makes musical sense because it can be constructed by adding more harmonics to the fundamental, and even the V^{13} is occasionally used for musical reasons. However, most of these chords, such as the IV^{11}, make no musical sense and would never be found in normal music. But they can be logically constructed using the abstract rules of Ci.

Ci and Cp both work with a network of Perceiver facts and Server sequences. In music, *chords* are the Perceiver facts and *melodies* are the Server sequences. In Cp, Server sequences are used to lead from one Perceiver location to another. Musically speaking, this means that the melody wends its way from one chord to another. This describes *harmony.* In contrast, Ci uses Perceiver thought to combine Server sequences. This type of writing is known musically as *counterpoint.* In counterpoint, two or more melodies are played at the same time. When the note of one melody is played at the same time as the note of another melody, then this *implies* a chord. These implied chords provide the Perceiver *glue* which ties the melodies together, and the melodies are combined in a way that the standard rules of harmony are not violated. The Brandenburg Concerti of J.S. Bach provide a good example of counterpoint. As far as Contributor thought is concerned, Ci and Cp are two versions of a single mental circuit. Similarly, musicologists regard harmony and counterpoint as two extremes in a spectrum of musical style, because most music contains both harmony and counterpoint, though certain composers and styles of music use more of one than the other.

Moving on, the *function* is the basic element of Cp. A function takes some 'input' and processes it in order to generate an 'output'. We saw in mathematics that Ci begins with the concept of the function and then uses abstract thought to generalize this definition.

The most abstract aspect of music is known as *form*—not to be confused with a Platonic Form. This generalization of a function can be seen in *sonata* form, the structure which generally describes the *first* movement of a symphony.

Sonata form contains the three basic sections of exposition, development, and recapitulation, or in the functional language of Cp, input, processing, and output. In Sonata form, Ci is used to expand upon these three basic elements. Remember that Ci treats Server sequences as a 'map' and uses Perceiver thought to manipulate and combine these Server sequences. The Server 'map' is presented during the *exposition* by playing the two Server sequences of two contrasting melodies in different keys. These Server sequences are then manipulated during the *development* by changing the keys in which they are played, altering the melodies, breaking the melodies down into fragments, or playing them against each other or against other melodies. All of this manipulation of Server sequences is done in a way that does not violate the Perceiver rules of harmony. Finally, the two melodies are restated during the recapitulation, but now both melodies are played in the home key. Thus the 'output' of the recapitulation takes the 'input' of the exposition and presents it in a way that has 'returned to home', with the 'input' connected to the 'output' by the 'processing' of the development. That describes the textbook version of Sonata form, which has been modified in various ways by composers.

The most rigorous musical combination of function and counterpoint can be found in the *fugue*, the musical form of which J.S. Bach was the master. Like Sonata form, the fugue also has an exposition, a development, and a final section. In a fugal exposition, the voices take turns playing the theme or subject, and when one voice is playing the subject, then another voice will play a countersubject. Similarly, the development is also more rigorous than in Sonata form, being composed mainly of counterpoint involving the subject and the countersubject. Like Sonata form, the final section of the fugue presents the subject again in the home key. But it may emphasize the feeling of 'returning to home' by having one voice start to play the subject before the previous voice is finished, known as *stretto*, or through the use of a *pedal note,* in which either the home note or the fifth (which is harmonically closest to the home note) is played for several bars as the subject is being recapitulated.

Music and Mental Networks

We have seen that music can be compared to a personal journey, as chords and melodies combine to lead Mercy thought on an emotional journey away from home and then back to home. Our understanding of mental networks can be used to expand upon this explanation. A musical composition is an *external* combination of Mercy emotion and structure that is formed when related musical notes are combined. A Mercy mental network, in contrast, is an *internal* combination of Mercy emotion and structure that forms when similar emotional Mercy experiences come together.

Because of this similarity, when a person hears a song, Mercy mental networks will probably be triggered. When a mental network is triggered, it wants to be 'fed' information that is compatible with its structure. If the structure of a song *matches* the structure of a triggered mental network, then that mental network will generate positive emotions. But if the structure of the song does *not* resonate with the triggered mental network, then that mental network will find the song emotionally threatening.

Personal identity is defined as the set of Mercy memories that repeatedly come to mind. If music triggers a Mercy mental network which is part of personal identity, then a person will find himself either *personally* attracted to the music or *personally* repelled from the music. When music resonates with a Mercy mental network that represents personal identity, then music will feel like a personal journey. This also explains why music is such a matter of personal taste, because each person has his own set of Mercy mental networks.

It has been shown that classical music can be used to 'repel' teenagers. For instance, I know of one law office that would play Bach solo cello sonatas all night outside the door to their building in order to stop drunks and teenagers from taking shelter in the entrance alcove. I was told by an employee of this firm that this technique was quite effective. We know that the music of Bach is full of abstract structure. If the average teenager finds math repulsive, he will also find music which reminds him of math personally repulsive.

Notice that music functions at both an *emotional* and a *hyper-emotional* level. The 'personal journey' represented by a song will produce Mercy emotions (and possibly Teacher emotions). But the *structure* of a song can lead either to the hyper-pleasure of holding a mental network together or the hyper-pain of threatening a mental network.

Because music can be used to 'feed' a mental network, a person can use music to stop a mental network from falling apart, and the structure of the mental network that is being supported can be determined by analyzing the structure of the music which the listener finds attractive.

This is an effective way of holding together a Mercy mental network that contains unpleasant memories. For instance, much of the music that resonates with today's youth is ugly, angry, chaotic, and dark. This tells us that personal identity within the mind of the listener must be similarly unpleasant. However, the typical person who listens to music that is ugly, angry, chaotic, and dark will respond with vigorous denial when these labels are used to describe his music. I suggest that there is a cognitive reason for this. Listening to such music holds personal identity *together*, preventing *hyper-pain*, while refusing to analyze and label the music stops Perceiver thought from constructing a mental map of *value*, avoiding the painful *emotions* of guilt and personal inadequacy.

As we know, Perceiver thought finds it difficult to function in the presence of Mercy emotions, and some of the most potent emotions come from the Mercy mental networks that represent personal identity. This explains why the typical person responds with antagonism when logical facts are used to analyze his musical taste, especially if these Perceiver facts make personal identity feel bad.

I have suggested that the path of religious education starts with personal honesty. I suggest that a willingness to analyze and evaluate musical taste is a good barometer of personal honesty. For instance, I remember asking one member of a 'Christian praise band' why he was putting his guitar signal through a *distortion* box, and I pointed out that the word 'distortion' was actually printed on this box. He first responded by claiming that the word 'distortion' did not mean distortion, and when the irrationality of this response sunk in, he insisted that I had no right to analyze his musical taste. I have mentioned in the main text that music can be an effective tool for either encouraging or destroying the path of religious education. If words about God are presented using a musical style that resonates with some aspect of childish identity, and if Perceiver thought is not being allowed to analyze this musical style, then Perceiver thought probably is not being used to analyze that part of childish identity, which means that personal honesty is not present. When such a non-verbal attitude is combined with a verbal message of unconditional divine acceptance, then one can conclude that the path of religious education is not being followed.

✵ Problems in Philosophy

Philosophy uses logic to analyze human thought. The theory of mental symmetry says that human thought is being carried out by a specific set of cognitive modules which are wired together in a specific manner. Thus, in the same way that the software which can be run on a computer is constrained by the hardware of that computer, so I suggest that the problems of philosophy ultimately have a cognitive explanation.

Therefore, I would like to take a brief look at some of the 'unsolved problems of philosophy' and see if the theory of mental symmetry can throw light on them. I should mention that I will not be attempting to solve these problems using logical analysis. The reason that these are unsolved problems is because they could not be tackled successfully by using logic. Instead, I will describe an underlying cognitive mechanism which either explains the reason for the problem or else helps to clarify the problem.

Most of these topics were taken from a Wikipedia list of "Unsolved Problems of Philosophy." I do not claim to be an expert in philosophy, but when I went through these topics, I realized that they dealt with issues which I had already analyzed during the process of developing my cognitive model. The fact that these philosophical problems can be addressed by the theory of mental symmetry provides a form of independent corroboration for the theory of mental symmetry.

Moore's Disbelief: How does one explain the sentence, "It's raining but I don't believe that it is raining."

This statement makes sense if one realizes that Perceiver facts come with a label of confidence. Perceiver mode may know a fact, but if the emotions of the situation are too intense, then Perceiver mode will lack the confidence that is required to assert that fact within the current situation. For instance, I may know that 'overeating leads to obesity', but not when I come face to face with a slice of double chocolate torte. In terms of the sample statement, Perceiver mode may know the fact that 'it is raining' but lack the confidence to believe in this fact within the current situation.

Computer scientists view Moore's disbelief as describing a situation in which a knowledge system tries to update its database in the light of new information but is unsuccessful. A similar situation can arise in the mind when emotional pressure prevents Perceiver mode from acknowledging new facts.

Sorites Paradox: Suppose that one has a heap of sand and that one removes sand from it one grain at a time. At what point does the heap stop being a heap? Or when does a bale of hay stop being a bale if one continues to remove straw from the bale?

This paradox can be explained if one recognizes the different mental roles that are being played by Perceiver mode and Facilitator mode. Perceiver mode performs object recognition by placing Mercy experiences within distinct Perceiver categories. Thus, Perceiver mode would use object recognition to distinguish between a heap and a non-heap, or between a bale and a non-bale. But when Perceiver mode recognizes an object, then this sets the mental context for mental reasonableness, which is evaluated by Facilitator mode—and Facilitator mode functions in a continuous, analog manner. Thus, Perceiver mode will recognize the heap or the bale, this will set the mental context for Facilitator mode, and Facilitator mode will then adjust the size of the heap or the bale by adding or taking away elements from it in an analog fashion, while continuing to assume the mental context of a heap or a bale. However, eventually a point will be reached where Perceiver mode will decide that the object has changed from one Perceiver category to another, which will then alter the mental context for Facilitator mode.

The Induction Problem: Why does induction work? What is the rationale for coming up with general conclusions based upon specific observations? Science uses induction very effectively to come up with general theories, but there seems to be no solid logical basis for using induction.

I suggest that the mind makes a logical jump when going from the normal circuits of concrete thought and abstract thought to the technical circuits of Cp and Ci. Perceiver mode and Server mode play the dominant roles in guiding the normal circuits of concrete thought and abstract thought. Perceiver mode places an *analog* label of confidence upon facts; Server mode puts an *analog* label of confidence upon sequences. Thus, as far as the Perceiver *person* is concerned, a fact is never certain. It can be 90% certain or even 99% certain, but never 100% certain.

The technical circuits of Cp and Ci are under the control of Contributor mode. It appears that Contributor mode only has a *digital* sense of Perceiver confidence and Server confidence. Thus, if the certainty of a Perceiver fact is below a certain threshold, then Contributor mode will treat this fact as unknown. Similarly, if the certainty of the Perceiver fact is above a certain threshold, then Contributor mode will treat the fact as known.

Logic and math are expressions of the technical circuit of Ci. Because Contributor mode has only a *digital* sense of certainty, when the mind makes the transition from normal thought to technical thought, it switches from a mode of operation in which confidence has an analog label to one in which confidence is either present or absent in a digital manner. Thus, the mind itself appears to make a logical leap when entering the technical circuit of Ci (with a similar leap occurring when entering Cp). When formal logic is then used to evaluate the basis for formal logic, it discovers that a logical leap has been made.

Now let us look at the process of induction. It begins with Perceiver mode observing the external world for facts and Server mode examining the external world for sequences. Suppose that Perceiver thought notices a repeated connection, or Server mode notices a repeated sequence. By seeing this pattern repeated or by observing the situation more carefully, it is possible to gain confidence in this data. If the mind acquires sufficient interrelated Perceiver facts and Server sequences, and if the level of confidence in these facts and sequences reaches a sufficient level, then this will permit the technical circuit of Ci to begin functioning, and once Ci starts to function, then the mind will make the jump from analog certainty to digital certainty, because the circuit of Ci will both assume and demand complete certainty.

Gettier Problem: This problem is illustrated by the story of the farmer and his cow. The farmer wants to know that his cow is safe in the field. So, he looks over the fence, sees a black and white shape, concludes that his cow is safe, and goes away satisfied. But in order to make sure, he asks his friend to check. His friend enters the field, sees the cow hidden behind a small hill, but also notices a piece of black and white paper caught in the tree—which the farmer assumed was his cow. So, did the farmer really *know* that his cow was safe?

I suggest that this is a concrete version of the induction problem. In the same way that the mind makes a logical leap from analog to digital certainty when entering the technical circuit of Ci, so it makes a similar logical leap when entering the technical mode of Cp. Induction builds a *theory* using incomplete information; it is driven by the Teacher emotions of a general theory. The farmer in this illustration is executing a *plan* based upon incomplete information; he is being motivated by the Mercy feelings associated with the bottom line of protecting his cow.

Thus, the information which the farmer has about his cow may be uncertain, but when he uses Cp to pursue a plan regarding his cow, then his mind makes a transition from analog certainty to digital certainty. As with the problem of induction, when technical thought retroactively examines the situation in detail, it realizes that its conclusions were not fully justified.

Cognitive style has a major bearing upon this assumption. The Perceiver person *is* aware of factual uncertainty. As a result, his natural tendency is to sit upon his information and never do anything with it, because he is never sufficiently certain. However, this also gives the Perceiver person an ability to make progress using uncertain information. The Contributor person and Facilitator person, in contrast, do not seem to be consciously aware of factual uncertainty. However, this mental 'blindness' gives the Contributor person the confidence that is needed to *use* information and not just acquire it. In a similar manner, this digital sense of confidence gives the Facilitator person the ability to blend and mix on the basis of a *fixed* set of constraints without doubting the constraints themselves, as illustrated by the sorites paradox.

The Is/Ought Problem: This problem was first formulated by the philosopher David Hume. In essence, how can one move from 'is' to 'ought'; how can one base a prescription of how the mind *should* behave upon a description of how the mind *does* behave.

Analyzing this problem is one of the main themes of this book. I suggest that the distinction between 'is' and 'ought' emerges from a conflict between the software of the mind and the hardware of the mind. The underlying problem is that the mind naturally develops inadequate mental software, which causes it to function in ways that use only part of the hardware. Thus, in order to use the hardware effectively, the software has to be reprogrammed. Restating this in the language of mental symmetry, input from the physical body leads naturally to the formation of mental networks that use some cognitive modules while disabling other cognitive modules.

For instance, here are some of the main 'is versus ought's that we have encountered in this book:

1) Emotional experiences from the physical body lead to a type of personal identity that uses identification and denial. This uses the Mercy module but disables the Perceiver module. The solution involves using Perceiver facts to redefine personal identity.

2) Perceiver thought tries to preserve its functioning by avoiding subjective emotions. This uses the Perceiver module but ignores the Mercy module. The solution requires building Perceiver confidence to handle emotional pressure, as well as going through a 'threshold of confusion'.

3) The technical circuits of Cp and Ci lock the mind into a specific context and prevent it from leaving that context. This emphasizes the Contributor module while downplaying input from Perceiver and Server modules. However, as Kuhn points out, mental development requires moving from one context to another.

4) Facilitator mode acts as the input filter for the mind, and it filters out information that violates the current context. If this filtering continues over the long term, then this will emphasize the Facilitator module while inhibiting most of the other modules. In order to change the context, information must be allowed past a mental filter which naturally rejects anything that is outside of the current context.

5) The distinction between words and actions leads to a separation between abstract thought and concrete thought. Abstract thought emphasizes the Teacher module while downplaying the Server module. Concrete thought emphasizes the Server module while disregarding the Teacher module. Mental development requires integrating these two forms of thought.

6) Overgeneralization leads naturally to a concept of God that is incompatible with mental content. This type of God uses the Mercy and Teacher modules, but disables the Perceiver and Server modules. The solution requires replacing an overgeneralized concept of God with one that is compatible with mental content.

Moral Luck: Suppose that two similar people accidently run a red light, and that in the one case, a pedestrian crossing the street is killed, while in the other case, no person is injured. Is the driver who killed the pedestrian morally more responsible than the one who did not encounter the pedestrian?

Thomas Nagel separates moral luck into three distinct categories (his fourth category appears to be similar to the other three). The example of the drivers and the pedestrian falls into Nagel's category of *resultant moral luck*.

Circumstantial moral luck is slightly different, and the example is given of citizens of Nazi Germany. Most of these citizens either performed or permitted reprehensible acts because they lived under Nazism. But if these citizens had been members of another society, then most of them probably would have lived entirely different lives. How do these circumstances affect moral responsibility?

I suggest that the tension between emotion and confidence can be used to provide at least a partial solution to these moral dilemmas. A Perceiver fact that is learned under emotional pressure, or a Server sequence that is followed under emotional pressure, is much more valuable than one that is learned in the absence of emotional pressure, because it carries with it the ability to 'operate under fire'. Even though the content of the moral rule may be the same, when a moral rule is backed up by mental confidence, then the mind is capable of implementing that rule in more emotionally charged situations. For instance, the surgeon may perform fairly straightforward skills of cutting and sewing, but he has acquired the mental ability to apply these skills even when faced with the emotional pressure of life and death.

Thus, the two drivers may have broken the same rule of running a red light, but the one who kills a pedestrian will probably end up learning his lesson much more thoroughly than the one who is lucky and gets away with just a warning. Similarly, acting in a moral fashion is much easier when the government itself is moral than when attempting to avoid being evil in the midst of an evil regime. Therefore, the individual who acts morally when surrounded by immorality gains much greater confidence than the one who simply goes with the flow when his surroundings are good. The moral lesson may be the same, but the level of confidence that is gained will be totally different.

The explanation for *constitutive moral luck* is slightly different. Education, genes, and upbringing all have an effect upon moral behavior. If a person is 'naturally good', then is his good behavior morally equivalent to that of the person who struggles to 'be good'? Part of the answer is provided by the previous paragraph. Obviously, when an individual who is naturally 'bad' manages to become 'good', then he has gained a greater level of mental confidence than the one who has no 'evil nature' to overcome.

The other part of the answer lies in cognitive styles. It appears that each cognitive style has its own natural strengths and weaknesses and must fight its own unique flavor of moral battles. The Server person, for instance, is 'naturally good'. But this goodness occurs at a low cognitive level. Thus, the mental challenge for the Server person is to go past merely good behavior to a more integrated form of mental functioning. The Exhorter person, in contrast, has a natural tendency to break the rules. However, he also is best at motivating people to break out of the status quo.

Material Implication: In formal logic, a statement such as, "If today is Saturday, then 1 + 1 = 2" evaluates as true. However, normal speech regards such a statement as absurd. Why?

The if-then statement plays a fundamental role in Contributor thought, because it combines a Server sequence with a Perceiver fact. Thus, one finds if-then statements being used both by the concrete circuit of Cp as well as the abstract circuit of Ci. However, these two mental circuits use the if-then statement in different ways, and that is where the confusion arises.

In concrete technical thought, Perceiver facts are used to define locations, and Server sequences are used to get from one location to another. This leads to the assumption that the 'if' is causally related to the 'then'. To concrete thought, "If it is Saturday, then we will go to the lake" makes sense, whereas, "If it is Saturday, then 1 + 1 = 2" does not make sense.

With abstract technical thought, Server sequences define the basic building blocks, and Perceiver facts are used to combine Server sequences in ways that lead to greater order. Thus, an if-then statement is defined through the use of a truth table, which indicates how to assign a Perceiver label of belief to the meaning of the final statement. An if-then statement is defined as true unless the 'if' is true and the 'then' is false. Using this approach, when the verbal sequence 'today is Saturday' is combined with the verbal sequence '1 + 1 = 2', this produces a true result because the 'then' is true. This contrast is explained in more detail in the appendix on math.

Counterfactuals: The mental reason for a counterfactual can be explained in a similar way. People often use counterfactuals in normal speech, such as "If it were raining, then I would go inside." But a counterfactual contains no logical information, because it is based upon a statement which is known to be false.

As with material implication, I suggest that we are dealing with a situation in which abstract thought and concrete thought are approaching an if-then statement from different perspectives. In the previous case, abstract thought came up with an interpretation of an if-then statement which did not make sense to concrete thought. With a counterfactual, I suggest that concrete thought is using an if-then statement in a manner which does not makes sense to abstract thought.

In the appendix that describes the mental circuit of Cp in more detail, we look at the mental mechanism behind *contingency planning.* Summarizing here, Perceiver facts organize emotional Mercy experiences in order to build a cognitive map of value. Exhorter mode will be naturally attracted to experiences within this cognitive map that have extreme emotions. The mind uses this Exhorter attraction to predict the good or bad experiences that could result from pursuing a certain course of action. The circuit of Cp will probe for possible disaster by altering the facts of a situation in various ways and then allowing Exhorter mode to be attracted to the possible emotional outcomes. For each undesirable experience that Exhorter mode uncovers, the circuit of Cp will then come up with a possible Server action for dealing with that possibility. The result is an if-then statement: If this goes wrong, then I will take that step.

For instance, suppose that I am planning a picnic for Saturday. One of the things that could go wrong is that it will rain. One possible response is to go inside. Thus, Cp finds counterfactuals very useful because they form an essential part of planning. However, Ci finds them useless because they deal with information that is not true, and therefore does not add to Teacher understanding.

Analytic Statement versus Synthetic Statement: Let us look first at the distinction which Kant made. According to Kant, "All triangles have three sides" is an analytic statement, because the conclusion is directly related to the subject: Triangles and sides both belong to the same context. In contrast, all "bachelors are unhappy" is synthetic, because 'bachelors' and 'unhappy' belong to different contexts.

Kant then focuses upon the *a priori synthetic statement*, which leads to his concept of the transcendental argument. For instance, according to Kant, the mind automatically perceives information in terms of space, time, and causality. These mental filters are *a priori* because they are used to 'justify' information, and they are *synthetic* because they are unrelated to the information that is being justified.

As was mentioned in the introduction, mental symmetry views Kant's transcendental biases as cognitive modules. For instance, the mind interprets information in terms of causality because the Contributor module works with cause-and-effect. Similarly, it looks for time because the Server module works with sequences. Thus, mental symmetry turns Kant's mental constraints into a cognitive model of interacting modules which can be used to analyze thought.

Now let us turn our attention to the controversy between Rudolf Carnap and Willard Quine. Carnap defined an analytic statement as one whose truth is based in meaning and theory, and a synthetic statement as one whose truth depends upon experience. Thus, "All bachelors are unmarried" is an analytic statement, while "Some bachelors are short" is a synthetic statement. Quine responded by suggesting that all statements are synthetic, because all meanings and definitions are ultimately based in real experiences.

Mental symmetry suggests that the mind is initially programmed with content from the physical body: Living within a physical body develops concrete thought, and concrete thought then leads to abstract thought. For instance, first the child encounters apples and oranges in real life. He then begins to learn math by adding physical objects together, such as apples or oranges. Later on he learns how to do math using variables which do not involve the use of physical objects. This progression from physical to concrete to abstract agrees with the assertion made by Quine. Because abstract thought is initially programmed by concrete thought, all analytic statements made by abstract thought are ultimately based in synthetic statements that are based in concrete thought.

However, concrete thought and abstract thought are two distinct mental circuits. Abstract thought may acquire its initial content from concrete thought, but once it begins to operate, then it can become disconnected from reality and start to function in an *autonomous* manner. In addition, abstract thought can begin to operate in a *technical* manner through the emergence of the circuit of Ci, in which abstract thought is guided by self-consistent rules within the domain of a paradigm. And, as Kuhn states, when a paradigm emerges, then the mind is driven (by Teacher emotion) to assert that abstract thought was *always* driven by this paradigm and that no other form of thought ever existed.

Thus, the theoretician is mentally driven to assert that he is capable of making analytic statements which are independent of synthetic statements. And in a sense he is correct, because the mental 'branch' upon which he is 'sitting' has cut itself off from the trunk, it functions separately from the trunk, and it (retroactively) claims that the trunk never existed—which sets up the mind for an eventual epistemological crisis.

Hard Problem of Consciousness: What exactly is consciousness? This is a very difficult question to answer. However, I suggest that mental symmetry can clarify this problem as well as explain why different people come up with different answers.

Mental symmetry suggests that consciousness is *not* the same for people who have different cognitive styles. Instead, each cognitive style is conscious in a different mode of thought. This means that it is not possible for one cognitive style to observe his own conscious awareness and then apply his findings to everyone. The Facilitator person is especially prone to making this cognitive error. On the one hand, he is conscious in a mode of thought which observes the rest of the mind, and so he is naturally drawn to the mental task of attempting to define consciousness. On the other hand, he uses a mode of thought which adjusts and mixes information from other cognitive modules in an analog fashion. Thus, he naturally rejects the concept that people fall into discrete categories of distinct cognitive styles.

Using Formal Logic to Analyze Human Thought: Many philosophers have tried to come up with a formal system of logic that can be used to analyze human thought. Mental symmetry suggests that this is an impossible task. The reason for this is quite simple. Formal logic is generated by the technical circuit of Ci—a subset of the mind that is functioning in a restricted manner. It is not possible to explain the *entire* mind by using a method of thought which only acknowledges a *subset* of the mind.

I suggest that this is a more generalized version of the error which Heidegger made when he attempted to explain human existence using only left hemisphere thought. He came up with a number of significant concepts, but his model was incomplete. One can tell that it was incomplete because he rejected most of the rest of philosophy as incorrect, and he had to come up with convoluted explanations in order to avoid referring to cognitive modules whose existence he was unwilling to acknowledge.

Notice how most of the philosophical problems that we have discussed result from attempting to use the technical circuit of Ci to interpret other modes of thought. In Moore's disbelief as well as in moral luck, Ci with its digital sense of certainty is trying to comprehend the interaction between confidence and emotion. The induction problem occurs when Ci examines the less rigorous thinking practiced by empirical science, while the Gettier problem results from Ci observing the semi-rational thinking of normal thought. With material implication, Ci is taking the if-then statement of Cp and turning it into something that no longer makes sense to Cp, while with counterfactuals, Ci is observing how Cp uses an if-then statement and finding it incomprehensible. Finally, the argument between analytic and synthetic boils down to a question of whether or not Ci is independent of Cp.

Demarcation Problem: In general terms, the problem of demarcation involves defining the limits to science. Addressing this question forms one of the main themes of this book. First, we see that the *method* of science can be analyzed in terms of cognitive modules: Perceiver facts are used to build general Teacher theories, which are then applied using Server actions. This leads to the emergence of the technical circuit of Ci, which defines what Kuhn calls normal science. Second, we see that the *topics* that are covered by science can be explained in terms of fundamental mental networks: By remaining objective, science can avoid triggering the Mercy mental network of personal identity. And by basing itself upon physical data, science can build upon the Teacher mental network of common sense. The *domain* of science is determined by the current size of these two mental networks, for science tackles topics if it has the instruments to perform physical observation and if it can avoid subjective bias.

If one extends the method of science to *include* the Mercy mental network of personal identity, then one enters the realm of psychology and religion. If one works out the mental steps that must be taken to apply the scientific method to the realm of the subjective, then one derives theological doctrine. But in order to notice this correspondence, theology must be translated into cognitive language. And the human mind only becomes capable of applying the scientific method to subjective matters if the mental networks that represent personal identity are rebuilt upon a rational foundation. Religion, by definition, focuses upon topics that are related to mental fragmentation and integration.

If one extends the method of science by *leaving* the Teacher mental network of common sense, then one enters the metaphysical realm of philosophy, which attempts to use Perceiver facts to build Teacher theories about mental topics that cannot be measured physically. As science acquires the ability to measure brain activity, then topics that used to be part of philosophy enter the realm of neuropsychology. Philosophy shares with science a focus upon using the technical circuit of Ci: Philosophy uses formal logic; science uses mathematics. If one develops a rational cognitive model, then it is possible to explain philosophical issues in terms of cognitive function, which we are attempting to do in this section. This leads us to the relationship between mind and brain, which will be discussed next.

Philosophy and religion overlap because including the Mercy mental network of personal identity usually also means dealing with non-physical data, while leaving the Teacher mental network of common sense also tends to bring one into contact with personal identity. However, religion usually starts by focusing upon personal identity, whereas philosophy begins by dealing with the metaphysical.

So far, we have described why science, religion, and philosophy are distinct, and how they can be reconciled. Historically speaking, science began as an offshoot of natural philosophy, which was seen as an aspect of religious philosophy. The scholasticism of the Middle Ages used rational thought to analyze two sets of 'revealed texts': The Bible was viewed as the primary source of religious truth, while the Greek writings were seen as the main source of secular truth. Analyzing these texts developed a method of rational thought that was compatible with the scientific method.

During the Renaissance, the focus of attention shifted from the scholasticism of revealed texts and metaphysical topics to the humanism of human existence and the natural world. This shift in attention was partially provoked by the crumbling of *existing* mental networks induced by events such as the Black Death, the Hundred Years War, and the corruption of the Catholic Church, as well as the formation of *new* mental networks as a result of travel and the discovery of the New World. Factors such as these encouraged thinkers to stop applying the method of scholasticism to the realm of religion and metaphysics and to start applying it to the realm of physical reality. As a result, modern science came into existence.

The Mind/body Problem: As we saw in the previous section, science tests its Perceiver facts by basing itself upon the Teacher mental network of common sense that results from living in the natural world. Thus, science deals with the brain and the body, because these can be physically observed and measured. The theory of mental symmetry is compatible with this approach because it uses cognitive modules that correspond to physical brain regions, it suggests that human thought is limited by the functioning and interaction of these cognitive modules, and it states that initial mental content is provided by the physical senses. Thus, one could say that the theory of mental symmetry is ultimately based upon physical evidence.

However, mental symmetry then crosses from the brain to the mind by suggesting that a cognitive model which is based in physical structure and physical input can be used to analyze mental topics that cannot be physically measured, including topics that involve strong personal feelings such as religion and personal identity.

In addition, even though human thought is compatible with the brain, is seeded by the physical body, and is constrained by brain architecture, programming the mind will lead to a mindset which believes in the existence of a non-physical realm and a personal identity which views self as being independent of the physical body.

In general terms, I suggest that the mind/body problem boils down to the issue of life after death, for the only way to prove that the mind is distinct from the body is for the mind to exist without the body, which is by definition life after death. Otherwise, any new scientific discovery about mental functioning can be interpreted as merely uncovering another aspect of either the physical body or the physical brain.

The theory of mental symmetry does not answer the question of life after death. But it does provide a cognitive model which can handle autonomous mental existence, it allows a person to form a personal identity that is based upon cognitive style and cognitive skills, and it provides a motivation to pursue the topic of non-physical existence through the development of Platonic Forms.

Artistic Essentialism: One could also describe this as *The Medium is the Message*, a phrase made famous by Marshall McLuhan. This is the idea that an artistic medium carries an inherent message which is independent of any verbal message conveyed through this medium.

The theory of mental symmetry provides a more rigorous way of applying this concept by looking at the cognitive modules that are being used by a certain artistic form and then comparing this with the cognitive modules that are being described by the verbal message.

For instance, the classic example given is that of a chase scene. Movies contain chase scenes, but poetry does not. A movie contains a continuing sequence of colorful visual images accompanied by environmental sounds. Such a medium emphasizes emotional Mercy experiences and physical Server sequences. Similarly, a chase scene also contains a sequence of emotional experiences. Thus, the medium matches the message. In contrast, poetry emphasizes similarity and reflection. It contains sequences of Teacher words which are mentally laid alongside one another through mechanisms such as meter and rhyme. This parallelism encourages Teacher mode to compare phrases in order to find hidden meanings—or possibly to collapse hidden meaning and create feelings of humor. In this case, the medium does not match the message, because in a chase scene there is very little verbal input, and there is no time for reflection.

Another example of the medium becoming the message can be found in the use of chanting to encourage meditation. Eastern meditation brings together Mercy emotions of personal identity with Teacher emotions of universality while avoiding Perceiver facts and Server sequences. Neurology tells us that beat involves aspects of the brain associated with Teacher mode, while tone involves brain regions connected with Mercy mode. Perceiver thought organizes notes into chords, while Server thought connects notes into phrases and melodies, and expands beat to create rhythm. Chanting combines Mercy tone with Teacher beat while avoiding the structure of scales, chords, harmony, phrases, rhythm, form, or melody. Thus, the medium mentally matches the message.

The Meaning of Art: If a musician plays a piece and misses several notes, is it still art? What exactly is art? As a musician, I have been pondering the meaning of art for years, especially when playing 'modern music'. For instance, I remember performing an orchestral work in which the 'soloist' was the rider of a snowmobile, who generated the musical notes of a melody by adjusting the throttle of his machine.

Based upon the previous section, I suggest that we can define art as input which resonates with existing mental networks. Therefore, a person appreciates art that provides his mind with input that is *consistent* with the structure and behavior of core mental networks, while he dislikes art which provides input that *collides* with the structure and behavior of core mental networks.

Because people have different mental networks, we can divide art into categories such as folk art, pop art, classical art, religious art, and modern art.

Folk art expresses the Mercy mental networks that are associated with culture and tradition. Any traditional society will have a form of folk art. When the mind is educated, then this develops new sets of mental networks which are expressed through classical art. Religious art resonates with mental networks that express concepts of God, heaven, hell, death, and other religious themes.

When objective science transforms a society through technology, then this causes new mental networks to emerge which will be reflected in new forms of art. On the theoretical side, education no longer focuses upon building general understanding. Instead, the goal is to produce the technical specialist, who generates incremental improvement in some narrow area of expertise. For instance, in order to get a PhD, a scholar must spend a significant amount of time doing original research, usually in some area of hyper-specialization. This leads to the formation of a mental network within his mind in some arbitrary fragment of knowledge which will end up motivating his behavior.

The mental result is that classical art gives way to 'modern art', which is technical novelty backed up by a mental network. In other words, the modern artist is expected to do something new—with conviction. The actual content of the artist's mental network that gives him this emotional conviction does not matter. What does matter is the fact that his actions are original and are being motivated by a mental network. For instance, if a painter is the first to place three stripes on a canvas and call it art, then it will be accepted as art, because it is novelty supported by a mental network. In 1990, the National Gallery of Canada paid $1.8 million for Barnett Newman's *Voice of Fire*—which consists of three stripes of paint. In a similar vein, I have officially 'played' a shortened version of John Cage's 4'33" in which the musicians of the orchestra sit still for four minutes and thirty-three seconds in front of a conductor. And the orchestra paid royalties to John Cage's estate for 'performing' this piece, because Cage was the first to come up with this idea and act as if it was art.

On the practical side, traditional culture is replaced by the consumer society, in which the consumer is presented with a cornucopia of new gadgets that satisfy his personal needs in an emotionally superficial way. As a result, folk art is replaced by pop art, a type of art that continually changes and which expresses itself superficially.

The combination of these two effects makes it much more difficult for the next generation to participate in society in a meaningful fashion. On the one hand, because *objective* thought suppresses childish Mercy mental networks, the young person who lives in childish Mercy mental networks feels alienated. On the other hand, because *technical* jobs require extensive training, the young person finds it difficult to find meaningful employment, especially if he lacks a formal education. This feeling of rejection will express itself through a form of art which expresses *rage against the system.*

Now let us return to the original question. If a person playing a piece by Chopin misses a few notes, is this still art? The folk art listener will focus upon the traditional melody contained within the composition of Chopin and will disregard the errors. The classical art listener will view it as a flawed performance of a classical work. The pop art listener probably does not know who Chopin is, while the young listener will leave the area when Chopin is playing because it does not resonate with his mental network of 'rage against the system'. Finally, the modern art listener might regard misplayed Chopin as a new form of art, but only if the musician is the first to make these types of mistakes and only if he makes these errors with sufficient emotional conviction.

✵ Quine's Web of Belief

I should begin by saying that I first read Willard Quine's book on the philosophy of science *after* I had finishing writing the main text, though I did do some rewriting after going through *The Web of Belief.* Thus, I suggest that his work provides an additional example of independent confirmation for the theory of mental symmetry. Quine writes concisely but clearly, and the concepts that he describes in *The Web of Belief* are sufficiently consistent with the theory of mental symmetry that it is almost possible to do a paragraph by paragraph translation from one to the other. Therefore, my analysis of *The Web of Belief* will combine his structure with mine: I will use Quine's chapter headings and describe Quine's concepts in the order in which he presents them, but I will explain these concepts using the language of mental symmetry followed by a quote from Quine. Thus, if a passage is enclosed in quotes, this means that it is taken from Quine's book. I will also attempt to address the problems which Quine raises in his book, as well as add the occasional theoretical explanation.

If building a theory of the mind is like assembling a picture puzzle, then it appears that Quine has identified about half of the pieces, defined their shapes, and arranged them neatly. But he has not assembled the puzzle. I apologize for the length of this appendix, but the only way to 'prove' that the theory of mental symmetry can explain scientific thought is by comparing mental symmetry *in detail* with a description of scientific thought written by someone who is acknowledged as having described scientific thought accurately. By 'proving', I don't mean following some chain of logic based upon quotes from Quine. Rather, my goal is to show that the theory of mental symmetry can be used to *explain* what Quine says in *The Web of Belief*, and I suggest that the *quality* of this explanation can be evaluated by using the 'six virtues of a good hypothesis' which Quine presents within his book.

Quine defines *science* fairly broadly: "What makes for science is system, whatever the subject. And what makes for system is the judicious application of logic. Science is thus a fruit of rational investigation." In other words, science uses Perceiver *logic* to construct a general Teacher *system.* Thinking scientifically means *acknowledging* Perceiver facts, which can be mentally difficult. If Perceiver thought is not allowed to function, then the result is superstition and magical thinking: "Science and reason have their enemies. Superstition and belief in magic are as old as man himself; for the intransigence of facts and our limitations in controlling them can be powerfully hard to take." Quine's goal is to describe the process of determining Perceiver facts, regardless of the associated Mercy emotions: "In the chapters ahead we will be interested in the ways of acquiring and sustaining right beliefs, be they pleasant or painful."

Belief

Mathematics deals with *absolute* certainty: "When it is a mathematical truth that is assailed there is likely to be a definitive way of settling the issue." Science, in contrast, works with *relative* certainty and reasonableness: "We will broach many of the criteria by which reasonable belief may be discriminated from unreasonable belief. But not only are the criteria not foolproof; they do not always even point in a unique direction."

Quine defines quite clearly what *belief* is and is not: "It is not a job to get on with. Nor is it a fit or mood, like joy or grief or astonishment. It is not something that we feel while it lasts. Rather, believing is a disposition that can linger latent and unobserved. It is a disposition to respond in certain ways when the appropriate issue arises." In other words, belief is not a Server action and it is not a Mercy emotion. Instead, it is an evaluation of Perceiver facts which mental symmetry refers to as a *label of Perceiver confidence*: "To believe that Hannibal crossed the Alps is to be disposed, among other things, to say 'Yes' when asked." The level of Perceiver confidence in a fact can change and will be affected by related facts: "The belief, like the charge, may last long or briefly...The belief that the cobbler is dependable gives way tomorrow to a contrary belief, while the belief in the bird is just forgotten. A disposition has ceased in both cases, though in different ways."

Mental symmetry says that belief is a label of *certainty* which Perceiver thought applies to facts. A Perceiver fact comes from *concrete* thought as Perceiver mode organizes Mercy experiences, and it affects *abstract* thought as Perceiver mode applies meanings to sentences. Quine says that belief *can* be non-verbal: "We also like to attribute a belief to a dumb animal, on the strength of his dispositions. So with the dog who wags his tail at the sound of a car in the driveway." But Quine focuses upon belief as a label attached to the meaning of a *sentence*: "We can retreat to the word-pair 'believes true' as relating men directly to sentences. We can retreat to this without claiming that believed things are sentences; we can simply waive that claim, and the philosophical question behind it. After all, our factual interest in what some speaker of English believes is fully satisfied by finding out what sentences the speaker believes to be true."

Perceiver thought can be confident that a fact is true, or it can lack the confidence that is needed to label a fact with certainty. But it can also be certain that a fact is *not* true, and a label of false can also be certain or uncertain: "It is important to distinguish between disbelief and nonbelief—between believing a sentence false and merely not believing it true. Disbelief is a case of belief; to believe a sentence false is to believe the negation of the sentence true. Nonbelief is the state of suspended judgment: neither believing the sentence true nor believing it false."

Using the language of mental symmetry, Quine defines *belief* as the label that Perceiver thought attaches to a fact, *truth* as a Perceiver fact which is correct, and *knowing* as a Perceiver belief which is both correct and mentally backed up by a network of related Perceiver facts: "Knowing is quite a special kind of believing; you can believe without knowing. Believing something does not count as knowing it unless what is believed is in fact true. And even if what is believed is true, believing it does not count as knowing it unless the believer has firm grounds for belief." However, as with belief, he focuses upon the *verbal*, abstract side of Perceiver thought: "Truth is a property of sentences; it is the trait shared equally by all that would be rightly affirmed. And knowledge, in its clearest sense, is what we have of those truths if our beliefs are solidly enough grounded."

Notice that a Perceiver belief is not the same as a Perceiver fact. The *fact* is the piece of information which is stored within Perceiver thought, while the *belief* is the label of certainty that Perceiver thought attaches to this fact, which can vary in an *analog* fashion all the way from 'definitely false' through 'uncertain' to 'definitely true'.

Perceiver facts acquire their labels of confidence from related Perceiver facts. Perceiver facts that are regarded as most certain become the *source* of labeling for related facts. Perceiver thought acquires these absolutes in one of two main ways: Perceiver facts that come from people with Mercy *status* may be regarded as most certain, or connections which are observed *repeatedly* may be regarded as certain. Science bases its knowledge in connections which are observed repeatedly in the *physical* world. In Quine's words, "Among our beliefs there are some of higher order—beliefs about beliefs—that often guide us in these assessments of evidence. We all hold, for example, that those gained from respected encyclopedias and almanacs are more to be relied on than those gained from television commercials. Further, we agree that what we think we see is usually there. Seeing is not quite believing, but it goes a long way."

When the certainty placed in a Perceiver fact is the result of Mercy emotions, then even obvious connections will be unnoticed because Perceiver thought is not functioning: "We may have little support for a belief tightly held, or much support for some belief that has not yet dawned upon us. In the goodness of her heart some dear old soul may retain implicit faith in the probity of her brisk family solicitor, though, if she would only put two and two together, she has clear evidence that he is mercilessly bilking her of her paltry patrimony."

Mental symmetry makes a distinction between automatic Perceiver processing and the 'internal world' of Perceiver thought. Facts form within automatic Perceiver thought *automatically* based upon sensory input, but these facts have only weak labels of confidence. These facts provide the *starting* point for the facts that reside within the internal world of Perceiver thought, which uses deliberate thought to assign labels to information. As Quine says, "As long as a belief whose causes are undetected is not challenged by other persons, and engenders no conflict that would prompt us to wonder about it ourselves, we are apt to go on holding it without thought of evidence. This practice is often reasonable, time being limited."

The Perceiver label that is given to a new fact will be influenced by the labels which have been assigned to all related facts: "It is in the light of the full body of our beliefs that candidates gain acceptance or rejection; any independent merits of a candidate tend to be less decisive."

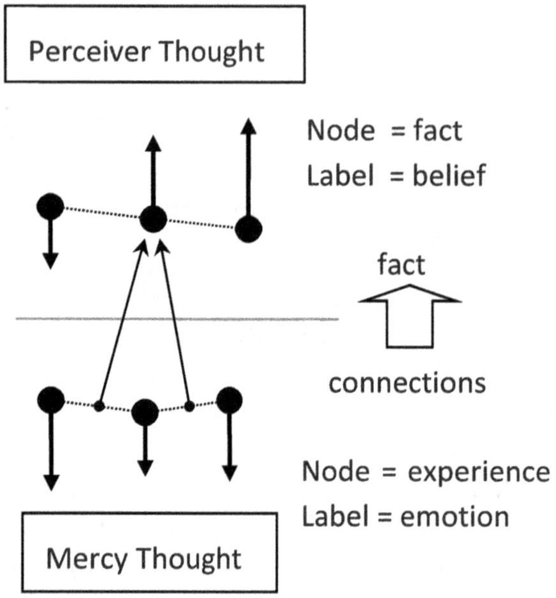

The relationship between these various elements can be portrayed in a diagram. In *Mercy* thought, experiences form the memory elements and a label of emotion is attached to each experience. The label of emotion that Mercy thought assigns to a new experience is determined by the emotions that have been assigned to *related* experiences. A Perceiver fact is a set of connections between Mercy experiences. In *Perceiver* thought, facts form the memory elements and a label of belief is attached to each fact. The label of confidence (or belief) which Perceiver thought assigns to a new fact is determined by the beliefs that have been assigned to *related* facts.

Summarizing Quine's chapter on belief, it appears to be a description of how Perceiver thought functions. I suggest that this type of thinking describes conscious thought for the Perceiver person. What is missing is the concept of cognitive modules.

<u>Observation</u>

For science, the ultimate source of Perceiver facts is the physical world. If a Perceiver fact corresponds to reality, then it is labeled as true. In Quine's words, "Such evidence as there is and ever was, collectively, for the whole overwhelming edifice of science, has consisted only in the direct evidence of many peoples' senses."

Science begins with concrete situations, but it makes a mental transition from concrete to abstract thought. In other words, it uses observations of the *real* world to build theoretical structures using the *abstract* raw material of Teacher words. Quine makes this transition when sidestepping the idea of belief and focusing upon belief in verbal *sentences*. Similarly, he bypasses the issue of observation and moves directly to the observation *sentence*: "Let us ask no longer what counts as an observation, but turn rather to language and ask what counts as an observation sentence."

Quine defines the *observation sentence* as a verbal description of an external situation which limits itself to facts that people share in common: "What makes it an observation sentence is that any second witness would be bound to agree with me on all points then and there, granted merely an understanding of my language." Thus, an observation sentence uses terms like 'stout man' or 'gray moustache', because everyone can see that these are true, but it would not say 'dean of the law school', because this refers to additional unseen knowledge.

Quine says that language is initially learned *ostensively*, in which a person *hears* someone whom he regards as an expert saying a sentence such as 'this is a chair' while simultaneously *seeing* a chair. The person's mind then associates the word 'chair' with the object of chair. In the language of mental symmetry, when a sequence of Teacher words is repeated, Server thought will gain confidence in this sequence of words, such as 'this is a chair'. Similarly, when a set of Mercy experiences is repeated, then Perceiver thought will gain confidence in the existence of an object, in this case the image of a chair. If the Server sequence is repeated at the same time that the Perceiver object is seen, then Contributor thought will conclude that the Perceiver object is the *meaning* of the verbal Server sequence and will connect the two together.

Quine adds that an observation sentence is one that *could* have been learned ostensively and that observation sentences form the basis for science: "Observation sentences are the bottom edge of language, where it touches experience, where speech is conditioned to stimulation. It is ultimately through them that language in general gains its meaning, its bearing on reality. This is why it is they that convey the basic evidence for all belief, all scientific theory." In other words, science is based upon sequences of Teacher *words* whose Perceiver meanings correspond to *physical* situations.

If Perceiver truth is based in observation sentences which describe *physical* facts that can be viewed by *many* people, then Perceiver truth is not relative, because all people can see the same objects and build Perceiver truth upon the same observations. In Quine's words, "An observation may be made by an individual; but, as we have emphasized, the truth of the observation sentence is an intersubjective matter...The hoary view contends that truth is relative to believer; there's truth for me and truth for you, and their reconciliation is generally neither possible nor desirable."

Perceiver facts about the physical world provide the basis for science, but when facts are used to build general theories, then the Teacher emotions produced by a general theory can make it difficult to acknowledge contradicting facts. Here Quine echoes Kuhn: "Even when observations persist in conflicting with a theory, the theory will not necessarily be abandoned forthwith. It will linger until a plausible substitute is found; the conflicting observations will stand unexplained, and the sense of crisis will mount."

Writing in the 1970s, Quine has an optimistic view of the scientist's ability to discover Perceiver facts about the external world and to adjust Teacher theories to account for Perceiver facts: "Scientists are so good nowadays at discovering truth that it is trivial to condone their methods and absurd to criticize them." Reading Quine's words in 2011, I think we can conclude that academic integrity is no longer something that can be taken for granted.

Summarizing, Quine describes the way in which science uses Perceiver facts from the external world to assign meanings to verbal sentences in abstract thought. Mental symmetry suggests that the *mental* structure that people share can *also* provide a basis for common truth, because the *same* mental circuits keep showing up in *different* fields of learning.

Self-Evidence

Mental symmetry says that the technical circuit of Ci can become divorced from reality, leading to the development of systems of logic and math that are rigorous and self-consistent, but no longer connected with observation of the real world. Quine describes these as *self-evident* beliefs: "What distinguishes these beliefs is that they look for support neither to other beliefs nor to observation. To understand them is to hold them."

Perceiver thought provides the glue which is used to construct systems of abstract thought. In speech, this glue is provided by Perceiver meaning: "Of a sentence that is obviously true and depends in no obvious way on observations or prior beliefs, one might then say that its truth is based solely on meanings—just because there is no other basis to point to."

Quine then introduces the logical statement: "Among the self-evident truths there are some that are called *logically true:* thus 'Every horse that is white is a horse.' This particular truth illustrates a general logical principle: 'Every *A* that is *B* is an *A*.' Our instance comes from the general principle by substitution: 'horse' for '*A*' and 'white' for '*B*'."

Quine is referring here to the use of *variables.* A variable could be described as a Perceiver object of a Perceiver object. Normally, Contributor thought attaches Server sequences of Teacher words to *specific* Perceiver meanings, such as 'horse' or 'white'. In contrast, a variable connects a Teacher word with a Perceiver fact which has a *general* meaning, such as 'A' or 'B'. Using variables allows the abstract circuit of Ci to become mentally independent of the concrete circuit of Cp.

Quine says that "The category of logical truths owes its importance mainly to the derivative notion of *logical implication.* This notion can be defined in terms of logical truth as follows: one sentence logically implies another when the compound sentence which we get by combining the two in the fashion 'If p then q' is logically true." In the language of mental symmetry, each statement is a Server sequence of Teacher words with a Perceiver meaning. This Perceiver meaning has an attached label of confidence which is either true or false. Each general statement such as 'if p then q' is associated with a truth table. This truth table provides the *Perceiver* rules for determining the label of confidence which will be attached to the meaning of the final compound statement.

Mental symmetry suggests that logic begins with the if-then statement because it is the basic building block for the practical circuit of Cp, and Ci acquires its initial structure from Cp. However, as is mentioned in the appendix on math, Ci interprets the if-then statement in a different manner than Cp. This makes it possible for Ci to *generalize* the if-then statement and come up with other ways to combine statements, using truth tables to come up with final labels. As Quine says, "The term 'implication', and its alternatives 'consequence' and 'deducible', have also a broader and vaguer application without the qualifier 'logical'. One sentence is said to imply another whenever, starting with the one sentence plus perhaps some self-evident truths, you can get to the other sentence by a series of self-evident steps...Logical implication is the well-defined core of implication, and the techniques governing it are the central business of logic."

Unlike facts about the real world, the technical circuit of Ci works with *digital* certainty. When facts are known for certain to be true or false, then it is possible to construct a chain of logic and end up with absolute certainty, just as a CD, DVD, or other form of *digital* media can be copied numerous times without losing any quality, while an *analog* recording loses some quality whenever it is reproduced. In Quine's words, "When a logical truth is too complicated to be appreciated out of hand, it can be proved from self-evident truths by a series of steps each of which is itself self-evident, in a word, it can be *deduced* from them."

Quine emphasizes that this sense of *digital* certainty makes formal logic possible: "However formal a proof procedure may be, the trustworthiness of the theorems that it generates still depends ultimately upon our conviction that each of the axioms is logically valid and our conviction that none of the rules of inference can lead from a form that is valid to a form that is not."

Mental symmetry says that the technical circuit of Ci restricts thought to a *limited* set of elements. A *set* is a limited collection of individual items, or in Quine's words, "These sets, or classes, are objects determined by their members, that is, by the objects that belong to them. So to specify just which members a set has is to specify the set." Like logic, math also uses the technical circuit of Ci. According to Quine, "Sets, or classes, are basic for mathematics; many of the fundamental portions of mathematics seem to require the notion of set for their systematic development."

Quine then spends some time discussing the fact that many mathematical systems contain inherent contradictions which cannot be eliminated. Mental symmetry suggests that following the technical circuit of Ci long enough will eventually lead to a crisis of knowing in which Ci discovers that its rigorous structure is based in some way upon a non-rigorous foundation.

Summarizing, Quine's description of formal logic can be explained in terms of the technical circuit of Ci.

Testimony

Speech can be used to convey *facts* to Perceiver mode and it can be used to give *instructions* to Server mode. In Quine's words, "Two basic ways in which language serves us are these: as a means of getting others to do what we want them to, and as a means of learning from others what we want to know. In the one way it affords us, vicariously, more hands to work with; in the other, more eyes to see with."

Science avoids Mercy emotions and acquires its Perceiver facts by observing the external world. Therefore, scientific speech tends to convey accurate Perceiver facts. As Quine says, "Observation sentences, taken narrowly, are comparatively foolproof. That is what makes them the tribunal of science. It is when we move to other sentences that the danger of mistaken testimony soars."

As Kant's concept of radical evil suggests, personal Mercy emotions can motivate a person to violate Perceiver rules for personal benefit: "The melancholy general point is that what a man gains from the law-abiding behavior of his fellows can be further augmented by his own violations. Take the case of a burning theater. A man's chance of escape is best if he bolts for the door and others file out in orderly fashion."

The mind has several mechanisms for evaluating facts that come from other *people*. First, we know that Perceiver thought places a label of confidence upon facts. When facts come from people, then Perceiver thought can also assign a label of reliability to a *person* based upon the accuracy of his Perceiver facts. If a person gives us information which is later shown to be inaccurate, then this will affect that person's Perceiver label of reliability, and other facts that came from him may have to be re-evaluated: "It can be useful to form the habit of filing in one's memory, as it were, the sources of one's information. For it can happen that sources once trusted will lose their authority for us, and one would then like to know which beliefs might merit reassessment."

When the Perceiver method of reliability is used, then authorities are chosen based upon the Perceiver facts that they know, combined with the Perceiver facts that they had the means to observe: "It might also be helpful to know how they came to hold it, and whether it concerns matters on which we should expect them to be well-informed. But more important still is the question of the belief's source, and of how, if at all, it was first established."

Second, Mercy thought assigns an emotional label to the mental network that represents a person. This *emotional status* can be used to evaluate what a person says. In this case, Mercy emotions are being used to *stop* Perceiver thought from functioning. This is the method of *blind 'belief'*: "One is sometimes called upon, notably in religion, to believe testimony in the face of strong contrary evidence. The Danish philosopher Kierkegaard remarked that the ability to do this is a test of one's faith. His ancient predecessor Tertullian even abjured reason altogether, declaring 'I believe because it is absurd.'"

Third, Facilitator thought acts as the *input filter* for the mind. In the right hemisphere, Perceiver thought sets the mental context for Facilitator filtering. Starting from this mental context, Facilitator thought will compare new facts with the *average* of existing facts. New information that is *similar* to the average will be accepted; information which *deviates* too much from the norm will be rejected. The default is for Facilitator thought to construct its average using information within *automatic* thought, leading to what is known as *common knowledge*: "For many claims, the typical endorsement is that they are 'common knowledge.' This is apt to be said of whatever is regarded by large numbers of persons to be true and by almost no one to be false." However, Facilitator thought can also *weight* its calculation of the average either by the *emotional* status of the sources, or by the Perceiver *reliability* of the sources.

When Perceiver thought is not functioning, either through passivity or when it is being overwhelmed by Mercy feelings, then a person will be unable to *test* his facts: "The ignorance of relevant truths is often accompanied by ignorance of that ignorance."

When Mercy emotions are used to mesmerize Perceiver thought, then it is possible to reinforce 'belief' by adding emotional pressure, because Mercy status is being used to determine Perceiver belief. For the person who uses Perceiver thought, this makes no sense because he realizes that Perceiver belief is *independent* of Mercy status: "The passage from Lewis Carroll brings out also the idea of *trying* to believe something. This is an odd idea even apart from believing the impossible."

It is also possible to use Facilitator filtering to emphasize facts that reinforce a Perceiver belief while downplaying facts which contradict that belief: "A more effective way is by casting about for favorable evidence. If it outweighs such unfavorable evidence as may turn up, or if wishful thinking saves you from noticing the unfavorable evidence, then your will to believe is crowned with success."

Finally, general Teacher theories of science may cause a person to believe in Perceiver facts which contradict Perceiver facts that are observed by the senses. In this case *abstract* thought is coming up with facts that make no sense to *concrete* thought: "Einstein claimed further that the speed of a ray of light is the same from any vantage point; the moving vantage point cannot, in pursuing the light ray, diminish the relative velocity. This again we accept on faith, for all its antecedent absurdity."

Hypothesis

Mental symmetry makes a distinction between *normal* thought and *technical* thought. One of the main differences between these two is in the matter of Perceiver *confidence*. The technical circuits of Ci and Cp work with *digital* certainty and treat Perceiver facts as either true, false, or unknown. Those who use technical thought may try to apply *digital* certainty to *all* of human thought and existence: "Some philosophers once held that whatever was true could in principle be proved from self-evident beginnings by self-evident steps. The trait of absolute demonstrability, which we attributed to the truths of logic in a narrow sense and to relatively little else, was believed by those philosophers to pervade all truth." But this attempt will lead inevitably to a crisis of knowing. First, technical thought will learn that facts from the real world cannot be learned with absolute certainty: "What then of the truths of nature? Might these be derivable still by self-evident steps from self-evident truths together with observations? Surely not." Second, technical thought will discover that rigorous thought itself is based upon a non-rigorous foundation: "Actually even the truths of elementary number theory are presumably not in general derivable, we noted, by self-evident steps from self-evident truths."

Technical thought will then realize that it is possible to work with uncertain information: "It is now recognized that deduction from self-evident truths and observation is not the sole avenue to truth nor even to reasonable belief." Making the transition from the uncertain information of normal thought to the digital certainty of technical thought requires taking a leap of faith. This leap of faith cannot be avoided, but it can be *minimized*: "In a word, hypothesis is guesswork; but it can be enlightened guesswork. It is the part of scientific rigor to recognize hypothesis as hypothesis and then to make the most of it."

The purpose of a hypothesis is to come up with a general Teacher theory that can explain *existing* Perceiver facts and Server sequences and predict *additional* facts and sequences: "What we try to do in framing hypotheses is to explain some otherwise unexplained happenings by inventing a plausible story, a plausible description or history of relevant portions of the world."

Quine then proposes six 'virtues' that can improve the chances of coming up with a good hypothesis, five of which are mentioned in this chapter:

"Virtue I is *conservatism*. In order to explain the happenings that we are inventing it to explain, the hypothesis may have to conflict with some of our previous beliefs; but the fewer the better." When facts are uncertain, then Perceiver thought cannot be used with absolute certainty, but it still can and should be used. In addition, it is *natural* for the Facilitator input filter to evaluate new facts by comparing them with the average of existing facts: "Conservatism is rather effortless on the whole, having inertia in its favor. But it is sound strategy too."

"Virtue II, closely akin to conservatism, is *modesty*. One hypothesis is more modest than another if it is weaker in a logical sense...Also, one hypothesis is more modest than another if it is more humdrum." Modesty relates to the Facilitator *input filter*. In the right hemisphere, the Facilitator filter accepts *facts* that are like existing facts, while in the left hemisphere, the Facilitator filter accepts *sequences* that are like existing Server sequences. In general terms, the Facilitator filter accepts that which corresponds to the *status quo*: "It tends to be the counsel of modesty that the lazy world is the likely world. We are to assume as little activity as will suffice to account for appearances."

I suggest that mental symmetry clarifies the relationship between conservatism and modesty: Conservatism uses Perceiver thought to work with *individual* facts, whereas modesty uses Facilitator thought to work with *averages* of facts and sequences. Obviously, these two are related, but they are not the same.

Virtue III is *simplicity*. Simplicity is driven by *Teacher* emotions. Teacher thought feels good when there is order-within-complexity, when the most information can be summarized by the simplest explanation. A smooth line is a *visual* example of simplicity: "What is simplicity? For curves we can make good sense of it in geometrical terms. A simple curve is continuous, and among continuous curves the simplest are perhaps those whose curvature changes most gradually from point to point."

Teacher thought builds *general* theories. Therefore, simplicity is emotionally most satisfying when it applies to the most *general* aspects of a theory: "There is a premium on simplicity in any hypothesis, but the highest premium is on simplicity in the giant joint hypothesis that is science, or the particular science, as a whole. We cheerfully sacrifice simplicity of a part for greater simplicity of the whole when we see a way of doing so."

"Virtue IV is *generality*. The wider the range of application of a hypothesis, the more general it is." Simplicity relates to *Server* mode; a Teacher theory is simple if the Server sequence that gives stability to the Teacher words is smooth and uncomplicated. Generality relates to *Perceiver* mode; a Teacher theory is general if Perceiver thought can link the Teacher theory to many different situations. Teacher emotions of order-within-complexity are affected by both simplicity and generality, but simplicity has a more fundamental influence, because when dealing with abstract thought, Server sequences are more basic than Perceiver facts. As Quine says, "Generality without simplicity is cold comfort. Thus take celestial mechanics with its elliptical orbits, and take also terrestrial mechanics with its parabolic trajectories, just take them in tandem as a bipartite theory of motion. If the two together cover everything covered by Newton's unified laws of motion, then generality is no ground for preferring Newton's theory to the two taken together. But Virtue III, simplicity, is."

Virtue V is *refutability*. Abstract thought uses Perceiver facts to build general Teacher theories. A hypothesis or theory is refutable if the Perceiver facts are *clearly* defined and the resulting Teacher theory is sufficiently *general*. When a Teacher theory is constructed out of Perceiver facts with vague meanings, then it is difficult to disprove: "A prime example of deficiency in respect of Virtue V is astrology. Astrologers can so hedge their predictions that they are devoid of genuine content. We may be told that a person will 'tend to be creative' or 'tend to be outgoing,' where the evasiveness of a verb and the fuzziness of adjectives serve to insulate the claim from repudiation." A Teacher theory that is insufficiently general is an *ad hoc hypothesis*: "Ad hoc hypotheses are hypotheses that purport to account for some particular observations by supposing some very special forces to be at work in the particular cases at hand, and not generalizing sufficiently beyond those cases." Ad hoc hypotheses are difficult to disprove because the Teacher theory is not general enough to extend beyond Perceiver facts that are known to be true.

When two general Teacher theories collide, then it may be possible to translate one into the language of the other, and one can end up a *subset* of the other. A subset theory is not wrong, but it has a smaller *domain* than the competing theory. For instance, I suggest that Quine's Web of Belief is a subset of the theory of mental symmetry. Quine uses Newton and Einstein to illustrate this concept: "We might say that the sphere of applicability of Newtonian mechanics in its original simplicity was shown, by the Michelson-Morley experiment and related results, to be less than universal; and then Einstein's theory comes as a generalization, presumed to hold universally. Within its newly limited sphere, Newtonian mechanics retains its old utility."

Summarizing, this chapter describes the guidelines that should be followed when *normal* thought uses uncertain Perceiver facts to construct general Teacher theories.

Induction, Analogy, and Intuition

As we have already seen, the Facilitator input filter compares new Perceiver facts and new Server sequences with the averages of similar Perceiver facts and Server sequences that already exist within the mind. Thus, the mind finds it reasonable that the status quo will continue: "Why do we expect toothpaste to exude when we squeeze the tube? We could cite general principles about what happens to liquids or soft solids under pressure, but we are more likely to support our expectation in terms of our past experience with tubes and their squeezings." Mental *context* is determined by the Perceiver cognitive module and the Server cognitive module; Facilitator filtering functions *within* this mental context. Thus, as was seen when looking at the philosophical problem of the sorites paradox, the results of Facilitator filtering do not directly alter facts within Perceiver mode or sequences within Server mode: "What happens in such simple activities is related to general principles only in ways which, for most of us, remain far in the background. Very far; for were toothpaste to fail to spurt forth on a given squeezing we would surely not want to rewrite our physics."

Quine then discusses a difficulty introduced by Nelson Goodman. In brief, the problem involves a hypothesis that applies at one time but not another. For instance, suppose that "every moment of one's life thus far has had the trait of being prior to 1978. By induction, then, may one conclude that all moments of one's life will share that trait?" Or, suppose that a person "observed that every past moment of his life had been followed by further living. By induction he might then have concluded that every moment of his life would be followed by further living, and hence that he would live forever."

It may be possible to clarify this dilemma by examining the difference between Perceiver facts and Server actions. Perceiver thought *observes* the *external* world, thus it makes sense to describe a situation using Perceiver facts that refer to *absolute* time, such as the end of 1978, and one can hypothesize that an external event *exists* even if no person is there to observe it. Server thought, in contrast, uses the physical body to *perform actions.* Thus, when referring to an action, one must use *relative* time, such as 'ten seconds after I turned on the motor' and not 'every moment I lived before 1978'. In addition, the ability to carry out an action depends upon the *condition* of the person, animal, or machine carrying out that action. Thus, if I live for ten minutes longer today, this is no guarantee that I can continue to hypothesize that I will 'live for ten minutes longer' *ad infinitum.*

Deduction uses the technical circuit of Ci to follow chains of logic in which each step is based in absolute certainty. In contrast, *induction* forms the hypothesis of a general Teacher theory by using Perceiver facts that have partial certainty. Deduction remains within the *technical* realm of absolute certainty guided by a general Teacher theory; induction begins with the messy Perceiver facts of observation and then uses *normal* abstract thought to build a general Teacher theory. In Quine's words, "Inference has two main species: deductive and inductive. The inductive, unlike the deductive, proceeds from the less to the more general; it gives you more than you began with.

These were looked upon as complementary and symmetrical ways of justifying knowledge. To pair them thus and picture them as symmetrical, however, is to lose sight of serious differences. In Chapter IV we reflected briefly on deductive inference as inference that can be carried out by a series of self-evident steps. Its central techniques are studied in logic and are well understood. Methods of inductive inference, on the other hand, are not sharply separable from strategies for framing hypotheses generally; and of such strategies no sharp and satisfactory theory is to be found, comparable to what logic provides for deduction."

Induction uses Perceiver facts to build a *general* Teacher theory; the Facilitator filter, in contrast, evaluates *specific* situations based upon past facts and sequences: "We might reserve the term 'induction' for inferences where the conclusion is general and explicit, since we have other terms for the leap from cases to cases."

Quine begins his description of *analogy* with an illustration that describes the operation of the *Agency Detector*: "Perhaps a person hears a new voice and, noticing that the voice resembles that of an old friend, speculates that the voice's owner will be like the old friend in other significant ways. Such an analogy is shadowy, but we all tend at times to build on analogies that are no better. When a feature of a newly encountered person or object strikes a familiar chord it is often fairly instinctive to project to the new person or object what experience has associated with that feature." In other words, a fragment of personal behavior is triggering the Mercy mental network which represents some person and that mental network is then attempting to remain active by continuing to interpret information.

What interests Quine is the *intuitive psychology* that emerges as Perceiver thought learns to classify and organize these various mental networks: "She learns to discriminate between associations that are worth building new beliefs on and those that are not. The more people she meets the better she is able to judge what expectations she can base on a person's voice. Her native flair for projectibility is developing in the light of experience." However, Quine recognizes that Perceiver thought finds it much easier to classify mental networks than it does to tear them apart and analyze them. (We saw this principle with Foucault's Renaissance Episteme.) "Even so she may remain quite unable to articulate any principles for her acquired discrimination. It is much easier to build beliefs and hypotheses than to describe the rationale behind their construction."

As far as *Perceiver* thought is concerned, analogy is simply a form of *object recognition*—noticing that one mental object is like another. And when a *new* fact reminds Perceiver thought of related facts, then the label of confidence that Perceiver thought gives to the new information will, as usual, be determined by the labels which have already been assigned to existing, related information: "One who derives a belief by analogy need not be prepared to offer any inductive support for it nor even notice that that belief rests on an analogy. It is the way of each of us most of the time to forge new beliefs from old ones without reflecting at all on the arguments that might be summoned in their behalf. Such beliefs may still be eminently reasonable."

Analogy can also function in the context of *abstract* thought. Perceiver thought is still performing the same basic step of *object recognition*, but in this case the mental object describes the Perceiver meaning of some general Teacher theory. In Quine's words: "Analogy can lead not only from particular experiences to particular expectations, but also from general hypotheses to general hypotheses...What is at work here is still analogy, but it is analogy now between two parallel laws rather than between particulars."

When analogy occurs within abstract thought, then there is implicit theory building. That is because an analogy is a Perceiver comparison, and Perceiver thought constructs general Teacher theories by comparing one set of Server sequences with another. Quine gives the example of comparing the function of one serum with that of another: "Say we have evidence that a serum prepared from a certain bacterial culture immunizes against the disease caused by those bacteria. If there is a closely related disease caused by bacteria that we regard as very much like those causing the first disease, then we may find it plausible that a correspondingly prepared serum will immunize against the second disease...What is at work here is still analogy, but it is analogy now between two parallel laws rather than between particulars."

Notice that analogy deals with *networks* of facts and not just individual facts. Using a picture puzzle as an illustration, analogy is like taking fragments of one puzzle and comparing them with fragments of another puzzle. When one checks an *individual* fact, then confidence in that fact grows as one finds the fact repeated in *many* different situations. In contrast, an analogy can be tested by comparing individual puzzle pieces within one fragment with corresponding pieces within the other puzzle fragment; the more pieces that match, the greater the certainty. In Quine's words, "The previous instances or premises, from which we are making the analogical inference, are apt to have been so chosen as to share a variety of features with the case to be inferred. On this account, we commonly have to make do with just one previous instance, as in the serum example, unlike the style of proper induction; and the single instance is apt moreover to carry sufficient conviction, thanks to the multiple resemblances."

The logic that is being used in this book is a *rigorous* form of analogy, something which lies between normal thought and technical thought. When one theory is translated into the language of another, then it becomes possible to compare them as with an analogy. Rigorous analogy compares the *details* of one theory with another to see if 'the analogy breaks down'; it takes one puzzle fragment and lays it atop a matching puzzle fragment from a different picture and then compares the *pieces* of one fragment with those of the other fragment to see if they match as well. If the analogy holds, even when looking at details, then one theory will end up being either a translation or a subset of the other, and one can combine both theories to form a single more general theory.

Moving on to the next point, once a network of Perceiver facts and Server sequences is in place, then this provides a mental 'highway system' along which Exhorter thought can travel. Any emotional 'destination', such as a general Teacher theory, that can be reached by this 'road system' will attract the attention of Exhorter thought. I suggest that this provides the mental mechanism for *intuition*. Intuition may be guided by facts, but it is not explicitly aware of those facts. As Quine says, "Sometimes, though we are quite convinced that a belief is right, we can think of no reasons at all for holding it. It is in such cases that we are apt to give credit to *intuition*." Because intuition is driven by emotions, it is often considered to be independent of facts: "Some people think of intuition as a mystical source of knowledge—a source disconnected from normal ways of reaching conclusions." But if one searches deeper, one sees that facts are still involved: "There may be no known evidence for the belief, but that need not mean that no relevant observations have been made. Perhaps the person hesitated just a fraction of a second before answering some question, or perhaps he momentarily exhibited a certain facial expression." And when new facts are learned, then they will indirectly affect intuition: "Nowadays, when offered seriously, the manufactured story is apt to be couched in terms from science to enhance its claim to authority." Intuition plays the major role in Teacher overgeneralization: "Still, when mechanism is unclear there is a lamentable tendency to embellish some scant story order to take up the slack. This is a tendency that has flourished from earliest times, the tendency to go to any needed lengths of invention rather than face ignorance." And intuition is the driving force in the first stage of learning: "The appeal to intuition is explicit and most insistent, understandably, among devotees of doctrines that are short on reasoned support."

Mental networks play a major role in both analogy and intuition. When some situation triggers a mental network, then that mental network will want to be 'fed' with additional compatible data. This emotion will lead to Exhorter urges which will provide the motivation for either exploring an analogy or using intuition. However, mental networks also make it more difficult to apply rigorous logic to analogy or intuition because Perceiver thought has to function in the presence of emotional pressure. Quine describes mental networks and the *pattern matching* that they carry out, but not their *emotional* aspect: "We respond to visual clues, organize them in a twinkling, and compare the result with what is stored in memory. That last phrase is one that is common in talk of computers. And indeed, machines are able to perform certain tasks of recognition...We know how they do it; they compare what is fed into them with what has been internalized in them through programming."

Summarizing, analogy and intuition describe less rigorous methods of moving from concrete to abstract thought. Analogy uses Perceiver thought to compare one situation or theory with another, which leads indirectly to more general conclusions, while in intuition Exhorter thought comes up with general conclusions by 'traveling' the mental 'highway system' of Perceiver facts and Server sequences.

Confirmation and Refutation

The chapter on hypothesis described how partially certain Perceiver facts are used to construct general Teacher theories. Let us look more closely at the roles which Teacher mode and Perceiver mode play in this process. The basic building block for Teacher thought is *words*, and Teacher emotion comes from *generality*, therefore Teacher thought is emotionally driven to make general statements, leading to the formation of verbal hypotheses. But each Teacher word has a Perceiver meaning. Therefore, when Teacher thought makes a verbal hypothesis, this implicitly ends up connecting Perceiver meanings. This creates *new* facts within Perceiver thought, because a Perceiver fact is defined as a set of connections. Perceiver thought will then assign a label of belief to these new facts by comparing them with existing facts. Summarizing, whenever Teacher thought forms a hypothesis, it will attempt increase the generality of this statement until Perceiver mode is reminded of a connection that Perceiver thought is certain is false.

For instance, using the example which is in Quine's book, 'This emerald is green' is a specific statement which corresponds to the specific Perceiver fact of seeing 'green' and 'emerald' combined. This is an *ad hoc hypothesis* which lacks generality. Teacher thought can generalize this to say that 'All emeralds are green', which will remind Perceiver thought of all encounters with emeralds. Because Perceiver thought has not encountered a situation in which 'green' and 'emerald' do not go together, there will be no conflict between emotionally driven Teacher generalization and belief driven Perceiver labeling. But the general form of this statement will lead to the *prediction* that 'emerald' and 'green' are *always* connected, which is the main feature of a general hypothesis.

Suppose that Teacher thought goes one step further and says that 'All gems are green'. This will remind Perceiver mode of the meanings of 'gem' and 'emerald' and how these are connected, as well as the fact that 'colorless' and 'diamond' are connected. The result will be a *counterexample*—a Perceiver connection that contradicts a general theory. Obviously, if Perceiver mode knows only a few facts, then Teacher thought will seldom find its general statements restricted, leading to Teacher *overgeneralization.*

A Perceiver fact that is consistent with a general Teacher theory does not *prove* the theory. Instead, it simply adds another fact which falls within the domain of the general statement, *confirming* it. In contrast, any Perceiver fact which is *inconsistent* with a general Teacher theory will force Teacher thought to limit the generality of its hypothesis to exclude that point. As Quine says, "A lawlike generalization is confirmed by each of its instances. The instance does not of course clinch the generalization, but adds to its plausibility. A generalization with even a single false instance, on the other hand, is irremediably false."

However, Perceiver belief in a contradicting fact must contend with Teacher emotions of *generality*. If Perceiver belief in this fact is weak, then this counterexample may be insufficient to cause Teacher thought to abandon its general statement. And Perceiver belief in a fact is determined by Perceiver belief in related facts. Thus, when Perceiver belief collides with Teacher generality, then this may cause a whole cluster of beliefs to be re-evaluated. As Quine says, "It would appear to be easier, therefore, to refute a false hypothesis than to establish a true one. If a hypothesis implies observations at all, we may stand ready to drop the hypothesis as false as soon as an observation that it predicts fails to occur. In fact, however, the refutation of hypotheses is not that simple...there is the matter of the supporting chorus. It is not the contemplated hypothesis alone that does the implying, but rather that hypothesis and a supporting chorus of background beliefs."

According to Quine, "A lawlike general sentence is one whose instances count toward its confirmation." For instance, every time that one sees a green emerald, this confirms the general hypothesis that 'All emeralds are green'. Defining a 'lawlike statement' is surprisingly difficult, and Quine is unable to come up with a satisfactory definition. However, I suggest that mental symmetry can throw some light on the situation, which we will take a few paragraphs to discuss, guided by Quine's dilemma.

Quine asks why inductive logic can be used to confirm a statement but not its contrapositive: "Note that all emeralds are green if and only if all ungreen things are nonemeralds. The two sentences logically imply each other; they are logically *equivalent.* Surely, then, whatever confirms the one must confirm the other. But 'All emeralds are green' is confirmed by its instances, the green emeralds, and these are not instances of 'All ungreen things are nonemeralds'. The instances of the latter are the ungreen nonemeralds, for instance chickens. Chickens do not confirm 'All emeralds are green', nor, therefore, can they be counted as confirming 'All ungreen things are nonemeralds'."

Why is it obvious that chickens do not confirm the hypothesis of 'All ungreen things are nonemeralds'? When one is searching for evidence that supports a hypothesis, then one is attempting to move *from* the uncertain realm of normal thought *to* the certain realm of technical thought. Technical thought works with a *limited* playing field. Therefore, in order to enter technical thought, one must be *able* to limit the playing field. This limiting will also *minimize* the leap of faith that the mind has to take when entering the realm of technical thought. The concept of 'emeralds' is inherently limited, because only a tiny fraction of all objects are emeralds. Therefore, each encounter with a green emerald will increase mental confidence in the relationship between 'emerald' and 'green'. In contrast, the set of 'ungreen things' is open-ended; it is difficult even to agree upon what constitutes a list of colors that are not green.

When one is moving between a statement and its contrapositive, then one is already *within* the realm of technical thought with its digital certainty. If one already *knows* statements with absolute certainty, then the statement 'All ungreen things are nonemeralds' is equivalent to 'All emeralds are green'. But when one is attempting to find evidence for a hypothesis, then one is still within the realm of *normal* abstract thought with its partial certainty. The two statements 'All emeralds are green' and 'All ungreen things are nonemeralds' may be equivalent for *technical* thought, but they are not equivalent for *normal* thought, because the category of 'emeralds' is inherently limited, while the category of 'ungreen things' is inherently open-ended. When one has only partial certainty, then attempting to gather evidence that will support a limited statement such as 'All emeralds are green' is *far* easier than attempting to gather evidence for an open-ended statement such as 'All ungreen things are nonemeralds'.

However, suppose that one is dealing with an if-then statement which is inherently limited, such as 'If a person ate the egg salad, then he got food poisoning'. In this case, we are dealing with a specific egg salad served to a specific group of people at a specific event. Because the entire situation is limited, evidence that is consistent with the contrapositive of 'If a person did not get food poisoning, then he did not eat the egg salad' will also tend to confirm the initial hypothesis.

In addition, one is also working with two different types of if-then statements. Both of these types of statements have a contrapositive which is true—but for different reasons. This is discussed at the end of the appendix on math in the section on logic, so we will summarize here. The statement 'If it is an emerald, then it is green' is based upon Teacher *domain*, which can be illustrated through the use of an Euler diagram. One can go from the 'if' of 'emerald' to the 'then' of 'green' because 'emerald' is a *subset* of 'green'.[52] In this case, the contrapositive of 'If it is not green, then it is not an emerald' is true because any point which lies outside of the larger circle depicting 'green' also lies outside of the smaller circle indicating 'emerald'. This type of if-then statement occurs when Ci takes the thinking of *normal abstract thought* and makes it technical.

In contrast, the statement, 'If a person ate the egg salad, then he got food poisoning" contains a *causal* link in which the 'if' leads to the 'then' through some Server action. Here, the contrapositive of 'If a person did not get food poisoning, then he did not eat the egg salad' is true because not getting sick implies that the egg salad was not present within the digestive system to do its debilitating deed. This type of if-then statement occurs when Ci takes the basic building block of *Cp* and translates it into the abstract language of Ci.

Putting these two factors together, I suggest that a statement is lawlike if it is *compatible* with technical thought. First, this means that the statement has limited scope and is clearly defined. Second, the structure of the statement must reflect the thinking of either Ci or Cp: Ci moves from one symbolic statement to another guided by Teacher domain; in this case, it must be possible for the 'if' to be a subset of the 'then'. For instance, 'If it is a noun, then it is heavy' does not qualify because the two concepts of 'noun' and 'heavy' involve completely different Teacher domains. A noun cannot be a subset of 'heavy' because the adjective 'heavy' does not apply to nouns.

Cp moves from cause to effect guided by some Server action; in this case some possible Server action, either by an agent or by Nature, leads from the cause to the effect. For instance, in the statement 'Whenever my toe hurts it rains', it is possible to connect humidity to a painful toe through a Server sequence of natural cause-and-effect. Even

---

52 Technically speaking, 'emerald' is only a subset of 'green' when referring to *color*. Thus, one should really say, 'All emeralds have the color of green', or 'If it is an emerald, then it has the color of green'. In other words, an if-then statement occurs within some mental *context* which is often assumed.

though the statement *may* not be true, it *could* be proven to be true by following Server sequences based in common sense and/or natural law.

One final point. Quine says that even though lawlikeness is difficult to define, it is easy to recognize: "In practice we seem to be able to recognize projectibility to our own satisfaction, and therewith lawlikeness, in most cases." I suggest that this is the result of *mental networks*. Studying formal logic or science will lead to the formation of Teacher mental networks. A statement will be recognized as *lawlike* if it triggers one of these Teacher mental networks in a way that is compatible with the structure of that Teacher mental network. Because lawlikeness is being judged by mental networks, the logician or scientist can *recognize* a lawlike statement even though he finds it difficult to define exactly what it is.

Let us move on now to Quine's *sixth virtue*: "*Precision* might be listed as Virtue VI, supplementary to the five virtues in Chapter VI. Like those virtues, precision conduces to the plausibility of a hypothesis. It does so in an indirect fashion. The more precise a hypothesis is, the more strongly it *is* confirmed by each successful prediction that it generates." A hypothesis is made by *normal* thought, which works with *partially* certain data and *partially* defined categories. Precision attempts to make data more certain and define categories more carefully. Obviously, if one knows more clearly *which* category data falls into, then it is easier to determine if it falls into the *right* category and supports the hypothesis, or falls into the *wrong* category and disproves it.

Remember that abstract thought uses Perceiver thought to compare Server sequences. Precision makes it easier to determine if one *physical* Server sequence is like another or not. According to Quine, "A notable boon of injecting quantity into hypotheses is *concomitant variation,* or *functional dependence*...Once such a hypothesis is devised, describing the fluctuation of one quantity explicitly as some function of the fluctuation of another quantity, the confirmatory power of a few successful predictions is overwhelming."

Server sequences can come from either *physical* sequences, as in the previous paragraph, or from sequences of Teacher *words*. Adding Perceiver precision to Teacher words defines the words more precisely: "Measure is not the sole source of precision. Another way of increasing precision is redefinition of terms. We take a term that is fuzzy and imprecise and try to sharpen its sense without impairing its usefulness." Perceiver thought works with *connections*. Thus, sharpening the definition of a word may change the items with which that word is connected: "In so sharpening we may effect changes in the term's application; a new definition may let the term apply to some things that it did not formerly apply to, and it may keep the term from applying to some of the things to which it had applied." When the Perceiver meanings of words are changed, then this will alter the examples and counterexamples that are triggered in Perceiver thought when Teacher thought uses these words to make general statements, which may make it possible to come up with Teacher theories that are more general: "Biologists gained precision and something more when they gave the common term 'fish' a sharp definition that banned whales; for the new distinction turned on biological characteristics that entered elsewhere into theory."

Philosophy focuses upon using the abstract *technical* circuit of Ci, and precision forms a major element of technical thought. In order to use technical thought, one must take words and give them more precise definitions: "When philosophers give a precise sense to what was formerly a fuzzy term or concept it is called *explication* of that term or concept...It is no wonder that philosophers seek explications; for explications are steps toward clarity. But philosophers are not alone in this."

Technical thought increases precision by adding *subcategories*. With numbers, this is done by adding decimal places. For instance, 8.67 is more precise than 8.6. Normal thought increases precision by improving *accuracy*. For instance, a micrometer is more accurate than a ruler, because distance can be controlled more closely with a micrometer than with a ruler. This distinction between *precision* and *accuracy* is taught in high school physics. Saying this another way, Ci works with *digital* certainty while normal thought uses *analog* certainty. The difference between these two could be compared to the analog waveform of a piece of music and the digital way in which this music is stored on a computer or CD. Any conversion from analog to digital requires the 'step of faith' of quantization. For instance, when using whole numbers to represent distance, any distance between 4.5 inches and 5.5 inches will be treated as five inches. This 'step of faith' can be minimized by adding *accuracy* to the analog measurements and *subcategories* to the digital categories.

When working with technical thought, one can add as many subcategories as required, because facts are clearly defined and belief is certain. However, one can only go so far in adding accuracy to normal thought, because each step of detail is only partially defined and has only partial certainty: "Precise hypotheses, we see, are hard to isolate for testing. They tend to carry other beliefs with them. Imprecise ones, on the other hand, can be hard to test because of difficulty in determining exactly what they imply."

If one *begins* with the concrete technical circuit of Cp, then it is possible to evaluate a hypothesis with arbitrary precision. A *game* is an example of Cp, in which the parameters are clearly defined. Thus, the technical rules of Ci can be applied because one is starting with Cp. As Quine says, "Some philosophers of science have tried to apply numerical probabilities as measures of the firmness of support. In games of chance the probability of hypotheses makes good sense; in fact, this is where the calculus of probabilities began." Putting this more clearly, Quine says, "The paradigm case of a hypothesis to which it makes clear sense to assign a probability is one that says of some fairly well specified and observable event that it will occur at some fairly well specified time."

However, if one begins with the poorly defined categories and uncertain labeling of the real world, then it is not possible to apply the rules of Ci: "We know what cards are in the deck...This available information consequently reduces the question to a count of combinations. In the wider world, however, how could we begin to calculate the probability of a hypothesis...there would be the problem of cataloguing all relevant information. Also there would be the far greater problem, which seems hopeless on the face of it, of compartmenting all alternative possibilities into what could be viewed as equal bits, preparatory to counting combinations."

Summarizing, this chapter focuses upon the effect that Perceiver facts have upon general Teacher theories in *normal* thought, and contrasts this with the relationship that exists in technical thought.

Explanation

When the mind is studying the physical world or using data from the real world to build or evaluate a hypothesis, then we are dealing with *normal* thought with all of its uncertainties. But when the mind *chooses* a theory or *commits* to a plan of action, then it becomes possible to make a transition from normal thought to technical thought. That is because choosing a theory or plan *restricts* the mind to the context of that theory or plan, *limits* action and thought to the elements of that plan, and *approaches* the theory or plan with an attitude of total certainty. One can choose a theory or commit to a plan without entering technical thought, but when one is dealing with a field as inherently technical as science during a period of time as technically oriented as Foucault's Modern episteme, then the one almost always implies the other.

Notice that choosing a theory or committing to a plan goes *further* than simply believing in a specific fact or deciding to do a specific action, because a fact or an action is merely one *single* element in a theory or plan, and technical thought requires a *network* of interconnected elements. A technical network of interconnected facts and sequences *may* have the emotional backing of some Mercy or Teacher mental network, but that does not have to be the case, since we are dealing here with Contributor mode and Contributor concentration.

Because choosing a scientific theory implies entering technical thought, a contradiction naturally arises between what science *is* and what science *does*—which Kuhn grasps but Quine apparently does not. Officially, science uses *normal* thought to deal with empirical data, and Quine describes applying normal thought to empirical data in exquisite detail in *The Web of Belief*. But when science *accepts* a paradigm, then it will usually enter *technical* thought with its limited world and digital certainty, even though, as Quine accurately describes, science is only justified in using normal thought. Thus, Quine describes in *The Web of Belief* what science *should* do, while Kuhn describes in *The Structure of Scientific Revolutions* what science *usually* does.

Mental symmetry suggests that it is *normal* for the mind to enter technical thought when it chooses a carefully defined paradigm, and that technical thought, by its very nature, *distances* the mind from the physical world of empirical data. This means that the *result* of science will disconnect the mind from the *source* of science. In other words, even though science *claims* that only sensory input and empirical data are worthy of rational analysis, when science enters technical thought, then it will go *beyond* the realm of sensory input and empirical data. The solution is for the scientist to *acknowledge* that he is using technical thought with its strengths and limitations, for he will then be more likely to recognize and respect normal thought with *its* strengths and limitations.

Moving on, hypothesis is tentative; it is a possible explanation; it is a general theory that normal abstract thought has constructed which could be used by technical thought. An explanation, in contrast, is a general theory which *has* been accepted by the abstract technical circuit of Ci. Ci takes a theory that has been accepted and *improves* it by adding technical details. Quine gives the example of tribesmen developing an explanation for the tides: "If some of our tribesmen are curious and observant they will improve their little law. They will correlate positions of the moon with low tides, and they will learn when to expect high tide while the moon is out of sight. They will notice that the high tide that comes moonlessly is a higher tide than the one with the moon overhead. In time they should recognize that the tides are maximized, both high and low, when the moon is new or full." Ci is emotionally driven by the Teacher emotions of order-within-complexity: "Explanation nourishes a desire for more of the same. We may respond to an explanatory law with a wish for a wider and deeper law to explain that law, and so on out."

In contrast, as Kuhn states, *generalizing* an existing paradigm is not a feature of normal science with its focus upon Ci, but instead requires an unusual approach, sometimes involving a person with the cognitive style of Teacher, such as Isaac Newton. Quine implies this: "If there happens to be one among the tribesmen with the genius of a Newton, some version of the law of gravitation might be thought of. Such a law would then explain the lesser law, and it would also make for a deeper and more powerful explanation of the tides themselves."

Technical thought is under the control of Contributor mode. At the most basic level, Contributor thought forms connections between Perceiver facts and Server sequences. Contributor-controlled technical thought emerges when there are sufficient interconnected Perceiver facts and Server sequences to permit Contributor thought to start functioning at a higher level. Contributor mode can approach the *same* network of facts and sequences from either the *concrete* viewpoint of Cp or the *abstract* viewpoint of Ci. For Cp, the basic building block is the connection of *cause-and-effect*—a Perceiver connection between the starting point and finishing point of a Server action. For Ci, the basic building block is the *word* or *phrase*—a Server sequence of words that is connected with a Perceiver meaning.

An *explanation* may involve *only* the abstract circuit of Ci. This occurs when explaining something like mathematics that uses only words and abstract symbols. But when one is explaining concrete *events*, then Cp gets involved as well, because Cp is the aspect of technical thought that deals with events. And when Cp becomes involved, then an explanation must respect the basic building block of Cp, which is the connection of cause-and-effect. In Quine's words: "What about a general statement and a singular instance thereof: does the one explain the other? Not always. Where it is some event or system of events that is to be explained, explanation has to do with cause...A hypothesis is explanatory of an event insofar as it advances us in our search for its causes." Or more explicitly: "What qualifies the hypothesis as explanatory is just that it suggests a causal connection."

An explanation of an event may include a *chain* of cause-and-effect links, essentially linking the end of one *Server* sequence to the start of another: "So, ideally, explanation discloses past events that are connected by causal chains to what is being explained, and it tells us something of those chains. How far back we will look for antecedent events will depend on what our interests are and on how deep our curiosity goes." However, an explanation may also use *Perceiver* facts to connect cause-and-effect links: "An explanation need not actually mention any event that is connected by a causal chain to what is explained. 'The time was short' is not thus related to 'He went by taxi.' What qualifies it as explanatory is that it helps us to infer something of the nature of the relevant causal chain."

The concrete circuit of Cp is *goal-oriented.* It is driven by the *purpose* of reaching some goal in Mercy thought, and it rearranges facts and actions in order to improve the bottom line of this Mercy goal. In other words, Cp functions *teleologically.* However, a purpose implies the presence of some *agent* who is attempting to reach the goal. Continuing with Quine's example of going by taxi, "the man wanted to include the quotation and he wanted to mail the manuscript before nightfall. Explanations of behavior that appeal thus to purposes, or reasons, are called *teleological.*"

The abstract circuit of Ci works with the *same* data as Cp, but it uses this data to build general theories in Teacher thought. When one takes a circuit that is *purpose* driven and generalizes it, one ends up with the concept of a *general purpose.* But if a purpose implies an agent, then who is the *agent* behind this general purpose? Quine describes this dilemma: "The trouble is that there is nobody whose purpose might have been operating anywhere in the causal chain. One proposed solution has been to assume Someone whose purpose was at work at the beginning of all causal chains. Here is a grand hypothesis, calculated to personalize the impersonal teleological explanations and so to accommodate them under the head of efficient cause after all. It is one of the classical arguments for the existence of God, and is known as the *argument from design.*" Mental symmetry suggests that combining the two technical circuits of Cp and Ci leads implicitly to the formation of a concept of God, and Quine agrees.

Quine also mentions why he regards a concept of God as an inadequate explanation: "It has been widely regarded as unsatisfactory because of problems it raises and leaves open regarding the mechanism of the creation and its overall purpose. Pleading the inscrutability of the ways of God has not appeased our appetite for explanation." However, I suggest that the theory of mental symmetry addresses these concerns. Mental symmetry distinguishes between a mental concept of God and a real God, and uses mental mechanisms to explain a concept of God. Mental symmetry also explains the 'inscrutable ways of God' in terms of mental mechanisms summarized by a general theory—and it uses the *same* mental mechanisms and general theory to explain scientific thought. As for the 'overall purpose of creation', mental symmetry again sidesteps that question and suggests that a mental concept of God has the overall purpose of encouraging and assisting a person to use his mind in a way that reaches its full potential.

Saying this in more general terms, it appears that everything in Quine's book on scientific thought can be explained in terms of mental mechanisms, and scientists love mechanisms, especially when they are presented in general terms. But Quine shies away from the *implications* of using scientific thought. However, if these implications can *also* be explained in terms of mental mechanisms, then what is the essential difference between scientific thought itself and the implications of scientific thought? Why accept one and reject the other if *both* can be explained equally well by the same mental mechanisms? Besides, if Quine begins his analysis of scientific thought by sidestepping the question of real observation and real belief and dealing only with the verbal description of observation and belief, why not take our cue from Quine and sidestep the question of a real God and focus upon the verbal description of God?

Quine proposes as a solution the theory of *evolution*, because this removes the need for *purpose*: "The seeing eye can evolve in the vertebrate, and hydrotropism in the willow, with never the intervention of purpose human or divine." Like Kuhn, Quine says that chains of cause-and-effect should be followed *back* in the direction of cause, but should not be followed *forward* in the direction of purpose. In Quine's words, evolution "reduces the teleological explanations of biology sweepingly to explanations in the proper causal sense. Easy answers like 'To see with' and 'So that their seeds will float away' become, thanks to Darwin, interpretable as shorthand allusions to long causal chains of natural selection."

The problem is that the circuit of Cp *does* follow chains of cause-and-effect primarily in the *forward* direction. Read almost any economic proposal—economic activity is a prime example of the operation of Cp—and it will contain a disclaimer with phrases such as 'this proposal contains forward-looking statements regarding strategy, plans, and objectives', and 'such forward-looking statements involve known and unknown risks, uncertainties, and other important factors beyond the control of the company', and 'the actual performance or achievements of this company could be materially different from such forward-looking statements'. Notice the various factors: The plan of Cp is being directed towards the future because the future can be changed. The warning is being given because the plan of Cp with its digital certainty is about to encounter the messy real world. The risk cannot be eliminated, but it can be reduced by adding details and contingencies to the plan.

When science insists that Cp should only look back and not forward, then Ci is shutting down the operation of Cp because Cp is by nature purpose-driven, and free will is being replaced by fatalism and determinism because everything is being explained in terms of events which have already occurred and therefore cannot be changed. Quine's description of human activity sounds depressingly deterministic: "A present purpose, however forward-looking, is a present state of a man's organism. It is caused by his heredity, by his training, and by an untold assortment of things that have happened to him early and late. Like everything that happens, it may be regarded as a history ultimately of combinations of elementary physical forces; and the man's activity in executing his purpose is more of the same."

As I mention in the main text, the theory of evolution is attractive to science because it appeals to *existing* natural scientific mechanisms: "Darwin's is an exemplary explanatory hypothesis, which appeals to plausible and independently discoverable processes." But while the mechanisms of evolution are plausible, the *application* of these mechanisms is implausible. In Quine's words, "Organisms show chance variations over the generations because of a process of genetic 'mutation'...These new traits then tend to be handed down to further generations if they are conducive to survival; otherwise they tend to disappear because their carriers tend to die before reproducing. Thus species that survive are to be expected to exhibit traits conducive to that survival, as with our tree." A mutation is, by definition, implausible, as is a 'chance variation'. Quine rightly questions theories of astrology because they avoid the virtue of refutability through the use of vague phrases such as 'tend to'. But Quine's description of evolution uses 'tend to' three times, in addition to an 'expected to'. It seems more plausible to explain teleology and a concept of God with mental mechanisms that *always* work, rather than explain teleology away, avoid the concept of God, and try to disable mental circuits by appealing to physical mechanisms which *might* work.

Moving on, I have mentioned that when the mind *uses* a theory or *commits* to a plan of action, then a mental transition is often made from normal thought to technical thought. Thus, it makes sense to apply the term *explanation* to a verbal analysis of a plan that was carried out or a theory that was spoken. In Quine's words, "Sometimes requests for explanation are demands for justification: 'Explain yourself!' Even here, to the extent that what is sought is an account of how some action came to be taken, it fits our scheme. The justificatory aspect is simply something additional. Other requests for explanation are not requests for explanation of events at all, but rather for elucidation: 'Explain your theory'; 'Explain what you just said'." Finally, a *machine* is a *physical* illustration of technical thought, composed of a network of objects that carry out functions. Thus, one can also say, "Explain how the pulleys and ropes are connected." The collection of Perceiver facts and Server sequences involved in such explanations may be limited, but if one listens to the person giving the explanation, one notices that he does not just give a simple answer, but rather spins a verbal web of interrelated facts and sequences, and his goal is accomplished when the listener accepts this explanation as satisfactory.

When the mind acquires a collection of interrelated Perceiver facts and Server sequences, then Contributor mode will begin to function by attempting to use technical thought: "In general we tend to believe not only that explanations exist, but that ones that would enlighten us exist. We believe, for instance, that crimes have solutions." An explanation of events will naturally include elements of Cp such as purpose, agents, and actions: "Solutions to crimes give explanations for them, explanations that meet special requirements: they identify the implicated persons, the methods used in the crime, and often the motives." And technical thought uses Contributor concentration to limit the range of thought: "Now just as some unsolved crimes have only a small number of reasonable suspects, it often happens that when we look for an explanation we reasonably believe that it will be found within certain narrow limits. We believe that one of some small number of conceivable explanations must be right."

When the mind goes from normal thought to the technical circuit of Ci, then it takes a 'leap of faith', because accepting a hypothesis as an explanation implicitly turns partial certainty into total certainty: "Often when we 'jump to conclusions' we are abusing it; we leap at the first explanatory hypothesis that comes to mind without duly surveying the field."

In science, Contributor mode takes a 'step of faith' when entering technical thought by extrapolating from reasonable hypothesis. However, technical thought can also be entered though a combination of Teacher overgeneralization and Facilitator reasonableness, resulting in a form of *science fiction*. Technical thought requires a collection of Perceiver facts and Server sequences to function, therefore the general *context* of science fiction must be one of logic, reason, and science. In normal thought, Perceiver facts limit the domain of Teacher theories. However, if Perceiver belief in some limiting fact or collection of facts can be questioned, then Teacher thought will become free of this factual constraint and will be able to come up with a more emotional Teacher theory, either by directly creating Teacher emotions of generality, or by indirectly triggering Mercy emotions produced by strange and wonderful Mercy experiences. As long as this factual questioning remains limited, then the Facilitator input filter will accept the modification as minimally counterintuitive. Thus, science fiction is a sort of pseudo-technical explanation in which Contributor mode enters Ci guided by the *context* of Perceiver facts and Server sequences but *motivated* by the Teacher overgeneralization that comes from questioning one or two of these facts or sequences.

Quine provides an example of science fiction: "Some purported event is described to us in a way that makes it seem not to fit comfortably with our other beliefs; for example, a discovery that there were rocketlike devices in medieval China. We are pressed to see the event as defying ordinary explanation...Before we know it some overwhelmingly ad hoc and monstrously immodest hypothesis, like a theory of visits from extraterrestrial beings, is thrust upon us. Just see how this would explain the discovery!"

The general point is that a little knowledge is a dangerous thing, because a person knows enough to enter technical thought but not enough to properly limit the overgeneralizing of raw Teacher thought. As Quine says, "Stubborn diseases or social ills invite rash or superstitious measures for want of sound ones. Responsible scientists may remain properly perplexed, whereupon an eager and impatient public hearkens to the irresponsible hypotheses that are so easily generated by uncritical if not unscrupulous minds."

Too *much* knowledge is also dangerous because one can 'lose sight of the forest for the trees'. Knowledge adds details to the technical thinking of Ci. But the overall goal of abstract thought is to build Teacher order-within-complexity. When a technical concept is unclear, the temptation is to use Ci to add more technical details. But by modifying the Teacher theory, it may be possible to discover greater order-within-complexity, which will make it possible to explain the concept more simply. For instance, as I was editing the appendix on Quine, I realized that some passages were unclear. My first tendency was to add more words in order to explain the concepts in more depth. But I then realized that the real problem was inadequate Teacher understanding. Adjusting my Teacher theory revealed greater order-within-complexity, making it possible to describe the order that lay behind the complexity in simpler terms.

The classic example is Ptolemy's geocentric model of the solar system. As Greek astronomers learned more about the paths of the planets, they realized that Ptolemy's model was inadequate. They responded by adding more technical details, embedding epicycles within celestial spheres. But viewing the sun as the center of the solar system made it possible to replace this complexity with a simpler explanation.

Quine puts it this way: "We must be wary, as Moliere taught us, of explanations couched in fancy language. It is a basic maxim for serious thought that whatever there is to be said can, through perseverance, be said clearly. Something that persistently resists clear expression, far from meriting reverence for its profundity, merits suspicion. Pressing the question 'What does this really say?' can reveal that the fancy language masked a featureless face."

Ci works with collections of Perceiver facts and Server sequences guided by *Teacher* emotions of order-within-complexity. It is easy for this thinking to be biased by *Mercy* mental networks, which also consist of Perceiver facts and Server sequences held together by emotion—the hyper-emotion of integration. As Quine puts it, "We should be wary of explanations that appeal to motives and character traits. Witness what might be offered as explanations for a man's electing to dedicate himself to some self-sacrificing career in which he serves the needs of others. It might be that his concern for other persons was so overwhelming that such a career was all he could consider, so we might explain his choice in terms of his love for fellow human beings."

If mental networks do form part of an explanation, then Perceiver thought must have sufficient confidence to be able to function despite the emotional pressure. If Perceiver thought has insufficient confidence, then it will become overwhelmed by the emotions and stop functioning. In Quine's words, "Attributing motives and character traits to persons as aids in explaining their behavior is legitimate only when such attributions can be regarded as hypotheses open to question in the light of further information. Talk about motives and character traits being as loose as it often is, we may too easily become intransigent about an attribution once it has been made. The belief that someone is a selfish scoundrel, once adopted, may be defended in the face of almost anything the person is seen to do."

Persuasion and Evaluation

This final chapter returns to normal thought and examines the way in which one person can influence Perceiver thought in another person. In this discussion, Quine assumes that Perceiver thought is functioning: "The force for truthfulness...has prevailed more in some circles than in others; and it has prevailed fully, we are glad to say, in the circle to which this little book is addressed. For this sincere circle, the business of convincing others reduces neatly to the business of convincing others of one's own beliefs."

Perceiver facts acquire their labels of belief from the beliefs of *related* Perceiver facts. Therefore, the easiest way to affect Perceiver belief in another person is by connecting with Perceiver facts that already exist within his mind: "We convince someone of something by appealing to beliefs he already holds and by combining these to induce further beliefs in him, step by step, until the belief we wanted finally to inculcate in him is inculcated." Obviously, such chains of logic work the best when dealing with the absolute certainty of technical thought: "The most striking examples of such arguments, no doubt, are mathematical."

A distinction can be made between *persuading* and *training*. One uses *persuasion* when it is known that Perceiver thought is functioning in the mind of the listener. Persuasion begins by looking for Perceiver facts in the mind of the listener that have strong labels of Perceiver certainty which are *related* to the topic. As Quine says, "In an effort merely to persuade someone of something, on the other hand, it would be presumptuous to argue for any preliminaries that he already accepts. We do well in such a case merely to seek a basis of shared beliefs broad enough to support the belief that we are trying to put over. We do well to appeal to a common ground of beliefs which are no more particular and detailed than necessary for agreement."

Primary education begins with blind faith in the teacher and the textbook. Therefore, one of the main goals of higher education is to teach Perceiver thought how to function: "If we were instructing a pupil in the generalization of the Pythagorean theorem, and not merely regaling a friend, we would press the pupil regarding the preliminary theorem about proportions between areas of similar figures. We would not merely acknowledge her acceptance of it and go on from there. Part of our responsibility to our pupil is to school her in critical and rigorous thinking. We would ask her to prove that preliminary theorem."

Science *ultimately* acquires its Perceiver facts from the external world, but people acquire most of their scientific facts *indirectly* from other people: "When we report an observation, we have the observation and others have only our testimony. Our observation reaches the other persons at one remove, and that one remove rubs out the guarantee that may be seen as stamped on observation. Thus, even though we have solid ground for a belief, there is this rub when we try to convince others." As a result, Perceiver thought is forced to assign a Perceiver label of reliability to people and to use this Perceiver label to evaluate the facts which they relate: "In Chapter V we noted what considerations might reasonably govern our credence of other people's testimony; and these apply now in reverse."

As with any Perceiver label assigned by Perceiver thought, this is an *analog* value which is based in repetition: "Our testimony gains in credibility also insofar as we have succeeded on past occasions in showing ourselves coolly judicious and moderately skeptical...Just as each of us forms hypotheses about the reliability and credibility of others, so do others form such hypotheses about us; and the best way to insure favorable ones is to earn them." However, one must remember that people are always *secondary* sources of truth: "The more honest and intelligent we are thought to be, the less supporting argument we are apt to have to produce in order to convince someone of something. In an extreme, indeed, such a reputation can be harmful to oneself and others, lulling both parties into inattentiveness to evidence."

It is possible to assign both a *Mercy* label of emotional status and a *Perceiver* label of reliability to the mental network that represents a person. When interacting logically, one must focus upon reliability and not emotional status. If one focuses upon emotional status, then the desire for Mercy emotions will make it more difficult for Perceiver thought to continue functioning. In Quine's words, "The desire to be right and the desire to have been right are two desires, and the sooner we separate them the better off we are. The desire to be right is the thirst for truth. On all counts, both practical and theoretical, there is nothing but good to be said for it. The desire to have been right, on the other hand, is the pride that goeth before a fall. It stands in the way of our seeing we were wrong, and thus blocks the progress of our knowledge. Incidentally it plays hob with our credibility rating."

As was mentioned, the label of belief that Perceiver thought assigns to a new fact is determined by the beliefs that have been assigned to *related* facts. Therefore, a new fact will not be accepted if it brings to mind related facts which are believed to be false: "Often there is also a negative element to contend with: actual disbelief of some of the needed premises." This can be overcome *directly* by connecting the new fact with sufficient additional facts that are believed, or *indirectly* by connecting related facts which are disbelieved with new factual information: "To overwhelm, we adduce such abundant considerations in favor of our thesis that we end up convincing the man in spite of his conflicting belief. He simply gives up the conflicting belief, deciding that there must have been something wrong with whatever evidence he once supposed he had for it. To undermine, on the other hand, we directly challenge his conflicting belief."

When Perceiver facts connect emotional Mercy experiences, then this forms a mental map of *value*. A mental map of value indirectly affects Server actions by defining an emotional topography of pleasant experiences to seek and unpleasant situations to avoid: "There is a domain, however, where the practical purpose, the influencing of action, continues to stand forth in very nearly its primeval starkness. This is the domain of values. To commend a past act is to urge the hearer to act likewise if occasion arises...But when we try to support our commendation of some act or object, we argue still for a belief: perhaps that the tidbit will titillate our interlocutor's palate, or that the painting or sonata will gratify the eye or ear, or that the act will have consequences to his or her liking."

And here it appears that Quine can go no further. He knows how Perceiver facts can be used to affect value by altering connections between emotional Mercy experiences, but he does not know how to analyze or define the emotional experiences themselves. That is a matter of *morality*, about which Quine limits himself to posing some suggestions: "There have been many theories that have sought to provide ultimate grounds for what is morally good or right. Some are religious theories, pure and simple; others have taken human desires or interests as their bedrock. Still others are cast in an abstract vein;

Immanuel Kant's, for example, turned on what maxims might admit of universal generalization for all people at all times...On the whole theories purporting to offer ultimate grounds for moral appraisal have had their troubles; surely none has commanded anything approaching universal assent."

We will finish by using Quine's six virtues of a good hypothesis to evaluate our explanation of Quine's book. Since we have taken essentially all of Quine's points and inserted them basically unmodified into the theory of mental symmetry, our explanation is conservative. And since Quine's views represent the scientific consensus, our explanation is modest. Our explanation has simplicity because it is held together by a single diagram of mental symmetry, and it is general because this same diagram can be used to explain a broad range of subjects. And we have attempted to be precise by using terms which are clearly defined. That leaves us with the virtue of refutability. I am proposing the theory of mental symmetry as an alternative to the theory of evolution. On the one hand, I am not sure how one can refute a theory that refers to implausible events which occurred in the prehistoric past. On the other hand, the field of the cognitive science of religion shows us that it is possible to come up with experiments that demonstrate cognitive mechanisms, even when dealing with something as 'non-scientific' as a mental concept of God.

www.ingramcontent.com/pod-product-compliance
Lightning Source LLC
Chambersburg PA
CBHW080234170426
43192CB00014BA/2456
* 9 7 8 0 9 8 7 9 7 8 5 0 9 *